User's Guide to Copyright

Sixth Edition

by **Michael Flint, Nicholas Fitzpatrick & Clive Thorne**

publishing

Tottel Publishing, Maxwelton House, 41–43 Boltro Road, Haywards Heath, West Sussex RH16 1BJ

© Tottel Publishing 2006
Previously published by LexisNexis UK.

A CIP Catalogue record for this book is available from the British Library.

ISBN 1–84592-068–6

Typeset by Columns Design Ltd, Reading, Berkshire
Printed by Antony Rowe Ltd, Chippenham, Wiltshire

Preface

This *User's Guide* is intended to help anyone whose job, business or studies brings them into contact with copyright issues, by giving them a general understanding of UK copyright law. In writing this sixth edition we have followed the tradition of the *User's Guide* by keeping clarity and practical advice at the top of our list of priorities. Part 1 outlines the law. Part 2 considers copyright in the context of a variety of occupations and activities. However, this is a much longer and more detailed work than the early editions: the direct result of an ongoing process of change in both the language of the Copyright Designs and Patents Act 1988 ('CDPA') and the way in which copyright is used.

It is worth remembering that, when the CDPA was written, the term 'digital' was more likely to describe the monochrome face of a wristwatch than a means of exploiting copyright. Since then, technology has driven us into a new age: the information age. Copyright has battled to keep pace, and in our turn we have battled to reflect the resulting changes in this *User's Guide*!

As the law has become more sophisticated, we believe the level of information our readers will demand has also increased in sophistication. This edition of the *User's Guide* is therefore extensively cross-referenced to statute, case law and now (for the first time) to academic articles which we hope will help those readers who need to look at particular issues in more depth. Our intention is that, as a result, this edition will prove to be useful for those engaged in academic studies. We are told the *User's Guide* is already very popular with non-specialist 'in-house' lawyers as well as copyright specialists in the UK and overseas.

So how is the sixth edition of the *User's Guide* different from earlier editions?

It has been fully updated to reflect the significant developments since our last edition. These are too many to list here, but the following are some highlights of issues we have included in our analysis:

- Emerging ideas for the future of copyright and subjects such as the 'creative commons'.

- The Copyright and Related Rights in the Information Society Directive 2001 and the 2003 Regulations (see the Glossary).

- The Enforcement of Intellectual Property Right Directive 2004.

- The Artists Resale Right Directive 2001.

- The Human Rights Act 1998 and copyright.

- Image rights, personality rights and copyright distinguished.

- Confidentiality, privacy and the Human Rights Act 1998.

- Performers' moral rights.

- Developments in the collective licensing of copyright.

- Extensively updated consideration of EU law, competition and copyright.

- The Registered Designs Regulations 2001.

- An extensive review of the latest case law.

- A new chapter dealing with 'network communications'.

We remain indebted to John Adams, Michael Edenborough and James Graham for the reproduction (in Appendix 5) of their table representing the duration of copyright.

We are also most grateful for the help of the following individuals who have contributed their expertise and support: Duncan Calow, Fiona Campbell, John Cloke, Stuart Levine, Lee McGuirk, Patrick Mitchell, Jon Ogle, Sam Szlezinger and Andrea Thompson.

This is for Evie and Emma.

Michael Flint
Nicholas Fitzpatrick
Clive Thorne December 2005

Contents

Contents

Contents

Contents

10 Ownership, transmission and licensing of copyright

Contents

Contents

Contents

Contents

24 Film and television production

Contents

Contents

How to use the *User's Guide*

Copyright is encountered by people in a great many walks of life: from television executives to authors, architects, artists, film producers, school teachers and museum curators. This *User's Guide* is designed to assist people whose work or studies involve them in day-to-day dealings with copyright. It can be used to acquire a general understanding of copyright and also as a reference work for dealing with general copyright problems.

Both laymen and lawyers tend to regard copyright as a difficult subject which is best left to the specialist. Certainly copyright legislation in the UK is structured in a complex way, and the significant changes introduced since the last *User's Guide* do nothing to make matters simpler. It is hoped that the format of this book will overcome some of those difficulties. The *User's Guide* is, however, only a guide and is not intended to take the place of a legal adviser where problems of complexity arise. Some matters contained in the CDPA (and subsidiary legislation made under the CDPA), are not discussed at all in this *User's Guide*, because they are of such a technical nature an expert legal adviser should always be consulted[1].

This sixth edition of the *User's Guide* has been extensively revised and updated. **Part 1** (Chapters 1 to 16) consists of a summary of the law of copyright. **Part 2** (Chapter 17 onwards) examines the way in which copyright law applies to certain organisations and occupations for which copyright plays an important role. This is the first edition of the *User's Guide* to consider in some detail the academic theory behind the law, and this is evidenced by the numerous references to underlying articles and other more theoretical texts. It is hoped that these editions will add value to those operating in academia, and also to those practitioners facing particularly complex or novel copyright-related issues.

The Table of Incidents of Copyright in **Appendix 4** sets out the essential incidents of copyright of each type of work entitled to copyright protection. The table is for general reference only: copyright law has many exceptions, and no simple table can deal with all of them. When considering specific points, the text must be used in addition to the table. However, the table serves as a quick guide, or checklist, when reading one of the chapters in **Part 2** which deals with a specific type of organisation or activity.

We recommend that **Part 1** is read in full. If this is not possible in a particular situation, a reader with little or no copyright knowledge should at least first acquaint himself with **paragraph 1.02**: the basic principles of copyright. You should also take care to follow up the references contained in the relevant chapters, and refer to the Table of Incidents of Copyright in **Appendix 4** regarding those types of works which are dealt with in the relevant chapter.

Most chapters in **Part 2** contain a paragraph of definitions of the terms used in that chapter. Although these may not make easy reading, it is important to know the technical meaning of the terms used in copyright, because sometimes the technical meaning conveys something different from the usual and ordinary meaning of the same expression[2].

The *User's Guide* is also extensively cross-referenced. The footnotes will enable you to refer back to case law, statutes, regulations and other parts of the *User's Guide* for further information on particular issues.

1   For example, the detailed rules regarding the Copyright Tribunal.
2   For example, under the CDPA, a 'film' is defined widely enough to include a CD-ROM.

Glossary of terms commonly used in the *User's Guide*

'the 1992 Regulations':   The Copyright (Computer Programmes) Regulations 1992, SI 1992/3233.

'the 1995 Regulations':   The Duration of Copyright and Rights in Performances Regulations 1995, SI 1995/3297.

'the 1996 Regulations':   The Copyright and Related Rights Regulations 1996, SI 1996/2967.

'the 1997 Regulations':   The Copyright and Rights in Databases Regulations 1997, SI 1997/3032.

'the 2000 Regulations':   The Conditional Access (Unauthorised Decoders) Regulations 2000, SI 2000/1175.

'the 2003 Regulations':   The Copyright and Related Rights Regulations 2003, SI 2003/2498.

'the Berne Convention':   The Berne Convention for the Protection of Literary and Artistic Works 1886.

'CDPA':   The Copyright, Designs and Patents Act 1988.

'DPA':   The Data Protection Act 1998.

'DMCA': The [U.S.] Digital Millennium Copyright Act 1998.

'the ECJ': The European Court of Justice.

'the EEA': The European Economic Area.

'the EU': The European Union.

'GATS': The General Agreement on Trade and Services.

'HRA': The Human Rights Act 1998.

'the Phonograms Convention': The Convention for the Protection of Producers of Phonograms against the Unauthorised Duplication of their Phonograms 1971.

'the Rome Convention': The Rome Convention for the protection of Performers, Producers and Broadcasting Organisations 1961.

'TRIPS': The Agreement on Trade Related Aspects of Intellectual Property Rights, Including Trade in Counterfeit Goods 1994.

'the UCC': The Universal Copyright Convention 1952.

'WIPO': The World Intellectual Property Organisation.

'the WIPO Treaties': The WIPO Copyright Treaty 1996 and the WIPO Performances and Phonograms Treaty 1996.

'the WTO': The World Trade Organisation.

Table of statutes

Paragraph references printed in **bold** type indicate where the Act is set out in part or in full.

Table of statutes

Table of statutes

Table of statutes

INTERNATIONAL ACTS

AUSTRALIA

UNITED STATES OF AMERICA

Table of statutory instruments

Those paragraph numbers in **bold** type indicate where a Statutory Instrument is set out in part or in full.

Table of statutory instruments

Table of cases

B

C

D

Table of cases

F

G

Table of cases

H

I

I

Table of cases

M

N

Table of cases

O

P

R

S

Table of cases

Part 1
Copyright law

Chapter 1

What is copyright?

Introduction

1.01 This chapter sets out the basic principles of copyright law in the UK. These principles are elaborated in the following chapters of the *User's Guide*, which have been extensively updated and improved in this edition. In order to assist your use of the *User's Guide*, we recommend you refer to the section 'How to use the *User's Guide*', set out above.

The basic principles of copyright

1.02

- *Copyright is a property right, which is protected in the UK by virtue of the Copyright, Designs and Patents Act 1988 (CDPA).*
- Copyright subsists only in material which falls within one of those categories of work prescribed by the CDPA as being capable of copyright protection. These are as follows:
  - (a) literary works;
  - (b) dramatic works;
  - (c) musical works;
  - (d) artistic works;
  - (e) sound recordings;
  - (f) films;
  - (g) broadcasts;
  - (h) the typographical arrangement of published editions[1].

Material which does not fall within any of these categories will have no copyright protection (i.e. it will not be a copyright work)[2].

- *There is no copyright in ideas,* only in the manner of their expression[3].
- *The material must be original* in order to be entitled to copyright protection[4].
- *The material must have involved the use of skill and labour by the author*[5].
- *The work must usually be reduced to a material form*[6].
- *Copyright is owned independently of the physical material which records it.* For example, the owner of the manuscript of a play is not necessarily the owner of the copyright in the play[7].
- *There are no formalities to copyright protection in the UK.* Material does not have to be published, nor does it have to be registered, for it to have copyright protection[8].
- *If material is entitled to copyright, then the right which vests in the copyright owner is the right to prevent others from doing certain restricted acts.* The restricted acts are specified by the CDPA in relation to each category of work and differ for each category. If something is done in relation to copyright material, which is not one of the restricted acts specified for that type of work, then there will not be a breach of copyright[9].
- *There are certain circumstances in which doing a restricted act without the authority of the copyright owner does not constitute an infringement of copyright*[10]. The most important of these general exceptions are:
  (a) the making of temporary copies and 'fair dealing'[11];
  (b) use of less than a substantial part of a work[12].
  There are many other important exceptions, some of which differ according to the type of works[13].
- *Copyright subsists for defined periods which differ according to the category of work.* The basic copyright period is usually the life of the author plus 70 years[14].
- *In most cases the author, maker, producer or publisher of a work and the director of a film is its first owner,* but there are special rules which can override this general provision[15].
- *The author or maker of the material must be a 'qualifying person':* basically a citizen or resident of the UK or one of the countries which is a party to the Berne Convention or the Universal Copyright Convention[16].
- *Authors and directors (and, for the first time during the life of this* User's Guide, *performers) enjoy 'moral rights'* which consist of the right to be identified as author, the right to object to the derogatory treatment of a work and (for authors and directors) the right to prevent false attribution of a work[17].

- *Performers and persons having recording rights* possess rights akin to copyright[18].
- Copyright should not be considered in isolation from other intellectual property rights[19].

1   CDPA s 1(1).
2   Column I of the *Table of Incidents of Copyright* sets out the different types of copyright works. **Chapter 2** will discuss in more detail what kinds of material are included within these categories.
3   **Paragraph 1.03** and **Chapter 3.**
4   **Paragraph 3.01** et seq.
5   Ibid.
6   **Paragraph 2.05.**
7   **Paragraph 10.01.**
8   **Paragraph 10.21.**
9   See Column III of the *Table of Incidents of Copyright* for the restricted acts applicable to each type of work. **Chapter 7** discusses the restricted acts in more detail.
10 **Chapter 9.**
11 **Paragraph 9.02** et seq.
12 **Paragraph 8.06.**
13 **Chapter 9** deals with these exceptions in more detail.
14 See Column II of the *Table of Incidents of Copyright*, **Chapter 6** deals with the duration of copyright in more detail.
15 Column IV of the *Table of Incidents of Copyright* outlines the rules as to who is the first owner of copyright in relation to each type of work. **Chapter 10** deals with ownership and transmission of copyright in more detail.
16 **Chapter 4** deals with qualifying persons and international copyright.
17 **Chapter 11** deals in detail with moral rights.
18 **Chapter 12.**
19 **Paragraph 1.04** and **Chapter 5.**

The nature of copyright

1.03   The nature of copyright was summed up succinctly by the bodies whose recommendations laid the basis for the 1956 Copyright Act and the CDPA respectively:

> 'Copyright is a right given to or derived from works, and is not a right in novelty of ideas. It is based on the right of an author, artist or composer to prevent another person copying an original work. There is nothing in the notion of copyright to prevent another person from producing an identical result (and himself enjoying a copyright in that work) provided it is arrived at by an independent process'[1].

'A writer writes an article about the making of bread. He puts words on paper. He is not entitled to a monopoly in the writing of articles about the baking of bread, but the law has long recognised that he has an interest not merely in the manuscript, the words on paper which he produces, but in the skill and labour involved in the choice of words and the exact way in which he expresses his ideas by the words he chooses. If the author sells copies of his article then again a purchaser of a copy can make such personal use of that copy as he pleases. He can read it or sell it second-hand, if he can find anyone who will buy it. If a reader of the original article is stimulated into writing another article about bread the original author has no reason to complain. It has long been recognised that only the original author ought to have the right to reproduce the original article and sell the copies thus reproduced. If other people were free to do this they would be making a profit out of the skill and labour of the original author. It is for this reason that the law has long given to authors, for a specified term, certain exclusive rights in relation to so-called literary works. Such rights were recognised at common law at least as early as the fifteenth century'[2].

Phrased another way: 'Copyright protection shall extend to expressions and not to ideas, procedures, methods of operation or mathematical concepts as such'.[3]

As the word implies, 'copyright' is literally a right to prevent other people copying an original work. It should be noted that it must be an original work, not just an original idea[4].

As for the word 'work', which appears frequently throughout this *User's Guide*, only those types of work which are specifically expressed as being entitled to receive copyright protection under the CDPA are so entitled. Not everything which could be described in the everyday sense as being a 'work' is entitled to copyright. In this *User's Guide* the word 'work' is used in the technical sense given to it by the CDPA[5].

Some writers have called for a simplification of UK copyright law, arguing that the complex structure of the legislation in the UK tends to undermine, rather than facilitate, the intentions of the copyright conventions and treaties which underpin copyright internationally.[6]

1   Gregory Committee on Copyright Law 1952.
2   Report of the Whitford Committee on Copyright and Design Law of 1977.
3   TRIPS Agreement, Sect 1 Act 9.2. For an interesting, if aged, discussion of the idea/expression dichotomy, see FW Grosheide, 'When ideas take shape' [1994] 6 EIPR 219. See also **paragraph 4.17** below.
4   This concept is considered further at **paragraphs 3.01** et seq. The reader should also note that a similar formulation was adopted internationally by the TRIPS Agreement and the WIPO Copyright Treaty, see **paragraph 4.18**.
5   A matter considered in more detail in **Chapter 2**, in particular **paragraph 2.12**.
6   E.g. Andrew Christie, 'A proposal for simplifying United Kingdom Copyright Law' [2001] EIPR, Issue 1.

Copyright and intellectual property generally

1.04 Copyright, patents and trade marks are diverse creatures which are, for convenience, usually grouped together under the headings of 'industrial property' or 'intellectual property'. It is certainly appropriate to include design copyright (which is registrable, unlike any other form of copyright) under these generic headings, but whilst copyright is a form of property, it is perhaps easier in practice to think of copyright together with principles such as passing off, breach of confidence and privacy[1].

1 See **Chapter 5**.

The CDPA

1.05 The law of copyright is contained in the CDPA which came into force on 1 August 1989. Much of the law relating to industrial designs (including the Registered Designs Act 1949, as amended) forms part of the CDPA[1].

Part II of the CDPA, which deals with rights in performances, gives protection to performers and persons having recording rights. Its effect is to create rights analogous to copyright.

1 Sch 4 to the CDPA. See further **Chapter 15**.

Statutory instruments

1.06 There are a number of rules and regulations contained in statutory instruments made under the CDPA. These have the effect in some cases of amending the CDPA and in particular of giving effect to various EU Directives[1]. The most important of these statutory instruments are the 1992 Regulations, the 1995 Regulations, the 1996 Regulations, the 1997 Regulations, the 2000 Regulations and the 2003 Regulations.

1 See **paragraph 1.08**.

Orders in Council

1.07 There are a number of Orders in Council extending the provisions of the CDPA to works originating outside the UK[1].

1 **Paragraph 4.09**.

EU law

1.08 The European Commission has adopted a number of Directives harmonising copyright laws (within the EU)[1]. The UK, like all EU Member States, must change its law to comply with these Directives by specified dates. Directives are binding on the Member States to which they are addressed although national authorities have the choice of the form and method of implementation into national law. The Commission may sue a Member State for non-implementation if the national authority has not incorporated the Directive into its law within the time limit specified in the Directive. Significantly, Directives are of *direct effect* in the sense that a citizen of a Member State may also sue his government before his or her national court for non-compliance with a Directive which has not been implemented within the requisite time period (provided the relevant provision is sufficiently clear, precise, unconditional and leaves no room for discretion in implementation)[2]. In the UK, EU Directives have been implemented by means of statutory instruments[3]. Since the EEA Agreement, EU legislation regarding copyright applies to all EEA States[4].

1 See **paragraph 14.03**.
2 *Van Duyn v Home Office: 41/74 [1975] Ch 358, ECJ.*
3 **Paragraph 1.06.**
4 See **paragraph 14.02**.

International conventions

1.09 The UK is party to a number of conventions dealing with international copyright recognition and other matters of an international nature[1].

1 **Paragraph 4.12** et seq.

Case law

1.10 There is a body of copyright-related common law consisting of the judgments delivered in relevant cases. Cases heard before implementation of the CDPA remain relevant.

Passing off, breach of confidence and privacy

1.11 The law relating to passing off, breach of confidence and privacy confers rights of action which can sometimes assist where copyright protection is not available. These are not matters which can, on the whole, be looked up in a statute[1], but have developed through a series of cases, and are contained in the judgments of those cases. They are based on common law and equity. As such these topics are in a constant state of evolution as judges modify the law in new cases which come before them[2].

1 Although the HRA and the DPA have had an impact on some of these issues.
2 **Chapter 5** discusses passing off and confidentially in detail.

The history of copyright in the UK

1.12 A short summary of the history of copyright may assist in understanding the present shape of the law.

Copyright effectively came into existence after the invention of printing. The first indications of copyright were the granting of licences by the Crown to printers giving them the right to print (i.e. copy), against the payment of fees to the Crown. In 1662 the Licensing Act was passed which prohibited the printing of any book which was not licensed and registered at the Stationers Company.

The first Copyright Act was passed in 1709. This gave protection for printed works for 21 years from the date of printing and unprinted works for 14 years. Again, books had to be registered at the Stationers Company.

The next important piece of copyright legislation was the Copyright Act 1842. This laid down the period of copyright as the life of the author and seven years after his death, or 42 years from the date of publication, whichever should be the longer.

The Copyright Act 1911 repealed the Copyright Act 1842 and itself remained in force until being repealed by the Copyright Act 1956. The 1956 Act re-enacted and continued in force some of the provisions of the 1911 Act.

In 1973, a departmental committee was set up, under the chairmanship of Mr Justice Whitford, to review the law of copyright and designs. Its report, *Copyright and Designs Law*, was published in 1977.

In 1981, the Government published its Green Paper *Reform of the Law Relating to Copyright, Designs and Performers' Protection*. In 1986 the Government published a White Paper *Intellectual Property and Innovation*. The White Paper dealt not only with copyright but also with patent and trade mark law. The Bill, which was to become the CDPA, was based upon most of the latter White Paper's proposals.

Since the CDPA came into force on 1 August 1989, very substantial changes have been made to it by the regulations referred to in **paragraph 1.06**. The effect of these regulations has been to:

- modify the law relating to computer programs;
- extend the period of copyright;
- change the law regarding the authorship of films;
- introduce wide-ranging provisions dealing with the rental and lending, satellite broadcasting and cable transmission of copyright works;
- extend performer's rights;
- introduce the publication right;
- introduce specific provision relating to the copyright protection of databases and to create a new sui generis database right;
- enhance the protection afforded to conditional access technologies;
- amend copyright law in light of developments in *information society* services.

The structure of the CDPA

1.13 The following outline of the CDPA (and indeed all following references to the CDPA in this *User's Guide*) deal with the CDPA as amended at 1 August 2005.

The CDPA is divided into seven parts: Part I Copyright; Part II Rights in Performances; Part III Design Right; Part IV Registered Designs; Part V Patent Agents and Trade Mark Agents; Part VI Patents; and Part VII Miscellaneous and General.

This *User's Guide* deals with Parts I and II in detail. It deals generally with Parts III and IV, not at all with Parts V and VI, and with Part VII only to the extent relevant to copyright users.

Part I of the CDPA is organised as follows:

- *Chapter I* deals with the subsistence, ownership and duration of copyright.
- *Chapter II* deals with the rights of copyright owners. The Chapter sets out and elaborates upon the acts which are restricted by copyright, and deals with issues of *'secondary infringement'* of copyright.
- *Chapter III* deals with acts permitted in relation to copyright works, i.e. those acts which can be performed without the consent of the copyright owner.
- *Chapter IV* sets out provisions dealing with moral rights.
- *Chapter V* considers 'dealings' with copyright works and describes how rights in copyright works and how moral rights may be assigned, licensed or passed on death.
- *Chapter VI* deals with remedies for infringement of copyright (both civil remedies and criminal sanctions).

- *Chapter VII* deals with licensing schemes and licensing bodies.
- *Chapter VIII* sets the provisions concerning the Copyright Tribunal.
- *Chapter IX* contains provisions dealing with the qualifications for, and extent of, copyright protection.
- *Chapter X* deals with Crown and Parliamentary copyright, other miscellaneous provisions dealing with, for example, folklore and, perhaps more importantly, the interpretation provisions in which terms not defined elsewhere in Part I are defined.

Part II of the CDPA deals with rights in performances[1].

Part VII is headed *Miscellaneous and General*. It deals with devices designed to circumvent copyright protection, the fraudulent reception of transmissions, the fraudulent application or use of trade marks, provisions for the benefit of the Hospital for Sick Children (the Peter Pan-saving provisions), and for certain international bodies. It also contains provisions dealing with the entry into force of the CDPA.

The *publication right*, which arises when a work is first published after its copyright period has expired, is not part of the amendments to the CDPA, but is to be found in reg 16 of the 1996 Regulations.

Similarly, the *database right*, which subsists in a database if there has been a substantial investment in obtaining, verifying or presenting the contents of the database, is not included as an amendment to the CDPA, but instead is set out in Part III of the 1997 Regulations.

1   Ss 180–212.

The future of copyright – convergence and the creative commons?

1.14   Every technical innovation affecting the distribution of copyright works challenges copyright law to change in order to address the new circumstances in which it operates. The development of the so-called *information society* is one such innovation. Copyright law has changed significantly in recent years to meet the challenges of the information society. Most notably, new definitions have sought to address new distribution networks on a 'technology neutral basis', and substantial changes have been made to the provisions of the CDPA which deal with technical measures designed to overcome copy-protection technologies, and to the exceptions and defences available against an allegation of copyright infringement[1].

These changes in UK copyright law take their lead from the WIPO Treaties, and also follow the lead of the United States' DMCA legislation (which has been criticised by some for shifting the balance of protection too far in favour of the rights holder at the expense of public interest in the 'fair use' of copyright works, whilst simultaneously failing to address the epidemic of unauthorised copyright use which has accompanied the development of peer-to-peer internet services[2]).

The digital agenda, as embodied by these latest changes, has been set around extending the exclusive rights of authors, protecting technical devices designed to restrict access to copyright works, and enhancing enforcement rights, whilst recognising that changes are required in order to foster the development of digital networks. However, the traditional basis for copyright law: the exclusive ability of the owner to prevent certain unauthorised uses of his work, remains largely intact[3]. Indeed, there have also been successful international efforts to expand the duration of copyright protection[4].

Yet many have argued that digital media, the convergence of computing, telephony and audio-visual technologies, and the ubiquity of the internet render obsolete the very basis of traditional concepts of copyright, requiring copyright law to change more fundamentally to cope with its new environment:

> 'Within a generation …copyright laws will change, so as to become unrecognisable. There will be a short burst of exclusivity, encouraging fast exploitation, followed by a short remuneration right for the lifetime of the creator …digital copyright at the turn of the millennium will have marked the end of an era'[5].

Lawrence Lessig[6], for example, has argued that the extended copyright term runs contrary to the public interest, by keeping works out of circulation entirely when digital networks create the possibility of a 'creative commons':

> 'the reason why it was so devastating to extend the term of existing copyrights is the huge amount of material that is basically unavailable right now because it's out of print …it is simply material that's locked up, unavailable'.

As a result, he argues, internet information repositories are prohibited from including vast amounts of information, including films that curators expect to disintegrate before their copyrights expire.

Lessig established the so-called 'Creative Commons' (its logo, cc in a circle, is a variation on the © symbol), an organisation through which authors may make available works on terms which are less restrictive than traditional copyright terms. Since it was set up in the US in December 2002, many millions of cc licences have been downloaded from www.creativecommons.org. Of course, the enforceability of these licences relies on traditional principles of copyright and contract law.

This issue of the 'lock up' of copyright works has also been addressed by a group of publicly-funded and non-profit organisations, who intend to make certain publicly funded content available for download to the public. In the UK, for example:

- The BBC, Channel 4, British Film Institute, and Open University have launched the 'Creative Archive Licence Group', with the aim of making their archive content (moving images, audio and stills) available for downloading using a 'Creative Archive' licence, a scheme which has some similarities to the Creative Commons licence referred to above: the aim is that users are permitted to share, watch, listen and re-use the content as long as they comply with certain terms and conditions of the licence, and they must agree that they will only use the material for non-commercial purposes. The BFI has, as we write, already launched its free video clips service under the terms of the Creative Archive Licence.
- Separately, the BFI recently also launched 'Screenonline', a service which provides access to national archives of film content to UK schools, colleges and libraries.
- The British Library provides free world-wide access to substantial numbers of rare and in many cases unique documents.
- On a pan-European level, as we write, discussions are underway to create an internet portal which will provide access to the digital collections of museums, libraries and archives across Europe[7].

Copyright principles also face challenge from principles of competition law[8], and from the implementation of human rights legislation in the UK[9].

There is not space in this *User's Guide* to do justice to the breadth of academic argument on these issues, although specific challenges will be discussed throughout the relevant sections of this work[10].

1   See **paragraphs 2.09, 7.07** and **Chapter 26**.
2   For a further discussion of peer-to-peer services, see **Chapter 26**.
3   With some notable exceptions, most obviously the compulsory collective licensing provisions relating to cable retransmissions, see **Chapter 26**.
4   E.g. in the US, the Sonny Bono Copyright Extension Act 1998.
5   Martin Kretschmer, 'Digital Copyright: the end of an era' [2003] EIPR 333.
6   Professor of law, Stanford University, author of 'The Future of Ideas' and 'Code and Other Laws of Cyberspace'.
7   A meeting of the National Representative Group (NRG) for eEurope Digitisation, held in Bristol 16–17 November 2005, launched the Dynamic Action Plan for European Ministers of Culture. The plan promotes the use of digital collections of museums, libraries and archives across Europe.
8   See **Chapter 14.**
9   The Human Rights Act 1998.

10 For further discussions on the future of copyright see Andrew Christie, 'A proposal for simplifying UK Copyright Law ' [2001] EIPR, Issue 1, and Shira Perlmutter, 'Convergence and the Future of Copyright', [2001] EIPR, Issue 2. For an interesting alternative take on copyright extension, see Adam Sutcliffe, 'Turning "Expired" Copyright into a Gold-mine' [1998] EntLR.

Stamp duty

1.15 Until 28 March 2000, documents which conveyed intellectual property (including copyright) attracted stamp duty. However, since that date, stamp duty is no longer applied to such documents[1].

1 Gordon Brown's 2000 Budget.

Copyright and freedom of expression: the Human Rights Act 1998

1.16 The nature of copyright is to reserve to the copyright owner the right to do certain 'restricted acts' in relation to his protected work. Within the parameters which will be investigated throughout this *User's Guide*, the copyright owner can use his property right in a work to restrain others from using it. In doing so, copyright limits the ability of others to express themselves (if doing so would involve using a copyright work without the authority of the owner in one of the ways restricted by copyright: e.g. copying).

There is a clear tension between the exclusive rights enjoyed by a copyright owner and the rights to freedom of expression enshrined in the European Convention on Human Rights, as enacted in the UK by the HRA, which entered into force in October 2000.

By Article 10 of the ECHR:

'1.   Everyone has the right to freedom of expression. This right shall include freedom to hold opinions and to receive and impart information and ideas without interference by public authority and regardless of frontiers ...

2.   The exercise of these freedoms, since it comes without duties and responsibilities, may be subject to such formalities, conditions, restrictions or penalties as are prescribed by law and are necessary in a democratic society ...for the protection of ...rights of others ...'.

This tension was investigated in the Court of Appeal decision in *Ashdown v Telegraph Group Ltd*[1]. In that case the *Sunday Telegraph* published a minute drafted by Paddy Ashdown which documented a confidential meeting between Mr Ashdown and the Prime Minister. The minute found its way to the *Sunday Telegraph* via a publisher to whom Mr Ashdown had entrusted a copy on a confidential basis. The *Telegraph* argued that their reproduction of the minute did not amount to an infringement since they should be entitled to enjoy one of the defences to infringement (either 'fair dealing' or 'public policy'[2]). Moreover, the *Telegraph* argued that the effect of the HRA was to require these defences to be applied in such a way as to preserve freedom of expression.

The court at first instance found against the newspaper, and the decision was upheld in the Court of Appeal. At first instance, Morritt VC found that the CDPA already balanced the rights of copyright owners and users. In other words, the legislation has (by initiating defences and exceptions to copyright infringement) balanced the competing demands of the right to enjoy property (i.e. copyright) and the right of freedom of expression. The Court of Appeal concluded that freedom of expression should not as a general rule have any effect on copyright enforcement. The Court did however recognise that rare circumstances arise where a freedom of expression will conflict with copyright protection, outside the ambit of the current exceptions set out in the CDPA. In those circumstances, the Court stated that it was necessary to apply the CDPA in a manner that accommodates the right of freedom of expression, looking closely at the facts of the case.

The decision exhibits the general reluctance of English courts to look outside the four walls of the CDPA itself as establishing an appropriate balance between the competing interests of property and freedom of expression. Nevertheless, it illustrates that copyright law is subject to re-examination in light of the Human Rights Act 1998, even if an active departure from existing copyright principles in favour of the freedom of expression would appear unlikely, except in rare circumstances.[3]

1   (2001) EMLR 44, CA.
2   See **paragraph 2.16** and **Chapter 9.**
3   For an interesting discussion of this issue, and a comparative study of the position under US and UK law, see 'Acknowledging the Conflict between Copyright Law and Freedom of Expression under the Human Rights Act' MD Birnhack (2003) ENTLR, Issue 2. It appears to the authors that there are circumstances where the expression is so intrinsic to the idea that arguably the HRA may operate to allow a different approach. This is particularly the case with artistic works. Would a modern English court now have difficulties, for example, with the issue in the US case *Rogers v Koons (960F2d301, (2nd Circuit) 1992)*, where the artist Jeff Koons was unsuccessful in defending a case of copyright infringement based on his use of a photograph, *Puppies,* to produce a sculpture which was intended to parody banal cultural images? He had claimed his use was 'fair use' under US law principles.

Chapter 2

Copyright works

Introduction

2.01   Copyright exists only in works which can be brought within one of the following categories:

- original literary, dramatic, musical and artistic works;
- sound recordings, films or broadcasts; or
- the typographical arrangement of published editions[1].

1   CDPA s 1(1).

Literary works

2.02   The CDPA outlines a 'literary work' as:

'any work, other than a dramatic or musical work, which is written, spoken or sung, and accordingly includes:

(a)   a table or compilation other than a database;
(b)   a computer program;
(c)   preparatory design material for a computer program; and
(d)   database.'[1]

The expression 'literary work' covers works which are expressed in words or numerals irrespective of quality. Where a work, such as a novel, goes through a number of draft stages the components of each draft stage is capable of constituting a copyright work in its own right, quite distinct from each other draft and the final published edition[2]. It should be noted that for the purposes of the CDPA, maps, charts and plans are not literary works but are deemed to be artistic works[3]. The borderline between literary works and artistic works is sometimes unclear. In the case of *ANACON Corpn Ltd v Environmental Research*

Technology Ltd[4], for example, Mr Justice Jacob held that circuit diagrams are both literary works and artistic works. He said:

> 'My first thought was that it would be absurd to regard a circuit diagram as a literary work, but the more one thinks about the ambit of that expression, as used in the [CDPA] Act, the more one is driven to the conclusion that provided that it is all written down and contains information which can be read by somebody as opposed to appreciate it simply with the eye, the more one sees that that is just what it is'.

Not everything that is 'written, spoken or sung' is entitled to copyright. There must be a degree of originality[5].

Although copyright is *not a right in novelty of ideas*[6], in the case of *Autospin (Oil Seals) Ltd v Beehive Spinning*[7], Mr Justice Laddie said:

> 'Copyright in a literary work gives protection not just to the words used but may also extend to the themes and ideas incorporated into it if they are efficiently substantial ... what the copyright protects is the relevant work and skill embodied in the work'.

The expression 'written, spoken or sung' was introduced by the CDPA. The inclusion of these words makes it clear that words spoken extempore (such as in an interview) will constitute a literary work at the time they are recorded. The author of such a literary work will be the speaker[8]. However, since such interviews are a common component of broadcasters' content, the CDPA contains an exception to copyright infringement for the benefit of broadcasters. Where a record of spoken words is made, in writing or otherwise, for the purpose of recording current events or broadcasting the whole or part of the work, the use of that recording (or copies of it) will not infringe the spoken literary work, provided that a number of conditions are met[9]. These are set out in detail elsewhere in this *User's Guide*[10].

Literary works also include databases. English courts have historically been more inclined to afford copyright protection to works like databases (although that expression was not introduced into the CDPA until 1997) than their European counterparts, and this tendency is evidenced by the low threshold of originality required by English courts for literary works to qualify as such[11]. Consequently a wide variety of sometimes quite mundane material has qualified as literary work. Examples include street directories, mathematical tables, lists of stock exchange prices, grids and sequences of letters for competitions and betting coupons.

The CDPA (as amended by the 1997 Regulations) also specifically protects databases as a separate class of literary work (distinct from tables and compilations). The CDPA (as amended) defines a database as:

'a collection of independent works, data or other materials which –

(a)   are arranged in a systematic or methodical way, and

(b)   are individually accessible by electronic or other means'[12].

The amended CDPA imposes a requirement that a database can only be considered an original literary work if it (by reason of the selection or arrangement of its contents) constitutes the author's own intellectual creation[13]. The significance of this requirement is considered further in **Chapter 3**, but it is worth noting here that in implementing the 1996 Directive, the Parliamentary draftsmen have subtly increased the burden on a person seeking to establish that a database (as opposed to a table or compilation) qualifies for copyright protection.

Whether or not a database qualifies for copyright protection under the CDPA, the 1997 Regulations also introduced an additional sui generis property right which subsists in a database if there has been a substantial investment in obtaining, verifying or presenting the contents of the database[14]. In brief, this right is infringed if a person extracts or re-utilises all or a substantial part of the contents of a database without the owner's consent[15]. The right expires at the end of 15 years from the end of the calendar year in which the making of the database was completed, except where the database is made public before the end of that period, in which event the right expires at the end of 15 years from the end of the year in which the database was made public[16].

Databases are now therefore subject to at least two possible tiers of protection. Compilations and tables receive yet another tier of protection. Unfortunately the result is a complex framework which brings with it a number of uncertainties[17].

1   CDPA s 3(1).
2   *Sweeney and another v MacMillan Publishers Ltd and another [2002] All ER(D)332.*
3   Dealt with in s 4 – the *'artistic works'* section, see **paragraph 2.06**.
4   [1994] FSR 659.
5   See **Chapter 3**.
6   See **paragraph 1.03**.
7   [1995] RPC 683.
8   See **paragraph 10.03**.
9   CDPA s 58.
10 See **paragraph 9.20**.
11 See **Chapter 3**.
12 CDPA s 3A(1).

13 CDPA s 3A(2).
14 Reg 13(1).
15 Reg 16.
16 Reg 17.
17 For a full analysis, of the database right, see **Chapter 16**.

Dramatic works

2.03 Dramatic works are defined in the CDPA as follows:

'dramatic work includes a work of dance or mime'[1].

This list is not exhaustive. Other works (e.g. radio plays, screenplays or even films) may also be dramatic works. A stage musical is a dramatic work. The 'book' of a musical comedy (i.e. the spoken words and lyrics) is both a dramatic and literary work. The music, considered separately from the book, is a musical work.

There must be some spoken words or action to perform or dance in order to differentiate a dramatic work from a literary work or a musical work. A description which is to be read, and is not written in a dramatic form, nor is intended for use in a dramatic way, would not be a dramatic work. On the other hand, the absence of dialogue (or indeed any spoken words) does not prevent a piece qualifying as a dramatic work. Dramatic incidents as well as spoken words are entitled to copyright.

The subject matter of the work must be sufficiently certain in order to qualify as a dramatic work. A screenplay will have dramatic elements (dialogue, directions etc), which are used to develop the plot. However the elements must be linked together in a way which is capable of performance. So, in one case, a television format was held to lack the necessary unity enabling it to be performed[2]. Similarly, in Canada, a sporting event was held not to be a dramatic work, notwithstanding that certain parts of the action were pre-planned[3].

In 2000, the Court of Appeal held that the ordinary and natural meaning of a 'dramatic work' could be summarised as:

'a work of action, with or without words or music, which was capable of being performed before an audience'.

So, the Court held, a film (as distinct from any dramatic work which may be recorded in the film)[4] may itself be capable of receiving protection as a dramatic work. Where a film contained a series of highly stylised 'jump shots', conveying the impression of a dance which was not actually capable of being performed and therefore not itself protectable as a dramatic work, the court held that the *film* itself (which was both a work of action and was quite capable of being performed) constituted a dramatic work in its own right and was capable of protection as such.[5]

1   CDPA s 3(1).
2   *Green v Broadcasting Corporation of New Zealand [1989] RPC 700*. See also **paragraph 2.14**.
3   *FWS Joint Sports Claimants v Copyright Board [1991] 22 IPR 429 (Fed Ct. of Appeal), Canada*.
4   See **paragraph 2.08**.
5   *Norowzian v Arks Ltd (No2) [2000] FSR 363, CA*, but also see the critique of this decision by Tom Rivers [2000] EIPR, issue 9.

Musical works

2.04   For the purposes of the CDPA, a musical work is:

'a work consisting of music, exclusive of any words or action intended to be sung, spoken or performed with the music'[1].

So, lyrics do not fall within the definition of a musical work, but instead are protected as literary works. However, musical annotations and directions on a score are part of the musical work.

In one recent case, the Court of Appeal needed to consider whether 'performing editors' of out-of-copyright musical works were themselves capable of constituting 'musical works' within the sense of Section 3(1) of the CDPA. The court rejected an argument to the effect that to be a 'musical work' the editors would need to create new musical notes. Instead a wider test was to be preferred: what is required in order to assess whether a musical work based on an earlier work is itself capable of protection as a musical work is not a note by note textual comparison, but rather a comparison of the sounds which result.[2]

1   CDPA s 3(1).
2   *Sawkins v Hyperion Records Ltd [2005] EWCA 565, CA*. See also **paragraphs 3.01 and 22.04**.

Literary, dramatic and musical works – fixation

2.05   For copyright to subsist in a literary, dramatic or musical work it must be recorded in writing or otherwise. In other words, it must be reduced to some tangible form[1]. 'Writing' is defined in the CDPA as:

'including any form of notation or code, whether by hand or otherwise and regardless of the method by which, or the medium in or on which it is recorded'[2].

The intention is that any tangible form of recording of the work is sufficient to satisfy the requirement. Copyright exists in these works only from the time the work is recorded. A dance does not have dramatic copyright until it has been filmed or written down in some form, such as the shorthand notation of Benesch[3]. Equally, a melody will not have copyright protection until it is recorded or written down. So a dance or melody that is not recorded can be performed without copyright infringement. The question as to who owns the copyright if a work is first recorded by someone other than the author is considered below[4].

The requirement of fixation does not apply to artistic works[5].

1   CDPA s 3(2).
2   CDPA s 178.
3   See **paragraph 23.09**.
4   See **paragraph 10.03**.
5   See **paragraph 2.06**.

Artistic works

2.06   Under the CDPA, 'artistic works' means:

'(a)   a graphic work, photograph, sculpture or collage, irrespective of artistic quality;

(b)   a work of architecture being a building or a model for a building; or

(c)   a work of artistic craftsmanship'[1].

It is worth noting that for an 'artistic work' to qualify for copyright protection, it need not, on the whole, have any artistic merit.

The CDPA sheds further light on the components of the definition of an artistic work[2]. So:

- a 'building' includes 'any fixed structure, and a part of a building or fixed structure';
- a 'graphic work' includes 'any painting, drawing, diagram, map, chart or plan' and 'any engraving, etching, lithograph, woodcut or similar work'[3];
- a 'photograph' means 'a recording of light or other radiation on any medium on which an image is produced or from which an image may by any means be produced, and which is not part of a film'. This is a very wide definition, including such things as holograms, although significantly limited to still rather than moving images; and
- a 'sculpture' includes 'a cast or model made for the purposes of sculpture'.

The expression 'collage' is not defined in the CDPA, although the meaning has been considered in one case which held that the expression did not extend to a collection of articles arranged around a swimming pool to form the set for a photographic shoot[4]. Again, 'painting' and 'sculpture' are not defined, and therefore these terms bear their natural meaning. In one case it was held that 'painting' did not include the facial make-up of the 1980s pop star Adam Ant, although in principle there is no reason why make-up should not be capable of receiving protection, provided it is sufficiently original[5]. Again, in one case moulds for functional items were held not to be sculptures[6].

What amounts to a 'work of artistic craftsmanship' is not defined in the CDPA and accordingly this expression should also be given its ordinary and natural meaning. Both artistry *and* craftsmanship are required. So, although a graphic work, photograph, sculpture or collage will be protected 'irrespective of artistic quality', a work of craftsmanship (e.g. pottery) will be protected *only* if it has artistic quality[7].

Only architectural works and works of artistic craftsmanship require any artistic quality in order to fall within the definition of 'artistic work'. In the case of *Merlet v Mothercare Ltd*[8], the court held that a cape designed to be worn by a baby was a work of craftsmanship, but not of artistic craftsmanship, and consequently was not protected as a copyright work. Walton J held that the test as to whether something is a work of artistic craftsmanship, once it is established that it is a work of craftsmanship, is whether or not the artist-craftsman *intended* to create a work of art. It will be easier for a recognised artist to satisfy the court of his intentions than someone who has never attempted to sell his creations. It is also easier to bring hand-crafted works within the meaning of the expression, than machine-made works.

It is more important to ascertain the intention of the artist in creating the work, rather than the reaction of the viewer to the completed work, for it is usual in copyright law to ignore the question as to whether or not the work has any merit. However, in the *ANACON* case[9], Mr Justice Jacob said that, 'the essential nature of a graphic work, it is a thing to be looked at in some manner or another. It is to be looked at in itself.'

Modern artists frequently use works in their art which do not fall within the technical definition of an artistic work described above (e.g. films, sound recordings, etc.). Where one of these other types of works is used in an artistic context, we recommend reference to the particular parts of this *User's Guide* dealing with those other works. If it is to receive copyright protection, a work of art which does not fall within one of the above types of artistic work, must fall within one of the other categories of protected work considered in this chapter.

The requirement of fixation does not apply to artistic works[10], so that an 'ephemeral work' (such as a sculpture created from rocks or debris below a tidal high water mark which is designed to be washed away by the next tide) is capable of being protected even if it is not recorded. 'Performance art' may receive protection as a dramatic work.

1   CDPA s 4(1).
2   CDPA s 4(2).
3   But query how this definition might cope with 'found' or 'ready made' pieces like those of Marcel Duchamp.
4   *Creation Records v News Group Newspapers [1997] EMLR 444*, see also **paragraph 7.03**.
5   *Merchandising Corp of America Inc v Harpbond Ltd [1983] FSR 32*.
6   *Metix (UK) Ltd v GH Maughan (Plastics) Ltd [1997] FSR 718*.
7   *George Hensher Ltd v Restawile Upholstery (Lancs) Ltd [1976] AC 64, HL*. The *Hensher* decision has proved difficult authority, as demonstrated in the case of *Vermaat (t/a Cotton Productions) v Boncrest Ltd (No 1) [2001] FSR 5*. For a summary of the relevant case law, see Simon Clark, 'What is a Work of Artistic Craftsmanship' Copyright World, November 2000. See further **Chapter 15**.
8   [1984] FSR 358.
9   See **paragraph 2.02**.
10 See **paragraph 2.05**.

Sound recordings

2.07   A 'sound recording' is:

'(a)   a recording of sounds, from which the sounds may be reproduced, or

(b)   the recording of the whole or any part of a literary, dramatic or musical work, from which sounds reproducing the work or part may be produced,

regardless of the medium on which the recording is made or the method by which the sounds are reproduced or produced'[1].

This is a technology-neutral definition intended to catch every type of sound recording which is made now or in the future.

There are a number of points to be noted in relation to this definition of sound recording:

● First it is not the physical disc or tape that receives copyright protection, but rather the *recording* itself.
● Secondly, the definition is not limited to a recording of sounds. The first part of the definition deals with traditional types of recording and includes recordings of any sound (e.g. birdsong). The second part is limited to recordings of literary, dramatic or musical works.

- Thirdly, sound recordings are copyright works quite distinct from the copyright in any compositions which they may record (which may be protected as literary, dramatic or musical works).
- Fourthly, sub-paragraph (*b*) of the definition has been included so as to include, for example, a recording made directly from a synthesiser of a musical work where the composer keys in his composition to the synthesiser without actually producing a sound at that stage, or of a literary or dramatic work where the synthesiser artificially reproduces the human voice. Computer produced samples, therefore, are entitled to protection as sound recordings. The same paragraph is worded in such a way that a computer program which can be played back so as to reproduce sounds in the form of a meaningless noise to the human ear, would not be protected because the noise will not constitute a sound reproducing a literary, dramatic or musical work.
- Fifthly, a sound recording does not qualify for copyright protection if, or to the extent that, it is a copy of a previous sound recording.[2]

The word 'record' does not appear in the CDPA (although it was defined in the 1956 Act, this definition is now irrelevant except in relation to recordings made before the CDPA came into force). Similarly, the word 'reproduction' is not defined in the CDPA. The absence of a definition is likely to widen, rather than limit, the meaning of the word.

1   CDPA s 5A(1).
2   CDPA s 5A(2).

Films

2.08   A film is 'a recording on any medium from which a moving image may by any means be produced'[1]. This too is a technology-neutral definition intended to cover all possible technical ways of recording moving images.

A film soundtrack is now treated as part of the film, following amendment of the CDPA by the 1995 Regulations[2]. Previously, the CDPA protected soundtracks separately simply as sound recordings, not as parts of films.

Copyright in a film is quite separate from the copyright in any literary, dramatic, musical or artistic work it may record. A film has copyright in its own right. So, the film of a live event or of abstract patterns (in which there is no copyright) will equally qualify as a 'film'.

Provided that a film constitutes a 'work of action' and is capable of being performed, recent case law suggests it will also receive protection as a dramatic work in its own right, quite distinct from the acts it records[3]. This is interesting because at one time, it was generally thought that under the CDPA a film could only be copied by means of a technical reproduction of the film itself[4]. This position is suggested by the wording of the CDPA, which talks of copying in the context of a film as copying an 'image forming part of the film'[5] and provides that a film (or part of a film) which is simply a copy of a previous film has no copyright protection[6]. The traditional view was that whilst re-recording the same incidents featured in a previous film may infringe the copyright in underlying works (e.g. a screenplay), it would not infringe copyright in the earlier film itself. Clearly, if a film is capable of receiving protection as a dramatic work in its own right, then replicating and re-shooting scenes from an earlier film is capable of infringing the earlier film (as distinct from the works appearing in it) if a substantial part is copied[7].

Copyright protection is not afforded to a film if, or to the extent that, it is a copy of another film[8].

Prior to the CDPA, the 1956 Act described 'films' as 'cinematograph films', an expression which carried a cumbersome definition. Films made before 1 June 1957 are not protected as cinematograph films at all, but as photographic works and dramatic works under the Copyright Act 1911. The law regarding old films can be complex and is beyond the scope of this *User's Guide*. Professional advice should be obtained when dealing with the copyright in such old films.

1   CDPA s 5B(1).
2   CDPA s 5A(2).
3   *Norowzian v Arks Ltd (No2) [2000] FSR 363, CA*, see also **paragraph 2.03**.
4   E.g. a still taken of the filmed image – see **paragraph 7.03**.
5   CDPA s 18(4).
6   CDPA s 5B(4); see below.
7   See **paragraph 8.06**.
8   CDPA s 5B(4).

Broadcasts

2.09 The CDPA, as amended by the 2003 Regulations, defines a 'broadcast' as:

'an electronic transmission of visual images, sounds or other information which—

(a)   is transmitted for simultaneous reception by members of the public and is capable of being lawfully received by them; or

(b)   is transmitted at a time determined solely by the person making the transmission for presentation to members of the public;

and which is not excepted by subsection (1A), and references to broadcasting shall be construed accordingly.

(1A) Excepted from the definition of 'broadcast' is any internet transmission unless it is—

    (a) a transmission taking place simultaneously on the internet and by other means;

    (b) a concurrent transmission of a live event, or

    (c) a transmission of recorded moving images or sounds forming part of a programme service offered by the person responsible for making the transmission, being a service in which programmes are transmitted at scheduled times determined by that person.'

Encrypted transmissions also constitute broadcasts, so long as the decoding equipment is available to members of the public by or with the authority of the person making the transmission or the person providing the contents of the transmission[1]. If the decoders are not made available to the public, then the transmission will not constitute a broadcast for the purposes of the CDPA.

A broadcast will not receive copyright protection if it infringes, or to the extent that it infringes, another broadcast[2].

The reception and immediate re-transmission of a broadcast is viewed as a separate broadcast to the one originally received[3].

The definition of 'broadcast' was substantially changed by the 2003 Regulations from that previously included in the CDPA. In order to give effect to the 2001 Directive, the CDPA no longer distinguishes a 'broadcast' (formerly meaning, in basic terms, a wireless transmission), from a 'cable programme service' (broadly, a wireline transmission). The 2003 Regulations removed the significance of this distinction, categorising both forms of transmission as 'communications to the public'.

The new definitions of 'broadcast' and 'broadcasting' relate to transmissions by any electronic means (wireless or wireline), provided that those transmissions are transmitted for simultaneous public reception or at a time determined by the broadcaster. So:

- True video-on-demand (VOD) services will therefore not be classified as broadcasts, since the user determines the time at which the transmission is made[4].

- Near on-demand services (whether provided by wireless or wireline means) appear most properly classified as broadcasts, since the service provider offers content over multiple channels at short intervals at a time determined by him[5].

- 'Enhanced' facilities included in broadcast streams such as multiple camera angles, drop down data streams or audio streams which are not truly 'interactive' features (given that they are usually broadcast simultaneously to all users as part of the primary transmission signal and individual streams then brought into view via user control of software in the set-top box) will constitute broadcasts for the purpose of the CDPA (as amended).

Content provided via websites will invariably be provided as a download or a stream.

Essentially, the CDPA now seeks to provide that only internet transmissions of conventional broadcast character will come within the definition of 'broadcast'. This means that the approach ensures that static web pages will not come within the scope of the concept but that copyright can subsist in images streamed via the internet at times determined by the person responsible for making the transmission.

Downloads occur when a user requests a transfer of, say, a music or video file sitting on a web server (i.e. an 'on demand' transfer) and will not therefore constitute a 'broadcast' for the purposes of the CDPA (as amended). However, 'streams' may or may not be classified as broadcasts. Streams (i.e. simultaneous display and downloads) occur when music or video is requested from a webpage and begins to play soon after the data transfer is initiated. The user's device is playing the content, essentially, as it receives it (although commonly part of the clip will be temporarily stored in the user's computer to 'buffer' against, for example, variations in transmission speed which might otherwise cause interruptions in the playout of the stream) rather than waiting for the entire clip to be transferred, and there is never a copy of the entire clip residing on the user's device as played parts are stored in transient memory rather than on any hard disk or other media.

An internet-delivered stream will constitute a broadcast for the purposes of the definition if the stream is delivered at scheduled times determined by the service provider. So:

- A real-time webcast where a user requesting the webcast joins the clip half-way through would be a broadcast for the purpose of a definition. So, if a user joining at 10.30pm a webcast of a music or sporting event which started at 10.00pm does not see the first 30 minutes of the event, that transmission will still constitute a broadcast.
- This should be contrasted with a stream that, when initiated, plays back music or a video clip and begins from the start 'on demand', which will not constitute a broadcast.

The words 'or other information' in the definition of 'broadcast' are designed to cover additional information included in the broadcast signal – for example, teletext transmissions or closed captioning. Other information might also include any 'pseudo-interactive' content, such as the 'enhanced' facilities described above.

Where users make available infringing copies of audio or video material via peer-to-peer services, their actions typically represent the provision of download facilities to others, and they would be treated in the same way as the operator of a traditional website hosting such content. This situation is complicated by more advanced peer-to-peer networks which permit a user to obtain a particular file more efficiently by copying different parts from different users simultaneously. However, despite technical differences in how different peer-to-peer systems facilitate the making available of a file to a very large number of other users, they involve individual transfers on-demand, which would not constitute broadcasting. A possible exception to this relates to the emerging technology of peer-to-peer internet radio and television, where users on the network make their spare bandwidth available for 'live' transmissions. Newer peer-to-peer software applications[6] also raise difficult issues. Where peer-to-peer technologies permit 'simultaneous' transmission by the internet and other means (e.g. television), or the 'concurrent' transmission of a live event, this raises arguments that such services may themselves amount to a 'broadcast'. It is likely that very great consideration will need to be given to the correct meaning of 'concurrent' or 'simultaneous' in the context of such services.

1   CDPA s 6(2).
2   CDPA s 6(6).
3   CDPA s 6(5A).
4   See **paragraph 7.07** and, generally, **Chapter 26**.
5   See **paragraph 7.07** and, generally, **Chapter 26**.
6   E.g. Coolstream, which allows users to upload files in streaming mode.

Cable programmes

2.10   The 2003 Regulations removed the previous definition of 'cable programme' included in the CDPA since, in the words of the Copyright Directorate of the Patent Office 'it is felt that there is no need to protect a "cable programme" as a species of copyright work other than where it is a "broadcast" as redefined, since any material included in an interactive cable service would seem already to be protected under other headings, i.e. as a literary, artistic, dramatic or musical work, sound recording or film.'[1]

1   Consultation Paper on implementation of the Directive in the UK, Patents Office, DTI, 7 August 2002.

Published editions of works [1]

2.11 Section 8 of the CDPA defines 'published edition' as meaning, in the context of copyright in the typographical arrangement of a published edition, 'a published edition of the whole or any part of one or more literary, dramatic or musical works'[2].

This definition expressly excludes editions which reproduce the typographical arrangements of previous editions of the same work[3] (i.e. duplicates of earlier editions). Without this exclusion, there could be perpetual copyright in a typographical arrangement because a new copyright period would commence with the publication of each new edition.

Because there is copyright in the typographical arrangements of published editions, publishers are able to sue for unauthorised copying of the published editions of literary, dramatic and musical works which do not themselves have copyright protection (because, for example, their copyright period has expired) where the typographical arrange-ments of the published editions of such works are themselves still in copyright. This is of particular importance to the publishers of novels, music, compositions etc where the works themselves are out of copy-right.

In one case, Marks and Spencer copied and distributed a significant number of press cuttings to its staff. The owner of the typographical arrangement in the cuttings, the Newspaper Licensing Agency, claimed copyright infringement. It was held that when considering typographi-cal arrangements of articles in a newspaper, the phrase 'typographical arrangement of a published edition' referred to the whole newspaper, not individual articles and that, in context, M&S had not copied a substantial part of the work[4].

1   For a history of typography, see Tariq Baloch, 'Typography in Law: From Mechanics to Aesthetics' [2001] Ent LR Issue 3.
2   CDPA s 8(1).
3   CDPA s 8(2).
4   *Newspaper Licensing Agency Ltd v Marks & Spencer plc [2000] NLJR 900, CA.*

Only 'works' protected

2.12 It is essential, when considering any copyright problem, to decide first whether the material which is being copied is within one of the categories of work set out in the CDPA.

The case of *Tavener Rutledge Ltd v Trexapalm Ltd*[1] illustrates the essential principle that copyright can only exist in a work which can be brought within one of the categories defined in the CDPA. Tavener Rutledge sold lollipops under the name 'Kojak pops' for about two years without any permission from the owners of the Kojak television series. Trexapalm Ltd were intending to sell lollipops under the brand name 'Kojak Lollies', having been granted an exclusive licence from the owners of the television series to use that name. Tavener Rutledge sought an injunction restraining the passing off of Trexapalm's lollipops as those of Tavener Rutledge. Mr Justice Walton granted the injunction and in his judgment said that although in the USA there might be rights in invented names or fictional characters, English law did not recognise any such copyright. Therefore, one could not look to copyright to protect the use of such a name. It should be noted that the law of passing off and/or trade mark infringement may afford protection in cases where copyright law does not apply because the material does not come within the definition of a work[2].

1   [1977] RPC 275.
2   See **Chapter 5** for an analysis of 'passing off'.

Real life events

2.13   There is no copyright in real life events, before they are reduced to writing or some other material form (such as the record of the telling of a story). However there *is* copyright in the *way* in which they are reduced into writing. So, in the case of *Harman Pictures NV v Osborne*[1], it was held that, although the events contained in a book by Cecil Woodham-Smith, entitled *The Reason Why* (an account of events surrounding the charge of the Light Brigade) were common to both that book and to John Osborne's screenplay for the film *The Charge of the Light Brigade*, there was, nevertheless, an infringement of the copyright in the book by the screenplay because the screenplay used the same characters and incidents in much the same order and arrangement as they appeared in the book. The case does not show that copyright exists in events, or that because someone has written down events he has a 'copyright' in those events. Copyright arose because of the *way* in which the events had been recorded into material form, which the court held had been copied by John Osborne. It follows that when real life events are resolved into material form, the result will be entitled to copyright but not the events themselves, as matters of fact[2].

Similar issues arise in the context of news reporting[3].

1   [1967] 2 All ER 324. See also *Ravenscroft v Herbert and New English Library Limited [1980] RPC193* and *Poznanski v London Film Production Ltd [1937] MacG Cop Cas (1936–45) 107* and **paragraph 8.04** below.
2   See also **paragraph 8.09**.
3   See **paragraph 18.05**.

Format rights

2.14   A programme format is essentially the formula by which a (usually episodic) television programme may be reproduced. The 'format' consists of the unifying elements of a series which are distinctive to the show and which are repeated from episode to episode. Common examples include game shows, chat shows and situation comedies. In the past, courts have been reluctant to extend protection to formats[1]. Notwithstanding that, in fact 'format rights' are commonly traded in the television industry. The popularity of 'reality TV' and the trade of such formats between UK and US-based companies has, in recent years, led to debates about the legal protectability of the formats of such shows as 'Survivor', 'I'm a Celebrity ...', 'Pop Idol' and 'X Factor'[2].

The chances of a protectable copyright work existing in a format are enhanced where the format creator maintains a detailed record of the format. The key will be whether the format is sufficiently detailed and cohesive to be capable of being performed. If so, the format may receive protection as a dramatic work. Case law in other jurisdictions has shown that some courts have been prepared to extend copyright protection to formats. In Holland, for example, the Dutch Supreme Court held that the format for 'Survivor' was capable of copyright protection, albeit that the claimants failed to show that it was infringed by the format of 'Big Brother'[3].

In Brazil, Endemol were successful in establishing that TV SBT's show 'Cas Dos Artistas' ('The Artist's House') infringed its format of Big Brother. The judge pointed to the 'whopping similarity' of the formats, after Endemol had provided significant information on its own format to TV SBT during contractual negotiations.

Of course, these cases are not binding authority in the English courts, and although they do demonstrate that certain jurisdictions are more sympathetic to the protection of formats than the court in *Green v Broadcasting Corporation of New Zealand*[4] the same is not true for the English courts, where Laddie J recently cited with approval the dicta of Lord Bridge in *Green*:

> 'The protection which copyright gives creates a monopoly and there must be certainty in the subject matter of such copyright in order to avoid injustice to the rest of the world.'[5]

Even if copyright protection is not available, it may (depending on the circumstances) be possible for the format creator to take action for a breach of confidentiality or passing off[6]. In practice, when format rights are traded, this is usually done through agreements which convey a variety of rights: including rights to confidential information, trade mark licences, 'know how', and contractual undertakings not to trade similar formats or cooperate with similar programmes within the same jurisdiction.

In March and April 1996 the Patent Office issued consultative documents proposing the introduction of copyright protection for the scheme or plan (i.e. a format) for a series of programmes recorded in a copyright work or works. The protection would only arise when the scheme or plan was 'sufficiently elaborated'. However, after assessing the outcome of a full consultative process, the Patent Office concluded that there was not sufficient industry support for the proposal and that the restricted acts of copying and adaptation together with the protection afforded by the laws of confidentiality and passing off provided sufficient protection for programme formats.[7]

1   See **paragraph 2.03**.
2   For a recent discussion, see 'Format Rights, Not so Simple for Simon' [2005] Ent Law Review, 16(2) 32–34. See also *Celador Productions Ltd v Melville, Boone v ITV Network and another, Baccini v Celador Productions Ltd & Others [2004] EWHC 2362* (re Who Wants to be a Millionaire), *Miles v ITV Networks Ltd and another [2003] All ER(D) 145* (re 'Dream Street').
3   *Castaway Television Productions Ltd and Planet 24 Productions Ltd in dispute with Endemol.*
4   See **paragraph 2.03**.
5   *IPC Media Ltd v Highbury-SPL Publishing Ltd [2004] EWHC 2984 (Ch).*
6   See **Chapter 5.**
7   For a further discussion of format rights, see Shelley Lane and Richard McD Bridge, 'The Protection of Formats under English Law', Parts 1 and 2, [1990] 3 Ent LR and 4 Ent LR and Peter Smith, 'Format Rights: Opportunity Knocks' [1991] 3 Ent LR.

Image personality rights and copyright distinguished

2.15   As celebrities have sought increasing levels of control over the exploitation of their image for commercial purposes, more focus has been placed on the phenomenon of 'image' or 'personality' rights. Unlike copyright, there is not a high degree of harmonisation between different national laws on the issue of whether 'image rights' per se are capable of protection. In England, for example, they go largely unrecognised[1]. If I own the photograph of a celebrity, I am free to exploit that photograph, provided that in doing so I do not infringe a right of privacy[2], engage in passing off[3], infringe a registered trademark or otherwise engage in misleading advertising.

My ability to exploit that photograph derives from my ownership of the copyright in the image. Copyright will subsist in a representation of the image of a celebrity as an artistic work[4]. If the image is taken from a photograph of the celebrity, then the first owner of copyright will be the photographer responsible for the picture, or their employer if they are an employee and the work is created in the course of their employment.[5] If the image is taken from a drawing of the celebrity, then the artist responsible for the drawing will be first owner of copyright in the image (again, unless they are an employee, in which case the employer is first owner of copyright).

1   For a discussion of image rights generally, see **paragraph 5.14**.
2   For a discussion of privacy, see **paragraph 5.07**.
3   See **paragraph 5.07 et seq**.
4   See **paragraph 2.06**.
5   See **paragraph 10.03**.

Public policy and the denial of protection

2.16   Since copyright is a property right conferred by statute, if a work qualifies for protection in accordance with the statute, public policy will not intervene to deny the existence of copyright, notwithstanding that the work may not be particularly meritorious[1]. The courts have however, recently utilised the language of public policy in order to deny copyright protection to the 'business logic' of a computer program where that logic had been followed, albeit that no textual copying of the program itself had taken place. The court held that 'as a matter of policy, to permit the 'business logic' of a program to attract protection through the literary copyright afforded to the program itself was an unjustifiable extension of copyright protection'[2].

Quite apart from the principles of copyright, the courts have an inherent jurisdiction to refuse to *enforce* copyright, where to do so would run contrary to public policy. The CDPA provides that 'nothing in this Part affects any rule of law preventing or restricting the enforcement of copyright, on grounds of public interest or otherwise'[3]. The courts have from time to time used this jurisdiction to deny copyright protection to works which are considered libellous, immoral, obscene, scandalous or irreligious, but have proved unwilling to allow public interest to be used as a general defence to copyright infringement[4]. So, where *The Sun* newspaper printed photographs taken from the security cameras of premises owed by Mr Al Fayed (showing the movements of Princess Diana and Dodi Fayed before their death) without authorisation, as part of a story which intended to convey that Mr Al Fayed had invented falsehoods about the events preceding their deaths, it was held that *The Sun* could not avoid copyright infringement by arguing there was a public interest in exposing those alleged falsehoods[5].

A work should also receive copyright protection, notwithstanding that the copyrights of others were infringed in making it[6]. Protecting an infringing work in this way may be advantageous to the owner of the work which has been infringed, since he may be entitled to an account of profits from the sales of the infringing work[7]. A typical example would be a sound recording which uses examples taken from other sound recordings without the authority of the copyright owners of those recordings.

1 See the *Hyde Park Residence* case below.
2 *Navitaire Inc v Easyjet Airline Co and another [2004] Ch D 30/7/2004.* See also **paragraph 7.03**.
3 CDPA s 171(3).
4 E.g. *Stockdale v Onwhyn (1826) 5 B & C 173.*
5 *Hyde Park Residence Ltd v Yelland [2000] 3 WLR 215, CA.* This decision has been met with criticism (see Robert Burrell, 'Defending the Public Interest' [2000] EIPR, issue 9, for an interesting survey of relevant case law).
6 *Redwood Music Ltd v Chappell & Co Ltd [1982] RPC 109.*
7 See **paragraph 8.12**.

Chapter 3
Originality

Generally

3.01 If a literary, dramatic, musical or artistic work is to be entitled to copyright it must be original[1]. Originality in this context refers to the way in which the work is reduced to a material form and not to the originality of the *idea* upon which the work is based. So, in *University of London Press Ltd v Universal Tutorial Press Ltd*[2], Mr Justice Peterson said:

> 'The word "original" does not in this connection mean that the work must be the expression of original or inventive thought. Copyright Acts are not concerned with the originality of ideas, but with the expression of thought, and, in the case of "literary work", with the expression of thought in print or writing. The originality which is required relates to the expression of the thought. But the Act[3] does not require that the expression must be in an original or novel form, but that the work must not be copied from another work – that it should originate from the author.'

Again, in *Bookmakers Afternoon Greyhound Services Ltd v Wilf Gilbert (Staffs) Ltd*[4], Mr Justice Aldous said that:

> 'It is settled law that the word "original" does not require original or inventive thought but only that the work should not be copied and should originate from the author'.

The test frequently cited by courts for determining originality in this sense is that of 'skill and labour':

> 'It is the product of the labour, skill and capital of one man which must not be appropriated by another, not the elements, the raw material, if we may use the expression, upon which the labour and

skill and capital of the first had been expended. To secure copyright for the product it is necessary that labour, skill and capital should be expended sufficiently to impart to the product some quality or character which the raw material did not possess, and which differentiates the product from the raw material.'

(Per Lord Atkinson, *MacMillan & Co v K & J Cooper*)[5].

Unfortunately, however, there is no simple test to determine the extent of the skill and labour which must be devoted to a literary, dramatic, musical or artistic work in order to confer copyright protection upon it: 'It is a question of degree and will depend on the work produced and all the circumstances of the case'[6].

So, for example, in the case of 'compilation' literary works, originality has been considered 'a matter of degree depending on the amount of skill, judgment or labour that has been involved in making the compilation'[7].

In the context of databases, the CDPA[8] now provides that: 'a literary work consisting of a database is original if, and only if, by reason of the selection or arrangement of the contents of the database the database constitutes the author's own intellectual creation'[9]. This requirement for 'intellectual creation' signals a departure from traditional tests of originality[10], reflecting the European tradition of not offering copyright protection to databases which do not have literary or artistic merit[11]. There is no judicial consideration as to whether or not this new test for the originality of databases will prove to be onerous. Some writers have noted that similar language in the Software Directive[12] was not included in the regulations which implemented the Directive into UK law. However, it is safer to assume that some higher degree of originality is required in connection with databases than is necessary to establish protectability in the context of a non-database-related copying of work.

Copyright has been found in football pools, timetables, lists of stock exchange prices[13], race cards[14] and mathematical tables[15] (to give but a few examples of cases where skill or labour has been applied to the compilation and organisation of information which is widely available). However, if such work is found to be a 'database', it will not qualify for copyright protection unless it meets the higher degree of originality test referred to above.

In the context of artistic works, the standard has been set differently. In *Interlego AG v Tyco Industries Inc*[16] Lord Oliver of Aylmerton, comparing the authorities concerning literary works (particularly compilations) and artistic works, stated:

'Originality in the context of literary copyright has been said in several well known cases to depend upon the degree of skill, labour and judgment involved in preparing a compilation ... skill, judgment or labour is likely to be decisive in the case of compilations. To apply that, however, as a universal test of originality in all copyright cases is not only unwarranted by the context in which the observations were made but palpably erroneous. Take the simplest case of artistic copyright, a painting or a photograph. It takes great skill, judgment and labour to produce a good copy by painting or to produce an enlarged photograph from a positive print, but no one would reasonably contend that the copy of the painting or enlargement was an "original" artistic work in which the copier is entitled to claim copyright. Skill, labour or judgment merely in the process of copying cannot confer originality'.

In the case of artistic works, the fact that a drawing is simple will not disqualify it for protection as an artistic work. In *British Northrop Ltd v Texteam Blackburn Ltd*[17] Megarry J had to consider whether drawings of such basic items as a rivet, screw, metal bar, washer etc were capable of being 'original' works. He said:

'A drawing which is simply traced from another drawing is not an original artistic work: a drawing which is made without any copying from anything originates with the artist ... It may indeed be that some thing may be drawn which cannot fairly be called a diagram or a drawing of any kind: a single straight line drawn with the aid of a ruler would not seem to me a very promising subject for copyright. But apart from cases of such barren and naked simplicity as that, I should be slow to exclude drawings from copyright on the mere score of simplicity. I do not think that the mere fact that a drawing is of an elementary and commonplace article makes it too simple to be the subject to copyright ... If simplicity were a disqualification, at some point there would come enough complexity to qualify. It is not that I am unable to see exactly where the [1956 Act] draws the line: it is that I cannot see that there is any intention to draw any line at all. Accordingly, I reject the defendants' contentions on this score.'

However, where a drawing contains only limited variations from an earlier drawing, the Courts have proved cautious in affording protection. In *Interlego AG v Tyco Industries Inc*[18] Interlego sought to establish that small but technically important additions to design drawings created a new originality. This was rejected by the Privy Council, which held that the test for originality would only be satisfied if the new drawings were visually and significantly different or differed materially in their visual aspects from previous drawings. Lord Oliver of Aylmerton said:

> 'What is important about a drawing is what is visually significant and the re-drawing of an existing drawing with a few minimal visual alterations does not make it an original artistic work, however much labour and skill may have gone into the process of reproduction ...'

The fact that a drawing is substantially derived from earlier drawings does not deprive the new drawing of originality *per se*. In the recent case of *SPE International Ltd v Professional Preparation Contractors (UK) Ltd*[19] it was held that although a substantial part of a drawing incorporated work from an earlier drawing, a substantial part was not so derived, and the differences in the new drawing did involve the expenditure of skill and effort necessary to confer on the new drawing (when considered as a whole) a quality which made it different from earlier drawings and was sufficiently original to deserve copyright protection.

More recently, it has been suggested that the dictum of Lord Oliver in *Interlego* should be confined to the subject matter of that case: technical drawings. In *Sawkins v Hyperon Records Ltd*[20], the Court considered the issue of copyright in musical works. The plaintiff had created new 'performing editions' of several works which were themselves out of copyright. He registered his new editions with MCPS and PRS, and when Hyperon Records wanted to use his editions on a CD format, he sued for copyright and moral rights infringement. The Court of Appeal upheld Dr Sawkin's claims, emphasising that the test for originality is that the work 'originates' from the efforts of the author, as distinct from being 'slavishly copied' from another work. This is essentially a restatement of the 'sweat of the brow' test favoured by earlier case law[21].

Originality in the context of musical works is considered in further detail elsewhere in this *User's Guide*[22].

It is worth noting that there is no requirement for originality in the case of sound recordings, films, broadcasts, cable programmes and typographical arrangements of published editions. This is because they usually all involve some other act or work. For example, a sound recording will be a record of another work (a literary, dramatic or musical) or of a non-copyright sound (such as a bell ringing). Literary, dramatic, musical and artistic works (which are not adaptations), on the other hand, may exist independently.

1   CDPA s 1.
2   [1916] 2 Ch 601.

3   I.e. the Copyright Act 1911.
4   [1994] FRS 723.
5   (1923) LR 51 Ind App 109, PC.
6   *Greyhound Services* case, above. For an interesting discussion in relation to original-
     ity in relation to the reconstruction of ancient texts, see Michael D Birnhack, 'The
     Dead Sea Scrolls Case: Who is the author' [2001] EIPR, Issue 3.
7   Per Lord Reid, *Ladbroke (Football) Ltd v William Hill (Football) Ltd [1964] 1WLR
     273 at 277, HL.*
8   As amended by the 1997 Regulations.
9   CDPA s 3A(2).
10   See *University of London Press Ltd* above which tended to see originality as
     meaning 'not a copy', rather than 'an intellectual creation'.
11   For further discussion of databases, see **paragraph 2.02** and **Chapter 16**.
12   Council Directive 91/250/EEC of 14 May 1991 on the legal protection of computer
     programs.
13   *Exchange Telegraph Co Ltd v Gregory & Co [1896] 1 QB 147.*
14   *Bookmakers' Afternoon Greyhound Services Ltd v Wilf Gilbert (Staffordshire) Ltd
     [1994] FSR 723.*
15   *Express Newspapers v Liverpool Daily Post and Echo [1985] FSR 306.*
16   [1988] RPC 343.
17   [1976] RPC 344.
18   [1989] AC 217.
19   [2002] EWHC 881.
20   [2005] EWCA Civ 565; see **paragraph 22.04**.
21   For a detailed analysis of this case see Richard Munden's commentary at IP & T
     Expert Commentary, 2005 [75].
22   See **paragraph 22.04**.

Titles and names

3.02   The title of a book, film or song will not have copyright
protection in the UK unless it is so elaborate that sufficient skill and
labour must have been involved in its invention so as to allow it to
qualify as a literary work in its own right[1].

It was held, in a case which decided that the name 'Exxon' was not
entitled to copyright protection, that for a name or title to have
copyright protection: 'it must have qualities or characteristics in itself,
if such a thing is possible, which would justify its recognition as an
original literary work rather than merely as an invented word'[2].

In *Rose v Information Services Ltd*[3], Mr Rose, the publisher of 'The
Lawyer's Diary', claimed he owned copyright in the title 'The Lawyer's
Diary 1986' which was infringed by the words 'Law Diary 1986'.
Dismissing the claim, Hoffmann J held that the words 'The Lawyer's
Diary' 'were a simple and accurate description of the product. They
were not a literary work of originality which qualified for literary
protection'. He said that if the plaintiff was entitled to copyright
protection it would be hard to see how the defendant could describe its

product in a commercially acceptable form without being said to infringe the plaintiff's rights. In effect the plaintiff would have acquired a monopoly of part of the English language.

1 See **paragraphs 3.01 and 5.08**.
2 *Exxon Corpn v Exxon Insurance Consultants International Ltd [1982] Ch 119, CA.*
3 [1987] FSR 254.

Photographs

3.03 Photographs present particular problems in the context of originality. The CDPA treats photographs as artistic works irrespective of their artistic quality[1]. A photographic enlargement of an existing photograph is not entitled to copyright protection in its own right if it is merely a copy (since it will lack originality)[2], but if a person takes a photograph of an identical scene to that shown in another photograph, the second photograph is entitled to copyright in just the same way as the first photograph. The test for originality in a photograph will be low, and will turn on whether requisite skill and labour have been invested in factors such as the way in which the shot is composed, the angle at which the camera is pointing at the scene, the setting of the aperture and the calculation of the exposure.

The question of originality becomes more complex when considering photographs of other copyright works (e.g. paintings). The traditional view has been that, provided skill and labour is expended in taking a photograph, copyright will not be denied because the subject of the photograph is another work:

'All photographs are copies of some object, such as a painting or a statue, and it seems to me that a photograph taken from a picture is an original photograph'[3].

One case, decided in the US, casts doubt on this traditional view. In *Bridgeman Art Library Ltd v Corel Corpn*[4] the New York District Court (Southern District) held that the photograph of a painting which was 'in the public domain' which had been taken in such a way as to faithfully reproduce the painting lacked sufficient originality to be protected as a copyright work. However, at least one recent UK case suggests that the UK courts will not follow the lead set by *Bridgeman*. *Antiquesportfolio.com plc v Rodney Finch & Co*[5] concerned copyright in photographic images of three-dimensional objects (i.e. antiques as opposed to paintings). The judge held the photographs were original and attracted copyright protection[6].

1 CDPA s 4.

2   See the dicta of Lord Oliver referred to in **paragraph 3.01**.
3   *Graves' Case (1869) 4 LR QB 715.*
4   36 F Supp 2d [9] and 25F Supp 2d 421 (SDN4) (1998).
5   [2001] FSR 345, [2000] All ER CD 950.
6   For a discussion of this and the *Bridgeman* case, see Simon Stokes, 'Creativity Challenges Copyright', Managing IP Feb 2002.

Abridgements and arrangements

3.04   There can be copyright in the abridgement of another copyright work, where the abridgement itself involves skill and labour, even though no original thought in terms of the content has been added[1]. Similarly, there can be copyright in the arrangement of a piece of music[2].

1   *Macmillan & Co v Cooper (1923) 40 TLR 186, PC.*
2   *Redwood Music Ltd v Chappell & Co Ltd [1982] RPC 109.*

Independent creation

3.05   Copyright does not carry a monopoly right over an idea, merely a right not to have a copyright work copied. So, if for example two people, acting independently of each other, produce identical directories, those directories will equally be entitled to copyright. Both works will be original in the sense that they owe their existence to the skill and labour of their compilers.

Identical subject matter

3.06   Similarly, if two different radio producers record a concert using their own equipment and quite independently of the other, there will be copyright in both recordings although the recordings will probably be identical in all material respects. On the other hand, a *copy* of one of those recordings would not in itself have copyright[1]. Another example is that of an artist who paints a true copy of another painting. The copy infringes the copyright of the original painting and the copy does not itself acquire a new copyright, because it lacks the quality of originality[2].

1   See **paragraph 2.07**.
2   See **paragraph 3.01**, the position is different however in relation to adaptations, see **paragraph 7.08**.

Chapter 4

Qualification for protection and international copyright

Qualification

General

4.01 For copyright to subsist in any category of work it is necessary for the qualification requirements of the CDPA to be satisfied[1]. A work which is entitled to copyright protection in another country and which has passed all the other tests entitling it to copyright protection in the UK will nevertheless be unprotected under UK copyright law unless it meets the qualification requirements of the CDPA.

In brief, there are three types of qualification, being qualification by reference to:

- the author; or
- the country in which the work was first published; or
- in the case of a broadcast, the country from which the broadcast was made[2].

1 These are to be found in Chapter IX, ss 153–162 of the CDPA; see **paragraphs 4.02–4.04**.
2 See **paragraph 4.07**.

Author: 'material time'

4.02 For the work to qualify for copyright protection the author must have been a qualifying person 'at the material time'[1]. What constitutes the 'material time' will depend upon the kind of work involved. The material time:

- *for unpublished literary, dramatic, musical or artistic works*, is when the work was made or, if the making of the work extends over a period, a substantial part of that period[2];

- *for published works*, is when the work was first published or, if the author died before that time, immediately before his death[3];
- *for sound recordings and films,* is when the sound recording or film is made[4];
- *for broadcasts,* is when the broadcast is made[5];
- *for published editions*, is when first published[6].

The question of when a literary, dramatic or musical work is made is considered elsewhere in this *User's Guide*[7]. The CDPA does not define when artistic works, sound recordings, films or broadcasts are made and therefore normal rules of construction will apply in respect of those categories of work.

1 CDPA s 154.
2 CDPA s 154(4)(a).
3 CDPA s 154(4)(b).
4 CDPA s 154(5)(a).
5 CDPA s 154(5)(b).
6 CDPA s 154(5)(d).
7 See **paragraph 2.05**.

Author: 'qualifying person'

4.03 The author of the work must be a 'qualifying person' at the material time. A 'qualifying person' is defined in some detail in the CDPA[1]. In brief, it means a British citizen, a British Dependent Territories citizen, a British National (Overseas), a British Overseas citizen, a British subject or a British protected person within the meaning of the British Nationality Act 1981.

The expression also includes individuals domiciled or resident in the UK or another country to which the CDPA has been extended[2]. Bodies incorporated under the laws of the UK or another country to which the provisions of the CDPA have been extended, also come within the definition[3].

In the case of literary, dramatic, musical and artistic works, with certain exceptions[4] the author must be a natural person (as opposed to a legal person, such as a limited company). A 'legal person' may be the first copyright *owner* of such a work (because the copyright owner of a literary, dramatic, music or artistic work or a film made by an employee in the course of his or her employment, is the employer subject to any agreement to the contrary)[5], but for the purpose of deciding whether a work qualifies for copyright protection by reference to its author, it is necessary to consider the nationality, residence or domicile of the first *author* not the first owner. So, even if the employing body corporate does not qualify, the work will be entitled to protection in the UK if the actual author qualifies.

The question of authorship is more complex in the context of other categories of work (i.e. sound recordings, films, broadcasts and typographical arrangements). English law has traditionally protected the 'maker' of these works (i.e. the person who assumes the financial risk in making the work) although, as the flavour of UK law is effected by the implementation of EU Directives, this position is changing[6].

1 CDPA s 154(1)(a) et seq.
2 CDPA s 154(1)(b), see **paragraph 4.08** below.
3 CDPA s 154(1)(c).
4 Discussed further at **Chapter 9**.
5 CDPA s 11(2).
6 See **Chapter 10** for a fuller discussion of authorship issues.

Qualification in country of first publication

4.04 All types of work, except broadcasts, qualify for copyright protection if they are *first published*[1]:

- in the UK; or
- in another country to which the relevant provisions of the CDPA have been *extended*[2]; or
- in another country to which the CDPA has been *applied* as regards that type of work[3].

A work will not be treated as 'first published' in a country which is not listed above simply because it is published elsewhere at the same time as it is published in one of the listed countries[4]. However, since it may be difficult to establish where publication first happened if a work is published in swift succession in several countries, the CDPA provides that publication will be deemed to be simultaneous if it takes place within 30 days following the first publication. So, if a work is published in the UK or another country to which the CDPA extends or has been applied within 30 days of its publication elsewhere, the publication will be regarded as simultaneous and the work will be entitled to copyright protection in the UK.

1 CDPA s 155.
2 **Paragraph 4.08** below.
3 **Paragraph 4.09** below.
4 CDPA s 155(3).

The meaning of 'publication'

4.05 So, qualification for copyright protection in the UK by reference to the country of first publication applies to literary, dramatic, musical and artistic works, sound recordings, films and published editions. What does 'publication' mean for these purposes?

'Publication' is defined in the CDPA as 'the issue of copies to the public'[1]. This definition applies to all categories of works except that a separate meaning is applicable in the context of 'the publication right'[2]. It is worth noting that in the case of literary, dramatic, musical and artistic works, publication specifically includes making available to the public by means of an electronic retrieval system[3]. A typical example of an electronic retrieval system is an on-line database.

A publication 'which is merely colourable and not intended to satisfy the reasonable requirements of the public' does not constitute publication. In *Francis, Day and Hunter v Feldman & Co* [4] sheet music of the song 'You Made Me Love You (I Didn't Want To Do It)' was printed in the USA. A few copies were sent to London and six were put on sale in a shop on Charing Cross Road within 30 days of the first copies being put on sale in New York (thus apparently satisfying the 30-day simultaneous publication rule referred to at **paragraph 4.04**). The court had to decide whether the copies offered for sale in London constituted publication. It held that the intention was to satisfy the reasonable demands of the public and therefore the song had been duly published in the UK. In each case the intention of the publisher, not necessarily the number of copies that are issued to the public, is important. The song had not been advertised and was not known in London, so six copies was sufficient to satisfy the reasonable demands of the public.

There is a special provision for architecture: the construction of a building is to be treated as publication of a work of architecture or an artistic work incorporated in a building[5].

1   CDPA s 175(1)(*a*).
2   See **paragraphs 6.20** et seq.
3   CDPA s 175(1)(*b*).
4   [1914] 2 Ch 728, CA.
5   CDPA s 175(3).

Acts not constituting publication

4.06   The CDPA specifically provides that some acts do not constitute publication[1]. These can be summarised as follows:

- *literary, dramatic and musical works*: performance or communication to the public of the work (otherwise than for the purposes of an electronic retrieval system)[2];
- *artistic works*: exhibition, the issue to the public of copies of a graphic work representing (or photographs of), a work of architecture in the form of a building or a model for a building, a sculpture

or a work of artistic craftsmanship, the issue to the public of copies of a film including the work, communication to the public of the work (otherwise than for the purposes of an electronic retrieval system)[3];

- *sound recordings and films*: playing or showing the work in public, or the communication of the work to the public[4].

1   CDPA s 175(4).
2   CDPA s 175(4)(a).
3   CDPA s 175(4)(b).
4   CDPA s 175(4)(c).

Broadcasts – qualification for copyright protection

4.07 Broadcasts qualify for copyright protection if they are made from or sent from the UK or another country to which the CDPA is extended or applied[1].

1   For further consideration of this issue see **paragraph 4.09**.

Extension of the CDPA overseas

4.08 The CDPA is extended to England and Wales, Scotland and Northern Ireland[1]. It has been further extended by Orders in Council to the Isle of Man. Guernsey and Jersey have now introduced their own Copyright Ordinances.

1   CDPA s 157.

Application of the CDPA overseas

4.09 Provision is made in the CDPA to enable the Government to *apply* the copyright protection afforded by Part I of the CDPA to works and people from countries to which the CDPA does not otherwise extend[1]. This is achieved by an 'Order in Council', implemented by statutory instrument. Orders need not apply protection uniformly to all classes of work. Indeed, the CDPA requires that an Order should *not* be extended to particular countries or classes of work unless the country in question is a member of the EU and/or one of the copyright conventions to which the UK is a party[2], except where satisfied that the country in question does or will give adequate protection to the class of works the Order relates to[3]. The intention is to give protection to works by authors from or first published in countries which give reciprocal protection to British works.

The latest such Order is the Copyright (Application to Other Countries) Order 1999[4], as amended by the Copyright (Application to Other Countries) Order 2003, and this Order applies protection to a variety of works from a number of different countries:

- First, the Order provides protection to literary, dramatic, musical and artistic works, films and published editions originating from Convention countries, EU member states, and other countries which are deemed to give adequate protection under their laws. The list of territories affected includes virtually all countries in the world.

- Secondly, the Order protects sound recordings originating from the same list of countries referred to above, although protection is excluded for the playing of the work in public, or the broadcast of the work, unless the country of origin is a signatory of the Rome Convention[5], an EU member state, or other country deemed to give adequate protection under its laws. Notably, the USA is excluded from protection, although this will change should the USA become a signatory to the Rome Convention.

- Thirdly, the Order protects broadcasts originating from a number of listed countries, which include the parties to the Rome Convention, the European Agreement on the Protection of Television Broadcasts and WTO/TRIPS[6], EU member states, and other countries which are deemed to give adequate protection under their laws. Broadcasts are not uniformly protected in all such countries. In a small number of countries (i.e. Singapore, Indonesia and the EU member states) protection is also extended to cable re-transmissions.

The CDPA also makes similar provision to extend rights in performances available under Part II of the CDPA to other countries[7]. The latest Order made under this section extends protection to the parties to the Rome Convention and the WTO/TRIPS Agreement[8].

This Order will be either replaced or amended by subsequent Orders adding or deleting countries to reflect membership of the international treaties, conventions and agreements which regulate international copyright protection.

1   CDPA s 159.
2   'I.e. Convention countries', as to which see **paragraphs 4.12** et seq.
3   CDPA s 159(3).
4   SI 1999/1751.
5   Cmnd 2425 – see **paragraph 4.17**.
6   See **paragraph 4.17**.
7   CDPA s 208.

8   The Performances (Reciprocal Protection) (Convention Countries) Order 1999,
    SI 1999/1752; see **paragraph 4.17**.

Denial of copyright protection

4.10   If a country fails to give adequate protection to British works,
then an Order in Council may be passed which restricts the copyright
protection in the UK afforded to works of authors connected with that
country[1].

1   CDPA s 160.

Territorial waters, continental shelf, ships, aircraft and hovercraft

4.11   The CDPA treats the territorial waters of the UK as part of the
UK. Things done in the UK sector of the continental shelf on structures
or vessels which are 'present there for purposes directly connected with
the exploration of the seabed or subsoil or the exploitation of the
natural resources' are deemed to have been done in the UK. So, if an oil
rig which is in British territorial waters is used for the duplication of
unauthorised video cassettes for commercial exploitation, or as a base
for a radio station which broadcasts without the broadcaster obtaining
licences for the broadcasts, there will be a breach of UK copyright
which could be the subject of civil and criminal proceedings in the
UK[1].

Similarly, the CDPA applies to things done on British-registered
ships, aircraft or hovercraft as it applies to things done in the UK,
wherever they are located[2].

1   CDPA s 161.
2   CDPA s 162.

International copyright: the Berne Convention and the Universal Copyright Convention

4.12   Copyright is a product of national law. It follows that 'international copyright' as such does not exist. There are as many potential
variations in the way a particular work may be protected in different
parts of the world as there are territories. In most cases, the owner of
copyright in a work who seeks to obtain relief against the illicit
exploitation of his work in another territory must enforce his rights
under the law of the territory in which the infringement takes place. In

an environment where works are generally exploited internationally, and commonly on a global basis (for example, via global networks such as the internet), it is vital that owners may effectively enforce their rights internationally. Territorial copyright has therefore become the subject of a number of international political agreements, regulating copyright issues and ensuring a degree of co-operation and legal uniformity between different territories regarding the works of their citizens. The three primary such international agreements are the Berne Convention, Universal Copyright Convention (UCC) and the TRIPS Agreement. Both the Berne Convention and the UCC have been subject to a number of amendments, principally necessary to update the law following technological developments. The last revisions of the Bern Convention were set out in the Paris Act of 1971, although more recently the Berne Convention was effectively revised by the WIPO Treaties as regards those countries which adhere to the WIPO Treaties[1].

Appendix 2 of this *User's Guide* lists the countries that adhere to the Berne Convention the UCC and TRIPS. Virtually all countries with any significant production of copyright works are parties to both Conventions and TRIPS.

The EU has also adopted a number of Directives intended to harmonise copyright law in the EEA[2].

1   Discussed at **paragraph 4.18** below.
2   See **paragraphs 1.08 and 14.03**.

The 'national treatment' principle

4.13   The key principle which guides both the Berne Convention and the UCC is the principle of offering *national treatment* to the works of foreign nationals of other Convention countries. In short: a Convention country will offer the same protection in its territory to the works of a foreign national originating from another Convention country as it will give to the works of its own nationals or which otherwise originate locally[1]. In practice the operation of this principle is restricted by two other principles: those of *minimum standards* and *reciprocity*[2].

1   Berne Convention Art 5(1) and UCC Art II(2).
2   See **paragraph 4.14**.

The principles of 'minimum standards' and 'reciprocity'

4.14   In certain respects the copyright protection offered by a Convention country to the work of a foreign national which originates outside that country may be more favourable than the protection afforded to the work of a local national or which otherwise originates locally. It is a requirement of both the Berne Convention and the UCC that members provide the nationals of other Convention countries with protection without any need to comply with local formalities such as deposit or registration notwithstanding that domestic nationals and/or works first published locally must comply with such provisions[1]. The most significant territory in which formalities are required is the USA. In this respect, for example, the literary work of a UK author first published in the UK may receive superior protection in the USA to the work of a US author first published in the USA if the latter has failed to comply with local formalities. However, under the UCC, a foreign national will only be deemed to have satisfied local formalities if the work in question bears an appropriate 'copyright symbol'[2].

1   Berne Convention Art 5, UCC Art III(I).
2   As to which see **paragraph 4.16**.

Differences between the Berne Convention and the UCC

4.15   The principal difference between the two Conventions is the minimum term of copyright protection they provide. Under the Berne Convention, the minimum period of copyright accorded to literary, dramatic, musical and artistic works is the life of the author plus 50 years. Under the UCC, the minimum term is the life of the author plus 25 years[1]. Both Conventions provide that signatories may provide for a greater degree of protection than that provided for in the conventions, and Convention countries often do.

1   Art 4(2).

Copyright symbol

4.16   It is important to note that under the UCC, if a work is to avoid the necessity of complying with domestic formalities which may operate as a precondition of copyright protection in other UCC countries[1], it is vital that from the time of first publication of the work in question, all copies published with the authority of the author or other copyright proprietor must bear the symbol '©' accompanied by the name of the copyright proprietor and the year of first publication. This notice must be placed in such a manner and location as to give reasonable notice of the copyright claim[2]. Failure to put this symbol on a work published in a Berne Convention country will not prejudice copyright in the other Berne Convention countries. However, it may result in the work losing copyright and going into the public domain in those UCC countries which are not Berne Convention countries and which require formalities as a condition to copyright protection.

1   See **paragraph 4.14**.
2   Art III(i).

Other international copyright conventions and agreements

4.17 The UK is a party to a number of other significant international agreements, including the following.

(a) The Rome Convention

4.18 In brief, the Rome Convention conveys rights protecting performers (with regard to the affixation and exploitation of recordings of their performances, phonogram producers (regarding the unauthorised reproduction of their phonograms – essentially audio records and cassettes) and broadcasters[1]. 'Broadcast' for these purposes means 'wireless' transmission, excluding cable transmission and re-transmissions (which were not contemplated). The minimum period of protection is 20 years from the end of the year of fixation, performance or broadcast (as relevant). Like the Berne Convention and the UCC, this Convention is based on the principle of 'national treatment'[2]. Again, like the UCC, the Rome Convention excuses phonogram producers from compliance with local formalities, provided that either the phonograms or their containers show a ℗ notice and the year of first publication. There is also a requirement to identify the producer, his successor in title or exclusive licensee[3]. The number and identity of the parties to this convention are shown in Appendix 2.

1   To authorise re-broadcasting, affixation and reproduction of their broadcasts, and the communication of their broadcasts to premises against payment of an admission fee.
2   See **paragraph 4.13**.
3   Art 11.

(b) The Phonograms Convention

4.19 This Convention focuses on measures to combat phonogram piracy. In essence, the Convention requires members to protect producers against the making and importation of unauthorised copies of phonograms for public distribution, and the public distribution of such phonograms. Like the Rome Convention, the Phonogram Convention requires a minimum 20-year period of protection[1], and similar notice requirements in order to fulfil local formality requirements. Unlike Rome, however, the level of protection is not based on 'national treatment'. Signatories are required to afford the minimum level of protection prescribed by the Convention to phonograms from other member states, even if local law is less protective.

1 Art 4.

(c) The WTO, TRIPS AND GATS

4.20 The agreement establishing the WTO was signed in Marrakesh, Morocco on 15 April 1994[1]. The principal *objectives* of the WTO are to raise standards of living, ensure full employment, expand production and trade and allow optimal use of the world's resources. The WTO *functions* include the development of an integrated multilateral trading system, the settlement of trade disputes, the provision of a forum for negotiations on trade relations, the review of trade policies and a greater coherence in global policy making. A list of countries which are members of the WTO is set out at **Appendix 2** of this *User's Guide*.

The TRIPS Agreement was entered into as part of and is annexed to, the WTO agreement. Both became effective on 1 January 1995. The aim of the TRIPS Agreement is to reduce distortions and impediments to international trade and to ensure adequate and effective intellectual property protection without creating barriers to trade. The ambit of the TRIPS Agreement includes copyright and related rights, trade marks, geographical indications (e.g. an indication of the region from which a product originates, such as Champagne), industrial designs, patents, topographies of integrated circuits, protection of 'know how' and the control of anti-competitive practices. Enforcement issues are also dealt with.

The Treaty is expressed not to derogate from existing Conventions. Its terms are based on the principles of 'national treatment'[2] and 'most favoured nations treatment' (i.e. that, subject to certain exceptions, any protection given by a member to the nationals of another country will be given to the other members of TRIPS). It is worth summarising the provisions of the TRIPS Agreement relating to copyright:

- *Principle* copyright protection is expressed to 'extend to expressions and not to ideas, procedures, methods of operation or mathematical concepts as such'[3].
- *Computer programs* whether in source or object code are protected as literary works[4].
- *Compilations* of data or other materials, whether in machine

readable or other form, which by reason of the selection or arrangement of its content constitute intellectual creations, are protected as such[5].

- *Rental rights* in computer programs, cinematographic works and phonograms are required to be protected for authors, phonogram producers and 'and any other right holders in phonograms' respectively, and their successors in title, subject to certain limitations[6].

- *Performers* should have the possibility of preventing the fixation of their performances, or the reproduction of a fixation, on a phonogram. With regard to live performances, a performer should have the possibility of preventing unauthorised (wireless) broadcast and 'communication to the public'[7].

- *Phonogram producers* should enjoy the right to authorise the reproduction of their phonograms[8].

- *Broadcasting organisations*: should have the right to prohibit the fixation of their broadcasts, the reproduction of fixations, the wireless rebroadcast of their broadcasts and the communication to the public of television broadcasts.

- *Term:* wherever the term for protection of a copyright work is not based on the life of a person, the term must be not less than 50 years from the end of the year of authorised publication, or, if not published within 50 years of its making, not less than 50 years from the end of the year of its making. Photographs and works of applied art are excluded from this provision[9]. For performers and phonogram producers the protection is set at 50 years from the end of the year of fixation or performance. For broadcasting organisations the term of protection required is at least 20 years from the end of the year of broadcast[10].

The General Agreement on Trade in Services (GATS) came into force in 1995 as a result of the Uruguay Round negotiations to extend the multilateral trading system of the WTO to services. All members of the WTO are signatories to the GATS and have committed to further rounds of GATS negotiations, the first of which started in 2000.

The members of the WTO are automatically members of the TRIPS Agreement.

1   'The Marrakesh Act'.
2   See **paragraph 4.13**.
3   Art 9.
4   Art 10.
5   Art 10.
6   Arts 11 and 14(4).
7   Arts 14(1).
8   Arts 14(2).

9   Art 12.
10 Art 14(5).

(d) The WIPO Treaties

4.21   The WIPO Treaties arose as a consequence of the need to update the provisions of the Berne Convention, Rome Convention and the Phonogram Convention in light of advances in technology and in line with the TRIPS Agreement.

The WIPO Copyright Treaty 1996 (in line with TRIPS) confirms the principle that copyright protection extends to expressions and not ideas, procedures of operation or mathematical concepts as such[1]. Computer programs and compilations (of data or other materials in any form, which constitute intellectual creations by reason of their selection or arrangement) receive protection. Authors of literary and artistic works also receive newly recognised rights: the exclusive right to authorise 'the making available to the public' of the original and copies of their work and the 'communication to the public' of their works (by wired or wireless means, e.g. by means of 'on demand' on-line transmission)[2] for authors of computer programs and films and works included in phonograms a limited right to authorise commercial lending rental[3]. The Treaty also contains provisions designed to ensure adequate remedies are available against infringers who would circumvent technical methods of preventing unauthorised use or, for example, remove rights management information (designed to track the use of a work for the purpose of calculating remuneration).

WIPO Performances and Phonograms Treaty 1996 protects performers and phonogram producers[4]. Parties are required to provide protection on the basis of 'national treatment'[5]. The Treaty recognises a number of rights in performances: namely performers' moral rights in affixations of their live aural performances on phonograms, and a performer's exclusive rights to authorise reproduction, making available to the public (again by wired or wireless means) and commercial rental of originals and copies of their performances embodied on phonograms[6]. Performers also receive the exclusive right to authorise the fixation of their performance and to authorise the broadcast and 'communication to the public' of affixed performances (except where the performance is already a broadcast performance)[7]. For phonogram producers, the Treaty provides similar exclusive rights to authorise reproduction, making available to the public (again by wired or wireless means) and commercial rental of originals and copies of their phonograms[8]. The Treaty provides for a single equitable remuneration right for performers and/or producers, leaving it to the discretion of signatories as to whether this is shared between producer and performer, or allocated to one or other of them[9]. In accordance with TRIPS, the minimum period of protection to be afforded to performers and phonogram producers is 50 years from the end of the year of affixation or (in the case of the rights of producers in published phonograms) publications[10]. As with the WIPO Copyright Treaty, this Treaty includes provisions targeted against the circumvention of technical methods of preventing unauthorised use or, for example, the removal of rights management information.

The WIPO Treaties did not address the issue of exhaustion of rights (which remains to be determined by national governments[11]), and whether reproduction includes the kind of temporary storage required for the operation of electronic systems. Nor was any protection of audio-visual performers provided for.

At the time of going to press, momentum was also growing for a new WIPO Treaty to update protections afforded to broadcasters in the digital age from those set out in the 1961 Rome Convention[12].

1   Art 2.
2   Arts 6 and 8.
3   Art 7.
4   Art 3.
5   Art 4.
6   Arts 5 and 7–10.
7   Art 6.
8   **Chapter 3**.
9   Art 15.
10   Art 17.
11   See **paragraphs 7.04 and 14.06**.
12   See **paragraph 4.17**.

Summary

4.22   For copyright users in the UK, the practical consequence of the UK's membership of the various international agreements is to achieve international protection for the works of UK authors, producers and performers. However, it is of vital importance, in order to ensure that such protection is available in as many territories as possible, for users to ensure from the outset that all copies of their work distributed with their authority bear the correct '©' or 'how a '℗' notices identified at paragraphs 4.16 and 4.18₁

1   The reader should note that the UK is party to a number of other Conventions and agreements which are not discussed in detail here but which include the Convention Relating to the Distribution of Programme-Carrying Signals Transmitted by Satellite 1974 (dealing with the transmission of broadcasts by satellite). The UK is also a member of a number of Conventions from the Council of Europe, including the

European Agreement Concerning Programme Exchanges By Means of Television Films 1958, the Agreement on the Protection of Television Broadcasts 1960, the European Agreement for the Prevention of Broadcasts Transmitted from Stations Outside National Territories 1965 and the European Convention Relating to Questions of Copyright Law and Neighbouring Rights in the Framework of Transfrontier Broadcasting by Satellite 1994.

Chapter 5

Breach of confidence and passing off

Confidence and copyright

5.01 As we have seen, copyright attaches only to the expression of ideas in one of a number of protected categories, not to ideas or information per se[1]. A right of confidentiality can fill the gaps where copyright protection is not available (e.g. because an idea for a library work has not been reduced to a written form). Confidential information is sometimes protected by reliance on contractual principles (i.e. as the basis of express or implied terms agreed between the parties), and sometimes by reference to principles of equity. More recent cases have also discussed the impact of the HRA and DPA on this area of law.

1   See **paragraphs 1.03 and 2.12**.

Breach of confidence – the essential elements

5.02 Three elements are needed to establish a breach of confidence:

- the information must be confidential;
- the information must have been communicated in circumstances which imported an obligation of confidence on the recipient;
- the defendant must have made or threatened an unauthorised disclosure or wrongful use of the information[1].

1   *Coco v AN Clark (Engineers) Ltd [1969] RPC 41 at 47.*

Confidential information

5.03 Confidential information need not be recorded in any material form, to qualify for protection. An idea expressed verbally is capable of qualifying for protection[1]. The information must, however, be secret, or private, or the information must have come into existence as a result of the expenditure of labour or money and must not already be in the public domain[2]. It must not be merely trivial, although it need not have commercial value. It must not be information which is so common that nobody knows from where it originated: it must be possible to trace its origins.

Examples of confidential information are: matrimonial confidences relating to the private and personal affairs of one spouse learned by the other during the course of marriage; information contained in private letters; notes of lectures which were given privately to students; details of an unpatented invention; information obtained in the course of employment; solicitors' precedents; plots of plays and novels.

The appearance of a film set is also capable of protection. In one recent case, *Creation Records v News Group Newspapers Ltd*[3], the appearance of a photographic set was also held to be the subject of an obligation of confidence, in circumstances where the set itself (an arrangement of several objects around a hotel swimming pool for the cover of an album by the rock band Oasis) was not capable of receiving copyright protection[4].

In *Fraser v Thames Television*[5], it was held that an idea communicated in the context of the television industry was capable of protection where it was established that the idea was communicated in confidence, was clearly identified, sufficiently original, was of potential commercial attractiveness and developed to a point at which it was capable of being realised.

However, the mere fact that information is held in encrypted form does not of itself render the encrypted material confidential. The issue is whether there is a relationship of confidentiality between the source and the decryptor. So, for example, where encrypted software was reverse-engineered, the fact of encryption did not impose an obligation of confidentiality[6].

It is worth giving further consideration to the position of employees regarding information obtained during the course of their employment. These principles were set out in the leading (and delightfully named) case of *Faccenda Chicken v Fowler*[7]. In brief, whilst in employment, an employee owes his employee an obligation of good faith and fidelity which prevents the employee disclosing material which he is told, or which is obviously, confidential, including 'know how' (i.e. the 'acquired skill and knowledge' which allows a skilled person to do his/her job). After the termination of his employment, the implied confidentiality obligation is less onerous, being essentially restricted to trade secrets. Courts require that in order to qualify for protection, the information must be identifiable with some precision, which renders employers in some difficulty in preserving the confidentiality of their general business dealings. An employee is entitled to use and put at the disposal of new employers all his acquired skill and knowledge[8].

The critical question recognised by the Court of Appeal in *Lancashire Fires Ltd v SA Lyons & Co Ltd*[9] is how to distinguish information which can be treated as an employee's 'acquired skill and knowledge' from that which is not. This may be a difficult question of judgment, in some cases. Know-how as to the way in which other employees do their work, which is secret to the employer concerned, will be treated as confidential information. Although an employer cannot use the doctrine of breach of confidence to prevent an employee earning his living by the exercise of his own trade, he can prevent an employee using lists of customers or clients which he takes with him when he leaves the employment.

1   *Fraser v Thames Television [1984] QB 44.*
2   This is particularly an issue where information may be confidential in some localities and not others, given the ease with which information can be disseminated globally via the internet – see *AG v Times Newspapers Ltd & Others: CA, 25 January 2001.* An injunction will not be available if the information is already in the public domain, see *D v L [2003] EWCA Civ 1169.*
3   [1997] EMLR 444.
4   See **paragraph 2.06**.
5   [1984] QB 44.
6   *Mars UK Ltd v Teknowledge Ltd [2000] FSR 138.*
7   [1987] Ch 117, CA.
8   See also *Ocular Sciences v Aspect Vision Care (1997 RPC 289)* where Laddie J emphasised the importance of properly pleading particulars of the confidential information relied upon.
9   [1996] FSR 629.

Confidential relationship

5.04   The courts have never laid down a simple concise definition of what constitutes a confidential relationship. A confidential relationship exists when it is reasonable to assume that the information was imparted in confidence.

As noted above, a confidential relationship can be created by contract[1]. However, confidential relationships may also be created in equity by virtue of the relationship of the parties to each other[2].

In the case of *D v L*[3], the claimant sought to restrain the use of tapes of private telephone conversations with his former partner made after the break up of their relationship in which she had secretly recorded details of his sexual proclivities. The Court of Appeal held the claimant was entitled to rely not only on the permanence of his relationship with his former partner but also the secret nature of his conversations with her as creating an equitable requirement on her not to use the information for any purpose other than that for which it was obtained[4].

If a playwright tells an impresario the plot of a play which has not yet been written, there is a breach of confidence if the impresario subsequently commissions another writer to write a play based on the same plot[5]. A similar situation would exist between a novelist and publisher.

If a photographer takes a portrait photograph of an individual, there is a confidential relationship which would not permit the photographer to sell copies of the photograph to third parties for his own gain. The right to privacy of photographs and films does not change the law as to breach of confidence in any regard[6].

Where students attend private lectures, they may not publish the contents of those lectures, because a confidential relationship is deemed to exist between students and lecturer.

In *Creation Records v News Group Newspapers Ltd*[7], an interim injunction was granted to prevent the publication of photographs of a photographic set which were taken by a press photographer who, it was argued, had surreptitiously photographed the appearance of a photographic set in circumstances where, it was claimed, photography was not permitted.

In *Murray v Yorkshire Fund Managers Ltd*[8], it was held that where certain confidential information was co-owned and one co-owner was excluded from the group of co-owners, he ceased to have any control over the information to prevent its use by a third party without his consent where no contractual, fiduciary or other special terms regarding its use had been agreed between the co-owners.

1　For example, a company may be required not to disclose the contents of drawings which it needs to manufacture goods under licence, nor the lists of contacts supplied by a manufacturer to a distributor.

2　A common example is to be found when negotiations are taking place intended to lead to a contract, and it is necessary to disclose some trade secret or unpatented invention to enable the parties to consider the proposed contractual terms. In such a case a confidential relationship may well be deemed to exist.

3　[2003] EWCA Civ 1169.

4　An injunction was however refused on other grounds, see below.

5　*Gilbert v Star Newspaper Ltd [1894] 11 TLR 4.*

6　See **paragraph 11.24**.

7　Referred to at **paragraph 5.03**.

8　[1998] 1WLR 951, CA.

Imparting confidential information

5.05 When it is established that information is confidential and that there is a confidential relationship, a person to whom the information is imparted pursuant to that relationship is under a general obligation not to disclose or use that information except as authorised by the person providing it. There are very few grounds upon which he is permitted to impart the confidential information to third parties. The only clearly established ground is that the information is such that it is in the public interest to disclose it to one or more persons, including even the press. Information of this sort may relate to crime, iniquitous behaviour, a breach of statutory duty or some other misdeed. In the case of *X v Y*[1], it was held that the public interest in preserving the confidentiality of hospital records identifying actual or potential AIDS sufferers, outweighed the public interest in the freedom of the press to publish such information.

If a third party uses a confidence which has been wrongfully imparted, then he also is liable to the person who originated the information. For example, if a writer, who learns the plot of a novel which is imparted to him through a confidential relationship before it has been written down, himself writes a novel incorporating that plot and arranges for it to be published, the publisher of the novel as well as the writer will be liable for breach of confidence.

The remedies for breach of confidence are damages and/or an injunction. It is interesting to note that where damages have been paid, the person to whom the information has been imparted can then use that information as if he paid for it. An account of profits and delivery up of material containing confidential information may also be ordered at the discretion of the court[2].

A failure to give full particulars of the confidential information relied upon and to rely upon wide and unsupportable claims of confidentiality has been held to amount to oppression or harassment[3].

1   [1988] 2 All ER 648.
2   See **paragraphs 8.12 and 8.13**.
3   Laddie J In *Ocular Sciences v Aspect Vision 1997 RPC 289.*

Confidentiality, privacy and the Human Rights Act 1998

5.06 Since the last *User's Guide*, the most significant developments in the law of confidentiality have moved hand-in-hand with developments arising from the Human Rights Act 1998.

Section 1 of the HRA specifies those Articles of the European Convention on Human Rights which are incorporated directly into

English law. These include Arts 8 and 10. Article 8 guarantees 'the right to respect for private and family life home and correspondence' and warns that there should be no interference with this right by a public authority except when the interference is in accordance with the law and is necessary in the interests of national security, public safety etc. Note that Art 8 refers to a public authority, which includes (inter alia) any court. Article 10 refers to the right of the media to freedom of expression.

Privacy and confidentiality were considered in *Michael Douglas and Catherine Zeta-Jones & anr v Hello! Ltd & ors*[1]. The couple had married in a private ceremony. Previously, they had agreed an exclusive agreement with *OK!* magazine to publish photographs of the wedding, which obliged the couple to arrange strict security. An infiltrator got past security, took photographs in secret and these were due to be published by a competitor magazine, *Hello!*

It was held that the equitable jurisdiction in confidence was based on 'the duty to be of good faith and on the moral principle of fair dealing', but that the scope of that cause of action must be evaluated in light of the HRA. That could be achieved by regarding the opposing rights under Arts 8 and 10 as being 'absorbed into an action for breach of confidence'. In that regard, there was no presumption that a right to freedom of expression should trump the right to privacy.

The court addressed the three components of a claim under the law of confidence taken from *Coco v A.N. Clark (Engineers) Ltd*[2] namely that: (a) the information itself must have the necessary quality of confidence about it (it must not be something which is public property and public knowledge), (b) that such information must have been received in circumstances imparting an obligation of confidence; and (c) the requirement for unauthorised use of that information to the detriment of the party communicating it. The court held that, in order to satisfy the 'quality of confidence' test, one should ask the question: 'Does the information have the basic attribute of inaccessibility?' To answer the question of whether the circumstances 'imposed an obligation', it was necessary to ask: 'would a reasonable man, standing in the shoes of the recipient of the information, have realised that information was being given to him in confidence?' The court held that, in respect of the third question, 'It cannot be doubted that the claimants suffered detriment from the publication by *Hello!*'

The court held that, in effect, the wedding was a 'valuable trade asset', that had 'a private character' and that attracted the quality of commercial confidentiality. *Hello!* had not acted in good faith nor by way of fair dealing, the publication was unconscionable and the claimants had suffered to their detriment.

The court heard evidence of the laws of privacy in Germany, France and Canada, but confirmed that there is no law of privacy in the UK, despite the HRA. Per Lindsay J: 'So broad is the subject of privacy and such are the ramifications of any free-standing law in the area that the subject is better left to Parliament. But that will only happen when a case arises in which the existing law of confidence gives no or inadequate protection; this case now before me is not such a case and there is therefore no need for me to attempt to construct a law of privacy and, that being so, it would be wrong of me to attempt to do so'[3].

As an aside, the judge also found that all three defendants were 'data controllers' for the purposes of the Data Protection Act. The unauthorised photographs are 'personal data' and publication of them in England is to be treated as an operation covered by the DPA, but held that damages under the DPA for distress would be nominal[4].

On appeal to the Court of Appeal, *Hello!*'s appeal against the judgment in favour of the claimants Zeta-Jones and Douglas based on privacy and commercial confidence was dismissed, but allowed in respect of *OK!* magazine. The Court took the view that confidential or private information which is capable of commercial exploitation but which is only protected by the law of confidence does not fall to be treated as property that can be owned or transferred[5].

The second significant recent case to examine the law of confidentiality and privacy was *Naomi Campbell v Mirror Group Newspapers*. This case concerned the publication of articles and photographs identifying Naomi Campbell as addicted to drugs and an attendee of Narcotics Anonymous. The judge at first instance had held[6] in favour of the supermodel and made an order for damages against the defendants for breach of confidence and breach of duty under the DPA[7]. However, the Court of Appeal ruled[8] that the covertly taken photographs of Ms Campbell outside an NA meeting did not, in themselves, convey any confidential information. Considering the totality of what was published, disclosure of Ms. Campbell's addiction could not amount to a breach of confidence, because disclosure was in the public interest. In relation to Miss Campbell's attendance at NA, publication was 'justified in order to provide a factual account of Miss Campbell's drug addiction that had the detail necessary to carry credibility.' The House of Lords thought differently, holding that whilst publication of the fact that Ms. Campbell had taken drugs and was seeking treatment was necessary to 'set the record straight' in light of her previous statements, the additional information (regarding NA) was an 'unjustified intrusion', such that Ms Campbell's rights under Art 8 outweighed any issue of freedom of expression[9].

As an aside, the Court of Appeal had also affirmed that the data had on the face of it been processed unfairly for the purposes of the DPA, rejecting the argument that the exemption under s 32 of the DPA applied[10].

More recently, the European Court of Human Rights had the opportunity to consider the issue of privacy further in *Von Hannover v Germany (Application 59320/00)*[11]. That case concerned paparazzi photographs of Princess Caroline of Monaco published in German tabloids. The ECHR held that the decisive factor in balancing the protections under Arts 8 and 10 should lie in 'the contribution that the published photos and articles made to a debate of general interest'. There was no such contribution in this case: there was no legitimate public interest in her private life, despite the fact she appeared in public, and, even if a public interest did exist, in this instance it should yield to the effective protection of her private life. As we write, it is too early to assess the impact of this case on UK privacy cases, although the English courts are obliged to give effect to the ruling.

It seems an inescapable conclusion from the most recent cases in this area that traditional notions of confidentiality have been expanded by the HRA, DPA and the ECHR. Notwithstanding the protestations of the court in the *Douglas* case, it does appear that, as a consequence, a general right of privacy is starting to emerge[12].

1   [2003] EWHC 786 (Ch).
2   Per Lindsay J. at para 229 (iii).
3   For a further discussion of this case, see Gayle Curry, 'Confidentiality OK' [2003] Ent LR Issue 6.
4   A detailed consideration of the DPA to beyond the scope of this *User's Guide*.
5   Mr Phillips and Clarke and Newberger LJJ (CA, 18 May 2005).
6   [2003] 1 All ER 224.
7   Section 32(1) states:

'Personal data which are processed only for the special purposes are exempt from any provision to which this subjection relates if:

(a)   the processing is undertaken with a view to the publication by any person of any journalistic, literary or artistic material,
(b)   the data controller reasonably believes that, having regard in particular to the special importance of the public interest in freedom of expression, publication would be in the public interest, and
(c)   the data controller reasonably believes that, in all the circumstances, compliance with that provision is incompatible with the special purposes.'

8   [2004] 2AC 457.
9   *Naomi Campbell v Mirror Group Newspapers Ltd [2004] UKHL 22.*
10   ibid.
11   [2004] EMLR 379, 16 BHRC 545.
12   For a recent discussion of case law on these issues, see Lorna Brazell, 'Confidence, Privacy and Human Rights: English Law in the Twenty-first Century' [2005] EIPR Issue 11.

Passing off, goodwill, territoriality and copyright

5.07 The tort (i.e. the wrongful act) of passing off protects the 'goodwill' established in a business. For these purposes, goodwill has been called 'the attractive force which brings in custom' to a business[1]. In one leading case the action was summarised by one proposition: ' no man may pass off his goods as those of another'[2].

For these purposes, goodwill is a local, territorial right:

'no trader can complain of passing off as against him in any territory … in which he has no customers, nobody who is in trade relationship with him'[3].

However, this position is qualified in the context of other EU countries[4]. The relationship between passing off and copyright is important because, like the law regarding confidentiality, an action in passing off can provide an alternative remedy where an actionable copyright infringement cannot be established (e.g. because A has copied something of B's which is not capable of copyright protection, such as a name, or because no actionable copyright infringement has taken place because, rather than copying a substantial part of B's work, A has created one which is confusingly similar). There is voluminous case law concerning passing off. However, the action is notoriously difficult to run, because cases usually turn on their facts and consequently require a detailed and expensive investigation of the factual background.

1   *IRC v Muller & Co's Margarine Ltd [1901] AC 217, HL.*
2   *Reckitt and Colman Products Ltd v Borden Inc [1990] 1 WLR 491* – see **paragraph 5.07.**
3   *Athletes Foot Marketing Associates Inc v Cobra Sports Ltd [1980] RPC 343.*
4   See **paragraph 14.08.**

Passing off: the essential elements

5.08 The essential elements of 'passing off' were considered in two leading cases. In *Erven Warnink BV v J Townend & Sons (Hull) Ltd*[1] ('the Advocaat case') five elements were identified as follows:

'(1)   a misrepresentation,

(2)   made by a trader in the course of trade,

(3)   to prospective customers of his, or ultimate consumers of goods and services supplied by him,

(4)   which is calculated to injure the business or goodwill of another trade (in the sense that this is a reasonable consequence) and

(5)   which causes actual damage to a business or goodwill of the trader by whom the action is brought or (in a quia timet action) will probably do so'.

These elements were restated in the case of *Reckitt Colman Products Ltd v Borden Inc*[2]. In that case Colman had developed goodwill in its 'JIF' lemon juice, which was packaged in a distinctive lemon-shaped container. Colman successfully applied for an injunction to restrain Borden selling lemon juice in a container with a deceptively similar 'get up'. The case stated a 'classic trinity' of three elements:

(1)   First, the plaintiff must establish his goodwill in his goods, name or mark in the mind of the purchasing public.
(2)   Secondly, the plaintiff must demonstrate a misrepresentation (or deception) by the defendant to the public, leading or likely to lead the public (whether international or unintentional) to believe that goods and services offered by him were the goods or services of the plaintiff.
(3)   Thirdly, the plaintiff must demonstrate that he has suffered, or is likely to suffer, damage as a result.

A number of cases have considered this 'classic trinity'.

In *Antec International Ltd v South Western Chicks (Warren) Ltd*[3], the plaintiff traded its product under the name 'Farm Fluid'. The defendant traded in the product *SWC Super Farm Fluid*. Unchallenged factual evidence was adduced to show that Farm Fluid was associated in the minds of farmers with Antec's product, and that farmers were likely to be confused by the defendant's product into believing some trading connection existed between the products, such that more than minimal damage was likely to result to Antec. On the other hand, the operators of a cable television channel called *The Box* were unable to obtain an interim injunction to prevent the launch of a television magazine, also called *The Box*, partly because the claimants could not claim to have built up goodwill in that name in the television context, where the term was descriptive of the nature of the product (the words being a slang expression for television)[4].

In *Mont Blanc Simplo GmbH v Sepia Products Inc*[5] the court had to consider the likelihood of confusion in the eyes of the public arising from the marketing of pens under a sign which was very similar to that of Montblanc. Montblanc's mark was distinctive and had acquired a reputation. The products were identical, although they may have been aimed at different ends of the market. Notwithstanding the absence of specific evidence of confusion, the court felt able to exercise its own mind as to the question of whether there was a likelihood of confusion, finding that all three elements of passing off had been shown.

The case of confusion in the context of supermarket 'look a like' products was considered in *United Biscuits (UK) Ltd v Asda Stores Ltd*[6]. United Biscuits manufacture the well-known Penguin chocolate biscuit. Asda marketed chocolate biscuits under the name 'Puffin' in similar packaging, which the court held was deceptively similar, notwithstanding that the court did not consider there was subjective intention to deceive.

In *Chocosuisse v Cadbury Ltd*[7] the Swiss chocolate manufacturers successfully used passing off to protect the words 'Swiss Chocolate' as describing chocolate made to a Swiss recipe with Swiss expertise by a Swiss manufacturer.

A politician, well known for his diaries, was entitled to an injunction to restrain a newspaper publishing a parody of his literary style where he could show that a substantial or large number of readers were misled, or were likely to be misled, as to the author, in a manner which was more than momentary or inconsequential. The court found that with a parody which contained, by definition, conflicting messages as to authorship, the court should consider the whole work to determine if the representation that the plaintiff was not the author was enough to ensure that a substantial proportion of readers were not misled. The court also held that although the plaintiff had to show damage or its likelihood, this could be presumed in the case of an established author[8].

In *Lyngstad v Anabas Products Ltd*[9] the pop group Abba could not prevent the use of the name *Abba* on T-shirts, badges, key rings and so on because, as they themselves had not marketed such goods under their name, they had not established any goodwill in trading in those goods – there was no common field of activity. Similarly, in the case of *Stringfellow v McCain Foods (GB) Ltd*[10] it was held that the marketing of frozen chipped potatoes under the name 'Stringfellow' would not injure the business of Stringfellows, the well-known London night-club.

Over the past 25 years the courts have recognised that the 'common field of activity' test no longer governs whether there is an actionable passing off, relying instead upon the principles set out in the Advocaat case. *Irvine v Talksport Ltd*[11] concerned a Formula One driver, Eddie Irvine. The defendant, a radio broadcaster, issued a brochure to potential advertisers that portrayed a manipulated picture of the claimant showing him holding a portable radio on which the words 'Talk Radio' were superimposed. Eddie Irvine sought damages in passing off. The defendant argued that the brochure was not such as to lead the public to believe the claimant had endorsed its business or that there was some other commercial arrangement between the parties (since the picture was obviously a spoof). The trial judge, Laddie J, and the Court of Appeal[12] held that there was an actionable passing off and awarded in damages the amount Irvine had claimed he would have charged by way of a licence fee for his image.

1   [1979] AC 731, HL.
2   [1990] 1 WLR 491, HL. Applied more recently in *Associated Newspapers Ltd and another v Express Newspapers [2003] EWHC 1322 (Ch)*.
3   [1998] FSR 738.
4   *Box Television v Haymarket Magazines Ltd [1997] 9 LS Gaz R 31*.
5   The Times, 2 February 2000.
6   [1997] RPC 513.
7   [1997] RPC 826, CA.
8   *Clark v Associated Newspapers Ltd [1998] 1WLR 1558*.
9   [1977] FSR 62, ChD.
10 [1984] RPC 501, CA.
11 [2002] EMLR 32.
12 [2003] EWCA Civ 423, CA.

Titles and passing off

5.09   The titles of films, songs, books or plays etc are not per se entitled to copyright protection unless they are so long, or so complicated, that they can be said to be the result of the application of labour and skill. In general it can be assumed that titles do not have copyright protection[1].

There are however many cases of titles being protected by actions in passing off, but such actions are not always successful. The case of *County Sound plc v Ocean Sound plc*[2] illustrates the way in which the courts apply the law of passing off in such cases. In that case, both of the parties to the action were local radio stations. Both stations were broadcasting 'golden oldie' records in programmes called *The Gold AM*, but the plaintiffs had begun their programme six months before the defendants. There was some overlap in the respective reception areas of the two stations, so the plaintiffs sued for an injunction to prevent the defendants calling their programme *The Gold AM*. The Court of Appeal held that the name *The Gold AM* could not acquire goodwill if it simply described the services of the programme unless the programme had been broadcast under that name, and no other, for a substantial period of time. Six months was held by the court to be far too short a period. The name was, in any event, considered to be merely descriptive of the type of programme being broadcast, but had their exclusive use of the name been for a much longer period of time, the plaintiffs might have overcome that hurdle[3].

1   See **paragraph 3.02** above.

2   [1991] FSR 367.
3   Titles, characters etc may also benefit from other protections, including registered
     trade marks. See Reuben Stone, 'Titles, Character names and catch phrases in the
     Film and Television Industry: Protection under the Trade Marks Act 1994 and
     Alternative Registration Systems' [1997] 2 Ent LR 34.

Dramatic sketches and passing off

5.10   Passing off can also be used, in certain circumstances, to prevent
the unauthorised reproduction of a dramatic work which has acquired a
reputation, but has never been written down. Thus, if a mime act or a
comedian's particular get-up and accessories are copied, an action in
passing off might be available to prevent performance by unauthorised
persons.

Examples of successful passing off actions

5.11   The following are some further examples of successful actions
for passing off.

- The owners of *The Eagle* magazine obtained an injunction to
  prevent the use of the name 'White Eagle Youth Holiday Camp' for
  a holiday camp[1].
- The publishers of *My Life and Loves* by Frank Harris obtained an
  injunction against the publishers of an abridgement of the same
  book under the same title[2].
- An employee obtained an injunction against his previous employer
  to prevent the employer publishing articles under the nom de
  plume that the employee had used for articles written for publication by the employer[3].
- A distributor of sherry obtained an injunction against another
  company which manufactured a drink under the title of sherry
  which was not made in the Jerez area of Spain[4].
- An author can prevent, through a claim in passing off, his name
  being used on a work he has not created[5].

1   *Hulton Press v White Eagle Youth Holiday Camp (1951) 68 RPC 126.*
2   *WH Allen & Co v Brown Watson [1965] RPC 191.*
3   *Forbes v Kemsley Newspapers (1951) 68 RPC 183.*
4   *Sykes v Fairfax & Sons [1978] FSR 312.*
5   *Clark v Associated Newspapers [1998] 1 WLR 1558.*

Examples of unsuccessful passing off actions

5.12   The following cases were ones in which actions for passing off
failed.

- The title of a song was used as a title of a film. The court decided that the action of passing off could not be used to defend the song title, because of the difference between a song and a film. There must be similarity between the goods which it is said are being passed off[1].

- The proprietors of *The Morning Post* were refused an injunction to prevent the publication of *The Evening Post*, on the grounds that *The Evening Post* was to be published at a place so far away from the place where *The Morning Post* was published, that there was no likely danger of confusion in the minds of the public[2].

- A broadcaster, 'Uncle Mac', was not entitled to an injunction against the manufacturers of 'Uncle Mac's Puffed Wheat', because there was no common field of activity between Uncle Mac the broadcaster and the manufacturers of puffed wheat[3].

- A playwright was unable to obtain an injunction against a film company to restrain the distribution of a film having the same name as that of a play, because the play and the film had no resemblance and the play was in any event unlikely to be filmed[4].

- The proprietors of *The Morning Star* sought an injunction against Beaverbrook Papers to prevent the publication of a new national newspaper to be called *The Daily Star*. The injunction was refused on the grounds that *The Morning Star* was established in the minds of the public as a political newspaper, whereas *The Daily Star* was intended to be a tabloid paper of an entirely different nature to *The Morning Star*. There was no danger of confusion between the two in the minds of the public[5].

- When the talk radio station *Talksport* broadcast commentary on Euro 2000 football matches which it had produced from outside the stadium (using commentators watching television monitors and ambient sound effects), describing this coverage as 'live', the BBC (which had acquired the exclusive right to broadcast live radio commentaries of the matches in the UK) took an action in passing off against *Talksport* to injunct its broadcasts. The court held that the BBC had established misrepresentation (i.e. the public was misled into believing the broadcast took place from the match), but rejected the suggestion that the BBC owned protectable goodwill which was infringed by *Talksport's* actions, or that there was actionable damage to any goodwill of the BBC[6].

1   *Francis Day & Hunter v Twentieth Century Fox Corpn [1940] AC 112, HL.*
2   *Borthwick v Evening Post (1888) 37 Ch D 449, CA.*
3   *McCulloch v Lewis A May (Produce Distributors) Ltd [1947] WN 318.*
4   *Houghton v Film Booking Offices (1931) 48 RPC 329.*

5   *Morning Star Co-operative Society v Express Newspapers [1979] FSR 113, DC.*
6   *BBC v Talksport Ltd (2000) Times, 29 June.*

Domain names and passing off

5.13   A series of cases has emerged dealing with passing off in the context of 'cyber squatting', the practice of registering internet domain names consisting of the names or marks of other businesses with the intention of selling the domain name on to that business. Under current procedures, domain names are registered in the UK on a 'first come first served' basis.

One of the first such cases in the UK[1] concerned a defendant which had, without authorisation, registered domain names of numerous well known enterprises, including Virgin, Sainsburys, Marks and Spencer and Ladbrokes. The domain names were up for sale. The plaintiffs sought an injunction to restrain passing off and trade mark infringement. The court found that the main purpose of the defendant's registrations was systematically to prevent registration by the owners of the goodwill in the name and extract money from the proper owner with the threat of either using the name or allowing someone else to do so. With regard to passing off, it was held that the proper owner was entitled to a final injunction to restrain such use, together with an order for the names to be assigned to the correct owners. In granting the injunction, the judge placed emphasis on the fact the court was entitled to infer from the evidence that the registration itself (without any trading using the name) amounted to equipping the defendant with an 'instrument of fraud' because it inherently led to passing off.

The *One in a Million* decision was generally welcomed as a valuable step toward discouraging the ransom on domain names by effectively creating a presumption of passing off in circumstances of 'cyber squatting'[2]. However, the decision does not create this presumption in all potential cases. In *French Connection Ltd v Sutton*[3] the defendant was an internet consultant who registered the domain name fcuk.com. French Connection had registered the same initials as a trade mark and used them in an advertising campaign, and applied for summary judgment for passing off. The application was refused because on the evidence, the judge was not satisfied there was no reasonable prospect of a defence to passing off (the defendant having claimed that the name was commonly used on the internet to denote pornography and that he had plans to use the name to attract traffic to his own site). The case illustrates that the courts will be reluctant to deal with 'cyber squatting' by way of summary judgment except in flagrant cases[4].

In *Marks & Spencer plc v Craig Cotterell,* Lightman J gave judgment against a serial cyber-squatter engaged in using fake web-sites for the purpose of 'phising' or using them for an ulterior fraudulent purpose. The claim was based upon trade mark infringement, passing off and copyright infringement in the literary and artistic content of the 'genuine' Marks and Spencer website[5].

1   *British Telecommunications plc, Virgin Enterprises Ltd, J Sainsbury plc, Marks and Spencer plc, Ladbroke plc v One in a Million Ltd [1999] 1WLR 903, CA.*
2   Although some have argued the case to be an unjustified extension of passing off principles. See Alexandra Sims, 'Rethinking One in a Million' [2004] EIPR, October 2004.
3   2 December 1999, unreported.
4   Domain names are considered in detail at **paragraph 26.62 et seq.**, together with details of ICANN and the ICANN dispute resolution procedure.
5   Lightman J, Chancery Division, 26 February 2001, unreported.

Image rights, personality rights and passing off

5.14   A celebrity may argue that the use of his name or image by an unauthorised person could amount to a 'passing off'[1]. This form of claim is only likely to increase in frequency as celebrities seek to impose greater controls on the exploitation of their image.

Again, in order to bring an action for passing off, a celebrity will need to show three requirements:

(a)   that his name or image is recognised by the public as distinctive specifically of goods or services connected with him;
(b)   that the relevant person has made a misrepresentation to the public by the use of the name or image such that the public is led to believe that the goods or services offered by that person are the goods or services of the player or connected with him; and
(c)   that the player suffers damage or is likely to suffer damage as a result of the misrepresentation.

A celebrity would typically only be able to show the first requirement of goodwill where he or she is already in the business of licensing his/her name or image for use in respect of goods or services. Until the *Irvine* case, the English Courts have proved reluctant to allow celebrities to succeed in a passing off action, by finding that there is unlikely to be any misrepresentation to the public. The misrepresentation which a celebrity would most likely seek to rely upon is that the use of their name or image will lead members of the public to believe that they have authorised the goods or services in question, contrary to the case. The English courts have traditionally rejected this argument on the basis that the mere use of a famous person's image would not lead members of the public to believe that the goods or services were provided by the character, nor that its quality was authorised by them. So, for example, in the case of *Haliwell & Ors v Panini*, the English court rejected the Spice Girls' application for an interim injunction to prevent Panini bringing out an unofficial sticker album of that pop group. The court rejected the claim of passing off, holding that the English public were unlikely to believe that the quality of the sticker album was authorised by the Spice Girls[2]. However, In *Alan McKenzie Clark v Associated Newspapers Ltd*[3] the well-known political diarist, politician and military historian successfully relied upon passing off and false attribution of authorship under s 84 CDPA to obtain judgment against the defendant for publishing a series of 'spoof' diaries entitled 'Not the Alan Clark Diary' and headed with his mug-shot photograph, which appeared regularly in the *Evening Standard*.

Other jurisdictions offer higher levels of protection for images. Indeed, the law in a number of jurisdictions has developed specifically in order to protect image/personality rights. Although we cannot provide comprehensive survey of these laws in this *User's Guide*, we believe the following examples to be informative.

1   See **paragraph 5.08**.
2   Unreported, SPA 6 June 1997. This should be contrasted with the sort of deliberate association referred to in the *Irvine* case referred to above; see **paragraph 5.08**.
3   1998 IWLR 1558.

(a) The United States

5.15 Image rights are known as the 'right of publicity'. The right of publicity is defined as the inherent right of every human being to control the commercial use of his or her identity. At least 27 US states recognise this right.

The right of publicity is a state-law created intellectual property right, infringement of which is a commercial tort of unfair competition. It is distinct from both trade mark and copyright law, false advertising and the right to privacy. It does not just apply to sportsmen and celebrities but is a right inherent to everyone to control the commercial use of their identity/persona and to allow them to recover damages and the commercial value of any unpermitted use of their image.

By way of example, the Californian Civil Code allows a person to take action where someone has knowingly used their name, voice, signature, photograph or likeness in any manner, on merchandising for advertising or selling products or services, without that person's prior consent. However, consent is not required if it is being used in connection with news, public affairs, sports broadcasts or accounts or any political campaign.

Image rights are further protected under US Federal Law, in particular s 43(a) of the Lanham Trademark Act. This prohibits the use of any word, term, name, symbol or device or any false or misleading description which is likely to cause confusion, mistake or deception as to the affiliation between one party and the goods/services of another[1].

1   McCarthy, *The Rights of Publicity and Privacy*, 2nd ed 6–3.

(b) France

5.16 French law provides some of the most significant levels of protection of image/personality rights. 'Personality rights', as they are known in France, are regarded as fundamental rights which are attached to the persona of the human being[1].

Under French law, a person is regarded as having an absolute property right in their image. This is the right to prohibit the production and distribution of an individual's likeness without their consent. However, what constitutes consent has given rise to several exceptions to this right. Of particular importance are:

  (i) where the image is incidental and was taken in a public place;
 (ii) when it concerns a current event and is published soon after; and
(iii) when it concerns the likeness of a public figure in his public life.
    However, publication must be made for the purpose of providing information and not for publicity or commercial exploitation.

1   Elizabeth Logeais, 'The French Right to One's Image – a Legal Lure' 1994 5 Ent Lr
    163 at 164.

(c) Canada

5.17 In Canada, image rights have been protected for some time by the tort of appropriation of personality. In particular, the Canadian courts recognised in the case of *Athans v Canadian Adventures Company Ltd* that a person has 'a propriety right in the exclusive marketing for gain of his personality, image and name, and that the law entitles him to protect that right if it is invaded'[1].

However, a celebrity will only have a cause of action where their image is used to suggest an endorsement of the product/services by that individual. If it is merely being used to illustrate, say, the sport in which he participates, then there will be no cause of action. In a number of Canadian provinces, image rights are further protected by their privacy laws, which prohibit the unauthorised use of a name of likeness in advertising and promotion of goods and services.

1   [1977] OR 2d425, 435.

(d) Australia

5.18   In Australia there is no proprietary right in one's own name or image which is equivalent to the US 'right of publicity' or the Canadian tort of 'appropriation of personality'. The position in Australia is very similar to that in England, whereby a celebrity must rely on a number of doctrines, such as passing off and the Trade Practices Act 1974[1].

Image rights are also protected by the law of passing off, which has traditionally been broader than that of England, and has been used successfully to protect the unpermitted use of personal identities in advertising and commercial promotion. In *Hogan v Specific Dunlop*[2], Paul Hogan, the star of the *Crocodile Dundee* films, established passing off by television advertisements for a shoe company which used images of him from the film. Since this case, the position in Australian law appears to be that a personality, who can be said to be in business, is free to grant or withhold his endorsement, such that unauthorised use of his image to imply an endorsement causes damage by depriving him of the fee he could otherwise have insisted on. However, there must be some misrepresentation, i.e. that the public would believe that that person was associated with the product or service[3]. Since the *Irvine* decision referred to earlier[4], it would appear that English law has moved in this direction.

1   V McMullen, 'Personality Rights in Australia' (1997) 8 Australian Intellectual Property Journal 86.
2   [1989]14 IPR 398.
3   Christopher Wadlow, *The Law of Passing Off*, 2nd ed, pp 298–299.
4   See **paragraph 5.08**.

Chapter 6

Term of copyright and publication right

Introduction

6.01   Copyright in a work, like its author, will not live forever. Public policy has set a balance between the private interests of authors and their estates, and the public interest in having access to works. For the copyright user, to know whether a work is still 'in copyright' (i.e. whether it still attracts copyright protection) is vital. Once copyright expires, it 'enters the public domain' and becomes freely exploitable.

Under the Conventions considered in **Chapter 4** above, we saw that international standards have been agreed regarding the duration of copyright. Of these, the longest period is set by the Berne Convention, which sets the minimum period of protection for literary, dramatic, musical and artistic works at 50 years 'post mortem actoris', or 'after the death of the author' (an expression often shortened to *pma*).

However, the Conventions only set minimum standards, and consequently the period of protection still varies from country to country. Within Europe, the effects of that variation were seen as an impediment to the common market. Consequently the standard was harmonised by the Duration of Copyright Directive 1993[1] to 70 years pma (being the longest copyright period previously afforded by an EU Member State, namely Germany). The Directive was implemented in the UK by the 1995 and 1996 Regulations which amended the CDPA. Prior to this, the UK standard had been 50 years pma.

The 1995 Regulations came into force on 1 January 1996 and increased copyright protection to 70 years pma. This affects the works of authors who died between 1925 and 1945, whose rights would otherwise have been extinguished.

The following table sets out a simple summary showing the copyright duration of works produced on or after 1 August 1989. Different rules will apply to works produced before this date.

Type of original work	Copyright duration
Literary, dramatic, musical or artistic works (including photographs)	70 years from the end of the year in which the author dies.
Works of unknown authorship	70 years from the end of the year it was written or 70 years from the end of the year it was made available to the public if it was made so available.
Sound recordings	50 years from the end of the year in which a sound recording was made and if not released immediately, then 50 years from the end of the calendar year in which it was released.
Films	70 years from the death of the last to survive of the principal director, the author of the film screenplay, the author of the film dialogue and the composer of the music specifically created for and used in the film.
Broadcasts	50 years from the end of the calendar year in which the broadcast was made. In the case of repeats, copyright expires at the same time as the original.
Typographical arrangements	25 years from the end of the calendar year in which the edition was first published.

Although the position in the UK regarding copyright works created after the implementation of the new regime is comparatively simple, the position becomes more complex for the user who needs to establish whether an older work which he wants to exploit is still in copyright. The 1995 Regulations contain complex transitional provisions which determine how old works will be treated under the new regime. These provisions mean that, depending on the age of the work, it may be necessary to apply one of a number of historic Copyright Act provisions in order to determine the copyright period remaining in the work.

In this chapter, we touch on the circumstances in which copyrights are revived or extended as a consequence of the amendments to the CDPA, and if so, who owns the revived or extended rights. We also consider what period of protection will apply to various categories of work or different ages.

In view of the complexity of the law regarding the duration of copyright, a tabular representation of the duration of copyright appears at the end of this *User's Guide*[2]. This tabular representation is by

Professor John N Adams and Michael Edenborough at James Graham, to whom the authors are greatly indebted for permission to reproduce it here[3].

1   93/98/EEC.
2   See **Appendix 5**.
3   For a comparison of terms of copyright protection internationally, see Peter Schonning, 'Survey of the Terms of Protection of Authors' Rights' [2000] Ent LR, Issue 4.

Revived and extended copyright

6.02   Works in which the copyright period expired before 31 December 1995 and which were therefore in the public domain, are now again protected by copyright, provided that the period of 70 years pma has not expired and that they were entitled to copyright protection in another EEA state on 1 July 1995[1]. Germany is an EEA state and had a copyright period of 70 years pma in place on 1 July 1995. So, provided that the work qualified for protection in Germany at that date, the work will gain the benefit of *revived* copyright. The qualification for protection in Germany is basically similar to the UK. The balance of the term of 70 years pma remaining at 31 December 1995 for works in which the copyright had expired is described as the *revived* copyright period[2].

The period of copyright of works still in copyright when the new provisions came into effect on 1 January 1996 is 70 years pma, because they get the benefit of the 20-year extension. The 20-year extension is described as the *extended* copyright period.

Performers' rights are also revived or extended and are known as 'revived performance rights' and 'extended performance rights'[3].

1   Reg 16(d) of the 1995 Regulations.
2   Reg 17 of the 1995 Regulations.
3   Reg 30 of the 1995 Regulations.

Ownership of extended copyright

6.03   Where the copyright in a work has been extended as a result of the extension of the copyright period to 70 years pma, questions arise as to who owns the copyright for the extended period, in works where the original copyright has granted licences or assigned his copyright. In that case, the owner of the extended copyright is the person who was the owner of the copyright in the work immediately before 1 January 1996[1].

If, however, that person was entitled to copyright for a period less than the whole of the copyright period under the CDPA (prior to amendment), then the extended copyright becomes part of the 'reversionary interest expectant on termination of that period'[2]. An *assignment* for a period less than the whole of the copyright period is permitted by the CDPA[3].

The provision with regard to *licences* of extended copyright is dealt with in a slightly different way – the licence will continue after the expiry of the old 1988 copyright period for the length of the extended copyright unless there was an agreement to the contrary[4].

1 Reg 18(1) of the 1995 Regulations.
2 Reg 18(2) of the 1995 Regulations.
3 CDPA s 90(2); see **paragraph 10.23**.
4 Reg 21(b) of the 1996 Regulations. See **paragraph 10.19** for a detailed consideration of this issue.

Ownership of revived copyright

6.04 The person who was the owner of the copyright in the work immediately before it expired is, from 1 January 1996, the owner of any revived copyright in the work[1].

1 Reg 19(1) of the 1995 Regulations. See **paragraph 10.20** for a detailed consideration of this issue.

Revived copyright: restricted rights of the owners

6.05 The rights of the owner of a work in which revived copyright subsists are limited. The holders of revived copyright cannot prevent exploitation. Their rights are simply to receive 'such reasonable royalty or other remuneration as may be agreed or determined in default of agreement by the Copyright Tribunal' in respect of such use[1].

In order to take advantage of this situation, the person who intends to use the work must give 'reasonable notice of its intention to the copyright owner stating when he intends to begin to do the acts'[2]. Failure to give such notice will result in his acts not being treated as licensed[3] and therefore will constitute an infringement of copyright against which he can be injuncted.

If notice has been given, the acts are treated as licensed and even though the royalty or other remuneration which is payable in respect of the acts has not been determined by the time the acts are carried out, there is not deemed to be a breach of copyright[4]. In other words it is not possible to injunct a person to prevent them doing acts which would infringe copyright if that person has given the necessary notice.

The reader should note that the 1995 Regulations contain specific provisions dealing with acts undertaken before revival of copyright, consideration of which is beyond the scope of this *User's Guide*.

1   Reg 24(1) of the 1995 Regulations.
2   Reg 24(2) of the 1995 Regulations.
3   Reg 24(3) of the 1995 Regulations.
4   Reg 24(4) of the 1995 Regulations.

Literary, dramatic, musical and artistic works

6.06   Copyright subsists in these works until the expiry of the period of 70 years from the end of the calendar year in which the author dies.[1]

1   There are exceptions for works of unknown authorship, computer-generated works and works of joint authorship, which are dealt with below, and for industrially applied artistic works, which are dealt with in **Chapter 15**.

Literary, dramatic, musical and artistic works unpublished at author's death

6.07   Until the CDPA came into force on 1 August 1989, the position with regard to literary, dramatic and musical works was that if:

● the work was not published;
● the work was not performed in public;
● records of the work were not offered for sale to the public; and
● the work was not broadcast or included in a cable programme

during the lifetime of the author, then the copyright in the work continued to subsist for a period of 50 years from the end of the calendar year which included the earliest occasion upon which one of those acts was done.

A graphic example of the continuation of copyright in such a work which was not published during the author's lifetime is to be found in the case of Boswell's Journals. These were discovered in a croquet box in a Scottish mansion in the 1920s. Although they were written in the eighteenth century, the copyright period ran in the case of each journal for 50 years from the date of publication of the journals. Therefore, some of these journals continued to be in copyright for many more years, even though they had been written in the eighteenth century.

Under the CDPA, before it was amended by the 1995 Regulations, copyright in literary, dramatic and musical works expired 50 years after the end of the year in which the author died, irrespective of whether or not they had been exploited in any way during the lifetime of the author. The only special provision was for works by authors who had died before 1 August 1989 and which had not been exploited in one of the ways mentioned above in their lifetime. Those works remained in copyright until the end of the fiftieth year after the year in which the CDPA came into force: the copyright in these works would therefore have expired on 31 December 2039. Unpublished anonymous works made between 1 August 1989 and 1 January 1996 enjoy perpetual copyright.

The position regarding artistic works (excluding photographs and engravings) was different under the 1956 Act in that the copyright period of the lifetime of the author plus 50 years applied, whether or not the work had been published or exploited in the author's lifetime.

Under the CDPA, as amended, and with effect from 1 January 1996, the copyright period for unpublished works is 70 years pma[1]. However, the old provisions continue to apply to works written before that date if those old provisions would have provided a longer period of protection[2]. For example:

- an author dies in 1960 leaving an unpublished work;
- the work is published in 1987.

Under the 1956 Act, copyright would have been 50 years from 1987. Thus copyright would have expired in 2037. Under the CDPA, as amended, the period would be 70 pma: thus copyright would expire in 2030 (1960 plus 70 years). Therefore the 1956 Act period will apply, and copyright will expire in 2037.

Engravings had the same treatment as literary, dramatic and musical works. If they were unpublished at the author's death, they continued in copyright until the expiration of 50 years from the end of the calendar year in which they were first published. If they had not been published at 1 August 1989, the copyright expires at 31 December 2039 or 70 years pma if longer.

1   CDPA s 12.
2   See reg 15(1) of the 1995 Regulations.

Pre-1989 photographs

6.08   The copyright in all photographs taken prior to 1 July 1912 has now expired.

The copyright in photographs taken between 1 July 1912 and 1 June 1957 subsisted until the expiration of 50 years from the end of the calendar year in which the photograph was taken.

The copyright in photographs taken after 1 June 1957 and before 1 August 1989 expires at the end of the fiftieth year from the end of the calendar year when the photograph was first published.

The copyright period in photographs taken during the period 1957 to 1989, which remained unpublished on 1 August 1989, is 70 years pma if that period is longer than the term provided for under earlier legislation. For unpublished photographs that was 50 years from the end of 1989, i.e. 2039.

Photographs taken on and after 1 August 1989

6.09 The copyright period for photographs taken after 31 July 1989 is the same as for all other artistic works (i.e. 70 years pma).

Date photograph is taken	Duration of protection
Before 1 July 1912	Copyright now expired.
Between 1 July 1912 and 1 June 1957	50 years from the end of the calendar year in which the photograph was *taken*.
Between 1 June 1957 and 1 August 1989	Expires at the end of the 50th year from the end of the year in which the photograph was first *published*. Any photograph taken but not published during this period will qualify for copyright protection for 70 years from the end of the year in which the author dies, if this period is longer than the term provided under the Copyright Act 1954. For unpublished photographs, that was 50 years from the end of 1989, i.e. until 2039.
After 31 July 1989	70 years from the end of the year in which the author dies.

Computer-generated works

6.10 Copyright subsists in computer-generated works until the end of the period of 50 years from the end of the calendar year in which they were made[1].

1   CDPA s 12(7).

Sound recordings

6.11 Copyright subsists in sound recordings until the end of the period of 50 years from the end of the calendar year in which the recording was made, and it then expires. However, if the sound recording was released during that 50-year period, the copyright period will be 50 years from the end of the calendar year in which it was released.

'Released' is defined in the CDPA as meaning when a sound recording is first published, played in public, or communicated to the public (although for these purposes no account is to be taken of any unauthorised act).[1]

Where the sound recording is produced by a person (which includes a company) who is not a national of an EEA state, the duration of copyright is that to which the sound recording is entitled in the country of which the producer is a national, provided that it is not longer than the period set out above in this paragraph[2].

Discussion has recently focused on whether this level of protection is appropriate: IFPI, for example, has pointed to the fact that Europe has one of the shortest periods of copyright protection for sound recordings in the world[3]. In the US, the 1998 Sonny Bono Copyright Term Extension Act affords a term of protection after the publication of a recording of 95 years, and, if the work has not been published commercially, protection can last for as long as 125 years. The result has been lobbying of the European Commission by IFPI on behalf of interested rights holders (including Cliff Richard, whose original 1950s hit recordings are now entering the public domain). A review of the level of protection in Europe is expected to take place during the life of this edition of the *User's Guide*. Proposals are expected in the UK.

1   CDPA s 13A(2), see also **paragraphs 22.02 and 22.19**.
2   See s 13A(4).
3   For an interesting discussion of this issue, see Juliana Koranteng, 'Fifty ways to lose your living' MIDEM News 2005.

Copyright in sound recordings made before 1 August 1989

6.12   The copyright in sound recordings made before 1 June 1957 subsists until the expiration of 50 years from the end of the calendar year in which the sound recording was made.

The copyright in sound recordings made between 1 June 1957 and 1 August 1989 expires at the end of the fiftieth year from the end of the calendar year when they were first published.

The copyright in sound recordings made during this period, which remained unpublished on 1 August 1989, expires on 31 December 2039, unless the recordings are published before 31 December 2039.

In this latter case the sound recordings will remain in copyright for a period of 50 years from the end of the calendar year in which publication takes place.

Films made before 1 June 1957

6.13 Because, before 1 June 1957, films were treated as dramatic works and photographs for copyright purposes[1], the period of protection was the life of the writer or writers of the screenplay plus 50 years and, for the photographic element, the period was 50 years from the end of the calendar year in which the photograph was taken.

1 There was no separate film copyright.

Films made between 1 June 1957 and 1 August 1989

6.14 The period of copyright for a cinematograph film made between these dates differed according to whether the film was registered under Part III of the Cinematograph Films Act 1938 or Part II of the Films Act 1960 as a 'British' film or whether it was not so registrable.

Copyright subsisted in a film which was so registrable, continued to subsist until the film was registered, and continued thereafter until the end of the period of 50 years from the end of the calendar year in which it was so registered. The copyright period for registered films remains unchanged.

In the case of films which were not registrable under the Films Act 1960, copyright continued until the film was published and thereafter until the end of the period of 50 years from the end of the calendar year which included the date of its first publication.

The position under the CDPA for films made before 1 August 1989 and which were neither registered nor published before that date, is that the copyright period will expire on 31 December 2039 unless they are released before 31 December 2039. In this latter case they will remain in copyright for a period of 50 years from the end of the calendar year in which they are released.

Films made after 31 December 1995

6.15 The copyright period for these films is 70 years from the end of the calendar year in which the death occurs of the last to die of the following persons:

- the principal director;
- the author of the screenplay;
- the author of the dialogue;
- the composer of music specially created for and used in the film[1].

If the identity of some but not all of these persons is not known, then the reference to the last to die is construed as a reference to the last known person to die[2].

Where the country of origin of a film is not an EEA state, and the producer and director of the film are not EEA state nationals, the duration of copyright is that to which the film is entitled in the country of origin provided that it is not longer than that set out above for EEA films[3].

If there are no persons falling within these categories, then the period is 70 years from the end of the calendar year in which the film was made[4]. This provision may for example, apply to films made (i.e. videos recorded) by security cameras if such films are entitled to copyright protection.

1   CDPA s 13B(2).
2   CDPA s 13B(3).
3   CDPA s 13B(7).
4   CDPA s 13B(4).

Broadcasts

6.16 Copyright subsists in broadcasts until the expiry of the period of 50 years from the end of the calendar year in which the broadcast was made[1]. The copyright period is not extended by repeats or reinstated by broadcasts made after the end of the copyright period[2].

1   CDPA s 14(2).
2   CDPA s 14(5).

Published editions

6.17 Published editions are, in effect, typographical arrangements of literary, dramatic, or musical works[1]. Copyright in published editions subsists for 25 years from the end of the calendar year in which the edition was first published[2].

1   See **paragraph 2.11**.
2   CDPA s 15(2).

Anonymous and pseudonymous, literary, dramatic and artistic works (except photographs)

6.18 A work is anonymous or pseudonymous[1] if the identity of the author is unknown, or in the case of a joint work, if the identity of none of the authors is known[2].

The identity of an author is regarded as unknown if it is not possible for a person to ascertain his identity by reasonable enquiry. If his identity is once known, it shall not subsequently be regarded as unknown[3].

The position with regard to anonymous and pseudonymous works made before 1 August 1989 is:

- if the work had been published before that date then the period is 50 years from the end of the year of 'publication';
- if the work was first made available to the public after that date, then it is 50 years from the end of the calendar year in which it was so made available.

The position with regard to anonymous and pseudonymous works made after 31 July 1989 and before 1 January 1996 is:

- if the work was made available to the public in that period – 70 years from the end of the calendar year in which it was made available;
- if the work was not made available to the public during that period it will enjoy perpetual copyright until it is so made available. If it is made available to the public, the period of copyright of 70 years will then begin to run.

The position with regard to anonymous and pseudonymous works made after 1 January 1996 is:

- if the work is not made available to the public, the copyright period is 70 years from the end of the year in which the work was made;
- if the work was made available to the public in that period, then 70 years from the end of the calendar year in which it was so made available.

Once the identity of the author is known, the normal 70 years pma rule will apply.

The expression 'made available to the public' includes, in the case of:

- *literary, dramatic or musical works* – performance in public or broadcasts of the works or their inclusion in a cable programme service;
- *artistic works* – exhibition in public;
- *films* – showing the work in public or including it in a communication to the public.

The use of the word 'include' in this definition means that other methods of making the work available to the public, such as publication in a written form, must also be taken into account.

If at any time before the end of this period it is possible for a person who had no previous knowledge of the fact to ascertain the identity by reasonable enquiry, then the full period of copyright will apply to the work.

The position with regard to pre-CDPA works was that the period commenced with 'publication' – a word defined in that context to mean making *copies* available to the public and, therefore, more restrictive than the expression 'making a work available to the public'.

1   CDPA s 9(3) uses the expression 'of unknown authorship'.
2   CDPA s 9(4).
3   CDPA s 9(5).

Unpublished works – the publication right

6.19   The publication right applies only to literary, dramatic, musical and artistic works and films[1]. Consequently, the word 'work' is used in this paragraph to refer only to *those* classes of works.

The publication right was introduced into the CDPA by the 1996 Regulations, as amended by the 2003 Regulations, and applies only from 1 December 1996.

A person who, *after the expiry of copyright protection*, publishes for the first time a previously unpublished work becomes the first owner of the publication right in that work, which is a property right equivalent to copyright[2].

'Publication' as used in this context has its own definition[3].

For these purposes 'publication' means:

'any making available to the public, in particular—

(a)   the issue of copies to the public;
(b)   making the work available by means of an electronic retrieval system;
(c)   the rental or lending of copies of the work to the public;
(d)   the performance, exhibition or showing of the work in public;
(e)   communicating the work to the public.'

This definition does not preclude any means of making available a work to the public which may be invented after the Regulations came into effect, or which may not be included in the particularised sub-paragraphs. An unauthorised act will not amount to publication[4].

Given that the publication right only arises in the case of works in which the copyright has expired before they are published, it is necessary for the Regulations to specify who can give the consent for an authorised act after the copyright has expired. For the purposes of the 1996 Regulations, an unauthorised act means 'an act done without the consent of the owner of the physical medium in which the work is embodied or on which it is recorded'[5].

It is important to bear in mind that the definition of an unauthorised act in relation to the publication right has no relevance whatsoever to the definition of an unauthorised act in relation to a work which is in copyright. Except in the context of the publication right, ownership of the physical medium in which the work is embodied or on which it is recorded (such as a canvas which bears a painting or a compact disc on which music has been recorded) carries with it no right whatsoever in copyright law[6].

The publication right will be of little value to owners of unpublished manuscripts and musical scores until the year 2040, because unpublished literary and musical works enjoyed perpetual copyright until the CDPA came into force and introduced a copyright period that was not dependant on publication[7]. There is, however, immediate copyright value in artistic works (including photographs) in respect of which the copyright period was not dependent on publication but was 50 years pma.

1   The publication right is also considered in detail at **paragraph 28.24**.
2   Reg 16(1) of the 1996 Regulations.
3   Wider than that set out in s 175 of the CDPA.
4   Reg 16(3) of the 1996 Regulations.
5   Reg 16(3).
6   See **paragraph 10.01**.
7   See **paragraph 6.04**.

The qualification for the publication right

6.20   A work qualifies for publication right protection only if:

- the first publication is in the EEA; and
- the publisher of the work is, at the time of first publication, a national of an EEA state[1].

It will be noted that these requirements are not in the alternative. Both must be satisfied.

1   See reg 16(4) of the 1996 Regulations.

Period of the publication right

6.21   The publication right expires at the end of the period of 25 years from the end of the year in which the work was first published[1].

There is no publication right in works in which crown copyright or parliamentary copyright subsisted but in which copyright expired before the works were published.

1   See reg 16(6) of the 1996 Regulations.

Application of copyright provisions to the publication right

6.22   Certain copyright provisions are applied to the publication right by reg 17 of the 1996 Regulations.

These provisions are:

- the rights of the copyright owner[1];
- the exceptions and defences to copyright actions[2];
- dealings with rights in copyright works[3];
- remedies for infringement[4];
- copyright licensing[5].

There are some minor variations in the way these provisions are applied to publication right which do not merit detailed discussion here[6]. Most deal with presumptions which can be made in the case of an action for infringement.

1   See **Chapter 7**.
2   See **Chapter 9**.
3   See **Chapter 10**.
4   See **Chapter 8**.
5   See **Chapters 10** and **13**.
6   Reg 17 of the 1996 Regulations.

Works of joint authorship

6.23   Works of joint authorship are works that are produced by the collaboration of two or more authors, in which the contribution of each author is not separate from the contribution of the other author or authors[1]. The term of copyright in such works is to be determined by reference to the date of death of the last surviving author. For example, in the case of literary, dramatic, musical or artistic works which are 'joint works', the term of copyright continues until the end of the period of 70 years from the end of the calendar year in which the last surviving author dies. All references to 'the author', when calculating the period of copyright in a joint work by reference to the death of the author, should be construed as references to the author who died last, when works are joint works.

1   CDPA s 10(1).

Works belonging to the Crown and government departments: position before the CDPA

6.24 The copyright term in literary, dramatic or musical works made by, or under the direction or control of the Crown, or a government department was as follows:

- where the work was unpublished, it continued to subsist so long as the work remained unpublished; and
- where the work was published, it subsisted until the end of the period of 50 years from the end of the calendar year in which the work was first published.

Copyright in artistic works made by or under the direction or control of the Crown or government departments, continued to subsist until the end of the period of 50 years from the end of the year in which the work was made. However, there was an exception in the case of engravings or photographs, in that the period of 50 years ran from the end of the year in which the engraving or photograph was first published.

As regards unpublished works, the CDPA applies, except to those works whose copyright protection would expire prior to 31 December 2039 if they were not subject to Crown copyright provision. In that event, copyright will expire on 31 December 2039.

Crown copyright

6.25 The basic position is that when a work is 'made by Her Majesty or by an officer or servant of the Crown in the course of his duties', if the work is entitled to copyright protection, the copyright will be owned by the Crown. In the case of a literary, dramatic, musical or artistic work, copyright will subsist for 125 years from the end of the calendar year in which it was made unless it is 'published commercially' during the period of 75 years from the end of the calendar year in which it was made. In that case copyright will subsist for 50 years from the end of the calendar year in which it was first so published. 'Commercial publication' is defined in the CDPA as:

'(a) issuing copies of the work to the public at a time when copies made in advance of the receipt of orders are generally available to the public; or

(b) making the work available to the public by means of an electronic retrieval system'[1].

The copyright period for works of Crown copyright which are not literary, dramatic, musical or artistic works is the same as that for non-Crown copyright works[2].

1   CDPA s 175(2).
2   CDPA ss 163–167 which concern Crown and Parliamentary copyright are only generally dealt with in this *User's Guide*.

Parliamentary copyright

6.26 The 70 years pma period does not apply to parliamentary copyright works or to works vesting in international organisations. The duration of Parliamentary copyright can be summarised as follows:

- *Acts of Parliament and Measures of the General Synod of the Church of England*: 50 years from the end of the calendar year in which the Royal Assent is given.
- *Works made by or under the direction or control of the House of Commons or the House of Lords*:
  - (a) literary, dramatic, musical and artistic works: 50 years from the end of the year in which the work is made;
  - (b) other works: the normal copyright period applicable to the relevant category of work under the CDPA.

Bills of either House cease to be in copyright when they receive Royal Assent (i.e. they become Acts of Parliament) or if they do not receive Royal Assent, on the withdrawal or rejection of the Bill or the end of the session. A Bill will regain its copyright protection if it is reintroduced in a subsequent session[1].

1   Parliamentary copyright is dealt with in ss 165–167 of the CDPA.

Copyright vesting in certain international organisations

6.27 The 'international organisations' in question are those to be specified in statutory instruments, of which the only one at present is the Copyright (International Organisation) Order 1989, which confers copyright protection on works originating with the United Nations, its Specialised Agencies or the Organisation of American States, which would not otherwise enjoy copyright in the UK. These works are protected for 50 years from the end of the calendar year in which they were made[1].

1   CDPA s 168(3).

'Peter Pan' and the Hospital for Sick Children

6.28 Sir James Barrie, who wrote the play *Peter Pan,* died in 1937. The copyright in the play expired on 31 December 1987, at which time the copyright was vested in the Trustees for the Hospital for Sick Children. The CDPA provides that notwithstanding the expiration of the copyright in the play, the Trustees are to continue to receive royalties payable in respect of any public performance, commercial publication, broadcasting or inclusion of the work in a cable programme which takes place after 31 July 1989[1]. The royalty is to be determined by agreement, or failing agreement by the Copyright Tribunal. The Trustees have no power to grant exclusive licences in *Peter Pan*. Their right is to receive royalties only. In short, the rights are comparable with those of revived copyright holders[2].

Anyone can perform or reproduce *Peter Pan* without needing to obtain permission from the Trustees, provided that they pay royalties.

1   CDPA s 301.
2   See **paragraph 6.05**.

Universities' and colleges' perpetual copyright

6.29 The perpetual copyright conferred on universities and colleges by the Copyright Act 1775 will now expire on 31 December 2039.

Chapter 7

Restricted acts and acts of secondary infringement

Introduction

7.01 Copyright is a property interest which allows the owner the exclusive right to undertake, and authorise others to undertake, a number of activities in relation to his work. By s 2 of the CDPA:

> 'the owner of copyright in a work of any description has the exclusive right to do the ...acts restricted by the copyright in a work of that description'[1].

Since the owner is exclusively entitled to permit these activities, anyone who undertakes a 'restricted act' without his authorisation will be strictly liable for a primary infringement of copyright regardless of the intention or knowledge of the infringer[2]. The ability to sell or license the right to perform these restricted acts is the basis of all copyright industries[3].

In addition to the basic restricted acts, a number of activities *may* amount to a breach of copyright if the person undertaking the activity has 'guilty knowledge'[4]. Doing these acts will constitute a *secondary* infringement of copyright.

If copyright material is used without the authority of the copyright owner in a manner which does not fall within the category of 'restricted acts', and does not amount to a secondary infringement of copyright, copyright law will not enable the owner to prevent that use.

The reader should note that different principles apply to those acts which may be controlled by the owner of the sui generis 'database right' in databases which do not receive protection as literary works[5].

1 See **Chapter 8** for a discussion of infringement issues.
2 See **paragraph 8.03**.
3 See **Chapter 10** for a discussion of issues regarding the transfer of rights.
4 See **paragraph 8.21**.
5 See **paragraph 2.02**. These principles are considered in detail in **Chapter 16**.

The restricted acts summarised

7.02 Under the CDPA, the restricted acts in relation to a work are:

- copying the work;
- issuing copies of the work to the public;
- renting or lending copies of the work to the public;
- performing, showing or playing the work in public;
- communicating the work to the public;
- making an adaptation of the work or doing any of the above acts in relation to an adaptation[1].

Significantly, 'copyright in a work is infringed by a person who without the licence of the copyright owner does, *or authorises another* to do, any of the acts restricted by copyright'[2]. For these purposes, facilitating the doing of an act is different from procuring the doing of an act[3]. So in one case (decided under the 1956 Act) it was held that 'sales and advertisements to the public generally of a machine which may be used for lawful or unlawful purposes, including infringement of copyright, cannot be said to "procure" all breaches of copyright thereafter by members of the public who use the machine'[4].

Some acts may involve multiple infringements. For example, it is worth noting that the functioning of the internet involves a variety of processes, several of which will involve restricted acts. Posting an audio-visual work on to an internet web-site will involve the 'uploading' of a work to a computer file server that is connected to the internet. Accessing this work will involve 'downloading' the work from the server. The transmission of images to the public via the internet or the immediate re-transmission of a broadcast signal containing work, made by means of the internet, will also amount to a 'communication to the public' of the work.

Briefly, there are at least four technical processes involved in 'webcasting':

- acquisition (capturing the data);
- digitisation and encoding (to make it compatible with one of the playback forms);
- hosting (storage on the hard drive ready for access by users); and
- delivery to the user.

These processes may involve the restricted acts of:

- copying (capturing the data, digitisation, uploading to the ISP server, downloading)[5];
- public performance (if the webcast is shown in public)[6];

- communication to the public.

Until recently, it was widely thought that the principles laid down in *CBS Songs Ltd v Amstrad Consumer Electronics plc* made it unlikely that a website which offers peer-to-peer software for download by others, but which does not itself directly engage in unauthorised copying, could be construed as 'authorising' the infringing activities of the software users. However, recent cases in the US and Australia (both common law jurisdictions) indicate a willingness of the courts in those jurisdictions to find that distributing such software may itself amount to infringing activity, raising the possibility that an English court may re-evaluate the Amstrad decision in light of peer-to-peer file sharing[7].

In *Universal Music Australia v Sharman License Holdings,* the Australian Federal Court found that Sharman Networks had infringed copyright by authorising its users to engage in unauthorised copying of music files. Sharman had encouraged users of its Kazaa software to 'Join the Revolution', and encouraged users to 'defy the record companies by ignoring copyright constraints'. Sharman was ordered to utilise filtering technologies which either stops users from sharing files that match a list provided by record companies, or which allows users only to see licensed works) and to put 'maximum pressure' on current users to upgrade to the filtered version.

1 CDPA s 16(1).
2 See s 16(2).
3 *Belegging-en Exploitatiemaatschappij BV v Witten Industrial Diamonds Ltd [1979] FSR 59 at 65, CA.*
4 *CBS Songs Ltd v Amstrad Consumer Electronics plc [1988] 2 All ER 484,* per Lord Templeman.
5 See **paragraph 7.03**.
6 See **paragraph 7.06**.
7 *MGM v Grokster, US Supreme Court, June 27, 2005,* and *Universal Music Australia v Sharman License Holdings FCA 1242 (5 September 2005).*

Copying

7.03 To some extent, what amounts to copying will depend on the work in question. The CDPA elaborates in relation to some categories of work as follows[1]:

- *Literary, dramatic, musical and artistic works*: Copying a literary, dramatic, musical or artistic work means *reproducing it in any material form*. This includes storing it in any medium by electronic means, such as on the memory of a computer[2]. For artistic works, copying includes making a three dimensional work from a two dimensional work and vice versa (e.g. making a drawing from a sculpture)[3]. A special exemption exists in relation to the taking of photographs in buildings[4].

- *Films and broadcasts*: Copying a film or broadcast includes making a photograph of the whole or any substantial part of any image forming part of it[5]. Although this is not an exhaustive definition, it is nevertheless vital, because it confirms that a 'video grab' (i.e. the reproduction of a still taken from a moving video image) will amount to copying, notwithstanding that the single image which is 'grabbed' may be a very insignificant part of the whole work[6]. Interestingly the CDPA contains no express provision confirming that these works will be copied if they are stored by electronic means (in contrast to the works referred to in the last paragraph), although this seems to be implicit.
- *Published editions*: Copying the typographical arrangement of a published edition of a work means 'making a facsimile copy', which includes copies that have been enlarged or reduced in size[7].

Special considerations apply in the context of photographs. A photograph can clearly be infringed where a facsimile copy is taken of it by some photographic means. However, a photograph can also be infringed if reproduced by another method (e.g. a painting). The test is whether a substantial part of the photograph has been replicated. If A sets up a scene to be photographed and B also photographs the same scene. B has not infringed A's photograph, since he has not copied the photograph, but the scene. There is no causal link between the works created by A and B[8].

No special guidance is offered in the CDPA with regard to the copying of sound recordings, although these, like the works discussed above, are subject to the general principles regarding infringement discussed in **Chapter 8**.

Although the CDPA does not specifically address the technological processes comprising the functionality of the internet, copying includes storing the work in any medium by 'electronic means'[9]. The word 'electronic' is very widely defined by the CDPA as meaning: 'actuated by electric, magnetic, electro-magnetic, electro-chemical, or electro-mechanical energy'[10] and would include computer hard drives, CD-ROMs and DVDs. So, when a digital copy is made of a work without the permission of the owner, the copier will infringe copyright.

In its original form, the CDPA makes it clear that copying will include copying which is transient or incidental to some other use[11]. In the digital environment this form of copying is integral to the operation of digital networks. Unlike most other means of communication (the fax machine excluded), downloading a digital transmission from a digital network like the internet, or uploading material from a digital storage device like a CD-ROM *inevitably* involves copying. In both cases a copy will be made on the memory of the user's computer and in the former case on any of a number of computers used in the process of conveying the information to the end user. This created complex legal problems for on-line service providers, who transfer (and in the process of so doing make 'cache' copies of) countless amounts of data that almost certainly contain unauthorised copies.

For that reason the CDPA has now been amended so as to specifically exclude the making of transient copies as part of networked communications from infringing copyright under certain circumstances[12].

Computer programs are protected as literary works[13], but a series of cases has limited the extent to which computer programs may be said to be infringed by anything other than straightforward textual copying. In one recent case, the court was invited to consider whether an online booking system created for Easyjet infringed the copyright of another booking system by appropriating the 'business logic' of the earlier system[14]. It was not disputed that the underlying software did not resemble that of the earlier system, except that it acted on similar inputs with similar results. The court was invited to draw an analogy with 'non-textual copying' in the context of the plot of a book[15]. The claim of non-textual copying failed. A computer program has no theme, events or narrative flow like a plot, simply a series of pre-defined operations intended to achieve a desired result, and no actual code had been copied. To extend the literary copyright in a computer program to restrain use of 'business logic' would be an extension of protection which ran counter to public policy[16].

1   CDPA s 17(2). See **paragraph 23.06** for a consideration of copying lighting designs in the context of plays, and **Chapter 28** regarding the copying of artistic works generally.
2   CDPA s 17(2).
3   CDPA s 17(3), see **paragraph 28.05**.
4   See **paragraph 9.24**.
5   CDPA s 17 (4).
6   See however the exceptions to copyright infringement considered at **Chapter 9** and in particular **paragraph 9.33**.
7   ss 17(5) and 178.
8   *Creation Records v News Group Newspapers Ltd [1997] EMLR 444*, see also **paragraph 2.06**.
9   CDPA s 17(2).
10   CDPA s 178.
11   CDPA s 17(6).
12   See **paragraph 9.02**.

13   See **paragraph 2.02.**
14   *Navitaire Inc v (1) EasyJet Airline Co (2) Bulletproof Technologies Inc (unreported, 30 June 2004, ChD, Pumfrey J).*
15   The court considered *Jarrold v Houlston [1857] 3 Kay & J 708.*
16   see **paragraph 2.16.**

The issue of copies to the public

7.04   Like copying, *issuing copies to the public* is an act restricted by the copyright in every category of copyright work. For the purposes of the CDPA, the phrase: 'issue to the public of copies of a work' means:

'(a)   the act of putting into circulation in the EEA copies not previously put into circulation in the EEA by or with the consent of the copyright owner; or

(b)   the act of putting into circulation outside the EEA copies not previously put into circulation in the EEA or elsewhere'[1].

For these purposes 'copies' will include electronic copies[2]. However the act of 'putting into circulation' suggests a *tangible* copy (such as a CD or DVD) which is itself circulated rather than, say, a computer file which is communicated from A to B via the internet, since any further circulation of that file would be of a further copy of that file, not the file itself.

The following activities do not qualify as issuing copies to the public for the purposes of this restricted act:

'(a)   any subsequent distribution, sale, hiring or loan of copies previously put into circulation (subject to rental or lending right); or

(b)   any subsequent importation of such copies into the UK or another EEA state,

except as far as paragraph (a) of section 18(2) applies to 'putting into circulation in the EEA copies previously put into circulation outside the EEA'[3].

This wording is confusing even for experienced practitioners, and has done nothing to ease the frequent misunderstandings amongst users in relation to this area of law. The current language arose from amendments made to the CDPA implementing the Rental and Lending Directive. Its intention was to introduce into the CDPA the concept of 'exhaustion of rights' between the Member States of the EU.

In accordance with Community principles, when goods have been circulated in any part of the Community there should, broadly, be no impediment to the movement of those same goods within any other part of the Community. This conflicts with the territorial nature of copyright law and the ECJ has developed a doctrine of European exhaustion of rights to address this issue[4]. Consequently, the first circulation of copies of a copyright work within the EEA with the authorisation of the owner is said to 'exhaust' the owner's right to control any further distribution, sale, hiring or loan *of those same copies* to the public within the EEA. The copyright owner cannot, for example, claim copyright infringement because copies he has authorised for sale in France are subsequently issued for sale into the UK, since this kind of 'parallel importing' is necessary to ensure the free movement of goods and services within the Community envisaged by the Treaty of Rome[5].

At the same time, the wording attempts to exclude any suggestion of adopting a policy of full 'international exhaustion of rights' (which would exhaust the right of a copyright owner to restrict the further distribution, sale, hiring or loan of copies of his work after the first authorised issuing of such copies to the public with his authorisation anywhere in the world, regardless of where that subsequent distribution takes place geographically). The Rental and Lending Directive, for example, specifically provides that the 'distribution right' in certain categories of work is not exhausted within the Community unless the first sale in the Community was made with the owner's consent[6]. A copyright owner can, for example, claim copyright infringement because copies he authorised for sale in the US were subsequently imported for sale into the UK. A doctrine of 'international exhaustion' has been discussed in the context of multilateral trade agreements, but its introduction currently remains unlikely since it would fundamentally attack the practice of exclusive territorial licensing practised in almost all industries involving the distribution of copyright works.

Two relatively recent trade mark cases are of interest since they track a similar debate in relation to exhaustion of rights. Consistent with the principles outlined above, in *Silhouette International Schmied GmbH & Co KG v Hartlauer Handelsgesellschaft GmbH*[7] the ECJ ruled out the possibility of a member state introducing a concept of international exhaustion of rights in the context of trade marks. However, in the UK, in a subsequent decision[8], Laddie J (whilst acknowledging that there is no international exhaustion of rights) observed that an owner may be said to have given implied consent to the importation of goods into the EEA where he has sold the goods outside the EEA without restricting the right of the purchaser to distribute and onward sell the goods in question. In practice then, it is important, in deciding whether rights have been exhausted in relation to particular goods within the EEA, to consider all the circumstances in which they were sold, including the nature of the goods, the terms of any contract of sale and the provisions of applicable law. For the user who wishes to ensure that no implied consent may be deemed to be given, it will be important to ensure that (for products circulated for distribution outside the EEA) any distribution agreement expressly limits the territory for sale and excludes importation of the products into different jurisdictions.

It should be noted that nothing in the CDPA limits the right of a copyright owner to prevent the issuing of *further* copies of the same work to the public. So, if the author of a book authorises his publisher to issue 1000 copies to the public in the UK and these are sold, the author's copyright is infringed if the publisher issues further copies of the book without the further authorisation of the author.

The effect of s 18 of the CDPA can be summarised as follows:

- Copies already circulating in the EEA with the consent of the copyright owner can be distributed, sold, hired or lent or imported into the UK or another EEA state without the copyright owner's authorisation.
- Copies already circulating outside the EEA but not circulated in the EEA, can only be sold, distributed etc in the EEA with the copyright owner's authorisation.
- Copies already circulating in the EEA without the copyright owner's consent (for example, where they were placed on the market in a member state where the copyright period had expired) may not be imported etc into the UK without the copyright owner's authorisation.
- The act of issuing copies to the public does not in itself exhaust any other right of the copyright owner to authorise 'restricted acts' (such as, for example, rental and lending or communication to the public).

1   CDPA s 18(2).
2   CDPA s 18(3).
3   CDPA s 18(3).
4   See **paragraph 14.06**.
5   See **paragraph 7.10** and **Chapter 14**.
6   Art 9(2).
7   *C-355/96: [1999] Ch 77*.
8   *Zino Davidoff SA v A & G Imports Ltd [2000] Ch 127*.

Rental and lending

7.05   The rental and lending right was introduced into the CDPA by the 1996 Regulations. The right exists only in respect of literary, dramatic and musical works, and artistic works (subject to certain exclusions regarding works of architecture in the form of buildings, or models of buildings, and works of applied, as opposed to fine, art), films and sound recordings[1]. 'Rental' for these purposes means:

'making a copy of the work available for use, on terms that it will or may be returned, for direct or indirect economic or commercial advantage'[2].

And 'lending' means:

'making a copy of the work available for use, on terms that it will or may be returned, otherwise than for direct or indirect economic or commercial advantage, through an establishment which is accessible to the public'[3].

In order to avoid doubt, the CDPA specifically provides that the expressions 'rental' and 'lending' do not include[4]:

'(a) making available for the purpose of public performance, playing or showing in public, or communication to the public;
(b) making available for the purpose of exhibition in public; or
(c) making available for on-the-spot reference use.'

Moreover, 'lending' is expressly stated to exclude 'making available between establishments which are accessible to the public'[5]. So, one public library may lend a book to another public library without infringing the restricted act of lending. Where lending by an establishment accessible to the public (for example, a public library) gives rise to a payment, the amount of which does not go beyond what is necessary to cover the operating costs of the establishment, there is no direct or indirect economic or commercial advantage for the purposes of the definitions of 'rental' and 'lending'. In other words, if the library is careful to establish that its charges are only sufficient to recover its costs, then the fact that a public library is being paid does not convert its 'lending' into 'rental'[6].

Since implementation of the Rental and Lending Directive, the authors of literary, dramatic, musical and artistic works, and film directors, also have a right to receive 'equitable remuneration' from the rental of their works, notwithstanding that the rental right itself is transferred by the author to, say, the producer of a film[7]. This right cannot be waived and cannot be assigned except to a collecting society (for the purposes of collecting it for the author). Any attempt in an agreement to exclude or restrict the right to equitable remuneration will be void[8].

The level of equitable remuneration is to be set by the parties; in the absence of agreement, the Copyright Tribunal may settle the amount[9].

In the film industry (where the rental of works remains commonplace) this provision has had a significant effect, with producers commonly attempting to reduce the uncertainty inherent in the vague notion of 'equitable remuneration' by adopting contractual devices intended, more or less, to absolve themselves and those taking title under them from any obligation to pay further amounts in respect of such rights.

Since a communication to the public (either as part of a broadcast or an on-demand service) is excluded from the definition of rental and lending, it follows that the author of the work included in such an electronic transmission will not by virtue of the transmission obtain a right to receive equitable remuneration. Rental and lending are intended to relate to the making available of hard copies, not files transmitted by means of networked computer systems.

1   CDPA s 18A(1).
2   CDPA s 18A(2)(a).
3   CDPA s 18A(2)(b).
4   CDPA s 18A(3).
5   CDPA s 18A(4).
6   See **Chapter 19**.
7   CDPA s 93B(1).
8   CDPA s 93B(5).
9   **Chapter 13**.

Performance, playing or showing of a work in public

7.06   The restricted act of 'performance' applies only to the copyright in literary, dramatic or musical works[1]. 'Performance' includes delivery (in the case of lectures, addresses, speeches and sermons), but also includes any method of visual or acoustic presentation, including presentation by means of a sound recording, film or broadcast of the work[2].

The 'playing or showing of a work in public' is also restricted in relation to sound recordings, films and broadcasts[3]. So, for example, to show the transmission of a film on a television set or other monitor 'live' before an audience, or to play a sound recording on a radio in public, will amount to a public performance, playing or showing of the work, (although the reader should note that there are significant qualifications to these principles considered fully below).

However, the CDPA specifically provides that:

'Where copyright in a work is infringed by its being performed, played or shown in public by means of apparatus for receiving visual images or sounds conveyed by electronic means, the person by whom the visual images or sounds are sent, and in the case of performance the performers, shall not be regarded as responsible for the infringement'[4].

This wording is 'technology neutral' and protects broadcasters, cable operators and internet service providers against any liability for making a 'public performance' if the service is displayed on a monitor in public.

The act of broadcasting itself is not a 'performance', notwithstanding that the broadcast will be received by the 'public at large'[5]. Communication to the public (including broadcasting) is a separate restricted act[6].

In determining whether a performance is 'in public' for the purposes of s 19 of the CDPA, the courts have repeatedly stated that the issue is a question of fact to be determined in each case. However, the meaning and scope of the words 'in public' is a question of law which in less obvious cases may need to be investigated.

The phrase has been the subject of numerous judicial decisions which stress that the determining factor in deciding whether a performance is in public should be 'common sense'[7]. Accordingly, while certain factors may be important in borderline cases[8], the courts will give very little weight to arguments based on such factors if a performance is clearly 'in public' in accordance with the ordinary meaning of the words[9].

The starting point for determining the meaning of 'in public' is that it is the character of the audience which is all-important: performance in public means a performance to an audience which is not domestic or quasi-domestic in character[10]. In the leading case[11] it is said that the question depends 'solely upon the character of the audience' and that factors such as whether visitors are present, whether an entrance fee is charged and the number of the audience are not decisive. However, it is clear from subsequent cases that these and other factors may help shed some light on whether the audience is domestic or quasi-domestic in a difficult case.

The question to be asked is whether the performance is 'part of the domestic or home life of the members of the audience' or whether the audience form a 'domestic circle' or whether the members of the audience are 'bound to one another by any domestic or quasi-domestic tie'. On the other side of the line lie performances which are part of the audience's 'non-domestic or outside life'[12]. An Australian case similarly puts the question as whether the 'persons coming together to form the audience are bound together by a domestic or private tie, or by an aspect of their public life.'[13]

The cases treat the issue of whether membership of the audience is open to the public as a strongly relevant factor and it is clear that this does not have to mean the public at large but can refer to a portion or section of the public. For example, where there was a performance at a private club which was sufficiently exclusive that most of the public could not afford the membership fees (or, indeed, satisfy the membership requirements) this was held to be a public performance – one of the reasons given was that a section of the public were 'able to become members'[14]. In an hotel, a live performance was 'in public', since any paying member of the public (whether paying for accommodation or dinner) was able to become a member of the audience[15].

Some of the more detailed analysis in the cases[16] looks at more economic arguments – essentially asking what the copyright owner's monopoly created by the exclusive right to authorise public performance is intended to cover. In *PRS v Harlequin Record Shops*, the judge recognised[17] the defendant's argument that 'a most important consideration is whether the performance injures the [copyright owner] or interferes with his proprietary rights' and 'whether the performance is given to audiences for performances to which the [copyright owner] would expect to receive a fee'. The fact that historically a fee has not been charged will not be decisive since 'one of the rights which [the copyright owner] possesses is the right to decide whether or not to charge a fee for performances'. In that case, the evidence was that a prudent record shop owner would be likely to pay for a licence rather than have performance stopped, and this was seen as relevant to whether the copyright owner would be injured; in another case the question of whether some of the audience members would be willing to pay for the performance was relevant to whether the copyright owner was suffering a loss[18].

The following audiences have been treated as non-domestic, so as to render a performance 'in public':

- the members of a proprietary club – where membership was exclusive but open to a section of the public who met the membership criteria[19];
- the members of a Women's Institute watching a play put on by another branch – membership was in theory open to all women in the catchment area of the branch[20];
- the staff in a factory – the general public not being able to attend[21];
- in an Australian case, a single person in an hotel room – on the basis that the viewer is there as a guest of the hotel and not as an individual in a private or domestic situation[22].

Furthermore, the viewing of films in prisons and oil rigs is generally regarded as 'in public', despite the fact that the residents of those places will live (for the time being at least) on the premises and despite the fact that no entrance fee is charged. It is suggested that the viewers are not there in their 'private and domestic' capacity but on another basis, i.e. the fact they have been incarcerated/employed there.

The CDPA contains an important qualification to the general principle regarding the performance of broadcasts. Where a broadcast is shown or played in public to an audience who does not pay for admission (such as for example, on a 'big screen' like those commonly displayed in sports and other bars) the copyright in the broadcast or in any sound recording or film which is included in the broadcast will not be infringed, provided the performance is before a non paying audience[23]. For these purposes, an audience is considered to be paying:

'(a) if they have paid for admission to a place of which that place forms part; or

(b) if the goods or services are supplied at that place (or a place of which it forms part) –

(i) at prices which are substantially attributable to the facilities afforded for seeing or hearing the broadcast of programme; or

(ii) at prices exceeding those usually charged there and which are partly attributable to those facilities'[24].

So, if a pub landlord charges increased beer prices instead of charging for admission to a room with a 'big screen', he will be deemed to be showing the broadcast to a paying audience and will be infringing copyright unless he obtains appropriate authorisations[25].

The CDPA specifies that a number of categories of people will not be regarded as having paid for admission, namely:

- residents and inmates;
- members of clubs and societies, where the payment is made only for membership and the provision of facilities for seeing or hearing the broadcast of cable programme, which is only incidental to the main purpose of the club or society[26].

What amounts to a 'broadcast' for these purposes is considered elsewhere[27].

It is important to note that, since implementation of the 2003 Regulations, this exception does *not* (except in certain limited cases, referred to below) permit the use of sound recordings without an appropriate licence if the recording is an 'excepted sound recording'. 'An excepted sound recording' is one:

'(a) whose author is not the author of the broadcast in which it is included; and

(b) which is a recording of music with or without words spoken or sung.'[28]

This essentially includes all commercial music. The only cases in which such music may be played in public as part of a broadcast without a licence is where the playing or showing of the broadcast in public:

'(a) forms part of the activities of an organisation that is not established or considered for profit;

(b) is necessary for the purpose of:

(i) repairing equipment for the reception of broadcasts;

(ii) demonstrating that a repair of such equipment has been carried out;

(iii) demonstrating such equipment which is being sold or let for hire or offered or exposed for sale or hire.'[29]

The effect of the amendments to s 72 of the CDPA made by the 2003 Regulations has therefore been to require that bars and other profit-making organisations that relay broadcasts (e.g. via radio or television) on the premises to customers who have not paid for admission will now require a licence in respect of the public performance of sound recordings contained in broadcasts in addition to their existing PRS licence for the public performance of the musical compositions in the broadcast. Previously, a PRS licence in respect of the public perform-ance of the musical works was all that was needed[30].

Performance is not a restricted act in the context of 'artistic works'[31].

1   CDPA s 19(1).
2   CDPA s 19(2).
3   CDPA s 19(3).
4   CDPA s 19(4).
5   This issue is considered in further detail in **paragraph 26.17**.
6   See **paragraph 7.07**.
7   *Ernest Tucker v PRS [1943] Ch 167*.
8   E.g. whether the general public is invited, whether an entrance fee is charged, whether guests are present, the number of persons present.
9   See e.g. *Ernest Turner*, above and *PRS v Harlequin Record Shops [1979] 2 All ER 828*.
10 *Jennings v Stephens [1936] 1 All ER 409*.
11 *Jennings v Stephens*, above.
12 *Jennings v Stephens*, above.
13 *Australian Performing Rights Association v Commonwealth Bank of Australia (1992) 25 IPR 157*.
14 *Harms Incorporated v Martan's Club [1927] 1 Ch 526*.
15 *PRS v Hawthorn's Hotel (Bournemouth) [1933] Ch 855*.

16 E.g. *Jennings v Stephens, Ernest Turner v PRS, PRS v Harlequin Record Shops*, above.
17 The judge appears to accept that these are valid arguments but was of the opinion that they would only be important in a difficult or borderline case – where the performance is clearly 'in public' then it was not proper to rely on them in order to turn a performance into something it is not.
18 *Harms v Martan's Club*, above.
19 *Harms v Martan's Club*, above.
20 *Jennings v Stephens*, above.
21 *Ernest Turner v PRS*, above.
22 *Rank Film Production v Dodds [1983] 2 NSWLR 553.*
23 CDPA s 72(1).
24 CDPA s 72(2).
25 See **paragraph 26.17**.
26 CDPA s 72(3).
27 See **paragraphs 2.09** and **2.10**.
28 CDPA s 72(1A).
29 CDPA s 72(1B).
30 See **Chapters 22 and 25 for a discussion of music and performance issues.**
31 See **paragraph 23.04**.

Communication to the public

7.07   The 2003 Regulations substantially amended the CDPA to deal with the provision of 'Information Society' services[1].

A new restricted act of 'communication to the public' was introduced. Communication to the public is an act restricted in a literary, dramatic, musical or artistic work, a sound recording or film, or a broadcast[2].

A 'communication to the public' means a communication to the public by electronic transmission, and in relation to a work includes the broadcasting of the work and making the work available to the public in such a way that members of the public may access it from a place and at a time individually chosen by them[3] (i.e. an on-demand, or other interactive service).

Previously, there was considerable debate about the legal status of an internet or mobile transmission, and how that transmission might be considered for the purposes of copyright law in the UK. The earlier definition of 'broadcast' was clearly not intended to capture 'point to point' transmissions, and the only relevant case in the UK which suggested that elements of the process of 'hypertext linking' could be construed as a cable programme service[4], was of somewhat limited authority.

The concept of communication to the public clearly covers the placement of material on a web-server for access by members of the public – whether by downloading or streaming – at a time individually chosen by them. Webcasts however may fall under the category of a broadcast, as tuning into an ongoing stream is analogous to tuning into a television or radio programme; and if they do not, they are certainly within the concept of a 'communication to the public'[4].

There has already been some controversy over the future interpretation of the communication right; in particular the 'making available' issue.

The EU Commission has taken the view that the critical copyright restricted act is the 'making available' of the work to the public, i.e. 'the offering of work on a publicly accessible site, which precedes the stage of its on-demand transmission. It is not relevant whether any person actually has retrieved it or not.' The Commission's view is that the term 'communication to the public' does not cover so-called near video on demand, where the offer of a non-interactive programme is broadcast several times in parallel at short intervals. On this view, BSkyB, for example, does not 'make available' films on the Sky Box Office channel. Interestingly, the Patent Office seems to disagree with the Commission, and takes the view that a delay of no more than 15 minutes is de minimis, and that a service such as Sky Box Office is effectively 'making available' films. In the view of the authors, the Commission's view is to be preferred on this issue.

To make a work available on an interactive basis some form of initial fixation (i.e. upload) must take place. To do this it follows that a certain amount of copying must take place. Many copies may be made in making a work available: on the initial server, at transmission points and at the reception point. What is not clear and what will need to be addressed are questions such as:

(a) Where and when does the making available take place, and which parties are making available?

(b) Are the parties responsible for the initial uploader and/or all the ISPs in the chain?

The Patent Office in its comments on the implementation of the 2003 Regulations stated that 'some right owner organisations suggested that the implementing legislation should seek to identify the points or points at which an act of 'making available' is to be regarded as having taken place. However, 'the Government does not feel that this is necessary or that it would be appropriate particularly given that the [2001 Directive] does not seek to expand upon this aspect'.

1   In order to give effect to these changes the definition of 'broadcasting' which previously existed in the CDPA was modified, and the references in the CDPA to 'cable programme services' and 'cable programmes' were deleted entirely.

2   CDPA s 20(1).

3   CDPA s 20(2).
4   *Shetland Times Limited v Wills [1997] FSR604.*

Adaptations or acts done in relation to adaptations

7.08   This restricted act applies only to literary, dramatic or musical works. The meaning varies dependent upon the category of work in question.

In relation to literary (other than computer programs and databases) and dramatic works 'adaptation' is specially defined as follows:

'(a)   a translation of the work;

(b)   in the case of a dramatic work, a version of the work in which it is converted into a non-dramatic work;

(c)   in the case of a non-dramatic work, a version of the work in which it is converted into a dramatic work;

(d)   a version of the work in which the story or action is conveyed wholly or mainly by means of pictures in a form suitable for reproduction in a book or in a newspaper, magazine or similar periodical'[1].

In the case of musical works, 'adaptation' means: 'an arrangement or transcription of the work'[2].

In relation to computer programs and those databases which receive copyright protection as such[3], an adaptation will mean any arrangement, altered version, or translation of the database or program in question[4].

In the case of computer programs, a 'translation' will include a version of the program which 'is converted into or out of a computer language or code or into a different computer language or code'[5].

An adaptation will itself have copyright if it has sufficient originality, even if the person making the adaptation has no licence from the copyright owner in the original work and is therefore infringing one of the restricted acts, such as copying, in making the adaptation. So, the CDPA provides that doing any of the other restricted acts to the adaptation, including making a further adaptation of the adaptation, will breach the copyright in that adaptation[6].

The restricted act of making an adaptation does not apply to artistic works, so that an artist can effectively imitate the style of another artist without infringing that artist's copyright. But he must not, in the process of so doing, make a copy of the original work.

1   CDPA s 21(3)(a), see also **paragraph 23.11**.
2   CDPA s 21(3)(b).

3   See **paragraph 2.02** and **Chapter 16**.
4   CDPA s 21(3).
5   CDPA s 21(4).
6   CDPA s 21(2).

Secondary infringement: importing, possessing, dealing with or providing means for making infringing copies

7.09   In addition to the 'restricted acts', the following acts will constitute 'secondary infringements' of copyright:

- *Importation*: the importation of an article (other than for private or domestic use) into the UK or any other country to which the CDPA extends or applies, if the importer knew or had reason to believe that the article was an 'infringing copy' of a work[1].
- *Dealing with infringing copies*: a person may not:
  (a) possess in the course of a business;
  (b) sell or let for hire, or offer or expose for sale or hire;
  (c) in the course of a business exhibit in public or distribute; or
  (d) distribute otherwise in the course of a business to such an extent as to effect prejudicially the owner of the copyright;

  an article which is or which he has reason to believe is an 'infringing copy' of a work[2].

  Possession in the course of business means possession in the ordinary course of a business, otherwise solicitors acting for copyright owners who are in possession of infringing video tapes which they had seized on behalf of their client would be liable for an infringement under this sub-section. In the case of *LA Gear Inc v Hi-Tech Sports plc*[3] it was held that where the articles were not on view and were only shown to those who requested a sight of them, they were not offered for sale nor exposed for sale. Moreover, a brochure and a price list had been prepared, but this, it was held, was inviting offers for sale rather than actually offering for sale.

- *Articles used to make infringing copies*: a person may not:
  (a) make;
  (b) import into the UK;
  (c) possess in the course of a business; or
  (d) sell or let for hire, or expose for sale or hire;

  an article specifically designed or adapted for making copies of that work knowing or having reason to believe that it is to be used for making 'infringing copies'[4].

- *Transmission of infringing copies:* the transmission of a work by means of a telecommunication system (otherwise than by communication to the public) knowing or having reason to believe that 'infringing copies' were made by means of the reception of the transmission in the UK or elsewhere[5]. E-mailing an infringing copy to a third party could also amount to a secondary infringement on the same basis.

The last of these acts of secondary infringement was introduced by the CDPA. For these purposes 'Telecommunication system' means 'a system for conveying visual images, sounds or other information by electronic means[6], and therefore has a very wide meaning. The most common case of secondary infringement likely to be encountered under this section is the sending of documents by fax machines. Although the sender does not make a copy on his machine he knows that a copy will be made on the recipient's fax machine.

'Dealing' with an article which is an infringing copy suggests the existence of physical 'articles' which infringe copyright. The question of what constitutes an 'article' for this purpose is difficult in the context of electronic copies. Arguably, a copy held on a hard disk of a computer, or even a temporary copy held on a computer's RAM could be an 'article'. However, it is difficult to envisage how the recipient of such a copy could 'deal' with it except by making further copies – in which case he would in any event commit a primary act of copyright infringement[7].

1   CDPA s 22.
2   CDPA s 23.
3   [1992] FSR 121, CA.
4   CDPA s 24(1).
5   CDPA s 24(2).
6   CDPA s 178.
7   See **paragraph 7.03**.

Infringing copies

7.10   The expression 'infringing copy' has a lengthy definition in the CDPA[1].

In the first place, an article is an infringing copy 'if its making constituted an infringement of the copyright in the work'[2].

An article made outside the UK, the making of which would have constituted an infringement of the copyright in the work had it been made in the UK, or a breach of an exclusive licence agreement relating to that work, will be an infringing copy if it has been, or is proposed to be, imported into the UK. For example, where a licence has been granted by a copyright owner resident outside the UK, to a person in the UK, giving that person the exclusive right to make copies in the UK, then copies which have been perfectly legally made outside the UK (either by the copyright owner himself, or other non-UK resident licensees), will become infringing copies if they are brought into the UK without the permission of the UK licensee[3].

There is an important exception to this rule, which is necessary by reason of the UK's membership of the EU. An article which may lawfully be imported into the UK by virtue of any enforceable Community right under the European Communities Act 1972 is not an infringing copy. Under Art 30 of the Treaty of Rome, goods must be able to circulate freely throughout the common market. Therefore, even if exclusive licences for the manufacture of goods have been granted to UK licensees, goods made elsewhere within the EEA can be imported into the UK without becoming infringing copies[4].

Various parts of the CDPA specify that copies made other than in accordance with various 'permitted' acts should be construed as 'infringing copies'[5]. For example, following the 2003 Regulations, any copy produced by a person in reliance on the 'time shifting' exception to copyright infringement will be treated as an 'infringing copy' if it is subsequently 'dealt with' (i.e. sold, let for hire, offered or exposed for sale or hire or communicated to the public)[6].

One recent case considered the issue of whether a transient copy of game software held on the RAM of a Sony Playstation games console without the authorisation of the copyright holder was capable of being considered an 'infringing copy' (in circumstances where it was necessary to establish that such a copy had been made in order to trigger those provisions of the CDPA which restrict the use of articles designed to circumvent technical anti-copying measures)[7]. The court found that the silicon RAM chip contained in the games console and on which the transitory copy was made was an article, and that whilst it contained an unauthorised copy it was also an infringing article: nothing in the CDPA suggests that an object containing an ephemeral copy should not be considered an article[8].

1   CDPA s 27.
2   CDPA s 27(2).
3   CDPA s 27(3)(b).
4   See also **paragraph 7.04** and generally, **Chapter 14**.
5   These include copies which are to be treated as 'infringing copies' by virtue of ss 31A(6) and (9), 31B(9) and (10), 31C(2), 32(5), 35(3), 36(5), 37(3)(b), 56(2), 63(2), 68(4), 70(2) and orders under s 141. See **Chapter 9**.
6   CDPA s 70(2)(2), see **paragraph 9.31**.

7   *Sony Computer Entertainment Inc v Ball, [2005] 3 FSR 160.*
8   ibid, p.161.

Secondary infringement: use of premises for infringing performances

7.11   A person who gives permission for a place of public entertainment to be used for the performance of a literary, dramatic or musical work which constitutes an infringing performance will be liable for the infringement unless, when he gives permission, he believes on reasonable grounds that the performance will not infringe copyright[1].

For these purposes, a 'place of public entertainment' includes premises which are occupied mainly for other purposes, but are, from time to time, made available on hire for the purposes of public entertainment[2]. This, for example, would include a pub which was occasionally used for live musical performances. If the performers did not have a licence from the owners of the music copyright, not only would the performers themselves be infringing the restricted act of performing a work in public, but the owner of the pub, if he knew or had reason to believe that the performers had not obtained a licence from the copyright owners, would also be liable for infringement of the copyright in the music.

It should, however, be noted that this act of secondary infringement applies only to performances of literary, dramatic or musical works and not, for example, to films or sound recordings.

1   CDPA s 25(1).
2   CDPA s 25(2).

Secondary infringement: provision of apparatus for infringing performances

7.12   Where any work is infringed by a public performance of the work (the restricted act applicable to literary, dramatic and musical works) or by the playing or showing of the work in public (the restricted act applicable to sound recordings, films, broadcasts or cable programmes) or by means of apparatus for playing sound recordings, showing films or receiving visual images or sounds conveyed by electronic means, the following persons are also liable for the infringement:

● the supplier of the apparatus or any substantial part of it;
● an occupier of premises who gave permission for the apparatus to be brought onto the premises;

- the person who supplied a copy of a sound recording or film used to infringe copyright.

In each case the person must be shown to have known or had reason to believe, that the apparatus was likely to be used so as to infringe copyright[1].

1   CDPA s 26.

Secondary infringement: knowledge and belief

7.13   In order to establish liability for secondary infringement the copyright owner must prove that the infringer had knowledge or reason to believe that he is dealing in an infringing copy. In *LA Gear v Hi-Tech Sports*[1] the Court of Appeal indicated that the existence of knowledge was an objective test. The plaintiff must demonstrate that the infringer must possess sufficient facts from which a reasonable man would arrive at the necessary belief or knowledge. For the avoidance of doubt written notice should always be given to the infringer who should have a reasonable time to evaluate the information.

1   [1992] FSR 121.

Chapter 8

Infringement of copyright and remedies

Primary and secondary infringement: a summary

8.01 When deciding whether a copyright infringement has occurred, it is necessary to establish that:

- the infringed work falls within one of the categories of work in which copyright exists[1];
- the term of copyright for the infringed work is still ongoing[2];
- a restricted act has been undertaken without the authorisation of the owner[3] (i.e. a primary infringement has been committed) and/or an act which amounts to a secondary infringement has been committed with 'guilty knowledge'[4]; and
- no exception or defence to copyright infringement is available to the defendant[5].

If any of the above elements are not established, an action for infringement will not succeed.

1 See **paragraph 2.01** et seq.
2 See **Chapter 6**.
3 See **paragraphs 7.02–7.08**.
4 See **paragraphs 7.09–7.13**.
5 See **Chapter 9**.

Proving infringement

8.02 Copyright does not convey any monopoly right in an idea[1]. If, say, a composer writes a melody identical to one created earlier by somebody else, this will not amount to an infringement if he has never heard the earlier melody.

When a person claims that a copyright infringement has occurred, he has the burden of showing that, on the balance of probabilities, this is the case. Except in obvious situations of piracy (when a whole work has clearly been reproduced without authorisation), it will usually be necessary to look at the surrounding facts to see if an infringement can be inferred. The claimant will need to show both that the degree of similarity between the works is substantial enough to suggest infringement[2] and that the claimed infringer had *access* to the infringed work. If substantial similarity can be shown, the practical burden of proof will be on the claimed infringer to rebut the claim that he had access, or to show that notwithstanding access he did not copy (e.g. because the two works were based upon a common public domain news story reported in the press[3]). Expert witnesses are often called, in difficult cases, to provide evidence regarding the level of similarity to assist the court in establishing whether copying has taken place.

In some cases, it is the copying of an unusual style or even mistakes which can provide a tell-tale give-away of copying. For that reason, it is common for the owners of copyright works (such as compilations) which require little originality in order to receive protection to deliberately insert false information for the purpose of detecting infringements. In *Waterlow Directories v Reed Information Services Ltd*[4], for example, the plaintiffs were alerted to an unauthorised use of their legal directory when mailings were received at a false 'seed' address, planted (if the reader will excuse the pun) by the plaintiff in its own directory from a competitor seeking to copy entries in order to compile its own database.

Again, in *IBCOS Computers Ltd v Barclays Mercantile Highland Finance Ltd*[5] the presence of copied mistakes in the coding of a computer program allowed a court to establish that copying had taken place.

1   See **paragraph 8.04**.
2   See **paragraph 8.06**.
3   See **paragraph 8.10**.
4   [1992] FSR 409.
5   [1994] FSR 275.

Intention: strict liability

8.03   A primary infringement of copyright carries strict liability. It is not necessary to show that the infringer *intended* to infringe another work. In one recent case, *Sony Music Entertainment (UK) Ltd v EasyInternetcafe Ltd*[1], the defendant operated an internet café which provided a 'CD burning' service allowing customers to download material from the internet onto CD-R. The café proprietor instructed its employees not to look at the files downloaded by customers. The café proprietor was sued for copyright infringement by the owners of musical tracks downloaded by customers. In his defence, the proprietor claimed (amongst other things) that he was an 'involuntary copier'. He did not know infringing acts were taking place. Although his copying devices were controlled by human employees, these were, in effect automatons. This argument was rejected by Mr Justice Peter Smith:

'If a high street printer copies material, which contains infringing copyright material (for example a pirated PhD thesis) the printer will be liable. He will not know that the material is infringing for obvious reasons. Nevertheless, he is liable. I do not see how it can be said to be different because he chooses not to know'.[2]

In the popular music industry, it is often said 'everybody copies everybody', since the structure of many popular compositions are based on a limited pool of cultural and musical references which are frequently reinvigorated by new treatments. Nevertheless, if a songwriter or composer draws on an influence so closely that his work is substantially similar, he will infringe copyright even if he does so unconsciously[3].

However, if someone who infringes a work can show that he did not know (or have reason to know) that the work was in copyright, this will have an impact on the remedies available to the claimant[4].

In the leading case of *Francis Day & Hunter Ltd v Bron*[5], it was claimed that the opening bars of a song, 'In a Little Spanish Town', composed in 1929, had been copied in a song entitled 'Why', composed in 1959. The evidence of the composer of 'Why' was that he had not seen or studied or, in his recollection, played the music of 'In a Little Spanish Town', nor had he ever to his knowledge heard it (although he admitted he might have heard it at a younger age). This evidence was accepted. The trial judge found that he had insufficient factual material concerning the similarity of the works. It was not right to draw an inference in the absence of direct evidence, and in the face of the composer's denial that he had sufficient knowledge or memory of 'In a Little Spanish Town', that he copied it without knowing that he was doing so, rather than to conclude that the similarity arose from coincidence. Accordingly, the judge held that the infringement of copyright was not established. The case went to appeal.

On appeal Wilmer LJ said:

'if subconscious copying is to be found, there must be proof (or at least a strong inference) of de facto familiarity with the work alleged to be copied'.

Diplock LJ (as he then was) said:

'If the existence of the copyright work has no causal connection with the production of the alleged infringing work, even though the latter be identical with the former, there is no infringement of copyright. In my view, however, it is equally clear law that neither intention to infringe, nor knowledge that he is infringing on the part of the defendant is a necessary ingredient in the cause of action for infringement of copyright. Once the two elements of sufficient objective similarity and casual connection are established, it is no defence that the defendant was unaware (and could not have been aware) that what he was doing infringed the copyright in the plaintiff's work'.

1   [2003] EWHC 62.
2   Per Mr Justice Peter Smith, *Sony Music Entertainment (UK) Ltd v EasyInternet-cafe Ltd.*
3   See **paragraph 8.06**.
4   See **paragraphs 8.12** et seq.
5   [1963] 2 All ER 16, CA.

Use of ideas and characters

8.04   Copyright, as we have seen, is concerned with the protection of form, not of ideas[1]. There is no infringement of copyright if the ideas in one work are used in another. It is sometimes said that there will be no infringement of a literary or dramatic work, even if the plot is followed in another work, provided different words are used. This is incorrect. The test is whether the copier, in following the original, made substantial use of the skill and labour of the original. Copyright exists not only in the series and order of certain selected works, but also in the organisation of the ideas and the manner of their presentation. In the case of a novel or play, the plot is presented by means of a series of dramatic incidents. If these incidents are reproduced, even with different language, an infringement will take place. The organisation and selection of these incidents to create the plot requires skill and labour. To determine whether the use of the plot in another work is an infringement will require an examination of the way (i.e. the form) in which the alleged infringer has presented his plot to determine whether he merely borrowed the concept of the plot and used his own skill and labour in expressing its form. In this context, the words from Mr Justice Laddie's judgment in *Autospin (Oil Seals) Ltd v Beehive Spinning*[2], are relevant[3].

A related question is: to what extent can the writer of, say, a novel, play or screenplay control the re-use of the characters, recast into different scenarios by other writers?

Although there is little by way of dicta considering this issue, in *Pozanski v London Film Production Ltd*,[4] a case based on the alleged plagiarism of a play based on Catherine the Great in a subsequent filmed work, the claimants argued that there was copyright (inter alia) in certain characterisations in the work, and that that copyright was infringed by the defendants when they followed the selection and treatment of the subject, scenarios and characters of the claimant. Crossman LJ held:

> 'I do not find myself driven to the conclusion that the selection or treatment was a copying of [the plaintiff's] selection and treatment. I find that if and so far as there are any similarities they are mainly in ideas which are not the subject matter of copyright, and the treatment and development of these ideas are quite different from the treatment and development in the [plaintiff's work].'

The conclusion that can be drawn from this is that an English court will not find that there is a breach of copyright where the idea or character is used from an original work and developed in a different direction for the new work. For example if a literary character is taken by another author and used for a different book which tells a different story entirely then this will not be copyright infringement, although such an action may result in an accusation of moral rights infringement (false attribution or derogatory treatment[5]), or a claim for 'passing off'.[6]

Of course where there is copying of a character and the same story is retold that may be a breach of copyright in the original literary work as a whole, provided a substantial part of the original work is taken.[7]

1   See **paragraph 1.03**.
2   [1995] RPC 683.
3   See **paragraph 2.02**.
4   (1937) MacG Cop Cas (1936–45) 107.
5   See **Chapter 11**.
6   See **Chapter 5** for a discussion of the law on 'passing off'.
7   See also **paragraphs 2.02** and **2.13**.

Parodies

8.05   A parody, which uses an idea from an existing work, but which also uses substantial new skill and labour, does not infringe the copyright in the original work. A parody, however, which uses the same work, will be an infringement[1].

There must be no reproduction of a substantial part of the original work. So, a parody of a song entitled 'Rock-a-Billy' using the words

'Rock-a-Philip, Rock' in the chorus of the parody in the same way as
the words of the song were used, was held not to infringe the copyright
in 'Rock-a-Billy'[2]. On the other hand, a label for a bottle substantially
the same as the Schweppes Indian tonic water bottle, except that the
name used was 'Schlurppes', was held to infringe the copyright in the
Schweppes label, even though it was accepted that the 'Schlurppes'
label was a parody[3].

1 See also **paragraph 1.16**
2 *Joy Music Ltd v Sunday Pictorial Newspapers (1920) Ltd [1960] 2 QB 60.*
3 *Schweppes Ltd v Wellingtons Ltd [1984] FSR 210.*

'Substantial part'

8.06 For copying to constitute an infringement, it must be substantial[1];

'What amounts to a "substantial" part for these purposes must be
assessed upon the basis of quality rather than quantity'[2].

If the most vital part of a work is copied (even though it may not be
a very large part), it will nevertheless be considered to be a substantial
part for the purpose of deciding whether or not there is an infringement.

The question is always whether the alleged infringer has used a
substantial part of the skill and labour of the original maker for the
making of the copy. To take a few examples:

- in the context of a literary work, four lines from Kipling's *If* used
  in a Sanatogen advertisement, were held to be a substantial part[3];
- in the context of a dramatic work, an episode in a full-length
  feature film consisting of dramatic events and accompanying
  dialogue, taken from four pages of a book of 126 pages, was held
  to be a substantial part[4];
- in the context of a musical work, an extract of 60 seconds' duration
  from 'Colonel Bogey' constituted a substantial part[5];
- in the context of a film, the copying of a style or technique (such as
  an editing technique) will not amount to an infringement of
  copyright unless a substantial part of the 'essence and originality'
  of the film has been appropriated[6];
- in the context of a published edition, cuttings from articles in
  various newspapers were held, in context, not to constitute a
  substantial part of the newspapers concerned[7].

In the context of a film, television broadcast or cable programme,
taking a photograph of the whole or any substantial part of any image is

an infringement[8]. 'Video grab' (the photographing of a still taken from a moving video image) will amount to copying, notwithstanding that the single image which is 'grabbed' may be a very insignificant part of the whole work[9].

The question of what constitutes a 'substantial part' was considered at length in the House of Lords' decision in *Designers Guild v Russell Williams*[10]. That case concerned a fabric design launched by the defendant under the name 'Marquante', in 1996, which was similar (but not identical) to the claimant's design 'Ixia' released in 1995. Four of five law lords gave reasoned judgments in favour of the claimant and their judgments offer limited guidance, although Lord Scott, finding for the claimant, restated with approval Laddie's test for determining whether an altered copy constitutes an infringement, as follows:

'Has the infringer incorporated a substantial part of the independent skill, labour etc. constituted by the original author in creating the copyright work?'[11]

Elsewhere, the judgments suggest that in an altered copying case, the finding of copying will usually depend on the extent and nature of the similarities between the work, and that if the similarities are enough to justify a conclusion that copying has occurred, then that infringing design must incorporate a substantial part of the original design.

Lord Hoffman suggests that the question is whether the alleged copy contains 'sufficient of the author's skill and labour as to attract copyright protection'. Although not expressly stated in his judgment, some writers have used this dictum as support for a new test for determining whether a substantial part has been copied: namely, 'Is the amount of material copied sufficient to constitute a copyright work in its own right as an original work?'[12]

1   CDPA s 16(3).
2   House of Lords in *Ladbroke (Football) Ltd v William Hill (Football) Ltd [1964] 1 WLR 273*.
3   *Kipling v Genatosan Ltd (1917–1923) Macg Cop Cas 203.*
4   *Farnald v Jay Lewis Production Ltd [1975] FSR 499.*
5   *Hawkes & Son Ltd v Paramount Film Service Ltd [1934] Ch 593.*
6   *Norowzian v Arks Ltd (No 2) [2000] FSR 363, CA* (see the further discussion of this case set out in **paragraphs 2.03** and **2.08**).
7   *Newspaper Licensing Agency v Marks & Spencer plc [2000] NLJR 900, CA*, see **paragraph 2.11**.
8   CDPA s 17(4); *Spelling Goldberg Productions Inc v BPC Publishing Ltd [1981] RPC 283, CA.*
9   See **paragraph 7.03** and the exceptions to copyright infringement considered at **Chapter 9** and in particular **paragraph 9.32**.
10   [2001] FSR 113.

Quotations

8.07 Where a work contains quotations from another work, but the quotations do not constitute a substantial part of the work from which they are taken, the use of the quotations will not constitute a breach of copyright. Whether or not they constitute a substantial part of the other work is a question of fact in each case[1].

1 See **paragraphs 8.06 and 18.06**.

Proof of damage unnecessary

8.08 In order to succeed in an action for infringement of copyright, it is not necessary to prove damage, although the fact that there has been damage caused by the infringement will inevitably affect the amount of damages awarded by a court. The plaintiff may in any event be able to sustain an account of profits from the infringer[1].

1 See **paragraph 8.12**.

Factual sources

8.09 A common problem arises where a work is based upon a factual event (e.g. a film or documentary based on real life events). Factual information is not, of itself, a 'work' capable of copyright protection[1]. Indeed, in a news context, there is a significant public interest in making information available as widely as possible. However, if the *expression* given to the story in one account is copied, then an infringement may be said to have occurred. The problem becomes acute for users who wish to create biographical films or other works based on events which are well documented in previous news reports or biographies. Such activities will often require the devotion of significant budgets, which may be at risk from claims of copyright infringement from earlier biographers whose works may be used as research tools. The question in these cases is no different from that stated above, namely: has the alleged infringer used a substantial part of the skill and labour of another? In practice it is common for film producers creating such a film to acquire the rights in an earlier biography, or to hire the consultancy services of a key figure in the factual events, in part to rebut any allegation of infringement, notwithstanding that the film may not be substantially based on these contributions.

Exceptions to copyright infringement also exist in the context of news reporting and these are considered further in **Chapter 9**.

1   See **paragraphs 1.02 and 2.13**.

Liability for infringement

8.10   Who is liable for infringement of copyright? The CDPA[1] provides that copyright in a work is infringed by any person who, without the license of the owner, does, or authorises another person to do, any of the restricted acts. In short liability falls upon any person who, without the consent of the owner of the copyright in question:

- does any of the restricted acts in relation to the work in the UK or any other country to which CDPA extends;
- authorises any other person to do any such act[2];
- commits any act of secondary infringement with guilty knowledge[3].

1   s 16(2).
2   See **paragraph 7.02**.
3   See **paragraphs 7.09–7.13**.

Remedies for infringement

8.11   There are two types of remedies for breach of copyright: civil remedies (damages, an injunction, an account of the profits gained by the defendant as a result of the infringement, delivery up of infringing articles, etc)[1] or criminal proceedings[2].

1   CDPA s 96 et seq.
2   CDPA s 107.

Damages and accounts of profits

8.12   If someone who infringes a work can show in the circumstances that he did not know (or have reason to know) that the work was in copyright, a claimant should not be entitled to damages for the infringement[1]. This is an objective test: would a reasonable man with the knowledge of the infringer have believed the work is in copyright?[2]

In *Infabrics Ltd v Jaytex Ltd*[3] Buckley LJ said:

'It is, in my opinion, incumbent upon anyone who proposes to make use of any artistic work in a way which might infringe copyright, if it subsists in the work, to make such enquiries and investigation as he reasonably can satisfy himself that the work is free of copyright ... If no adequate enquiries or investigations are made it must, it seems to me, be difficult to suppose that the person proposing to use the work has no grounds for suspecting that it may be subject to copyright'.

The defence of not knowing, or having reason to believe, therefore, is unlikely to be available, except in those cases:

● where the work is very old and might be out of copyright; or
● where it is the sort of work which it would be reasonable to assume did not have copyright protection; or
● where it is of foreign origin and is unlikely to be entitled to protection under UK law.

In each case, the court will take into account all the relevant circumstances. The defence has not been made available in circumstances:

● where the defendant knew, believed or suspected that copyright subsisted, but belonged to someone other than the plaintiff[4];
● where the defendant makes a mistake as to the owner of the copyright from whom authorisation must be obtained, and obtains consent to publish from the wrong person[5];
● where the defendant proves that the publication occurred in circumstances where it is common practice to publish without the owner's consent[6];
● where the defendant assumes that, because the work was published anonymously, it is not entitled to copyright protection.

On the other hand, under certain circumstances the court, in assessing damages for infringement, has power to award additional damages (i.e. damages which go beyond the actual damage suffered as a result of the infringement). The court must have regard to all the circumstances and, in particular, to the flagrancy of the infringement and to the benefit which accrued to the defendant by reason of the infringement[7]. What is not clear is whether these damages should be compensatory or punitive[8].

In the case of *Cala Homes (South) Ltd v Alfred McAlpine Homes East Ltd*[9], it was held that:

● the power to award additional damages is not limited to cases where the infringer knows or has reason to believe that copyright has been infringed (which is not the same thing as not knowing that the work in question was in copyright);

- it is not necessary that there should be both flagrancy and benefit accruing to the defendant;
- additional damages are designed to allow the court to register in terms of a financial penalty its disapproval of the behaviour of the infringer.

In the case of *Redrow Homes Ltd v Bett Bros*[10] it was held that additional damages can be awarded if there is an award of damages, but not if there is only an award of account of profits (see below). The additional damages are not available if the claimant does not seek compensatory damages.

If an infringement is careless rather than deliberate, additional damages will not be appropriate[11]. Nor are additional damages available where a clip was broadcast by the defendant in the belief that its broadcast was permissible, in the public interest, and did not compete with the rights-holder's use of the work[12].

Instead of damages, a claimant can apply for an account of profits. This is an 'equitable' remedy and as such, the remedy may not be awarded if the claimant has not himself acted equitably. So, by way of example, an account of profits may not be ordered by the court when there has been a delay on the part of the claimant in claiming the account. However, the fact that damages would be an adequate remedy is not of itself enough to deter the request. The aim is to prevent an infringer from being unjustly enriched by his activities. The remedy is most useful, and likely to be available, in the cases of simple, deliberate infringement. The account of profits which will be applied for is of net profit[13].

A claimant is not entitled to claim for both damages and an account of profits. In the case of *Minnesota Mining and Manufacturing Co Ltd v C Jeffries Pty*[14], the plaintiff was allowed discovery of the defendant's accounts before having to make an election as to whether to claim damages or an account of profits.

1 CDPA s 97(1).
2 *LA Gear Inc v Hi-Tec Sports plc [1992] FSR 121.*
3 [1980] FSR 161, CA.
4 *John Lane Bodley Head Ltd v Associated Newspapers Ltd [1936] 1 KB 715.*
5 *Byrne v Statist Co [1914] 1 KB 622.*
6 *Banier v News Group Newspapers Ltd [1997] FSR 812.*
7 CDPA s 97(2). 'Flagrancy' implies scandalous conduct, deceit etc, including deliberate and calculated copyright infringements, and 'benefit' implies a financial benefit in excess of the damages he would otherwise have to pay. *Ravenscroft v Herbert [1980] RPC, 193.*

8   Although not a decided point, obiter dicta of Lord Clyde *in Redrow Homes Ltd v Bett Bros* (see footnote 10 below) suggests his view that these damages were aggravated, at 209F per Lord Clyde. Amounts awarded by courts under s 97(2) have typically been modest.
9   [1995] FSR 818.
10 [1999] 1 AC 197, HL overruling *Cala Homes*.
11 *Noah v Shuba [1991] FSR 14* per Mummery J.
12 *ProSieben Media AG v Carlton UK Television Ltd [1998] FSR* 43.
13 *Pike v Nicholas (1869) 5 Ch App 251.*
14 [1993] FSR189 (Aus).

Delivery up and forfeiture

8.13   In addition to damages or an account of profits, the owner (or exclusive licensee) of copyright may apply to the court to require a person who has been dealing with articles which infringe the copyright to deliver up to him the infringing copies (for example, books, records etc), as if he had been the owner of them since the time when they had been made[1]. Generally this right must be exercised by applying for a court order within six years from the date on which the infringing copy or article in question was made[2]. This limitation is subject to two caveats. First, if the copyright owner is under a 'disability' then an application may be made at any time within six years after the date on which he ceased to be under the disability (for these purposes 'disability' means insanity or minority). Second, if the copyright owner was prevented by fraud or concealment from discovering the facts entitling him to apply for an order, an application may be made at any time within six years after the copyright owner could, with reasonable diligence, have discovered the facts.

The owner has a similar right to delivery up of any article specifically designed or adapted for making copies of a particular copyright work, provided that the person against whom the order is sought, knew or had reason to believe, that the article would be so used[3].

Alternatively, the court can order the disposal of infringing copies[4]. Again, this remedy is at the discretion of the court and will not be awarded if the harm it does to the infringer would be out of proportion to the interests of justice served by making the order[5].

1   CDPA s 99(1)(a).
2   I.e. prior to expiry of the limitation period by such action, Limitation Act 1980.
3   CDPA s 99(1)(b).
4   CDPA s 114, 204 and 231.
5   *Ocular Sciences Ltd v Aspect Vision Care Ltd [1997] RPC 289.*

Injunctions and interim injunctions

8.14 An injunction can be obtained to restrain a copyright infringement, although an injunction will not be available if the court consider that damages would provide adequate relief in the circumstances.

An interim (or 'interlocutory') injunction may be available to restrain an infringement pending trial, provided that the claimant is able to establish that he has a sufficiently serious claim which is not frivolous or vexatious, and that on the balance of convenience the likely damage from the claimed infringement will exceed the harm caused to the claimed infringer by the injunction[1].

1   *NWL Ltd v Woods [1979] 1 WLR 1294.*

Who may sue?

8.15 An action for copyright infringement may be brought by the owner of the copyright, or by a person to whom an 'exclusive licence' has been granted[1].

For the purposes of CDPA, an 'exclusive licence' means a licence in writing, signed by or on behalf of an owner or prospective owner of copyright, authorising the licensee to the exclusion of all other persons (including the licensor), to exercise a right which would be exercisable exclusively by the owner of the copyright[2]. So, for example, if two publishing houses are given licences to publish a work in the UK (neither, therefore, having an exclusive licence), any action against a third party publisher who publishes an infringing work in the UK must be brought by the original owner – not by one of the two licensed publishers.

1   CDPA ss 96 and 101; see **paragraph 10.30**.
2   CDPA s 92(1).

Technical provisions concerning plaintiffs and defendants in civil actions

8.16 Chapter VI of CDPA contains provisions regarding the rights of plaintiffs and defendants in relation to civil actions, some of which have been mentioned above, which are generally of a technical nature and of importance mainly to the lawyers into whose hands an action for infringement has been entrusted. For example, ss 101 and 102 deal with the rights and remedies of exclusive licensees in infringement proceedings; ss 104–106 deal with presumptions which apply in proceedings for infringement of copyright and which apply in the absence of evidence to the contrary being forthcoming. These sections and similar issues of a technical nature are not, therefore, dealt with in detail here.

Criminal proceedings

8.17 The provisions of CDPA regarding penalties and summary proceedings in respect of dealings which infringe copyright are set out in ss 107–110 of CDPA.

In brief, any person who:

'(a) makes for sale or hire; or

(b) imports into the UK, otherwise than for his private and domestic use; or

(c) possesses in the course of business with a view to committing any act infringing the copyright; or

(d) in the course of a business:

  (i) sells or lets for hire, or

 (ii) offers or exposes for sale or hire, or

(iii) exhibits in public, or

(iv) distributes, or

(e) distributes otherwise than in the course of a business to such an extent as to affect prejudicially the owner of the copyright;

an article which he knows or has reason to believe is, an infringing copy of a copyright work shall be guilty of an offence.'[1]

In addition, any person who makes, or has in his possession, an article specifically designed or adapted for making infringing copies of a particular copyright work, is guilty of an offence, if he knew or had reason to believe it was to be so used[2].

Furthermore, a person who infringes copyright in a work by communicating the work to the public in the course of business, or otherwise than in the course of a business to such an extent as to affect prejudicially the owner of the copyright, commits an offence if he knows or has reason to believe that, by doing so, he is infringing copyright in that work[3]. This provision, which was implemented by the 2003 Regulation, facilitates, for example, criminal proceedings against large-scale 'uploaders' of infringing material to peer-to-peer internet services.

Where copyright is infringed (otherwise than by reception of a communication to the public):

• by the public performance of a literary, dramatic or musical work; or

- by the playing or showing in public of a sound recording or film,

any person who caused the work to be so performed, played or shown is guilty of an offence if he knew or had reason to believe that copyright would be infringed[4].

A Law Commission consultation paper in 1999 provisionally recommended that the consent of the Director of Public Prosecutions should be required prior to any private prosecution for copyright infringement. Following responses opposing this suggestion, however, the Law Commission decided not to pursue this point, and private prosecutions may still be taken. In circumstances of genuine piracy, this remedy can be an effective weapon in the hands of copyright holders.

1   CDPA s 107(1).
2   CDPA s 107(2).
3   CDPA s 107(2)(A).
4   The reader should note that the Patent Office issued a consultation paper in February 2000 concerning improvements to these provisions (see www.patent.gov.uk\dpolicy\crimprov.html); further consultative processes will follow.

Penalties in criminal proceedings

8.18   The penalty on summary conviction for the offences set out in (a), (b), (d)(iv) and (e) of **paragraph 8.17**, or of communicating the work to the public (again as detailed in **paragraph 8.17**) above is a fine not exceeding the statutory maximum, at present £5,000, or imprisonment for a term of six months (or three months in relation to an infringing communication to the public), or both[1]. If convicted on indictment the penalty is an unrestricted fine and/or imprisonment for up to ten years (or two years in relation to an infringing communication to the public). The other offences set out in **paragraph 8.17** must be dealt with summarily and the penalty on conviction is imprisonment for a term not exceeding six months or a fine not exceeding 'level 5 on the standard scale' (at present £5,000), or both.

The court may order that any article in the possession of a person who is charged with an offence under s 107, whether he is convicted of it or not, but which appears to the court to be an infringing copy, or to be an article used or intended to be used for making infringing copies, is to be delivered up to the owner of the copyright in question or such other person as the court may direct[2].

1   CDPA s 107(4) and s 107(4A).
2   CDPA s 108.

Notice to HM Revenue & Customs

8.19 The copyright owner of a published literary, dramatic or musical work can give notice to HM Revenue & Customs:

- that he is the owner of the copyright in the work; and
- that during a period specified in the notice he requests Customs to treat as prohibited goods printed copies of the work which are infringing copies[1].

The owner of the copyright in a sound recording or film may give notice in writing to Customs that he is the copyright owner of the work and that infringing copies of the work are expected to arrive in the UK at a time and place specified in the notice. He may request by the notice that Customs treat the copies as prohibited copies. During the period that a notice is in force (and there is no limit) the only copies that may be imported are those for private and domestic use.

1   CDPA s 111.

Company directors and officers liable for infringement

8.20 Where an offence is committed under s 107 of the CDPA by a company, and it is proved that the offence was committed with the consent or connivance of a director, manager, secretary or other similar officer of the body, or a person purporting to act in any such capacity, that person as well as the company, is guilty of the offence and liable to be proceeded against and punished accordingly[1].

1   CDPA s 110(1).

'Knowing or having reason to believe'

8.21 In cases of secondary infringement and criminal prosecutions, it is necessary to show that the defendant knew or had reason to believe that there was an infringement or offence committed. What constitutes 'reason to believe' will depend on the circumstances in each case and the owner can assist his case by positive action. When a copyright owner becomes aware that pirated copies of his work are on the market he would be well advised to give notice to traders of that fact with such details as are available to enable traders to identify the pirated versions. Proof of receipt of such a notice or information should constitute 'reason to believe' that the trader was dealing with a pirated copy and therefore guilty of secondary infringement and liable for a criminal offence. Consequently such a notice can be a powerful disincentive to further trading in the article in question.

The Enforcement of Intellectual Property Rights Directive

8.22 The European Commission the European Parliament and Council agreed, on 26 April 2004, the terms of the Enforcement of Intellectual Property Rights Directive[1].

In response to rising levels of piracy and counterfeiting, the Directive aims to harmonise national laws in relation to the enforcement of intellectual property rights and build upon member states' international obligations[2].

The deadline by which member states must implement the Directive into national law is 29th April 2006[3].

The Directive is based on 'existing best practice' in member states (i.e. it adopts the best practices already used by member states and seeks to harmonise them). It covers infringements of all intellectual property rights, both copyright and industrial property, such as trade marks, designs or patents[4].

Article 4 stipulates that rights holders, other persons authorised to sue on those rights, for example licensees, collective rights-management bodies and trade associations, can seek redress under the Directive if their rights have been infringed.

The Directive is limited to civil sanctions for commercial or large-scale infringement, rather than one-off infringements by individuals. It contains no criminal sanctions, although member states are free to implement them if they wish. The measures, procedures and remedies it will extend throughout the EU include, among others, injunctions to halt the sale of counterfeit or pirate goods, provisional measures such as precautionary seizure of suspected offenders' bank accounts, evidence-gathering powers for judicial authorities and powers to force offenders to pay damages for lost income to rights holders. In certain circumstances, if the infringer has acted unintentionally and without negligence, then compensation may be awarded to the rights holder if other measures will cause the infringer disproportionate harm. A right of information allows judges to order certain persons to reveal the names and addresses of those involved in distributing the illegal goods or services, along with details of the quantities and prices involved. Member states are encouraged to introduce preventative measures such as the publication of judicial decisions and the development of professional codes of conduct.

As many of the sanctions already exist in the UK, the Directive is unlikely to have a great impact on UK copyright law.

More generally, the Directive forms part of a broad-based approach by the European Commission to tackle counterfeiting and piracy. The Directive complements Council Regulation 1383/2003 under which customs officials have been given increased powers to stop the flow of and seize counterfeit and pirated goods[5].

1   2004/48/EC.
2   In particular, TRIPS.
3   For further information, see the UK Patent Office website, http://www.patent.gov.uk/about/enforcement/eu.htm, and the Europa Patent Office, http://www.europa.eu.int/comm/internal_market/en/indprop/piracy/index.htm.
4   Art 1.
5   Council Regulation 1383/2003 replaced Regulation 3295/94 on the export and re-export of goods infringing intellectual property rights with effect from 1 July 2004, and the UK has dealt with the changes in the Goods Infringing Intellectual Property Rights (Customs) Regulations 2004 (SI 2004/1473).

Chapter 9

Exceptions and defences to copyright actions

Acts permitted in relation to a copyright work

9.01 Public policy demands that several categories of use are specifically permitted by CDPA in relation to copyright works. A user who undertakes one of these 'permitted uses' will not infringe copyright in the work, notwithstanding that his activity would otherwise appear to be a restricted act. At the heart of these permitted uses is the concept of 'fair dealing'. The most important permitted uses are:

- making of temporary copies;
- fair dealing for purposes of research or private study;
- fair dealing for purposes of criticism, review and news reporting;
- incidental inclusion of works;
- making a single copy available for personal use (by the visually impaired);
- certain educational uses;
- certain uses by libraries and archives;
- certain uses for the purposes of public administration (such as use for Parliamentary and judicial proceedings).

In addition, there are a number of specific exceptions relating to computer programs, database designs and typefaces, as well as a number of miscellaneous exceptions which are considered below and elaborated on in the relevant chapters in **Part 2** of this *User's Guide*.

Apart from the activities referred to above, recent case law suggests that the courts will not recognise any other general 'public interest' defence to copyright infringement[1]. This reflects the fact that what is being protected is a statutory property right in a work, as opposed to, say, the confidentiality in information passed in the course of a confidential relationship[2].

The 'fair dealing' exceptions to copyright infringement were substantially amended by the 2003 Regulations, which implemented the 2001 Copyright Directive[3].

The 2001 Directive radically overhauled the exceptions to copyright infringement which EU member states could include in local law. However, of the 20 exceptions which the EU permit to be included, only one is *mandatory* on member states: the exemption for transient copies (referred to below). Of the remaining non-mandatory exceptions, the UK Patent Office has elected not to expand the pre-existing exceptions available in the UK under CDPA (although several of those exceptions have altered in scope[4]). The fact that a widely differing scope of exceptions is now available across different Member States has had the effect of perpetuating a lack of harmonisation on important issues (most obviously in relation to private copying[5]) across Europe[6].

The 2001 Directive implemented the so-called 'three-step test' to determine the circumstances in which exceptions to copyright infringement are permissible[7]. Specifically, under the 2001 Directive, exceptions and limitations may only be applied:

- in special cases;
- which do not conflict with the normal exploitation of the work or other subject-matter; and
- which do not unreasonably prejudice the legitimate interests of the rightsholder[8].

In the UK, the Patent Office was lobbied by rights holders to directly incorporate this test in UK law, as a means of limiting the scope of the exceptions available in the UK. However, the Government elected not to do so, on the basis that the 'three-step test' was relevant in framing the exceptions, rather than in the application of the exceptions once incorporated into UK law.

Broadly, the changes made to the UK law on fair dealing implemented by the 2003 Regulations are simple to summarise:

- *Fair dealing for the purposes of research and private study:* the 'research' element must now be non-commercial and subject to acknowledgement. The 'private study' element must also include study for a non-commercial purpose[9].
- *Fair dealing for the purpose of criticism, review and news reporting* must now be in relation to work 'lawfully made available to the public'. The provisions on source acknowledgement have also been altered[10].
- *The other fair dealing exceptions* (for things done for the purposes

of instruction and examinations, recording of broadcasts by educational establishments, reprographic copying by educational establishments, copying by librarians or archivists, recordings of folk songs) have been modified to operate only for 'non-commercial purposes'[11].

- *A new exception* has been introduced to permit observing, studying and testing functions of computer programs[12].

1   See **paragraph 2.15.**
2   As to which see **paragraph 5.05.**
3   Directive 2001/29/EC of the European Parliament and of the Council of 22 May 2001 on the harmonisation of certain aspects of copyright and related rights in the information society.
4   See below.
5   2001 Directive, Art 5(2)(b). The private copying exemption, which provides for a system of 'fair compensation' for rights holders, forms the basis for the levy systems in operation in certain other European jurisdictions.
6   For a further examination of the 'non mandatory' exemptions, see Carstan Schaal, 'The Copyright Exceptions of Art 5(2)(a) and (b) of the EU Directive 2001/29' [2003] Ent Lr, Issue 5. Harmonisation of these exceptions is on the agenda for the Commission's review of the 2001 Directive, scheduled for completion in 2007.
7   The 'three-step test' is found in international treaties (e.g. Art 13 of the TRIPS Agreement and Art10, WIPO Copyright Treaty). For a further discussion of the 'three-step test' see Ute Decker, 'The Three Step Test', Copyright World, February 2001.
8   2001 Directive Art 5.5.
9   See **paragraph 9.03** below.
10 See **paragraph 9.04.**
11 See **paragraph 9.10 et seq.**
12 See **paragraphs 9.03, 9.13 and 30.15 et seq.**

Mandatory exception: making of temporary copies

9.02   Copyright in a literary work (other than a computer program or a database), or in a dramatic, musical or artistic work, or the typographical arrangement of a published edition, or in a sound recording or a film, is *not* infringed by making a temporary copy which is:

'transient or incidental, which is an integral and essential part of a technological process and the sole purpose of which is to enable-

(a)   a transmission of the work in a network between third parties by an intermediary; or
(b)   a lawful use of the work;

and which has no independent economic significance.'[1]

The purpose of this exception, is to enable the temporary acts of reproduction (browsing, caching, etc) which are integral to the operation of the digital networks such as the internet. The exception was considered mandatory by the Commission because it is necessary to enable transmission systems to function effectively[2].

It is worth noting that the exception does not apply to computer programs or databases, a position which the Patent Office has agreed to monitor.

1   CDPA s 28A.
2   For a detailed discussion of caching and the mandatory exception, albeit predating the 2003 Regulations, see P Bernt Hugenholtz, 'Caching and Copyright: the Right of Temporary Copying' [2000] EIPR, Issue 10.

Fair dealing

Research and private study

9.03   Fair dealing for 'research for a non-commercial purpose' is a defence available only in respect of the infringement of literary, dramatic, musical and artistic works. No fair dealing with these works will constitute an infringement of copyright in the work, provided that it is accompanied by a sufficient acknowledgement[1]. No acknowledgement is required if impossible 'for reasons of practicality or otherwise'[2].

Similarly, fair dealing with a literary, dramatic, musical or artistic work for the purposes of *private study* does not infringe copyright in the work[3]. For these purposes, 'private study' excludes any study which is directly or indirectly for a commercial purpose[4]. Where fair dealing involves copying (and fair dealing can involve actions other than copying, such as, for example, broadcasting) and if the copying is done by somebody other than the researcher, or the student himself, then the exception does *not* apply:

- if a librarian, or a person acting on behalf of a librarian, does anything which is not permitted under any regulations made by the Secretary of State relating to copying by libraries and archives[5];
- in any other case, if the person doing the copying knows, or has reason to believe, that the copying will result in copies of substantially the same material being provided to more than one person, at substantially the same time and for substantially the same purpose. So, for example, a person researching a legal matter may not make copies of a textbook dealing with that issue to provide to a number of his colleagues who are also researching the same issue[6].

Nor is it fair dealing:

- to convert a computer program expressed in low-level language into a version expressed in high-level language; or

- incidentally, in the course of so converting the program, to copy it[7];
- to observe, study or test the functioning of a computer program in order to determine the ideas and principles which undertake any elements of the program[8].

However, if certain conditions[9] are complied with, it is not an infringement of copyright to do these acts[10].

Guidelines issued by the Patent Office indicate that all research done by businesses operating for profit are likely to be considered as being conducted for a commercial purpose. Even research undertaken by non-profit organisations will fall outside the exception if it is for a commercial purpose. This is a particular issue for universities, whose facilities have increasingly been used on a 'contracted-out' basis by commercial companies in support of their commercial activities. However, the impact extends beyond these activities, and would include, for example:

- work done for spin off companies owned by a university;
- work undertaken by an author contributing to a scholarly journal for which the author is paid or receives royalties;
- work undertaken to prepare for a paid conference speech.

In short, the impact of this change in law is, therefore, to require many people conducting commercial activities to obtain licences in order to continue activities they had previously undertaken without the necessity for a licence.

The Society of Authors publishes influential guidance as to what it would consider to be fair dealing for the purposes of criticism and review in relation to a literary work, which may provide a useful rule of thumb for publishers. In brief this amounts (in the case of poems) to no more than one quarter of the whole poem or 40 lines (whichever is shorter) and, (in the case of prose) to 400 words for a single extract, or 800 words over a series of extracts each of no more than 300 words[11].

1   CDPA s 29(1C).
2   CDPA s 29(1B).
3   CDPA s 29(1G).
4   CDPA s 29(1).
5   This question is dealt with in more detail in **Chapter 20**.
6   CDPA s 29(3).
7   CDPA s 29(4).
8   CDPA s 29(4A).
9   CDPA s 50B (decompilation) and s 50BA (observing, studying and testing).
10 This is discussed more fully in **Chapter 30**.
11 See **Appendix 1**.

Criticism, review and news reporting

9.04 Fair dealing is permitted with any work for the purpose of criticism or review of that or another work or of a performance of a work, provided that it is accompanied by a sufficient acknowledgement *and provided that the work has been made available to the public*[1].

The words in italics were added by the 2003 Regulations, and effectively limit the ambit of this exception. It will no longer be permissible, for example, for a biographer to include previously unpublished letters in his work without licence in reliance on this exception[2].

The amended CDPA includes a non-exhaustive list of circumstances which will be deemed included within the scope of the phrase 'made available to the public'. This includes the issue of copies to the public, making the work available by an electronic retrieval system, rental and lending, performance, exhibition, playing or showing the work in public, or the communication of the work to the public. In each case, however, when determining whether the work has been made available to the public, no account is to be given to an unauthorised act[3].

Case law has given the words 'criticism' and 'review' their dictionary definitions. Criticism may extend to matters other than literary criticism, such as ideas contained in the work, or events surrounding it[4]. So, in one case, Channel 4 successfully argued that the inclusion of a clip from the film *A Clockwork Orange* in a programme considering the merits of the decision to withhold the work from distribution in the UK, was fair dealing. The question in each case will be whether the use is genuinely one of criticism or review.

In the context of news reporting, the CDPA provides that:

'(2) Fair dealing with a work (other than a photograph) for the purpose of reporting current events does not infringe any copyright in the work provided that (subject to subsection (3)) it is accompanied by a sufficient acknowledgement.

(3) No acknowledgement is required in connection with the reporting of current events by means of a sound recording, film or broadcast where this would be impossible for reasons of practicality or otherwise.'[5]

So, in the case of *BBC v BSB Ltd*[6] it was held that the showing of excerpts from BBC broadcasts of World Cup football matches, to which the BBC had the exclusive broadcasting rights in the UK, constituted fair dealing for the purpose of reporting current events. The excerpts varied in length from 14 to 37 seconds and were used in successive news bulletins over a period of 24 hours following the match in question. They were accompanied by a verbal report of the incidents and an acknowledgement of the source of the film. Scott J accepted that for the purposes of the CDPA, fair dealing is largely 'a matter of impression'.

It is worth noting that a photograph can be reproduced for the purposes of criticism or review, but not for the purpose of reporting current events. The intention of the legislation is to prevent, for example, newspapers or magazines reproducing photographs for reporting current events which have appeared in competitors' publications. On the other hand a painting can be reproduced for this purpose, if, for example, it had been stolen and the reproduction was for the purpose of illustrating the report of the theft.

Also, the reproduction of stills taken from a film and printed as if they are photographs in order to report a current event may be fair dealing, provided a sufficient acknowledgement is made[7].

The terms 'criticism' and 'review', or 'reporting current events' were recently described as of wide and indefinite scope so that 'any attempt to plot their precise boundaries was doomed to failure'[8]. Consequently, these broad concepts are often relied upon as a first line of defence against many claims of copyright infringement. A good example of this phenomenon was the recent case of *IPC Media Ltd v News Group Newspapers Ltd*[9]. The case concerned the an advert published by the Sun newspaper which included a reproduction of the cover of a TV listings magazine belonging to the claimant, alongside a picture of a publication owned by the defendant. The aim was comparative advertising, although the defendant argued that its use of the claimant's material was for the purpose of 'criticism and review' of the claimant's product. The court held that the use was not 'fair'. It was using the copyright material to advance its own commercial interests at the expense of the other. All that was required to criticise the claimant's product was to identify it, which did not require the reproduction of its cover.

1   CDPA s 30(1).
2   It may still be possible to do so in reliance on the 'news reporting' exemption in appropriate circumstances.
3   CDPA s 30(1).
4   For example, *Time Warner Entertainments Ltd v Channel 4 Television Corpn plc [1994] EMLR 1*.
5   CDPA s 30.
6   [1992] Ch 141.
7   *Hyde Park Residence Ltd v Yelland [2000] 3 WLR 215, CA.*
8   *Pro Sieben Media AG (formerly Pro Sieben Television AG) v Carlton UK Television Ltd and Twenty Twenty Television Ltd [1999] EMLR 109, CA.*
9   Unreported, Ch D 24 February 2005.

Substantial use in relation to fair dealing

9.05 It is not necessary to decide whether use of a work constitutes fair dealing, until it has been determined that a substantial part of a work has been used[1]. Once that is established, it is necessary to examine whether the use is in fact fair dealing.

1 See **paragraph 8.06**.

Use must be fair: motive and substantial part

9.06 The expression 'fair dealing' is not defined in the CDPA, although it is clear that for a defence of fair dealing to succeed, the use must be fair in the circumstances. A number of factors have been considered relevant to determine fairness, but three are particularly important:

- the number and extent of quotations and extracts used;
- the use made of them; and
- the proportion the extracts bear to the new work[1].

The test for fairness is objective. The question is not whether the alleged infringer honestly believes his activities fall within one of the 'fair dealing' provisions, but whether the court does. The fairness of his motivations and intentions are important, but the focus of the court's concern should be the likely affect on the claimant[2].

The amount and significance of the material taken is key. The court must consider whether, on balance, the nature and the extent of the copying was within the bounds of what was reasonable and appropriate. This will clearly vary widely depending on the circumstances, but as a rule of thumb, the more substantial the copying is, the less likely a defence of fair dealing is likely to succeed. In *PCR Ltd v Dow Jones Telerate Ltd*[3], for example, a news reporter's use of quotes from another's report in the course of reporting a current event was not fair dealing, because she used more material than was reasonable or appropriate to report the event in question.

Another difficult area is that of art criticism. A large market has developed in glossy 'coffee-table' books, reproducing works of art. Many of these books have been published on the assumption that the subject artworks can be reproduced without authorisation from the copyright owner, because the use is for the purpose of criticism and review. Frequently such books include a modest amount of art criticism to support the images in the book. In each case it will be necessary to consider whether, in context, the use is fair. In cases where artists, or their descendants, and the Design and Artists Copyright Society have challenged this form of use, they have achieved some success[4].

In other jurisdictions the operation of internet search engines has raised issues as to what sort of use may be 'fair'. In *Leslie A Kelly v Arribasoft Corp*[5], the court was asked to consider whether the inclusion of images in a visual search engine infringed copyright in the images. The search engine in question (unusual, in that it used visual images rather than text) produced a lot of 'thumbnail' versions of images relating to a search inquiry, produced by maintaining an indexed database of millions of images, obtained via the use of 'crawler' software (trawling the internet for relevant images). Some 35 of the claimant's images appeared on the defendant's database. The judge found a prima facie case of copyright infringement, but considered that the defendant's use of the images would be 'fair use'. It is unlikely the same decision would result in the UK however, since 'fair dealing' defences are more narrowly defined in the UK than the general US doctrine of 'fair use'; nevertheless, in light of the implementation of the Human Rights Act 1998, such an outcome is not impossible[6].

Under the CDPA, a criticism or review which uses part of an unpublished work is able to rely on the defence of fair dealing.

In the context of news reporting, one recent case identified three principles which should be considered central in establishing whether the dealing is 'fair':

- the motive of the infringer;
- the extent and purpose of the use;
- whether the extent of use was necessary in order to report the current event in question[7].

In the same case, the fact that certain stills which had been used by a newspaper had not previously been published or physically distributed, and had been misappropriated, was considered important in finding that use was not fair dealing: 'Misappropriation and use of other people's property is not likely to be regarded as fair dealing'[8].

1   Lord Denning, *Hubbard v Vosper [1972] 2 QB 84, CA.*
2   *Pro Sieben Media AG (formerly Pro Sieben Television AG) v Carlton UK Television Ltd and Twenty Twenty Television Ltd,* above.
3   [1998] EMLR 407.
4   A case involving the descendants of Matisse (supported by DACS) against the publisher Phaidon resulted in a settlement on terms preventing Phaidon printing such books without a licence, and required a payment of retrospective licence fees.
5   US District Court, Central District of California, 18 March 2004.
6   See **paragraph 1.16.**
7   *Hyde Park Residence Ltd v Yelland [2000] 3 WLR 215, CA,* per Aldous LJ.
8   Ibid, per Mance LJ.

Sufficient acknowledgement

9.07 A 'sufficient acknowledgement' is required when there is a fair dealing for the purposes of criticism, review or reporting current events or the reading in public of extracts from literary or dramatic works. For these purposes 'sufficient acknowledgement' means an acknowledgement which identifies the work by title or other description, unless:

- in the case of a published work, it is published anonymously;
- in the case of an unpublished work, it is not possible for a person to ascertain the identity of the author by reasonable inquiry[1].

1   CDPA s 178.

Incidental inclusion

9.08 Copyright works are often included incidentally in other works. In fact, for example, filmed images often include a huge variety of diverse material. The incidental inclusion of any work in an artistic work, sound recording, film or broadcast does not infringe the copyright in the earlier work and nor will issuing the resulting work to the public, or playing, showing the work or its communication to the public[1].

This 'incidental inclusion' exception is very important to those users who make works potentially featuring a large number of visual images or sounds (such as photographers and film producers). However, where musical works are included, the position is qualified. A musical work, or words spoken or sung with music, or so much of a sound recording or broadcast as includes a musical work or such words, will not be treated as incidentally included in another work if it is deliberately included[2]. The producer of a television transmission from a concert hall, for example, could not claim to incidentally include the music performed at the concert in his programme. However, if music is played on loud speakers for the benefit of the audience at a sporting event, the inclusion of the music in the transmission of the event will be 'incidental inclusion' because it cannot be excluded. On the same basis, if music can be incidentally heard whilst a commentator sums up a match, there will be no infringement.

What 'incidental' means will depend on all the circumstances of the case. In *FA Premier League Ltd & Ors v Panini*[3] the defendant, without authorisation from the claimant, published a sticker album featuring images of footballers in their playing strip bearing the logos of the club and the FA Premier League. The claimant had exclusively authorised another person to include such logos in another sticker album. The defendant claimed its use of the club strip was 'incidental'. The court held that the following factors were relevant:

- 'incidental inclusion' does not only mean unintentional or non-deliberate inclusion;
- in considering whether the inclusion was an infringement, it is necessary to consider how the artwork which includes the relevant material was created;
- an inclusion can be incidental, notwithstanding that the material was an integral part of the final work.

The test of whether the use of the work was incidental should include a consideration of why the material was included. Was there a commercial reason?

On these tests, the court held for the claimant. In order for the stickers to be collectable, the players had to appear in their strip. The inclusion of the relevant material was therefore essential, not incidental[4].

1   CDPA s 31(1) and (2).
2   CDPA s 31(3).
3   [2003] EWCA Cw 995.
4   It was considered that in any event, the sticker albums were probably literary works, to which the defence under s.31 does not apply.

Visually impaired persons

9.09 A number of provisions were added to the CDPA by the Copyright (Visually Impaired Persons) Act 2002[1] providing exemptions from copyright infringements for the benefit of the blind:

- If a visually impaired person (VIP) lawfully possesses a copy of a literary, dramatic, musical or artistic work, or a published edition which is not 'accessible' to him because of his impairment, it will not be an infringement of copyright for an accessible copy to be made for his personal use[2].
- Such 'accessible copies' must be accompanied by a statement that they are made pursuant to s 31A of the CDPA, a sufficient acknowledgement, and may not be charged at a price which exceeds the cost of making or supplying the copies[3].
- The CDPA also provides that if a person holds an 'accessible copy' and is not a VIP or a person who lawfully possesses a legitimate copy and intends to transfer the accessible copy to a VIP, then the accessible copy will be deemed an infringing copy[4], and any transfer of an accessible copy to another person will infringe copyright unless the transferor has reasonable grounds to believe

the transferee is a VIP or a person who lawfully possesses a legitimate copy and intends to transfer the accessible copy to a VIP[5]. If an accessible copy is subsequently 'dealt with' (i.e. sold, let for hire, offered or exposed for sale or hire, or communicated to the public) it will be treated as an infringing copy[6] for the purpose of that and subsequent dealings.

- If an 'approved body' (i.e. an educational establishment or a body that is not conducted for profit[7]) lawfully possesses a copy of a commercially published literary, dramatic, musical or artistic work, or a commercially published edition, it will not be an infringement of copyright for the body to make, or supply, accessible copies for the personal use of VIPs[8].

- Again, such 'accessible copies' must be accompanied by a statement that they are made available pursuant to s 31B of the CDPA, and a sufficient acknowledgement[9]. The approved body must not make a charge for supplying the copy in excess of the cost of making and supplying the copy[10].

- An approved body, if an educational establishment, must ensure that the copies are only used for educational purposes[11]. The copy must be copy protected (unless the owner agrees otherwise)[12]. The copy will be treated as an infringing copy if the approved body ceases to be entitled to make or supply it[13]. If the copy is subsequently dealt with it will be treated as an infringing copy for that and subsequent dealings[14].

- Additional provisions apply to the making of intermediate copies by approved bodies[15].

- The provisions regarding approved bodies do not apply if a licensing scheme operated by a licensing body is in force under which licences may be granted by the licensing body permitting the making and supply of copies of the work in that form, and the scheme is not 'unreasonably restrictive'[16].

- The Secretary of State may make an order if it appears to him that the making of copies by approved bodies or under the licensing scheme referred to above has led to increased copyright infringement[17].

1   Enacted in SI 2003/2499, effective from 31 October 2003.
2   CDPA s 31A(1). NB this exception does not apply to musical works or databases if making the accessible copy would involve recording a performance of the music or infringing copyright in the database – s 31A(2). Nor does it apply if 'accessible copies' have already been made commercially available with the authority of the copyright owner – s 31A(3).
3   CDPA s 31A(4).
4   CDPA s 31A(6).
5   CDPA s 31A(8).

6   CDPA s 31A(9) and (10).
7   CDPA s 31B(12).
8   CDPA s 31B(1). NB This exception does not apply to musical works or databases if making the accessible copy would involve recording a performance of the music or infringing copyright in the database – s 31B(2). Nor does it apply if 'accessible copies' have already been made commercially available with the authority of the copyright owner – s 31B(3) and (4).
9   CDPA s 31B(5).
10   CDPA s 31B(6).
11   CDPA s 31B(7).
12   CDPA s 31B(8).
13   CDPA s 31B(9).
14   CDPA s 31B(10).
15   CDPA s 31C.
16   CDPA s 31D(1).
17   CDPA s 31D(1) (et al).

Education, libraries and archives

9.10   A number of exceptions set out in the CDPA specifically relate to educational activities[1] and these may be summarised as follows[2]:

- things done for purposes of instruction or examination[3];
- anthologies for educational use[4];
- performing, playing or showing works in course of activities in educational establishment[5];
- recording by educational establishments of broadcasts[6];
- reprographic copying for educational establishments of passages from published works[7];
- lending by educational establishments[8].

As discussed above[9], it is now a feature of the CDPA that these uses must be non commercial in nature.

1   ss 32–39; these exceptions are considered in detail in **Chapter 19**.
2   See **paragraphs 19.03–19.14**.
3   CDPA s 32.
4   CDPA s 33.
5   CDPA s 34.
6   CDPA s 35.
7   CDPA s 36.
8   CDPA s 36A.
9   See **paragraph 9.01**.

Libraries and archives

9.11   The CDPA also provides a number of exceptions to copyright infringement applicable in the context of libraries and archives[1]:

- copying by librarians: articles in periodicals[2];

- restriction on production of multiple copies of the same material[3];
- lending of copies by libraries or archives[4];
- copying by librarians: supply of copies to other libraries[5];
- copying by librarians or archivists: replacement copies of works[6];
- copying by librarians or archivists: certain unpublished works[7];
- copies of work required to be made as a condition of export8;
- legal deposit libraries[9].

These exceptions are considered in detail elsewhere in this *User's Guide*[10].

1   See **paragraphs 20.03–20.07**.
2   CDPA s 38.
3   CDPA s 40.
4   CDPA s 40A.
5   CDPA s 41.
6   CDPA s 42.
7   CDPA s 43.
8   CDPA s 44.
9   CDPA s 44A.
10 See **Chapter 20**.

Public administration

9.12   The CDPA sets out a number of uses which may be applied to copyright works for the purposes of public administration without the licence of the copyright owner[1]. The provisions are detailed but can be summarised as follows:

- *Parliamentary and judicial procedure:* copyright is not infringed by anything done for the purposes of Parliamentary or judicial proceedings or for the proceedings of a Royal Commission or statutory enquiry[2].
- *Public inspection:* material open to public inspection pursuant to a statutory requirement or on a statutory register may, under certain circumstances, be copied[3].
- *Public issues:* material which is communicated to the Crown in the course of public business may be copied by the Crown[4].
- *Public records:* material comprised in public records within the meaning of the Public Records Act 1958, the Public Records (Scotland) Act 1937, the Public Records (Northern Ireland) Act 1923 or in Welsh public records (as defined in the Government of Wales Act 1998) may be copied[5].
- *Statutory authority:* when the doing of a particular act is specifically authorised by an Act of Parliament, then the doing of that act does not infringe copyright[6].

This is a short summary of complex provisions and a user who proposes to make or issue copies to the public in reliance on these public administrative exceptions is recommended to undertake a detailed review of the CDPA.

One point of general interest is that where material which is open to public inspection contains information about matters of general scientific, technical, commercial or economic interest, copyright is not infringed by the copying or the issuing to the public of copies of that material, although the authority of the person who is required to make the material open to public inspection must be obtained[7].

1   ss 45–49.
2   ss 45 and 46.
3   CDPA s 47.
4   CDPA s 48.
5   CDPA s 49.
6   CDPA s 50.
7   CDPA s 47(3).

Computer programs: lawful users

9.13   A person who may lawfully use a copy of a computer program will not infringe copyright by making back-up copies 'which it is necessary for him to have for the purposes of his lawful use'[1]. The CDPA, defines a 'lawful user' as a person who has a right to use the program 'whether under a licence to do any acts restricted by the copyright in the programme or otherwise'[2]. If the user is entitled by this provision to make a back-up copy, then any term or condition in an agreement which purports to prohibit or restrict him from doing so will be irrelevant, and void[3].

Similarly, a lawful user of a computer program will not infringe copyright by 'de-compiling' the program, provided that a number of conditions are met[4], nor is it an infringement of copyright for a lawful user of a copy of a computer program to observe, study or test the functioning of the program in order to determine the ideas and principles which undertake any element of the program if he does so while performing any of the acts of trading, displaying, running, transmitting or storing a program which he is entitled to do[5].

Lastly, copyright is not infringed by a lawful user who copies or adapts a computer program, 'provided that the copying or adapting – (a) is necessary for his lawful use, and (b) is not prohibited under any term or condition of an agreement regulating the circumstances in which his use is lawful'[6].

1   CDPA s 50A.

2   CDPA s 50A(2).
3   ss 50A(3) and 296A; see **paragraph 30.17**.
4   These conditions are considered in detail at **paragraph 30.18**
5   CDPA s 50BA; see **paragraph 30.19**.
6   See **paragraph 31.40**.

Databases

9.14   The CDPA provides that:

'It is not infringement of copyright in a database for a person who has a right to use the database or any part of the database, (whether under a licence to do any of the acts restricted by the copyright in the database or otherwise) to do in the exercise of that right, anything which is necessary for the purposes of access to and use of the contents of the database or of that part of the database.'[1]

The term in any contract which purports to prohibit or restrict the user of a database from undertaking this permitted act, will be irrelevant and void[2].

1   CDPA s 50D(1).
2   ss 50D(2) and 296B.

Designs

9.15   The CDPA contains a number of permitted acts in relation to design documents and models, designs derived from artistic works and things done in reliance on registration of designs, which are not considered in detail in this *User's Guide*[1].

1   ss 51–53.

Typefaces

9.16   The CDPA makes a special exemption for the use of a typeface (which is protectable as an artistic work) in the ordinary course of printing. Since this is particularly relevant to printers and publishers, this exception is discussed in more detail elsewhere in this *User's Guide*[1].

1   See **paragraph 17.14**.

Works in electronic form

9.17   The purchaser of a copy of a work in 'electronic form' may copy or adapt the work, or make copies of the adaptation, in connection with his use of the work, provided that it has been purchased on terms which (expressly or impliedly) allow him so to do, or else he is permitted to by virtue of any rule of law[1].

For the purposes of the CDPA, 'electronic' means actuated by electric, magnetic, electro-magnetic, electro-chemical or electro-mechanical energy and 'in electronic form' means in a form usable only by 'electronic means'[2].

If the seller has not imposed any express terms which prohibit the transfer of the purchaser's copy, or imposed obligations which continue after a transfer, or prohibit the assignment of any licence, or terminate any licence on a transfer, then anything the purchaser is allowed to do may also be done by a subsequent transferee without infringement of copyright. However, any copies or adaptations made by the purchaser which are not transferred must be destroyed, because they will be treated as infringing copies for all purposes after the transfer. If there are express terms (which themselves lay down the terms on which the transferee may do things which the purchaser was permitted to do) then the transferee is bound by those latter terms. Normally, a transferee is not bound by the terms of sale between the transferor and his vendor. This is a special provision introduced by the CDPA, and applies only in these particular circumstances[3].

The same rules apply when the originally purchased copy is no longer usable and what is transferred is a further copy used in its place[4]. The provisions also apply on subsequent transfers.

Section 56 was introduced into the CDPA primarily to deal with computer programs, but the definition of 'electronic form' is wide enough that it will cover any types of work (such as musical works, films or sound recordings) which are carried on CD-ROMs, DVDs, magnetic tapes or compact discs or any other electronic carriers.

Usually, there are very clear express terms, both on the covers and on the actual carrier in the case of films on video tape or DVD and sound recordings on compact discs, to the effect that they may not be copied. However, in the case of computer programs, the express terms of sale normally clearly state what may be done with them and these should be referred to if the purchaser wishes to rely on the exceptions contained in s 56 dealing with works in electronic form.

The CDPA contains additional provisions relating to the making of back up copies, decompilation and observing, studying and testing the functioning of computer programs[5].

1   CDPA s 56.
2   CDPA s 178.
3   CDPA s 56(2).

4 CDPA s 56(3).
5 See **paragraph 9.11** and **Chapter 30**.

Miscellaneous permitted acts

General

9.18 A number of 'miscellaneous' acts are specifically permitted by the CDPA in respect of copyright works[1]. Some of these are of particular relevance to specific industry sectors and will be discussed further in Part 2 of this *User's Guide*, however, because they are of broad application, it is worth noting these exceptions here.

1 ss 57–75.

Anonymous or pseudonymous literary, dramatic, musical and artistic works

9.19 When it is not possible by reasonable enquiry to ascertain the identity of an author and it is reasonable to assume that copyright has expired or that the author died 70 or more years ago, then there is no infringement by any act done in relation to that work. This does not apply to Crown copyright works and works vested in international organisations[1].

If the work in question is a joint work, then the exception only applies if it is not possible to ascertain the identity of any of the authors[2].

This exception is particularly relevant in the context of the quotations[3].

1 See **paragraphs 6.25 and 6.28**.
2 CDPA s 57.
3 See **paragraph 18.06**.

Use of notes or recordings of spoken words

9.20 The definition of a literary work in the CDPA includes a work which is spoken or sung[1]. If, for example, a journalist tapes an interview, the words spoken by the interviewee have copyright as they are recorded and the copyright belongs to the interviewee[2].

However:

'where a record of spoken words is made, whether in writing or otherwise for the purpose:

(a)   of reporting current events; or

(b)   of communicating to the public the whole or part of the work;

it is not an infringement of any copyright in the words as a literary work to use the record or material taken from it (or to copy the record, or any such material, and use the copy) for that purpose'[3].

This exception is subject to the following proviso, namely that:

'(a) the record is a direct record of the spoken words and is not taken from a previous record or a broadcast;

(b) the making of the record was not prohibited by the speaker and, where copyright already subsisted in the work, did not infringe copyright;

(c) the use made of the record or material taken from it is not of a kind prohibited by or on behalf of the speaker or copyright owner before the recording was made; and

(d) the use is by or with the authority of a person who is lawfully in possession of the record'[4].

In short, provided that the interviewee does not object to the making of the recording and it is used only for the purpose of recording current events or broadcasting, then the journalist will be able to use the record without infringing the copyright in the spoken words. But the copyright in the spoken words as recorded by the journalist will belong to the speaker.

1   See **paragraph 2.02**.
2   See **paragraph 2.05**.
3   CDPA s 58(1).
4   CDPA s 58(2).

Public reading or recitation

9.21   The reading or recitation in public by one person of a reasonable extract from a published literary or dramatic work does not constitute an infringement of the copyright in the work, provided that it is accompanied by a sufficient acknowledgement[1]. Similarly, copyright in a published literary or dramatic work is not infringed by the making of a sound recording of such a reasonable extract from it, or by its communication to the public, or a reading or recitation of such extract, provided that the recording or communication to the public consists mainly of material in relation to which it is not necessary to rely on this exception[2].

It is interesting to note that the CDPA provides that the communication to the public must not consist 'mainly of material in relation to which' it is necessary to rely on the exception. This can be read as meaning that the programme must not consist of the readings of a series of reasonable extracts from a number of different literary and dramatic works (not necessarily readings of extracts from a particular work). No definition of what amounts to a 'reasonable extract' is offered by the CDPA.

1   CDPA s 59(1). See also **paragraph 23.14** for a consideration of the use of extracts in dramatic performances.
2   CDPA s 59(2).

Abstracts of scientific or technical articles

9.22   If a scientific or technical article appears in a periodical accompanied by an 'abstract' indicating the content of the article, the copyright in the article or the abstract will not be infringed by copying the extract or issuing copies of it to the public. This exception does not apply to the extent that a licensing scheme is established under the CDPA[1] to grant licences to undertake this activity[2].

1   CDPA s 143.
2   CDPA s 60.

Recordings of folksongs

9.23   The words and music of a song may be recorded for the archive of a body designated by Order of the Secretary of State, provided that the song is unpublished and of unknown authorship at the time the recording is made, and provided that the recording does not infringe any other copyright (e.g. another sound recording) or the rights of performers[1]. Copies of such recordings may be made and supplied by archivists on conditions prescribed by the Secretary of State, including a requirement that the archivist is satisfied the recording is needed for research and private study, and no person is given more than one copy of any particular recording[2].

1   CDPA s 61(1) and (2).
2   CDPA s 61(3) and (4). A number of bodies have been designated for this purpose and these are considered in further detail at **paragraph 20.11**.

Representations of artworks on public display

9.24   The CDPA contains specific provisions relating to buildings, sculptures, models for buildings and works of artistic craftsmanship (i.e. an artistic work which is not a painting, sculpture, drawing, engraving, photograph or work of architecture) where permanently situated 'in a public place or in premises open to the public'[1]. The copyright in any such work is not infringed by:

'(a)   making a graphic work representing it;

(b)   making a photograph or film of it; or

(c)   making a broadcast of a visual image of it.'[2]

Copyright will not be infringed by issuing to the public, or the communication to the public of anything made pursuant to this exception[3].

So, a film or television broadcast (live or pre-recorded), for example, may make use of buildings and other such works which are in public parks, houses which are open to the public (whether or not an admission fee is charged), galleries, museums, etc. without any express licence from the owner of the copyright in those works. If the works are situated on private premises, permission will be required from the owner of the premises in order to enter them for the purpose of making the television broadcast or film, but this is unrelated to any question of copyright.

Models of buildings (or parts of buildings) are frequently used as sets in the film and television industry. A licence from the copyright owner of a building still 'in copyright' must be obtained before making such a model, because the exception does not extend to making models, which would infringe the restricted act of copying.

The Design and Artists Copyright Society (DACS) was formed with the intention of protecting artists whose works are used in films and broadcasts (among other uses). Further information may be obtained from DACS[4].

1   The CDPA does not define what does or does not qualify as being 'in a public place'. For example, there is no clarification as to whether a work of art situated on private property, but clearly visible from public land, could be construed as 'being in a public place'.

2   CDPA s 62(2). See also **paragraph 28.11**.

3   CDPA s 62(3).

4   See **Appendix** 1.

Advertisements for sale of artistic works

9.25   Copyright in an artistic work is not infringed by making copies to advertise its sale. However, a copy made for this purpose will be an infringing copy if it is subsequently dealt with (i.e. sold, let for hire, offered or exposed for sale or hire, exhibited in public, distributed or communicated to the public) for any other purpose[1].

1   CDPA s 63.

Subsequent works by the same artist

9.26   There are clear public policy reasons why copyright should not be used to inhibit an artist's creative development. The author of an artistic work who no longer owns the copyright in his earlier work, will not be deemed to infringe his earlier work by copying it, unless he repeats or imitates the main design in his earlier work[1].

1   CDPA s 64.

Reconstruction of buildings

9.27   Anything done for the purpose of reconstructing a building will not infringe copyright in the building itself, or in any drawings or plans by which the building was constructed[1].

1   CDPA s 65. See **paragraph 28.12**.

Lending to the public

9.28   The rental or lending of a literary, dramatic, musical, artist work (other than a work of architecture or applied art) or a film or sound recording will infringe copyright in the work unless it is authorised[1]. However, the Secretary of State may order compulsory licensing subject to reasonable payment[2]. This power has not been exercised as at the time of writing.

1   CDPA s 18A. See **paragraph 7.05**.
2   CDPA s 66.

Miscellaneous permitted acts: films

9.29   Copyright in a film will not be infringed by any act which is done at a time when, or in pursuance of arrangements made at a time, when:

'(a)   it is not possible by reasonable inquiry to ascertain the identity of any of the persons [by reference to whose life the copyright period is ascertained][1] and
(b)   it is reasonable to assume–
   (i) that the copyright has expired, or
   (ii) that the last to die of those persons died 70 years or more before the beginning of the calendar year in which the act is done or the arrangements are made.'[2]

This exception will not apply where the film is Crown copyright or is the copyright of an international organisation, pursuant to s 168 of the CDPA[3].

1   See **paragraph 6.15**.

2   CDPA s 66A(1).
3   See paragraph **10.09**.

Sound recordings

9.30   The amended CDPA also provides that: 'It is not an infringement of the copyright in a sound recording to play it as part of the
activities of, or for the benefit of, a club, society or other organisation if
the following conditions are met'[1]:

'The conditions are:

(a)   that the organisation is not established or conducted for profit
      and its main objects are charitable or are otherwise concerned
      with the advancement of religion, education or social welfare,

(b)   that the sound recording is played by a person who is acting
      primarily and directly for the benefit of the organisation and
      who is not acting with a view to gain,

(c)   that the proceeds of any charge for admission to the place
      where the recording is to be heard are applied solely for the
      purposes of the organisation; and

(d)   that the proceeds from any goods or services sold by, or on
      behalf of, the organisation-
      (i) in the place where the sound recording is heard, and
      (ii) on the occasion when the sound recording is played,

are applied solely for the purposes of the organisation'[2].

This modifies the position prior to the 2003 Regulations, which
allowed the free playing of sound recordings in 'not for profit' clubs
even if, say, the premises had been licensed to a third party. Now if such
venues are hired out for a fee and commercial music is played, a licence
will be required in the relevant sound recordings from Phonographic
Performance Limited (PPL)[3].

1   CDPA s 67(1).
2   CDPA s 67(2).
3   See paragraph **22.29**.

'Ephemeral recordings' for broadcasts[1]

9.31   The technical process of preparing a broadcast may involve
various technical acts of copying. The CDPA provides for this[2] by
making it clear that where a person is authorised (by licence or
assignment) to include a literary, dramatic, or musical work (or an
adaptation of one of those works), an artistic work, sound recording or

film in a broadcast, he will be deemed to be authorised to undertake a number of acts for the purpose of his broadcast, namely:

- for literary, dramatic, musical works and adaptations to make a sound recording or film[3];
- for artistic works to make a photograph or film[4];
- for sound recordings and films to make a copy[5].

These are the so-called 'ephemeral rights'. It should be noted that the ephemeral right does not extend to making further reproductions from the original recording. Moreover, the recording, photograph, copy or film made by the licensee must be destroyed within the 28-day period beginning on the day on which the recording is first used for broadcasting the work, and may not be used for any other purpose[6]. If the owner of the copyright agrees, the 28-day period can be extended.

The ephemeral right does not vest any rights beyond the right to make a recording, photograph, film or copy (as relevant), which must be destroyed within 28 days. If, therefore, a television station is given a licence to broadcast a play expressly limited to its area, then the ephemeral right exception would additionally entitle it to pre-record the play, but it would not be entitled to use the recording for any other purpose (for example, such as transmitting to another area or selling the tape to a station in another country).

Retaining the recording beyond the 28-day period infringes the copyright in the material which has been recorded, entitling the owner of the copyright to damages for breach of copyright and to destruction, or delivery up, of the offending recording[7].

1   See also **paragraph 26.15**.
2   CDPA s 68.
3   CDPA s 68(2)(a).
4   CDPA s 68(2)(b).
5   CDPA s 68(2)(c).
6   CDPA s 68(3).
7   CDPA s 68(4).

Supervision of broadcasts and other services

9.32   The Broadcasting Acts 1990 and 1996 and the Communications Act 2003 contain provisions for the making of copies of transmission services by regulatory bodies (now OFCOM and the Governors of the BBC) for the purposes of maintaining supervision and control. The making of such copies does not require a licence from the authors.

Time shifting

9.33 A record of a broadcast may be made *in domestic premises* for private and domestic use, solely for the purpose of enabling it to be viewed or listened to at a more convenient time, without infringing the copyright in the broadcast, or works included in it[1].

The requirement that the copy must be for 'private and domestic use' was found in one recent case to prevent the operator of a commercial copying service from relying on this defence in making copies for customers of material taken from the internet:

'... the interposition of the defendant in the copying exercise for commercial gain is fatal to this defence. The copying is done by the defendant and the defendant is not copying it for the purpose of private and domestic use. It is copying for the purpose of selling [a CD-R]'[2].

For the same reason, the words 'in domestic premises' were added to the provisions of the CDPA by the 2003 Regulations. It is now clear that 'time shifting' is not a defence which can be used to excuse activities which take place on commercial premises.

The availability of a 'time shifting' defence to persons downloading from the internet was thrown into sharp focus by the *EasyInternetcafe* decision[3]. In particular there was a concern that the defence could aggravate the impact of unauthorised peer-to-peer copying. However, the 2003 Regulations added a new sub-section, to prevent individuals who copy broadcasts in domestic premises, purportedly for 'private and domestic use', being able to rely on the section where such a copy is subsequently 'dealt' with. Under s 70(2)(2) of the CDPA (as amended) such copies will be treated as infringing copies for the purposes of that dealing and if that dealing infringes copyright, copies shall be treated as infringing copies for all subsequent purposes. 'Dealt with' is defined to mean sold or let for hire, offered or exposed for sale or hire or communicated to the public.

The 2003 Regulations also limited the ambit of this exception to the copying of *broadcasts* only. This can be distinguished from the position prior to the 2003 Regulations, whereby the 'timeshifting' exemption extended to both broadcast and cable programme services[4]. The *Easy-Internetcafe* decision had found (based on the authority of the *Shetland Times* case) that the unauthorised downloading of copyright material from the internet may be excused by the 'time-shifting' exception set out in s 70 because the processes of the internet could be construed as a cable programme service[5]. It is now clear that some, but by no means all, applications of the internet are caught by the definition of 'broadcast' (which is intended to capture only services 'transmitted for simultaneous reception by members of the public' or 'at a time determined solely by the person making the transmission'[6]). The functioning, for example, of an internet-based peer-to-peer service would not typically appear to amount to a broadcast for the purposes of the CDPA (as amended), since material is made available 'on demand'. It follows that since the implementation of the 2003 Regulations copying material from internet-based services without authorisation is no longer permitted by 'time-shifting' except in those circumstances (such as the 'live' streaming of an event or a scheduled internet communication)[7] which may now be construed as broadcasts under the CDPA. Some writers have commented that the process of 'capping' television programmes (by recording them onto digital files for communication and download via peer-to-peer networks) could be construed as 'time-shifting' for the purposes of the CDPA. The authors would respectfully disagree that that reflects the current position under English law. The fact that the material included in a download started life as an authorised broadcast may excuse the making of a copy by the 'uploader', but would not excuse the further distribution of that copy by the uploader via a peer-to-peer network, nor the download of a file made available 'on demand' over such a network[8].

It is worth noting that 'at a convenient time' does not mean 'at only one other convenient time' since, on the general rule of statutory construction, the singular will imply the plural and vice versa unless the context so requires.

1   CDPA s 70.
2   Mr Justice Peter Smith, *Sony Music Entertainment (UK) Ltd & Others v EasyInternetcafe Limited (unreported, 28 January 2003, Peter Smith J)*.
3   Ibid.
4   See **paragraph 2.10** for a discussion of cable programmes
5   **See paragraph 7.07** for a brief discussion of the *Shetland Times* case.
6   See **paragraph 2.09.**
7   See **paragraph 2.09.**
8   The same may not be the case in relation to peer-to-peer streaming services.

Photographs of broadcasts

9.34 Taking photographs, for private and domestic use, of images from a broadcast is permitted and does not infringe the copyright in the broadcast or in any film included in it[1].

1   CDPA s 71.

Transmissions to public and non-paying audiences

9.35 Where a broadcast service is shown or played in public to an audience who does not pay for admission (such as, for example, on a 'big screen' like those commonly displayed in sports and other bars) the copyright in the broadcast, or in any sound recording (other than an 'excepted sound recording' – essentially commercial music) or film which is included in the broadcast will not be infringed, provided the performance is before a non-paying audience[1]. This provision is considered in detail elsewhere in this *User's Guide*[2].

1   CDPA s 72(1).
2   See **paragraphs 7.06 and 26.17**.

Reception and retransmission of wireless broadcast by cable

9.36 Under certain circumstances, a wireless broadcast made *from the UK* (i.e. not from elsewhere in the EEA) may be received and immediately retransmitted by cable, without infringing copyright in the broadcast, or works included within the broadcast[1]. The circumstances are that:

- The re-transmission by cable is because of a 'relevant requirement' (essentially a 'must carry' obligation imposed by the Communication Act 2003).
- The broadcast is made for reception in the area in which it is retransmitted by cable[2].
- The broadcast is part of a qualifying service (i.e. regional and national ITV services, Channel 4, 5, S4C, S4C Digital, BBC broadcast services and the teletext services which accompany these services and any others the Secretary of State may require)[3].

For these purposes, a retransmission by cable will include microwave transmissions between fixed points[4.]

The intention of these provisions is to enable cable retransmission to bolster reception levels in areas of poor broadcast reception, and to enable cable operators to comply with their 'must carry' obligations for basic channels. It is important to note that if the broadcaster has failed to clear the necessary rights in works which he includes in his service, the fact that a retransmission takes place under this provision is relevant when considering damages[5]. So, if a cable operator relays the broadcast of a local ITV contractor, no licence need be obtained by the cable operator for including either the broadcast or the works in it, in his cable programme service. The ITV contractor must, however, have obtained licences to permit the broadcasting of the works.

An application to settle the royalty or other sum payable for the reception and retransmission of wireless broadcast by cable may be made to the Copyright Tribunal by the copyright owner or the person making the broadcast[6].

The issue of retransmitting broadcasts which emanate from elsewhere in the EEA is considered in detail elsewhere in this *User's Guide*[7].

1   CDPA s 73.
2   CDPA s 73(2)(b).
3   CDPA s 73(2)(b) and (6) see also **paragraph 26.19**.
4   CDPA s 73(13).
5   CDPA s 73(3).
6   CDPA s 73A.
7   See **paragraph 26.20**.

Sub-titling broadcasts

9.37   The CDPA provides that broadcasts may be copied, and those copies issued to the public, without infringing copyright in the broadcasts, or the works included in them, if the purpose of so doing is to sub-title or otherwise modify the broadcasts for the purposes of providing the deaf, physically or mentally handicapped, with copies. Only a body nominated by Statutory Instrument is permitted to copy and sub-title for this purpose[1]. The Copyright (Sub-titling of Broadcast and Cable Programmes) (Designated Body) Order 1989 nominates the National Sub-titling Library for Deaf People as such a body.

1   CDPA s 74

Recording of broadcasts for archival purposes

9.38   Broadcasts may be copied for archival purposes. Again, these copies may only be made by designated bodies nominated by Statutory Instrument[1]. The Copyright (Recording for Archives of Designated Class of Broadcasts and Cable Programmes) (Designated Bodies) Order 1993 nominates the following as such bodies:

● the British Film Institute;
● the British Library;
● the British Medical Association;
● the British Music Information Centre;
● the Imperial War Museum;
● the Music Performance Research Centre;
● the National Library of Wales;
● the Scottish Film Council.

1   CDPA s 75.

Adaptations

9.39 Where one of the permitted acts is performed in relation to an adaptation of a literary, dramatic or musical work, then the copyright in the work from which the adaptation was made is not infringed any more than the copyright in the adaptation itself[1].

1   CDPA s 76.

Revived copyright: action taken before copyright revived

9.40 No act done before 1 January 1996 will be regarded as infringing revived copyright in a work[1]. Moreover, if arrangements were made before 1 January 1995 but after copyright had expired in a work to undertake an activity which would have infringed copyright in a work had it been in copyright, then those actions will not be an infringement[2]. There is no explanation in the 1995 Regulations as to what is meant by 'arrangement' (e.g. there is no indication that the arrangement must be in writing).

Similarly, it is not an infringement of revived copyright in a work to:

- issue to the public after 1 January 1996 copies of the work made before 1 July 1995, if at the time when they were made copyright did not subsist in the work[3];
- do anything after 1 January 1996 in relation to a literary, dramatic, musical or artistic work or a film made after that date or made in pursuance of arrangements made before 1 January 1996 which contains a copy of that work or is an adaptation of that work if:
  - (a) the copy or adaptation was made before 1 July 1995 and at a time when copyright did not subsist in the work; or
  - (b) the copy or adaptation was made pursuant to arrangements made before 1 July 1995 at a time when copyright did not subsist in the work[4].

It should be noted that these latter provisions deal only with copies and adaptations. A film of a book is not a copy or adaptation for this purpose, but results from the exercise of the restricted act of making a film;

- do, after 1 January 1996, anything which is a restricted act in relation to the work (such as making a film of a book) if the act is done at a time when, or done in pursuance of arrangements made at a time when, the name and address of a person entitled to authorise the act cannot by reasonable enquiry be ascertained[5].
- do any of the acts restricted by copyright in respect of a revived

copyright work provided that payments of a reasonable royalty are made to the copyright owner or such other remuneration as may be agreed or determined in default of agreement by the Copyright Tribunal[6].

1 1995 Regulations, reg 23(1). As to revived copyright, see **paragraphs 6.04 and 6.05**.
2 Reg 23(2)(a).
3 Reg 23(2)(b).
4 Reg 23(3).
5 Reg 23(4).
6 Reg 24.

Chapter 10

Ownership, transmission and licensing of copyright

Distinction between copyright and objects

10.01 It is important to distinguish between ownership of copyright, and ownership of the object on which the copyright work has been reduced to material form. It is a common misapprehension that the owner of the object is also the owner of the copyright. For example, if an artist draws a picture in a fan's autograph book, the copyright in the drawing would not belong to the owner of the autograph book. Although he would be entitled to retain physical possession of the object (i.e. the book), the copyright in the drawing would remain with the artist.

Basic rules of authorship and ownership

10.02 The basic rules as to authorship and ownership of a copyright work are that the author is the person who creates the work, and the first owner of copyright in the work will be the author[1].

Even if a literary, dramatic, musical or artistic work is specifically commissioned, the copyright ownership will remain with the author unless there is a specific contractual provision vesting the copyright with the person commissioning the work[2].

However, there are special rules regarding the authorship of sound recordings, films, broadcasts and typographical arrangements and also in relation to works of joint authorship[3]. There are also exceptions to the basic ownership rules in the case of Crown copyright, Parliamentary copyright and the copyright of certain international organisations and works made by employees[4].

1   CDPA s 11(1).
2   In contrast with the position prior to the CDPA, see **paragraph 10.16**.

3 See **paragraph 10.08**.
4 See **paragraphs 10.09 and 10.14**.

Literary, dramatic, musical and artistic works and computer-generated works

10.03 The basic rules of authorship and ownership of copyright works apply to literary, dramatic, musical and artistic works. However, the person who *creates* the work may not be the same person who *records* it for the first time. In each case the question will be who is responsible for the expression that is recorded? In the case of a literary or a dramatic work, it is commonly said that the person who creates the language will be the author, but that will not always be the case. In each case it will be a question of determining on the facts who is responsible for the protectable elements. So:

> 'a mere copyist of written matter is not an 'author' ... a person to whom the words are dictated for the purpose of being written down is not an 'author'. He is the mere agent or clerk of the person dictating, and requires to possess no art beyond that of knowing how to write'[1].

To take a number of examples:

- *The secretary*: If a secretary records the words dictated by someone else, the person dictating the text will be the owner of copyright[2].
- *The reporter*: If a reporter takes down the words of another, but uses his own skill and labour to turn those words into an original article, he will be the author[3].
- *The story collaborator*: If a person collaborates on a literary or dramatic work, it is possible that he will acquire copyright in his contribution. If the work consists of detailed elements of plot construction and characterisation, for example, which are sufficiently distinct and original to amount to protectable works[4], then this will receive protection[5]. The circumstances in which a contribution will receive copyright protection in these circumstances are uncommon.

The CDPA makes special provision for 'computer-generated works', the author of which will be the person by whom the arrangements necessary for the creation of the work are undertaken[6].

For these purposes a computer-generated work means a literary, dramatic, musical or artistic work which is 'generated by computer in circumstances such that there is no human author of the work'[7]. A typical computer-generated work would be a list of names and addresses, such as to be found in a classified directory, where a computer rather than a person sorts the names and addresses into a certain order and manner. Such a list will itself have copyright. The person (probably a company) which employed the people who obtain the names and addresses and input the data, will be the copyright owners.

Particular issues relating to the ownership of artistic work[8], especially photographs, are considered elsewhere in this *User's Guide*[9].

1   *Walter v Lane [1900] AC 539*, per Lord James.
2   *Donoghue v Allied Newspapers Ltd [1938] Ch 106.*
3   *Express Newspapers plc v News (UK) plc [1990] FSR 359.*
4   See **paragraph 2.03**.
5   See **paragraph 8.04**.
6   CDPA s 9(3). NB This is to be distinguished from the position in certain jurisdictions, where the person commissioning software is the first owner of copyright in the program (e.g. New Zealand). See Earl Gray and Fiona McKenzie, 'Works for hire when software is commissioned, who owns the copyright', Copyright World July/ August 2003.
7   CDPA s 178.
8   For further discussion of databases, see **paragraph 2.02 and Chapter 16**.
9   See **paragraph 28.14**.

Sound recordings

10.04   The author of a sound recording is the person who creates the sound recording (i.e. the producer). 'Producer' is defined in the CDPA as meaning: 'the person by whom the arrangements necessary for the making of the sound recording … are undertaken'[1].

1   CDPA s 178.

Films made after 30 June 1994

10.05   The authors of a film made after 30 June 1994 are the producer and the principal director[1]. A film is treated as a work of joint authorship unless the producer and principal director are the same person. 'Producer' is defined as for a sound recording[2] (i.e. the person by whom the arrangements necessary for the making of the film are undertaken). There is no definition of 'director' or 'principal director' in the CDPA. It should be noted that since 30 June 1994, the rule that the employer is the first owner of the copyright in a work made by an employee in the course of his employment also applies to films[3].

Copyright	First owner
Film	In a film made since 1 July 1994 the producer and director are the first owner. In a film made before 1 July 1994 the first owner is invariably the producer
Sound recording – the soundtrack when not accompanying the film	As above
Musical work – musical score, songs in the film	Composer/songwriter
Literary work – i.e. script, song lyrics	Author of the work
Dramatic work – provided the film constitutes a work of action and is capable of being performed	Author of the work
Design right in the set design	Set designer
Rights in performance	Actors

1   CDPA s 9(2)(ab).
2   See **paragraph 10.04**.
3   See **paragraph 10.11**.

Broadcasts

10.06   The author of a broadcast is the person 'making the broadcast'[1]. If the broadcast consists of the relay of another broadcast by reception and immediate re-transmission, then the author of the original broadcast will also be the author of the relay broadcast[2].

Under the CDPA, the person making a broadcast, broadcasting a work or including a work in a broadcast is:

- the person transmitting the programme, if he has responsibility to any extent for its contents; and
- any person providing the programme who makes, with the person transmitting it, the arrangements necessary for its transmission,

and in this context references to a programme include references to any item included in a broadcast[3].

1   CDPA s 9(2)(b).
2   CDPA s 9(2)(b).
3   CDPA s 6(3), see **paragraph 26.03**.

Typographical arrangements of published editions

10.07 The publisher is the author of the typographical arrangement of a published edition[1].

1 CDPA s 9(2)(d).

Works of joint authorship

10.08 Works of joint authorship are those produced by the collaboration of two or more authors in which the contribution of each is not distinct from that of the others. A song, the words of which are written by one person and the music composed by another (e.g. a composition by Elton John and Bernie Taupin) will not be a work of joint authorship. If the lyricist and composer actually work together in writing the words, then the words will be a joint work, so long as the contributions of the two were not distinct from those of each other. If, therefore, one of the writers composes the chorus and the other the verses (e.g. as in the case of a number of Lennon and McCartney compositions), because their respective contributions would be distinct, there would not be a joint work[1].

In one case, the members of the band Spandau Ballet claimed a right to participate in publishing royalties from the band's songs which had been written by Gary Kemp. One of the arguments advanced by the other band members was that they were joint authors because of their contributions in rehearsal. Park J held that the other band members' contribution (which was to the performance and interpretation of the compositions) was not 'the right kind of skill and labour' required. Although there had been improvisation of some elements of the songs in rehearsal, the melody, choral structure, rhythm and groove had been created by Mr Kemp[2].

The question of who will be a joint author is sometimes a difficult one. In the case of *Cala Homes (South) Ltd v Alfred McAlpine Homes East Ltd*[3] the employee of a building company gave a very detailed brief to a firm of technical draughtsmen as to the design of certain houses and even as to the choice of material. He did not, however, actually put pen to paper. Mr Justice Laddie held that:

'to have regard merely to who pushed the pen is too narrow a view of authorship. What is protected by copyright in a drawing or a literary work is more than just the skill of making marks on paper or some other medium. It is both the words or lines and the skill and effort involved in creating, selecting or gathering together the detailed concepts, data or emotions which those words or lines have fixed in some tangible form which is protected. It is wrong to think that any the person who carries out the mechanical act of fixation is an author. There may well be skill and expertise in drawing clearly and well but that does not mean that it is only that skill and expertise which is relevant. Where two or more people collaborate in the creation of a work and each contributes a significant part of the skill and labour protected by the copyright, then they are joint authors'.

Accordingly, Mr Justice Laddie held that in spite of the fact that the builders' executive did not actually draw the designs, he was a joint author.

Nevertheless, it is essential that there is 'direct responsibility for what actually appears on the paper', and to that extent, at least one subsequent case has noted that the facts of *Cala* are exceptional. In *Ray v Classic plc*[4], the court set out three criteria for joint ownership: collaboration, significant creative input, and a constitution which is not distinct from that of other authors' work. The question is: *can the putative author be said to have contributed the right kind of skill and labour, and if so, was his contribution enough to amount to joint authorship?* In one recent case for example, a member of a team had worked on the development of a software program. It was held that his case for joint authorship would hold prospects of success only if he made a substantial contribution to the detailed idea or program structure. In circumstances where he had little input into the actual coding, his claim failed[5].

The difficulties of joint authorship were considered in detail in the recent case of *Brighton v Jones*[6], a case which concerned the play *Stones in His Pockets*, written by Marie Jones. After the play was commissioned from Ms Jones, she wrote an initial version in 1996, later rewriting it in 1999. The second version was a commercial success. The claimant, Ms Pamela Brighton, directed initial productions of the 1996 script and in the process gave Ms Jones contributions which improved the script. Ms Brighton's contributions also included manuscript notes in respect of some scenes which were followed, albeit not word for word, by Ms Jones.

The court reviewed the relevant case law, and emphasised:

- That a person does not have to actually write in order to qualify as a joint author (per *Cala Homes*) (although Park J pointed out in that case that there was 'close instruction' by the joint author which amounted to direct responsibility for what appeared on paper).
- There must be a 'significant and original' contribution[7]. The contribution need not be equal to other authors but (per *Hadley v Kemp*) it would be surprising if a 'slight contribution' was enough.

- That the contribution must be to the work. A contribution to the performance or interpretation of the work is not enough (per *Hadley v Kemp*).

The court held that the claimant's contribution did not give rise to joint authorship status. It was always Jones who created the words. Further, any copying from the claimant's manuscript notes was de minimus[8].

Some writers have suggested that the proliferation of interactive works presents a special problem for the law regarding joint authorship. In recent years, for example, the development of broadband internet-based gaming services has resulted in a new generation of on–line multi–player games, based on complex interactive environments formed by the game provider, but populated by thousands of characters the attributes of which are, at least in part, determined by the game–player himself. Such games usually utilise a 'client/server' architecture. In short, one computer program operates on the player's personal computer, and another operates on a centralised server to which gamers obtain 'live' simultaneous access. The server-based software determines the parameters (or 'logic') of the game (the virtual environment), whilst the software based on the player's personal computer stores the player's game-based information and communicates that to the server. Players can, within the parameters pre–set by the server software, 'create' original items (names, characteristics, even assets such as originally designed buildings etc). However, on the principles set out above, it does not appear to the authors possible for game players to acquire, by virtue of their input, any position of joint authorship of the game which they join. Nevertheless, it is possible for the player to generate valuable assets (and indeed such assets have been traded on on–line auction sites such as eBay). For that reason, the terms and conditions which game players are required to accept before joining such digital environments are likely to include a full assignment of any intellectual property rights which might be generated by the player in participating in the game.[9]

A film is to be treated as a work of joint authorship unless the producer and principal director are the same person[10].

In **Chapter 26** the issue of joint authorship in the context of broadcasts is considered further[11].

1   See **paragraph 22.06**.
2   *Hadley v Kemp [1999] EMLR 589*.
3   [1995] FSR 818.
4   *Ray v Classic FM plc [1998] FSR 622*.
5   *Pierce v Promco SA [1999] ITCLR 233*.
6   [2004] EWHC 1157(Ch) May 18 2004.
7   Per *Godfrey v Lees, [1995] EMLR 307*.

8 For a detailed discussion of the case see comment, Thorston Lauterbach, [2005] EIPR 119 and (for a less than objective view) see Les Christy, ' "Stones in His Pockets": how a tragi-comedy became a legal farce', ENT LR Vol 15, Issue 7, August 2004.
9 For a fuller discussion of these interesting issues, see Angela Adrian, 'Who owns the Copyright in Multi-Author Interactive Works' [2003] Ent LR, Issue 2. For a discussion of copyright ownership in 'Copyleft' schemes, see Andrew Stokes, 'Authorship, Collaboration and Copyright: A new view from the United Kingdom' [2002] Ent LR Issue 6.
10 CDPA s 10(1A).
11 See **paragraph 26.03**.

First ownership of Crown copyright

10.09 The above rules do not apply to Crown copyright or parliamentary copyright or to copyright of certain international organisations. In the case of Crown copyright, the Crown is the first owner of the copyright in a work made by an officer or servant of the Crown, in the course of his duties[1].

In the case of parliamentary copyright, where a work is made by or under the direction or control of the House of Commons or the House of Lords, the House by whom, or under whose direction or control the work is made, is the first owner of any copyright in the work and, if the work is made by or under the direction or control of both Houses, then the two Houses are joint first owners of copyright[2]. There are some variants to this rule relating to the ownership of copyright in parliamentary Bills which are beyond the scope of this *User's Guide*.

Modifications to s 165 of the CDPA were introduced by the Parliamentary Copyright (Scottish Parliament) Order 1999[3], so that its provisions apply (as modified) to works made by or under the direction or control of the Scottish Parliament.

Certain international organisations are the first owners of copyright in original literary, dramatic, musical or artistic work made by their officers or employees[4].

1 CDPA s 163.
2 CDPA s 165(1)(b).
3 SI 1999/676.
4 CDPA s 168.

Ownership of the publication right

10.10 The publication right is discussed at **paragraphs 6.19 et seq** above. The owner of the publication right is the person who publishes for the first time a previously unpublished work in which the copyright has expired, with the consent of the owner of the physical medium in which the work is embodied or on which it is recorded[1]. Thus, if a book publisher publishes a collection of photographs taken in the nineteenth century with the consent of the owners of the actual photographs, the owner of the publication right would be the publisher, not the owners of the photographs.

1   1996 Regulations, reg 16(1).

Works created in the course of employment

10.11   The most common exception to the rule that the person who creates a work is its first owner arises in respect of works created in the course of employment.

When a literary, dramatic, musical, artistic work or film[1] is created by an employee in the course of his employment, under a contract of service, the employer is the first owner of the copyright in the work subject to any agreement to the contrary[2]. So for example, if an advertising executive writes the text of an advertisement in the course of his employment, the copyright in that text vests with his employer[3].

Under the CDPA an employee who produces a copyright work in his own time will own his own work. However, some contracts of employment vest in the employer the copyright in all works written during the period of employment, whether or not they are written during the course of employment. For the employee who wishes to retain rights in works created in his own time, it will be vital to ensure his employment contract adequately deals with the question of the ownership of such work.

1   But not a sound recording – see **paragraph 10.13**.
2   CDPA s 11(2).
3   See **paragraph 30.03**.

Contracts of service and contracts for services distinguished

10.12   In brief, the distinction between 'contracts of service' and 'contracts for services', is that between employees and freelancers. Employment contracts must impose an obligation on the employee to provide his services personally, and include a 'mutuality of obligations' (so that both parties have obligations to one another during the whole period of the agreement, such as an obligation to do work where it is available and to receive payment – even if it is only a retainer)[1]. The expression 'contract of service' has been a subject of considerable judicial examination. In each case it will be necessary to assess the situation on the facts. A number of points are relevant in considering whether an arrangement is a contract of service as distinct from a contract for services:

- Does the 'employer' have the right to control not only what, but how and when work is done?
- Is the worker employed as part of the business of the employer and is his work integral to the business?
- Does the worker provide his own equipment, hire his own helpers or take any degree of financial risk?
- Does he take responsibility for investment or management, and will he profit from soundly managing his task?
- How is the worker remunerated (wages or salary?), is he paid during illness or holidays? Is he free to work for others?

The rule of thumb here is that the greater the degree of individual responsibility the worker has in respect of these matters, the more likely he is to be an independent contractor[2].

1   For example, *Express and Echo Publications Ltd v Tanton [1999] IRLR 367, CA* and *Clark v Oxfordshire Health Authority [1998] IRLR 125, CA.*
2   *Market Investigations Ltd v Minister of Social Security [1969] 2 QB 173.*

Assignment by terms of employment

10.13   The provisions regarding first ownership by employers referred to at **paragraph 10.11** apply only to literary, dramatic, musical and artistic works and films. So, an individual record producer who undertakes the arrangements necessary for a record to be made, will be the first owner of the copyright in the sound recordings he produces, whether or not he does so in the course of this employment. Consequently, for any record company employing his services and wishing to own the product of those services, it is all the more vital that an agreement, setting out a full assignment of the producer's rights in his work, is entered into. The terms upon which a person is employed can vary the provisions of the CDPA.

In any event, where an author is hired on a 'contract for services', such as a freelance consultancy agreement, it is vital (and common practice) that where the prospective owner wishes to make further use of a copyright work produced by the consultant, he must indicate the ownership position of the work and take appropriate rights. In *Ray v Classic FM plc*[1], a radio station wished to make use overseas of a database which it had engaged the defendant to prepare for its UK station. The consultancy agreement was silent as to ownership of the database. Although the court held that some right to use the work was implicit in the arrangement, it refused to imply these rights extended to the additional use sought. The case provides a salutary reminder of the need for good professional advice in drawing up such agreements, even when they appear to be basic.

However, in one recent case, the court *was* prepared to imply a beneficial assignment of copyright to the commissioner of artwork. In *Griggs Group v Ross Evans*[2] the court granted a declaration to a person commissioning artwork from the defendant, because it was necessary to imply a term requiring such a beneficial assignment in order to give business efficiency to the commissioning arrangement. An exclusive licence would be insufficient for the purpose:

> 'Where a freelance designer is commissioned to create a logo for a client ...the designer will have an implicit task if he were to contend that he is free to assign the copyright to a competitor ...in order to give business efficiency to the contract, it will rarely be enough to imply a term that the client shall enjoy a ...licence ...'.

Griggs represents a departure from the approach of *Ray v Classic FM*[3].

1   [1998] FSR 622.
2   *R Griggs Group Ltd, R Griggs and Co Ltd and Airwair Ltd v Ross Evans, Raben Footwear Pty Ltd, Ronny Leopold Lewy and Gary Lewy [2003] EWHC 2914, (Ch), [2005] EWCA Gull CA.*
3   See Baines, 'Copyright in commissioned works a cause for uncertainty' [2005] EIPR for a further discussion of the case.

Ownership in works created before 1 August 1989

10.14 The general rule is that the ownership of copyright at the time of its creation is determined by reference to the law in force at that time. This means that for works created during the life of the 1956 Act[1], ownership is determined by the terms of that Act, and that for works created during the life of the 1911 Act[2], the 1911 Act remains relevant. Earlier works are governed by still earlier Acts. Under the 1956 Act there were significant differences in the first ownership rules to those contained in the CDPA. The 1996 Regulations also changed the rules as to the ownership of films with effect from 1 July 1994. What follows is a discussion of particular issues arising in respect of older works[3].

1   I.e. from 1 June 1957 to 31 July 1989.
2   I.e. from 1 July 1912 to 31 May 1957.
3   **Paragraphs 10.15–10.18.**

Films made before 1 July 1994

10.15 The first owner of a film made after 1 June 1957 and before 1 July 1994 was the person by whom the arrangements necessary for the making of the film were undertaken.

Before 1 July 1957 films were not protected as a separate category of protected work as such, and ownership vested in the owners or their component parts (i.e. the writers of the screenplay, composers of the musical score, and the cinematographer). Specialist expert advice should be sought if it is important to ascertain the first owner of such a film, as the law involved is beyond the scope of this *User's Guide*.

Commissioned works: pre-CDPA

10.16 Before the CDPA, the copyright in photographs, portraits and engravings which were made under commission from a third party, vested in the person who commissioned the work. It was necessary that the commission was made for valuable consideration (i.e. money or money's worth). This provision could be varied by agreement. For example, artists who painted portraits under commission might require the person commissioning the portrait to enter into an agreement providing that certain aspects of the copyright should remain vested in the painter.

It should be noted that this exception applied only to photographs, portraits and engravings. This produced some strange anomalies. If a painter was commissioned to paint a picture of a house by the person who owned it, the copyright in the painting remained in the artist, unless there was an express agreement to the contrary. The person commissioning the painting was entitled to own the painting and keep it in his house; but he would not have been entitled to license reproductions of it for magazines etc. That right remained with the artist. Similarly, if a theatrical impresario commissioned a musical play from a freelance composer and writer, the rights in the play would not have vested in the impresario, unless he took an express assignment. Alternatively, he could have employed the composer and writer as full-time employees under contracts of service, in which case copyright would have vested in the impresario as employer[1].

1   See **paragraph 10.11**.

Photographs: pre-CDPA

10.17 Before the CDPA there was a special exception regarding the ownership of copyright in photographs. The owner in this case was the person who owned the material on which the photograph was processed. In the case of an ordinary photograph this was the negative. If an instant camera was used, then the owner of the roll of film would be the owner of the copyright in the photograph. The owner of the copyright was not the person who took the photograph. It will be recalled, though, that the copyright in a photograph commissioned by a third party vested in the person who ordered the taking of the photograph[1]. This rule overrode the provision that the owner of the material upon which the photograph was taken was the owner of the copyright in it.

1   See **paragraph 10.16**.

Sound recordings: pre-CDPA

10.18   Prior to the CDPA, the rules as to the ownership of copyright in sound recordings were similar to those which applied to photographs. That is to say, the owner of the material upon which the recording was made was the owner of the sound recording. There was an exception in the case of soundtracks of films (which the 1956 Act excluded from the definition of sound recordings), the copyright in which vested in the owner of the copyright in the film.

On the other hand, the rule regarding ownership of commissioned recordings differed from that applicable to photographs. If a sound recording was commissioned, the ownership remained with the person who owned the record at the time when the recording was made and not with the person who commissioned the record – unless the contract between them provided otherwise.

Ownership of extended copyright

10.19   The period of 'extended copyright' is that 20-year period following the date on which copyright would have expired under the CDPA, before the period of protection was extended from 50 years to 70 year pma by the 1995 Regulations[1].

The owner of extended copyright is the person who was the owner of the copyright in the work immediately before 1 January 1996. However, if his ownership was for a period of less than the whole of the 50 years pma under the original 1988 provisions, then the extended copyright will be owned by the person who owned the balance of the original 50 years pma period[2].

By way of illustration:

● A assigns the film copyright in his novel in 1960 to XYZ

Films Ltd. A dies in 1965. Therefore, the original copyright period would have expired in 2015 but it is now extended to 2035. XYZ Films Ltd owns the extended copyright.

- A assigns the copyright in his original screenplay to XYZ Films Ltd in 1960 on condition that if a second film is not made by the year 2000, the rights will revert to him. The other facts are as above. In this case, A's heirs have the benefit of the extended copyright because it is part of the reversionary interest expectant on the termination of the original period granted to XYZ Films Ltd.

1 See **paragraph 6.02**.
2 1995 Regulations, reg 18.

Ownership of revived copyright

10.20 The person who was the owner of the copyright in a work immediately before it expired[1] is from 1 January 1996 the owner of any revived copyright in the work[2]. However, if the former copyright owner had died before that date, or in the case of a company had ceased to exist, then the revived copyright vests (in the case of a film) in the principal director of the film or his personal representatives and (in any other case) in the author of the work or his personal representatives.

By way of illustration:

- A assigns the copyright in a novel to X in 1935. A dies in 1940. Copyright expires in 1990 (50 years pma). X is therefore the former copyright owner and will own the revived copyright from 1 January 1996.

- A assigns the copyright in a novel or any other copyright work, except a film, to X in 1935. A dies in 1940. Copyright expires in 1990. X dies in 1993 or, X being a company, is struck off the register in 1993 (mere winding-up proceedings are not enough for the company to cease to exist). X having been the former copyright owner, the revived copyright will vest in the heirs of A and not in the heirs of X.

- A directs a film and B photographs it in 1940[3]. XYZ Films Ltd as assignee and employer owned the rights in the services of A and B. It therefore owned the dramatic and photographic rights in the film and effectively was copyright owner of the film. A dies in 1943 and B dies in 1944, therefore, the term of dramatic copyright in the film expires in 1993 and the photographic copyright in 1994. XYZ Films Ltd is the owner of the revived copyright. If XYZ Ltd has been struck off the Companies House register in 1995, the heirs of A, (the director of the film) will become the owners of the revived copyright in the entire film[4].

1 'The former copyright owner'.
2 1995 Regulations, reg 19.
3 See **paragraph 2.08** – as the film was made before the 1956 Act came into force, it would have been protected as a dramatic and artistic work, not as a film.
4 See also **paragraph 6.04**.

Registration

10.21 There is no copyright registry in the UK, but many years ago it was necessary to register copyright material at the Stationers Hall[1]. The Stationers Company maintained a register of copyrights (being originally the right to print) from the sixteenth century. The Registry finally ceased to be of any importance when the Copyright Act 1911 came into force. It is sometimes thought that it is necessary to register one's work with a lawyer or bank in order to establish copyright. This misconception arises probably because it is useful to have some evidence of the date when the work came into existence, in case a very similar work comes into existence elsewhere at a later date. The ability to prove the date upon which a work came into existence can be of considerable value in an infringement action. The Stationers Hall Registry still exists, although since 1 January 2000 works may no longer be registered there. The Registry continues to maintain its database in relation to works previously registered, which can be valuable in establishing the date upon which a registered work came into existence. This may equally be accomplished by sending a copy of the work to oneself (or to a bank, solicitor etc) by registered mail or recorded delivery and leaving it sealed. Outside the UK, the great majority of the Berne Convention countries[2] do not maintain copyright registries. However, in some Southern African countries, for example, the registration of copyright is important in determining ownership of copyright in infringement actions. In the UK, the Producers Alliance for Cinema and Television, PACT, also operates a registration scheme[3].

1 See **paragraph 1.12**.
2 See **Chapter 4** and **Appendix 2**.
3 See **Appendix 1**.

Assignments and exclusive licences: what do 'sole' and 'exclusive' mean?

10.22 The transmission of copyright may be effected by assignment, by will, or by operation of law, as personal or movable property[1].

Equally the owner can grant contractual rights (i.e. licences) to undertake restricted acts in respect of his copyright work. If that licence is exclusive (in the sense that it authorises the licensee to do a particular act to the exclusion of all others, including the grantor himself) then the CDPA provides that the exclusive licensee will have enhanced rights not available to other licensees[2].

The expressions 'sole' and 'exclusive' are often used together in intellectual property licences. However, whilst the word 'exclusive' has the clear statutory meaning referred to above, 'sole' is not defined in intellectual property legislation at all. Instead, it has been suggested that a 'sole licence' is one that grants rights to the licensee at the exclusion of everyone except the licensor[3]. This accords with the meaning of 'sole' in other areas, for example in agency contracts[4]. This is contradictory to the meaning of an 'exclusive licence' (above), in the sense that a 'sole licence' allows the licensor to exploit rights under a licence, whereas an 'exclusive licence' expressly prevents it. The definitions also overlap in the sense that they both prevent the rest of the world (outside the licensor and licensee relationship) from exploiting the rights.

'Sole' and 'exclusive' were historically used in legislation such as the Copyright Act 1842[5], but seem to have been superseded by a more precise definition of 'exclusive' in legislation and a more precise definition of 'sole' in practice.

In consequence, the words 'sole' and 'exclusive' should not be used together in copyright licences.

1 CDPA s 90(1).
2 See **paragraph 10.30**.
3 Ruth Annand and Helen Norman (1994) *Blackstone's Guide to the Trade Mark Act*, p.198.
4 The appointment of a person to be the sole agent for the sale of property does not debar the owner from selling the property himself (*Bentall, Horsley & Baldry v Vicary [1931] 1 KB 253*) but if another agent sells the property the 'sole agent will be entitled to damages estimated on the probability that he would have earner his commission (*Hampton & Sons v George [1939] 3 All ER 627*).
5 See also *Re Jude (1906) 2 Ch 601*.

Assignments limited to part of copyright

10.23 A copyright owner may want to transfer particular rights in his work to different people (e.g. because they possess particular skills necessary to exploit those rights fully). A novelist, for example, may want to allow publisher A to reproduce his novel and sell those copies to the public, and film producer B to adapt his novel into a screenplay (i.e. a dramatic work) to be recorded on film. Alternatively, a promoter of a sports event may require the television broadcaster who records the event to assign him the right to exploit such television feed (signal) or recording in all media other than television, recognising that other licensees may be better placed to exploit it in other media (e.g. the internet). Indeed the promoter may go one step further and allow the television broadcaster to exploit the TV rights in a certain part of the world only, say the United Kingdom, and require the rights in respect of exploitation in the rest of the world to be assigned to the promoter for onwards licensing to overseas broadcasters.

The law recognises that copyright may be sold off in these separate packages. In fact, in the drafting to the CDPA, the House of Lords amended the Bill and used the word 'things' instead of 'acts', so that it was clear that an assignment could subdivide the various restrictive acts. The example used in the debate was from the publishing industry: it would not be necessary to assign the copying rights as a whole, one could assign paperback rights separately from hardback rights and each would be a legitimate copyright[1]. The CDPA provides that the owner can enter partial assignments which apply:

- to one or more but not all of the things the owner is exclusively entitled to do with regard to the work; or
- to part, but not the whole of the period during which the copyright subsists.

So, for example, a novelist may assign to publisher A the right to distribute copies of his book for a period shorter than the life of copyright, after which the rights revert to the novelist. However, he could not assign to the publisher the right to distribute copies of the book in only part of the UK (since a geographical limitation is not contemplated by the CDPA[2] as one by which copyright for the UK can be divided). So, a document purporting to assign copyright in Surrey, for example, will not be an effective assignment, although it could take effect as a licence.

1 Hansard HL Vol 495 Columns 667 and 668.
2 At s 90(2).

Assignments and exclusive licences must be in writing

10.24 Legal assignments and exclusive licences of copyright must be in writing and signed by or on behalf of the assignor; although a non-exclusive licence need not be in writing[1].

1 CDPA ss 90(3) and 92(1).

Assignment of future copyright

10.25   It is possible to assign copyright which has not yet come into existence. Indeed this is entirely usual when, for example, a film producer commissions a writer to create a screenplay[1].

1   CDPA s 91(1); see **paragraph 24.03**.

Assignments of extended or revived copyright made before 1 January 1996

10.26   Where an agreement made before 1 January 1996 purports to assign the extended or revived copyright to another person, that will be an effective assignment, providing that it is signed by or on behalf of the prospective owner of the copyright. The assignment does not have to be of the whole of the extended or revived copyright, but may be a partial assignment[1].

So, if a copyright owner learning of the intentions of the EU in say, 1994, decided to sell the additional 20 years of copyright by assignment, provided that he was indeed the person legally entitled to do so, such an assignment would be effective to pass the extended or revived copyright to the purchaser.

In any event it is common to find wording in agreements for the sale, for example, of film rights or musical compositions, which have very wide language capable of encompassing extended or revived copyright. In *Redwood Music Ltd v Francis Day and Hunter Ltd*[2] the judge had to consider a large number of assignments of songs in order to determine whether the wording was wide enough to include the reversionary copyright. If the wording of an assignment shows a clear intention to assign not only the copyright for the period under current legislation, but also any extensions etc, then a court may hold that reg 20 will be effective even though the words 'extended' or 'revived copyright' do not appear in the granting clause in the assignment. It is probable that the words 'extended' or 'revived' will have been used, however, because lawyers working for entertainment industry companies have long been aware of the way in which copyright legislation can be changed and will usually take steps to ensure that if there is any additional copyright period their companies will gain the benefit from it. The problem is not a new one. Germany, for example, extended its copyright period from 50 years pma to 70 years pma after the Second World War.

In the recent case of *Novello & Co Ltd v Keith Prowse Music Publishing Co Ltd*[3] the court had to consider the issue of a purported assignment, made by the author during his lifetime, of a reversionary interest in a copyright work made during the currency of the Copyright Act 1911 (which prohibited such assignments except by will)[4]. The author made the assignment during the currency of the 1956 Copyright Act, under which such assignment was valid[5]. The claimant's case rested on the application of transitional provisions of the 1956 Act which, it was claimed, rendered such an assignment ineffective. The court held that since the CDPA now governed the existence and enforceability of copyrights it was necessary to look at the transitional provisions of that Act, which preserved the legal effect of such pre-commencement assignments, with the effect that the assignment made under the Copyright Act 1956 was valid[6].

1   1995 Regulations, reg 20.
2   [1978] RPC 429.
3   Unreported, CA (Civ Div) 14 December 2004.
4   CDPA s 5(2) of the Copyright Act 1911.
5   By s 36 of the Copyright Act 1956.
6   Sch 5 para 25 to the CDPA.

Presumption of transfer of rental right to film producers by authors

10.27   Where an agreement concerning film production is concluded between an author of a literary, dramatic, musical or artistic work (excluding the author of a screenplay or any dialogue or music specially created for the film) and a film producer, the author is presumed to have transferred to the film producer his rental right[1].

This provision came into effect on 1 December 1996, and the presumption applies in relation to agreements concluded before 1 December 1996. However, the exclusion of the presumption in relation to the screenplay, dialogue or music specially created for the film does not apply to films made before 1 December 1996.

1   CDPA s 93A(1).

Right to equitable remuneration where rental right is transferred

10.28   The 1996 Regulations introduced a right for authors to receive 'equitable remuneration' from the exploitation of their rental rights under certain circumstances. The amount of equitable remuneration is to be agreed, or failing agreement, is to be determined by the Copyright Tribunal[1].

The right applies only to authors who have transferred their rental right concerning a sound recording or a film to the producer of the sound recording of the film[2]. In such an event, the author retains the right to equitable remuneration and that right cannot be assigned by the author during his lifetime or except 'by operation of law'[3]. This last phrase means that the right could pass, (for example, to third parties as a result of a bankruptcy of the author, or to his trustees, if he ceases to be of sound mind).

The equitable remuneration is payable by the person for the time being entitled to the rental right (usually the distributors of the film or sound recording)[4].

1   CDPA s 93B.
2   CDPA s 93B(4).
3   CDPA s 93B(2).
4   CDPA s 93B(3).

Distinction between assignments and licences

10.29   The first key difference between an assignment and a licence is that an assignee becomes the owner of the copyright (i.e. he becomes owner of the *property* in the copyright conferred by the CDPA). By contrast, a licence does not convey any property rights, only the *personal* contractual authority of the copyright owner to exercise certain rights to which the owner is otherwise exclusively entitled. Even so, a licence granted by a copyright owner will bind anyone to whom the owner may subsequently assign his copyright, except for a purchaser in good faith for valuable consideration without actual or constructive notice of the licence or someone who acquires rights from such a purchaser[1]. So:

- If an owner O assigns his copyright to A and later purports to assign the same copyright to B, the later purported assignment is ineffective to transfer any rights, since O has already divested himself of the rights and has nothing to left to assign. B's only remedy will be against O (i.e. a contractual claim), whether or not B had notice of the earlier assignment to A.

- If O has granted an exclusive licence to A and later assigns his copyright (including the rights exclusively licensed to A) to B, the licence will not be binding on B unless B has actual or constructive notice of A's licence. If B has not had notice, A's only remedy will be against O (i.e. a contractual claim).

- Equally, if a licensee assigns his rights to a third party, and his own head licence is terminated, the assignment of rights he has entered into will fail, as will, for example, any sub-license agreement entered into by the assignee. If the head licence is terminated by reason of a breach by the assignee or one of his sub-licensees it will make no difference that the terms of the assignment and/or sub-licence neglected to mention the restriction which brought about termination. The assignee and sub-licensee's rights fail since a licensee cannot itself grant more than he has been granted[2].

The second key difference between assignments and licenses is that, as a general rule, only the property owner can enforce copyright against third parties. Since a licensee's rights are contractual, the basic rule of 'privity of contract' under English law is that he can only enforce them against the licensor. In essence, 'privity of contract' means that only the parties to an agreement can sue or be sued under its terms. So, if a contract between A and B purports to grant rights over A in favour of C, C cannot usually enforce the obligation against A unless it is possible to construe some direct agreement between A and C, such as a collateral agreement. Moreover, if B brings proceedings for breach of contract against A, he can only claim damages for his own loss, he cannot claim the loss of any third party on that third party's behalf. This position is modified in two key respects:

(a) *Exclusive licensees*: first, under the CDPA an exclusive licensee has enhanced statutory rights[3].
(b) *Third party beneficiaries*: second, third parties may now benefit from any contract in accordance with the terms of the Contracts (Rights of Third Parties) Act 1999, which received royal assent in the UK on 11 November 1999. In essence, this Act gives a third party the right to enforce the term of a contract which confers a benefit on him. For the third party to be able to enforce his rights, he must be expressly identified in the contract (by name or as a member of a class answering a particular description); however, the third party need not be in existence when the contract is made. For example if a contract refers to the conferral of rights on suppliers, such suppliers may not yet have been chosen and appointed by the parties.

The third party can only enforce a term of a contract subject to and in accordance with the other relevant terms of the contract. In other words, the term being enforced should not be construed in isolation from the rest of the contract. The third party will be entitled to all the remedies the other parties are entitled to, therefore, conversely the third party will also be under a duty to mitigate any loss it may suffer under any breach of contract.

Crucially, the parties to a contract cannot vary or remove the third party's rights under the contract once the third party's rights have crystallised. Those rights are deemed to have crystallised when the third party has communicated his agreement to the term of the contract, or when the party against whom the term is enforceable by the third party (i.e. the promissor) becomes aware that the third party has relied on the term, or when the promissor can reasonably be expected to have foreseen that the third party would rely on the term and has in fact relied on the term. For that reason, since the 1999 Act, most licence agreements will normally contain a clause such as:

'The parties confirm that it is not their intention that the terms of this Agreement should create any right enforceable by third parties pursuant to the Contracts (Rights of Third Parties) Act 1999.'

The 1999 Act applies to any contract entered into on or after 11 November 1999, although for contracts entered into before until 11 May 2000, the Act only applies to contracts where the contract expressly invokes it.

1   CDPA s 90(4).
2   *Monty Python Pictures Ltd v Paragon Entertainment Corpn [1998] EMLR 640.*
3   As to which see **paragraph 10.30**.

Exclusive, non-exclusive and implied licences

10.30   Although no licence conveys property rights, under the CDPA an exclusive licensee does have certain rights akin to those of an owner. In short, an exclusive licensee 'has, except against the copyright owner, the same rights and remedies in respect of matters occurring after the grant of the licence as if the licence had been an assignment'[1].

So, if an owner exclusively licenses to A the right to exploit the owner's copyright in a work within the UK, and B later, without authority, purports to exercise some of those rights during the life of A's licence, then both the owner and/or A could take action against B to prevent B's infringing activity. A non-exclusive licensee on the other hand would usually have no standing against a third party[2], with the effect that if he wishes to enforce his rights against a third party, the co-operation of the copyright owner will be required. Commonly, licences of copyright contractually require an agreed level of co-operation in such matters from the licensor.

Although formalities are required in respect of the creation of an exclusive licence[3], none are required to create a non-exclusive licence.

If the terms of a licence are not reduced to writing, or otherwise specifically agreed, a licence to use material may still be implied in the circumstances. In a contractual setting, a licence, like any other term, will only be implied in order to give 'business efficacy' to the arrangement, not because it would be reasonable to do so. The question will be whether the party would, had they been reminded by an 'officious bystander' during their negotiations of the need for the licence, have agreed it was necessary[4]. The extent of the licence recognised will be the minimum necessary to give effect to the initially intended arrangement. In other words, the courts will not intervene to improve on the commercial deal, but it will impose a term necessary to give effect to it. So, where A and B agree terms by which B will supply work for a particular use to A under terms which allow B to retain copyright, a licence for the particular use will be implied, but that licence will not extended to other uses not contemplated by the parties at the time of contract[5]. It may also be possible to imply the existence or terms of a licence from a course of conduct or industry custom, on the same principles which apply to other contractual terms. So, in one recent case, the claimant owned a music track sought by the defendant for inclusion on a compilation CD. The defendant sent the claimant a deal memo marked 'subject to contract' which the claimant signed and returned, with an invoice, a copy of the track and label copy for the track as a 'cleared' track. The claimant then had a change of heart, telling the defendant not to use the track. The defendant, who had not yet paid for the track, acted to his detriment in reliance on his assumption that the track was 'cleared' (e.g. by manufacturing copies of the album including the track). The court held that, although the 'subject to contract' deal memo was not an offer capable of acceptance, the sending of the track and label copy constituted a bare licence to reproduce and the claimants were estopped from denying the licence.[6]

1 CDPA s 101(1).
2 Subject to the points made at **paragraph 10.29**.
3 **See paragraph 10.24**.
4 *Liverpool City Council v Irwin [1977] AC 239.*
5 *Ray v Classic FM plc [1988] FSR 622.*
6 *Confetti Records and Others v Warner Music UK Ltd (t/a East West Records) [2003] EWHC 1274 (Ch).*

Licences of uncontemplated technologies

10.31 When licensing copyright works, it is necessary to ensure that the drafting is sufficiently wide to catch the specific uses envisaged for the work. Any copyright licence should clearly state the rights to be granted. However, questions sometimes arise as to whether a particular technology or distribution mechanism, which was not specifically contemplated by the parties to a copyright licence at the time of signature, will be included in the licence. This has been the subject of numerous disputes (e.g. in the context of video, CD, and more recently the internet). In each case, the answer will depend upon the manifest intention of the parties as that may be understood by construing the contract. The key to establishing this intention is to determine the meaning the agreement would convey:

'to a reasonable person having all the background knowledge which would reasonably have been available to the parties in the situation they were in at time of the contract'[1].

Is the plain wording of the grant wide enough to catch the technology concerned? If it is, then the technology may be deemed included within the licence even though it was not specifically in the contemplation of the parties at the time of entering into the agreement, nor could have been (since it had not been invented). So, by way of example, a grant of 'the exclusive right of production' in 1880 was held to include producing a film of the work, even though film had not been invented[2].

In the context of digital media, although there have been no recorded UK cases considering this issue, courts in other jurisdictions have sometimes proved reluctant to find that electronic formats can be construed as simply caught within traditional media definitions. Many of these cases have considered issues of re-use of originally printed material in on-line environments.

In *Random House v Rosetta Books*[3]. Random House attempted to injunct Rosetta from marketing on-line 'ebooks', on the basis of Random House's contention that a grant of 'book rights' included the right to put versions of the works on-line. The court in New York found that they were different kinds of work. An ebook could not be equated with a paper book.

Similarly, in France, the courts have taken the view that on-line publication cannot be equated with print publication for the purposes of determining whether a grant of rights was sufficiently wide to permit the re-use of materials on internet and other on-line services[4].

If the contractual wording is ambiguous, then it will be necessary to consider all the terms of the agreement to establish whether these terms suggest that the parties did not intend to include the disputed right. If particular terms do not make sense in the context of the new medium, or if payment provisions are unworkable, then these are likely to be taken as indications that the parties did not intend to grant the rights.

One common device employed to overcome this kind of problem is to use 'technology-neutral' wording such as 'all methods of transmission known or hereafter devised' in licences. Some caution is urged in relation to the use of such words, since certain jurisdictions do not consider this kind of wording to bind the parties regarding technologies not in their contemplation at the time of contract. In Germany, for example, Art 31(4) of the Copyright Law renders void any grant which purports to license the right to use a work by means unknown as at the time of contract. Clearly, in any event, for a licensor, this type of wording is to be avoided if possible.

1   *Investors Compensation Scheme Ltd v West Bromwich Building Society [1998] 1 WLR 896, HL* (per Lord Hoffman).
2   *Serra v Famous Lasky Film Service Ltd (1921) WN 347.* There are a number of other examples, including *Barstow v Terry [1924] 2 Ch 316, Hospital for Sick Children v Walt Disney Productions Inc [1968] Ch 52* and *JC Williamson Ltd v Metro Goldwyn Mayer Theatres Ltd (1937) 56 CLR 567.*
3   New York District Court, [2001] 01 Civ. 1728 (SHS).
4   *Le Progres, Tribunal de grande instance, Lyon, 21 July 1999, Cour d'appel de Lyon, 9 December 1999.*

Licences of extended or revived copyright

10.32   The copyright owner can grant a licence of extended or revived copyright before the date upon which it has arisen (i.e. before the expiry of the original copyright period). However such a licence is vulnerable to the purchase of the copyright by a purchaser in good faith without actual or constructive notice who is not aware of the licence and therefore is not bound by it[1]. Licences which were in existence immediately before 1 January 1996 and which were not due to expire before the end of the old copyright period, continue to have effect during the period of any extended copyright[2]. This is, however, subject to any agreement which might exist to the contrary.

These same provisions apply to waivers or assertions of moral rights and to 'any term or condition of an agreement relating to the exploitation of a copyright work'. Therefore, if five years before the end of the copyright period, the heirs of an author granted a licence of the television rights in a novel to a television company, unless there was some wording indicating a different intention, that licence would be effective not only for the five-year term but for the full 20-year extended copyright period.

Any copyright licence which is imposed by the Copyright Tribunal is equally effective in similar circumstances[3].

1   See **paragraph 10.29**.
2   1995 Regulations, reg 20(2).
3   1995 Regulations, reg 21(2).

Other forms of transmission – insolvency and death

10.33 When the owner of copyright becomes bankrupt, his copyright passes by operation of law to the trustee in bankruptcy, without any assignment in writing by execution of law[1]. Copyright can be bequeathed by will like any other property.

1 CDPA s 90(1).

Reversion of works assigned before 1 June 1957

10.34 If a copyright work was assigned or licensed before 1 June 1957[1] it may be affected by a provision originally contained in the Copyright Act 1911 which remains in force in respect of works assigned or licensed before the Copyright Act 1956 came into force. Under the provisions of the 1911 Act, assignments or licences made by the author of a work in his lifetime are only effective (whatever the terms of the assignment or licence) for the period of his life and 25 years after the death. Grants made by his executors or heirs of his copyright are not affected by these provisions.

There is an exception in the case of 'collective works'. This expression applies to encyclopedias, newspapers, anthologies etc.

Although it is not settled law, it is probably the case that authors who had made assignments before 1 June 1957 could assign the reversion after that date. This is certainly the case under the CDPA in respect of assignments of the reversion made after 31 July 1989.

1 I.e. when the Copyright Act 1956 came into force.

Dealings with copyright within Europe

10.35 There is an inherent tension between the exclusive (and territorial) rights which vest in a copyright owner and the tendency of European law to seek the elimination of market barriers within the EU. The result has been a considerable body of legislation and case law. It is vital for users who enter into agreements for the exploitation of copyright works within the EU to appreciate the impact of these developments, which are considered in detail in **Chapter 14**.

Moral rights

10.36 Moral rights are not assignable[1].

1 CDPA s 94. For further discussion of these rights see **paragraph 11.28**.

Performers' property rights

10.37 The transmission of performers rights is dealt with elsewhere in this *User's Guide*[1].

1 See **paragraphs 12.11–12.14**.

Partners

10.38 Unless a partnership deed states anything to the contrary, the copyright in all work produced during the currency of a partnership is a partnership asset, and, like other assets, is owned and passes in accordance with the general provisions of the partnership deed concerning assets. To avoid dissemination of shares in copyright, it is usually desirable to provide that, upon the death or retirement of a partner, his share in the copyright should vest in the surviving partners. Alternatively, partners could, in their wills, leave their shares in the copyright to their surviving partners.

Chapter 11

Moral rights

Introduction

11.01 Continental European jurisdictions, in contrast to their Anglo-Saxon counterparts, have long distinguished between an author's *economic* rights (broadly equating to his right to control the exploitation of his work and thereby receive compensation by selling rights to others) and his *moral* rights (essentially rights to remain linked to his creation, such as to be recognised as author and to object to treatments of his work which would tend to undermine his integrity). Prior to the CDPA, these rights received no statutory protection in the UK[1].

The CDPA introduced moral rights into UK law for the first time, providing four categories of rights[2]:

- the right to be identified as author (or director) – the *paternity right*[3];
- the right to object to a derogatory treatment of work – the *integrity right*[4];
- the right not to have work falsely attributed – the *false attribution right*[5];
- the right of privacy to certain photographs and films – the *privacy right*[6].

1 Although certain common law rights, such as passing off – see **Chapter 5** – served similar functions.
2 Chapter IV, ss 77–89.
3 CDPA s 77 and **paragraphs 11.02–11.11** below.
4 CDPA s 80 and **paragraphs 11.12–11.20** below.
5 CDPA s 84 and **paragraphs 11.21–11.23**.
6 CDPA s 85 and **paragraphs 11.24–11.26**.

Paternity right – in outline

11.02 The paternity right essentially provides its owner with the right to be identified as the author (or in the case of films, the director) of his work to the viewer, listener or purchaser of a copy of his work, whenever the work is exploited. The details of the right differ depending on the category of work in question, and it is worth considering each category in turn. Significantly, the author (or director) is required to specifically assert this right in order to gain protection[1].

1   See **paragraph 11.08**.

Paternity right: who is protected?

11.03 The authors of literary, dramatic, musical or artistic works and the directors of films have the right to be identified as the author (or director) of their work. Producers of sound recordings and authors of broadcasts and typographical arrangements have no paternity rights. All the works must be entitled to copyright protection[1].

1   CDPA s 77(1).

Paternity right: literary and dramatic works

11.04 In the case of literary works or dramatic works[1], the author has the right to be identified when his work is:

- published commercially;
- performed in public;
- communicated to the public;
- included in copies of a film or sound recording which are issued to the public[2].

1   Excluding words intended to be sung with music – see **paragraph 11.05**.
2   CDPA s 77(2).

Paternity rights: musical works and lyrics

11.05 The author of musical works and lyrics has the right to be identified when:

- his work is published commercially[1];
- copies of a sound recording of his work are issued to the public; or
- a film of which the soundtrack including his work, is shown in public, or copies of such film are issued to the public[2].

1   See **paragraph 11.07** for a discussion of 'commercial publication'.
2   CDPA s 77(3).

Paternity right: artistic works

11.06 The author of an artistic work has the right to be identified as the author of the work whenever:

- his work is published commercially;
- his work is exhibited in public;
- a visual image of his work is communicated to the public;
- a film including a visual image of his work is shown in public or copies of such a film are issued to the public;
- (in the case of a work of architecture in the form of a building or model for a building, a sculpture or work of artistic craftsmanship) copies of a graphic work representing it, or a photograph of it, are issued to the public[1].

1   CDPA s 77(4).

Paternity rights: commercial publication

11.07 'Commercial publication' for these purposes means, so far as literary, dramatic, musical or artistic works are concerned:

'(a)   issuing copies of the work to the public at a time when copies made in advance of the receipt of orders, are generally available to the public; or

(b)   making the work available to the public by means of an electronic retrieval system.'[1]

This excludes works which are published only after subscriptions have been received for the work (which is often the case, for example, in respect of academic works).

The reference to electronic retrieval systems makes it clear that commercial publication will occur if copies are never distributed to the public but the work is instead made available on, say, an online database.

1   CDPA s 175(2).

Paternity right: the need for assertion

11.08 There is no infringement of the right of paternity unless the right has been asserted by a statement to that effect by the author or director in an assignment of the copyright in a work, or by an 'instrument in writing signed by the author or director'[1].

For artistic works, the right may be asserted in relation to the public exhibition of the work 'by securing that, when the author or other first owner of copyright parts with possession of the original, or of a copy made by him or under his direction or control the author is identified on the original or copy, or on a frame or mount or other thing to which it is attached'[2].

In relation to copies of a work, the right may be asserted by a statement signed by the person granting the licence to make copies to the effect that the author asserts his right to be identified if the copy is exhibited in public. This is useful to artists who make prints, for example, rather than paintings or drawings[3].

1 CDPA s 78(2).
2 CDPA s 78(3)(a); see **paragraph 28.21**.
3 CDPA s 78(3)(b).

Paternity right: the persons bound by an assertion

11.09 Where an assertion of paternity is made in an assignment, the assignee and anyone claiming through him is bound by it, whether or not he has notice of the assertion[1]. Anyone acquiring the copyright in literary, dramatic, musical or artistic works or films should make enquiries as to whether or not the right has been asserted. The purchaser may want to examine the original assignment of copyright from the author, or at least take appropriate warranties that no rights have been asserted.

Where the right is claimed by an instrument in writing, only those people to whose attention the assertion has been brought are bound[2].

In the case of works of art, where the assertion is made on parting with possession of the original, or a copy made under the control of the author or first owner of copyright, then anyone into whose hands that original or copy comes is bound, whether or not the identification is still present or visible[3].

Where the assertion is made by inclusion in a licence to make copies of an artistic work, then the licensee is bound. Moreover, anyone into whose hands a copy made pursuant to the licence comes, is bound, whether or not he has notice of the assertion[4].

The right of paternity should always be asserted promptly, because in an action for infringement the court must take into account any delay in asserting the right[5].

1 CDPA s 78(4)(a).
2 CDPA s 78(4)(b).
3 CDPA s 78(4)(c).
4 CDPA s 78(4)(d).
5 CDPA s 78(5).

Paternity right: exceptions

11.10   The right to be identified as the author of a work does not apply to:

- computer programs, the design of typefaces or any computer generated work[1];
- anything done with by or with the authority of the copyright owner, where the copyright in the work originally vested in the author's (or director's) employer (i.e. done in the course of employment)[2];
- a number of acts which, by virtue of other provisions of the CDPA, do not infringe copyright[3], including:
  - (a) fair dealing for the purpose of reporting current events by means of sound recordings, films or broadcasts [4];
  - (b) incidental inclusion of work in an artistic work, sound recording, film or broadcast [5];
  - (c) use in connection with setting, communication or answering examination questions[6];
  - (d) use in connection with parliamentary and judicial proceedings, Royal Commissions and statutory inquiries[7];
  - (e) use of design documents or model recordings for anything other than artistic works and typefaces to make an article to the design[8];
  - (f) use of a design derived from an artistic work[9];
  - (g) use in connection with acts permitted when copyright may be assumed to be expired in anonymous or pseudonymous works and other specific permitted acts[10];
- works made for the purpose of reporting current events[11];
- publication of literary, dramatic, musical or artistic works in a newspaper, magazine or similar periodical, and encyclopedia, dictionary, yearbook or other collective work of reference if the work is made for the purpose of the publication or is authorised for inclusion by the author[12];
- Crown copyright or parliamentary copyright works, or works in which copyright originally vested in an international organisation, except where the author or director has been identified on published copies[13].

1   CDPA s 79(2).
2   CDPA s 79(3).
3   See **Chapter 9**.
4   CDPA s 79(4)(a), see **paragraph 9.03 et seq**.
5   CDPA s 79(4)(b) see **paragraph 9.08**.
6   CDPA s 79(4)(c) see **paragraph 9.10**.
7   CDPA s 79(4)(d) and (e) see **paragraph 9.12**.

8   CDPA s 79(4)(f) see **paragraph 9.15**.
9   CDPA s 79(4)(g) see **paragraph 9.15**.
10 CDPA s 79(4)(h) and **paragraph 9.19**.
11 CDPA s 79(5).
12 CDPA s 79(6).
13 CDPA s 79(7).

Duration of right of paternity

11.11   The right of paternity subsists so long as copyright subsists in the work[1].

1   CDPA s 86(1). Reference should be made to **Chapter 6** to ascertain the period of copyright attributable to the type of work concerned.

Right to object to derogatory treatment (the 'integrity right')

11.12   Authors or directors of relevant work[1] have the right in certain circumstances not to have their work subjected to derogatory treatment[2].

For these purposes, 'treatment' means an addition to, deletion from or alteration to or adaptation of the work. However, translations of literary or dramatic works, or arrangements or transcriptions of musical works which involve no more than a change of key or register do not constitute 'treatment'[3].

A 'treatment' is derogatory if it amounts to distortion or mutilation of the work, or is otherwise prejudicial to the honour or reputation of the author or director[4].

In the case of *Tidy v Trustees of the Natural History Museum*[5], in considering whether the reduction in size of the plaintiff's cartoons by the museum established a derogatory treatment, the court treated the question as being whether this was a distortion or was otherwise prejudicial to the author's honour or reputation[6].

1   As described in **paragraph 11.13**.
2   Section 80(1)(a).
3   Section 80(2)(a).
4   Section 80(2)(b).
5   (1997) 39 IPR 501.
6   For a discussion of the integrity right and case law, see 'Training the law: the right of Integrity in Britain', Stina Teilmann, [2005] EIPR, January 2005. See also **paragraph 27.21**.

Integrity right: who is protected?

11.13   The integrity right protects authors of literacy, dramatic, musical or artistic works and the directors of films. As with the paternity right, the producers of sound recordings, authors of broadcasts and typographical arrangements are not protected by this right[1].

1   See **paragraph 11.03**.

Integrity right: literary, dramatic and musical works

11.14   In the case of literary, dramatic and musical works, the author has the right to object to a derogatory treatment when that treatment is:

- published commercially[1];
- performed in public;
- communicated to the public
- included in copies of a film or sound recording issued to the public.[2]

1   See **paragraph 11.07**.
2   CDPA s 80(3).

Integrity right: artistic works

11.15   The integrity in an artistic work is infringed whenever:

- a derogatory treatment of the work is published commercially or exhibited in public[1];
- a visual image of a derogatory treatment of the work is communicated to the public;
- a visual image of a derogatory treatment of the work is included in a film which is shown in public, or when copies of the film are issued to the public;
- (in the case of works of architecture in the form of a model for a building, a sculpture or a work of artistic craftsmanship) copies of a graphic work representing or a photograph of the derogatory treatment of the work are issued to the public[2].

It should be noted that the right does not arise where a building is erected which would constitute a derogatory treatment of the work if it had been issued to the public in the form of a graphic work or a photograph. However, in these cases the architect, if he is identified on the building, may require the identification to be removed[3].

1   See **paragraph 27.21**.
2   CDPA s 80(4).
3   CDPA s 80(5).

Integrity right: films

11.16   The integrity right is infringed whenever a film which constitutes a derogatory treatment of the work is:

- shown in public;
- communicated to the public;
- issued to the public[1].

A film soundtrack is both part of a film and a sound recording[2]. Authors of sound recordings and of film soundtracks do not have the right to object to a derogatory treatment of work. It is worth noting that only the director of the film or the authors of the literary, dramatic, musical or artistic copyrights in the film soundtrack would have the right to object to the derogatory treatment of a soundtrack.

1   CDPA s 80(6); see **paragraph 24.05**.
2   **See paragraph 2.08**.

Integrity right: no need for assertion

11.17   Unlike the paternity right, authors of copyright, literary, dramatic, musical or artistic works and directors of copyright films are not required to assert the integrity right. It is binding on all third parties, unless it falls within one of the exceptions or exclusions discussed below[1].

1   See **paragraph 11.18**.

Integrity right: exceptions

11.18   The right to object to a derogatory treatment of a work does not apply:

- to computer programs or any computer-generated work[1];
- to works made for the purpose of reporting current events[2];
- to the publication of literary, dramatic, musical or artistic works in a newspaper, magazine or similar periodical, or an encyclopaedia, dictionary, yearbook or other collective work of reference (or a subsequent edition of such works) if the work is made for the purpose of the publication or is authorised for inclusion by the author[3];
- to a number of acts which, by virtue of other provisions of ss 57 or 66A of the CDPA, do not infringe copyright (namely use in connection with acts permitted when copyright may be assumed to be expired in anonymous or pseudonymous works and films)[4];
- to acts done to avoid committing an offence, complying with a statutory duty and (in the case of the BBC) avoiding the inclusion in a broadcast of anything offending good taste or decency, or likely to encourage or incite crime or to lead to disorder or offend public feeling, provided that a sufficient disclaimer is included

where the author or director of the work has been identified (either at the time of the act or previously)[5];

- to works in which copyright originally vested in the author's (or director's) employer (i.e. done in the course of employment), to Crown copyright or parliamentary copyright works, or works in which copyright originally vested in an international organisation, provided that a sufficient disclaimer is added where the author or director has been identified either at the time of the act or previously on published copies[6].

1   CDPA s 81(2).
2   CDPA s 81(3).
3   CDPA s 81(4).
4   CDPA s 81(5).
5   CDPA s 81(6).
6   CDPA s 82. Although beyond the scope of this *User's Guide*, it is worth noting that other jurisdictions have, notwithstanding the International Standards established by the Berne Convention, looked at local definitions of authorship in order to determine the beneficiary of the paternity right. See, for example, the 'Asphalt Jungle' case, concerning a colourised version of a John Huston film in which the French courts protected Huston's moral rights, notwithstanding that Huston made the film as a 'for hire' employee of a US studio (MGM).

Integrity right: secondary infringement

11.19   The right to object to a derogatory treatment can also be subject to 'secondary infringement'. Secondary infringement of copyright is considered in detail elsewhere in this *User's Guide*[1]. Briefly, the possession, sale, hire, offering for sale or hire, exhibition or distribution of an 'infringing article' in the course of business will constitute secondary infringement. Distribution other than in the course of business will also constitute a secondary infringement where that distribution is such as to 'affect prejudicially the honour or reputation of the author or director'[2]. For these purposes an 'infringing article' means a work, or copy of a work, which has been subjected to a derogatory treatment and which has, or is likely to be, subjected to one of the incidents giving rise to infringement referred to above[3].

1   See **paragraphs 7.09 et seq**.
2   CDPA s 89(1).
3   See **paragraph 11.12**.

Duration of right of integrity

11.20   Like the paternity right, the integrity right continues so long as copyright subsists in the work[1].

1   CDPA s 86(1); see **paragraph 11.11**.

False attribution of work

11.21 Of the moral rights set out in the CDPA, the right to prevent false attribution of work was the only right to be found in earlier UK legislation. The right consists of the right not to have a literary, dramatic, musical or artistic work falsely attributed to a person as being the author, or to have a film falsely attributed as having been directed by a person other than the director.

For these purposes 'attribution' means a statement (either express or implied) as to who is the author or director[1].

The right to prevent false attribution also applies where a literary, dramatic or musical work is falsely represented as being an adaptation of the work of another person. In the case of an artistic work, it applies where the work is falsely represented as being a copy made by the author of the artistic work[2].

It should be noted that the right does not apply to the authors of sound recordings, broadcasts, or typographical arrangements of published editions.

1   CDPA s 84(1).
2   CDPA s 84(2).

Infringement of the right to prevent false attribution

11.22 The right to prevent false attribution will be infringed by a person who:

- issues copies of a literary, dramatic, musical or artistic work or a film in which there is a false attribution[1];
- exhibits an artistic work (or copy of such a work) containing a false attribution[2];
- either performs in public, or communicates to the public any literary, dramatic or musical work, or shows in public, broadcasts, as being the work of, or directed by, a person, knowing or having reason to believe the attribution is false[3];
- issues or displays to the public material (such as advertising materials) containing a false attribution regarding any of the acts mentioned in the three paragraphs listed above[4];
- (in the course of business) possesses or deals with copies of a literary, dramatic, musical or artistic work or a film in which there is a false attribution (and in the case of artistic works possessing or dealing with a work which itself contains a false attribution) knowing or having reason to believe it contains an attribution and that the attribution is false[5];
- (in the course of business) deals with an artistic work as the

unaltered work of the author, if the work has in fact been altered after the author parted with possession of it, or else deals with a copy of the altered work as being the unaltered work of the author, where he knows or has reason to believe this is not the case[6].

1   CDPA s 84(2)(a).
2   CDPA s 84(2)(b).
3   CDPA s 84(3).
4   CDPA s 84(4).
5   CDPA s 84(5).
6   CDPA s 84(6).

Duration of the right of false attribution

11.23 The right continues to subsist for 20 years after a person's death[1].

1   CDPA s 86(2).

Right to privacy of photographs and films

11.24 Under the Copyright Act 1956, a person who commissioned the taking of a photograph became its copyright owner[1]. Under the CDPA the owner of the copyright in the photograph is the photographer. He is, therefore, able to sell copies of the photograph or to license newspapers and magazines to reproduce it, even though the person who had commissioned the photograph might not wish it to be seen publicly. The effect of the right to privacy is to mitigate against the inherent right of the copyright owner to deal with the photograph.

The right applies only to persons who have commissioned the taking of a photograph or the making of a film for private and domestic purposes[2] and conveys a right so long as copyright subsists in the work, to prevent copies of the work being issued to the public, being exhibited or shown in public or communicated to the public. Any person who does, or authorises the doing of, any of these acts without the permission of the person who commissioned the photograph, infringes only the right of privacy[3].

It should be noted that it is the commissioner who has the right to sue for the infringement of the right to privacy and not, say, another person who may be in the photograph or film[4].

1   See **paragraphs 10.14 et seq** for a discussion of the copyright treatment of works pre-dating 1 August 1989.
2   CDPA s 85(1).
3   Ibid.
4   Ibid.

Exceptions to right to privacy

11.25 The right is not infringed in the following circumstances:

- the incidental inclusion of a photograph or film in an artistic work, film or broadcast[1];
- the use of a photograph or film for parliamentary or judicial proceedings[2];
- the use of a photograph or film by royal commissions or statutory enquiries[3];
- any acts done in relation to a photograph or film under statutory authority[4]; and
- the use of photographs or films which are anonymous or pseudonymous works, where the acts are permitted on the basis of assumptions as to the expiry of the copyright on death of the author[5].

1 CDPA s 85(2)(a).
2 CDPA s 85(2)(b).
3 CDPA s 85(2)(c).
4 CDPA s 85(2)(d).
5 CDPA s 85(2)(e).

Duration of the right to privacy of photographs and films

11.26 The right subsists so long as copyright subsists in the work[1].

1 CDPA s 86(1).

Extended and revived copyright – exercise of moral rights

11.27 Moral rights continue to subsist as long as copyright subsists in a work. Moral rights are therefore exercisable during extended and revived copyright periods[1]. Any waiver or assertion which existed immediately before the expiry of copyright continues to have effect during the revived copyright period.

If the author of a work or the director of a film died before 1 January 1996, the rights are exercisable by his or her personal representatives.

1 See **paragraphs 6.02–6.05**.

Assignment and transmission of moral rights

11.28 None of the moral rights are assignable. However, on the death of a person entitled to the paternity right, or the rights of integrity or privacy, the right will pass to such person as his will or other testamentary disposition specifically directs[1]. If there is no specific direction as to who is to inherit these moral rights, then, if the copyright was part of the author's estate (that is to say the copyright has not been disposed of before the death of the testator), the moral rights will pass to the person to whom the copyright passes. If neither of the first two situations are applicable, the personal representatives of the person entitled to the moral right have the right to exercise such right[2].

As regards the right to prevent false attribution, this is actionable after a person's death only by his personal representatives. The right cannot be transferred by will or other testamentary instrument[3].

We have seen elsewhere that copyright may be partially transferred (either by dividing the right to do different things with the work between different people, or by transferring rights for only part of the period of copyright[4]). Where on death, the right to undertake different acts are bequeathed to different people (eg where a novelist wills the publishing rights in his work to A and the film rights to B) the moral rights may be exercised by different people as follows:

- the paternity right may be asserted by any of them[5];
- the integrity right and the right to privacy can be exercised by any of them, and any consent or waiver issued by one right holder will not affect the position of any other[6];

It should be noted that not only can the author or director himself transmit the moral rights on death to such person as he sees fit by his will, but so also can that person who inherits the moral rights. Accordingly, it does not follow that the author's family will be entitled to exercise the moral rights on the death of the author.

1 CDPA s 95(1)(a).
2 CDPA s 95(1)(b) and (c).
3 CDPA s 95(5).
4 See **paragraph 10.23**.
5 CDPA s 95(3)(a).
6 CDPA s 95(3)(b) and (c).

Consents and waivers of moral rights

11.29 Although moral rights may not be assigned, there will not be an infringement if the person entitled to the right has consented to the doing of an act which would otherwise constitute an infringement[1].

Similarly, the rights may be waived by instrument in writing signed by the person giving up the right[2]. The waiver can relate to a specific work, to works of a specified description or to works generally, and may relate to existing or future works[3]. For example, a waiver might be given by an artist to an advertising agency which commissions him to create art works for advertisements, which relates to his works already in existence and those which he might make in the future.

The waiver may be conditional or unconditional, or be subject to revocation[4].

If the instrument in writing states that the waiver is made in favour of an owner or prospective owner of the copyright in a work or works to which it relates, then the waiver will be presumed to extend to the licensees and successors in title of the owner of copyright unless the instrument indicates a contrary interest[5]. So, if the author of a screenplay waives his moral right in favour of the film company to which he is assigning the copyright, that waiver will benefit any other companies who become licensees of that film company, or who purchase the rights in the screenplay from the film company.

Moral rights may also be waived informally, or as part of the general law of contract, as well as pursuant to an instrument in writing. If an artist sells a painting and tells the purchaser that he has the right to do anything with the picture that he sees fit, and this forms part of the contract of sale, the purchaser will be able to rely on the contract as a waiver of the moral right. The CDPA does not interfere with the operation of the general law of contract or estoppel in addition to such informal waivers[6].

1   CDPA s 87(1).
2   CDPA s 87(2).
3   CDPA s 87(3)(a).
4   CDPA s 87(3)(b).
5   CDPA s 87(3).
6   CDPA s 87(4).

Joint works

11.30   The meaning of the expression 'a work of joint authorship' is considered elsewhere[1]. In brief:

- the *paternity right* must be asserted by each joint author for himself[2];
- the *integrity right* is a right of each joint author, and any waiver issued by one joint author will not effect the position of any other[3];
- the *false attribution right* is infringed by any false statement as to authorship of a joint work, or by the attribution of a work by a single author as one of joint authorship[4]; and
- the *right of privacy* vests in each commissioner where the work was jointly commissioned, and the waiver by one commissioner will not affect the rights of any other[5].

In relation to films which are jointly directed, the position will be the same as for joint authors. For these purposes 'jointly directed' means 'made by the collaboration of two or more directors and the contribution of each director is not distinct from that of the other director or directors'[6].

1   See **paragraph 10.08**.
2   CDPA s 88(1).
3   CDPA s 88(2) and (3).
4   CDPA s 88(4).
5   CDPA s 88(6).
6   CDPA s 88(5).

Application of moral right to parts of works

11.31   The rights of paternity and privacy in photographs and films apply in relation to the whole or any *substantial* part of a work, whereas the rights to object to the derogatory treatment of a work and to false attribution apply in relation to the whole or any part of a work[1]. So, notwithstanding that the paternity right has been asserted, a short extract from a book can be quoted without identification. Similarly, a part of a photograph or a film, taken or made for private and domestic purposes, can be copied and issued to the public or exhibited etc without the commissioner's consent provided it is not a substantial part[2].

On the other hand, if even the smallest part of a work (other than a sound recording, broadcast or typographical arrangement of a published edition) is the subject of derogatory treatment or false attribution, there will be a breach of both those moral rights.

1   CDPA s 89.
2   What constitutes a 'substantial part' of a work as considered at **paragraph 8.06**.

Works made before 1 August 1989

11.32   The moral rights provisions of the CDPA apply only to acts which are done after the commencement of the CDPA. However, they apply to all works which were in copyright at the commencement of the CDPA, with certain important exceptions (see below). The provisions of the 1956 Act as to false attribution of authorship continue to apply in relation to acts done before commencement of the CDPA.

The exceptions are as follows:

●   The paternity right and the integrity right do not apply to literary, dramatic, musical and artistic works the authors of which died before 1 August 1989. Nor do they apply to films made before commencement of the CDPA.

- As regards literary, dramatic, musical and artistic works, moral rights do not apply, in cases where the copyright first vested in the author, to anything done pursuant to an assignment of copyright or a licence which was made or granted before 1 August 1989 and the act done is pursuant to such assignment or licence. For example, the author of a screenplay of a film, who has assigned or licensed the right to make a film based on the screenplay, cannot object to any changes made to his screenplay for the purpose of making a film under that assignment or licence.

- In cases where the copyright first vested in a person other than the author (of which the most common example is the work made in the course of employment where the copyright vests in the employer), there is no infringement of the paternity right or the integrity right if the act is done by or with the licence of the copyright owner.

- Under the 1956 Act a record could be made of a piece of music under what was known as a 'statutory licence' by serving an appropriate notice and paying a statutory licence fee. Moral rights do not apply to anything done in making a record of a piece of music pursuant to such a licence.

- The right of privacy of photographs and films[1] does not apply to photographs taken or films made before commencement of the CDPA.

1   Paragraphs 11.24 et seq.

Moral rights in performances

11.33   The WIPO Performances and Phonograms Treaty 1996 provided that, quite independent of the economic rights afforded to performers in respect of their performances[1], performers should also benefit from similar 'moral rights' protections to those already enjoyed by author's and described throughout this chapter.

Two rights are provided for in the Treaty:

- The first is a right to claim to be identified as the performer of a performance[2];
- The second is to object to any distortion, mutilation or other modification of his performance which would be prejudicial to his reputation[3].

The Treaty requires that these rights should apply to live aural perform-ances, and their recorded performances ('fixed on phonograms'). There is no definition of the word 'aural' in the Treaty, but in the consultation documents circulated by the UK Government, it has been taken to mean the 'sound element' of a performance.

To implement these provisions in the United Kingdom, and permit ratification of the Treaty, further changes are required to the CDPA, and following its consultation process, the UK has, as we write, publish draft Regulations[4].

Although the Regulations are not, as we write, in force, it is anticipated they will enter into effect on 1 February 2006. Conse-quently, it is worth considering their provisions in some detail.

(a) The identification right

11.34 The *'identification right'* will be implemented by new s 205C to the CDPA. When a performance is given in public or broadcast live, or a sound recording of the performance is communicated or issued to the public, the performer has a right to be identified[5]. For these purposes 'communication' means communication by electronic trans-mission.

The right may be satisfied (for live performances) by identifying the performer in the relevant programme and/or (for copies of any record-ing of the performance issued to the public) by identifying the per-former in or on the copies.

For a live performance, the person who organises or promotes the performance who will have to give effect to the right to be identified. Guidance issued by the UK Patent Office indicates that this require-ment will 'have to be met by those who regularly organise perform-ances in concert halls or theatres, or those who only occasionally organise or promote a performance in a village or church hall or other venue'.

The draft Regulations also make provision for performances given by groups[6]. In short, there will be no right for performers to be individu-ally identified where a performance is given a group performance[7], provided the group itself is identified. This reflects the perceived practical difficulties associated with dealing with large groups, and with live performances where not all performers are identified.

As in the case of authors' paternity rights, the identification right will need to be asserted[8].

Exceptions to the identification right set out in the draft Regulations[9] are similar to those applicable to authors' and directors' moral rights[10] (e.g. performances given for reporting current events, incidental inclu-sion, for purposes of examination and for parliamentary proceedings).

However, additional exceptions apply in respect of circumstances where it is not reasonably practicable to identify the performer[11] and/or where the performance is 'given for the purposes of advertising any goods or services'[12].

According to documentation issued by the Patent Office the latter right is necessary 'because listing performers featured in advertisements would be a substantial hindrance on advertisers and provide little benefit to performers'. However, in that regard, it is questionable whether, as drafted, the Regulation will achieve its desired effect: many cases recordings used in advertisements are commercial recordings. In respect of such recordings, it will in most cases be difficult to argue that the original performance was rendered for advertising purposes.

(b) The integrity right (i.e. right to object to derogatory treatment)

11.35 This right is infringed where a performance is broadcast 'live', or if a sound recording of the performance is played or communicated to the public with any distortion, mutilation or modification which is 'prejudicial to the reputation of the performer'[13].

The right is similar to the integrity right afforded to authors and directors[14].

The exceptions to the integrity right allows modifications for the purpose of reporting current events, or which are consistent with 'normal editorial or production practice', or which are done to avoid committing an offence, complying with a duty under an enactment or, in the case of the BBC, to avoid offending good taste or decency, which is likely to encourage crime or lead to disorder, of which offends public feeling[15].

(c) Other provisions in relation to performers moral rights

11.36 If implemented in their draft form, the Regulations will:

- provide that performers moral rights will subsist for the same duration as performers property rights[16];
- provide for similar provisions in relation to waiver and consent, non-assignability, transmission on death and remedies which are applicable to the moral rights applicable to authors and directors[17].

---

1   See **Chapter 12** for a full discussion of performer's rights.
2   Akin to the paternity right referred to at **paragraph 11.02 et seq.**
3   Akin to the integrity right (i.e. the right to object to derogatory treatment) referred to at **paragraph 11.12 et seq.**
4   The (draft) Performances (Moral Rights, etc) Regulations 2005.
5   The circumstances in which the right arises are set out in sections new ss 205C(1)(a) to (d) of the CDPA, and the rights are to be elaborated in new ss 205C(2)(a) to (d) of the CDPA.

6   New ss 205C(3) and (4).
7   'Group' meaning two or more performers known by a particular collective name, new s 205C(4) of the CDPA.
8   New s 205D of the CDPA.
9   New s 205E of the CDPA.
10   See **paragraph 11.10**.
11   New s 205E(2).
12   New s 205E(4).
13   New s 205F.
14   See **paragraph 11.12 et seq**.
15   New s 205G.
16   New s 205I. See **paragraph 12.17 et seq**.
17   New ss 205J, K, L, M and N.

Chapter 12

Rights in performances

Introduction

12.01 Prior to the CDPA, the Performers Protection Acts 1958 to 1972 imposed criminal liability on persons making certain uses of performances without the consent of the performer. A panoply of international obligations also provides minimum protections for performers[1]. Part II of the CDPA addressed the UK's international obligations, and has itself been amended by European legislation, implemented by the 1995 Regulations and the 1996 Regulations[2].

Essentially, performers now receive protection under two regimes in the CDPA: performer's non-property rights and recording rights, and performers' property rights.

- *Performers' **non-property** rights and recording rights* comprise the right to consent to the recording or live broadcast or transmission of a performance, or to the use of the recording, or to the importation, possession or dealing with a recording[3].
- *Performers' **property** rights* comprise the right to authorise the reproduction, distribution and rental and lending of copies of a recorded performance[4].

In addition, the performer is entitled to equitable remuneration from the playing, broadcast, cable transmission or rental of a commercially produced sound recording[5].

The 2003 Regulations inserted a new right into the CDPA, providing an exclusive right for performers to control the 'making available' to the public of a recording of a performance.[6]

---

1 See **paragraph 4.17**.
2 Implementing the Rental and Landing Right Directive (92/100EC), the Cable and Satellite Directive (93/83/EC) and the Term of Copyright Directive (93/98/EC).
3 CDPA ss 182–184, see **paragraphs 12.06–12.10**.

4 CDPA ss 182A–182C, see **paragraphs 12.11–12.13**.
5 CDPA ss 182D and 191G.
6 CDPA s 182CA, see **paragraph 12.14**.

Relevant performances

12.02 For these purposes, 'performance' means:

'(a) a dramatic performance (which includes dance and mime);
(b) a musical performance;
(c) a reading or recitation of a literary work; or
(d) a performance of a variety act or any similar presentation.

which is, or insofar as it is, a live performance given by one or more individuals'[1].

The ambit of these categories has been subject to debate in recent years. In the context of sporting performances, for example, the traditional view is that these are not capable of protection by way of a performance right. There may be an exception to this where activity is closely choreographed (e.g. an ice dance) so as to amount to a work or dance or mime. More difficult are some of the 'trade mark' movements and actions which have increasingly come to characterise, for example, the goal mouth celebrations of soccer players. In all but the most exceptional cases, these kinds of activities will not be of a character which are capable of being protected as a performance[2].

1 CDPA s 180(2).
2 See, generally, **Chapter 2**.

Persons entitled to rights in performances

12.03 Rights are conferred on a performer (who must give his consent to the exploitation of his performance) and the person who has recording rights in relation to a performance (who has rights in relation to recordings which are made without his consent or that of the performer)[1].

1 CDPA s 180(1).

Recordings of performances

12.04 A 'recording' is a film or sound recording which is:

'(a) made directly from a live performance;

(b)   made from a broadcast of the performance; or
(c)   made, directly or indirectly, from another recording of the performance'[1].

1   CDPA s 180(2).

Qualifying performances

12.05   A performance will not qualify for protection unless it is given by 'a qualifying individual ... or takes place in a qualifying country ...'[1].

For this purpose, a 'qualifying country' means the UK, another member state of the EEA or a country to which the protection has been extended by an order made pursuant to the CDPA[2]. Such an order will only be made in respect of countries which provide reciprocal protection. A body corporate will be a qualifying person if it is formed under the law of the UK or another qualifying country and has in any qualifying country a place of business at which a substantial business activity is carried on. In determining whether a substantial business activity is carried on at a place of business in any country, no account is to be taken of dealings in goods which are at all material times outside that country. So, a manufacturing company which exports all its goods would be treated as having a substantial business activity in the country of manufacture, but a film distributor which never imported prints into the UK would not be so treated.

A 'qualifying individual' means 'a citizen or subject or an individual resident in, a qualifying country'[3].

1   CDPA s 181.
2   CDPA s 206(1).
3   CDPA s 206(1).

Non-property rights

Recording, broadcasting and transmission of performances

12.06   A performer's *non-property* rights are infringed by a person who, without his consent:

'(a)   makes a recording of the whole or any substantial part of a qualifying performance directly from the live performance;
(b)   broadcasts live the whole or any substantial part of a live performance;

(c)   makes a recording of the whole or any substantial part of a qualifying performance directly from a broadcast of the live performance'[1].

Although 'substantial part' is not defined, the expression is used in the same context in relation to copyright works[2]. These provisions do not apply to recordings which were made without consent for private or domestic use[3].

1   CDPA s 182(1).
2   See **paragraph 8.06**.
3   CDPA s 182(2).

Use of recordings made without consent

12.07 A performer's *non-property* rights are also infringed by a person who:

'(a)   shows or plays in public the whole or any substantial part of a qualifying performance; or

(b)   communicates to the public the whole or a substantial part of a qualifying performance;

by means of a recording which was, and which that person knows or has reason to believe was, made without the performer's consent'[1].

1   CDPA s 183.

Importing, possessing or dealing with illicit recordings

12.08 It is an infringement of a performer's non-property rights to possess for business purposes or deal with illicit recordings without his consent. Being a form of secondary infringement, it is necessary to show that the person against whom the infringement was alleged neither knew, nor had reason to believe, that the recording was illicit[1].

Again, any claim for damages for infringement will be limited to a reasonable payment for the act complained of where the infringer can show that the illicit recording was innocently acquired by him, or his predecessor in title[2]. For these purposes, a recording is 'innocently acquired' where the acquirer did not know and had no reason to believe it was an illicit recording[3].

1   CDPA s 184(1).
2   CDPA s 184(2).
3   CDPA s 184(3).

Persons having recording rights

12.09 The 'recording rights' apply only to persons who have the benefit of an exclusive recording contract, meaning a contract made between a performer and another person under which that person is entitled, to the exclusion of all other persons (including the performer), to make recordings of one or more of his performances with a view to their commercial exploitation[1].

Only qualifying persons are entitled to exercise the recording right. A person to whom the benefit of an exclusive recording contract is assigned or licensed will also benefit from the right, provided that he also is a qualifying person. For these purposes a 'qualifying person' means:

'a qualifying individual or a body corporate or other body having legal personality which (a) is formed under the law of a part of the UK or another qualifying country; and (b) has in any qualifying country a place of business at which substantial business activity is carried on'[2].

Accordingly, an American record company (assuming that the USA is not a qualifying country) which has an exclusive recording contract will not itself have the benefit of the protection of this part of the CDPA. But such benefit will be acquired by persons licensed by the record company to make recordings with a view to their commercial exploitation. This could equally apply to an assignee from a company which was not a qualifying person, if such assignee itself was a qualifying person. So, the UK subsidiary company of an American recording company could enforce the rights under an exclusive recording contract assigned to it by the American holding company.

1   CDPA s 185(1).
2   CDPA s 206(1).

Infringement of recording rights

12.10   The recording rights are similar to those accorded to performers and are subject to the same qualifications and defences available to the persons against whom partial action for infringement is brought. The rights of a person holding 'recording rights' in a performance will be infringed by a person who, without his consent or the consent of the performer, 'makes a recording of the whole or any substantial part of the performance, otherwise than for his private and domestic use'[1]. It is worth emphasising that a performer can give consent to the recording of his performance even though the effect of so doing would be to put him in breach of his exclusive recording contract. The person making the recording pursuant to the consent of the performer will not be liable for infringement of the recording right, either to the performer or to a recording company which has an exclusive recording contract with the performer, even though that record company was not aware of the fact that the consent had been given by the performer[2].

1   CDPA s 186(1).
2   CDPA s 187.

Property rights

The reproduction right

12.11 A performer's *property rights* are infringed by a person who, without his consent, makes, otherwise than for his private and domestic use, a copy of a recording of a whole or any substantial part of a qualified performance[1]. It is irrelevant for these purposes whether the copy is made directly or indirectly[2].

1   CDPA s 182A(1).
2   CDPA s 182A(2).

The distribution right

12.12 A performer's property rights are also infringed by a person who, without his consent, issues to the public copies of a recording of the whole or any substantial part of a qualifying performance[1].

This restricted act has the same ambit as the restricted copyright act of 'issuing copies to the public'[2].

It should be noted that references to the issue of copies of a recording of a performance include the issue of the original recording of a live performance[3].

1   CDPA s 182B(1).
2   See **paragraph 7.04**.
3   CDPA s 182B(4).

Rental or lending of copies to the public

12.13 Performers are accorded a rental and lending right in relation to recordings of their qualifying performances in the same way as copyright owners[1].

There is a presumption of the transfer of this rental right, in the case of film production agreements:

'where an agreement concerning film production is concluded between a performer and film producer, the performer shall be presumed, unless the agreement provides to the contrary, to have transferred to the film producer any rental right in relation to the film arising from the inclusion of a recording of his performance in the film'[2].

This presumption can be implied even where the agreement between the performer and the film producer is made by intermediaries such as agents or unions.

1   CDPA s 182C, see **paragraph 7.05**.
2   CDPA s 191F.

The making available right

12.14   A performer's rights are infringed

'by a person who, without his consent, makes available to the public a recording of the whole or any substantial part of a qualifying performance by electronic transmission in such a way that members of the public may access the recording from a place and at a time individually chosen by them.'[1]

This is the so-called 'making available' right afforded to performers under the 2003 Regulations and now reflected in the CDPA[2]. Its purpose is to allow performers to exercise control over the making available of their work over 'on demand' electronic systems.

This is one of the few new rights incorporated into the CDPA by the 2003 Regulations. Previously under s 182(D) of the Act the performer had no right to prevent the public performance, broadcast or 'inclusion in a cable programme service' of a recording of his performance. He was merely granted the right to equitable remuneration for such uses[3]. This new exclusive right enables performers to control the making of recordings of their performances available to the public. It will, no doubt, also mean that in commercial contracts such as recording agreements, companies will require an assignment of the exclusive right.

1   CDPA s 182 CA(1).
2   CDPA s 182 CA(2).
3   See **paragraph 12.15** below.

Equitable remuneration

12.15   The CDPA provides that:

'Where a commercially published sound recording of the whole or any substantial part of a qualifying performance:

(a) is played in public; or

(b) is communicated to the public otherwise than being made available to the public by electronic transmission in such a way that members of the public may access the recording from a place and at a time individually chosen by them;

the performer is entitled to equitable remuneration from the owner of the copyright in the sound recording'[1].

This means that *no* equitable remuneration right exists in relation to the making available of such sound recordings by 'on demand' systems. However, a remuneration right is preserved for all other communications to the public.

It is important to note that this equitable remuneration is payable to performers *by the owners of the copyright* in the sound recording, whereas authors of copyright works must look to payment from the person for the time being entitled to the rental rights[2].

The performer of a qualifying performance also has a right to receive 'equitable remuneration' from the rental of sound recordings or films in respect of which he has transferred his property right[3]. As with authors' rental rights[4] this right cannot be assigned except to a collecting society (for the purposes of collecting it for the author)[5]. Any attempt in an agreement to exclude or restrict the right to equitable remuneration will be void[6].

The level of equitable remuneration is to be set by the parties and, in the absence of agreement, the Copyright Tribunal may settle the amount[7]. As with the authors of copyright works, this provision is particularly significant in the film industry, where producers tend to adopt contractual devices intended to absolve themselves and those taking title from them from any obligation to pay further amounts in respect of such rights[8].

1 CDPA s 182D(1).
2 See **paragraph 7.05**.
3 CDPA s 191G(1).
4 See **paragraph 7.05**.
5 CDPA s 191G(2).
6 CDPA s 191G(5).
7 CDPA s 191G(4).
8 See **paragraphs 7.05 and 10.28**.

Exceptions to rights in performances

12.16 The exceptions which are applicable to copyright infringement also broadly apply to rights in performances[1].

1 CDPA s 189, see **Chapter 9** above.

Duration of rights in performances taking place after 1 January 1996

12.17 The period of the rights conferred by Part II of the CDPA as amended by the 1995 Regulations is:

'(a) 50 years from the end of the calendar year in which the performance took place, or

(b) if during that period a recording of the performance is released, 50 years from the end of the calendar year in which it is released[1].'

A recording is 'released' when it is first published, played or shown in public, broadcast or included in a cable programme service, but no unauthorised act is to be taken into account in determining whether a recording has been released[2].

Where a performer is not a national of an EEA state, the duration of the right in relation to his performance is that to which the performer is entitled in the country of which he is a national, provided that does not exceed the period set out above. Therefore, nationals of those countries where the period of protection for a performance is 25 years will only receive a 25-year protection in the UK, unless this is overridden by an international agreement to which the UK is a party[3].

1   CDPA s 191(2).
2   CDPA s 191(3).
3   CDPA s 191(4).

Duration of rights in performances given before 1 January 1996

12.18 Although the CDPA also provided for a 50-year term of protection for performances, the introduction by the 1995 Regulations of a period of 50 years from the end of the calendar year in which a recording is released, has had the effect of extending the period of protection for certain unpublished performances or recently published performances. The new period applies not only to performances which take place on or after 1 January 1996, but also to:

● existing performances which first qualify for protection after 31 December 1995 by virtue of the new provisions;

● existing performances which qualify for protection under the provisions of the CDPA before it was amended by the 1995 Regulations;

- existing performances in which protection has expired in the UK but which would have been protected in another EEA state on 1 July 1995.

It follows that there are extended performance rights for a large majority of recordings, since the only recordings in which there will not be any extension are those where the recording was released in the same calendar year as the live performance took place.

Where the 50-year period from the end of the calendar year in which the performance took place has expired, but a record has been released during that period, there will be revived performance rights.

Assignability of performers' non-property rights

12.19   These rights are not assignable or transmissible[1], although when the person entitled to the performer's rights dies, the rights will be exercisable by the person to whom he wills it, or in the absence of any will, by his personal representatives[2].

1   CDPA s 192A(1).
2   CDPA s 192A(2).

Assignability of recording rights

12.20   These rights are not assignable or transmissible[1], although they are exercisable by the licensee or assignee of an exclusive recording agreement if he is a 'qualifying person'[2].

1   CDPA s 192B(1).
2   CDPA s 192B(2); see **paragraph 12.09**.

Assignability of performers' property rights

12.21   Performers' property rights can be transferred by assignment, testamentary disposition, or by operation of law, as personal movable property[1].

Like a copyright assignment, an assignment of performers' property right, is not effective unless it is signed in writing on behalf of the assignor[2]. An assignment may be partial or limited, as in the case of a copyright assignment[3].

As in the case of a copyright licence, a licence of performer's property rights is binding on successors in title to the performer's property rights, except a purchaser for value without actual or constructive notice of the licence, or a person taking rights from such a purchaser[4].

1   CDPA s 191B(1).
2   CDPA s 191B(3); see **paragraph 10.24**.
3   CDPA s 191B(2).
4   CDPA s 191B(4).

Entitlement to extended and revived performers' rights

12.22 Because parties to agreements made before the period of protection of performance rights was extended or revived did not anticipate the survival of these rights beyond the original 50-year period, the 1995 Regulations now legislate as to who may exercise these rights during the extended or revived period. In brief:

• *Extended performers' rights* are exercisable by the person who was entitled to exercise them immediately before 1 January 1996, that is to say the performer, or (if he has died) the person entitled to exercise those rights, being either a beneficiary or a personal representative[1].

• *Revived performers' rights* are exercisable:
   (a) in the case of rights which expired after 1 August 1989, by the person who is entitled to exercise those rights immediately before they expired;
   (b) in the case of revived pre 1988 performers' rights, by the performer or his personal representative[2].

1   1995 Regulations, reg 31(1).
2   1995 Regulations, reg 31(2).

Consents

12.23 In relation to performers' non-property rights and recording rights, consents may be given either in connection with a specific performance, a specified description of performance, or performances generally, and either in connection with past or future performances[1].

The consent must be given (in the case of performer's non-property rights) by the performer or (in the case of the recording rights) by the person entitled to the recording rights. In the case of recording rights however, consent can also be given by the performer (even if that leaves the performer in breach of an exclusive recording contract)[2]. A consent given by the person entitled to recording rights will bind any successor in title or licensee to the exclusive recording contract[3] and a consent given by a performer will bind any person to whom the right to consent may at any time pass[4].

Consents given in respect of extended performers' rights will continue to subsist during the period of the extended performance rights if they subsisted on 31 December 1995 and were not to expire before the period of protection expired.

There is an implication that consents can be given by properly authorised persons on behalf of performers or persons having exclusive recording rights[5] but if it is decided for convenience to rely on a consent from a person other than the performer, then a copy of the written authority to give such consent should be obtained.

The Copyright Tribunal can give consent in a case where the identity or whereabouts of the person entitled to the reproduction right in a performance cannot be ascertained by reasonable enquiry or where the performer unreasonably withholds consent[6]. In March 1992, for example, the Tribunal gave consent to S4C to make a recording from a previous recording of *Under Milk Wood* by Dylan Thomas made by the BBC in 1954 on behalf of individual performers' whose whereabouts could not be established by reasonable enquiry. This ability is particularly important to broadcasters, for whom increased channel capacity has meant digging further into archives for transmittable material.

1   CDPA s 193(1).
2   See **paragraph 12.10**.
3   CDPA s 193(2).
4   See **paragraph 12.21**.
5   CDPA s 201.
6   CDPA s 190.

Civil remedies for infringement of performers' non-property rights

12.24   The right of action for infringement of a performer's non-property right is to sue for breach of statutory duty. The remedies, therefore, include damages, orders for the delivery of illicit recordings and the right to seize illicit recordings[1].

A right to seize illicit recordings was introduced into the CDPA to deal with the problem of street traders selling pirated or bootlegged audio cassettes and videos from a mobile barrow, who may be untraceable before formal proceedings can be instituted or the police have had an opportunity to make an arrest under the criminal provisions contained in Part II of the CDPA. A person having performers' rights or recording rights can himself authorise other people to seize and detain illicit recordings which are found exposed, or otherwise immediately available, for sale or hire[2]. Before anything is seized, however, notice of the time and place of the seizure has to be given to the local police station in a prescribed form[3]. The person exercising the right can enter premises to which the public have access. Nothing may be seized which is in the possession, custody or control of a person at a permanent or regular place of business, and no force may be used.[4] So, for example, a rights holder could enter a covered market and seize goods, but not from a trader who trades regularly in that market.

At the time when anything is seized, a notice in a prescribed form detailing the person by or on whose authority the seizure is made and the grounds for making the seizure, must be left at the place where it was seized[5].

1   CDPA ss 194–196.
2   CDPA s 196(1).
3   CDPA s 196(2).
4   CDPA s 196(3).
5   CDPA s 196(4).

Civil remedies for infringement of performers' property rights

12.25   The remedies for infringement of performers' property rights are the same as those for infringement of any other property right (i.e. damages, injunction, account of the profits gained by the defendant from the infringement, etc)[1].

As in the case of copyright infringement, an award of damages for infringement of performers' property rights will be affected by the circumstances. So, a claimant will not be entitled to damages where it is shown that at the time of the infringement the infringer did not know or have reason to believe the rights subsisted in the recording to which the action relates[2]. On the other hand, the court may award additional damages taking into account the flagrancy of the infringement and any benefit accruing to the infringer from the infringement[3].

1   CDPA s 191I, see **paragraphs 8.11 et seq.**
2   CDPA s 191J(1), see **paragraph 8.12.**
3   CDPA s 191J(2), see **paragraph 8.12.**

Infringement of extended and revived performers' rights

12.26   No act done before 1 January 1996 is to be regarded as infringing revived performance rights in a performance[1]. With regard to acts done after that date, it is not an infringement of revived performers' rights:

- to do anything pursuant to arrangements made before 1 January 1995 at a time when the performance was not protected[2]; or
- to issue to the public a recording of a performance made before 1 July 1995 at a time when the performance was not protected[3];
- if the name and address of a person entitled to authorise the act cannot by reasonable enquiry be ascertained[4].

For these purposes, 'arrangements' means 'arrangements for the exploitation of the performance in question'[5].

There are special provisions set out in the 1995 Regulations with regard to films and sound recordings made before 1 January 1996, if the recording of the performance was made before 1 July 1995.

1   1995 Regulations, reg 33(1).
2   Reg 33(2)(a).
3   Reg 33(2), (6).
4   Reg 33(4).
5   Reg 33(5).

Revived performers' rights: restricted rights of the owners

12.27 As in the case of revived copyright, the holder of revived performers' rights has restricted rights. In short, the rights holder's consent will be deemed given, subject to the payment of 'such reasonable remuneration as may be agreed or determined in default of agreement by the Copyright Tribunal'[1], and provided that the person wishing to use the right gives reasonable notice of his intention to do so to the rights holder, stating when he intends to begin his acts[2]. Failure to give notice will mean that consent will not be deemed given[3]. If notice is given, the person providing notice can begin exploitation, even if the amount of reasonable remuneration remains to be agreed[4].

1   1995 Regulations, reg 34(1).
2   Reg 34(2).
3   Reg 34(3).
4   Reg 34(4), by way of comparison, see **paragraph 6.05** dealing with revived copyright.

Criminal liability

12.28 In addition to civil liability, criminal liability attaches to a person who, without sufficient consent, makes for sale or hire, imports other than for private and domestic use, possesses in the course of business with a view to committing an infringing act or (in the course of business) sells, lets for hire, offers or exposes for sale or hire or distributes a recording which he knows or has reason to believe is an 'illicit recording'[1].

For these purposes, 'illicit recording' means a recording of the whole or any substantial part of a performance made otherwise than for private purposes without (in the case of performers' rights) the consent of the performer, and (in the case of recording rights) without the consent of the person holding the recording right, or the performer[2].

Similarly a person will commit an offence by causing the showing or playing in public or communicating to the public, of a recording of a performance made without sufficient consent, where the person knows or has reason to believe the rights have been infringed[3].

1   CDPA s 198(1).
2   CDPA s 197.
3   CDPA s 198(2).

Performers' moral rights

12.29   During the life of this edition of the *User's Guide* the CDPA will be amended to introduce a regime of moral rights for performers. These are considered elsewhere in this *User's Guide*[1].

1   *See* **paragraph 11.33**.

Chapter 13

Collecting societies, copyright licensing schemes and the Copyright Tribunal

Collecting societies

13.01 Copyright confers on its owner exclusive rights to exploit a copyright work. However, in some instances, individual licensing of rights may run against the public interest (e.g. because the public interest favours wide availability of a work) or even against the interests of the owner himself (e.g. because the difficulty in clearing rights in large numbers of works from individual users may be so arduous as to act as a disincentive for the user to exploit or properly clear particular works, or because an individual copyright owner is likely to have an inferior bargaining position when negotiating against a major user of copyright works, such as a broadcaster).

The undoubted benefits of collective licensing in some circumstances have led to the creation of numerous bodies, throughout the world, with the specialist function of licensing particular rights in copyright works on behalf of member owners, collecting the resulting revenues received from users, and distributing those revenues to members (net of deductions). These bodies are frequently called 'collecting societies'. Members either transfer the rights to be licensed on their behalf to the society, or appoint the society as their agent to enter into licenses on their behalf. Since a number of collecting societies consequently control rights in huge numbers of works, they provide both an efficient method of negotiating acceptable licence terms and fees for the member, and a convenient source of rights clearances for users. Some societies negotiate 'blanket' agreements which allow use of works for a fixed fee or tariffs for classes of use.

To date, collecting societies have been most commonly used in the licensing of music. In the UK the primary societies and their functions are, in brief:

- *The Performing Right Society* (PRS): which takes an assignment of and primarily administers for its members public performing rights and broadcasting and cable transmission, rights in musical works, the right to include such works in cable programme services, the right (in certain cases) to record musical works onto the soundtrack of films (i.e. 'synchronisation rights') and the right to authorise third parties to do the above[1].

- *The Mechanical Copyright Protection Society* (MCPS): which acts as agent for its members in licensing rights to make sound recordings of musical works, issue copies of those recordings to the public, importing those copies, or authorise third parties to do the above[2].

- *Phonographic Performance Limited* (PPL): which takes an assignment or acts as exclusive agent for its members in licensing public performing rights and broadcasting and cable transmission rights and the 'dubbing' right in sound recordings (i.e. the right to copy, produce, reproduce or make records embodying sound recordings for the purpose of exercising the performing right) and authorising third parties to do the above[3].

It is worth noting, however, that the trend toward collective licensing which started with music has proliferated to include a number of other uses, such as reprography of literary works, and the rental and cable retransmission of audio-visual works. As we advance toward the information society, the volume of copyright and performance usage increases, and the technology for tracking and managing copyright uses improves, the importance of collecting societies as a convenient source for clearing copyright will only grow. Nowhere will they be more important that when considering internet exploitation[4].

Other collecting societies operating in the UK include the Authors' Licensing and Collecting Society Ltd (ALCS), the British Equity Collecting Society Ltd (BECS), ComPact Collections Ltd (ComPact), the Copyright Licensing Agency Ltd (CLA), the Design and Artists Copyright Society Ltd (DACS), the Director's and Producer's Rights Society (1992) Ltd (DPRS), the Educational Recording Agency Ltd (ERA), the Newspaper Licensing Agency Ltd (NLA), the Performing Artists' Media Rights Association Ltd (PAMRA), and Video Performance Ltd (VPL), all of which administer different rights on behalf of the various members. The function of these societies will be considered in further details in the various chapters focusing on copyright use[5].

Notwithstanding the public function of collecting societies, their collective control of copyright works represents a potentially monopolistic control which has the potential to distort the market. The CDPA therefore contains provisions dealing with 'licensing schemes' and 'licensing bodies' and establishes the Copyright Tribunal to deal with issues arising in respect of such schemes and bodies. The OFT, the Competition Commission and the Courts also undertakes important controls under the Competition Act 1998, the Enterprise Act 2002 and the EC Treaty, considered below[6].

The period since the last *User's Guide* has seen increasing speculation as to the future of collecting societies, in a digital environment where DRM will increasingly facilitate complex, automated individual rights arrangements without the same need for the collective licensing in which collecting societies are rooted.[7]

Unlike other areas of copyright, the EU has not provided a single harmonised framework for collecting societies. However, the collective management of rights has been under increasing scrutiny from the EU Commission. In 2004, the EU started a consultation exercise relating to the issue[8].

The key issues with which the Commission is concerned are increasing competition amongst collecting societies, and transparency in the functioning of their operations. In particular, the Commission is interested in examining the reciprocal arrangements between different societies operating in different territories, and the issue of providing a 'one stop shop' on a multi-territorial contractual basis.[9]

Following the consultation process referred to above, on 12 October 2005 the EU Commission adopted a recommendation on the management of online rights in musical works. The recommendation proposes measures for improving the licensing of copyright for online services on a pan-European basis. The Commission has taken the view that the existing territorial licensing models used by the music publishing collecting societies have retarded the development of internet-based music services. The recommendation indicates that right-holders and commercial users of copyright should have a choice as to their preferred model of licensing: proposing that territorial restrictions and customer allocation provisions in existing collective licensing contracts should be removed, and if right-holders do not want to permit their repertoire to be represented on this basis, they should engage in direct pan-European licensing. The recommendation also deals with issues of governance, transparency, dispute settlement and accountability.

The Internal Market and Services Commissioner, Charlie McCreevy, has indicated that unless these recommendations lead to improvements in the market, 'tougher action' will be taken[10].

1   See **paragraphs 22.07**.
2   See **paragraph 22.08**.
3   See **paragraph 22.22**.
4   See **paragraph 26.28**.

5 See **Part 2** further information can be obtained from the societies themselves. The reader should also note the list of contact addresses set out in **Appendix 1**.
6 See **paragraph 13.09**.
7 See Harman Cohen Jehoram, 'The Future of Copyright Collecting Societies' [2001] EIPR, Issue 3, for a further discussion of this and related issues.
8 Communicate the Management of Copyright and Related Rights in the Internal Market
9 For an excellent discussion of these issues, see Maria Mercedes Trabboni, [2005] Ent. L.R. Issue 6.
10 Commission recommendation on management of online rights in musical works, IP/05/1261, 12 October 2005.

Licensing bodies

13.02 For the purposes of the CDPA, a 'licensing body' means a 'society or other organisation which has its main object, or one of its main objects, the negotiation or granting of copyright licences and where those objects include the granting of licences covering works of more than one author'[1].

1 CDPA s 116(2).

Licensing schemes

13.03 Under the CDPA, a 'licensing scheme' means:

'a scheme setting out:

(a) the classes of case in which the operator of the scheme, or the person on whose behalf he acts, is willing to grant copyright licences; and

(b) the terms on which licences will be granted in those classes of case[1].'

A scheme will include anything in the nature of a scheme whether it is described as a scheme or as a tariff or by any other name[2]. The PRS, for example, publishes detailed tariffs of the fees payable for the public performance of music in virtually any type of venue where music is currently performed in public.

1 CDPA s 116(1).
2 CDPA s 116(1).

Referral of licensing schemes to the Copyright Tribunal

13.04 Schemes which cover works by more than one author and which relate to licences for:

- copying the work;
- rental or lending of copies of the work to the public;
- performing, showing or playing the work in public; or
- broadcasting the work or including it in a cable programme service

can be referred to the Copyright Tribunal[1]. Proposed licensing schemes can be referred to the Copyright Tribunal by an organisation which is proposing to operate the scheme and the Tribunal can either confirm or vary the proposed scheme[2].

The terms of a proposed licensing scheme may also be referred to the Copyright Tribunal by an organisation which claims to represent persons claiming they need licences of the kind the scheme will apply to[3]. If the Tribunal does not think the reference is too premature[4], it may decide to confirm or vary the proposed scheme as it deems reasonable[5].

Once a licensing scheme is in operation, it may also be referred to the Tribunal by a person claiming to require a licence of the kind to which the scheme will apply (or an organisation claiming to represent such people)[6]. Again, the Tribunal may confirm or vary the scheme as it determines to be reasonable[7].

Subject to certain constraints, the Tribunal may hear further references in respect of schemes and cases it has already made orders in respect of[8].

Applications may also be made to the Tribunal by persons who claim to have been refused, or refused within a reasonable time, a licence covered by a scheme[9] or, in cases not covered by a scheme, or by persons who claim to have has been unreasonably refused a licence, or refused one within a reasonable time, or upon reasonable terms[10]. Again, the Tribunal can, if it considers appropriate, make an order that the applicant is entitled to a licence on terms according with the scheme or as the Tribunal considers reasonable[11].

Orders may be made for limited or indefinite periods[12].

1   CDPA s 117.
2   CDPA s 118(1).
3   CDPA s 118(1).
4   CDPA s 118(2).
5   CDPA s 118(3).
6   CDPA s 119(1).
7   CDPA s 119(3).
8   CDPA s 120.
9   CDPA s 121(1).
10   CDPA s 121(2).
11   CDPA s 121(4).
12   CDPA ss 118(4), 119(4), 120(5) and 121(5).

References to the Copyright Tribunal with respect to licensing by licensing bodies

13.05 It is also possible to refer licences to the Copyright Tribunal which do not relate to a licensing scheme, but are nevertheless granted by a licensing body. A copyright user may, for example, need a licence from a licensing body for a use which does not come within schemes and therefore requires a tailor-made licence. Licences to television broadcasters which are negotiated on an ad hoc basis are examples of such individual licences.

Again, references may be made regarding licences given by licensing bodies which fall outside the ambit of licensing schemes, cover works by more than one author, and which authorise copying, rental or lending of copies to the public, performing, showing or playing the work in public, or broadcasting the work[1].

A prospective licensee may refer the terms on which a licensing body proposes to grant a licence to the Tribunal. Again, if the Tribunal does not think the application is too premature[2], it can consider the application and make an order confirming or varying the terms as it considers reasonable[3].

Where an existing licence is due to expire, a licensee can apply to the tribunal on the ground that it is unreasonable in the circumstances that the licence should cease to be in force[4]. The Tribunal has the power to order that the licensee should continue to benefit from the licence on reasonable terms[5].

Subject to certain limitations, licensing bodies and licensees may apply to have an order reviewed[6].

As in the case of licensing schemes, orders may be made for limited or indefinite periods[7].

1   CDPA s 124.
2   CDPA s 125(2).
3   CDPA s 125(3).
4   CDPA s 126(1).
5   CDPA s 126(4).
6   CDPA s 127.
7   CDPA ss 125(4) and 126(5).

Unreasonable discrimination

13.06 In deciding what is 'reasonable', the Copyright Tribunal has regard to the availability and terms of other schemes, or the granting (and terms) of other licences in similar circumstances, with the aim of securing that there is no unreasonable discrimination between licensees and potential licensees[1].

1   CDPA s 129.

Specific cases of licensing schemes

13.07   The CDPA contains special rules with regard to certain types of copyright licences[1]. These rules deal with the matters with which the Tribunal must have regard when an application or reference has been made to it in such cases. These include:

- licences for reprographic copying[2];
- licences for educational establishments in respect of works including broadcasts[3];
- licences to reflect conditions imposed by promoters of events[4];
- licences to reflect payments in respect of underlying rights[5]; and
- licences in respect of works included in re-transmissions of broadcasts[6].

These detailed provisions go beyond the scope of this *User's Guide*.

A statutory right to use sound recordings in broadcasts was also added to the CDPA by the Broadcasting Act 1990[7]. The right relates to 'needletime' (meaning the time in any period in which recordings may be included in a broadcast)[8]. If a licensing body refuses to grant (or procure the grant of) needletime (either unlimited or as otherwise requested by the user) on acceptable payment terms, or refuses to alter a current licence to provide unlimited needletime (or the amount requested by the user), that person will be treated as if he has a licence provided that he gives sufficient advance notice of his intention to use and his proposals for payment[9], complies with the reasonable conditions of the licensing body, provides the licensing body with information regarding his use as reasonably required by the body and pays to the body the amounts established by the procedure established under the CDPA. That amount will either be an amount ordered by the Copyright Tribunal, the amount required by the licensing body or (in the absence of an Order from the Tribunal or a reasonable requested fee from the licensing body), the amount notified by the user under the notice procedure referred to above[10].

1   CDPA ss 130–135A.
2   CDPA s 130.
3   CDPA s 131.
4   CDPA s 132.

5   CDPA s 133.
6   CDPA s 134.
7   CDPA s 135A (as amended by the 2003 Regulations).
8   CDPA s 135A(5).
9   CDPA s 135B.
10 CDPA s 135C.

Collective administration of cable retransmission right

13.08   Under the CDPA (as amended by the 1996 and the 2003 Regulations) owners of literary, dramatic, musical or artistic works, sound recordings or films only exercise their cable retransmission rights 'as against a cable operator' through a licensing body[1]. Such rights only apply to the grant or refusal of authorised cable retransmission of a wireless broadcast from another EEA member state in which the work is included[2]. The reason for the collective administration of these rights is that it was felt counterproductive to the development of the European market for cable retransmission to allow such rights holders an effective veto over this form of exploitation and to facilitate owner rights clearance for cable operators.

If an owner of one of these rights has not transferred management of such rights to a licensing body, the body managing rights of the same category is deemed to be mandated to exercise his right[3]. The copyright owner in such cases will have the same rights and obligations against and to the licensing body as a copyright owner who has transferred management of retransmission rights to that body. However, these rights must be exercised within three years from the date of the cable retransmission concerned[4].

Significantly, the requirement to licence collectively does not extend to broadcasters. The maker of a broadcast is entitled to individually licence any rights exercised by him (whether in relation to the broadcast and any works included in it)[5].

A number of the collecting societies now seek to administer cable retransmission rights on behalf of their members[6].

1   CDPA s 144A(1)
2   CDPA s 144A(2).
3   CDPA s 144A(3).
4   CDPA s 144A(5).
5   CDPA s 144A(6).
6   For example, ComPact; see **paragraph 13.01** and **Appendix 1**.

Competition Commission

13.09   Under the Fair Trading Act 1973 the OFT could examine scale or complex monopolies and make a reference to the Competition

Commission (ex Monopolies and Mergers Commission) to establish if a monopoly exists and its effect on the public interest. Copyright licenses could be examined under these powers.

As of 20 June 2003 the Enterprise Act 2002 replaced the above provisions with a new 'market investigation' procedure. The OFT can refer a market to the Competition Commission if it has 'reasonable grounds for suspecting that any feature, or combination of features of a market in the UK for goods or services prevents, restricts or distorts competition in connection with the supply or acquisition of any goods or services in the UK or a part of the UK'. The Secretary of State has a reserve power to refer if the OFT does not.

The CC will determine whether there is an adverse effect on competition and if so it has a duty to apply remedies.

Section 144 of the CDPA deals with the situation which can arise (under the Enterprise Act 2002) where the Competition Commission have reported that conditions exist in respect of licences granted by an owner of copyright in a work, which restrict the use of the work by a licensee, or the right of a copyright owner, to grant other licences in such a way that it is an abuse of a monopoly. In addition, the Competition Commission may recommend that the refusal of a copyright owner to grant licences on reasonable terms in certain circumstances constitutes an abuse of a monopoly. In these cases there is power to cancel or modify such conditions, or provide that licences in respect of the copyright are to be made available as of right. If the government decides to exercise these powers, then the terms of a licence available as a result of such exercise are to be settled by the Copyright Tribunal if the relevant parties cannot reach agreement and the persons requiring the licence make an application to the Copyright Tribunal.

Chapter 14

EU law, competition and copyright

Introduction

14.01 The impetus for the recent changes to UK copyright law has its origins in Europe, and at the root of all European legislation is the Treaty of Rome[1]. The Rome Treaty was most recently amended by the Treaty on European Union[2], and by the Treaty of Amsterdam[3]. The main objective of this European legislation is to improve the life of Europeans by establishing a common market and other common policies[4]. EU law most noticeably has affected copyright in the following ways:

- directives which have the effect of harmonising copyright law throughout the EEA[5];
- regulations which have the effect of direct law in all member states of the EU;
- the provisions of arts 28–30 (formerly arts 30–36) of the Treaty of Rome, which seek to eliminate restrictions on the free movement of goods;
- the provisions of arts 49–55 (formerly arts 59–66) which seek to eliminate restrictions on the free movement of services;
- the provisions of Art 81 (formerly Art 85) which prohibits agreements which restrict or prevent or distort competition;
- the provisions of Art 82 (formerly Art 86) which seek to prevent abuse by private enterprises which have a dominant position in a particular market.

This chapter will consider European Law as it impacts on copyright, and (given the importance of competition law to the copyright industries discussed in **Part 2**), we will also touch on some general issues arising under EU and UK competition law which are relevant to those industries.

1   25 March 1957.
2   February 1992.
3   Signed in Amsterdam 2 October 1997, OJ [1997] C-340.
4   Treaty of Rome, arts 2 and 3 et seq.
5   See **paragraph 1.08**.

The EU and the EEA

14.02   The EEA was established by the EEA Agreement[1]. The member states of the EU and the EEA are set out in Appendix 3 of this *User's Guide*. It is worth highlighting that since the last edition of the *User's Guide* a further 10 countries have been admitted to the EU: Cyprus, Czech Republic, Estonia, Hungary, Latvia, Lithuania, Malta, Poland, Slovakia and Slovenia. These 'Acceding Countries' are aligning their legislation to comply with EU law.

The provisions of the Treaty of Rome relevant to copyright now apply not only to EU member states but also to Iceland, Norway and Liechtenstein. The 1995, 1996, 1997, 2000 and 2003 Regulations apply and refer to the EEA rather than the EU, because the Directives they implemented were applicable to all EFTA countries.

1   Signed in Oporto 2 May 1992 as amended by the Brussels Protocol of 17 March 1993.

Directives

14.03   The following directives impacting on copyright should by now have been implemented in the national laws of member states:

- Directive on Semi-Conductor Topographies[1];
- Directive on Computer Programs[2];
- Directive on Rental Lending and Neighbouring Rights[3];
- Directive on Satellite Broadcasting and Cable Transmission[4];
- Directive on Copyright Duration[5];
- Directive on the Legal Protection of Databases[6];
- Directive on the Legal Protection of Services based on, or consisting of, Conditional Access[7];
- Directive on Copyright and Related Rights in the Information Society[8].

All have been implemented in the UK[9].

In addition two new directives (not yet implemented in the UK) are worthy of mention:

- The Enforcement of Intellectual Property Rights Directive[10]; and

● The Artist's Resale Right Directive.[11]

1 87/54.
2 91/250.
3 92/100.
4 93/83.
5 93/98.
6 96/9.
7 98/84/EC.
8 2001/29/EC.
9 See **paragraph 1.06.**
10 2004/48/EC, see **paragraph 8.22.**
11 2001/84/EC, see **paragraph 28.22.**

Regulations

14.04 The only regulation that has been issued that has any impact on copyright law is Council Regulation 3295/94 of 22 December 1994 laying down measures to prohibit the release for free circulation, export, re-export or entry for a suspensive procedure of counterfeit or pirated goods.

Freedom of movement of copyright material

14.05 Article 28 of the Treaty of Rome prohibits quantitative restrictions on imports between member states, and measures which have an equivalent effect. Once goods are placed on the market in the EEA, they must be allowed to circulate freely. The CDPA (as amended by the 1996 Regulations which implemented the Rental and Lending Right Directive) recognises this principle[1].

Article 30 contains an exception to Art 28 for measures 'justified on grounds of ...the protection of commercial property'. Copyright falls within this category.

One leading case on the application of Art 28 is *Deutsche Grammophon GmbH v Metro*[2]. In that and other cases it was held that a German company could not prevent the re-importation into Germany of goods marketed in France by its French subsidiary. Such a restriction on importation went beyond the specific object of the copyright. The definition in each case will depend upon examining the interests of the copyright owner deserving of protection and the means of remunerating him in the light of market conditions at the time[3].

1 See **paragraphs 7.04 and 14.06.**
2 78/70: [1971] CMLR 631, ECJ.
3 158/86: *Warner Bros v Christiansen [1990] 3 CMLR 684, ECJ.*

Exhaustion of rights

14.06 It follows that the principles of Art 28 of the Treaty of Rome, and the territorial rights afforded by copyright, are in conflict. In part, that conflict is resolved by the harmonisation initiatives of the EU[1], but most significantly, the issue has also been addressed by the development of the doctrine of 'exhaustion of rights' by the ECJ.

The essence of the principle of European exhaustion of rights is considered elsewhere in the context of its implementation into the CDPA[2]. However, it is worth noting here that the exhaustion of one right in a copyright work does not exhaust all rights in respect of that work. As we have noted in other parts of this *User's Guide*, copyright is a bundle of rights. Particular rights can be separately licensed or assigned. So, whilst the issue of copies of a video or a record into the EU market with the authorisation of the owner will exhaust his right to sell etc those copies within the EU, it will not exhaust, say, the right to authorise the performance, playing or showing of the work embodied on those copies in public, or the rental of those copies[3].

1 See **paragraph 14.03.**
2 See **paragraph 7.04.**
3 For example *Metronome Musik GmbH v Music Point Hokamp GmbH: C-200/96 [1998] ECRI-1053, ECJ.*

Freedom of movement of services

14.07 Article 49 provides for the abolition of restrictions on the freedom to provide services within the EEA in respect of nationals of member states who are established in a state other than that of the person for whom the services are intended. The exception provisions of Art 30[1] do not apply to Art 49.

In *Coditel SA v Ciné Vog Films SA*[2] the owner of the film *Le Boucher* granted a licence to the German television channel ARD to broadcast the film. At the same time, Ciné Vog had an exclusive licence in the theatrical distribution and television broadcast rights in the film for Belgium.

The Coditel companies are cable television operators in Belgium. They retransmitted the German broadcast to their cable subscribers.

Ciné Vog sued Coditel on the grounds that the cable retransmission infringed Ciné Vog's exclusive rights. Coditel claimed that Arts 49–55, providing for the free movement of services, constituted a defence to Ciné Vog's claim since if Ciné Vog succeeded, there would be a restriction on the movement of services, television having been established to be a service for the purposes of Art 49. The ECJ held, however, that the performance of the film was an essential element in the copyright in the film which went to the 'specific subject matter' or 'object' of the copyright and in the circumstances could be protected by a geographically limited licence. What *Coditel* established was that copyrights which depend on performance such as broadcasts may be licensed on a geographical basis within the EC without infringing Art 49. In other words, although the distribution right in goods may be exhausted by the first distribution of the goods within the EU which is authorised by the owner, the same does not apply to performances.

1   See **paragraph 14.05**.
2   262/81: [1983] 1 CMLR 49, ECJ. In a subsequent case, the ECJ considered the compatibility of an exclusive licence with Art 81.

Passing off

14.08   Actions to prevent persons from representing that their goods or services are those of someone else, or are connected with someone else, can have the effect of restricting the movement of goods between member states.

For the purpose of passing off actions, the whole of the EC is to be regarded as a single country, so that provided that the plaintiff has established the reputation for his goods in one member state, he can bring actions of passing off against defendants in other member states, although the plaintiff may never have marketed his goods in the member states in respect of which the actions commenced[1].

1   See **Chapter 5** for an analysis of 'passing off' generally.

EC competition law and copyright: Arts 81 and 82 of the Treaty of Rome[1]

14.09   Article 81 prohibits agreements between undertakings which restrict, distort or prevent competition in the EU or a substantial part of it.[2] Article 82 prohibits the abuse by one or more undertakings of a dominant position in the EU or a substantial part of it. The provisions only apply where trade between member states is affected.

There are no specific exemptions dealing with copyright or other intellectual property interests.

1   As amended, see **paragraph 14.01**.
2   The ECJ has held that a single member state constitutes a substantial part of the EU: *Vereeniging van Cementhandelaren v EC Commission: 8/72 [1972] ECR 977*. In appropriate cases, part of a member state could satisfy this test.

Parallel provisions in UK law

14.10 In the UK, the Competition Act 1998 has introduced two main prohibitions, which are closely modelled on Arts 81 and 82[1]. The first, the Chapter I prohibition, prohibits agreements which are intended to or may have the effect of, preventing, restricting or distorting competition within the UK and which may affect trade within the UK. Provisions which have such an effect will be void, unless they are exempted under certain EC or UK block exemptions or individual exemption. The second, the Chapter II prohibition, prohibits a dominant company from abusing its position in a way which may affect trade within the UK or part of it. There is no possibility of exemption from the second prohibition. Under s 60 of the Competition Act 1998, the UK courts and authorities are obliged, where possible, to interpret UK law in a manner which is consistent with EC jurisprudence. The principles set out below are therefore likely to apply to the CDPA[2].

1   In addition to the Competition Act 1998, the monopoly provisions of Part IV of the Enterprise Act 2002 may affect the exercise of intellectual property rights of companies subject to investigation under those provisions. They are dealt with at **paragraph 14.28** below.
2   In particular, jurisprudence under the previous law, the Restrictive Trade Practices Act 1976 which was repealed upon the coming into force of the Competition Act 1998 (subject to transitional arrangements), to the effect that copyright licences do not constitute restrictions on the licensee should be regarded as no longer good law.

Article 81(1) – agreements restricting competition

14.11 A detailed review of Art 81 is beyond the scope of this *User's Guide*. In general its effect is to prohibit agreements between undertakings which appreciably restrict competition, if the restriction may affect trade between member states. Article 81(1) contains the following examples of such restrictions. These are agreements which:

'(a)   directly or indirectly fix purchase or selling prices or any other trading conditions;

(b)   limit or control production, markets, technical development or investment;

(c)   share markets or sources of supply;

(d)   apply dissimilar conditions to equivalent transactions with other trading parties, thereby placing them at a competitive disadvantage; or

(e)   make the conclusion of contracts subject to acceptance by the other parties of supplementary obligations which, by their nature, or according to commercial usage, have no connection with the subject of such contracts'.

In addition to 'agreements' between undertakings, Art 81(1) also prohibits decisions by associations of undertakings and concerted practices, if they 'have as their object or effect the prevention, restriction or distortion of competition within the Common Market'.

Appreciable effect

14.12 The ECJ has held that an agreement will only infringe Art 81(1) where the effect on trade between member states and the restriction of competition is appreciable. The Commission has declared that agreements involving undertakings operating at the same level of trade (ie horizontal agreements) and having an aggregate market share of no more than 10%, and agreements between parties at different levels of trade (vertical agreements) and having an aggregate market share of no more than 15%, will not generally be considered as having an appreciable effect on trade between member states[1].

1   Commission, Notice on Agreements of Minor Importance.

Effect of infringing Art 81(1)

14.13 Provisions of agreements which infringe Art 81(1) will be void and unenforceable by virtue of Art 81(2). Such unenforceable provisions might render the entire agreement unenforceable, if the provisions in question are fundamental to the agreement as a whole. In other cases, the unenforceable provisions may be severable. Whether the provisions are fundamental or can be severed will usually be a matter for a court having jurisdiction in respect of the agreement and will be decided under the governing law of the agreement.

Parties to an agreement which infringes Art 81(1) may be subject to fines imposed by the Commission. The fines imposed on each party can amount to up to 10% of that party's total annual worldwide turnover (including the turnover of any parents or subsidiaries)[1].

Any third party who suffers loss as a result of the infringing provisions may be entitled to sue for, and recover, damages in the national courts.

1   In practice, fines are imposed in respect of serious infringements of Arts 81(1) and 82; in particular, market partitioning and price fixing.

The possibility of exemption

14.14 Before 1 May 2004, the parties to commercial agreements that infringed Art 81(1) could notify them for an exemption to the Commission, which was empowered to grant exemptions if the criteria in Art 81(3) were met. The key advantage for parties to agreements of notifying their agreements was that for the period from the date of notification they could not be fined (unless the Commission took the unusual step of withdrawing the immunity), although the other consequences of infringing Art 81(1) – fines and actions in local courts by adversely affected third parties – were unaffected.

Since 1 May 2004, it is no longer possible for parties to an agreement to seek an exemption, and they must assess for themselves whether their agreement is caught by the prohibition contained in Art 81(1) and, if so, whether they satisfy the criteria for an individual exemption under Art 81(3). In order to meet the exemption criteria, it is necessary that the agreement:

'contributes to improving the production or distribution of goods or promoting technical or economic progress while allowing consumers a fair share of the resulting benefit'[1].

However, the exemption criteria are not met if the agreement or decision:

'(a) imposes on the undertakings concerned restrictions which are not indispensable to the achievement of these objectives;

(b) affords such undertakings the possibility of eliminating competition in respect of a substantial part of the products in question.'[2]

Guidelines have been published by the Commission to assist with the application of Art 81(3)[3] to an agreement and the Commission has also published a number of block exemptions which exempt an entire class of contractual arrangements, provided they fall entirely within the scope of the block exemption. There is no applicable block exemption for most agreements concerning copyright. However, as explained below, the technology transfer block exemption[4] which came into force on 1 May 2004 applies to bilateral software copyright licensing agreements and ancillary provisions relating to copyright provided that the market share thresholds[5] are met. The block exemption does not cover non-software copyright. However, the Commission explains in the accompanying Guidelines that it will apply the principles set out in the block exemption to licences of copyright for the purposes of reproduction and distribution of the protected work (but not to the licensing of rights in performances and other related rights)[6].

1   Art 81(3).
2   Ibid.
3   Commission Notice *Guidelines on the Application of Article 81(3) of the Treaty* (2004/C 101/08).
4   Regulation 772/2004/EC, Official Journal L123, 27.04.2004, pages 11–17.
5   For agreements between competitors, the block exemption applies if the combined market share of the parties does not exceed 20% on either the relevant product market or the relevant technology market. For agreements between non-competitors, the relevant figure is 30%.
6   Guidelines on the application of Art 81 of the EC Treaty to technology transfer arrangements, Official Journal C101, 27.04.2004, pages 2–42, paras 51–52.

Exclusive copyright licences and Art 81

14.15   A key question in the case of copyright licences is the extent to which exclusivity can be granted without infringing Art 81(1), or, if Art 81(1) is infringed, the circumstances in which an exemption is justified.

In determining the application of Art 81(1) to licence agreements, the Commission considers:

• whether the agreement restricts competition that would have existed in the absence of the agreement; and
• whether any individual provisions of the agreement are more restrictive than would appear to be objectively necessary.

The position under Art 81(1) was considered in the *Coditel (No 2)* case[1]. The ECJ held that an exclusive licence of film rights could infringe Art 81(1) where it created artificial and unjustifiable economic barriers or generally restricted competition. This means that an exclusive licence will infringe Art 81(1) only in exceptional circumstances. For example, Art 81(1) would be likely to be infringed where the agreement, assessed in the context of other similar agreements in the industry, substantially foreclosed the market, for example by materially affecting the ability of third parties to enter or expand their activities in the market.

In one case, exclusive 15-year licences to broadcast a large number of films in the MGM/UA film library were granted to a group of public German television broadcasting organisations (ARD). The Commission granted an exemption to the agreements but only after ARD agreed to modify its licence to permit the licensor to grant licences in respect of its films to other broadcasters within the same geographical area during fixed periods varying from two to six years (known as windows)[2]. The

Commission expressed its concern that an exclusive licence of large quantities of content, such as, in this case, an entire library, would amount to an artificial barrier to competition. Other television stations would be unable to obtain the rights to a large pool of titles, including those which the licensee elected not to show. The German case was unusual in the sheer quantity of programming covered by the licence and the duration of the exclusivity granted to the broadcasters. Where exclusivity is granted for particular windows and the licensor remains free to licence the particular programmes to third parties outside such windows, and where the exclusivity only applies to a particular distribution platform, the risk of interference by the authorities will be less likely, especially where there are competing suppliers of programming.

This was applied in *Telenor/Canal+/Canal Digital COMP 38.287,* in which Canal+ sold its 50% shareholding in the satellite pay TV distribution platform Canal Digital to the other shareholder, Telenor and to ensure the continuity of the service, the parties entered a long-term exclusive agreement for the DTH satellite distribution of Canal+'s premium pay TV and pay-per-view services. The Commission was able to exempt the agreement after the parties agreed to reduce the duration of the exclusivity rights. The Commission also required the parties to eliminate restrictions which were not related to the pay TV market, particularly rights of first refusal concerning the acquisition and marketing of premium content through new media platforms.

The grant of exclusive rights has been extensively examined in the context of premium sports rights and, prior to 1 May 2004, the Commission had granted several exemptions under Art 81(3)[3]. In this context, in reviewing the effect of exclusivity in licences of premium content licences, the Commission has been concerned as to the effect of those rights on downstream markets, and particularly new media rights. In the cases examined by the Commission, the restrictions found by it have been a result of joint selling or the pooling of rights by sellers, resulting in the concentration of rights and the risk that a single buyer could acquire all the rights.

In the *UEFA* exemption, the Commission's concerns were that the rights were licensed in each national market to a single broadcaster for three years (with only limited sublicensing), clubs were prevented from licensing their own rights in many cases and new media rights were not exploited.

In order to satisfy the requirements of Art 81(3), the Commission required the licences granted to be limited in scope and duration. UEFA agreed to offer 15 different packages for a period of three years (including three live packages), and provided for the co-exploitation of new media rights by the clubs and the leagues for certain rights to be exploited by the clubs alone.

Similarly, in the UK, the FA Premier League agreed a settlement with the Commission that allowed it to offer licences for several packages for three seasons' duration (including near-live and terrestrial highlights packages). The settlement allows deferred rights to be exploited by both the FAPL and the clubs (though there are limitations on the clubs' ability to 'bundle' their rights with those of other clubs and thereby create packages for the competition). As part of the settlement, the number of matches to be broadcast in the 2004 to 2007 seasons will increase by approximately 30%. Further, from 2007, no single buyer will be able to acquire exclusive rights to all of the pooled live rights packages.

The *UEFA* and *FA Premier League* exemptions indicate that the Commission is likely to be concerned about licensing structures which:

- grant key rights – especially live rights – to a single broadcaster in a national territory; and
- leave rights unexploited by the seller of the rights, but do not permit the clubs to exploit them.

As these cases demonstrate, exclusive licences which are likely to last for an excessively long duration or cover an excessive amount of programming may be in breach of Art 81(1) and outside the exemption criteria under Art 81(3). The term of any licence and quantities of programming are, however, only one of several factors which will be considered. The Commission will look more generally at the context in which a licence may be expected to operate, particularly at the scope of the rights covered by the licence, the structure of the markets in question and the availability of alternative programming.[4]

1   *Coditel SA v Ciné Vog Films SA (No 2) (Coditel (No2)) Case 262/81 [1982] ECR 3381.*
2   Film purchases by German television stations IV31.734 (89/536/EEC) Official Journal L284, 03.10.1989, pages 36–44.
3   UEFA COMP 37.368, FAPL COMP 38.453, DFB COMP 37.214.
4   The Commission's focus on sports rights was given added impetus by the Sector Inquiry into New Media report in May 2005, which found that rights holders' practices of exclusive licensing, cross platform bundling and collective selling were restrictring the availability of sports rights on 3G services; see EC Issues paper, 'On the Preliminary finding of the Sector Inquiry into News Media', May 2005.

Other common restrictions in copyright licences

14.16 Whether contractual provisions concerning copyright will constitute appreciable restrictions of competition will depend upon the context including effect of the agreement on the market and should be the subject of specialist legal advice. The following generalisations can be made.

- *Territorial restrictions*: taking as an analogy the treatment afforded to other intellectual property rights and on the basis of the Technology Transfer Block Exemption, in licences permitting the manufacture of goods, a prohibition on the licensee conducting an active sales policy outside the licence territory will be exempted. In some cases, restrictions on passive sales may be acceptable[1]. As far as restrictions on the licensor are concerned, an obligation not to license the same rights to others or to exploit such rights directly itself within the licensee's territory (provided that the duration of the obligation is not excessive) would also meet the exemption criteria. Complete territorial protection is also permissible for performance copyrights[2].

- *Pricing and output restrictions*: contractual provisions that restrict either party's ability to set the price at which it sells products to third parties will generally infringe Art 81 and not satisfy the exemption criteria[3]. Provisions that amount to output restrictions are also likely to be problematic[4].

- *No challenge provisions:* a provision in a copyright licence under which the licensee is not allowed to challenge the validity or existence of the copyright which is the subject of the licence was traditionally regarded as void under Art 81(1) and not capable of being exempted under Art 81(3)[5]. However, in the Technology Transfer Block Exemption, such a provision is outside the Block Exemption and requires a separate assessment (ie consideration as to whether the provision is an appreciable restriction of competition, and, if so, whether it meets the exemption criteria).

- *'Non competition' covenants*: under the previous Technology Transfer Block Exemption, 'non-competition' covenants (under which the licensee usually undertakes not to use any competing technology or manufacture or distribute any competing products) were black-listed. They are now permitted up to the 20 or 30% market share level.

- *Royalties for unprotected rights*: in general, charging royalties on a product which is not protected by the licensor's intellectual property rights will infringe Art 81(1) and will not be capable of exemption under Art 81(3)[6].

- *'Most favoured nations' provisions*: in general, a 'most favoured nations provision', that is, a provision which requires one party to grant the other the benefit of any more favourable terms which the licensor may grant other licensees during the term of the agreement, will not be regarded as infringing Art 81. There may however be circumstances in which such a provision has the effect of restricting competition: for example because it deters a licensor (who is required to upgrade a licensee to better terms granted to another licensee) from granting other licences or because the effect of the most favoured nations provision across a particular market is to blunt competition. In 2004, the Commission carried out an investigation into the contracts entered into between eight Hollywood studios and European pay TV broadcasters containing most favoured nations provisions which the Commission considered had the effect of aligning prices of broadcast rights. The investigation was closed as regards six studios when they agreed to amend their contracts[7].

- *Restriction of licensee's ability to exploit its own technology*: under the Technology Transfer Block Exemption, a provision in an agreement between competitors which had the effect of restricting the licensee's ability to exploit its own technology was black listed and thereby prevented the agreement from benefiting from the block exemption.

1 See the Technology Transfer Block Exemption which allows a restriction on the licensor and the licensee in a non-reciprocal agreement from active and passive selling into the other party's exclusive territory or customer group (Art.4(1)(c)(iv)). In an agreement between non-competitors, the period during which a licensee can be protected from passive sale into its territory is two years (Art.4(2)(b)(ii)).
2 See *Coditel (No 2). Case 262/81 [1982] ECR 3381.*
3 Limitation of output in reciprocal arrangements are blacklisted under the Technology Transfer Block Exemption (Art.4(1)(b)).
4 See for example, the UEFA and Premier League cases referred to above.
5 *Neilson-Hordell/Richmark*, XII Annual Report on Competition Policy (1982), point 88–89.
6 See *Neilson Hordell/Richmark*, XII Annual Report on Competition Policy (1982), point 88–89.
7 Press Release IP/04/1314.

Co-operative joint ventures and Art 81

14.17 In part because of the cost of establishing and operating television services, there have been a significant number of mergers and joint ventures in the media sector. Although a detailed discussion of this issue is beyond the scope of this *User's Guide*, it is worth noting that joint ventures which are of a co-operative nature rather than a form of merger[1] may infringe Art 81(1) where the joint venture parties are actual or potential competitors who would otherwise be competing; and/or the agreement contains restrictions on the parties' commercial freedom which are not ancillary to the creation or operation of the joint venture actual or potential competitors.

In the context of the developing new media markets, the Commission has been rigorous in its consideration of co-operation agreements, preventing all restrictions not necessary to the parties' core business or the efficiencies to be generated, that may foreclose entry into the new market[2].

1 These are subject to a separate regime under the EC Merger Regulation. See **paragraphs 14.24–14.27** below.
2 *Telenor/Canal+/Canal Digital COMP 38.287.*

Article 82 – abuse of a dominant position

14.18 Article 82 applies to companies occupying a 'dominant position' when they abuse that position. No exemptions are available to companies which abuse a dominant position.

Abuses by one or more undertakings of a dominant position within the EU or in a substantial part of it are prohibited to the extent that they affect trade between member states. Such abuses are not exhaustively defined, but, Art 82 specifies a number of examples of abuse:

'(a)   directly or indirectly imposing unfair purchase or selling prices or unfair trading conditions;
(b)   limiting production, markets or technical development to the prejudice of consumers;
(c)   applying dissimilar conditions to equivalent transactions with other trading parties thereby placing them at a competitive disadvantage;
(d)   making the conclusion of contracts subject to acceptance by the other parties or supplementary obligations which, by their nature or according to commercial usage, had no connection with the subject of such contracts'.

Like Art 81, Art 82 has been subject to a large number of decisions before the ECJ and of the Commission and a detailed review is beyond the scope of this *User's Guide.*

Meaning of 'dominance'

14.19 Dominance is considered to exist where a company has the ability to act independently of competitors, customers and consumers. It is not assessed purely in terms of market share, although market shares of 30% and over may be indicative of dominance. This largely depends on the structure of the market, the position of key participants within the market and the existence of barriers to entry. To assess market share it is necessary to define the relevant product market. Regard should be had, when assessing the definition of the market, to other products which are substantially interchangeable with the relevant products in question.

In one case, the ECJ considered the circumstances in which a record producer would be considered as dominant:

'the manufacturer should have the power to impede the maintenance of effective competition over a considerable part of the relevant market, having regard in particular to the existence of any producers marketing similar products and to their position on the market. If recording artists are tied to the manufacturer by exclusive contracts consideration should be given, inter alia, to their popularity on the market, to the duration and extent of the obligations undertaken and to the opportunities available to other manufacturers of sound recordings to obtain the services of comparable performers.'[1]

Markets may develop over time. For example, at one stage there was a market for all television broadcasting, but at a later date, that market having developed, there are separate markets for pay television and free television. As the media sector develops, these markets have been more narrowly defined in terms of premium content sport and film.[2]

1 *Deutsche Grammophon Gesellschaft mbH v Metro SB-Großmärkte GmbH & Co KG, 1971 ECR 487, paras 17–18 (Case 78–70).*
2 *Telenor/Canal+/Canal Digital COMP 38.287.*

Meaning of 'abuse'

14.20 It is the *abuse* of the dominant position, rather than the dominant position itself, which is prohibited by Art 82. The ECJ has held that the concept of abuse 'is an objective concept relating to the behaviour of an undertaking in a dominant position which is such as to influence the structure of a market'[1]. Yet the distinction between conduct which is permissible and conduct which amounts to abuse can be a difficult one to make. It will be a question of fact and degree in each case, and will depend on such factors as normal industry practice, the effect on competitors, and customers, the intention of the dominant firm and the proportionality of the conduct.

1 *Hoffmann-La Roche & Co. A.G. v EC Commission: 85/76 [1979] ECR 461 at 541.*

Examples of 'abuse'

14.21 Examples of behaviour which has in the past been held to be abusive include:

* imposing unfair prices (eg, excessive, predatory or discriminatory prices);
* imposing unfair trading conditions;
* discriminatory treatment of equivalent transactions and/or persons;
* refusal to supply;
* bundling of goods and/or services.

Collective licensing societies raise specific issues under Art 82. These are considered in **Chapter 13**.

Refusal to licence

14.22 The leading case on the circumstances in which a refusal to license intellectual property rights will infringe Art 82 is the *Magill TV Guide* case[1]. The case arose out of the refusal in the 1980s of the BBC, RTE and ITP (the owners of copyright in TV listing information for the terrestrial television in UK and the Republic of Ireland) to license their TV programme schedules for publication to Magill TV Guides other than on a restrictive basis. At the time each broadcaster produced a guide based on their own television information, and therefore no comprehensive guide existed. Magill wanted to produce a comprehensive weekly television guide covering the services of all broadcasters and complained to the Commission that the refusal to license meant they were unable to do so.

The Commission found that there had been an abuse of a dominant position under Art 82 and this was confirmed on appeal by the CFI and, on a subsequent appeal, by the ECJ. The ECJ held that a dominant's firm's refusal to grant a licence does not in itself constitute an abuse of a dominant position. However, a refusal to grant a licence may amount to abusive conduct where:

* the refusal to license prevents the creation of a new product for which there is potential customer demand;
* there is no objective justification for the refusal; and

- the effect of the refusal is to reserve a secondary market to the dominant firm.

In *Magill*, the TV companies were reserving to themselves the secondary market of weekly television guides by excluding all competition in the market. This was denying access to the information essential for the compilation of a comprehensive weekly guide.

At the time of the *Magill* judgment, it was suggested that the principles established by the court were an application of the 'essential facilities' principle. That is, the principle which was developed in the context of access to port facilities to the effect that a company in a dominant position which also controls access to infrastructure which is essential to competing in the market must have a valid reason ('objective justification') for refusing access to the infrastructure. However, when the issue was reconsidered in the *IMS Health* case, the ECJ did not base its judgment on essential facilities principles[2].

The *IMS Health* case concerned a refusal by IMS to grant a licence to a competitor, NDC, to use the copyright in a database known as the '1,860 brick structure' which had become the standard way of analysing sales of pharmaceutical products in Germany. NDC used a similar structure for the market studies it sold. IMS successfully sued NDC for copyright infringement and thereafter NDC sought, and was refused, a licence of IMS's copyright. NDC complained to the Commission that IMS was abusing its dominant position.

The German court referred to the ECJ the question of whether the refusal was an abuse of a dominant position. The ECJ found that the following circumstances will be considered sufficient to justify a compulsory licence:

- there must be no objective justification for the refusal to license;
- the use of the intellectual property rights in question must be indispensable to operating on the relevant market and the refusal of a licence must eliminate all competition on that market;
- the person seeking the licence must have intended to produce new goods and services that would have met specific consumer requirements not met by the copyright owner's goods and services;
- there must be at least potential consumer demand for the new goods and services.

In other words, the refusal to licence must prevent the introduction to the market of a new and innovative product for which there is demand from consumers[3].

Most recently, the Commission has found that Microsoft abused its dominant position by refusing to provide information needed by third party providers of operating systems which the Commission considered indispensable to achieve interoperability with Microsoft PC operating systems[4]. This decision is currently on appeal to the CFI[5], with Microsoft claiming that the Commission erred in its finding that the information was indispensable and that the *Magill* criteria has been wrongly applied. In particular, Microsoft has said that it will argue that their IP rights constitute an objective justification for their refusal to supply the information requested. The CFI's judgment will hopefully provide clarity to the application of *Magill* and the essential facilities principles in the context of Intellectual property.

1   Official Journal L78, 21.03.1989, pages 43–51; *Joint Cases C-241/91 P and C-242/91 P Radio Telefis Eireann (RTE) and Independent Television Publications Ltd (ITP) v Commission of the European Communities [1995] ECR 743.*

2   *IMS Health GmbH v NDC Health GmbH, 2004 ECR 0000 (Case C-418/01).*

3   For a detailed analysis, see Christopher Stothers, 'IMS Health and its Implications for Compulsory Licensing in Europe' [2004] EIPR 476. See also Burton Ong, 'Anti-competitive Refusals to grant Copyright Licences' [2004] EIPR November 2004.

4   *Microsoft: COMP 37.792.*

5   T-201/04.

Tying

14.23   The Commission's decision in the *Microsoft* case also found that Microsoft had been acting abusively by tying, the first time this abuse had been found in a case concerning intellectual property rights[1]. The decision relies on principles enunciated by the Commission in other decisions[2] based on Art 82(d). The Commission considered that as the Windows operating system is all-pervasive in the market for PC operating systems, Microsoft is able to abuse its super-dominant position by securing the secondary market of Media Players by 'tying' the sale of Windows Media Player with the Windows operating system as a single package. Essentially, the super-dominant nature of the 'tying' product (Windows) means that the 'tied' product (Windows Media Player) will foreclose the market in media players and software to competition.

This is a new application of the principle of 'tying' as it is the first time it has been applied in the context of IP. Microsoft have appealed the Commission decision on the basis that the two product markets identified are not separate and that the assertions of foreclosure are speculative. The decision of the CFI should help to identify how the concept of typing will be applied to copyright.

1   *Microsoft: COMP 37.792.*

2   *Case C-333/94 Tetra Pak [1996] ECR 5951 and Hilti AG v Commission of the European Communities (C53/92 P) [1994] ECR I-667.*

The EC Merger Regulation

14.24   The EC Merger Regulation (ECMR) requires the pre-notification of certain mergers and joint ventures, known as concentrations with a Community dimension. A concentration with a Community dimension occurs where either:

(a)   two or more previously independent undertakings merge; or
(b)   one undertaking acquires direct or indirect control of another; and

one of the turnover criteria are satisfied.

With effect from 1 March 1998 there are two alternative turnover tests which are designed to catch larger, cross-border mergers.

Full-function joint ventures

14.25   The ECMR treats the formation of certain joint ventures as akin to a merger – these are 'full-function joint ventures'. In other words, joint ventures which have sufficient resources and assets to conduct business on a lasting basis.

A key issue which arises in the television sector[1] is whether, if the joint venture enters into agreements with the parent companies either for supplies to the joint venture or sales from it, this will prejudice the full-function nature of the joint venture. If this is the case for an initial start-up period which does not exceed three years, it would not affect the full-function character of the joint venture. If supplies to the joint venture from the parents are intended to be made on a longer-term basis, the question will depend upon a proportion of the joint venture's supplies which are supplied by the parents and to the extent to which the joint venture adds value to what is supplied. As far as supplies by the joint venture are concerned, the effect on the full-function status of the joint venture will depend upon the proportion of the joint venture's production which is supplied to the parents and whether supplies are made on an arm's-length basis.

1   A significant contribution to the joint ventures in the television sector that is often made by joint venture parties is licences of copyright material to which the parties own the rights.

Substantive issues

14.26   Under the ECMR, the Commission is empowered to prohibit concentrations that it considers will significantly impede effective competition in the Common Market or a substantial part of it, in particular because it creates or strengthens a dominant position[1]. The Commission generally has 25 days from the date of filing[2] to determine whether it has 'serious doubts', in which case a full 90-day investigation can be commenced.

In the television sector, mergers and joint ventures which raise competition issues fall into one of three categories: (i) where the parties are actual or potential competitors in the same market or segment; (ii) where the parties have a vertical relationship such as content providers and carriers; and (iii) where the parties carry on business in the sectors which are separate but converging.

In each case the test will be whether the transaction will significantly impede effective competition in the EU. If the merging parties have a vertical relationship such as content providers and carriers, the Commission would have to consider how the transaction would affect the access of competitors to content and carriage. The transaction may for example make it difficult for a third party carrier to access sufficient content or alternatively it may be difficult for a third party content provider to have its content broadcast.

The Commission's approach has been to protect competition on converging and vertical markets to prevent foreclosure and to protect the interests of third parties. This is demonstrated by two Commission decisions: *Nordic Satellite Distribution*[3] and *MSG Media Service*[4]. In the first of these, the Danish and Norwegian national telecommunications companies sought a joint venture with Kinnevic, a television media conglomerate, to provide satellite transmission and distribution services by cable and direct-to-home broadcast. The Commission prohibited the agreement on the basis that the purpose of the venture would mean that the downstream activities of the joint venture would reinforce both the upstream and downstream market positions of the parents. In the 1994 decision of *MSG Media Service,* the Commission prohibited a joint venture that would provide pay TV broadcasters with infrastructure, booking and marketing services for the operation of commercial pay television. The Commission found that the joint venture would create a dominant position on three markets – the market for administrative and technical services, the market for pay TV and the market for cable networks and that effective competition would be significantly impeded as a result.

More recently, the Commission demonstrated a more pragmatic approach. In *NewsCorp/Telepiu* it approved the merger between the two satellite pay TV platforms in Italy, subject to a complex package of conditions which apply until 2011[5]. The transaction concerned the acquisition by News Corporation of sole control of Telepiu and the subsequent merger of Telepiu with Stream, a pay TV platform controlled by News Corporation. The Commission's appraisal indicated that the transaction would have led to the creation of a lasting near-monopoly in the Italian pay TV market, raised barriers to entry for satellite pay TV and created a monopolist position in Italy as regards the acquisition of premium programme content (particularly, exclusive rights to certain football matches and premium films). This would have foreclosed third party access to premium content which drives pay TV subscriptions. However, in view of the dire situation of the industry, it was extremely unlikely that two operators could have survived in the Italian pay TV market. For this reason and because of the disruption that the potential closure of Stream would cause to Italian pay TV subscribers, the Commission decided to approve the concentration, subject to appropriate conditions. The alternative was considered to be the closure of Stream by its owners.

The commitments accepted by the Commission had the aim of ensuring that the transaction does not have the effect of foreclosing third party access to premium content, the technical platform, the conditional access system and that the combined platform had no involvement in alternative means of transmission.

In *Sony/Bertelsmann*[6], the Commission approved the merger of the two companies' recorded music businesses (including the discovery and development of artists and the recording and marketing of their music) into a 50/50 joint venture named Sony BMG. The Commission initially thought that the merger might create or strengthen a collective dominant position between the remaining four major record companies (Universal, SonyBMG, Warner and EMI) in the market for recorded music. This was based on the fact that following the concentration, Universal, SonyBMG, Warner and EMI would account for about 80% of the recording market in Europe as a whole, and in most national markets in the European Economic Area. The two largest players, SonyBMG and Universal, would account for approximately half of the recorded music market, although Universal would remain larger than SonyBMG. The Commission was also concerned about the vertical integration of the parent companies in other markets (television, for example, for Bertelsmann, and music downloading services/portable music players, for Sony).

Ultimately, the Commission was unable to substantiate its concerns. Whilst it found evidence of relatively close price parallelism, there was insufficient evidence indicating coordinated pricing or that by reducing the number of major recording companies from five to four, the concentration would lead to a collective dominant position in the national markets for recorded music in the future. It also considered that the vertical issues did not give rise to significant competition concerns.

1   It should be noted that prior to 1 May 2004, the Commission was only empowered to prohibit concentrations if they created or strengthened a dominant position in the EU or a substantial part of it. The cases referred to in the text were decided on that basis. The change was made because it was considered that before 1 May 2004, the commission had no power to block a merger creating or strengthening a non-collusive oligopoly which could adversely affect competition, even in the absence of dominance by the merging parties.
2   This period can be extended by 10 days in certain circumstances.
3   Case IV/M. 490.
4   Case IV/M. 649.
5   Case IV/M. 2876.
6   Case COMP/M.3333.

Ancillary restraints

14.27   A decision by the Commission declaring a concentration as compatible with the Common Market will also cover any contractual restrictions which are 'ancillary' to the transaction – that is, are necessary for and directly related to its implementation. This would include non-competition covenants and transitional supply arrange-ments although it will depend upon the circumstances. However, the Commission rarely accepts that exclusive arrangements or arrange-ments that adversely affect the position of third parties can be ancillary. Provisions which are not ancillary to the transaction are subject to Art 81.

Monopoly provisions of the Enterprise Act 2002

14.28   Under UK law, investigations under the monopoly provisions of Part IV of the Enterprise Act 2002 may affect the intellectual property rights of companies investigated under those provisions. This legislation came into force on 20 June 2003 and replaced the procedure under the Fair Trading Act 1973. The OFT may make a market investigation reference to the Competition Commission (CC) (formerly the Monopolies and Mergers Commission (MMC)) where it has reason-able grounds for suspecting that any feature, or combination of features, of a market in the UK for goods or services prevents, restricts or distorts competition in connection with the supply or acquisition of any goods or services in the UK or a part of the UK. This may mean the market structure of the product or service in question, or the conduct of suppliers or customers, whether intentional or not. The CC will then determine whether there is an adverse effect on competition and where this is found to be the case, the CC has a duty to apply the remedies it considers appropriate.

Although there have been no recent investigations by CC into any area related to copyright, the MMC in 1995 in its *Report on the Supply of Video Games* in the UK, found that Sega held a scale monopoly position for hardware and software and that Sega and Nintendo were in a complex monopoly situation. The MMC found that a number of Sega and Nintendo's activities went against the public interest, including their discriminatory price structure for software and hardware; the imposition of restrictive conditions in licensing arrangements with competing software publishers such as restrictions on the quality of games which may be published and requiring approval of games, programs and concepts before publication; and the imposition of restrictions on video game rental.

The MMC recommended that the licensing arrangements of Sega and Nintendo should be modified to include the removal of a number of licence conditions, in particular the requirement that Sega and Nintendo control the manufacture of games cartridges.

Chapter 15

The protection of designs

Introduction

15.01 Designs created after 1 August 1989 are governed by the CDPA, which introduced a new code for design protection consisting of:

- a strengthened Registered Designs Act 1949 (described as the 1949 Act) which is set out in its entirety in Sch 4 to the CDPA;
- a new UK national unregistered design right which is set out in Part III of the CDPA; and
- limited copyright protection for designs derived from artistic works.

These have now been supplemented by an amended Registered Designs Act 1949 stemming from Directive 98/71/EC on the legal protection of designs (which was intended to harmonise registered design rights within member states of the European Union) and also by the introduction of European Community Registered and Community Unregistered Design rights by way of European Council Regulation 6/2002 which has direct effect within the member states of the European Union.

Part I: Pre-CDPA protection

15.02 The pre-1988 law of design protection was based on an interaction between copyright protection and the Registered Designs Act 1949. The scope and extent of copyright protection for articles made to design drawings was ultimately set out by the House of Lords in *British Leyland Motor Corpn Ltd v Armstrong Patents Co Ltd*[1]. The case concerned an exhaust system copied by Armstrong Patents Co from British Leyland's exhaust system by means of reverse engineering. It was held that the copied exhaust system infringed British Leyland's copyright in the design drawings for their exhaust system. Under the 1956 Act, the copyright in an artistic work extended to the reproduction of a purely functional object by means of indirect copying of a design drawing of the object. This was so even though the design might not be capable of registration as a registered design under the 1949 Act. In giving its majority decision, the House of Lords recognised the harshness and anti-competitive nature of the existing law. It introduced an exception to copyright protection which became known as the 'spare parts exception', based upon the principle of derogation from grant. The effect of this was that British Leyland's design copyright was subject to the right of a purchaser of a car manufactured by them, and, of any subsequent owner of the car, to keep the car in good repair, which required that the purchaser had access to a free market in spare parts for the car. British Leyland were not entitled to use their copyright so as to maintain a monopoly in the supply of spare parts.

In summary, following the *British Leyland* decision and before the CDPA, copyright protection for industrial designs was as follows:
- design drawings themselves, if original, were protected as artistic works for life plus 50 years;
- non-functional designs, ie which were capable of registration under the 1949 Act, were entitled to copyright protection for 15 years from the date of first marketing of articles made to that design;
- solely functional designs which were not capable of registration as registered designs, eg the British Leyland exhaust pipe, were protectable for the life of the designer plus 50 years;
- spare parts were subject to the *British Leyland* spare parts exception.

The law as interpreted in *British Leyland* was much criticised by the judges in that case and in the subsequent Privy Council decision of *Interlego AG v Tyco Industries Inc*[2] because of the extreme period of protection given to functional designs which would normally be less meritorious for protection than aesthetic designs which could be registered under the 1949 Act. The life plus 50-year period of protection for functional designs was commercially unnecessary and hindered competition.

1 [1986] AC 577.
2 [1989] AC 217.

Part II: Post-1988 protection

15.03   The scheme of the CDPA was:

- to extend the period of protection for aesthetic designs registered under the 1949 Act to a longer maximum period of 25 years from the existing 15-year maximum period of protection;
- for a new unregistered design right to have no more than a 15-year period of protection; and
- for industrially exploited artistic works to have copyright protection for 25 years.

Under the transitional provision of the CDPA existing design copyright for designs created before 1 August 1989 could extend for a maximum of ten years until 1 August 1999. In addition, licences of right would be available in the final five-year term of the maximum outstanding period of copyright protection. Licences of right would be available from 1 August 1994.

Differences between Registered Design protection under the 1949 Act and Unregistered Design protection

	Registered Design	Unregistered Design Right
1	Subject to official examination at Designs Registry.	Arises automatically subject to qualification.
2	Registrable at Designs Registry.	Not registrable.
3	Must be novel.	Need not be novel but a requirement of 'original' creation; must be created independently and not be 'commonplace'.
4	Infringement does not require copying.	Infringement requires copying.
5	Maximum term 25 years.	Maximum term 15 years.
6	Governed by Registered Designs Act 1949 as amended.	Governed by Part III of CDPA.
7	In general the rights granted can overlap with unregistered rights.	

Part III: Copyright in industrially applied artistic works

Industrial copyright

15.04 Articles which are themselves artistic works still acquire copyright protection if they are original and can be brought within the definition of artistic works in s 4 of the CDPA.

Section 4(1) provides:

'In this Part "artistic work" means–

    (a)   a graphic work, photograph, sculpture or collage, irrespective of artistic quality,

    (b)   a work of architecture being a building or a model for a building, or

    (c)   a work of artistic craftsmanship'.

Section 4(2) defines further the concept of a 'graphic work', which is expressed to include paintings, drawings, diagrams, maps, charts or plans as well as engravings and etchings, whilst a sculpture is expressed to include a cast or model made for the purposes of sculpture.

15.05 Of most practical importance are works of artistic craftsmanship and sculptures manufactured industrially in three-dimensional form ('industrial' in this context means mass-produced).

Examples include jewellery, designer clothes, designer crockery, cutlery and furniture. The scope of works of 'artistic craftsmanship' was construed narrowly by the House of Lords in *Hensher v Restawile*[1], where the subject matter was a suite of furniture. A level of artistic intent or attainment by the designer is necessary for protection to be available in this category of copyright. In a subsequent case[2], where a raincape was held not to be a work of artistic craftsmanship, the test was interpreted as to whether the designer possessed the conscious purpose of creating a work of art.

The nature of the work produced industrially appears not to matter provided that it constitutes a reproduction of a substantial part of the artistic work. Thus in *Oakley Inc v Animal Ltd*[3] Peter Prescott QC (sitting as a Deputy High Court Judge) referred to the example of the author of a sculpture (an artistic work) licensing the reproduction of the sculpture as mass-produced garden gnomes. The gnomes would be subject to copyright protection for a term of 25 years.

By s 52(2) of CDPA the period of protection for artistic works manufactured by an industrial process is limited to 25 years from the date of marketing such articles in the UK or elsewhere.

1   [1976] AC 64.

2   *Merlet v Mothercare plc [1986] RPC 115, CA.*
3   [2005] EWHC 210 Ch.

Part IV: The harmonised UK registered design system

15.06   The system of design registration established in the Registered
Designs Act 1949 was generally continued by the 1988 Act. Schedule 4
to the CDPA incorporates an amended Registered Designs Act 1949 in
its entirety. The main change introduced by the CDPA was to extend the
maximum period of protection for registered designs to 25 years instead
of the previous 15 years maximum and is consistent with the 25-year
period of copyright protection for 'artistic works applied industrially'
under s 52 of the 1988 Act.

The underlying purpose of the registered design system was originally to provide a system of registration for aesthetic designs applied
industrially.

The 1949 Act was amended by the Registered Designs Regulations 2001 ('the 2001 Regulations'), which came into force on
9 December 2001. The 2001 Regulations were intended to implement
the Registered Design Harmonisation Directive 98/71/EC. The 2001
Regulations amend the 1949 Act on a line-by-line basis, but have been
criticised as being 'like a sculptor crafting a cat out of a dog'.

In *Oakley Inc v Animal Ltd*[1] an attack was made on the validity of the
2001 Regulations on the basis that the Secretary of State in implementing them had acted ultra vires her power under the European Communities Act 1972. In a judgment of constitutional importance Mr Peter
Prescott QC (sitting as a Deputy High Court Judge) rejected this
contention in respect of the 2001 Regulations in their entirety but
nevertheless found that regs 12(2) and 12(3) were ultra vires, so that the
amended law did not apply in respect of applications for regulation
after 28 October 2001 and before 9 December 2001. Thus the law
existing prior to the 2001 Regulations in respect of validity and rights
given by registration, the period of protection and the terms of pre-
existing times will apply to applications for registration made before
9 December 2001.

1   [2005] EWHC 210 Ch.

Definition of design

THE OLD LAW BEFORE THE 2001 REGULATIONS

15.07   By s 1(1) of the 1949 Act, 'a design' was defined as meaning:

'Features of shape, configuration, pattern or ornament applied to an article by any industrial process, being features which in the finished article appeal to and are judged by the eye'.

It should be noted that the definition was amended by the CDPA to remove the qualifying adverb 'solely' from the phrase 'judged by the eye'.

What is registered is not the design itself but the article incorporating the design. The design must therefore be registered separately for various kinds of articles incorporating the same design. In *Sifam v Sangamo*[1] 'an article' was held to be 'anything intended to be sold separately'.

The meaning of the phrase 'appeal to and are judged by the eye' was considered in *Amp Inc v Utilux Pty Ltd*[2], where the House of Lords held that an electrical terminal clip for use inside a washing machine was a (solely) functional design which did not 'appeal to' nor was 'judged by the eye'. The House of Lords set out a number of general propositions, including the following:

- the eye to be considered is the 'eye of the customer' and not the 'eye of the judge';
- an article may still appeal to the eye even though it is not of aesthetic quality or a work of art;
- the intention of the designer is of value but it is not conclusive; and
- a solely functional article does not possess features judged solely by the eye since the only issue of interest to purchasers is whether the article will meet its intended function.

The issue of registrability was considered further by the Privy Council in *Interlego AG v Tyco Industries Inc*[3]. The case involved the design of children's building blocks. It was argued by Interlego that the designs of the blocks were dictated (solely) by function, which, under the 1956 Act, would have entitled the design to copyright protection for a period of life plus 50 years rather than the shorter 15-year period from the date of first marketing if it could be shown that the design of the bricks was capable of registration under the 1949 Act. The Privy Council held that an article qualified as a design under the 1949 Act if its features or configurations, taken as a whole, had 'eye-appeal' even though there were some features which were dictated by purely functional require-ments. The shape of the bricks was found to have not only eye-appeal but also significant features of outline and proportion which were not dictated by any mechanical function which the brick had to perform as part of the construction set. In summary, therefore, unless every feature of the design is dictated by the function which the article is to perform, the design of the article is in principle capable of registration as a registered design under the 1949 Act.

A further amendment was made by the CDPA to s 1(3) of the 1949 Act to the effect that a design shall not be registered if the 'appearance of the article is not material, that is, if aesthetic considerations are not normally taken into account to a material extent by persons acquiring or using articles of that description, and would not be so taken into account if the designs were applied to the article'. This amendment has the effect of removing from protection under the 1949 Act many household articles which might otherwise be registrable on the basis that their design is not dictated by function. For example, the case of *Gardex v Sorata*[4], where the design of the underside of a shower tray was held to be registrable, would now be decided differently.

1   [1973] RPC 899.
2   [1972] RPC 103.
3   [1989] AC 217.
4   [1986] RPC 623.

THE NEW LAW AFTER THE 2001 REGULATIONS

15.08   The definition of a design has been broadened to cover:

'the appearance of the whole or a part of a product resulting from the features of, in particular, the lines, contours, colours, shapes, texture or materials of the product or its ornamentation'. (Section 1(2).)

'A product' is defined as:

'any industrial or handicraft item other than a computer program; and, in particular, includes packaging, get-up, graphic symbols, typographic type-faces and parts intended to be assembled into a complex product'. (Section 1(3).)

A 'complex product' is defined as:

'a product which is composed of at least two replaceable component parts permitting disassembly and reassembly of the product'. (Section 1(3).)

Under the new law:

(a)   Spare and replacement parts can generally now be registered provided that the parts remain 'visible' during 'normal use' by the end user of the 'complex product' comprised of the assembled parts provided that the parts themselves satisfy the criteria for registrability (s 1B(8)).

(b)   The concept of 'dictated solely by function' is reintroduced. In general, a design can now be registered irrespective of any aesthetic merit, ie designs with an element of functionality may be registrable, though designs 'dictated solely by the product's technical function' may not be registered (s 1C(1)). This resurrects the reasoning of the House of Lords in *Amp v Utilux*[1].

(c) There is a 'must fit' exception in respect of features which must necessarily be reproduced in their exact form and dimensions so as to permit the product incorporating the design, or to which the design is applied, to be mechanically connected to another product so either can perform its function, e g auditorium seating with interlocking features which provide for multiple assembly (s 1C(2) and (3)).

(d) There is an exclusion for designs which are contrary to public policy or to accepted principles of morality (s 1D).

1   [1972] RPC 103.

Exclusions from registrability

15.09   Prior to the 2001 Regulations, the 1949 Act expressly excluded the following from registration[1]:

• Methods or principles of construction, i e the process which gives the article its appearance. For example, weaving of a basket has been held to be a method of construction, whilst the surface ribbing on a hot water bottle has been held to be a design feature rather than a production feature.

• Features dictated by function (see above).

• Features of shape which are dependent upon the appearance of another article of which the article is intended by the author of the design to form an integral part. The effect of this exception is that designs for spare parts, such as car body panels which must fit both with the rest of the body structure and with the design of the car body as a whole, are not normally capable of registration. This should be contrasted with car accessories such as mirrors or alloy wheels, which are likely to be sold separately and registrable in their own right. This so-called 'must match' exception was therefore introduced to prevent the registration of a design whose purpose is to enable the article to which the design has been applied to fit with some other article. This section was considered by the House of Lords in *Re Ford Motors Designs*[2] in which their Lordships excluded from registration articles which had 'no independent life as an article of commerce'.

• Designs contrary to law or morality. Section 4(1) of the 1949 Act excludes designs from registration which in the opinion of the Registrar would be contrary to law or morality. This section was considered in *Masterman's Design³*, where the court on appeal from the Registrar held that the design of an obscene model doll of a Scotsman wearing a kilt did not offend against morality.

- Designs excluded under r 26 of the Registered Design Rules 1989, including sculptures, wall plaques, medallions and printed matter primarily of a literary or artistic character.

1   At s 1.
2   [1995] RPC 167.
3   [1991] RPC 89.

Novelty

15.10   Under the law prior to the 2001 Regulations a design might only be registered if it was 'new' under s 1(2) of the 1949 Act.

'a design shall not be regarded as new for the purposes of this Act if it is the same as a design–

(a)   registered in respect of the same or any other article in pursuance of a prior application, or

(b)   published in the UK in respect of the same or any other article before the date of the application, or if it differs from such a design only in material details or in features which are variants commonly used in the trade.'

For registered design purposes, the word 'published' means disclosed to the public. This can be distinguished from copyright law which uses the word in a number of different defined ways.

It has been held that the whole design need not be new to qualify for registration. It should be noted that the concept of 'new' is not the same concept as 'originality' in copyright. The design will not be new if it differs only in immaterial respects or by way of common trade variants from a prior design.

A consequence of the requirement of novelty is that registration may be the subject of attack because the design is not new. Because prior publication of the design would defeat novelty, provision is made that prior publication does not arise in certain circumstances including:

- disclosure in breach of a duty of confidentiality or in breach of good faith;
- disclosure with the proprietor's consent at an exhibition certified by the Secretary of State for Trade; or
- communication of the design to a government department to allow its merits to be assessed.

Under the 2001 Regulations applicable to registrations applied for from 9 December 2001:

(a) The design must be 'new' and have 'individual character' (s 1B(1)).

(b) The novelty of a design will now be defeated by prior disclosure anywhere in the world not as formerly just in the United Kingdom (s 1B(5)).

(c) The prior disclosure need not be of an identical design. A similar design differing in 'immaterial details' may be effective prior art, destroying the novelty (s 1B(2)).

(d) By way of defence, a 12-month 'grace period' has been introduced to allow a designer to market a design and ascertain its commercial value, before incurring the cost of registration (s 1B(C)).

(e) It may nevertheless be prudent to apply for registration as soon as the design is in a state capable of registration in order to obtain priority against a possible third party application for registration of a conflicting design.

(f) In considering whether a design has 'individual character' it is necessary to consider the overall impression it produces on the informed user and show that it differs from the overall impression produced on him by any design which has been made available to the public before the date of application for the registration. It is expressly provided that the degree of freedom of the designer in creating the design shall be taken into account (s 1B(3) and (4)).

Proprietorship

15.11 Registration of a design under the 1949 Act may only be applied for by a person claiming to be its original proprietor. Section 2(1) of the 1949 Act provides that the author of the design shall be treated as the original proprietor save that where a design is created in pursuance of the commission, the person commissioning the design shall be treated as the original proprietor. Where the design is created by an employee in the course of his employment, his employer is treated as the original proprietor. The author of the design is defined as the person who creates it. Provision is made for computer-generated designs (where there is no human author) so that the person who makes the arrangements which are necessary for the creation of the design, is the author. Registered designs and the rights to apply for registration are capable of assignment (s 2).

The term of protection

15.12 A registered design lasts initially for five years from the date of application but can be renewed for a maximum of four further periods of five years, to a maximum term of 25 years (s 8).

Infringement

15.13 Section 7 of the 1949 Act gives the registered proprietor an exclusive right to use the design and any design which does not produce on the informed user a 'different overall impression'. It is expressly provided that in considering the 'different overall impression on the informed user the degree of freedom of the author in creating the design shall be taken into consideration.'

Use of the design is taken to 'include' a reference to:

- the making, offering, putting on the market, importing, exporting or using of a product in which the design is incorporated or to which it is applied; or
- stocking such a product for these purposes.

The rights created are monopolistic, so that under s 7A, acts which offend against the exclusive right of the registered proprietor constitute an infringement. It is also an infringement to make anything, such as a drawing or a mould, which could enable an article to be made which infringes the design. It is not an infringement to do acts privately and for non-commercial purposes or for experimental or teaching purposes.

Proceedings may not be brought for infringement before the certificate of registration is granted.

Remedies for registered design infringement

15.14 Actions may be brought in the High Court (Patents Court) or the Patents County Court. A successful claimant would normally be entitled to:

- damages for infringement (which would probably be assessed at a separate damages inquiry); or
- an account of the profits made by the infringing defendant;
- an injunction restraining further infringement; and
- an order for the delivery-up or destruction of articles which infringe the design.

Defences to an action for infringement

15.15 A defendant to a claim for infringement would normally wish to consider defending the action on the basis that:

- the articles complained of did not infringe the design; and
- to counterclaim that the registered design was invalid because it lacked novelty so that the register should be rectified by removal of the design and marked with an indication of its invalidity.
- A limited defence is available for 'innocent infringement'.

Unjustified threats

15.16 Section 26 of the 1949 Act provides remedies for groundless threats of registered design infringement. Extreme care should be taken to ensure that an action for infringement is not threatened. 'Mere notification' of the design does not constitute a threat. A person threatened can:

- claim against the proprietor or any person (including professional advisers) making the threat, that the threats are unjustified; and
- seek an injunction to restrain continued threats; and
- seek damages to compensate for any loss suffered.

The courts have construed widely what constitutes a threat. The writer of a letter, even if acting in a professional capacity (eg a solicitor), may also have a personal liability in addition to the client. It is normally prudent therefore to do no more in open correspondence addressed to the infringer than notify of the existence of the registration.

Application for registration

15.17 An application for registration must be made by the proprietor or by an agent acting on his behalf on forms published under the Design Rules. Details of the design are normally provided by drawings, samples or photographs. A statement of novelty must be signed. The Registrar upon receiving the application must satisfy himself that the design is new. The searches are not conclusive and are not undertaken in great depth. Even if the Registrar at the time of application considers the design to be new, it may later be attacked in separate revocation proceedings in the Courts or in the Designs Registry or by way of counter claim in the infringement action. Appeals from the Registrar's decisions lie to the Registered Designs Appeal Tribunal.

Part V: UK national unregistered design right

15.18 Unregistered design right, or 'design right' as it is more commonly known, was introduced by the CDPA as a means of providing residual protection for purely functional designs such as toys, furniture, pottery, cutlery and industrial gadgets which would not qualify for protection under the 1949 Act. The scope of design right, however, is sufficiently wide so as to encompass aesthetic designs which might also be registered under the 1949 Act. The right is something of a hybrid, incorporating elements from copyright, registered designs and patent law. Overall, a registered design confers stronger rights. Ways in which a registered design differs from an unregistered design right include the following:

- the protection given by design right applies automatically to qualifying designs without the need for action by the proprietor of the design, an unregistered design comes into effect automatically. By contrast a registered design requires action by the proprietor;
- the main purpose of design right is to give relatively short-term protection (generally 10 years from the date of first marketing) to industrial designs, as opposed to a registered design which gives a relatively long-term protection to artistic design.
- registered design protection is a monopoly right, whilst unregistered design protection requires copying to establish infringement.

Definition of design right

15.19 Section 213 of the CDPA provides that design right is a property right subsisting in an original design. For this purpose, design is expressed to be the design of 'any aspect of the shape or configuration (whether internal or external) of the whole or part of an article'. The proprietor can choose to assert design right in the whole or any part of his product. A recent case used the analogy of a teapot so that the right vests in the teapot as a whole or in parts such as the spout, handle or lid or even part of the lid. It would appear that even if the part lacked 'visual significance' it would still be protected.

An unfortunate side-effect, which was surprisingly approved by the Court of Appeal in *A Fulton v Totes Isotoner (UK) Ltd*[1], is that infringement may be established in part only of the design, even though the infringing article when looked at as a whole could not be regarded as a reproduction of the protected design when looked at as a whole. It was particularly unfortunate because the Patents County Court had already found that the alleged infringing article (an umbrella case) when taken as a whole did not infringe the claimant's registered design of the whole umbrella case. The practice has grown up of pleading unregistered design infringement not merely in the design as a whole but in 'cropped' parts of the design. It has the somewhat unjust effect of a defendant not being able to evaluate the merits of the claim against it, nor of establishing whether its design infringes, until the claim against it is properly pleaded.

1   [2004] RPC 16.

Exceptions to design right

15.20   Unregistered design right does not subsist in the following:

- A method or principle of construction; see further *A. Fulton Co Ltd v Grant Barnett*[1], where Park J. considered that the design (of an umbrella case) was based on the shape or configuration produced by methods of construction of the design.
- Features, shape or configuration of an article which enable the article to be connected to or placed in, around or against another article so that either article may perform its function or which are dependent upon the appearance of another article of which the article is intended by the designer to form an integral part. These exceptions constitute the well-known 'must fit' and 'must match' exceptions.
- Surface decoration – see for example *Cow & Co v Cannon*[2], in respect of hot water bottle surface ribbing, but contrast with *A. Fulton Co Ltd v Grant Barnett*[3], where Park J surprisingly found that the raised edges of an umbrella case were not surface decoration but features of shape and configuration.
- A juxtaposition of colours. In *Lambretta Clothing Co Ltd v Teddy Smith (UK) Ltd*[4] the Court of Appeal held that a juxtaposition of colourways for the design of a tracktop could not be 'an aspect of shape or configuration' under s 213(2). The Court also held that the juxtaposition of colours did not have protection as a registered design nor under artistic copyright.

1   (2001 RPC 257).
2   (1959 RPC 240).
3   (2001 RPC 257).
4   (2005 RPC 6).

The 'must fit' and 'much match' exceptions

15.21   Features of articles that are dictated by the need to fit or interface with each other so that the two together can perform their intended function, e g car mechanical parts such as an exhaust pipe, or which are dictated by the appearance of another part with which it is required to form an integral whole, such as car body parts, are excluded from design right protection. These exceptions are influenced by the

British Leyland spare parts exception. In *Ocular Sciences Ltd v Aspect Vision Care Ltd*[1] the court held that the design of contact lenses were excluded from protection because they were designed to fit with the eyeball, which was an 'article', albeit living.

The exceptions were considered in depth by Mann J in *Dyson Ltd v Qualtex (UK) Ltd*[2], a case involving duplicate spare parts and accessories for Dyson vacuum cleaners. The judge appears to have rejected the applicability of a 'general right to repair' based upon *British Leyland* and concluded that spare parts should not be subject to some special regime but were to be treated like other commercial articles.

In considering the 'must-match' test, he held that the test to be applied was:

> 'whether there is dependency of the kind, or to the extent, which would make the overall article in question radically different in appearance if [the substitute article] were not the shape it is …The saleability of the item can be used as a sort of guide to assessment or a cross-check in any particular case.'

In considering the 'must fit exception' (which the judge pointed out was a shorthand which did not form part of the wording of s 213) the judge approved and applied *Ocular Sciences*. Thus interconnecting elements of the design will be excluded from protection even if they have another functional role in the design.

1   [1997] RPC 289.
2   [2004] EWHC 2981.

Originality

15.22   Although s 213 of the CDPA refers to design right subsisting in an 'original' design, 'original' is not defined. Section 213(4) states that a design is not 'original' if it is 'commonplace in the design field in question at the time of its creation'. The concept of 'commonplace' was considered in *Ocular Sciences Ltd v Aspect Vision Care Ltd*[1], where it was suggested that 'any design which is trite, trivial, common-or-garden, hackneyed or of the type which would excite no peculiar attention in those in the relevant art, is likely to be commonplace'.

This was considered further by the Court of Appeal in *Farmers Build Ltd v Carrier Bulk Materials Handling Ltd*[2], which held that 'originality' should be considered in the 'copyright sense' (ie not copied visibly from an earlier design). If the court is satisfied that the design has not been copied from an earlier design, then it is 'original' in the 'copyright sense'. The court then has to decide whether it is 'commonplace'. For that purpose it is necessary to ascertain how similar that design is to the design of similar articles in the same field of design made by persons other than the parties of persons unconnected with the parties.

It has not been established whether prior art necessary to establish the design field in question should be limited to the UK, or worldwide. The current leading authority Judge Fysh in the Patents County Court in *A Fulton v Totes Isotoner*[3] took the somewhat surprising view that it was limited to the UK, even though the designs in dispute were created in the Far East. Moreover, unregistered design right protection is given to designs created by designers outside the UK.

1   [1997] RPC 289.
2   [1999] RPC 461.
3   [2004] RPC 16.

Ownership of design right

15.23   Generally the designer is the first owner of design right and is defined as the 'person who creates it'. In the case of a computer-generated design, the person who makes the arrangements necessary for the creation of the design is the designer. If the design has been created in the course of employment or by commission, the employer or the commissioning party is expressed to be the first owner. If a design qualifies for protection on the basis of having been first marketed in the UK, the person (provided he is a qualified person) first marketing the articles is regarded as the first owner of the design right.

Qualification for design right protection

15.24   Complicated provisions contained in ss 217–221 of the CDPA govern the qualification for design right protection. Generally, only designs created in the UK, the EC and certain limited designated countries (mainly British dependent territories) are entitled to protection. In particular, designs created in nations such as the USA and Japan, and EEA nations such as Norway, would not normally qualify for design right protection. For a design to be protected:

- the designer must be a qualifying person; or
- the design must have been created by an employee of or commissioned by persons who were qualifying persons.

If neither of these tests apply, the first marketing of articles made to the design must have been undertaken by a qualifying person and in a qualifying country.

Qualifying person

15.25 A person will qualify if he is:

- a citizen, or subject of, or habitually resident in a qualifying country; or
- a company or other legal entity:
  (i) formed under the law of any part of the UK or a qualifying country; and
  (ii) having in any qualifying country a place of business where a substantial business activity is carried out.

Recording of the design

15.26 The right does not subsist until the design has been recorded in a design document or an article has been made to the design.

Duration of the design right

15.27 Design right lasts for 15 years from the creation of the design document or ten years from the date on which articles made to the design were placed on the market in the UK. In the last five years of the design right term, licences of right are available, which, in default of agreement, are settled by the Patent Office.

Rights granted by design right

15.28 The owner of design right is granted the exclusive right (without territorial limitation) to reproduce the design for commercial purposes by making articles to the design or by making a design document recording the design for the purpose of enabling such articles to be made.

The right is infringed by a person who does or authorises another to do anything which is within the exclusive right of the design right owner. The infringement may be direct or indirect and it is immaterial whether or not any intervening acts lead to the infringement. Provision exists for secondary infringement of design right by the import or dealing in articles in which design right exists with the knowledge by the infringer that the article is an infringing article. Infringement was considered in *C & H Engineering v Klucznik*[1], a case involving pig-fenders. The court compared the infringement in its entirety with the design and held that because the infringement embodied other features there was no infringement. There must be a copying of the design so as to reproduce articles exactly or substantially to that design.

1   [1992] FSR 421.

Remedies for infringement

15.29 The usual remedies for infringement of intellectual property rights are available including damages, injunctions and accounts of profit. In addition, in cases of flagrant infringement and taking into account any benefit accruing to the defendant, the court has jurisdiction to award additional damages. This is a similar concept to additional damages under s 97 of the CDPA in relation to flagrant infringement of copyright. Provision exists for delivery-up of infringing articles and for the disposal of infringing articles.

Part VI: European Community Registered and Unregistered design rights

15.30 These new rights are governed by Commission Regulation 2245/2002/EC implementing Council Regulation (EC) No 6/2002. This is binding in its entirety and directly applicable in all Member States. There is therefore no national implementing legislation. The Regulation creates directly enforceable rights. The Regulation is in key aspects identically worded to the Registered Design Harmonisation Directive 98/71/EEC.

In order to be protectable as a Community Design the following requirements must be satisfied:

1   The definition of 'design' must be satisfied (Art 3a).
2   The 'design' must relate to a 'product' (Art 3b).
3   The 'design' must not relate to functional features (Art 8).
4   The 'design' must be 'new' (Art 5).
5   The 'design' must have 'individual character' (Art 6).
6   The 'design' must not be contrary to public policy or morality (Art 9).

Definition of 'design'

15.31 Under Art 3(a) this is defined as 'the appearance of the whole or part of a product resulting from the features of, in particular, the lines, contours, colours, shape, texture and/or materials of the product itself and/or its ornamentation'.

Definition of 'product'

15.32 Under Art 3(b) this is defined as meaning:

'any industrial or handicraft item, including inter alia parts intended to be assembled into a complex product, packaging, get-up, graphic symbols and typographic typefaces, but excluding computer programs.'

It should be noted:

1. The definition is widely worded and includes parts intended to be assembled into a complex product, eg packaged kit-form kitchen units;
2. The inclusion of typographic typefaces reflects old-style printing plates, even though typefaces are now generally electronic.

Exclusion of technically functional features

15.33 This exclusion contained in Art 8 encompasses features of appearance of a product which are 'solely dictated by its technical function'. This is a similar exclusion to that arising in pre-1988 design copyright law. Thus the electric terminal considered in *Amp v Utilux*[1] would not attract protection. A similar interpretation was accorded by the ECJ in the trade mark case of *Philips v Remington*[2], where the court held that:

'the grounds for refusal of [trade mark] registration ...is to prevent trade mark protection from granting its proprietor a monopoly on technical solutions or characteristics of a product ...'.

1   [1972] RPC 103.
2   [2003] RPC 14.

Novelty

15.34 The requirement of novelty in Art 5, ie 'that it is new', applies to both Registered and Unregistered Community designs. The requirement of 'novelty' in UK national design right is discussed in **paragraph 15.10** above.

The operative date for establishing novelty in respect of Registered Community designs is the date of filing the application. In the case of Unregistered Community designs, it is the date on which the design 'has first been made available to the public'.

Individual character

15.35 This is an additional requirement to novelty.

Article 6 of the Regulation provides that a design shall be considered to have individual character:

'if the overall impression it produces on the informed user differs from the overall impression produced on such a user by any design which has been made available to the public'.

It is expressly provided that the 'degree of freedom of the designer in developing the design' shall be taken into consideration.

It should be noted that 'overall impression' is the key issue to be decided by an 'informed user'. This is akin to the patent law concept of a 'person skilled in the art' and suggests that the court in considering the validity of the design should rely upon expert evidence rather than reaching its own conclusion.

The date at which novelty and individual character is to be assessed will be either the date at which the unregistered Community design was first made available to the public or in the case of registered Community design the date when the application is filed.

Term of protection

15.36 Unregistered community design has a three-year term, beginning from the date when it was first made available to the public within the Community (Art 11).

Registered Community design has a term of up to 25 years from its filing date, based upon five-year increments (Art 12).

Infringement – Article 19

15.37 Registered Community design right gives exclusive rights to the design. Infringement arises in respect of the use of a design or any design 'which does not produce a different overall impression on the informed user'. In the case of unregistered Community design there is an additional requirement of 'copying', ie that 'the contested use results from copying the protected design'. Copying will not arise if the 'contested use' results 'from an independent work of creation by a designer who may be reasonably thought not to be familiar with the design'.

This suggests that UK courts will approach infringement of unregistered Community design in similar terms to their approach to copyright and unregistered (national) design right: ie independent creation will provide a defence. Some assistance is given by Laddie J. in *Mattel Inc. v Woolbro (Distributors) Ltd*[1], where in a case of unregistered Community design infringement the court admitted evidence of 'similar fact' evidence of copying.

1   [2004] FSR 12.

Application for registered Community design

15.38 Application is made to OHIM in Alicante or at the UK Designs Registry. The application must be in a prescribed form, containing details of the identity of the applicant with a representation of the design to be registered. There is no substantive examination of the design applied for. There is a possible appeal to the OHIM Board of Appeal.

Chapter 16

The protection of databases

Introduction

16.01 A database is simply a collection of information which is organised in a particular way. The word 'database' was not even mentioned in UK copyright legislation until 1997, although English courts have historically been more inclined to afford copyright protection to works which may be described as 'databases' than their other European counterparts[1]. In the UK the courts usually protected such works as 'tables or compilations'[2]. The disparity in the legal protection afforded to databases in different member states was the primary reason for the Directive on the Legal Protection of Databases[3], which was implemented in the UK by the 1997 Regulations. In brief, the 1997 Regulations protected databases as a new category of literary work protected by copyright, and also introduced an additional *sui generis* property right in databases, 'the database right'. The provisions dealing with databases as literary works were added to the CDPA by way of amendments. The provisions dealing with the sui generis right on the other hand are only to be found in the 1997 Regulations.

The owner of a database may therefore look to at least two possible tiers of protection (i.e. copyright and the database right) for his work. Compilations and tables receive yet another tier of protection. This is over and above any copyrights which exist in any material included on the database. Unfortunately the result is a fairly complex framework[4].

1   See **paragraph 2.02**.
2   Ibid.
3   The Database Directive, 96/9/EC.
4   For an interesting comparison of EU and US database protection, see Jeremy Dickman, Andrew Deutsch and Alex Battison, 'Don't Bet on It', Copyright World, April 2005.

Definition of a 'database'

16.02 For the purpose of the CDPA (as amended) a 'database' means 'a collection of independent works, data or other materials which: (a) are arranged in a systematic or methodical way, and (b) are individually accessible by electronic or other means'[1]. This closely follows the definition in the Database Directive. In this context the phrase 'or other means' suggests that databases are protected notwithstanding that they do not use electronic storage methods. So, a paper filing system or a newspaper may be capable of protection as a database.

The wording of the Database Directive recites a number of categories of work which are intended to be excluded from the definition, including computer programs used for making or operating electronic databases, recordings, films, literary and music works[2]. Under the Database Directive, a music compilation is also expressed to be outside the meaning of database[3].

1   CDPA s 3A(1).
2   Recitals 17 and 23.
3   Recital 19.

Databases as literary works

16.03 The fact that English courts have traditionally adopted a low test for originality than other European jurisdictions is discussed in detail elsewhere in this *User's Guide*[1]. For the present purposes, however, we would emphasise that in the UK 'originality' has been treated as more akin to 'originating from' than 'the intellectual creation of'. The expenditure of 'skill and labour' in the creation of a work is usually sufficient.

However, reflecting the European sensibility guiding the Database Directive, the amended CDPA imposes a requirement that a database can only be considered an original literary work if it (by reason of the selection or arrangement of its contents) 'constitutes the author's own intellectual creation'[2]. No similar criteria apply to the test of establishing whether a table or compilation should receive copyright protection. So, the effect of the 1997 Regulations was to increase the burden on a person seeking to establish that a database (as opposed to a table or compilation) qualifies for copyright protection. How onerous it will prove to establish that the database is his 'intellectual creation' has yet to be established before the English courts[3].

Nevertheless the requirement of 'intellectual creation' is an additional hurdle for rightholders. A database which is entirely the production of mechanical processes or a software program will not be protected by 'database copyright'.

Given the restrictive approach taken by the ECJ to 'database rights' in the context of sporting data (in particular horse racing data and football fixture lists), it seems likely that the creators of such data may place increasing reliance on 'database copyright' as a means of protection.

As with other literary works (except computer-generated works), the author will be the person who creates the database[4]. If the database is computer-generated, its author is the person by whom the arrangements necessary for the creation of the database are undertaken[5].

Broadly, a database which receives copyright protection may be infringed in all the ways a literary work may be infringed[6]. However, several special provisions also exist in relation to copyright databases as a consequence of the 1997 Regulations:

- *Infringing acts*: as with computer programs, the restricted act of adaptation in the context of a copyright database means an 'arrangement or altered version of the database, or a translation of it'[7].

- *Fair dealing:* use of a copyright database for research and private study may only be 'fair dealing' if the source of the material is indicated and if the research is not 'undertaken for a commercial purpose'[8].

- *Permitted acts*: copyright in a database is not infringed if a person who has the right, by licence or otherwise, to use the database (or any part of it) and does any act in exercising his rights which is necessary for the purpose of accessing and using the content of the database (or part). Significantly, this permitted act cannot be prohibited or restricted by a contract between the owner and user. Any term which purports to do so will be deemed void[9].

1   See **paragraph 3.01**.
2   CDPA s 3A(2).
3   See **paragraph s 2.02 and 3.01**.
4   See **paragraph 6.04**.
5   CDPA s 9(1), see **paragraph 10.03**.
6   CDPA s 9(3), see **paragraph 10.03**.
7   See generally **Chapters 7, 8 and 9**.
8   CDPA s 21(2)(ac), see **paragraph 7.08**.
9   See **paragraph 9.02**.
10   CDPA ss 50D and 296B, see **paragraph 9.12**.

The database right

16.04 Regardless of whether a database is capable of receiving copyright protection as a literary work, it will be protected by the sui generis 'database right' if 'there has been a substantial investment in obtaining, verifying or presenting the contents of the database'[1]. This formulation emphasises the nature of the protection offered by the database right, which is intended to protect the economic rather than the intellectual investment in its creation. Since the database right is independent of copyright, its ambit is fully delineated by the 1997 Regulations. To a large degree, the issues which arise are similar to those arising in relation to copyright and for that reason the following paragraphs are structured in a similar way to our consideration of copyright issues elsewhere in this *User's Guide*.

The meanings of the expressions 'obtaining', 'verification' and 'substantial investment' were considered in the recent case of *The British Horse-racing Board Ltd v William Hill Organisation Ltd*[2].

The BHB is the governing body for horse-racing in the UK, and oversees the compilation of a database which contains information relating to the registration of racehorses in the UK. The database is maintained on an outsourced basis using approximately 80 technicians. The information contained in the database is exploited by the granting of licences (e.g. to on- and off-course bookmakers and media organisations) which in turn make it available to the industry and to the public before and on the race day.

In advance of each day's horse-racing in the UK, data including race times and lists of runners and riders will have been forwarded to various subscribers in electronic form by way of a 'declarations feed'. Without this information, bookmakers would in all likelihood be unable to accept bets on races.

William Hill used this data throughout its betting offices and via the internet. William Hill took no licence to use the data on its website.

The information on the William Hill website encompasses only a small part of the information contained within the BHB database and is also arranged in a different way. The information obtained from the BHB database could also be found elsewhere in media such as newspapers.

The BHB issued proceedings against William Hill in the English courts on the basis that the latter had infringed the former's database right. The BHB claimed that William Hill's daily use of the information was an extraction or re-utilisation of a substantial part of its database. Alternatively, if the amount of information was considered insubstantial, the BHB argued that repeated extraction and re-utilisation violated Art 7(5) of the Database Directive (see below)[3].

The Court of Appeal referred 11 questions concerning the interpretation of the Directive to the ECJ.

The ECJ held that to qualify for protection under the Database Directive, there must be a 'substantial investment' (qualitative and/or quantitative) in creating the database. The relevant investment is restricted to that involved in 'the obtaining, verification or presentation of the contents'; that is the 'seek[ing] out existing independent materials and collect[ing] them in the database'. It does *not* include the actual 'creation as such of independent materials'.

The court had the following to say on the meaning of 'obtaining', 'verification' and 'substantial investment' for these purposes:

- *'Obtaining'*: this term does not cover the actual production or generation of the data, but rather its collection and screening. Therefore, the selection of horses for specific races relates to data rather than database creation, and falls outside the scope of 'obtaining'; it cannot be taken into account when assessing whether there was substantial investment in the creation of the database.

- *'Verification'*: again, this term is to be interpreted so as to apply only to data which already forms the contents of the database, not the checking of data before it becomes part of the database. It is essentially a matter of monitoring the materials in a database for completeness and accuracy and includes ensuring the database is up to date. As the checks carried out before entering a horse in a race are made at the stage of creating the list for the race in question, they constitute investment in the creation of data, and not in the verification of the contents of the database in which the list appears.

- *'Substantial investment'*: the ECJ took the view that the collection, arrangement, organisation and verification of information in a database could, even if the maker was also the creator of the raw data, amount to substantial investment. However, the process undertaken by the BHB was not viewed as involving no 'investment' on its part[4].

More recently, the Court of Appeal heard arguments (made for BHB) that the ECJ had misunderstood the primary facts concerning BHB's database by virtue of the distinct steps taken in generating the database: BHB's investment had been mainly in gathering and verifying existing independent materials[5]. The Court held that the ECJ had ruled out BHB's attempts to 'deconstruct the nature of the ultimate database' in this way, and refuted BHB's arguments[6].

1   1997 Regulations, reg 13(1).
2   *Case C-203/002 Reference for a preliminary hearing under Article 234 EC, from the Court of Appeal on the case of British Horse-racing Board Limited & Others v the William Hill Organisation Ltd.* The reader should note that, as a consequence of this decision, the Commission is (inter alia) considering reviewing or repealing the database right.

3   See **paragraph 16.08.**
4   For an analysis of the ECJ's judgement on the BHB and Football Fixtures cases, see Davidson and Hugenholtz, 'Football Fixtures, Horseraces and Spin-offs. The ECJ authenticates the Database Right' [2005] EIPR 1.
5   Counsel for BHB, Peter Prescott QC, unsuccessfully sought to distinguish the BHB 'pre-race data' from three other references to the ECJ made in the context of football fixtures on the basis that football fixture lists are 'actually created by the relevant football authority', the BHB data was only 'gathered in' rather than 'created'.

The football fixtures references were: *Fixtures Marketing v OPAP Case C-444/02 [2005] IPLT 453, Fixtures Marketing v Oy Veikkaus Case C-46/02, [2005] IPLT 490 and Fixtures Marketing v Svenska Spel Case C-338/02 [2005] IPLT 520.*

6   Judgment of the CA, *(1) BHB, (2) The Jockey Club (3) Weatherleys Group Ltd and William Hill Organisation Ltd [2005] EWCA (CW) 863.*

Database right: ownership

16.05   The first owner of a database right is the 'maker' of the database[1]. Again, in line with the aim of protecting the 'risk taker' behind the database, 'maker' is defined for these purposes as the 'person who takes the initiative in obtaining, verifying or presenting the contents of a database and assumes the risks of investing in that obtaining, verification or presentation'[2]. If all these functions are undertaken by more than one person, then the database will be considered a work of joint authorship so that the database right will vest jointly in all those persons[3].

As with copyright works, the first owner of the database right in work undertaken by an employee in the course of his employment will (in the absence of an agreement to the contrary) be the employer[4]. It seems likely therefore that the case law considering the ambit of the analogous copyright principle will also be relevant here[5]. The Crown is deemed to be the maker of a database where the database is made by an officer or servant of the Crown in the course of his duties[6]. Similarly, if a database is made by or under the direction of the House of Commons or the House of Lords, the owner will be deemed to be the relevant House. If both, the Houses of Parliament will be joint makers[7].

1   1997 Regulations, reg 15.
2   1997 Regulations, reg 14(1).
3   1997 Regulations, reg 14(5).
4   1997 Regulations, reg 14(2).
5   See **paragraphs 10.11 and 10.12.**
6   1997 Regulations, reg 14(3).
7   1997 Regulations, reg 14(4).

Database right: qualification

16.06   The qualification criteria for the database right differ significantly from copyright works. The database right is a creature of EU law and thus protection is only afforded to works which, in essence, qualify as of European origin. To qualify for the database right, the maker (or one of the joint makers) of the database must, at the material time, be a natural person who is a national of or resident in an EEA state, a body (e.g. a limited company) incorporated under the laws of an EEA, or a partnership or other unincorporated body formed under the laws of an EEA state[1]. Where the maker is an incorporated body, or a partnership or other unincorporated body, there is an additional requirement that it has its 'central administration or principal place of business' in the EEA, or that its registered office is in the EEA and its operations 'are linked on an ongoing basis with the economy of an EEA state'[2].

1   1997 Regulations, reg 18(1).
2   1997 Regulations, reg 18(2).

Database right: duration

16.07   The right continues until expiry of the later of 15 years after the end of the year of its completion, or 15 years after the end of the year it is first made available to the public (provided that period starts within 15 years after the end of the year of its completion)[1]. So if a database is completed on 31 December 2000, but not made available to the public until 31 December 2015, the database right will survive until 31 December 2030. It is in the nature of most databases that they are periodically reviewed and updated. If the revision is sufficient to qualify for protection in its own right[2] then it will receive a database right of itself for its own period of protection[3].

1   1997 Regulations, reg 17.
2   I.e. there is sufficient investment; see **paragraph 16.04**.
3   1997 Regulations, reg 17(3).

Database right: restricted acts and infringement

16.08   Under the terms of the Database Directive, the maker of a database has a right to 'prevent extraction and/or re-utilisation of the whole or of a substantial part, evaluated qualitatively and/or quantitatively, of the contents of that database'[1].

The Directive continues by stating that additionally:

'the repeated and systematic extraction and/or re-utilisation of insubstantial parts of the contents of the database implying acts which conflict with a normal exploitation of that database or which unreasonably prejudice the legitimate interests of the maker of the database shall not be permitted.'[2]

Under the CDPA (as amended by the 1997 Regulations), the database right is infringed if a person *extracts* or *re-utilises* all or a substantial part of the contents of a database without the owner's consent[3].

For these purposes, 'extraction' is defined as: 'the permanent or temporary transfer of those contents to another medium by any means or in any form', and 're-utilisation' means 'making those contents available to the public by any means'[4].

So, copying a substantial part of a qualifying electronic database of telephone numbers onto a computer hard disk, or printing out hard copies, or converting, say, a database of addresses into labels to be attached to envelopes, would amount to 'extraction' and infringe the database right if undertaken without the owner's consent. Similarly, including an extract in a broadcast or distributing copies to the public would constitute '*re-utilisation*' and so infringe the database right in the absence of consent.

The ECJ in *BHB v William Hill* also discussed what constituted 'extraction', 're–utilisation' and 'substantial part':

- '*Extraction*' and '*re-utilisation*': these concepts are to be given a wide definition. The terms must be interpreted as referring to any act of appropriating and making available to the public (without the database maker's consent) the results of the maker's investment. The terms do *not* imply direct access to the database concerned. To do so would leave the database maker without protection from unauthorised copying from a copy of the database.'

  However, the protection provided within the concepts of 'extraction' and 're-utilisation' does *not* cover the mere consultation of a database by an unauthorised third party. Therefore, if a database (or part of it) is made accessible to the public, the maker's sui generis right does not allow him to prevent third parties from consulting that database. However, simply because the contents of a database is made available to the public by its maker or an authorised third party, it does not mean that the maker loses its right to prevent acts of extraction and/or re-utilisation of the contents.

- '*Substantial part of the contents of that database*': whether the part of the database that has been extracted or re–utilised is substantial can be judged by reference to quantitative and/or qualitative assessments.

In order to decide whether the part is quantitatively substantial the court will first consider its size relative to the entire database. If it is 'significant', the investment in the database's creation becomes important; if this is substantial, then the investment in the part in question will be, proportionately, equally substantial.

In a qualitative assessment, the scale of investment in the obtaining, verification or presentation of the *actual part* in question is relevant. This is regardless of whether that part represents a quantitatively significant portion of the contents of the protected database. Neither the intrinsic value of the data contained within the part nor the investment in the creation of the data itself is relevant to the question of whether or not that part is qualitatively substantial.

As the materials on the William Hill website which derived from the BHB database represented 'only a very small proportion' of the whole database, they did not amount to a quantitatively substantial part.

As the materials extracted and re-utilised by William Hill on its website did not require the BHB to put in investment *independent* of the resources required for their creation, it was held that they did not represent a qualitatively substantial part of the BHB database.

The ECJ also concluded that the inclusion of the concept of an 'insubstantial part' in the Database Directive was designed to prevent circumvention of the protection since repeated and systematic extractions and/or re-utilisations of insubstantial parts of the contents of a database can have the same cumulative effect on the maker's investment as a single extraction and/or utilisation of a substantial part. If such unauthorised acts would lead to the reconstitution of the database or a substantial part of it, then they are prohibited irrespective of their purpose.

The unauthorised extraction and re-utilisation of materials from the BHB database was repeated and of a systematic nature. However, the ECJ held that there was no prospect of William Hill reconstituting and making available to the public the whole or substantially the whole BHB database so as to seriously prejudice BHB's investment in the database.

1   Database Directive, Art 7(1).
2   Database Directive, Art 7 (5).

3   1997 Regulations, reg 16.
4   1997 Regulations, reg 12(1).

Database right: avoiding contractual limitations

16.09   A term which purports to limit the extraction or re-utilisation of a database by a 'lawful user' (i.e. a person having a right to use the database, either because of licence or otherwise) is void[1].

1   1997 Regulations, reg 19(2).

Database right: exceptions to infringement and permitted acts

16.10   Fewer exceptions to database right infringement are provided by the 1997 Regulations than are provided in relation to copyright infringement. There is, for example, no exception for 'fair dealing' for the purpose of criticism, review or news reporting, or in relation to libraries and archives. However, extraction of a substantial part of a database which has already been made available to the public is permitted if the person making that extraction is otherwise a lawful user of the database (e.g. it has licence from the owner), the source is indicated, and the extraction takes place for the purpose of providing an illustration for teaching or research (other than for commercial purposes)[1]. A number of other exceptions to database infringement are set out in the 1997 Regulations. Essentially, these relate to public administration. So, the database right is not infringed by things done in relation to Parliamentary or judicial proceedings, Royal Commissions and statutory inquires, or by extraction from databases open for public inspection or on official registers. Similarly, there are limited rights enabling the Crown to extract and re-utilise substantial parts of databases communicated to it by the owner for a public purpose, if that use could reasonably have been anticipated by the owner, enabling the use of public records and undertaking acts for which statutory authority has been granted[2].

At least one writer has argued that one unintentional effect of the 1997 Regulations is to undermine the reporting and library exceptions to copyright generally[3].

1   1997 Regulations, reg 20(1).
2   1997 Regulations, Sch 1.
3   See John Adams, Opinion [1999] EIPR Issue 8.

Database right: assumptions and presumptions

16.11   The database right will not be infringed by an extraction or re-utilisation of substantial parts of a database if:

'(a)   it is not possible by reasonable inquiry to ascertain the identity of the maker, and

(b)   it is reasonable to assume that the database right has expired'[1].

Also, there is a rebuttable presumption that where a name purporting to be the maker's name, or a year of first publication, is recorded on copies of a database, it will be correct, and that (in essence) that author has not created the database during the course of one of a number of specific relationships (such as employment) by which a third party is the first owner of the database right[2].

1   1997 Regulations, reg 21(1).
2   1997 Regulations, reg 22.

Database right: remedies

16.12   With the exception of the lack of any right to require delivery up or seizure, the remedies available for infringement are the same as copyright infringement, as are the rights of exclusive licensees[1]. There are no express criminal remedies.

1   1997 Regulations, reg 23; see **paragraphs 8.11** et seq.

Database right: licensing

16.13   Licensing schemes and bodies are considered in detail elsewhere in this *User's Guide*[1]. The 1997 Regulations provide for licensing bodies to conduct schemes in relation to the database right, which will be subject to the jurisdiction of the Copyright Tribunal[2].

1   See **paragraphs 13.02** et seq.
2   1997 Regulations, regs 24 and 25.

Database right: transitional provisions

16.14   The 1997 Regulations apply to all databases, whenever created[1], although acts done prior to commencement on 1 January 1998, or afterwards pursuant to pre-existing agreements, will not infringe the database right[2]. Also, copyright databases which were created on or before 27 March 1996 and were still in copyright immediately prior to 1 January 1998, will continue to receive copyright protection during the full copyright term[3]. For databases completed on or after 1 January 1993, which receive a database right as of 1 January 1998, that right will continue for 15 years following 1 January 1998[4].

1   1997 Regulations, reg 27.
2   1997 Regulations, reg 28.
3   1997 Regulations, reg 29.
4   1997 Regulations, reg 30.

Part 2

Copyright in use

Chapter 17

Publishers and printers

Introduction

17.01 Publishers and printers deal mainly with literary and artistic works and, to a lesser degree, with dramatic and musical works. This chapter highlights some of the special copyright problems they encounter. However, much of **Part 1** of this *User's Guide* is applicable to publishers[1]. Please note that issues regarding newspapers, magazines and periodicals are dealt with separately[2]. Electronic publishing is also dealt with separately[3].

1 References to those paragraphs particularly applicable to publishers and printers are listed in **paragraph 17.16.**
2 See **Chapter 18**.
3 See **Chapter 26**.

Definitional Issues

17.02 'Literary work' is defined by the CDPA as meaning:

'any work, other than a dramatic or musical work, which is written, spoken or sung, and accordingly includes:

(a)   a table or compilation other than a database; and
(b)   a computer program;
(c)   preparatory design material for a computer program; and
(d)   a database'[1].

'Writing' is defined as including 'any notation or code, whether by hand or otherwise, and regardless of the method by which, or medium in or on which, it is recorded, and "written" shall be construed accordingly'[2].

Other significant activities include 'adaptation'[3] and 'publication'[4].

Definitions applicable to 'artistic works' (relevant in the case of book illustrations) are considered in detail elsewhere in this *User's Guide*[5].

1   CDPA s 3(1).
2   CDPA s 178.
3   See **paragraph 7.08**.
4   CDPA s 21(3)(a) and see **paragraphs 4.05 and 4.06**.
5   See **paragraph 2.06**.

Ownership

17.03   The owner of copyright in a book is the author, even if the book is specially commissioned[1]. If the publisher wishes to be the first owner (and this has certain advantages for him) of a book he has commissioned, then the commissioning agreement must provide that copyright is assigned to the publisher[2]. Future copyright can be assigned even though it is not in existence at the time when the assignment is made[3].

In practice, books often contain contributions from several people, including illustrators, photographers, editors, designers and typesetters as well as a primary author. In the book publishing industry it is, in most cases (the educational sector is a common exception), unusual for the publisher to acquire more than an exclusive licence from authors who are not staff writers. In the case of contributions by staff members, the copyright in any literary, dramatic or artistic work which is produced in the course of employment will belong to his employer without requiring any special assignment[4]. Nevertheless, publishers should have written contracts of employment with staff writers, illustrators and editors who make contributions to avoid disputes as to whether their work was in fact done in the course of employment[5].

In some cases, the use of artistic works as illustrations may be cleared on a collective licensing basis through the Design and Artists Copyright Society[6].

1   See **paragraph 10.02**.
2   See **paragraph 10.22**.
3   See **paragraph 10.25**.
4   See **paragraphs 10.12** et seq.
5   See **paragraph 10.13**.
6   See **Appendix 1**.

Quotations and acknowledgements

17.04   When including quotations in a book, the question for the author/publisher is: 'Does the quotation used constitute substantial part of the original work?'[1]. If it does, then it will be necessary to obtain a licence from the author of the original work to use the quotation[2].

If the use falls within the fair dealing exception of criticism or review, it will still be necessary to make a 'sufficient acknowledgement' to the author of the original work[3]. However, if the quotation is so short as not to constitute a substantial use of the original work, it is not necessary to make a sufficient acknowledgement, even if the use would constitute fair dealing.

The common, but not uniform practice, is for the publisher and not the author to decide whether an acknowledgement for a quotation from another work is required. If so, the publisher will usually seek consent for the use of the quotation from the publisher of the work quoted, even though, as a matter of law, he may not consider any consent or even any acknowledgement is necessary.

1 See **paragraph 8.07**.
2 Unless the quotation is used for the purpose of criticism or review in the book, so that the use is 'fair dealing'; see **paragraphs 9.03 et seq.**
3 See **paragraph 9.07**.

Foreign authors

17.05 Where there is any doubt as to the ownership of a work written by a foreign author, legal advice should be sought in the country concerned. In the case of works written by authors resident in, or citizens of, the USA, or which have first been published in the USA, it is advisable to arrange for a search to be made at the Library of Congress in Washington. There are a number of firms in Washington specialising in this service. The charges are a few hundred dollars, the precise amount depending upon the urgency and complexity of the search[1].

1 See **Appendix 1** for details of one such firm: Thompson and Thompson.

Assignments and licence

17.06 An assignment of copyright from an author invariably offers better protection for a publisher of a copyright work than a mere licence[1]. However, when a publisher takes rights from an author it is unlikely that, unless there are unusual circumstances, or in certain sectors such as educational publishing, he will require (or in any event obtain from a well-advised author) more than an exclusive licence.

When a publisher takes rights from another publisher, it is advisable to undertake 'due diligence' to ensure that the principal publisher has the rights which he purports to own (e.g. requiring him to provide a copy of his agreement with the author). If it is intended to make any use of the work in the USA, a search at the Library of Congress should also be made[2].

In most cases an assignment from one publisher to another will apply only to some of the restricted acts applicable to the book. In practice the document describing itself as an assignment should be used, whenever this is intended by the parties.

When an assignment or licence comes to an end (remembering that an assignment can be limited in point of time)[3] there is an issue as to what happens with any stock remaining unsold. If the publisher continues to sell copies after the expiry of his assignment or licence, he will infringe the restricted act of issuing copies to the public[4]. It is therefore vital that any limited term licence of assignment deals adequately with the need for a 'sell-off' period after the end of the term.

If a publisher takes an assignment or licence of publishing rights, he will not necessarily be obliged to publish the book, but an obligation to publish may be inferred under certain circumstances. If a publisher enters into a contract with an author under which he is given the exclusive rights to the author's works over a period of time and the publisher does not accept any obligation to publish the works during that period but only to pay a royalty in the event of publication, then the court may hold that such a contract is unenforceable as being 'a restriction of trade' or oppressive against public policy. The reason for this is that such a contract, if enforced against an author, would prevent him from earning his living by writing books for other publishers, even though the publisher with whom he had entered into a contract was refusing to publish his works.

It is therefore vital for both parties to a publishing agreement to express the extent of the publisher's obligation to publish (or otherwise to exploit) the author's work.

1   See **paragraph 10.22**.
2   See **paragraph 10.21**.
3   See **paragraph 10.23**.
4   See **paragraph 7.04**.

Ownership of manuscripts

17.07 The manuscript of a work will belong to the author, unless there is an agreement to the contrary. Ownership of the manuscript is unrelated to ownership of copyright[1] in the work embodied in the manuscript. Even if there is an outright assignment of the publishing rights, the publisher will have no rights over the manuscript although, leaving the manuscript with another person may eventually result in a deemed abandonment of the property on the manuscript. On the other hand, the person owning the manuscript has no right to publish it, as long as it is in copyright.

If an author fails, or refuses, to deliver a manuscript in accordance with the terms of a publishing agreement, the publisher is entitled to sue him for damages or, if it can be shown that the author in fact completed the book, the publisher can obtain an order of the court requiring the author to deliver the manuscript. If the author has not yet written the book, the rights of the publisher are limited to damages. A court will not order an author to write a book. Today publishers normally require manuscripts to be delivered in electronic form, and often require the author to maintain a back-up copy.

1   See **paragraph 10.01**.

Reversionary copyright

17.08   Assignments and licences of copyright made by authors before 1 July 1957 become ineffective on the expiration of 25 years from the date of the death of the author even if the author did not die until after June 1957. At that point in time the rights in the work revert to the estate of the author, irrespective of the existence of any assignments made in the author's lifetime. Publishers, therefore, should always obtain confirmatory assignments from the executors or administrators of the estates of those authors now dead and who assigned works to them before 1 July 1957. Alternatively, if the author is still living they can now obtain such a grant from the author himself.

Publishing agreements not considered

17.09   It is beyond the scope of this *User's Guide* to consider the terms of publishing agreements generally, although in any event, most problems arising under publishing agreements are likely to be matters of contract rather than copyright. A common difficulty with both new and existing contracts is determining how far traditional 'volume form' grants of rights for print on paper extend into new forms of digital exploitation[1].

1   See **paragraph 10.31**.

National libraries: obligation to deposit

17.10 The publisher of every book published in the UK is required to deliver, within one month after the date of publication, at his own expense, a copy of the book to the British Library Board. In addition if he receives a written demand before the expiration of 12 months from the date of publication, the publisher is required within one month after the receipt of the written demand to deliver at his own expense a copy of the book to each of the following libraries: the Bodleian Library, Oxford; University Library, Cambridge; the National Library of Scotland; the Library of Trinity College, Dublin; and the National Library of Wales, Aberystwyth[1].

Copies of trade publications do not have to be delivered to national libraries.

Foreign books printed abroad and published in England are not usually required to be delivered, unless the British publisher has his name printed in the book as a publisher.

A publisher who fails to comply with these requirements is liable to a fine.

1 See Copyright Act 1911, s 15 and the National Library of Wales (Delivery of Books) (Amendment) Order 1987, SI 1987/698.The Legal Deposit Libraries Act 2003 introduced arrangements for the deposit of electronic publications. A voluntary core of practice applies until formal regulations are agreed under that Act.

Importation of books

17.11 A book which has been published outside the UK may not be imported (except for private or domestic use) if the importer knows or has reason to believe that it is an 'infringing copy' (i.e. a copy the printing of which in the UK would have infringed the copyright of the copyright owner or an exclusive licensee of the right to make copies of the work in the UK). This is a 'secondary infringement' of copyright, the details of which are considered in detail elsewhere[1]. It should be noted that this principle is subject to the important qualification that importation of copies from another EEA state where they have been distributed with the authorisation of the owner, will not infringe copyright due to the operation of the doctrine of 'exhaustion of rights' in Europe[2].

1 See **paragraphs 7.09 et seq.**
2 See **paragraph 7.04 and 14.06.**

International copyright protection

17.12 It is most important to include the © symbol followed by the name of the copyright owner and the date of first publication on all books.

Firstly, this will assist in securing the widest possible copyright protection for the work in those countries which have adhered to the Universal Copyright Convention[1]. The notice must be placed in such manner and location as to give reasonable notice of claim of copyright. In effect this means proximate to the title page. It is not considered advisable to place the notice at the end of the work, although no precise position is stipulated in the Convention[2].

Secondly, such a notice assists in proving in an infringement action that the alleged infringer knows that the work was in copyright (it is a defence in secondary infringement actions to show that the defendant did not know that the work was in copyright)[3].

1   **Appendix 2** lists those countries.
2   See **paragraphs 4.16 and 4.18**.
3   See **paragraph 8.21**.

Published editions of work

17.13 The copyright in a published edition of a book is quite distinct from the copyright in the work itself. See the Table of Incidents of Copyright in **Appendix 4** for the period of copyright, the restricted acts, general exceptions and first owner of published editions. The publisher is the owner of the typographical arrangement, not the printer[1].

1   CDPA s 9(2)(d), and see **paragraph 10.07**.

Typefaces: exception for use of typefaces in printing

17.14 The design of a typeface is entitled to copyright protection as an artistic work[1]. However, the CDPA permits the use of typefaces which are in copyright[2] if the typeface is used in the ordinary course of typing, composing text, typesetting or printing[3]. It is not an infringement of copyright to possess a typeface for the purposes of such use or to do anything in relation to material printed by using a typeface which is in copyright[4].

However, where persons make, import, possess or deal with equipment for printing in a particular typeface, then notwithstanding this general exception, the copyright owner of the typeface can obtain remedies under the 'secondary infringement' provisions of the CDPA[5].

Where articles specifically designed or adapted for producing material in a typeface entitled to copyright protection have been marketed with the licence of the copyright owner, the copyright in the typeface expires 25 years from the end of the calendar year in which the first such articles were marketed[6].

1 **Paragraph 2.06.** Software used to display electronic fonts will also usually be protected by copyright. Users should apply such software in compliance with the relevant licence agreement. See **paragraph 18.11.**
2 CDPA s 54.
3 CDPA s 54(1)(a).
4 CDPA s 54(1)(b) and (c); see also **paragraph 9.16.**
5 See **paragraphs 7.09 et seq.**
6 CDPA s 55.

Moral rights

17.15 Authors will almost certainly wish to assert their right to be identified (the *paternity right*)[1]. This should be stated in the contract with the publisher[2]. Contracts by publishers with their sub-licensees should oblige the sub-licensees to comply with the obligation to identify the author in the same terms as those contained in the contract with the author.

The author will also usually have the right to object to the derogatory treatment of his work (the *integrity right*)[3]. Unlike the paternity rights, this right does not need to be asserted[4]. A lurid and unsuitable cover to a book may be regarded by its author as a derogatory treatment. Similarly, inappropriate artistic works in the form of photographs or illustrations to a book may be subject to the same objections. Unless the author specifically waives the integrity right in his contract with the publisher, his consent should be obtained to the covers, artwork and to any editing of the work. A publisher may seek a waiver but agree specific contractual approvals.

It is worth noting that the rights of paternity and integrity do not apply to publications in encyclopaedias, dictionaries and other collective works, which are specifically excluded from the application of these rights[5].

The right of privacy of photographs may also be relevant where publishers are including photographs in a book[6]. It is not the subject of the photograph who can object to the inclusion of a photograph on the grounds of the moral right of privacy, but the person who commissioned the taking of it. It may not always be easy to find out beyond doubt whether a photograph was specially commissioned. Therefore, publishers should seek warranties from the author, photographer or other person who is providing the photograph to the publisher to the effect that it was not commissioned, other than by the person providing the photograph himself. If the photograph was commissioned by someone else, then a waiver should be sought from that other person for the use of the photograph in the book. It should be remembered that the right to privacy of photographs only arises in the case of photographs which have been commissioned for private and domestic purposes which will narrow the field considerably. Moreover, it does not apply to photographs taken before 1 August 1989. With regard to works which were not published before 1 August 1989, but which were the subject of a contract between the publisher and the author, the manuscript of which has been delivered prior to that date, moral rights will not apply[7].

With regard to books for which there was a publishing contract completed before the commencement date, but which were not completed prior to that date, or, the work having been completed, there was no agreement entered into prior to that date, moral rights will apply. Even though the assignment may not contain an assertion of the paternity right, the CDPA permits the author to assert his rights subsequent to the assignment by an instrument in writing[8]. Therefore, if a publisher wishes to make changes to a work which was completed before 1 August 1989, but for which no agreement was entered into before that date, he should seek legal advice.

1 See **paragraphs 11.02 et seq.**
2 See **paragraph 11.08**.
3 See **paragraphs 11.12 et seq.**
4 See **paragraph 11.17**.
5 See **paragraph 11.18**.
6 See **paragraph 11.24**.
7 See **paragraph 11.32**. Privacy is considered further **in paragraph 5.06**.
8 See **paragraph 11.08**.

Generally

17.16 Reference should be made to the Table of Incidents of Copyright in **Appendix 4** for the period of copyright, restricted acts, general exceptions, and rules as to first owners applicable to literary works, artistic works, photographs, engravings and published editions of works[1].

The special problems faced by publishers in the field of copyright arise mainly in connection with assignments and licences. The problems of infringement and plagiarism which have to be faced by publishers every time they consider publishing a book are not special to publishers and reference should be made to **Part 1** for a general discussion of infringement[2].

1   The following paragraphs in **Part 1** of this *User's Guide* are also particularly
     relevant when dealing with literary works in the context of publishing:
       Definition of literary works – **2.02**;
       Definition of artistic works – **2.06**;
       Definition of graphic work – **2.06**;
       Copyright in published editions – **2.11**;
       Qualification for copyright protection – **4.01**–**4.05**;
       Fixation – **2.05**;
       Publication – **4.05**;
       Term of copyright and publication right – **6.01**–**6.06** and **6.17**–**6.30**;
       Restricted acts in literary, dramatic, and musical works – **7.02 et seq**;
       Principal exceptions and defences – **9.01**;
       Fair dealing and sufficient acknowledgement – **9.03 et seq**;
       Ownership in literary, dramatic, musical and artistic works – **10.03**;
       Ownership in published editions – **10.07**;
       Ownership in works by joint authors – **10.08**;
       Assignments and licences – **10.22 et seq**;
       Moral rights and false attribution of authorship – **11.01 et seq**.
2   See **Chapters 7 and 8**. In addition, reference should be made to **Chapter 3** as to
     originality, and **Chapter 5** as to passing off (especially in relation to titles).

Chapter 18

Newspapers, magazines and periodicals

Introduction

18.01 The main copyright issues which face the editors, journalists and other persons involved with newspapers, magazines and periodicals, concern the ownership of the copyright in the separate contributions and the quotation or re-use of copyright material from elsewhere. In the digital age, most 'print media' publishers have developed significant digital products (both 'on-line' and 'off-line'), and consequently the importance of ensuring the copyright has been adequately dealt with in publishers' arrangements with contributors has never been greater. Newspapers, magazines and periodicals will be 'compilations' of other works and as such are protected in themselves, independent of the copyright in their contents[1]. If the separate contributions which make up the whole qualify for copyright protection under the principles we have outlined in **Part 1**, they too will each be entitled to their own separate copyright. A newspaper will also constitute a 'published edition' and the typographical arrangement of the newspaper will be entitled to copyright protection. When considering what constitutes a 'published edition' for these purposes, it is necessary to consider the newspaper as a whole, not as individual articles[2].

1   See **paragraph 2.02**.
2   See **paragraph 2.11**.

Definitional Issues

18.02 There is no single definition of 'newspaper', 'magazine', or 'periodical' in the CDPA, and, therefore, normal usage should be applied. A newspaper or magazine is a publication which is published on a regular basis. In practice, it is unlikely that there will be much difficulty in determining whether or not a particular publication falls within the expression. If a learned journal, for example, was published on an occasional, rather than a regular basis, with an identical format, it might be a periodical. But such a publication, published without any regularity, and without similarity as to format (even though having the same title) may well not be a periodical for the purposes of copyright law.

Contributor's copyright

18.03 The Copyright Act 1956 contained a special provision as to the ownership of copyright in contributions to newspapers, magazines and similar periodicals. It provided that in the case of a literary, dramatic or artistic work which was made by an author in the course of his employment under a contract of service or apprenticeship by the proprietor of a newspaper, magazine or similar periodical, and made for the purpose of publication in a newspaper, magazine or similar periodical, the proprietor of the newspaper, etc, was entitled to the copyright in the work – but only in so far as the copyright related to publication in *any* newspaper etc.

The CDPA removed this special provision. The rules regarding the ownership of copyright in material produced by newspaper employees are now the same as for any other literary, dramatic, musical or artistic works produced by employees. All the copyright in works produced by such employees in the course of their employment under a contract of service vests in the employer, in the absence of any agreement to the contrary[1].

It is matter of degree in every case whether a person providing services is an independent contractor or is working under a contract of service. A writer who contributes one article a week to a newspaper, who works from home and who has reasonable choice as to the form and content of the article, may well not be working under a contract of service[2].

The ownership of the copyright in photographs is considered in detail elsewhere in this *User's Guide*[3].

The principle is the same as for text: the copyright in a photograph by a staff photographer working under a contract of service for a newspaper will usually belong to the newspaper. But copyright in photographs submitted by outsiders will vest in the person who 'created' the photograph. In the absence of special arrangements, it will not belong to the person who commissioned it[4]. Attention should also be given by publishers to the right of privacy in certain photographs[5].

Increasingly, the power of individuals to negotiate special terms, and the complexity of benefits packages made available to both employees and independent contractors, can make the question as to which category the arrangement falls into difficult to determine. Serious consequences can ensue for a publisher that does not address the issue correctly in its contractual arrangements[6].

1   See **paragraphs 10.12 et seq.**
2   See **paragraph 10.13**.
3   See the Table of Incidents of Copyright in **Appendix 4**, and **paragraphs 27.03 and 27.19**.
4   See **paragraphs 10.03 and 10.17**.
5   See **paragraphs 11.24 et seq.**
6   See **paragraphs 10.12 et seq.**

Freelance and unsolicited contributions

18.04 In the real world of newspaper publishing, the counsel of perfection in relation to 'contracts for services' will be difficult to apply in the case of work submitted by freelancers. Such work is frequently delivered under short deadlines. In these circumstances, imposing assignments or express licences of copyright may be impracticable. If there is no express agreement, it may be possible to imply a licence to use the material. The publisher, however, must be very circumspect about relying on implied licences. The key weakness is that a court will only uphold an implied licence to the extent that it is necessary to give business efficacy to the initial arrangement[1].

Similarly, it is risky to rely upon industry custom and practice. In *Banier v News Group Newspapers Ltd*[2], a newspaper relied unsuccessfully upon industry practice as a defence to a damages claim where it used a photograph without an express licence, on the basis that the photograph was needed urgently and the licence fee would be paid after the fact. Relying on industry practice will be all the more dangerous in the context of an industry, such as the newspaper industry, where standard practice is being rewritten by the movement toward digital media and electronic publishing. An implied licence may well be inadequate for the publisher wishing to make additional uses of material over and above its initial inclusion in a print publication (such as including it on an archival database or adding it to an on-line news service). One method of swinging the balance in favour of the publisher on these issues is to issue 'standard terms of acceptance' to contributors who have no written contract. In the UK the National Union of Journalists and bodies representing photographers have, however, led vocal campaigns against 'digital rights grabs'.

When an unsolicited contribution (such as a letter to the editor) is received by a newspaper, it is again a matter of construction as to whether or not the author intends the letter to be published. If there is an intention to publish, then a licence giving the newspaper the right to publish the work may be implied, but again this implied licence will be narrow in scope, its extent depending upon the circumstances.

1　See **paragraph 10.30**.
2　[1997] FSR 812.

The news

18.05　Copyright arises not because of originality of an idea or item of news, but because it is reduced to a material form. Copyright attaches to the form rather than to the idea[1]. It follows that there is no copyright in unwritten news and the only copyright which attaches to the news is the manner in which it is presented. The courts have given protection in certain cases to news agencies which sell news, but on grounds of breach of contract, or of breach of confidence, rather than copyright infringement[2].

It is common for news publishers to receive input from news and photo agencies, which form a valuable source of information and copyright material. This material will be provided under the terms of licence arrangements allowing specified uses. For the publisher, the extent of his reproduction and distribution rights under the licence will be of key concern[3], as will his ability to edit the material at his discretion. Given the general issues which arise in relation to the licensing of copyright material, a well-advised publisher will seek appropriate protections from the licensor, such as warranties that he has the right to make the material available, and suitable indemnification against breach.

It is also common practice for journalists to rewrite news stories from the information contained in other articles. In these cases, the question will be whether a 'substantial part' has been copied, or whether a defence to copyright infringement may be established on the basis of fair dealing[4].

Since the last edition of the *User's Guide*, case law has begun to reconsider the doctrine of confidentiality in the context of the Human Rights Act 1998 (including, inter alia, the balancing of 'freedom and expression' concerns (Art 10 of the ECHR) and 'privacy' concerns (Art 8 of the ECHR)), and also to consider the extent to which the Data Protection Act 1998 may be used to inhibit the publication of personal information regarding celebrities. This case law is considered in detail elsewhere in this *User's Guide*[5].

1　See **paragraphs 1.03 and 2.13**.
2　See **Chapter 5**.

3   See **paragraphs 7.02 et seq**.
4   See **paragraphs 8.06 and 9.02 et seq**.
5   See **paragraph 5.06.**

Quotations

18.06   Newspapers often quote or otherwise use other copyright material. The fact that a newspaper, having used its best endeavours to trace the owner of the copyright in the quotation, is unable so to do, does not give that newspaper the right to publish a copyright work. Copyright will be infringed if a substantial part of the original work is published. 'Substantial' does not necessarily mean substantial in proportion to total length. If it is the most important part of the original work, then a relatively short extract could be a substantial part[1].

If a substantial part is published, no effort having been made to trace the copyright owner, a newspaper can be subject to heavy damages. On the other hand, if the newspaper proprietor, having made reasonable enquiries, is unable to ascertain the identity of the author, the copyright in the work which is being quoted will not be infringed, provided that:

* copyright has expired; or
* the author died 70 years or more before the beginning of the year of publication of the relevant issue of the newspaper etc[2].

This exception does not apply to Crown copyright, nor to a work of joint authorship which is still in copyright where it would have been possible to identify one of the authors.

1   See **paragraph 8.06**.
2   CDPA s 57; see **paragraph 9.19**.

Fair dealing: reporting current events

18.07   Fair dealing with a literary, dramatic or musical work is not an infringement of the copyright in the work if it is for the purpose of reporting current events in a newspaper, magazine or similar periodical, provided it is accompanied by a sufficient acknowledgement[1].

A 'sufficient acknowledgement' means an acknowledgement identifying the work in question by its title, or other description, and also identifying the author. However, it is not necessary to identify the author if the work was published anonymously, or if in the case of an unpublished work it would not be possible to identify the author by reasonable enquiry[2].

The fair dealing provisions in the CDPA, regarding the reporting of current events, do not extend to photograph, so newspapers may not publish a photograph of some current event taken by another newspaper and then attempt to avoid a breach of copyright action by claiming the benefit of the fair dealing provisions[3].

1 See **paragraph 9.04**.
2 See **paragraph 9.07**.
3 See **Chapter 9** for a fuller discussion of these issues.

Fair dealing: criticism and review

18.08 The fair dealing provisions of the CDPA also extend to the use of all kinds of copyright works for the purpose of criticism or review provided that the work has been 'lawfully made available to the public' (following the implementation of the 2003 Regulations). Again it is necessary that the work be accompanied by a sufficient acknow-ledgement but the CDPA (as amended by 2003 Regulations) confirms that an acknowledgment is not required in certain circumstances[1].

1 See **paragraph 9.07**.

Use of notes or recordings of spoken words

18.09 The copyright in the words of an interviewee will vest in the interviewee, notwithstanding that they may be recorded by the inter-viewer. However, the CDPA contains a specific provision to the effect that it is not an infringement of the copyright in spoken words, as a literary work, to use a record of them for the purpose of reporting current events provided that certain conditions are met[1].

Where the contribution of the interviewer qualifies for copyright protection, its use will also require proper authorisation.

1 See **paragraph 9.20**.

Pseudonyms

18.10 Although there is no copyright in a title[1], if a contributor to a newspaper uses a nom de plume, on leaving that newspaper he can take the nom de plume with him. Therefore, newspaper proprietors some-times provide in contracts of service that the contributor shall have no right to use the nom de plume, except for articles written for the commissioning employer's paper.

1 See **paragraph 3.02**.

Digital issues and newspapers, magazines, periodicals

18.11 Newspapers, magazine and periodicals commonly employ digital methods for transmitting information in the process of producing and exploiting their publications, and during the life of this *User's Guide* the availability of news material on an 'on-line' basis will increase significantly. All significant newspaper publishers in the UK now have an on line presence. In terms of copyright, the real significance of all this for the publisher is to ensure that the arrangements by which he has acquired content are sufficient to enable him to include and exploit that content as part of his 'on-line' service[1], and to allow him to manipulate the content to the extent necessary for him to include it on the on-line service. Increasingly this may require the interpolation of the material with other material as part of an interactive presentation. Paying close attention to the wording of licence agreements is more necessary than ever[2].

Inevitably, the ability to exploit newspaper and similar formats 'on-line' also enables the publishers to use films and sound recordings in his service in a way previously unavailable. Issues regarding the use of films and sound recordings in on-line services are considered in detail elsewhere in this *User's Guide*[3].

Publishers should note that not merely the content, but also any software element of its electronic publication is properly cleared (eg, search engines, screen displays, software enabling manipulation etc).

Particular problems also arise in the context of the use of software for generating fonts. The CDPA provides that no copyright infringement occurs where a typeface is used in the ordinary course of typing, composing text, typesetting or printing. Nor is it an infringement to do anything in relation to material produced by such use, or to possess articles for the purpose of such use. It follows that an electronic copy which is typeset using font software will not, per se, render the publisher liable for infringement.

However if, say, the electronic transmission of material involves the transfer of font software itself, this may result in an infringement. So, for example an infringement may arise where software for generating fonts is transferred to a publisher by a person transferring a copy digitally. The publisher should therefore seek assurances from any persons making digital transfer of copy that (where font software is to be transferred) an appropriate authorisation has been obtained from the owner to allow such transfer to take place.

1   As to licensing and assigning copyright, see **Chapter 11**.
2   For a further analysis of the moral right of integrity, see **paragraphs 11.12 et seq** .
3   See **Chapter 27**.

Chapter 19

Schools, universities and other educational establishments

Introduction

19.01 Schools, universities, and all kinds of educational establishments (which for convenience are together called 'schools' in this chapter) make extensive use of copyright material. Literary, dramatic, musical and artistic works, recordings, films and broadcasts (both television and radio) are all used in schools.

In brief, the CDPA specifies certain acts in relation to each category of copyright material, which if done without the permission of the copyright owner, constitute an infringement of copyright. These acts are called 'restricted acts'[1].

The use of copyright material in schools involves doing many of these 'restricted acts'. In particular, copying works in a material form, performing works in public, making adaptations (for example, translations), causing recordings to be heard in public and causing films to be seen and heard in public are all activities regularly undertaken in schools.

However, the CDPA does contain certain special provisions which exempt schools from the restricted acts in certain circumstances. The fair dealing provisions of the CDPA also apply to educational use[2].

1 See **paragraphs 7.01 et seq.**
2 See **paragraphs 9.03–9.08**.

Definitional issues

19.02 The CDPA defines an 'educational establishment' as:

- any school; and
- any other description of educational establishment specified by statutory instrument[1].

The Copyright (Educational Establishments) Order 2005[2] sets out the classes of universities, colleges and institutes of further education that come within the definition – effectively all educational institutions are included.

The CDPA defines a 'school' as:

'(a) in relation to England and Wales, having the same meaning as in the Education Act 1996;

(b) in relation to Scotland, having the same meaning as in the Education (Scotland) Act 1962, except that it includes an approved school within the meaning of the Social Work (Scotland) Act 1968;

(c) in relation to Northern Ireland it has the same meaning as the Education and Libraries (Northern Ireland) Order 1986.'[3]

In practice, virtually every school in the UK is covered by the above Acts and the Order.

1   CDPA s 174(1).
2   SI 2005/223.
3   CDPA s 174(3).

Copying of literary, dramatic, musical and artistic works and published editions

19.03 It is an infringement of copyright to make a copy of any type of copyright work without the copyright owner's permission, unless there are provisions in the CDPA which permit copying in the relevant circumstances[1]. However the CDPA contains certain exceptions regarding the use of copyright material for educational purposes[2]. In brief, literary, dramatic, musical or artistic works may be copied, without infringing their copyright, in the course of instruction, whether at an educational establishment or elsewhere, provided that the reproduction is made by a teacher or a pupil, is *not* by the use of a reprographic process, is accompanied by a sufficient acknowledgment and provided that the instruction is for a non-commercial purpose [3].

A 'reprographic process' is defined as a process:

'(a) for making facsimile copies; or

(b) involving the use of an appliance for making multiple copies'[4].

The definition expressly includes, in relation to a work held in 'electronic form' (for example, a magnetic tape or CD-ROM) any copying by electronic means. It does *not* include the making of a film or sound recording.

A literary work in the form of a computer program or a tape recording of the reading of a play may not be copied as this would constitute copying 'a work held in electronic form by electronic means'. On the other hand, a teacher may himself film and make a sound recording of a live performance of a play.

Copyright is not infringed by anything done for the purposes of an examination[5].

The licensing of schools by the Copyright Licensing Agency is considered elsewhere in this *User's Guide*[6].

1   See **Chapter 9**.
2   CDPA ss 32–36.
3   CDPA s 32(1).
4   CDPA s 178, see **paragraph 21.01**.
5   CDPA s 32(3) see **paragraph 19.07**.
6   See **paragraph 21.10**.

Reprographic copying

19.04   Although unauthorised copying by means of a reprographic process is not permitted under the CDPA[1], limited reprographic copying by educational establishments of passages from published works is permitted, provided that they are accompanied by sufficient acknowledgement and the instruction is for a non-commercial purpose. No acknowledgement is required if it is impossible for reasons of practicality or otherwise[2]. The exception applies only to published literary, dramatic or musical works and their typographical arrangements[3].

Provided that the reprographic copies are made by or on behalf of an educational establishment for the purposes of instruction, then copies can be made of not more than 1% of any work in any quarter. A quarter is any period from 1 January to 31 March, 1 April to 30 June, 1 July to 30 September or 1 October to 31 December[4]. Copying is not permitted if, or to the extent that, licences are available which authorise the copying in question and the person making the copies knew or ought to have been aware of that fact[5]. This is a reference to blanket licences such as that entered into between the Copyright Licensing Agency and the Local Education Authorities Associations in England and Wales. However, these blanket licences may not restrict educational establishments from copying less than 1% of any work in any quarter.

1   CDPA s 32(1); see **paragraph 19.03**.
2   CDPA s 32(1) and 32(1A).
3   CDPA s 36(1) and 36(1B).
4   CDPA s 36(2).
5   CDPA s 36(3).

Recordings made by schools

19.05 Virtually all schools are equipped to make sound and video recordings. Sound recordings, films and broadcasts are protected by copyright in their own right (as distinct from the rights in the musical, dramatic, literary works, etc. which they record or contain). As for the restricted acts applicable to films, sound recordings and broadcasts, see the Table of Incidents of Copyright in **Appendix 4**.

The making of copies of films and sound recordings infringes their copyright, but there are a number of general exceptions, which are dealt with in more detail in **Chapter 9**. In particular there are certain special exceptions for the making of reproductions in material form of sound recordings and cinematograph films by schools.

Copying of sound recordings, films and broadcasts

19.06 The copying of these works by 'educational establishments' is permitted in three circumstances.

Firstly, they may be copied by making a film or film soundtrack in the course of instruction in the making of films or film soundtracks, provided that the copies are made by the person who gives or receives instruction and is accompanied by a sufficient acknowledgement and is done for a non-commercial purpose[1]. Accordingly this exception is applicable only to film schools or to other educational establishments which have special courses on the making of films or film soundtracks. For example, a school would not be permitted to make a copy of a film of *Henry V*, or even of a part of the film, in connection with lessons on that play as part of an English literature course.

Secondly, these works may be copied in connection with examinations[2].

Thirdly, there is a broader exception for the recording of broadcasts which may be recorded by educational establishments (or on their behalf) for the educational purposes of the establishment without infringing the copyright in the broadcasts themselves, or in any works included within such broadcasts, provided that it is accompanied by a sufficient acknowledgement and is done for a non-commercial purpose[3].

In addition, copyright is not infringed where a recording of a broadcast, or a copy of such a recording (whose making was not itself an infringement of copyright by virtue of the exception referred to above) is communicated to the public by a person situated on the premises of an education establishment, provided that it cannot be received outside the premises[4]. However, these exceptions do not apply unless the copying is done in accordance with the provisions of a licensing scheme.

Two such schemes have been certified.

The licensing scheme operated by the Educational Recording Agency Limited (ERA) was certified by the Copyright (Certification of Licensing Scheme for Educational Recording of Broadcasts and Cable Programmes) (Educational Recording Agency Limited) Order 1990[5], in accordance with s 143 of the CDPA. This covers the copyright works of:

- the Author's Licensing and Collecting Society Limited;
- the BBC;
- Channel 4 Television Corporation;
- Channel 5 Broadcasting Limited;
- the Design and Artist's Copyright Society Limited;
- the British Phonographic Industry Limited (which controls virtually all sound recordings sold in the UK);
- the Independent Television Network Limited (all the ITV companies);
- the MCPS[6];
- S4C (the Welsh language fourth television channel);
- the Open College.

Licences under this scheme must be obtained from the ERA. The Copyright (Certificate of Licensing Scheme for Educational Recording of Broadcasts) (Open University Educational Enterprises Limited) Order 2003 provides for schools and educational establishments to obtain licences at the fees specified in the Order to record off-air Open University television programmes.

Both schemes require the payment of fees of varying scales according to the type of programme recorded and the type of educational establishment making the recording. The provisions of the schemes are too detailed to be set out in this *User's Guide*.

1 CDPA s 32(2).
2 See **paragraph 19.07**.
3 CDPA s 35(1).
4 CDPA s 35 (1A).
5 As amended in 1993, 1994, 1996, 1998 and 1999.
6 See **Chapter 22**.

Examinations

19.07 The provisions of the CDPA are less restrictive as regards the use of the copyright works for examination purposes. Briefly, copyright is not infringed by anything done for the purposes of an examination by way of setting the questions, communicating the question to the candidates, or answering the questions, provided that the questions are accompanied by a sufficient acknowledgement (unless impossible for reasons of practicality or otherwise)[1]. This applies to all types of copyright work and is not limited to literary, dramatic, musical or artistic works; however, this does not apply to the making of a reprographic copy of a musical work for use by an examination candidate in performing the work[2].

1   CDPA s 32(3) and 32 (3A).
2   CDPA s 32(4).

Fair dealing

19.08   In considering the restrictions on copying, the fair dealing provisions[1] are relevant. In brief, 'fair dealing' with a literary, dramatic, musical or artistic work or published edition for the purposes of research for a non-commercial purpose (provided that it is accompanied by a sufficient acknowledgement) or private study, does not constitute an infringement of the copyright in the work[2].

There is no definition in the CDPA of 'private study'; and it is arguable that the exception does not apply to study at schools which is not 'private study'. It is clear that the Society of Authors and the Publishers Association take this view, in that they have said only single copies may be made.

Accordingly, it is almost certainly an infringement for a teacher to use any duplicating process to make copies of parts of works or whole works and circulate them to his pupils – except for the purposes of an examination.

1   See **paragraphs 9.03–9.07**.
2   See **paragraphs 9.03–9.07**.

School performances of plays, music

19.09   It is not a 'public performance' (for the purposes of copyright infringement) for a literary, dramatic or musical work to be performed before an audience which consists of teachers and pupils and others directly connected with the activities of an educational establishment, provided that the performance is given either:

'(a)   by the teacher or pupil in the course of the activities or of the establishment; or

(b) at the establishment by any person for the purpose of instruction'[1].

Similarly, the copyright in a sound recording, film or broadcast will not be infringed by playing or showing it before such an audience at an educational establishment for the purpose of instruction[2]. The CDPA provides that parents (or guardians) of pupils are not per se to be taken to be persons connected with the activities of the school[3]. If, however, such parents or guardians have special activities relating to the school (e.g. as members of the board of governors), they could be regarded as being directly connected with the activities of the school. Nevertheless, if a school gives a performance of a play for the benefit of the parents without the express consent of the copyright owner of the play, this would be a copyright infringement. Accordingly, when a school wishes to perform a play otherwise than in accordance with the conditions set out above, it must obtain a licence from the owner of the rights.

1   CDPA s 34(1).
2   CDPA s 34(2).
3   CDPA s 34(3).

Performers' rights

19.10   If an educational establishment wishes to make a film or sound recording of a live performance of a play or musical work or the reading of a literary work, the right of performers, as well the rights in any copyright literary, dramatic or musical work which is performed, will need to be properly cleared[1].

1   See **Chapter 12**.

Ownership of copyright by teachers

19.11   Teachers at all educational establishments produce a considerable amount of material which is entitled to copyright protection. This includes examination papers, teaching notes, lecture papers and the like. The author of a literary, dramatic, musical or artistic work is the first owner of the copyright unless the work was created under a contract of service, in which case the employer will own the copyright[1]. There are a number of exceptions from this rule[2]. So, when a teacher prepares an examination paper in the course of his employment and he is an employee working under a contract of service, the copyright in that examination paper will usually belong to his employer without any formal assignment. If however, the teacher works outside his normal working hours to prepare lectures and notes for an entirely new course of study which he is subsequently invited to give to the school, the position will be less clear-cut, but the teacher may well have an argument that the copyright material was not produced in the course of employment. Each case would need to be considered on its merits[3].

1   See **paragraphs 10.11 et seq**.
2   These are more fully discussed in **Chapter 10**.
3   Reference should be made to **Chapter 10** in relation to the ownership of copyright and to the Table of Incidents of Copyright under the column headed 'First owner'.

Schools' collections

19.12   The inclusion of short passages from published literary or dramatic works in collections, anthologies etc which are intended for the use of schools will not infringe copyright in such works, provided that the following conditions are complied with:

* only a short passage from the literary or dramatic work may be included in the collection;
* the collection must be described in its title, and in any advertisements issued by, or on behalf of the publisher, as being intended for use in schools;
* the literary or dramatic work from which the passage is taken must not have been published originally for the use of schools;
* the collection must consist mainly of material in which no copyright subsists;
* the inclusion of the passage must be accompanied by a sufficient acknowledgement if the work had not been intended for use by educational establishments[1];
* no more than two excerpts from the work of the same author may be included in collections published by the same publisher over any period of five years[2].

This exception is not one that will often be encountered by schools. It is designed more for the protection of publishers and authors.

1   See **paragraph 9.07**.
2   CDPA s 33(2).

Use of computer software by schools, universities etc

19.13 Computer software is protected as a literary work[1]. It follows that the right to copy in the course of instruction referred to in **paragraph 19.03** will apply equally to computer programs.

1 See **paragraph 2.02**.

Lending by educational establishments

19.14 Although lending a work is a restricted act, copyright is not infringed by lending of copies of a work by an educational establishment[1].

1 CDPA s 36A, see **paragraph 7.05**.

Chapter 20

Libraries and archives

Introduction

20.01 Copyright works commonly lent by libraries include literary, dramatic, musical and artistic works, and sound recordings. When videograms and DVDs are lent by libraries, the library is involved in the lending of films and therefore the provisions of the CDPA relevant to films are relevant[1].

Reference should be made to the Table of Incidents of Copyright in **Appendix 4**, and the restricted acts relating to each type of copyright work[2]. As a consequence of the changes made to the CDPA by the 1996 Regulations, lending to the public is now a restricted act applicable to literary, dramatic and musical works, films and sound recordings and artistic works other than:

'(a)   a work of architecture in the form of a building or a model for a building, or

(b)   a work of applied art'[3].

The principal areas of copyright law with which the librarian should familiarise himself are those dealing with lending rights, the making of copies by libraries, the publication of works held by libraries which have previously been unpublished and the fair dealing provisions of the CDPA. There are special exceptions for libraries in relation to the making of copies and the copying of unpublished works which are amplified by regulations made under the CDPA, the Copyright (Librarians and Archivists) (Copying of Copyright Materials) Regulations 1989[4]. In this chapter these regulations are referred to as 'the 1989 Regulations'.

1   See **paragraph 2.08**.
2   See **Chapters 7 and 9**.

3   CDPA s 18A(1)(b).
4   SI 1989/1212.

Definitional issues

20.02   There is no definition of 'library' in the CDPA or the 1989 Regulations, although the latter do contain a list of relevant libraries. These 'prescribed libraries' include the libraries of schools, universities, establishments for further education, public libraries, parliamentary libraries, government department libraries and libraries conducted for or administered by any establishment or organisation whose purpose is encouraging the study of bibliography, education, fine arts, history, languages, law, literature, medicine, music, philosophy, religion, science or technology. Only these libraries may make copies of articles in periodicals or parts of published works[1].

'Public library' is defined by the CDPA to mean:

'a library administered by or on behalf of:

(a)   in England and Wales, a library authority within the meaning of the Public Libraries and Museums Act 1964;

(b)   in Scotland, a statutory library authority within the meaning of the Public Libraries (Scotland) Act 1955;

(c)   in Northern Ireland, an Educational Library Board within the meaning of the Education and Libraries (Northern Ireland) Order 1986'[2].

'Lending' is defined as meaning:

'making a copy of the work available for use, on terms that it will or may be returned, otherwise than for direct or indirect economic or commercial advantage through an establishment which is accessible to the public'[3].

Lending and rental do not include:

'(a)   making available for the purpose of public performance, playing or showing in public, or communicating to the public;

(b)   making available for the purpose of exhibition in public; or

(c)   making available for on-the-spot reference use'[4].

The expression 'lending' does not include making the work available between establishments which are accessible to the public, or lending the original[5].

'Rental' means:

'making a copy of the work available for use on terms that it will or may be returned for direct or indirect economic or commercial advantage'[6].

The CDPA contains no list of archives of the kind referred to above in the context of libraries.

1   See **paragraphs 20.03 et seq.**
2   CDPA s 178.
3   CDPA s 18A(2)(b).
4   CDPA s 18A(3).
5   CDPA s 18A(4).
6   CDPA s 178.

Copying by libraries – generally

20.03   The restricted act of copying a work applies to all categories of works[1]. However, the CDPA and the 1989 Regulations provide for a number of exceptions which permit the copying by librarians of copyright material. None of these exceptions apply to libraries or archives 'conducted for profit', so any references in this chapter to libraries or archives are to *prescribed* libraries or archives.

The expression 'conducted for profit' in relation to a library or archive, means a library or archive which is established or conducted for profit or which forms part of, or is administered by, a body established or conducted for profit. Therefore, the libraries of solicitors' and accountants' offices, pharmaceutical companies and the like, will be libraries 'conducted for profit'[2].

Librarians and archivists are entitled to make copies of articles in periodicals and parts of published works to supply to other libraries[3], to make copies to replace copies of work[4], and to copy certain unpublished works[5]. The CDPA outlines the conditions of making such copies and these conditions are set out in further detail in the 1989 Regulations[6].

A general exception which is not limited to libraries permits the copying of articles of cultural or historical importance or interest which cannot lawfully be exported from the UK unless a copy is made of them and deposited in an appropriate library or archive[7].

1   See **paragraph 7.03**.
2   1989 Regulations, reg 3(1).
3   CDPA s 41.
4   CDPA s 42.
5   CDPA s 43.
6   CDPA ss 38–44 and the 1989 Regulations.
7   CDPA s 44.

Copying by librarians: articles in periodicals and parts of published works

20.04 Provided that certain conditions are complied with, the librarians of prescribed libraries may make and supply copies of articles in periodicals or parts of literary, dramatic or musical works from published editions to persons requiring copies. This is the so-called 'library privilege', and is subject to a number of conditions, which may be summarised as follows:

- *Research and private study:* the librarian must be satisfied that the copy is required for research for a non-commercial purpose or private study and will not be used for any other purpose[1].
- *Declaration*: the person requiring the copy must deliver to the librarian a signed declaration in writing[2].

  The librarian is entitled to rely on the declaration in order to satisfy himself that the copy is required for the purposes of research or private study only, unless he is aware that it is materially false. Previously it was possible for people to obtain a number of copies of the same article by producing declarations signed by different people. The 1989 Regulations made this a breach of copyright.

- *Multiple users*: in order to ensure that copies are not made by libraries for whole classes of students, the librarian must be satisfied that the requirement of the person seeking the copy and that of any other person, are not similar. That is to say, the librarian must ensure that the requirements are not for copies of substantially the same article, or part of a work, at substantially the same time and for substantially the same purpose[3]. He must also be satisfied that the requirements of the person seeking the copy and that of any other person are not related. In other words, that they 'do not receive instruction to which the article or part of the work is relevant at the same time and place'[4]. So, if two schoolchildren from the same class ask for copies of the same article, the librarian should not supply copies to either of the children, unless he makes further examination to ensure that the reason they are asking for copies of the article is not because the article is relevant to work set by the school for the class of which both children are members.

- *Articles from periodicals*: in the case of articles from periodicals, only one copy of the article may be furnished[5]. Nor may more than one article contained in the same issue of a periodical be supplied to the persons seeking the copy. There is no express exclusion in the CDPA or the 1989 Regulations which would prevent someone coming back at different times and signing different declarations which would enable him to obtain copies of more than one article from the same publication.

- *Published works*: in the case of the supply of copies of part of a published work, no more than one copy of the same material may be supplied. Only a reasonable proportion of any work may be supplied[6].

The requirement that a person may only be furnished with a copy of a reasonable proportion of any work raises some difficult questions. The word 'work' is not defined in the CDPA. A book is a single literary work. On the other hand, a poem, short story or a letter is also a single literary work. If a book consists of a collection of letters, the librarian should satisfy himself that the copy which is being sought is a reasonable proportion of a letter reproduced in the book, or a reasonable proportion of the whole book.

- *Payment*: the person seeking the copy must pay a sum not less than the cost (including a contribution to the general expenses of the library) attributable to its production[7].

There is no significance as to the method of copying used. To make a copy by any means, including a handwritten copy, will breach the CDPA and the 1989 Regulations, unless there is compliance with the above requirements.

1   CDPA ss 38(2)(a) and 39(2)(a).
2   The form of the declaration is set out in Sch 2 to the 1989 Regulations and is reproduced at **Appendix 6**.
3   CDPA s 39(2).
4   1989 Regulations, reg 4(2)(b)(ii).
5   CDPA ss 38(2)(b) and 39(2)(b).
6   CDPA ss 38(2)(b) and 39(2)(b).
7   CDPA ss 38(2)(c) and 39(2)(c).

Copies for other libraries

20.05   A copy of an article from a periodical, or of the whole or part of a published edition of a literary, dramatic or musical work may be copied by a prescribed library and supplied to another prescribed library, subject to the following conditions[1]:

- only one copy of the article or of the whole or part of the published edition may be supplied[2];
- the library to which the copy is to be supplied must furnish a written statement to the effect that it is a 'prescribed library' and

that it does not know and could not by reasonable enquiry ascertain, the name and address of a person entitled to authorise the making of a copy[3];

• the library seeking the copy must pay for the copy a sum not less than the cost (including a contribution to the general expenses of the library) attributable to its production.

It should be noted that in the case of the supply of copies from one library to another, a copy of the whole work may be made – the restriction as to copying a part only, which applies in the case of copies supplied to ordinary persons, does not arise.

1   CDPA s 41.
2   CDPA s 41(1)(a).
3   1989 Regulations, reg 6(2)(c).

Copying to replace copies of works for libraries and archives

20.06   A librarian or archivist may make a copy from any item in the permanent collection of the library or archive in order to preserve or replace that item in the collection or in the permanent collection of another prescribed library or archive[1]. However, the following conditions must be complied with:

• the item in question must be an item in the permanent collection which is to be used wholly or mainly for the purposes of reference on the premises or is an item which is available on loan only to other libraries or archives[2];

• it must not be reasonably practicable for the librarian or archivist to purchase a copy of that item for replacement purposes[3];

• where the copy is to be made for supplying another library, then that other library must be a prescribed library. Moreover, that other library must furnish a written statement to the effect that the item which is to be replaced has been lost, destroyed or damaged and that it is not reasonably practicable for it to purchase a copy of that item. The written statement must also say that the copy will only be used as a replacement[4];

• in the case of copies being supplied to other libraries, the other libraries must pay for the copies a sum equivalent to but not exceeding the cost (including a contribution to the general expenses of the library or archive) attributable to its production[5].

The provision that it is not reasonably practicable to purchase a copy of the item to be replaced, presumably extends to looking at cost as well as availability.

1   1989 Regulations, reg 6(1), (2).
2   1989 Regulations, reg 6(2)(a).
3   1989 Regulations, reg 6(2)(b).
4   1989 Regulations, reg 6(2)(c).
5   1989 Regulations, reg 6(2)(d), as amended by the 2003 Regulations.

Copying by librarians or archivists of certain unpublished works

20.07   Libraries and archives may make and supply copies of the whole or part of a literary, dramatic or musical work from a document in the library or archive to a person requiring the copy, provided that it is unpublished and that the following conditions are fulfilled[1]. The conditions are:

- the person requiring the copy must satisfy the librarian or archivist that he requires the copy for the purposes of research for a non-commercial purpose or private study and will not use it for any other purpose[2];
- he must deliver to the librarian or archivist a declaration in writing in the form that is set out in Sch 2 to the 1989 Regulations[3];
- no more than one copy of the same material may be supplied to the same person[4];
- the person requiring the copy must pay a sum not less than the cost (including a contribution to the general expenses of the library or archive) attributable to its production[5].

If the work had been published before the document was deposited in the library or archive and the librarian or archivist is, or ought to be aware of that fact, the exception does not apply and the library or archive will be in breach of copyright in supplying the copy[6].

Similarly, no copy may be supplied of an unpublished work if the copyright owner has prohibited copying of the work and the librarian or archivist is aware, or ought to be aware of the prohibition[7].

1   CDPA s 43.
2   CDPA s 43(3)(a).
3   Reproduced at the end of this chapter, reg 7(2)(a)(ii).
4   1989 Regulations, reg 7(2)(b).
5   1989 Regulations, reg 7(2)(c).
6   CDPA s 43(2)(a).
7   CDPA s 43(2)(b).

Copies of work required to be made as a condition of export

20.08 Under certain circumstances, the grant of an export licence for an article of cultural or historical importance or interest may only be granted subject to the condition that a copy of the article is made and deposited in an appropriate library or archive[1]. Where such a condition is imposed on export, then it is not an infringement of copyright to make that copy. This may be a copy of any type of copyright work and is not limited to literary, dramatic, musical or artistic work. Moreover, the copy does not have to be deposited in a prescribed library if another library would be more appropriate[2].

1   CDPA s 44.
2   For further information contact the Department for Culture, Media and Sport, Export Licensing Unit (see **Appendix 1**).

Copies of published editions

20.09 A separate copyright exists in 'published editions in the typographical arrangements' of literary, dramatic and musical works. Where a library is permitted to make copies under the conditions set out above, such copyright is not infringed by the making and supplying of such copies.

Copying of artistic works by libraries and archives

20.10 With the exception of the condition referred to at **paragraph 20.08** (conditions of export), the above exceptions only apply to artistic works to the extent that they constitute illustrations accompanying a literary, dramatic or musical work. A painting is a single artistic work. A book which consists of little more than reproductions of a work of an artist or photographer is itself a literary work. However, where the words are only simple descriptions of the artistic works reproduced in the book, could it be said that the paintings or photographs are 'illustrations accompanying' the book? As a matter of law, the library exceptions leave these issues unresolved.

Copying by libraries and archives of sound recordings, films, broadcasts and cable programmes

20.11 Only the exception permitting copies to be made for deposit in libraries or archives as a condition of export referred to at **paragraph 20.08** applies to these types of works. However, there are two special provisions which permit the making of all copying of sound recordings of folk songs and recordings of broadcasts or cable programmes to be made for the purpose of being placed in archives:

(a) *Recordings of folk songs*: the words and music of a song may be recorded for the archive of a body designated by Order of the Secretary of State, provided that the song is unpublished and of unknown authorship at the time the recording is made, and provided that the recording does not infringe any other copyright (e.g. another sound recording) or the rights of performers[1]. Copies of such recordings may be made and supplied by archivists on conditions prescribed by the Secretary of State including a requirement that the archivist is satisfied the recording is needed for research for a non-commercial purpose and private study and no person is given more than one copy of any particular recording[2]. A number of bodies were designated by the Copyright (Recordings of Folksongs for Archives) Order 1989[3]. These are as follows:

- the Archive of Traditional Welsh Music, University College of North Wales;
- the Centre for English Cultural Tradition and Language;
- the Charles Parker Archive Trust;
- the European Centre for Traditional Regional Cultures;
- the Folk Lore Society;
- the Institute of Folk Lore Studies in Britain and Canada;
- the National Museum of Wales, Welsh Folk Museum;
- the National Sound Archive, the British Library;
- the North West Sound Archive;
- the Sound Archives, British Broadcasting Corporation;
- the Ulster Folk and Transport Museum;
- the Vaughan Williams Memorial Library, English Folk Dance and Song Society.

(b) *Recording of broadcasts for archival purposes*: recordings of broadcasts may be made for the purpose of being placed in an archive[4]. The archives are specified in the Copyright (Recording for Archives of Designated Class or of Broadcasts and Cable Programmes) (Designated Bodies) Order 1993[5], and are the National Film Archive of the British Film Institute and the Scottish Film Archive of the Scottish Film Council. All broadcasts (other than encrypted transmissions) may be copied for these purposes.

1   CDPA s 61(1) and (2).
2   CDPA s 61(3) and (4).
3   SI 1989/1012.

4   CDPA s 75.
5   SI 1993/74, as amended by the 2003 Regulations.

Delivery of books to museums

20.12   The provisions of the CDPA regarding the delivery of copies of books to the British Museum and other National Libraries are dealt with elsewhere in this *User's Guide*[1].

1   See **paragraph 17.10**.

Microfilm copies for libraries

20.13   Libraries may only make microfilm copies of works if they can meet the conditions set out above for the purpose of replacing items in a permanent collection[1]. Only literary, dramatic or musical works and the illustrations accompanying them may be microfilmed. Because the exception applies for the purpose of preserving items in permanent collections, libraries may make microfilm copies even though the items which are to be copied have not been lost, destroyed or damaged. However, they cannot make copies of items which it is reasonably practicable to purchase. Thus, it would not be permissible for a library to make copies of works which are in print without a licence from the copyright owner, even though the purpose of the copying was merely to make microfilm copies for preservation purposes.

1   See **paragraph 20.07**.

Libraries in the digital environment

20.14   Inevitably, publishers are anxious that the privileges granted to libraries are not used, in an environment in which information can be so readily made available on line, to expand unreasonably the use of material under a claim of privilege. States may provide limitations to the exclusive rights of reproduction, communication to the public and distribution provided for under the Directive.

When the 2001 Directive was implemented into UK law a small number of material changes were made to the CDPA, including adding the qualification 'for a non-commercial purpose' to the definition of 'research' in the exclusion relating to research and private study. The Directive made specific reference to the 'three-step test' in determining whether exclusions were fair and reasonable. Found at Art 9(2) of the

Berne Convention, this provides that governments can allow exceptions to a copyright holder's exclusive rights: in certain special cases (step 1) which neither conflict with a normal exploitation of the work (step 2) nor unreasonably prejudice the legitimate interests of the copyright holder (step 3).

The UK government declined to incorporate the expression into UK law, saying that the concept was already present in all the UK exceptions. Publishers, however, argue that without this explicit limitation, library privilege in the field of electronic delivery is not in conformity with European law. Arguably, step 1 is met by limiting library privilege to 'research for non-commercial purposes and private study'. In the case of steps 2 and 3 though it is argued that online has changed the relevant market. The library privilege delivery of photocopies may not directly have had a significant impact on e.g. the sales of journal subscriptions, but many publishers argue that online library privilege document delivery will conflict with licensed document delivery including the development of new pay per view services.

Publication of unpublished works kept in libraries

20.15 The publication right is the right to publish an unpublished work after the expiry of copyright protection, and is considered in detail elsewhere in this *User's Guide*[1]. The right applies to unpublished works owned by libraries in the same way as it does to copies owned by individuals.

1 See **paragraphs 6.20** et seq.

Lending of books by libraries

20.16 The 1996 Regulations implementing the Rental and Lending Right Directive introduced the restricted acts of rental and lending[1].

The CDPA provides that the copyright in a work of any description is not infringed by the lending of a book by a *public library* if the book is in the public lending right scheme[2].

The use of the words 'work of any description' makes it clear that the book may contain not only a literary work but also artistic, dramatic and musical works. It is probably stretching the meaning too far to suggest that sound recordings or films (in a form, say, of discs) attached to the book constitute a part of the book.

Prescribed libraries or archives which are not conducted for profit can in any event lend any kind of copyright works without infringing their copyright[3].

1   See **paragraph 7.05**.
2   CDPA s 40A(1).
3   CDPA s 40A(2).

Rental of sound recordings and films by public libraries

20.17   Libraries are not treated differently from any other bodies with regard to the rental of sound recordings and films. 'Rental' is distinguished from 'lending' by the fact that it involves the renter obtaining an economic or commercial advantage[1]. If a public library to which no membership fee is payable loans sound recordings and films with or without making any charge whatsoever for such loans, it will infringe the restricted acts of renting or lending works to the public. If such a library sets up a club for which a membership subscription is payable, it will infringe the restricted act if it lends records or films to the members, because that will constitute making copies available in the course of a business as part of a service for which payment was made[2].

1   See **paragraph 20.02**.
2   See also **paragraph 7.05**.

The statutory lending right

20.18   Although the introduction of the lending right to the CDPA has had the effect of removing the right of public libraries to lend sound recordings and films without charge without infringing copyright, there is a provision in the CDPA which entitles the Secretary of State to make an Order (i.e. a statutory instrument) to provide that 'lending to the public of copies of literary, dramatic, musical or artistic works, sound recordings or films shall be treated as licensed by the copyright owner subject only to payment for such reasonable royalty or other payment as may be agreed or determined in default of agreement by the Copyright Tribunal'. This does not apply to situations which are covered by licensing schemes[1].

1   See **Chapter 13**.

The public lending right

20.19   The Public Lending Right Act 1979 conferred on authors of printed books which have an ISBN a right, known as the 'public lending right' ('PLR'), to receive payment for the free lending of their books by public libraries. The PLR is not a copyright, rather it is the right of authors to receive remuneration from a fund established under the Act ('the Central Fund'), in respect of such of their books as are lent out to the public by local library authorities in the UK. The scheme is administered in accordance with the rules set out in the Public Lending Right Scheme 1982 (as amended). The Fund does not receive moneys obtained from the public by a charge or levy exacted by libraries, it is funded by a grant from the Treasury.

The duration of the PLR is the life of the author plus 70 years[1].

The scheme provides for the PLR:

- to be established by registration (a significant distinction from copyright);
- to be assignable to up to four persons or otherwise capable of being dealt with by will etc (as is copyright) except that authors must assign their entire entitlement and not just a part;
- to be capable of renunciation[2].

The only libraries to which it applies are local authority library collections of books held by them for the purpose of being borrowed by the public (including mobile local authority libraries)[3].

The author's entitlement to PLR is dependent on, and the amount payable to each author calculated by reference to, the number of occasions on which books are lent out. This is ascertained by the returns from 16 selected libraries in various parts of the UK. PLR is payable to authors, not copyright owners. To be eligible, authors must reside in the European Economic Area. The division of PLR between the co-authors of a book is a matter for negotiation and agreement between them. In the absence of agreement to the contrary, the Registrar will divide their PLR entitlement equally between them. Each separate editor of a book is entitled to PLR payments. Each volume in a series is treated as a separate book.

In order to be eligible for PLR registration a book must:

- be written by an eligible author (one eligible author among the co-authors is sufficient);
- not have more than three co-authors on the title page;
- not be wholly or principally a musical score;
- be printed and bound (paperbacks are regarded as bound volumes);
- not be a newspaper, magazine, journal or periodical;
- be published by copies having been issued for sale;
- not be Crown copyright; and
- show on its title page an author who is an individual and not a company or association.

PLR years run from 1 July to 30 June. Registration is effected by completing a form, deposing to it as a statutory declaration and sending it to the Registrar of PLR[4].

1   Public Lending Right Act 1979 s 1(b) as amended by SI 1997/1576.
2   Public Lending Right Act 1979 s 1(b).
3   Public Lending Right Act 1979 s 3(4).
4   The Registrar's address is given in **Appendix 1**.

Chapter 21

Reprography

Introduction and definitional issues

21.01 Multiple copying and facsimile machines are ubiquitous business tools. The CDPA deals with these 'reprographic processes' in detail. For the purposes of the CDPA:

'a "reprographic process" means a process:

(a) for making facsimile copies; or

(b) involving the use of an appliance for making multiple copies;

and includes, in relation to a work held in electronic form, any copying by electronic means, but does not include the making of a film or sound recording'[1].

'Reprographic copy' and 'reprographic copying' refer to copying by means of a 'reprographic process'[2].

'Facsimile copy' includes a copy which is reduced or enlarged in scale[3].

1 CDPA s 178.
2 Ibid.
3 Ibid.

Infringement of copyright by copying

21.02 When a copy of printed material is made by a reprographic process, this will involve copying both the content and the typographical arrangement. It follows that in addition to infringing the copyright in the literary, dramatic or artistic work which is copied, the copyright in a typographical arrangement will also be infringed[1].

1 See **paragraph 7.03**.

Liability

21.03 A person who makes an unauthorised copy, unless making it under instructions as an employee, is liable for copyright infringement to the owner of the work copied, unless one of the exceptions mentioned below applies[1]. The owner of a machine used to make an infringing copy will be liable for a 'secondary infringement' of copyright if he knows that the machine is being used for the making of infringing copies[2].

Accordingly, those persons in the business of making copies are liable for copyright infringement if they are making unauthorised copies of copyright material.

1   See **paragraph 8.03.**
2   See **paragraph 7.09.**

Damages for making unauthorised copies

21.04 If a person charges a fee to the public at large for making copies, and takes no care to ensure that the copies are being made with the licence of the copyright owners, he may be liable for significant damages. The damage caused to a copyright owner by just one or two copies being made in a 'copying shop' of his material will not normally be significant. However, the court is given power by the CDPA to award such additional damages as it may consider appropriate in the circumstances. The circumstances to which the court must give consideration include the flagrancy of the infringement and the benefit shown to have accrued to the defendant by reason of the infringement[1].

1   See **paragraph 8.12.**

Avoidance of liability

21.05 How should a company which is in the business of offering the service of making copies, protect itself? Persons seeking to make copies may be asked to sign declarations to the effect that the person submitting the document has licence or consent of the copyright owner to make the copy or, alternatively, that the copy is for the purposes of research or private study[1].

Such a declaration should contain an indemnity in favour of the owner of the copying machine against any proceedings or damages incurred by the owner in case of any breach of copyright being proven in respect of the copy.

Although this form of declaration will not constitute a defence against an action for breach of copyright where there is an actual infringement, it will go some way to assist in ensuring that the court does not award damages at large under the provisions of the CDPA as per **paragraph 21.04** above.

1   See **paragraph 21.06**.

Fair dealing and reprography

21.06   The CDPA provides that no 'fair dealing' with a literary, dramatic or musical work for the purposes of research for a non-commercial purpose or private study will constitute an infringement of the copyright in the work, provided that it is accompanied by a sufficient acknowledgment[1]. The fair dealing exception also extends to the typographical arrangement of any published edition which is copied for the purposes of research or private study[2].

However this does not give the user a free hand to make copies for research or private study without regard to the extent of the copies. It is necessary to consider the detailed criteria for showing that making the copy constituted 'fair dealing'[3].

1   See **paragraph 9.07**.
2   CDPA s 29(2).
3   Ibid.

Judicial proceedings

21.07   Copying for the purposes of judicial proceedings is not an infringement of copyright[1]. Lawyers make a great many copies for many purposes and, if they use outside copying agencies, then such agencies will be well advised to take care that the firms of solicitors, for whom the copies are being made, state in writing that either the works are not in copyright; or that the permission of the copyright owner has been received for the making of the copies; or that the copies are being made for the purposes of judicial proceedings.

1   See **paragraph 9.12**.

Reprography by libraries

21.08   The provisions for making copies of articles and periodicals and of literary, dramatic or musical works by libraries only apply when the copies are made or supplied by or on behalf of the librarian of the library[1].

1   See **paragraphs 20.04 et seq**.

Micro-fiches, micro-copies, etc

21.09 Copying is copying whatever the size or shape of the result. There is no difference, so far as the law of copyright is concerned, between micro-copies and same-size copies[1].

1 See **paragraph 21.01**.

Copyright Licensing Agency

21.10 The Copyright Licensing Agency is a collecting agency established by publishers and authors with the purpose of collecting and sharing revenue from licences granted for the right to copy books, journals, magazines and periodicals on reprographic machines. The constituent members of the CLA are the Authors Lending and Copyright Society Limited (ALCS) and the Publishers Licensing Society Limited (PLS), between whom the income is shared equally on behalf of authors and publishers. The CLA has issued licences to over 30,000 colleges and schools, to over 2,400 independent schools and to higher educational establishments – universities, language schools etc. It has distributed £106 million since 1982 and includes as its members 120,000 authors and 1,500 book, journal, magazine and periodical publishers.

The licences extend to books, journals, magazines and periodicals published in the UK and 17 other countries. Not more than 5% or one complete chapter of a book, or one article from a journal, magazine or periodical may be copied in full, and up to 30 copies of the same extract, or the number required for a class of students and their teacher, are permitted. The licence does not extend, for example, to published music and newspapers. Specific works, or all the works, of an author can be excluded from the blanket licence at the author's or publisher's request. The precise terms of the licences should be referred to as they vary slightly and are subject to periodic renegotiation.

The CLA also issues licences to professions, industrial and commercial enterprises and associations. Surveys are carried out and the statistical data gathered is used as the basis for the distribution of licence fees to authors and publishers, which take place on a regular basis.

All other European countries have arrangements which are more or less similar to those of the CLA to ensure that authors are recompensed for the copying of their works. The US also has a similar structure in place. These various international organisations (including the CLA) are also members of the International Federation of Reproduction Rights Organisation[1].

1   See www.ifrro.org for further information.

Copyright ownership distinct from material ownership

21.11   The ownership of copyright in a copyright work is quite independent of the ownership of the material upon which the copyright work is recorded – whether it be paper, film, etc[1]. If the person who is seeking to have a copy made owns the physical paper, book, etc, which he requires to be copied, it does not automatically entitle him to have that work copied without infringing the copyright in it.

Whether or not any rights of copyright are acquired by the person buying the physical material will depend upon the circumstances. However, in the absence of any express agreement on the issue, a licence of copyright may sometimes be implied. If a book contains standard forms and precedents for example, for use in the preparation of commercial agreements, then it seems clear that the forms are intended to be as a source and that some licence to copy may be implied by the sale of the book. However the licence will be limited (it may not for example extend to creating alternative form and precedents based upon those supplied, for resale as part of another book). The issues surrounding implied licences are considered elsewhere in this *User's Guide*[2].

1   See **paragraph 10.01**.
2   See **paragraph 10.30**.

Copyright ownership distinct from material ownership

Chapter 22

The music industry: publishers and composers and the record industry

Introduction

22.01   The commercial music industry exploits copyright works of all descriptions, but in this chapter we will focus in particular on the two primary categories of work involved, namely *musical compositions* (i.e. music and possibly lyrics, which are separately protected by the CDPA as *musical* and *literary* works respectively) and *sound recordings* (i.e. the recorded versions of musical compositions). Additionally musical compositions and sound recordings may be included in films, broadcasts or other 'communications to the public' (e.g. internet transmissions or in mobile devices), and where physical copies are sold to the public, the packaging will also usually carry artistic and literary material[1]. Issues which arise in connection with the exploitation of public performances, such as concerts, are considered elsewhere[2].

Copyright issues raised by the exploitation of music are consistently the most puzzling to those who do not work within the industry. There are several reasons for this, including the following:

- *Conceptual issues*: users at first usually have difficulty with the conceptual problem that, when considering the exploitation of a music product, there will almost always be a number of independent copyrights to deal with (i.e. a musical composition which comprises of a musical work and a literary work in the words of a song, and a sound recording). These copyrights may be owned or controlled by different entities, each with separate concerns.
- *Collective licensing*: of all media industries, the music industry remains the one most dependent upon the use of licensing schemes and licensing bodies to administer copyrights on behalf of owners. Without those schemes, the task of clearing rights from a myriad of separate owners would be prohibitively time-consuming for the

heaviest users of music (such as broadcasters). These schemes and bodies have separate constitutions, rules and practices. The three most significant to the UK industry are the PRS, MCPS and PPL[3].

- *Industry dynamics*: the relationship between major talent and industry is volatile. Record companies are fond of referring to the rule of thumb that of ten 'acts', only one will ever recoup for the company the costs invested in developing, recording and promoting the act. Historically, therefore, artist recording contracts have contained exclusivity and product delivery options in favour of the company which tie up an artist's services for the entirety (or at least the best part) of his likely career. Increasingly, these contracts have been challenged in the courts as a 'restraint of trade'[4]. Although a detailed discussion of this issue is beyond the scope of this *User's Guide*, it is worth noting that such decisions have thrown doubt on longer terms contracts.

- *Digitisation*: the position of the industry is not static. Since sound lends itself most easily to use in the context of digital media, the industry has been forced to deal head on with the challenges posed by digitisation. The difficulty of tracking uses, the ease of piracy, the potentiality for new industry models to replace traditional distribution methods, have all led to considerable soul searching in the sector in recent years. Established artists may increasingly use 'on-line' transmission and mail order mechanisms to avoid the need for a record company and its traditional distribution methods and both legitimate and illegitimate digital download services have had a significant impact on the traditional distribution models used by the music industry.

In developing an understanding of how copyright effects the industry, it is easiest to distinguish between the issues arising in connection with the exploitation of musical works (usually called 'the publishing rights') and sound recordings of musical works (usually called 'the record rights').

The publishing rights are usually controlled by specialist music publishers who acquire rights from authors/composers, and in certain respects by collecting societies. The performing right in compositions and the right to include those compositions in broadcasts are usually vested in the PRS by the author/ composer, and the so-called 'mechanical' rights are usually licensed for the publisher by the MCPS[5]. It is rare for any publishing rights to be retained by the composer of a musical work.

Similarly the record rights are usually controlled by specialist record companies who will generally be either the first owner of the copyright in the sound recordings (as producer), or else acquire ownership from the producer by way of an assignment[6]. The record company will therefore have the right to exploit the copyright in the sound recording by authorising the 'restricted acts'[7]. Again, certain of the record rights may be administered on behalf of the record company by a collecting society[8].

Broadly, then, the principal characters in the music industry are the publishers and the record companies.

The performing and broadcasting rights in a significant proportion of all music videos are vested in Video Performance Ltd (VPL), although major record companies will do direct deals with broadcasters in some cases (e.g. Music Television, or MTV, following that broadcaster's well publicised dispute with VPL).

1   As to these categories of copyright work generally, see **Chapter 2**.
2   See **Chapter 25**.
3   These are described in more detail at **paragraph 13.1**.
4   For example *Panayiotou v Sony Music Entertainment (UK) Ltd [1994] EMLR 229*.
5   See **paragraphs 13.1 and 22.02**.
6   See **Chapter 10**.
7   Generally, see **Chapter 7**.
8   The performing right is usually administered by PPL, see **paragraphs 13.1 and 22.22**.

Definitional issues

22.02   'Publisher' is not defined in the CDPA. However, in the music industry the expression commonly means the company in which the copyright in a musical composition (except the performing rights) is vested. Although to the layman, publishing may imply publishing sheet music and other printed material, that activity is only a small part of the business of a music publisher. The major part lies in pushing for records to be made, music to be performed live, the use of the music on television and in films and in collecting and distributing income from record companies and the PRS (in respect of performances). Sheet music *is* published, but in the case of popular music usually only after the music has been successful in another medium (such as on record).

A musical work will be taken to have been 'published' if copies are issued to the public (e.g. sheet music) or if it is made available to the public by an 'electronic retrieval mechanism'[1].

Although this latter expression is not defined in the CDPA, it includes by its natural meaning computer databases, electronic publishing systems (such as teletext) on-line databases such as the internet and also compact discs. So, the sale of a recording containing a performance of a musical work will constitute publication of the musical work.

'Publication' in relation to a sound recording, is not defined by the CDPA. A 'publication' which is 'merely colourable' and not intended to satisfy the needs of the *public*, does not constitute publication and is to be disregarded[2].

It is important to note that the CDPA states that the performance or the communication to the public of a musical work or sound recording does *not* constitute publication[3].

The duration of the copyright in a sound recording is affected by the date on which it is released. For these purposes, 'released' means 'When it is first published, played in public, communicated to the public'.

No account is to be taken of an unauthorised act in determining whether a sound recording has been released'[4].

A number of other definitions from the CDPA are relevant in relation to the exploitation of music and are considered in detail elsewhere in this *User's Guide*. These include the definitions of the works in question (i.e. musical works, literary works and sound recordings)[5], and of the acts restricted by copyright in relation to those works (i.e. copying, issuing copies to the public, rental or lending, performing, communicating to the public etc)[6].

Although the expression 'mechanical rights' is not used in the CDPA, it is used extensively by the industry. It means the right to make copies of a musical work and includes the right to record on the soundtrack of films and taped television programmes.

Again, the expressions 'dubbing rights' and 'synchronisation rights' are not defined in the CDPA but are extensively used by the music industry to refer to the right to record, respectively sound recordings and musical works (including songs), on the soundtracks of films.

1   See **paragraph 4.05**.
2   See **paragraph 4.05**.
3   CDPA s 175(4)(a) and (c), see **paragraph 4.06**.
4   CDPA s 13A(2), see **paragraph 6.11**.
5   See **paragraphs 2.02, 2.04, and 2.07**.
6   See **paragraphs 7.02** et seq.

Part I: Publishers and composers

Restricted acts in musical works

22.03   The restricted acts (that is to say, the rights which only the owner of the music or persons licensed by him can exercise) in a musical work are:

- *copying the work* (i.e. reproducing the work in any material form, including in writing, by printing, recording on disc, tape or film or storing the work in any medium by electronic means);
- *issuing copies of the work to the public*;
- *renting or lending* copies of the works to the public;
- *performing in public* (it is immaterial whether a public performance of a musical work is given by a live performer or takes place by some mechanical means, such as by playing a record, exhibiting a sound film or operating a radio or television set in a public place);
- *communicating the work to the public* (by radio or television or by way online and mobile music services);
- *adapting the work* (which includes making arrangements or transcriptions)[1].

As we have seen, in the case of a musical composition, the lyric is not a part of the musical work, but is a literary work, with its own separate copyright[2]. The restricted acts applicable to a literary work are essentially the same as those for musical works, but see the Table of Incidents of Copyright in **Appendix 4** for the copyright attributes of musical and literary works. Essentially the lyrics of a song receive the same copyright treatment as the music.

It is customary for a composer (and in this chapter, for convenience, composer includes lyricist, unless there is an express reference to the lyricist) to assign or licence the entire copyright in his compositions to a publishing company, with the exception of the right to perform the music which he assigns to the PRS. The publisher may choose to delegate control over the right to make recordings of the work ('the mechanical rights') and the collection of mechanical royalties to the MCPS as agent.

1   See **paragraphs 7.02** et seq.
2   See **paragraph 2.04**.

Quality and originality

22.04   The CDPA does not require that a work should be of any minimum standard or quality in order for it to be entitled to copyright. However, it must be original[1]. The extent of originality is a problem which sometimes arises in connection with music. If only five bars are original out of 50, it is unlikely but not impossible that the work will be regarded as an original work (e.g. unless where these five bars contain the key melody of an exceptional quality which converts what is otherwise a minor change, into an important new variation of the other 45 bars).

There can be copyright in the arrangement of a piece of music, but it must be shown that labour and skill have been applied to the production of the arrangement. Recently, in *Sawkin v Hyperion Records Ltd*[2] it was held that:

'A claim to copyright in a new version of a musical work was not to be rejected simply because the editorial composer had made no significant changes to the notes, whether by correction or addition. That was too rigid a test, and not one which properly respected the reality of what music was. Where the material produced was based on an existing score, the test was whether the new work was sufficiently original in terms of the skill and labour used to produce it'.

A new arrangement of an old composition which is out of copyright may be entitled to copyright in its own right. Similarly, arrangements for one instrument of a piece of music written for a different instrument may have a new copyright. In one case for example, the court was satisfied that the composition of the piano score of an opera involved such skill and labour as to justify the creation of a new work of copyright[3].

The test for originality of an arrangement is not high. In *Godfrey v Lees*[4] approving *Redwood Music v Chappell*[5] it was held that:

'the degree of originality required is merely that the manner of expression in permanent form is such that it can be seen to have originated from the arranger rather than having been copied from the original but that, subject to that, an arrangement can attract copyright notwithstanding that it is no more than a straightforward arrangement of a well-known song employing for the purpose well-known musical devices and clichés'.

Where the arrangement is of a piece of music which is still in copyright, although the arrangement may itself be a new work with its own copyright, there will still be the need to acquire a licence from the owner of the original work before the new arrangement can be used.

1 See **paragraphs 3.01** et seq.
2 *Sawkins v Hyperion Records Ltd (2004) EWHC 1530 (Ch)*.
3 *Wood v Boosey (1868) LR 3 QB 223, Exch.*
4 [1995] EMLR 307.
5 [1982] RPC 109.

Material form

22.05   In order for copyright to subsist in a work, it is necessary for the work to be recorded, in writing or otherwise[1].

The making of a sound recording of a musical work is a sufficient reduction to material form to confer copyright on the musical work. However, until it has been recorded or written down, there is no copyright in a piece of music. It is immaterial whether it is recorded by or with the permission of the composer.

So, the recording of a work which has not previously been recorded, which is made without the composer's or author's permission, will not constitute a copyright infringement, because copyright does not subsist in a work until it has been first recorded. It does not follow however that the person making the recording is the owner of the work. The owner is the *author* (i.e. the person who creates the work), and the person making the recording cannot claim to be anything more than the author of the *recording*. An unauthorised recording of a musical and literary work has the effect of giving copyright protection to the work, but the owner of that copyright is the composer or author[2].

1   See **paragraph 2.05**.
2   See **paragraph 10.03**.

Ownership

22.06   The first owner of a musical work is the author (i.e. the composer), unless the work is composed in the course of employment under a contract of service, in which case his employer will be deemed the first owner of any copyright material the author creates in the course of his employment, in the absence of any agreement to the contrary[1]. Because a song is two separate works in copyright law – the words are a literary work and the music is a musical work – a song is not a work of joint authorship between the composer and the librettist. There can be joint authors of the lyrics and joint authors of the music[2]. In *Godfrey v Lees*[3] it was held that a claimant to joint authorship must establish that he had made a significant and original contribution to the creation of the work and that he had done so pursuant to a common design. One recent case considered in detail the question as to whether the work of 'jamming' musicians can be said to contribute as original contribution to a song, meriting copyright protection as joint authors[4].

Music is often commissioned for stage musicals, for films, for television, for radio etc. If the composer is not in the employment of the person who commissioned the work, copyright will remain with the composer and the person commissioning will receive only a licence to use the work for the purpose for which it was expressly commissioned. If more than that is required, then the composer must grant an assignment or licence in writing, signed by the composer, in favour of the person giving the commission[5].

Since it is possible to assign copyright in work which has not yet been created, it is common for agreements with composers to assign the rights in the composer's work before the music is composed[6].

In practice, many composers are in the full-time employment of single purpose companies which are owned or controlled by the composer. These 'loan out' companies are usually established for reason of tax planning, rather than for copyright reasons. When acquiring rights from a 'loan out' company, the acquirer should make sure that he also obtains a relationship which is legally enforceable directly against the composer. Traditionally this has been achieved by obtaining a separate 'inducement letter' in favour of the acquirer and signed by the composer himself.

It is the practice of some music publishing companies to employ composers whenever possible on long-term exclusive contracts, so that the copyright in everything they write over a period of years belongs to the publisher. The courts have held that such contracts are unenforceable if the publishing company has no obligation to exploit the works of the composer, and the contract provides that the composer is compelled, without any – or with only minimal – remuneration to continue to write for the publishing company. So, contracts under which composers are to work exclusively for a publisher over a period should always be the subject of legal advice, on both sides.

1 See **paragraph 10.12**.
2 See **paragraph 10.08**.
3 Ibid.
4 Ibid.
5 See **paragraphs 10.23** et seq.
6 See **paragraph 10.25**.

Performing rights – the Performing Rights Society

22.07 The PRS takes an assignment from its member publishers and composers of the right to perform their works in public and the right to communicate their works to the public. The Society refers to these rights collectively as the 'performing right'[1].

Composers and publishers enter into membership contracts when they join the PRS, under which the performing rights in the works already composed and published by them, and all works composed (or published) by them in the future, whilst they are a member of the PRS, automatically vest in the PRS. Having taken this assignment, the PRS is able to licence others to exploit the performing rights (or some of them). Taking into account music licensed by overseas affiliates of PRS, the PRS repertoire consists of virtually every piece of published music in copyright[2].

The PRS grants:

- 'blanket' licences authorising radio and television cable and satellite broadcasters to broadcast, website owners to simultcast and ringtone suppliers to supply any works in the PRS repertoire.
- 'blanket' and sometimes one-off licences authorising the live performance or public playing of music on premises (e.g. live, DJ, jukebox). The licence is normally granted to the proprietor of the premises at which the music is to be publicly performed, or to the promoters of the musical entertainment. It is not usually granted to performers, as such[3].

PRS licences are granted in consideration for royalties out of which (following the deduction of administrative expenses) it then distributes in accordance with the terms and conditions of the PRS. PRS fees are divided between its members, which consist not only of composers but also of publishers. It is the practice of the Society to divide fees on the basis of fractions of 12 or multiples of 12 rather than on a percentage basis. Where there is *no* publisher, PRS fees pass entirely to the composer, or, in the case of a song, are shared between the lyric writer and the composer. Where there is a publisher, then the composer is entitled to 6/12ths and the publisher 6/12ths of the moneys paid in respect of the song by the PRS, although the composer and the publisher may agree a different division amongst themselves. PRS's rules do not permit it to allocate to a composer less than half of the net fee available for distribution in respect of the work, but the publisher may require by contract that the composer account to him for a proportion of the writer's share of fees. On the other hand, PRS will honour distribution agreements whereby the publisher permits the composer to receive a larger share than 6/12ths. If, however, the publisher is entitled to 6/12ths by the agreement of the composer and lyric writer, then the shares of the latter are preferred to reduce to 3/12ths each.

(PRS handles performing rights in music and also in the lyrics in musical compositions. It does not however deal with:

- performances during divine service in churches and other places of worship[4];

- musicals, operas, ballets, etc which are performed on stage in their entirety or in excerpts;
- performance rights in music specifically composed for *son-et-lumière* productions or plays or other dramatic or theatre productions[5].

These latter two rights (i.e. not relating to the divine service) must be cleared directly from the owner (usually a publisher). For a full account of rights administered, please see the PRS members handbook, sections D and E.

When it is not being 'dramatically' performed in the context as part of a musical, opera, ballets or other dramatico-musical work, the PRS will control the performance rights in the music written for such productions (e.g. where the music is interpolated into another production).

PRS permits its members to withdraw and self-administer their live performance rights. It also has a Live Concert Service under which it administers the live performance rights in the UK for a fixed service charge per night per set and per act with an undertaking to make payment within 60 days of the completion of the UK tour. It is only available to PRS members where the live performance generates a performer's royalty of £1,000 or more.)

PRS works in close association with similar bodies outside the UK, both in licensing those bodies to collect royalties in respect of the works administered by the PRS when they are performed outside the UK, and also in collecting performing right royalties in respect of works performed in the UK, but which are owned by the foreign societies.

On 1 January 1998 the PRS's and MCPS's common 'back room' functions were formally transferred to a jointly owned company, The MCPS-PRS Alliance Limited, formerly named Music Copyright Operational Services Ltd (the Alliance). However the PRS's and MCPS's respective repertoires and memberships remain vested in those bodies for the purposes of licensing and distribution functions.

The potential of the Alliance to achieve greater economies of scale is being realised with the increased use of music in new media. The Alliance has developed a licensing scheme (known as 'the joint online licence') for the provision of online and mobile music services to the public for private use. The joint online licence grants online and mobile music services a worldwide interim licence of mechanical rights and performing rights in the repertoires administered by the MCPS and the PRS respectively[6]. The development of the joint online licence is seen by the Alliance as 'an attempt to meet the needs of online music providers, whilst safeguarding the interests of its members'. The licence covers 'most audio-only methods of supplying music online, including downloads, webcasts and individual streams of individual works' and limited audio-visual uses including 'promo' music videos and live concert performances. It does not permit music used with advertising, the supply of mobile ringtones or the simulcasting of traditional scheduled broadcast services. These uses are either covered by other blanket licensing schemes or are to be directly approved by the copyright owner. Apple iTunes, AOL UK and Napster 2.0 are examples of some of the more high profile services who have recently signed up to the joint online licence.

The Alliance has also introduced the limited online exploitation licence (known as the 'LOEL') for small-scale online operations. This licence covers limited use of the MCPS and PRS repertoire in the form of 'streamed' (play only) 30 second clips and/or as audio-only 'streamed' programming on a website.

More information on both the joint online licence and the LOEL can be found on www.mcps-prs-alliance.co.uk.

The PRS also licences public performance rights in compositions for the internet and authorises the communication to the public of its repertoire in online services and mobile music services (e.g. mobile ringtone suppliers)[7]. Licences can be obtained from the Broadcast Department[8].

1   Although it intends to do so, at the time of going to press the Society had not yet updated its membership agreement and corporate documents to accord with the language introduced by the UK and Copyright and Related Rights Regulations (SI 2003/2498). For example, the PRS defines the 'performing right' in its Articles of Association as '(a) the right to perform the work in public; (b) the right to broadcast the work or include it in a cable programme service; (c) all rights in the nature of the rights under (a) and (b) above including any extension or modification of those rights which by virtue of any present or future enactment exist or may exist) ...'. The Society believes this language is broad enough to include the right to communicate to the public.

2   Although the PRS repertoire also includes unpublished works.

3   See **Chapter 25**.

4   Although the PRS has rights it currently chooses not to charge. This is a concern which is revocable at any time by the PRS, see **paragraph 25.05**.

5   Source: PRS website at www.prs.co.uk.

6   The rights granted to online and mobile music services under the joint online licence are limited by numerous exceptions, limitations and restrictions. A copy of the most recent version of the joint online licence is available on www.mcps-prs-alliance.co.uk.

7   The current Ringtone Licence (available on www.mcps-prs-alliance.co.uk) issued by the PRS to mobile ringtone suppliers grants licensees the right to communicate to the

public (as that act is described in the CDPA) in the UK its repertoire for the purposes of delivering a ringtone to a mobile telephone and allowing consumers to preview a ringtone before purchasing the ringtone.

8   For further details see www.prs.co.uk.

Mechanical rights: the Mechanical Copyright Protection Society

22.08   Mechanical rights are the rights to make copies of a musical work. The right is exercised when a record company makes a CD or when a TV producer makes a programme including music, as well as in a host of other media, including videos, novelty toys, interactive games, CD-ROMs and all online applications and mobile devices where music is used. The MCPS acts as an agent for the licensing of the mechanical rights (and distribution, rental and lending) on behalf of writers and publishers in the UK and, through its overseas affiliates and sub-publishing agreements, copyright owners overseas. The MCPS also licenses the sound recording rights in production music on behalf of library publishers.

Unlike the PRS, the MCPS does not own the mechanical rights. Its membership agreement is an exclusive agency agreement and is subject to certain optional exclusions. MCPS licenses all audio-only products (record company CDs, music-only DVDs, cassettes and vinyl etc) and retail video products (VHS and non music-only DVDs), but the major and larger independent publishers usually license TV and radio adverts and film synchronisation directly.

About two-thirds of MCPS revenue is derived from licensing record companies.

There are essentially two types of licence available to record companies:

* a sales agreement (AP1), where the record company accounts to the MCPS on shipments on a quarterly basis; and
* a manufacturing agreement (AP2), where the record company accounts on pressings at the time of release or re-release[1].

Provided the works to be licensed are in the MCPS repertoire, the record company will receive a licence except in the case of a first recording where the copyright owner has the option of granting specific prior consent. In these cases, the record company will be notified by MCPS that the work is subject to 'First Licence Refusal'. MCPS will also inform the record company of any works which are not claimed at the time of the licence but which are likely to be subject to a subsequent claim. In these cases, the record company is required to retain the appropriate licence fees in a separate Copyright Control account.

In 2004, after a lengthy negotiation, the BPI, on behalf of the record companies, and the MCPS agreed licensing terms for DVD-Video music products (known as the DVD1 Agreement). The royalty rates agreed with the MCPS are inclusive of both the mechanical and synchronisation rights. Record companies also have automatic access to all the MCPS repertoire without the need for prior approval from copyright owners for the use of each individual musical work[2].

MCPS enters into blanket licences with radio, television and cable stations on behalf of its members. The scope of these licences is usually limited to 'convenience copying' by the broadcaster allowing him to retain copies for longer than the period allowed under 'ephemeral copying' exceptions set out in the CDPA[3]. Licences may also be obtained by broadcasters from the MCPS for the synchronisation of MCPS library music and recordings in broadcaster produced programming (such as promotional materials), and for the broadcast of library recordings.

In addition to the joint online licence and the LOEL offered by the Music Alliance[4], the MCPS continues to operate a number of other blanket online licensing schemes (these are generally in the form of interim or trial licences) covering 30 second clips, audio and audio-visual webcasts, internet radio, mobile telegrams and mobile ringtones.

MCPS calculates royalties, invoices, and carries out audits and generally exercises control, to ensure that its members receive the royalties due to them. This is done by means of agreements with various record companies.

Over one-half of the total revenue of the MCPS is derived from record companies. The other half is split between radio and television receipts, sound film, background use and miscellaneous and overseas receipts. The recording rights in connection with these other uses, is not automatic. Separate licences are required if the use made of the music is not simply making a phonogram.

1   The MCPS also offers an AP2A licensing agreement to record companies. This is similar to an AP2 licensing agreement but it allows the record company greater credit terms.
2   **Paragraph 9.30.**
3   The DVD1 agreement provides for the licensing of standard DVD-Video (i.e. music products that are predominantly audio-visual and contain no more than two audio-only music tracks) at 6.25% of PPD (published dealer price), mixed audio and audio-visual product (i.e. music DVDs that contain more than two audio-only music tracks and more than two audio-visual music tracks e.g. a DVD release packaged with a CD) at 7.25% PPD and audio products with limited audio visual tracks (music DVDs that contain audio-only music tracks and no more than two audio-visual music tracks e.g. many DVD singles) at 8.5% of PPD. Source: www.bpi.co.uk.
4   See **paragraph 22.07.**

Sheet music

22.09 Royalties earned from the performance of music and the making of recordings of music are collected by the relevant collection societies[1], but there is no collection society for sheet music royalties. The publisher merely receives a percentage of the sales from the retailer and accounts to the composer, in accordance with the agreement struck between the composer and the publisher. The usual industry royalty in respect of sales of sheet music is 10% of the recommended retail sales price, although sometimes the royalty is based on wholesale prices.

1   See **paragraphs 22.07 and 22.08**.

Publication of music overseas

22.10 In order to ensure ease of enforcement and in some cases to ensure that music does not lose its copyright when published overseas, all copies of the score and phonograms should bear the © symbol accompanied by the name of the copyright owner and the year of first publication[1].

When music is published in the USA, it should be borne in mind that, unlike the UK, there is a system for the registration of copyright, although registration is not necessary in order to obtain copyright protection for UK works[2].

Publishing arrangements overseas are frequently undertaken by foreign affiliates of local publishers. Where this is the case, the composer should seek the maximum transparency in the publishing arrangements to ensure that he is aware of, and approves, the arrangements by which revenue will flow back to him.

1   See **paragraph 4.16**.
2   See **paragraph 4.14**.

Period of copyright

22.11 Copyright subsists in musical works for the life of the composer and the period of 70 years from the end of the calendar year in which he died. In the case of computer-generated musical works the copyright expires 50 years from the end of the calendar year in which the work was made[1].

In the case of assignments of music effected before 1 June 1957[2] the rights assigned will revert to the estate of the composer at the expiration of the period of 25 years after his death irrespective of any assignments or licences made by the composer in his lifetime. Until 1 June 1957 the only persons who could deal with this so-called 'reversionary period' of 25 years following the first 25 years after the death of the author until the full 50-year period had expired, were the executors of the composer or the persons who inherited the copyright in his compositions but now composers or lyricists can deal with these rights in their lifetime.

There are certain important exceptions from these provisions and when dealing with copyright works which were written by composers or lyricists who are now deceased, legal advice should be taken to ensure that the person purporting to sell the rights is, in fact, the true owner.

1   See **paragraph 6.06 and 6.10**.
2   The date upon which the Copyright Act 1956 came into force.

Infringement

22.12 There can be no infringement of copyright unless a 'substantial part' of the work has been reproduced, adapted, copied, etc. The test of what amounts to a 'substantial part' is qualitative, not quantitative. If from a very large piece of music a composer makes use of 15 bars, being not particularly important, or significant bars, such use may not constitute the use of a substantial part of that work. On the other hand, it may be that the same work has five bars – which establish, for example, the main theme so that use of these bars will constitute the use of a substantial part[1].

1   See **paragraph 8.06**.

Exceptions

22.13 If a substantial part of the work has been used, it is then necessary to see if any other exceptions could apply to the use. The mandatory exception introduced by the 2003 Regulations in relation to the 'making of temporary copies' and fair dealing is discussed in detail elsewhere in this *User's Guide*[1]. A number of other exceptions apply to musical works and these are also considered elsewhere[2]. In summary, the CDPA provides that no 'fair dealing' with a musical or literary work for the purposes of:

- making temporary copies with no independent economic significance for technical reasons (e.g. browsing and caching); or
- private study; or
- research if undertaken for a non-commercial purpose; or

- criticism or review, whether of that work or another work (provided that it is accompanied by a sufficient acknowledgement and provided that the work has been made available to the public); or
- reporting current events (provided that it is accompanied by sufficient acknowledgement) except in the case of reporting by means of a film, sound recording or broadcast,

will amount to an infringement of the work[3].

1   See **paragraphs 9.02–9.06**.
2   See generally **Chapter 9**.
3   See **paragraphs 9.02** et seq.

Incidental inclusion of musical works in other works

22.14   Copyright in a work is not infringed by its incidental inclusion in an artistic work, sound recording, film or broadcast. But a musical work or lyrics are not to be regarded as incidentally included in another work if they are deliberately included[1].

1   See **paragraph 9.08**.

Moral rights in musical works

22.15   The author of a musical work or lyrics has a right to be identified whenever:

- the work is published commercially;
- copies of a sound recording of the work are issued to the public;
- a film, the soundtrack of which includes the work, is shown in public or copies of such a film are issued to the public[1].

The right includes the right to be identified whenever a musical work has been adapted and must be asserted[2].

The author also has right to object to a derogatory treatment of his musical work. 'Treatment' in relation to a musical work means any addition to, deletion from or alteration to or adaptation of a work, other than an arrangement or transcription of a musical work involving no more than a change of key or register. In the case of *Morrison Leahy Music Ltd v Lightbond Ltd*[3] the court held that taking parts of five different George Michael songs and putting them together amounted to 'treatment'[4].

1   CDPA s 77(3), see **paragraph 11.05**.
2   See **paragraph 11.08**.

3   [1993] EMLR 144.
4   See **paragraph 11.12**.

Part II: The record business

Copyright in recordings distinguished from copyright in underlying material

22.16   We emphasised in Part I of this chapter that in order to understand the relationship between copyright and the exploitation of music, it is important to understand that there are separate copyrights in the sound recording, and in the material which is 'fixed' on the recording[1]. A sound recording is a copyright work in its own right[2], but if a producer wishes to capture the performance of a musical composition on his sound recording, he will be copying that composition. That process of copying will require authorisation from the owner of the composition[3] because copying is a restricted act in relation to musical (and all other varieties of copyright) works[4]. Where a musical work is recorded in a material form for the first time this will also satisfy the prerequisite to copyright protection in the musical work itself by fixing the work[5]. So, if a composer records a performance of his new composition, two copyrights will simultaneously come into existence: namely the copyright in the sound recording itself, and in the musical composition fixed on the recording.

The recording of a musical composition will also involve a performance of the work. A performer has rights in his performance which are analogous to copyright. These rights are very significant to the music industry, but they are equally important to other industries (such as the film and television industry) which involve the recording of performances and in this *User's Guide*, performances are therefore dealt with in a separate chapter[6].

1   **Paragraph 22.01**.
2   See **paragraph 2.07**.
3   Usually a music publisher, see **paragraphs 22.01** et seq.
4   See **paragraph 7.02**.
5   See **paragraph 2.05**.
6   **Chapter 12**.

Restricted acts in sound recordings

22.17   The acts restricted by the copyright in a sound recording are:

- copying the sound recording;
- issuing copies of the sound recording to the public;
- renting or lending the sound recording to the public;
- playing the sound recording in public[1];
- communicating the sound recording to the public[2].

So, if a record embodying a recording (for example, the soundtrack of a film) has been made with the licence of the owner of the sound recording, and that record is itself, for example, played in public, there will be a breach of the copyright in the first record.

1   Although note that exceptions are applicable to the public performance of broadcasts; see **paragraph 7.06**.
2   See **Chapter 7**.

Ownership

22.18   The author and the first owner of a sound recording is the producer of the recording[1].

A recording is taken to have been made at the time when the first record embodying the recording is produced. By 'produced' this does not, for example in the case of a disc, mean pressed in a factory, but 'produced' in the sense that a record producer records, mixes and balances the various tracks, and arranges the recording equipment to record a live performance.

It should be noted that the provisions regarding ownership in relation to musical works, whereby the employer of the composer becomes the owner of the copyright, do not apply to sound recordings[2].

It can be argued that the producer of the sound recordings in some circumstances is an individual rather than the company entering into the contracts for the making of the recording. To avoid doubt, all individuals who are involved with the production should be required to enter into agreements at an early stage assigning all present and future copyright in relation to the recording to the production company.

The ownership of the copyright in sound recordings can be assigned and licensed like other copyright materials[3].

1   I.e. the person who makes the arrangements for the recording, see **paragraph 10.04**.
2   See **paragraphs 10.04 and 10.11**.
3   See **paragraphs 10.22 et seq**.

Period of copyright

22.19   The copyright in a sound recording produced by a national of the EEA subsists for a period of 50 years from the end of the calendar year in which the recording is made. If, however, it is released before the end of that period, copyright expires 50 years from the end of the calendar year in which it is released. A sound recording is released when it is first published, played in public or communicated to the public. In this context, publication means the issue to the public of records embodying the recording of any part thereof[1].

Where the producer of the sound recording is not a national of an EEA state, the duration of copyright in the UK of the sound recording is that to which the sound recording is entitled in the country of which the producer is a national, but not longer than that accorded to sound recordings produced by EEA nationals.

Record companies these days are increasingly searching their archives for recordings which, for one reason or another, have not previously been issued. The term of copyright for records made:

- before 1 June 1957,
- after 1 August 1989,

is 50 years from the end of the calendar year in which they were made, or if released during that period, 50 years from the end of the calendar year in which the recordings were released[2].

The remastering of analogue recordings onto digital formats raises an issue as to whether the producer of the remastered recording is entitled to a new period of copyright protection in respect of the remastered recording. We have noted elsewhere in this *User's Guide* that originality is not necessary in order to receive protection for a sound recording[3], but copyright will not subsist in a new sound recording (including a digitally remastered recording) which is, or to the extent that it is, a copy taken from a previous sound recording[4]. On that basis it seems unlikely that a re-master could acquire a new period of copyright protection.

1 See **paragraph 6.11**.
2 See **Chapter 6** for a detailed discussion of the term of copyright.
3 See **paragraph 3.01**.
4 CDPA s 5A(2).

The statutory licence

22.20 Section 8 of the Copyright Act 1956 provided that after the owner of the copyright in a musical work had permitted records of it to be made in, or to be imported into, the UK for retail sale, then subject to compliance with certain conditions, anyone else could make recordings of that work for retail sale. Certain conditions had to be complied with, including the payment by the manufacturer of a royalty of 6.25% of the ordinary sales price of a record.

Mechanical royalties

22.21 With the repeal of the 1956 Act, and with no provision for a statutory licence in the CDPA, the position of the record companies vis-à-vis the music publishers is like that of all other copyright users (i.e. they must negotiate licences for the use of the right to record the music and issue copies of the recordings). The jurisdiction of the Copyright Tribunal has jurisdiction in cases where the parties are unable to agree upon a licensing scheme. MCPS licences are subject to the jurisdiction of the Copyright Tribunal not only in respect of mechanical recording licensing, but also in respect of all other licences such as broadcasting mechanicals.

Following a reference to the Copyright Tribunal by the British Phonograph Industry (BPI) on behalf of record companies, which was heard in 1991 and 1992, a rate of 8.5% of the dealer price of recordings is now payable instead of the 6.25% of retail price[1].

1   See **Chapter 13** for an analysis of the Copyright Tribunal.

Phonographic Performance Limited, the Performing Artists Media Rights Association, the Association of United Leading Artists and the British Equity Collecting Society Limited

22.22 Just as MCPS exists to assist composers and publishers in the collection of mechanical royalties and PRS exists to collect the fees payable for the performance of music embodying musical compositions, PPL licenses the public performance and broadcasting of records.

PPL operates by taking an assignment of that part of the copyright in sound recording embodied in records belonging to the members of PPL (so long as they remain members) which enables PPL to authorise the public performance and broadcasting of the sound recording.

PPL issues licences to broadcasters (both television and radio). It is worth noting that this includes all forms of television and radio, and simulcasts of UK radio broadcasts by means of the internet. However, PPL is not currently able to license sound recordings for use on the internet or mobile services apart from simulcasts of radio broadcasts and clearance for other internet uses of recordings must be obtained directly from the record companies concerned.

PPL also licences discotheques, night clubs, public houses, hotels, cafés, restaurants, clubs, halls, dance teachers, aerobic and keep-fit dancing classes, mobile discotheques, football, greyhound and speed-way tracks, sports clubs, shops, stores, boutiques, shopping precincts, amusement parks, amusement arcades, theatres, cinemas, leisure centres, swimming pools and local authority properties.

The members of PPL are the record companies themselves. PPL operates by dividing up between its members the licence fees it receives in proportion to the use made of such tracks. Prior to the coming into force of the 1996 Regulations on 1 December 1996 which, amongst other things, gave rental and lending rights to performers[1], PPL paid 12.5% of the revenue it collected to the Musicians Union (on an ex gratia basis). PPL also pay 20% to featured artists contracted to EU record companies (again on an ex gratia basis).

The fees which PPL charges for the licences it issues depend on a number of factors, including the size of the premises, and the likely size and type of audience. PPL has agreed that 50% of relevant income will be paid to performers for equitable remuneration. Currently, the 50% of relevant income attributed to musicians is divided as to 65% to featured performers and as to 35% to session musicians.

PAMRA was established to act as the collecting society for performers equitable remuneration by the Musicians Union, Equity, REPRO and the Incorporated Society of Musicians. The Association of United Recording Artists has been set up to represent featured artists in the popular music field by the International Managers Forum.

1   See **Chapter 12**.

Video Performance Limited

22.23   VPL is the UK organisation set up by the music industry in 1984 to administer the broadcast, public performance and dubbing rights in short form music videos. VPL represents the copyright owners of music videos and currently has some 800 members comprising mainly, but not exclusively, of record companies. There are approximately 45,000 short form music videos registered with VPL. VPL takes an assignment from its members of the public performance right and dubbing right in their videos, and also a non exclusive right to grant licences of the broadcasting and cable right and related dubbing right in such videos. It grants to users the right to publicly perform videos (e.g. in video juke boxes), include videos in broadcasts and cable programme services, and copy, or dub, videos for the purpose of exercising the above rights. VPL issues blanket licence agreements and its charges are negotiable. Since the highly publicised dispute between MTV and PPL, clearances can also be obtained direct from the record companies direct.

Rental and lending of sound recordings

22.24 The CDPA provides that the Secretary of State may, by order, provide for a compulsory licensing scheme for the lending to the public of sound recordings, subject only to the payment of such reasonable royalty or other payment as may be agreed or determined in default of agreement by the Copyright Tribunal. A likely instance where such an order would be made would be the refusal of record companies to allow public libraries to loan out their output of sound recordings[1].

1 **Paragraph 7.05** deals with rental and lending, **paragraph 20.17** with the lending of sound recordings by libraries.

Agreements with performers

22.25 Contracts between recording companies and performers are very complex, providing for different royalties for different types of records. Thus, different royalties may be paid according to whether the record is a disc or for 'club' recordings where the records are issued at below the normal retail price for foreign sales of the records. As in the case of contracts between the composers and the publishers, the contracts between performers and record companies may be unenforceable if they operate as an unreasonable restraint of trade (e.g. because the term is too long, the performer cannot terminate if the company does nothing to exploit the rights or the payment provisions for the performer are unreasonably low, etc). Equally, contracts between performers and their managers may be unenforceable[1]. If, for example, the performer is not separately advised, the contract may be held to be unenforceable on the grounds that the recording company or manager exercised undue influence over the performer. Professional advice should always be sought on such arrangements.

1 For example, *O'Sullivan v Management Agency and Music Ltd [1985] QB 428, CA.*

Performers' equitable remuneration for sound recordings – public performance and broadcasting

22.26 Following the 1996 Regulations and the 2003 Regulations, the CDPA provides that:

'where a commercially published sound recording of the whole or any substantial part of a qualifying performance:

(a) is played in public, or

(b) is communicated to the public (otherwise than by its being made available to the public by a person without the performer's consent[1]),

the owner of the copyright in the sound recording is liable for the payment of the equitable remuneration to the performers in the sound recordings'[2].

The right to receive equitable remuneration can only be assigned by the performer to a collecting society and then only for the purpose of collecting it on his behalf. However, it can be transmitted under the performer's will or on his intestacy to his heirs or passed to his trustee in bankruptcy.

The amount of equitable remuneration is to be agreed, or failing agreement, to be determined by the Copyright Tribunal. Therefore, any attempt to avoid payment of the equitable remuneration by waiving it or transferring it to the record company is void and ineffective. Moreover, any provision in a performer's contract designed to prevent him or her from questioning the amount of equitable remuneration or from taking the matter to the Copyright Tribunal will equally be ineffective.

There is nothing to prevent the parties stating in a performer's agreement that the amount of the equitable remuneration has been agreed at a certain figure or royalty. However, either party – not just the performer – can query the amount at a later date based upon the actual success, or lack of success, of the recording[3].

1 CDPA s 182CA – the 2003 Regulations introduced the right of a performer to authorise or prohibit the 'making available right'. Considered further at **paragraph 12.14**.
2 CDPA s 182D.
3 Equitable remuneration is considered further at **paragraph 12.15**.

Performers' equitable remuneration for sound recordings – rental

22.27 Where a performer has transferred his rental right concerning sound recording to the producer of the sound recording, he retains the right to equitable remuneration for the rental. The right may not be assigned by the performer, except to a collecting society for the purpose of enabling it to enforce the right on a performer's behalf. It can be transmitted by will or by operation of law (for example, bankruptcy). The person into whose hands it passes can further assign or transmit it.

The equitable remuneration is payable by the person for the time being entitled to the rental right, that is, the person to whom the right was transferred or any successor in title of his. This will normally be the production company but the production company will seek to arrange for the right to be transferred to the record company that will be exploiting the recordings and receiving rental payments, if any.

The amount payable by way of equitable remuneration is to be agreed between the parties or failing agreement can be referred to the Copyright Tribunal. Any attempt to exclude or restrict the right of equitable remuneration is void.

No right to equitable remuneration arises:

- in respect of any rental of a sound recording before 1 April 1997; or
- in respect of any rental after 1 April 1997 of a sound recording made in pursuance of an agreement entered into before 1 July 1994 unless the performer or a successor in title of his has before 1 January 1997, notified the person by whom the remuneration would be payable that he intends to exercise that right. The great majority of performers that have such an entitlement either notified personally or had notices sent in on their behalf before 1 January 1997[1].

1   CDPA s 191G.

Exceptions

22.28   The requirement that there must be the use of a substantial part of a work before there is an infringement of copyright applies equally to sound recordings as it does to musical works[1].

The mandatory exception introduced by the 2003 Regulations in relation to the 'making of temporary copies' applies to sound recordings. The 'fair dealing' exceptions under the CDPA also apply to sound recordings, but in a modified manner. So, although fair dealing for the purposes of research for non-commercial purposes and private study do not apply to sound recordings[2], fair dealing, for the purposes of criticism, review and news reporting, does. No acknowledgement is required in the case of the use of a sound recording for the purposes of reporting current events[3].

The 'incidental inclusion' exception also applies to sound recordings[4], and the CDPA also contains specific exceptions dealing with parliamentary and judicial proceedings[5].

A sound recording in the form of an audio cassette or compact disc is a work in 'electronic form', because it is in a form usable only by electronic means[6]. Thus the exception permitting the transfer of copies of works in electronic form[7] which applies when such works are sold without express terms forbidding such transfer, applies. Record companies should ensure that the packaging and the cassettes and discs themselves carry statements that the copying of them is not permitted.

1   See **paragraphs 8.06 and 22.12** above.
2   See **paragraphs 9.02 and 9.03 et seq.**
3   See **paragraph 9.07.**
4   **Paragraph 9.08.**
5   See **paragraph 9.12.**
6   CDPA s 178.
7   CDPA s 56.

Playing of sound recordings for purposes of club, society etc and the playing of sound recordings in public places

22.29   A specific exemption from copyright infringement exists in relation to the playing of sound recordings at certain clubs and societies not established for profit and whose main objectives are charitable[1]. Following heavy lobbying by the record industry, this exemption has been restricted in the 2003 Regulations by the introduction of additional provisos to the exemption. The exemption will not apply (i.e. a PPL licence will be required) if such clubs and societies pay a third party to play sound recordings or if they use the proceeds of any goods or services sold while sound recordings are playing for any purpose other than for the purpose of their organisation[2].

Prior to the 2003 Regulations, bars and other profit-making organisations were exempt from copyright infringement in relation to the public performance of sound recordings contained in television and radio broadcasts relayed on their premises to customers who did not pay for admission. Following the 2003 Regulations such bars and profit-making organisations are required to obtain a PPL licence in relation to the free public showing or playing of television and radio broadcasts[3].

1   See **paragraph 9.30.**
2   CDPA s 67(b) and (d).
3   CDPA s 72.

Labelling

22.30   It is essential that records, when issued, bear a label indicating the name of the copyright owner and the year in which the recording was first published.

The labeling or marking of sound recordings in this way enables the copyright owner to gain the benefit of the presumption as to copyright ownership[1].

1   See **paragraph 4.16**.

Infringement of copyright in sound recordings

22.31   If a sound recording has been made in infringement of copyright outside the UK, importing such a sound recording will constitute an infringement of the copyright in the sound recording itself[1].

To sell, hire or offer for sale or even exhibit for sale in public, records which have been made without the licence of the owner of the copyright in the record will constitute an infringement of the copyright in the record. Where a pirated record is imported into the UK, the company importing it is liable for infringement of copyright. Similarly, where a pirated record is offered for sale, the shop offering it for sale is liable for breach of copyright. If the person, against whom the breach of copyright is alleged, can show that he did not know and had no reason to believe that the record concerned had been made in infringement of the copyright in the original recording, he will not be liable for breach of copyright. In other words, genuine ignorance of the original piracy is a complete defence[2].

1   See **paragraph 7.09**.
2   A full analysis of 'secondary infringements' is considered in **paragraphs 7.09** et seq.

Parallel importation of sound recordings

22.32   If copies of a record made outside the UK (for example, in the USA) by or with the licence of the owners of the sound recording and musical composition copyrights in the USA, are imported into the UK, the UK licensee of the copyright owner can take action against the importer.

This does not apply to recordings made in or imported into the EEA. A record which has been lawfully imported into or manufactured in one EEA country can be freely sold in all other EEA countries irrespective of the fact that the copyright owner may have granted exclusive licences to different companies in different EEA countries[1].

1   See also **paragraphs 7.04 and 14.06**.

Use of recordings by other media

22.33   The use of recordings in sound and television broadcasts and films are considered in detail elsewhere in this *User's Guide*[1].

1   See **paragraphs 24.03 and 24.11**.

No moral rights for performers in sound recordings

22.34   Moral rights do not apply to sound recordings or to performers. Accordingly, as yet there is no statutory obligation to identify the producer (author) of a sound recording or any of the performers and they cannot object to the derogatory treatment of their work[1].

1   Moral rights are discussed in **Chapter 11**.

International copyright

22.35   Records should bear the a ℗ symbol together with the date of first publication and the name of the owner of the copyright in the recording together with the names of the performers in order to ensure that the recording and the performers are properly protected in the countries which are parties to the Rome Convention and to the Phonogram Convention. In addition, the © symbol together with the date of first publication and the name of the owner of the copyright in the phonogram sleeve or tape container should be placed on the sleeve or container. This will ensure that the copyright in the artwork is protected in those few countries which are parties to the Universal Copyright Convention but not also parties to the Berne Convention[1] and which require formalities as a prerequisite to copyright protection ˙

The placing of the copyright notice on the packaging of the actual disc, cassette, etc also assists in civil and criminal infringement suits where it is necessary to prove that the defendant knew that the material infringed was in copyright[2].

1   See **paragraphs 4.16 and 4.17**.
2   See **paragraph 8.21**.

Private recordings

22.36   Anyone who copies a sound recording embodying a music composition at home, for whatever use, is infringing the copyright in the recording, although there may be no infringement of the copyright in the musical work contained in the recording (provided that one of the fair dealing exceptions can be applied). This breach of copyright commonly takes place and it is not practically possible to take proceedings against infringers when the infringement is on such a massive scale. In recognition of this fact, other European jurisdictions compensate lost revenue to the recording industry by raising a levy on blank tape sales, although no levy is in operation in the UK.

Chapter 23

Drama, ballet and opera production

Introduction

23.01   The works entitled to copyright protection which are incorporated in ballet, opera, live theatre (plays, revues, musicals, pantomimes and the like) productions are many and various and the following is a non-exhaustive list:

- *Artistic works* set designs, costumes, properties, back projection of slides, photographs;
- *Dramatic works* sketches, pantomimes, revues, mime, libretti, choreography;
- *Musical works* music, songs;
- *Sound recordings* records, tapes, cassettes;
- *Films.*

Various other elements of the production, such as sound design also may arguably be capable of protection, subject to the general prerequisite to copyright protection[1].

Reference should be made to the Table of Incidents of Copyright **in Appendix 4** to ascertain the period of copyright, the restricted acts and the rules for identifying the first owner, applicable to each of these types of works.

1   See **Chapters 2 and 3**.

Definitional issues

23.02   What constitutes a 'dramatic work' is considered in detail elsewhere in this *User's Guide*[1].

As to what amounts to a 'performance', the CDPA contains two definitions. In relation to issues regarding rights in performances per se, 'performance' means:

'(a) a dramatic performance (which includes dance and mime); or
(b) a musical performance;
(c) a reading or recitation of a literary work; or
(d) a performance of a variety act or any similar presentation, which is, or so far as it is, a live performance given by one or more individuals'[2].

When discussing the *restricted act* of performance in relation to copyright works, *performance* includes delivery in the case of lectures, addresses, speeches and sermons and in general any mode of visual or acoustic presentation including presentation by means of a sound recording, film, or broadcast of the work[3].

This latter definition is not an exhaustive list. Consequently, when considering the *restricted act* of performance, the word has its natural meaning, provided that the above categories of delivery are considered.

1 See **paragraph 2.03**.
2 CDPA s 180(2); see also **paragraph 12.02**.
3 CDPA s 19(2), see **paragraph 7.06**.

Set designs, costumes, properties and the like

23.03 All these works are in principle capable of being protected as artistic works. The first owner of an artistic work is the author, unless the work is made by an employee in the course of his employment[1]. So if a theatre company employs a set designer to work full-time at designing its sets and costumes, the copyright in the sets will belong to the company, in the absence of any agreement to the contrary. If, on the other hand, the set designer is engaged on a freelance basis or commissioned for the purpose of preparing the designs for one production only, the copyright in the designs will belong to the designer, although there will be an implied licence permitting the company to use the designs for the purposes of its production.

As a general rule, in order to avoid the potential pitfalls of relying on employer/employee or implied licences, it is wise to enter into a written contract with the designer clearly expressing how the copyright is to be owned and dealt with[2]. There is a difference between an assignment and a licence of copyright[3]. In short, an assignment is the outright purchase of a particular part of the copyright, whilst a licence is a limited contractual grant.

If the entire copyright for all purposes is to pass to the company, this should be stated and put in writing, signed by both parties. However, many designers seek to retain copyright in their designs.

It should be noted that copyright ownership is quite distinct from the ownership of the physical record of the original designs themselves, and of the sets, costumes, etc made from the designs. Whilst the theatre companies may own the physical sets and costumes, the use to which they may be put will depend upon the copyright position[4].

When anything less than an outright assignment of copyright is taken, care should be taken to spell out the rights which are granted. For example, it should be stated clearly whether or not the theatre company has the right to use the designs, not only for the original production, but also for other productions of the same play; or, possibly, any other productions whatsoever; whether it may assign the designs to any other company to use in their productions of the play; whether the rights include the right to use the designs in television or film versions of the production; whether the production may be presented outside the UK without additional payment. The period during which the company will be entitled to use the sets and costumes should also be set out.

If it is intended that the rights to be granted to the company are to be limited to the one production for which the designer has been commissioned to prepare designs and further limited so that they can only be used by the company itself, then consideration should be given as to whether the company should be given options to use the designs in other contexts (in a revival of the production or in films or television versions of the production) on payment of an additional sum.

1   See **paragraph 10.11**.
2   Issues regarding implied licences are dealt with at **paragraph 10.30**.
3   See **paragraphs 10.22 et seq**.
4   See **paragraph 10.01**.

Use of existing artistic works in the theatre

23.04   If a painting, photograph, sculpture or other artistic work is used as part of the set, there will be no breach of copyright, because such a use is not an infringement of any of the restricted acts applicable to artistic works[1]. However, if it is necessary to reproduce the artistic work for the purposes of the production, for example by preparing a slide for projection or blowing up a photograph – then this will entail making a copy of the artistic work, which is a restricted act[2]. Accordingly, in such circumstances it is necessary to obtain a licence from the owner of the copyright in the photograph or other artistic work which is to be used. But if a slide is obtained or a photograph is projected without having been reprinted, no authorisation is required.

If a film is projected as part of the scenic effects of the production, a licence will be required from the owner of the film, since this will amount to a performance of the film[3].

If it is necessary to adapt (in the ordinary sense of the word) an artistic work or a film for the purposes of designing a set, the adaptation will not constitute an infringement of the copyright in the artistic work or film. However, the adaptation may amount to a 'derogatory treatment' for moral rights purposes[4]. If there is any doubt that a use will infringe another's moral rights, a waiver should be sought from the owner of the moral rights in question[5].

1　See **paragraph 7.03**.
2　See **paragraph 7.03**.
3　See **paragraphs 7.06 and 23.02**.
4　This issue is considered in further detail in **Chapter 11**.
5　See **paragraphs 11.29**.

Rights of the director

23.05　Unlike the director of a film, the director of a play, opera or ballet acquires no copyright interest in the production as a result only of his direction[1]. Obviously, if he creates dialogue he will own the copyright in the resulting 'literary work'[2] (always depending on the nature of his agreement with the producers).

If the director writes down his stage directions, they cannot be copied in a new written version of the play without his licence.

If the production is filmed, and another stage director copies the stage directions (such as the movement of actors) then this may also infringe copyright in the 'dramatic work'[3].

1　See **paragraph 10.05**.
2　See **paragraph 2.02**.
3　See **paragraph 7.03**.

Lighting designs

23.06　The lighting designer's plots are drawings, and entitled to copyright protection as artistic works[1]. To the extent that they consist of written instructions, they are entitled to protection as literary works or as part of the whole dramatic work[2].

The making of copies is a restricted act applicable to literary, artistic and dramatic works. It follows that copies of the lighting designs cannot be made without the consent of the copyright owner. However the actual use of lighting designs for the purpose of a production in a theatre does not constitute reproduction in a material form necessary to establish copyright infringement[3].

The restricted act of performing the work in public is not applicable to artistic works. In any event it is unlikely that the use of the designs amounts to a performance. By analogy, following the instructions of a board game can hardly be said to be performing them. Therefore, an unauthorised person who obtains a copy of a lighting design and uses it for the purposes of his own production will not be infringing the copyright in the designs. It follows that if a lighting designer does not restrict the use of his designs in the contract under which he is engaged to prepare them, even though he may retain the copyright in them, he is unlikely to be able to sue for unauthorised copying of the designs themselves, nor for unauthorised use. Ideally, a lighting designer should carefully spell out in any contract of engagement the limits of the uses of his designs permitted to the theatre company engaging him. He should state clearly on all copies that any copying of the designs requires his written consent. All copies should be numbered and they should be circulated to as few people as possible.

1   See **paragraph 2.06**.
2   See **paragraphs 2.02 and 2.03**.
3   See **paragraphs 7.03 and 27.05**.

Expressions not ideas, have copyright

23.07   Copyright protects the expression of ideas, not ideas themselves[1]. So, using the idea or concept of a designer and reconstructing completely new designs from new drawings is not of itself breach of copyright. If a production is set entirely in white, for example, another designer might also produce designs in white for the same play. Provided the new designs are different from the old ones, there would be no copyright infringement.

1   See **paragraphs 1.03 and 8.04**.

Plays, sketches and other live theatrical entertainments (except ballet and opera)

23.08   All these works are dramatic works and reference should be made to the Table of Incidents of Copyright in **Appendix 4** as to the attributes of copyright appropriate to dramatic works.

Mimes, choreography and choreology

23.09   Works of dance or mime are 'dramatic works'[1] and reference should be made to the Table of Incidents of Copyright[2] in order to ascertain the copyright incidents of choreographic works. In order to receive protection, these types of works must be recorded, in writing or otherwise.

If recorded in writing, the form of the writing is immaterial. The CDPA defines writing as including 'any form of notation or code, whether by hand or otherwise'[3]. Thus, choreology (which is the reduction of choreography to writing) is protected as a dramatic work. It does not matter what type of choreology is used: the shorthand notation of Benesch, the longer, more academic and elaborate Laban system or even a choreographer's personal notes in his own invented system.

However, a simple way of ensuring that a dance, mime or other form of dramatic work that is not easily reduced to writing acquires copyright is to film it.

1   See **paragraph 2.03**.
2   See **Appendix 4**.
3   CDPA s 178, see **paragraph 2.05**.

Ownership of dramatic works

23.10   The first owner of a dramatic work is the author, unless he is an employee who creates the dramatic work in the course of his employment, in which case the employer will be the first owner in the absence of any agreement to the contrary[1].

1   See **paragraph 10.11**.

Adaptations of dramatic works

23.11   For the purposes of the CDPA, an adaptation of a dramatic work is:

- *in the case of a non-dramatic work*, a version of the work (whether in its original language or a different language) in which it is converted into a dramatic work[1];
- *in the case of a dramatic work*, a version of the work (whether in its original language or a different language) in which it is converted into a non-dramatic work[2];
- *a version* in which 'the story or action is conveyed wholly or mainly by means of pictures in a form suitable for reproduction in a book, or in a newspaper, magazine or similar periodical'[3];
- *a translation* of the work[4].

It is a breach of copyright in relation to a dramatic work to make an unauthorised adaptation, so that a licence is required from the copyright owner of an original play before a translation of the play can be made. There will be a separate copyright in the translation, but it cannot be used unless the owner of the copyright in the original play grants a licence.

1   CDPA s 21(3)(a)(ii).
2   CDPA s 21(3)(a)(ii).
3   CDPA s 21(3)(a)(ii).
4   CDPA s 21(3)(a)(i).

Plots

23.12   Plots themselves are not per se entitled to copyright. However, where in addition to the basic plot, the dramatic incidents, the order of incidents, characters, etc are also used, there may well be a breach of copyright[1].

1   See **paragraph 8.04**.

Use of real life incidents in the theatre

23.13   If a play is based upon real life incidents or upon an unwritten story told to the author by some other person, there is no question of breach of copyright in those incidents or that story[1]. However, the playwright who uses information which has been told to him by another person should always bear in mind the laws relating to breach of confidence[2].

1   See **paragraph 2.13**.
2   See **Chapter 5**.

Exceptions

23.14   There is no 'fair dealing' provision in the CDPA that makes it possible to quote from other works in a play and claim that the use of the other work was merely a 'fair dealing'. Even giving an acknowledgement does not assist in this regard. On the other hand, before there is infringement of a work, a 'substantial part' of the work must be reproduced in the play[1]. Reading in public by one person of any reasonable extract from a published literary or dramatic work, if accompanied by a suitable acknowledgement, does not constitute an infringement of the copyright[2]. However it is unlikely that a court would hold that the performance of part of another dramatic or literary work in the course of a play amounts to a reasonable extract. On the other hand the reading of reasonable extracts of works as part of a 'platform performance' would probably come within the exception. It would be unwise to rely on this provision for the usual varieties to dramatic performance. A licence should always be obtained from the copyright owner when part of another copyright work is incorporated in a play[3].

1   For what constitutes a 'substantial part' see **paragraph 8.06**.
2   CDPA s 59(1), see **paragraph 9.21**.
3   The exceptions to copyright infringement (including 'incidental inclusion') are considered in detail in **Chapter 9**.

Moral rights

23.15   Moral rights generally are discussed in **Chapter 11** of this *User's Guide*.

Improvisations

23.16   An improvisation is a play which is not written down, although there may be written guidelines. Except to the extent to which the play is recorded, there will be no copyright protection for it until such time as it is recorded. Upon being recorded, the copyright will vest in the creator, not the scribe[1]. Also, if it is clearly stated on tickets and programmes that recording a performance would be a breach of confidence and that admission is conditional upon no unauthorised reproduction, there will be a right of action for breach of confidence and breach of contract against anyone who tries to make an unauthorised use of the production[2].

1   See **paragraph 10.03**.
2   See generally **Chapter 5**.

Deposit requirements – the Theatres Act 1968

23.17   The Theatres Act 1968 introduced a provision that a copy of every play must be deposited with the British Museum not later than one month after the date of the performance of the play. No charge may be made to the British Museum for the copy so delivered. It is a criminal offence to fail to deposit copies at the British Museum[1].

1   Theatres Act 1968, s 11.

Opera and ballet

23.18 These types of entertainment both use music and constitute dramatic works[1]. The comments made above regarding plays apply equally to opera and ballet[2].

However, there is an important difference between opera and ballet performances and other presentations including music. Although in general the performing rights in music are vested with the PRS[3], this is not usually the case with opera and ballet in respect of which the performing rights are usually retained by the composer. Therefore, when a company wishes to present an opera or a ballet, it is necessary to obtain not only a licence to perform the choreography and the libretto, but also an individual licence from the composer or his publisher to perform the music.

1 See **paragraph 2.03**.
2 See **paragraph 23.09** as to choreography.
3 As to which, see **paragraphs 13.01 and 22.07**.

Filming or broadcasting opera, ballet and live theatre

23.19 Including a dramatic work in a broadcast without authorisation infringes the copyright in the dramatic work, since it is a restricted act in relation to copyright works[1].

To make a film or sound recording of a dramatic work without permission will be an infringement of any copyright in the work[2]. In addition, when the film is shown to the public, this will constitute performing the work in public[3]. Therefore, it is essential to check the original grant from the author of the play before the theatre company permits any television or sound broadcast or feature film or video tape or similar audio/visual record to be made of its production of the play.

1 See **paragraph 7.07**.
2 See **paragraph 7.03**.
3 See **paragraph 7.06**.

Music incorporated in live theatre productions (except ballet and opera)

23.20 The performance of music in a play requires authorisation from the copyright owner. Where the performance is of 'pre-existing' music (i.e. music not specifically written for the production), rights should be cleared through the PRS. Where the music is specifically written for a play, would-be licensees should approach the individual rights owner. If a recording of music is used, a licence will also be required from the owner of the copyright in the sound recording itself (as distinct from the owner of the copyright in the music). This latter right may, but will not necessarily, be vested in PPL[1]. Enquiries should be directed to that body in the first instance, which will grant a licence to the theatre management, if it does own the performance rights in that record. If a sound recording of music is to be made especially for the production, the company should approach the MCPS for a licence[2].

1   See **paragraph 22.22**.
2   See **paragraph 22.08**.

Contracts with theatre owners

23.21   Copyright is relevant to the contract with the theatre owner, because the CDPA specifically provides that the copyright in a dramatic or musical work is infringed by any person who permits a place of public performance to be used for a performance in public of a work where the performance constitutes an infringement of the copyright[1]. It follows that the owners of theatres and other places used for public performances should at least insist upon a warranty by the theatre management that they have a licence granted by the owner of the copyright to perform the dramatic or musical work in public.

1   See **paragraph 7.11**.

Dealing with dramatic works

23.22   In summary, agreements for the right to perform a dramatic work can either be copyright licences or copyright assignments, the most important distinction being that by taking an assignment, the company acquiring the rights has no fear of losing them by a subsequent sale of the same rights by the author. In the case of a licence, if there is a subsequent sale of the same right to a bona fide purchaser who has no notice of the earlier licence, then the licence will be defeated by the subsequent assignment[1].

There is no copyright registry in the UK and no registration system[2]. So when an assignment or licence is granted, the person to whom it is granted cannot easily check to ensure that there has been no previous grant of the same rights. In the case of dramatic works which have already been performed in the USA or have been written by a resident of the USA, it is worthwhile making a search at the Library of Congress registry in Washington DC. This can be effected quite quickly by letter or fax to appropriate agents or to the Library of Congress itself[3].

It follows from the above that a theatre producer is best advised to obtain an assignment of rights, and although most writers prefer to grant licences only the custom of the theatre business favours limiting grants to licences.

1   A detailed analysis of the means of licensing and transferring rights in dramatic and other works is contained in **Chapter 10**.
2   See **paragraph 10.21**.
3   See **Appendix 1** for the names of relevant organisations in the USA.

Points to be covered in licences of dramatic works

23.23   A grant of rights in a dramatic work should deal specifically with the following points:

- *The date by which the first performance must take place*: it is usual to provide that unless the first performance takes place by a certain date the licence will lapse.
- *The precise rights granted*: if it is intended that the play is to be performed by professional actors only in the West End of London, with a right to tour before and afterwards, the licence should say so. Sometimes any rights to overseas tours or foreign presentations, or the right to license presentations of the production overseas are expressed to arise only after a qualifying number of performances have taken place in the UK.
- *Sub-licences*: if it is intended that the management is to have the right to grant sub-licences either in the UK or abroad to other companies to perform its production of the play, this again should be clearly stated.
- *Whether the agreement constitutes a licence (exclusive or non-exclusive) or an assignment of copyright.*
- *The period of the grant*: it is common to provide for a fixed period subject to extension if the work is performed for a minimum number of performances.
- *Royalty provisions*: there should be a clear statement as to what happens in the event of any failure to pay royalties. That is to say, are the unpaid royalties to be treated simply as a recoverable debt, or are all the rights in the play granted to the management liable to revert to the copyright owner in such circumstances?
- *The right to arrange for film, television or radio performances of the work, should be set out*: normally the producer is not given any such rights, except those necessary to enable it to advertise the

work. It is nevertheless not uncommon to include a provision, in the case of new works, that after a certain number of performances the producer is entitled to a share of the proceeds of any grant of the film and television rights that the owner of the copyright might make.

- *The right of the management to make any changes in the text or title of the play*: in most cases a new play is changed in varying degrees during the course of rehearsals. Sometimes these changes are made by the director, or even by members of the cast. If they are written down by the director, then the copyright in them will vest in the director. Accordingly, the agreement should provide that the copyright in all changes should belong to the copyright owner. Similarly, the management should ensure in its agreement with the director, the individual producer and any other people who might contribute to the play, that the copyright in the changes will vest in the management.

   Even if the right to make changes is granted, if such changes amount to a derogatory treatment of the work, the dramatist (or other person to whom the moral rights in the play have been transmitted if the dramatist is deceased) will have the right to sue for infringement of the moral right to object to derogatory treatment of the work[1]. A specific waiver or approval should therefore be sought.

- *Holdbacks*: if the author reserves rights to himself (and it is common for agreements granting the right to create a stage play to reserve, for example, film and television rights), the producer may seek restrictions upon how these are exercised. The nature of these restrictions will depend upon the negotiating positions of the parties. At one end of the spectrum, the author may agree not to exploit these rights at all whilst the stage play is being exploited. This kind of holdback is becoming less common, and may be counterproductive since the theatrical production might well benefit from the promotional opportunities created by, say, a film of the work. On the other hand, the producer has a legitimate concern to ensure that exploitation of these rights harmonises with his own plans, and for that reason consultation rights with regard to the exploitation of such rights are common.

1   See **Chapter 11**.

Chapter 24

Film and television production

Introduction

24.01 In this chapter, we consider copyright issues created by the process of producing films. The CDPA defines 'film' very broadly, as 'a recording on any medium from which a moving image may by any means be produced'[1]. For this reason, most of the comments made in this chapter will apply equally to the production of feature films, television productions (other than live transmissions) or the creation of original content for, say, the internet.

Although quite distinct industries, there are many similarities between the production process of television and film projects. In essence, in each case 'production' consists of three broad phases:

- *Development*: initially, the producer will acquire control in the copyright (if any) of the work he wishes to use as a basis for his project (e.g. a novel, play, original screenplay, treatment or format) and find suitable cast, director and other personnel, locations and facilities, funding and distribution. Frequently, the producer will seek funding for this initial stage from a third party financier, and in exchange will usually enter into some limited assignment of the rights he has acquired in order to secure this loan investment. In the case of the film industry this finance will often come from a public funding body or from a broadcaster with interests in the film industry.

- *Production*: next, *pre-production* consists of those steps necessary immediately before filming can begin (including set design and building, final casting, hiring crew, securing locations, equipment and facilities etc). If all goes well, pre-production should end with the commencement of the production phases proper, in which performances of the principal cast will be recorded ('principal photography'). After the completion of the photography of the shooting script, production will give way to *post-production* during which, broadly, the film which has been recorded will be edited, effects added in the studios, sound effects dubbed, music added to the soundtrack (both in terms of original music commissioned for the film and 'licensed in' tracks). In the case of television projects the production process may well take a different shape, in particular where a series of programmes is commissioned by a broadcaster.

- *Exploitation*: the production stage will end on delivery of the finished film or programme to its distributor (or broadcaster). Where the project is a television programme, its exploitation life may consist of single or repeat showings on television. On the other hand the project may be intended for the fullest possible international exploitation in all media. In the latter case, it will be common for the producer to appoint a 'sales agent' or intermediate distributor to handle the sale of rights internationally, who will commonly sell rights on to distributors on a territorial basis.

1   See **paragraph 2.08** and CDPA s 5B(1).

Definitional issues

24.02   Copyright works of all kinds are relevant to film production[1]. The definition of 'film' under the CDPA itself is very wide, and since the 1995 Regulations were implemented, the CDPA also protects the soundtrack of the film as part of the film itself[2].

Although the practical steps necessary to create a feature film, a television series, a one-off television special or a music video may be very different, for copyright purposes they will all be films and most of the comments in this chapter will apply to all these works.

The restricted acts, with the exception of adaptation, are all relevant when considering the infringement of copyright in films[3]. In particular, the reader should note the technical meaning of 'broadcast' and 'cable programme service' in this context[4].

The authors of a film are the producer and the director[5]. For these purposes, the producer is 'the person by whom the arrangements necessary for the making of the film are undertaken'[6].

1   See **paragraph 1.02**.
2   See **paragraph 2.08**.
3   See **Chapter 7**.
4   See **paragraphs 2.09 and 2.10**.
5   **Paragraph 10.05**.
6   CDPA s 178; see **paragraph 10.05**.

The elements of production

24.03　The producer must acquire sufficient rights to enable him to create and exploit his film in any and all media[1]. Except in the context of licensed music and sound recordings, it is customary for the producer to acquire these rights by way of assignment[2]. The basic elements of a film are as follows:

(a) *Underlying works* (e.g. the novel, play, biography, story board, treatment, format, original screenplay, research etc). It is customary for the producer to take an irrevocable assignment of the underlying works used for the film. However, in some cases, a full assignment of all rights will not be available (e.g. print publication rights, with certain limitations, are usually reserved to the author, and in the case of a novel, will be a primary means of exploitation for the writer). In any event, to make and exploit his film, the producer will need to acquire the right to:

- *adapt* the work (e.g. from a novel into a screenplay for film or television, or possibly to create a novelisation of a screenplay);
- *copy* the work (e.g. by creating the film and trailers, and possibly prequels, sequels remakes, spin-off's etc);
- *issue copies to the public* (e.g. in the form of video cassettes and discs etc containing the film embodying a copy of the work, for sale to the public, or by the publication of screenplay, or a 'book of the film', synopses etc);
- *perform, play or show the work in public* (e.g. by performing it as part of the films or other works created by the producer in front of audiences in cinemas, or alternatively on stage);
- *communicate to the public* the film or films he creates (by all forms of transmission media, although radio rights in the underlying work are commonly reserved and may be subject to some form of hold back or other limitation on exploitation). It will be important to ensure the assignment is clearly drafted to include all forms of transmission)[3];
- *rent or lend copies of the work to the public* (e.g. by video rental);
- *make alterations to or manipulate the work* (i.e. a waiver of the author's moral right of integrity)[4].

The agreement will also deal with issues such as credit and equitable remuneration for rental and lending[5].

If the owner is not the author, it will be necessary to establish a complete 'chain of title' by which the present owner may establish how he acquired the rights. This chain will need to track dealings with the rights from the first owner of copyright through to the current owner. The owner will be expected to provide copies of all relevant documentation, and provide warranties and indemnities as to its completeness and his ownership of the rights.

At an early stage, the producer will commonly seek to reduce his costs by taking an exclusive option to acquire the necessary rights from the owner within a period (usually one year, with a right to extend for a similar period) against payment of a fee. The fee may vary widely, but one rule of thumb is 10% of the projected purchase price of the work. It will be vital to the producer to ensure that having paid his option fee, he can ensure that a mechanism is in place whereby the owner must transfer the rights to him on pre-agreed terms when the opinion is exercised. Consequently the full terms of the assignment are usually negotiated simultaneously with the option and the agreed wording appended to the option itself.

If the underlying work is 'in the public domain', either because copyright protection in it has expired or because the work was not of a kind which was capable of attracting protection[6], there will be no legal reason to acquire any rights in the underlying works. In the case of copyright works it will be necessary to assess carefully whether the copyright has expired in all intended countries of exploitation[7].

(b) *The screenplay*: except in the unlikely circumstance that the producer acquires rights to an original screenplay which requires no rewriting, it will be necessary to hire the services of a writer. Again, the producer must ensure that he has all the rights he requires in the screenplay. If the writer is an employee of the producer pursuant to a contract of service, the producer will be the first owner of copyright in the writer's work, provided that it was created during the course of his employment and provided that there is no agreement to the contrary[8]. Nevertheless, the writer's agreement will usually contain a confirmatory assignment to avoid the possibility of arguments later on[9]. Since the agreement will (hopefully) be entered into prior to delivery of the work, such assignments usually include all 'future copyright' created by the writer in relation to the screenplay[10].

The same agreement will need to address the issue of moral rights (to which the writer will be entitled unless he worked as an employee[11], in respect of which a waiver will usually be obtained[12]), credit, such issues as 'equitable remuneration' for rental and lending, and other service obligations. In the case of writers, an agreement between the Writers Guild of Great Britain and the Film Production Association of Great Britain, a predecessor to the Screenwriter's Credit Agreement 1974, the predecessor to the Producers Alliance for Cinema and Television (PACT) will provide a mechanism for establishing the credit to be applied in any particular instance[13].

(c) *Musical compositions – copying the music as part of the film*: the use of music in film is a complex area, but in brief, the inclusion on the soundtrack of each composition (i.e. copying) will need to be authorised, as will the exploitation of the film including the compositions. The producer does not clear all these rights himself, but will need (when he is negotiating contracts with publishers) to ensure that he had cleared sufficient rights to enable him to make the film, and (when he is negotiating with distributors) to ensure that the burden of obtaining other authorisations is properly placed on the distributor and not inadvertently accepted by the producer[14].

(d) *Sound recordings – copying sound recordings as part of a film*: again, if a film is to include previously recorded versions of musical compositions, this will involve obtaining authorisations to dub these sound recordings in addition to a grant of rights from the owners of the musical compositions[15].

(e) *Sets designs, costume designs, locations etc*: various copyright works will be created or used during the course of making a film. Many of these will be protectable as original artistic works[16]. Similarly, the producer may make use of pre-existing footage, photographs etc. Again, the producer must ensure that he has taken all the rights he needs to exploit these works to enable him to make his film, usually by way of assignment. Commonly, artistic and other copyright works of various descriptions will be caught on film (for example the artist works embodied in buildings passed during a street scene), and where they are 'incidentally included' there will be no breach of copyright[17]. In some circumstances it may be permissible to include copyright works without infringing copyright (e.g. fair dealing); the issues associated with making such uses of works are considered elsewhere in this *User's Guide*[18].

(f) *Performances*: performers such as actors and musicians now have 'non-property rights' and 'property rights' akin to copyright in their performances. In brief, a performer's engagement terms should also contain the fullest possible grant or assignment of these rights and confirm the consent of the performer to the affixation and exploitation of his work in all media[19].

(g) *The director*: the director is an author and (except where he produces the work in the course of his employment[20]) will be a first owner of the copyright of the film together with the producer[21]. Additionally the director may contribute to any of a number of other creative elements of the film (including the screenplay). Consequently, the producer must ensure that an adequate transfer of copyright, and waiver of moral rights[22], in the film (and all other products of the director's services on the film) is properly effected.

1   Of utmost importance for those acquiring rights is the need to ensure that rights agreements clearly include digital media, such as the internet.
2   See **paragraph 10.23**.
3   The above rights correspond to the restricted acts referred to at **paragraph 7.02**.
4   See **paragraph 11.29**.
5   See **paragraph 7.05**.
6   See **paragraph 2.12**.
7   As to which see **Chapter 6**.
8   See **paragraph 10.11**.
9   See **paragraph 10.13**.
10   See **paragraph 10.25**.
11   See **paragraph 11.29**.
12   See **paragraph 11.29**.
13   For further information contact PACT or the WGGB, whose addresses are set out in **Appendix 1**.
14   These issues are considered in detail in **paragraph 24.10** and the paragraphs referred to in that paragraph.
15   These issues are considered in detail in **paragraph 24.11** and the paragraphs referred to in that paragraph.
16   See **paragraph 2.06**.
17   One important qualification to this principle being that a musical work or such other work as includes a music work will not be held 'incidentally included' if it is deliberately included, see **paragraph 9.07**.
18   See **Chapter 9**.
19   See **Chapter 12**.
20   See **paragraphs 10.11 et seq**.
21   See **paragraph 10.05**.
22   See **paragraph 11.29**. Note that during the life of this edition of the *User's Guide* moral rights will also be introduced for performers; see **paragraph 11.33**.

Issues when acquiring rights – ancillary rights

24.04   Commonly, ancillary rights will mean merchandise, comics, books, clothes and the like of all kinds and in all languages. Even if the producer does not acquire all publishing rights in the work, he will always require the right to distribute and translate synopses of the work to assist sales etc. It will not always be clear whether these will infringe the copyright in underlying works, but since these may feature substantial parts of copyright works included in the film (such as drawings or stills of characters, or extracts or adaptations of the screenplay) the producer will want to ensure that he has the fullest rights to exploit 'ancillaries' based on the project. For major projects the producer will be anxious to protect its interest in such works by registering trade and service marks, although a detailed consideration of this issue is beyond the scope of this *User's Guide*[1].

1   Merchandising rights are considered in further detail in **Chapter 31**.

Issues when acquiring rights – moral rights

24.05   Moral rights are discussed in detail elsewhere in this *User's Guide*[1].

The paternity right, the integrity right, and the right to object to false attribution are all available to the authors of literary, dramatic, musical or artistic works, and film directors[2]. Since the film-making process involves manipulating and adapting the content provided by all the various creative people involved (e.g. by editing, applying effects, reducing the duration of the film, removing or altering material for censorship purposes, modifying the aspect ratio of the image for television exploitation, etc), it is customary to obtain a waiver from the owner of the integrity right, and often all moral rights. It is worth noting that the integrity right of an author in respect of works created by him as an employee in the course of his employment, where the act is done with the authority of the copyright owner, is not infringed unless the author or director has been identified at the time of the act or has previously been identified in or on published copies of the work. Even then, a claim of infringement can be avoided if 'sufficient disclaimer' is given[3].

In France, it has been held[4] that the colourisation of a black and white film may constitute derogatory treatment. The cutting of a film into a shorter version to fit a television slot may well constitute a derogatory treatment, although in most cases, this will be expressly permitted by the terms of the director's contract with the producer.

If an author or director wishes to assert his paternity right, he must do so in writing at the time of the assignment (not afterwards)[5]. It is advantageous for the author or director to make the assertion in the assignment of copyright, since otherwise it will only be binding on those to whose attention it is brought[6]. The right will not in any event apply where the work is made by an employee during the course of his employment[7].

The right to prevent false attribution of a work applies equally to the director of a film as to the authors of literary, dramatic, musical and artistic works. So, if a producer re-cuts a film such that the director no longer regards it as his own work, he may argue an infringement of this moral right[8].

If a producer wishes to make use of a film or photograph made for private and domestic purposes he will require authorisation not only from the copyright owner, but also from any third party who commissioned it[9]. It should be noted that moral rights do not apply to films made before 1 August 1989[10]. However, they do apply to acts done to literary, dramatic, musical and artistic works which were in existence before that date, provided their authors were still alive as at that date. An act undertaken pursuant to a licence or assignment entered into prior to 1 August 1989 will not infringe moral rights[11]. In short, if a producer acquired rights prior to 1 August 1989, he need not worry about moral rights in relation to the exercise of his right under the licence or assignment.

1 See **Chapter 11**. Please also note that during the life of this edition of the *User's Guide* moral rights will be afforded to performers for the first time; see **paragraph 11.33**.
2 **Paragraphs 11.03 and 11.13**.
3 See **paragraph 11.18**.
4 In 1991, by the Supreme Court of France, re 'The Asphalt Jungle' by John Huston.
5 See **paragraph 11.08**.
6 See **paragraph 11.09**.
7 See **paragraph 11.10**.
8 See **paragraph 11.21**.
9 See **paragraph 11.24**.
10 I.e. commencement of the CDPA.
11 See **paragraph 11.32**.

Issues when acquiring rights – performers' rights

24.06 Performers' rights are dealt with in **Chapter 12**. Essentially, performers receive *performers' non-property rights and recording rights* and *performers' property rights*. The former include the right to consent to the recording or live broadcast or transmission of a performance, or to the use of the recording, or to the importation, possession or dealing with a recording[1], and the latter comprise the right to authorise the reproduction, distribution, rental and lending of copies of a recorded performance[2]. Significantly, the Copyright Tribunal may grant consent on behalf of a performer whose whereabouts cannot be ascertained by reasonable inquiry or where he unreasonably refuses consent[3].

Although no permission is required to record on film the actions of people which do not amount to protectable performances, there is a clear danger that filming in such circumstances may amount to a breach of confidence (depending on the circumstances)[4]. Commonly, producers will obtain wide releases, or 'quitclaims' from persons they record confirming that use of their appearance will not infringe their rights.

1   See **paragraphs 12.06–12.10**.
2   See **paragraphs 12.11–12.13**.
3   See **paragraph 12.23**.
4   See **Chapter 5**.

Issues when acquiring rights – rental rights and equitable remuneration

24.07   Rental rights of authors and qualifying performers are dealt with in detail elsewhere in this *User's Guide*[1]. Briefly, these rights are presumed to be transferred in film production agreements (except for the author of a screenplay, dialogue or music created for the film). The authors of literary, dramatic, musical and artistic works, and film directors, and qualifying performers, also have an inalienable right to receive equitable remuneration from the rental of their works notwithstanding that the rental right itself is transferred by the author or performer to, say, the producer of a film. The level of equitable remuneration is to be set by the parties and in the absence of agreement, the Copyright Tribunal may intervene. In the film industry (where the rental of works remains commonplace), producers generally attempt to pre-estimate the equitable remuneration[2].

1   See **paragraphs 7.05, 10.28 and 12.13**.
2   See **paragraphs 7.05 and 10.28**.

Issues when acquiring rights – films as dramatic works

24.08   In 2000, the Court of Appeal held that a film[1] may itself be capable of receiving protection as a 'dramatic work' in its own right[2]. It follows that if a producer wishes substantially to duplicate the scenes and content of an earlier film, he should consider the need not only to acquire necessary rights in the underlying material from its owner, but also in the earlier film.

1   As distinct from any dramatic work which may be been recorded in the film.
2   See **paragraph 2.03**.

Issues when acquiring rights – works of joint authorship

24.09   The producer will need to be cautious where he wishes to acquire rights in works in which there have been contributions from other people, such as story collaborators or script editors, to ensure that all potential authors have assigned their rights, or entered into binding agreements confirming they have no rights (including moral rights) over the material to be acquired. Although it will be unusual for such persons to acquire copyright, they may do if their contributions to the protectable parts of the resulting work are sufficiently distinct and original[1]. Such contributions are a common source of copyright claims in the film and television industry.

1   See **paragraphs 3.01, 10.03 and 10.08**.

Issues when acquiring rights – musical compositions

24.10   Music used in films may either be used in the background, or 'featured'. It may take the form of jingles, themes, incidental music, scores, songs etc. It may be pre-existing music which is 'licensed in' for the film, or it may be specifically commissioned by the producer from a composer. It may be performed live (e.g. where the film features a concert performance) or as part of recordings. In any event, the producer will need to obtain the right to synchronise the musical compositions to the soundtrack of the film and to any trailers which he may produce to promote the film[1]. This right will usually need to be obtained from the relevant music publisher, except in the case of specially commissioned music, in respect of which PRS members assign their right to the PRS and it is common to require the composer to procure the co-operation of the PRS in granting the synchronisation right. If the composer agrees, the PRS will transfer the synchronisation right in such musical compositions to the producer, provided that the PRS obtains the producer's agreement regarding the payment of fees in respect of the performance of the film including the musical composition in the USA. Further details may be obtained from the PRS[2]. The mechanical right (i.e. the right to copy the musical composition onto carriers such as video cassettes and discs by which copies of the film will be sold to the public) will also need to be cleared, and this may be administered on behalf of the publisher by MCPS[3].

Frequently, the standard synchronisation licence issued by publishers will restrict the use of the film embodying the musical compositions to 'linear' use, which will be problematic when considering those forms of exploitation available in the context of digital media which include a non-linear capability. The producer should be careful to ensure that if he is giving undertakings regarding the rights he will clear in the music he wishes to use as part of his film, he does not commit himself to obtaining 'non-linear' rights unless this has been specially agreed with the publisher concerned and any effect on consequent clearance costs has been built into the budget.

The exploitation of the film including musical compositions will also involve engaging in other acts restricted by copyright in relation to the musical compositions: namely the performance of the work (i.e. by exhibition of the film in cinemas etc) and its inclusion in broadcasts and cable programme services. These rights must also be cleared, although usually by the distributors and exhibitors of the film, not the producer. It is important for the producer to ensure that his agreements with distributors properly reflect the rights to be cleared by the distributor[4].

1   I.e. to authorise the restricted act of copying, see **paragraph 7.03**.
2   See **Appendix 1**.
3   See **paragraph 22.08**.
4   The right to perform compositions and include them in broadcasts and cable programmes are considered in **paragraphs 22.07 and 25.13**.

Issues when acquiring rights – sound recordings

24.11   Unless the musical compositions to be included in a film are performed 'live' on the soundtrack for the film (such as, for example, in the case of a concert), it will also be necessary to obtain the right to dub, or copy, the sound recording featuring the musical compositions onto the film soundtrack, and, again, the right to copy the recording onto carriers such as video cassettes and discs by which copies of the film will be sold to the public. Where the music is specially commissioned for the film (i.e. from a composer) it is probable that the producer will take an assignment over the recording so that it owns these rights in the recording. Where the producer 'licences in' commercial recordings both rights will be vested in the relevant record company.

Whether the recordings are specially commissioned by the producer, or are pre-existing recordings licensed in for the film, it will be necessary to ensure that all rights (e.g. performers' rights) are properly cleared, and the producer should ensure that his 'dubbing licence' with the record company, includes suitable warranties and indemnities that, for example, that the rights of the musicians performing on the recording have been properly cleared by the record company.

The exploitation of a film whose sound track includes sound recordings of musical compositions will also involve engaging in other acts restricted by copyright in relation to those sound recordings: namely 'playing the work in public' (i.e. by exhibition of the film in cinemas etc[1]) and its inclusion in broadcasts and cable programme services. As with the musical compositions embodied in such sound recordings, these rights will usually be obtained by the distributors and exhibitors of the film, not the producer. Again, it is important for the producer to ensure that his agreements with distributors properly reflect the rights to be cleared by the distributor[2].

1   See **paragraph 7.06**.
2   The right to play sound recordings and include them in broadcasts and cable programmes are considered in **paragraph 22.22** and **Chapter 25**.

Sequels, prequels and remakes

24.12   We have mentioned elsewhere that there is no copyright in an idea[1], although it is possible that copyright infringement may occur as a consequence of the appropriation of plot or characters. In any event, the owner of an earlier work may well have a legitimate claim for passing off[2]. The producer will want to ensure that the position regarding derivative works based on the work he acquires is clearly dealt with in his contract with an author (usually the producer will take the right to create his own sequels, prequels and remakes of his film, and will want to have some right to acquire, or at least to have a favourable opportunity to negotiate for, any author written sequel to a novel he acquires).

1   **Paragraph 8.04**.
2   See **Chapter 5**.

Co-productions

24.13   Many European films are created as 'co-productions', where two or more producers divide responsibilities for the development, financing, production and distribution of the film. Since the authors of a film are the producer and the director[1], the producer for these purposes meaning 'the person by whom the arrangements necessary for the making of the film are undertaken'[2], it will be necessary to carefully distinguish in the co-production arrangements how ownership will be shared between the producers. It is common for co-producers to divide exploitation of the film between them along territorial lines. If this is the case, particular attention should be paid in any contract to those transmissions which are not territorially limited[3].

1   **Paragraph 10.05**.
2   See **paragraph 24.03**.
3   For example, satellite transmissions, as to which see **paragraph 26.21 et seq**.

Infringement

24.14   The acts restricted by copyright in relation to films are:

- *Copying*: this will include taking a photograph of the whole or a substantial part of an image (i.e. 'video grab')[1].
- *Issuing of copies to the public*: this applies to the first act of putting particular copies of the work into circulation within the EEA[2].
- *Rental and lending*[3].
- *Playing or showing in public*: however, where a film is shown or played in public to an audience who does not pay for admission (such as for example, on a 'big screen' in a bar) the copyright in a film which is included in the transmission will not be infringed, provided the performance is before a non-paying audience[4].
- *Communicating to the public*[5].

It is worth noting that the restricted act of adaptation is not applicable to films[6].

An infringement will only take place if a 'substantial part' of a work is copied although the test is qualitative not quantitative[7].

1   See **paragraph 7.03**.
2   See **paragraph 7.04**.
3   See **paragraph 7.05**.
4   See **paragraph 7.06**.
5   See **paragraph 7.07**.
6   The acts which may only be undertaken with the authority of the copyright owner are considered in detail in **Chapter 7**.
7   See **paragraph 8.06**.

Permitted acts

24.15   A number of acts may be undertaken in relation to films without informing copyright, and broadly, these are the same as those applicable to other categories of copyright work[1]. It is worth noting that special provision is made to deal with acts undertaken when it is reasonable to assume the copyright in the film has expired[2].

1   See **Chapter 9**.
2   See **paragraph 9.29**.

Duration

24.16   The basic rules for establishing the author and period of copyright of copyright works are set out in **paragraphs 10.05, 10.16 and 6.13–6.15**. It should be noted that the copyright treatment given to film will vary significantly depending upon when it was made. Films made before 1 June 1957, for example, did not receive copyright protection in their own right at all.

International issues – local formalities and foreign registrations

24.17 Producers should ensure that in order to receive the widest possible international protection for their films, the '©' symbol, the name of the copyright owner and the year of first publication appear on all film prints and negatives[1].

It is worth noting that although compliance with local formalities is not required under the terms of the Berne Convention[2], it is common (given the significance of the US market) for producers to ensure that the underlying work and screenplay are registered at the US Copyright Office[3], since registration acts as effective notice to third parties of the rights of the producer. Options and assignments may also be registered and it is customary for writer's agreement and option/assignment agreements in the USA to attach a short form confirmatory document which is supplied to the US Copyright Office for registration. Searches of the Register by title may reveal existing interests recorded against the title, and will enable the producer (and financiers) to become aware of other projects with similar titles. Such a search is usually an item required for the delivery of the film and is also required by film insurers. A registry of titles is also operated by the Motion Picture Association[4]. Registration does not confer copyright or other protection on a title, although a search may assist the producer in bringing his product to the market without causing confusion. As we have considered elsewhere, a title is unlikely to be sufficiently original to receive protection as a literary work[5].

1   Issues of international copyright are considered in detail in **Chapter 4**.
2   See **paragraph 4.15**.
3   See **Appendix 1**.
4   See **Appendix 1**.
5   See **paragraph 3.02**.

Chapter 25

Public performance: discotheques, concert halls, cinemas, theatres, clubs, hotels, etc

Introduction

25.01 The owners, occupiers and managers of places of public performance are concerned with copyright because the performance of a literary, dramatic or musical work in public and the playing or showing of a sound recording, film or broadcast in public may infringe the copyright in such works[1]. In each case a licence is required from the respective copyright owners for the public performance of these works. An exception exists in relation to the free public showing or playing of a broadcast, and this is considered in further detail below[2].

1   See **paragraph 7.06**.
2   See **paragraph 25.10**.

Definitional issues

25.02   The CDPA defines 'performance' as including:

'delivery, in the case of lectures, addresses, speeches and sermons'. It also includes ...any mode of visual or acoustic presentation, including any such presentation by means of a sound recording, film, or broadcast of the work'[1].

A 'place of public entertainment' is defined as including:

'any premises which are occupied mainly for other purposes, but are from time to time made available for hire to such persons as may desire to hire them for purposes of public entertainment'[2].

It should be noted that both these definitions are inclusive, rather than comprehensive. So, premises which are mainly occupied for the purposes of the CDPA for public entertainment are also included as places of public entertainment.

'In public' is not defined. However, the Gregory Committee Report on Copyright said:

'So far as we can see, the courts have generally interpreted the term "performance in public" as a term in contradistinction to a performance which takes place within the domestic circle'[3].

It is an infringement of copyright to authorise persons to do acts in relation to a work which are designated as restricted acts. As we have seen, public performance is designated as a restricted act in relation to certain works[4].

The expression *'to authorise'* is not defined in the CDPA, but under the Copyright Act 1911 the courts held it to mean: 'sanction, approve and countenance'[5].

The restricted act of performance, showing or playing a work in public is considered in further detail elsewhere in this *User's Guide*[6].

1   CDPA s 19(2).
2   CDPA s 25(2).
3   See **paragraph 12.29** for a further consideration of 'public' in this context.
4   See **paragraph 7.06**.
5   The question of authorising infringement was considered in detail in *CBS Songs Ltd v Amstrad Consumer Electronics plc [1988] 2 All ER 484, HL*.
6   See **paragraph 7.06**.

The public performance of music and sound recordings

25.03 In considering any question involving the performance of music, it is essential to distinguish between the performance of a record (i.e. a sound recording) and the performance of any music (and associated lyrics) embodied in that record. In the case of a live performance, the only consent required is from the owner (or owners) of the relevant copyright in the musical compositions. Lyricists and composers in the UK, almost without exception, assign the performing right in their music to the Performing Right Society (PRS)[1]. Moreover, foreign composers and lyricists usually have similar arrangements with their national music collecting agency, which themselves have reciprocal collection arrangements that include the PRS. Consequently, it is the PRS that grants the licences to perform music in public.

When a record is performed in public, two consents are required (i.e. one from the owner of the copyright in the music itself and the other from the owner of the copyright in the sound recording). In the great majority of cases, the owners of the copyright in the sound recordings which are issued for sale to the public, assign the right to perform such recordings to Phonographic Performance Limited (PPL)[2]. So, in the case of a performance of a record on, say, a juke box in a public house, two licences are required: the PRS licence to perform the *musical composition* and a licence from PPL to play the *recording* of the music in public.

1   See **paragraphs 13.01 and 22.07.**
2   See **paragraphs 13.01 and 22.22.**

PRS public performance licences

25.04   The general practice of the PRS is to grant licences to the companies and persons who are responsible for managing places where music is performed, either live or by means of a record, broadcast, film etc. It should be noted that the licence is not normally granted to the persons actually performing the music or to the people who actually play the records, but to the person who controls the premises where the music is performed (in theory, the person performing the music could be the person actually playing the record, such as a customer who selects a record on a juke box).

The following are some examples of the places and performances for which the PRS grants licences. Its charges are available on request.

Place	Examples of performances covered
Bingo clubs and halls	30 minutes before sessions commence, short intervals and during dispersal of bingo players at end of session
Cinemas	Film soundtracks, music for intermission and playout relaying to foyer of music audible in auditorium
Restaurants, cafes and hotels and community buildings	Featured music (dances, discotheques etc), background music (e.g. TV, radio etc). All musical performances
Factories, offices and canteens	Background music at work stations in factories, works offices and similar premises Background music in canteens associated with the above
Clubs	Featured music Live performances Recorded music (discotheques and karaoke) Background music by means of radio, television and record players Juke boxes

Public houses	Featured music – live performances Recorded music Background music – television; radio; radio and TV; record; tape

The PRS issues music licences to almost every place where it is conceivable that music could be performed in public, ranging from aircraft to roller-skating rinks and pop festivals to football grounds, speedway stadia, retail shops, ice rinks, holiday centres etc. If music is played to the public (whether or not they pay for admission), there will be a breach of copyright unless a licence has been granted by the PRS. As we have seen above, the word 'public' would include members of clubs. What constitutes the public is a question of law depending on the facts of each case, but it is only when a performance takes place in a truly domestic context that it can safely be regarded as not being a public performance. Whenever there is any doubt, an application should be made to the PRS for a licence.

Exceptional cases where no licence is required

25.05 The PRS makes voluntary exemptions as a matter of policy from the general rule that a licence is required for a public performance, as follows:

- no licence is currently required for music in services of worship in churches or other places of worship;
- no licence is required for performances of musical works in the course of the curriculum at all recognised educational institutions where the audience is limited to persons who are teachers in, or pupils in attendance at, the school or who are otherwise directly connected with the activities of the school.

Opera and ballet 'Grand Rights'

25.06 Performances of opera, operetta, musical plays, revues, panto-mime[1] and ballet, insofar as they consist of words and music written expressly for such works (i.e. 'dramatico-musical works'), also require licences from the copyright owner, but in most cases the PRS is not the owner of the performing right for Grand Rights works such as these. Accordingly, in the case of opera, operetta, musical plays, revues and ballets etc it may be necessary to negotiate directly with the composer, his publisher or agent.

1   See **paragraph 19.09**.

Division of PRS fees

25.07 The revenue collected by the PRS, after deduction of its administration costs, is split up between its writer and publisher members, and the writers and publishers who are members of similar societies in foreign countries to which PRS is affiliated.

The division of PRS royalties between composers, lyricists and publishers is determined by reference to the Society's rules and to the relevant publishing and sub-publishing contracts[1]. In order to enable the Society to make as equitable a distribution as possible between all the interested parties, it is a condition of many of its licences that lists of the works actually performed or broadcast are furnished to it at regular intervals. The Society divides its revenue among the interested parties by reference to these returns and to other programme information to which it has access. Major terrestrial radio and television broadcasters are required to submit complete returns. Smaller broadcasters' usage is analysed on a sample basis. As regards premises where public performances take place, returns are required only in respect of live performances[2], and (except for concerts of serious music) only when the annual royalty is a specified minimum annual sum. As this is subject to change, enquiry should be made of the PRS as to the currently applicable minimum.

Managers of premises which have PRS licences should ensure that the performers assist them in completing the programme forms.

It should be noted that the PRS repertoire includes not only works by British composers but also works by foreign composers. There is an international network of performing right societies who collect on behalf of each other throughout the world.

1　See **paragraph 22.07**.
2　These returns are also analysed on a sample basis. Other statistical information on public performance repetoire is collected by means of a survey carried out by a market research company.

Recorded music – PPL licences

25.08 Whilst a PRS licence is required for both live and recorded performances (because the licence is given in respect of the use of the composition itself), a PPL licence is required in respect of the performance of a sound recording of the composition. Where a sound recording is caused to be heard in public as part of the activities of, or for the benefit of, a club, society or other organisation which is not established or conducted for profit and whose main objects are charitable or otherwise concerned with the advancement of religion, education or social welfare then the act of recording or playing the work in public does not constitute an infringement of the copyright in the recording. However if a charge is made for admission and any part of the proceeds of the charge are applied otherwise than for the purposes of the organisation, the exception does not apply[1].

PPL grants licences in much the same way as the PRS and application should be made to PPL for a quotation for their fee in each case[2].

1   See **paragraph 9.30**.
2   See **Appendix 1** for PPL's contact details.

Juke boxes

25.09   In the majority of cases the PRS and PPL grant licences to the operator of the juke box (i.e. the person who rents out the juke box and supplies it with records). The remainder are licensed to site occupiers who own their own juke boxes.

Video juke boxes are licensed by Video Performance Ltd[1].

1   See **paragraph 22.23**.

Public performances of broadcasts

25.10   There is copyright in a broadcast quite distinct from and additional to the copyright in any teleplay, music, films etc, which is the subject matter of the broadcast, and the acts restricted by the copyright in a broadcast include playing or showing the work in public[1]. However, the CDPA contains significant exceptions to this right of 'playing or showing' a broadcast in public[2].

Significantly, the copyright in a film or sound recording forming part of a broadcast is not infringed by the public performance of the broadcast to an audience who have not paid for admission. If the inclusion of such film or sound recording in the broadcast was not authorised by the copyright owner of the film or sound recording the fact that it was heard or seen in public by the reception of the broadcast is taken into account in assessing the damages for the wrongful inclusion of the film or sound recording in the broadcast[3]. The rights in any literary, dramatic or musical works included in a public performance of a broadcast are infringed, whether or not the audience was a paying audience, unless the licence from the owners of such rights permitted such public performance.

Residents or inmates of places and members of clubs or societies where the provision of facilities for seeing or hearing broadcasts is only incidental to the main purposes of the club or society will be deemed by the CDPA to be a non-paying audience and it should be noted that this broadcast exception for clubs or societies is wider than the exception for records, in that there is no provision that the club or society must not be one established or conducted for profit and that it must be one whose main objects are charitable[4].

To take an example, where a piece of recorded music is contained in a broadcast which is played or shown in public, there will be three copyrights involved:

- *First, the copyright in the musical composition*: since the broadcast of the composition is a restricted act in relation to that composition, a licence is required from the PRS. The definition of performance in the CDPA includes *presentation* of a work by means of a broadcast[5]. Public performance is a separate restricted act.

- *Secondly, there is a copyright in the record (i.e. the sound recording)* which is infringed if there is no licence for the playing of the record in public (whether or not the audience is a paying audience) from the owner of the performing right in the record (the PPL, in most cases). If the sound recording is included in a broadcast which is played or shown to a paying audience, then a PPL licence will be required. However, as we have seen, copyright in a sound recording is not infringed by the public performance of the broadcast to a non-paying audience unless the author of the sound recording is not the author of the broadcast and it is a recording of music with or without words spoken or sung[6].

- *Thirdly, the copyright in the broadcast itself*: if the broadcast is to be seen or heard in public by a *paying audience*, then a licence is required from the broadcaster. In the case, for example, of a pub where the audience is *not a paying audience*, a licence will be required from the PPL for the performance of the record and from the PRS for the performance of the music itself. However, no licence is required in respect of the public performance of the broadcast to a non-paying audience.

In summary, the practical effect of all this is that:

- A PRS licence is always required in respect of public performances of a musical composition so far as the copyright in the composition itself is concerned.

- A PPL licence is required in respect of the performance to any audience of sound recordings by radio or television.

- A licence is required from the broadcaster provider when television broadcasts are seen and/or heard in public by paying audiences, but not if there is no paying audience.

1　CDPA s 19(3), see **paragraphs 2.09, 2.10 and 7.06**.
2　See **paragraph 7.06**.
3　CDPA s 72(4).
4　See **paragraph 7.06** for a detailed discussion of this issue.
5　CDPA s 19(2) and see **paragraph 25.02** above.
6　See **paragraphs 7.06 and 25.11**.

Meaning of paying audience

25.11　An audience is treated as having paid for admission to a place if they have paid for admission to a place of which that place forms part[1]. For example, in the case of a leisure park which charges for admission, if a television set is playing in a bar or restaurant in the leisure park, the persons in that bar or restaurant will be deemed to be a paying audience as regards the broadcasts shown on that television set.

An audience is also deemed to be a paying audience if goods or services are supplied at the place where the performance of the broadcast takes place (or a place of which it forms part) at prices substantially attributable to the facilities afforded for seeing the broadcast[2]. If a venue is providing dinner and showing a broadcast of a boxing match but the price of the dinner exceeds that which is normally charged at that place for the dinner alone, the customers will be deemed to be a paying audience.

If the goods or services provided at a place (or a place of which it forms part) where the broadcast is being performed are supplied at prices exceeding those usually charged there and which are partly attributable to those facilities, the customers will be deemed to be a paying audience[3]. So, if a public house charges more than its usual prices for its drinks on an evening when it is showing the final match of a football championship on the television set in the bar, or a surcharge on its drinks in a room off the bar where the television set is performing, the playing of the television set will be deemed to be a showing or playing of the broadcast in public to an audience who have paid for admission.

In the case of hotels, the exception for residents of the place where the broadcast is played or shown in public[4] should be borne in mind. There does not appear to be any decided case as to whether or not a normal hotel guest is a resident. If, in law, he is deemed to be a resident (which is probably the case), then the performance of television sets in the guests' rooms does not constitute public performance to a paying audience, even though the hotel's charges for room use are surely charges for admission. The separate charge made by many hotels for viewing pay TV channels will make the guests a paying audience as regards those broadcasts only.

1   CDPA s 72(2)(a).
2   CDPA s 72(2)(b)(i).
3   CDPA s 72(2)(b)(ii).
4   CDPA s 72(3).

Plays and dramatico-musical works

25.12 The copyright in a play, opera or ballet is infringed by performance without a licence from the copyright owner[1]. There is no industry collection body for the performing rights in plays as such. Yet, whenever a play, opera or ballet is performed in public (except in schools as part of an educational curriculum), a licence from the copyright owner is required. In the case of the exercise of amateur performances there are commercial companies which license the performing rights to amateur bodies for most plays[2].

If it is desired to perform a play which is in copyright, but the copyright owner cannot be traced, the performance of the work will, nevertheless, be an infringement of copyright. It can be prevented by injunction or can be the subject of a suit for damages. In the case of plays (unlike music) it is the company performing the play which is licensed and not the occupier of the premises.

The music in dramatico-musical works (e.g. stage musicals) must be the subject of a performing right licence but although the rights may be vested in the PRS, the licence is granted by the publisher of the music[3].

1   See **paragraph 25.06**.
2   For example Samuel French and Warner Chappell.
3   The PRS directors have issued directions under the Articles of the PRS to the effect that the PRS will not administer performance rights in musical works performed in the context of dramatico-musical works. These rights are effectively referred to the publisher (or author if unpublished); see PRS Article 7(6).

Cinemas

25.13 There is a copyright in the original play (dramatic work) or novel (literary work) upon which a film is based; in the screenplay; in any music in the soundtrack; and in the film itself as a copyright quite distinct from the rights in the 'ingredients' which make up the film. It is customary for the producer of a film to obtain from the owners of the basic literary or dramatic work and of the screenplay all rights necessary to enable the film in which they will be incorporated, to be performed[1]. Furthermore, the distributor takes from the maker of the film a licence or an assignment of the performing rights in the film. However, the right to perform *music* which is included in the sound-track of the film is vested in the PRS. The PRS does not grant a licence to the owner of the film, or to the distributor, of the right to perform the music. As in the case of any other music which is recorded (and, of course, music on the soundtrack of a film is recorded music), the PRS grants a licence to the operator of the cinema in which the film is shown.

A licence will also be required by the cinema operator in respect of any music which is performed before and after the exhibition of the films, or during any intermission, or in the foyer of the cinema[2].

1　See **paragraph 24.03**.
2　Ibid.

Owners' and occupiers' liability

25.14　The CDPA provides that the copyright in a literary, dramatic or musical work is infringed by any person who permits a place of public entertainment to be used for a performance in public of the work, where the performance constitutes an infringement of the copyright of the works[1].

However, the person who gives permission for the place to be used for the infringing performance will not be liable if, at the time permission is given, he believes on reasonable grounds that the performance would not infringe copyright[2].

There is an additional liability in respect of infringing public performances which are by means of sound recordings, films or the use of equipment for 'receiving visual images or sounds by electronic means' – an expression which includes the use of television sets to receive broadcasts. In such cases the occupier of premises who gives permission for the apparatus used for the performance to be brought onto the premises is liable for the infringement. He can avoid liability if he can show that, when he gave permission, he did not know and had no reason to believe that the equipment was likely to be used to infringe copyright[3].

The person giving permission for the premises to be used for a performance or the occupier permitting performing apparatus to be used on the premises should check whether there are current PRS and PPL licences and that they are applicable. If there is no appropriate licence, then one should be obtained.

1　See s 25(1) and **paragraph 7.11**. See **paragraph 25.02** above for the definition of 'place of public entertainment'.

2   See **paragraph 7.11**.
3   See **paragraph 7.12**.

Copyright Tribunal

25.15   The PRS and PPL have a very powerful position by virtue of the fact that they control the performing rights in almost all the compositions and sound recordings which are currently in copyright and for which there is any public demand. Accordingly, under the CDPA the Copyright Tribunal has the ability to determine disputes arising between licensing bodies and the persons requiring performing right licences. It is beyond the scope of this *User's Guide* to discuss the mechanics of the tribunal in detail, suffice it to say that any person or company seeking a performing right licence for live or recorded music considers that the terms being asked are excessive, then the matter can be referred to the Copyright Tribunal[1].

1   See **Chapter 13**.

Performers' rights

25.16   Performers are accorded property and non-property rights in their performances by the CDPA. Although these are not technically rights in copyright, they are akin to copyright. Infringement of these rights can give rise to claims in both civil and criminal law[1].

To summarise (although these are detailed provisions which we would recommend be considered in full):

- *Performers' non-property rights and recording rights* comprise the right to consent to the recording (which includes making a copy which is transient or is incidental to some other use of the original recording) or live broadcast or transmission of a performance, or to the use of the recording, or to the importation, possession or dealing with a recording[2].
- *Performers' property rights* comprise the right to authorise the reproduction, distribution, rental and lending of copies of a recorded performance[3]. In addition, the performer is entitled to equitable remuneration from the playing, broadcast or rental of a commercially produced sound recording[4].

It follows that anyone wishing to exploit rights in a recorded performance should obtain the necessary consents required under the CDPA[5], and obtain an assignment of performer's property rights[6].

A simple consent and form of assignment, directly referring to the CDPA, should be included in any letter, agreement or formal contract with performers when it is intended to record, film, broadcast or include their performance in a cable programme. If there is no such contract, then the consent and assignment wording could be incorporated in the receipt given for payment of fees, which the performer should sign, but we would counsel against this approach.

It is not necessary to obtain a performer's consent or assignment (and indeed there is no breach of the provisions of the CDPA) if the recorded performance is only 'incidentally included' in the film or record, or if the record is only to be used for the purpose of recording current events[7]. For example, a television news item on a pop music festival which incidentally included some film of a performance at the festival would not require a consent from the performers (subject to the usual limitations on fair dealing discussed in detail elsewhere in this *User's Guide*)[8]. Similarly if, for example, someone is being interviewed and the performance is being conducted in the background, or if a film is made about the building or design of a theatre which incorporates some shots of a performance, there may not be any infringement of copyright[9].

If it is intended to record or film a performance by an orchestra or group, the conductor of the orchestra or leader of the group can only give a consent and assignment under the CDPA on behalf of other members of the orchestra or group if he is duly authorised to do so. Evidence of such authority should *always* be obtained before accepting the signature of anyone claiming to be authorised to sign a consent or assignment on behalf of other performers.

In addition, if the organiser of a public performance knows, or has reason to believe, that someone has exclusive recording rights over their performances, his written consent should also be obtained, although strictly speaking in law only the consent of the performer is necessary[10].

The kinds of performance to which the CDPA applies are considered in further detail elsewhere in this *User's Guide*[11].

During the life of this edition of the *User's Guide* (although not in force at the time of going to press), the CDPA will be amended to provide, for the first time, for moral rights benefiting performers. These are discussed elsewhere in the *User's Guide*[12].

1   These rights are considered in detail in **Chapter 12**.
2   CDPA ss 182–184; see **paragraphs 12.06–12.10**.
3   CDPA ss 182A–182C; see **paragraphs 12.11–12.13**.
4   CDPA ss 182D and 191G.
5   See **paragraph 12.20**.

6   See **paragraph 12.21**.
7   See **Chapter 12**.
8   See **paragraphs 9.03** et seq.
9   See **paragraph 9.08**.
10 See **paragraph 12.10**.
11 See **Chapter 12**.
12 See **paragraph 11.33**.

Chapter 26

Networked communications: broadcasting, cable, internet and mobile transmissions

Introduction

26.01 Technology is in the process of transforming how copyright works are made and exploited: nowhere more so than in the context of network communications.

In past editions of the *User's Guide* we have focused on different types of communication under separate chapter headings (broadcasting, cable, electronic publishing, internet). In copyright terms, since the implementation of the 2003 Regulations, with their 'technology neutral' definitions of 'broadcast' and 'communication to the public'[1], the distinction has not altogether lost its significance (a considerable part of the CDPA remains devoted to dealing with the particular issues associated with 'wireless broadcasts' and those are dealt with below in this chapter), but that distinction is much reduced. During the life of this *User's Guide*, the practical distinction between these different modes of communication will also become increasingly blurred. In a single word, this is 'convergence': the ability for similar services to be conveyed by different delivery systems, and the combination of formerly discreet delivery systems such as the television, the computer and the telephone (more correctly now 'mobile devices' in their broadest sense).

Under the CDPA, as amended by the 2003 Regulations, the only *transmission* which is capable of receiving protection as a copyright work in its own right is a 'broadcast'[2] (i.e. the programme-carrying signal, whether carried by wireless or wired means).

Since the 2003 Regulations were implemented, the owners of copyright works have the exclusive right to authorise the 'communication to the public' of their works (including by way of broadcast)[3]. Communication to the public is a concept not without difficulties, but one which was clearly intended by legislators to encompass the process of making works available to the public by means of all 'information society' services, whether as part of a 'linear' transmission made at a time scheduled by the sender, or at a time dictated by the recipient as part of an interactive 'on demand' service. A 'communication to the public' will now be caught by the provisions of the CDPA regardless of the nature of delivery mechanism by which it is conveyed.

It is necessary to distinguish the 'communication to the public' (whether it is a broadcast or otherwise) from the information which may be conveyed by that transmission. If that information consists of copyright works, those works will be entitled to separate copyright protection[4]. By way of example, if a broadcast of a film which has a commercial sound recording included on its soundtrack is made, there are at least five copyrights involved:

- copyright in the screenplay on which the film is based (a dramatic work);
- copyright in the music on the soundtrack (a musical and, where there are lyrics, literary work);
- copyright in the recording of the music on the soundtrack (a sound recording);
- copyright in the film (a film);
- copyright in the broadcast by which the film is transmitted.

If the film is included on an 'on demand' service, the transmission signal carrying the work will not be protected as a separate copyright work, although the operator of the service will be entitled to other rights designed to inhibit the fraudulent reception of its services and the circumvention of protection measures[5].

The dominant medium in terms of 'on-line' distribution still consists of the worldwide network of computers, known as the internet. The internet operates by 'packet switching'. Packets of information are routed by point-to-point transmissions between computers, the transmissions being made in accordance with certain protocols (the protocol used for the internet is the Transmission Control Protocol/Internet Protocol, or TCP/IP). Packets of information are usually no larger than 1,500 bytes and one transmission may consist of large numbers of such packets. The 'backbone' of the internet comprises a series of high-speed cables capable of quickly communicating vast amounts of information between networks locally and internationally via access points housing purpose constructed routing computer systems. The development of the worldwide web and web browsers in the early 1990s formed the basis for the modern internet. Consumer access to the internet is most commonly effected through Internet Service Providers, which commonly also provide their own proprietary services as well as internet access. Those proprietary services, as well as other on-line services available on the internet through web sites, will equally comprise 'digital products' in the sense referred to later in this chapter.

In the context of mobile communications, wireless protocols and technologies (such as the Wireless Access Protocol (WAP), General Pocket Radio Services (GPRS), the Global System for Mobile Communications (GSM), Personal Communications Networks (PCN), and Universal Mobile Telecommunications Systems (UMTS)) offer consumers greater flexibility in terms of how the internet is accessed (e.g. from portable wireless devices), as well as offering the delivery of mobile networked communications which are, to a greater or lesser extent, controlled by their network operator.

Since technology is changing so rapidly, it would be unwise to investigate too closely in this *User's Guide* the latest developments, although we will mention a few since they represent an important example of the possibilities for convergence between the television, computing and telephone based communications:

- *TV over DSL* (*TVODSL*) refers to the delivery of audiovisual content, typically sent as data 'packets', over copper wires, cable or fibres and using DSL technology which form part of a private network (usually leased or owned by the operator of that network) available only to those who are customers of the relevant network operator. The wires, cables and fibres usually form part of the existing telecommunications network in a territory. Operators of TVODSL systems reserve a guaranteed amount of constant bandwidth capacity for TV content – the network recognises, and prioritises the delivery of, any TVODSL data packet with the consequence that, unlike the internet, there are no bandwidth bottlenecks for content and no unpredictability of service. Existing telecoms operators throughout Europe are the leading figures in each territory, since they usually own the infrastructure. Many have either launched a TVODSL service (e.g. France Telecom in December 2003) or are trialling services with a view to a launch in the short term. At present, it is unclear as to how telecoms operators will structure their services commercially. However, they may: remain a carrier and offer PC-based content (i.e. steer away from 'television'-style offerings); join forces with a pay television operator and focus on delivery to televisions (via a set top box); allow pay television operators to retain ownership of channels retailed over TVODSL (e.g. 'Sky by Wire' on the HomeChoice network); offer TVODSL services together with conventional television services (e.g. a hybrid box allowing access to 'free' television channels whilst also facilitating TVODSL for access to, say, an 'on-demand' back catalogue of content; create a new brand and offering entirely; or offer 'multi-play' offerings (e.g. voice, internet and TVODSL for a single periodic charge). As we write, for example, Hong Kong Cable uses a web browser in order to guide the user to the point of accessing the TVODSL content. Although the content itself is not delivered over the web, the user experience has a PC-like feel to it.

- *TV over the internet* (*IPTV*) refers to the delivery of broadcast-quality, full-screen television to users over a network of interconnecting computers using IP protocols. IPTV is different to a TVODSL offering because, although it may be delivered over the same infrastructure, it does *not* use a private network to deliver the content to users, i.e. IPTV uses the public network of computers to distribute content to viewers. It may, however, be viewed on both televisions and computers (or both) dependent on the form of IPTV. In the UK, the internet can deliver live content, but the amount of data necessary means only small-screen, low resolution viewing is possible. The internet can also deliver small-screen non-live content, or full-screen non-live content with a long download period. However, companies are gearing up for IPTV. Wanadoo is planning to offer a broadband home gateway which will offer voice, internet access and IPTV/VOD (in due course). In other territories, progress has been quicker. Fastweb is at the forefront of the IPTV deployment in Europe, Italy being the leading territory. IPTV development depends entirely on the internet's ability to carry substantial quantities of content efficiently and without 'breaking down'. Within the network of inter-connecting computers, there remain blockages and 'narrow' spots where the transmission of content is slowed or delayed. As compression and broadband technology improves, so will the viability of IPTV. The key difference between TVODSL and IPTV is that content made available via IPTV will not have the security benefit of being transmitted via a private network. Accordingly, rights owners and broadcasters will need to ensure that their premium or territory-restricted content is protected so it is not available for viewing outside of the desired territories.

- *Personal video records* (*PVRs*) are essentially set top box devices which use a hard disc to store data comprised in the broadcast signal to allow viewers to record and manipulate (e.g. fast forward, rewind or skip programming) and potentially redistribute (on a peer-to-peer basis) the broadcast signal. The result is an 'intelligent' next generation video recorder, offering the possibility of true

VOD. These devices are, as we write, already widely available in the UK via BSkyB's 'Sky+' set top box.

- *Mobile devices* have traditionally only received cellular mobile signals, but reception, transmission and sharing of information have become possible in a variety of ways. Cellular networks have themselves increased power and speed (2G to 2.5G to 3G). Technologies which enable the mobile sharing of data have been developed (e.g. WiFi, WiMax and Mobile-Fi offer additional ways to attach mobiles to the internet), and the ability to broadcast content to mobile telephones will become a reality during the life of this *User's Guide*. In this regard, several broadcast standards exist: DVB-H (a similar standard to digital terrestrial television broadcasting – DVB-T), DMB (a 'multimedia' variation on DAB) etc. Developments in handsets mean that mobile phones are achieving an enhanced level of physical connectivity (e.g. through the use of memory cards) and will develop an increasing capacity of the storage of data as well as a device for simple communication (offering the opportunity to use the mobile telephone as a truly 'converged' device for the storage, reception and distribution of copyright material)[6].

1   See **paragraphs 2.09 and 7.07.**
2   The CDPA was amended by the 2003 Regulations to remove the concept of a 'cable programme' as a distinct protectable copyright work, and to expand the concept of a 'broadcast' to include wired as well as wireless transmissions, See **paragraphs 2.09 and 2.10.**
3   See **paragraph 2.09.**
4   In much the same manner as the copyright works recorded on a film are entitled to separate protection to the film itself, see **Chapter 24**.
5   See **paragraphs 26.39 et seq**.
6   Technology convergence has been anticipated by Government not only through changes to the CDPA but also through the Communications Act 2003. The 2003 Act aims to introduce greater flexibility to respond to the 'technological and market changes driving modern media and communications'. The Act established a new regulator, OFCOM. The powers and duties of the ITC (and the Radio Authority, Office of Telecommunications, Broadcasting Standards Commission and Radiocommunications Agency) have been transferred to OFCOM, and the former authorities have ceased to exist. There is an explicit requirement on OFCOM to review the application and operation of its functions so as not to impose unnecessary burdens or maintain burdens which have become unnecessary (so-called 'light touch' regulation). OFCOM and its regulatory regime will not have direct powers over internet content whether fixed or mobile. Certainly, there is little or no mention of the internet, although the Government has also drafted the 2003 Act in technology-neutral language, aiming to be non-platform specific. The 2003 Act states that only a 'television licensable content service' would be regulated and these exclude true two-way and on-demand services i.e. just what you'd expect to find on a mobile (though neat distinctions between broadcast and on-demand media may not always

be so technically straightforward to maintain). Further regulatory changes are likely to follow the much debated review of the Television Without Frontiers Directive.

Definitional issues

26.02 The definitions of 'broadcast' 'wireless broadcast', 'wireless telegraphy' and 'communication to the public' in the CDPA (as amended by the 2003 Regulations) are considered in detail elsewhere[1]. Essentially, the definition of 'broadcast' has been amended such that, rather than catch only wireless transmissions of images, sounds and 'other information' which are capable, and intended, for reception by the public (as was the case prior to the 2003 Regulations), it will now catch wired transmission too, provided that these wireless or wired transmissions are not 'on demand'. The 'public' element will be satisfied even though broadcasts are encrypted provided that decoding equipment is made publicly available with suitable authority.

The definitions of 'cable programme' and 'cable programme service' have now been removed from the CDPA, by the implementation of the 2003 Regulations. Instead, the concept of wired transmissions to which the previous definitions referred has been subsumed into the definitions of 'broadcast' and 'communication to the public' that are referred to above[2].

The ability to obtain copyright protection for a work is in part dependent on establishing that the work falls within one of those categories of work for which copyright protection is available. A typical television programme will receive sui generis protection under the CDPA as a 'film'. However, more complex interactive 'digital products' which may be communicated to the public do not sit easily within any of the defined protectable copyright 'works' referred to in the CDPA. The word 'digital' cannot be found in the CDPA, but in this chapter we will use the expression 'digital product' to refer to any product which is an amalgam of copyright works designed for exploitation by means of digital media (such as a multimedia presentation on a web site).

Numerous terms of art are used in the broadcasting and cable industries and in the context of other digital transmission media, and it is impossible in the context of this *User's Guide* to attempt a comprehensive list, but it is worth clarifying some terms, some of which are not defined in the CDPA. So:

Affiliation Agreement means the agreement between a cable operator and a programme provider (often also called by the industry 'a cable operator's agreement').

Analogue means the direct electrical representation of pictures or sound, as opposed to digital which is a binary coded representation.

Analogue Television means a television system, or a television receiver, which makes use of signals transmitted as analogue waveforms.

Bandwidth means the range of frequencies occupied by a signal or the range of frequencies over which a signal receiver operates.

Basic Tier means the programmes which are supplied to a subscriber for the basic monthly rental (effectively the advertising supported independent channels and any community or similar programmes originated by the cable operator).

Broadband means a service or a connection which enables the movement of sufficient information to enable the conveyance of very complex data (such as that required to generate moving audio visual pictures) at speed. Services with a band width of 2 Mbits or greater are usually considered 'broadband'.

Broadcast Television means free or pay 'over-the-air' conventional broadcast television which is capable of reception by the general public by means of standard home antennae and/or aerials including terrestrial microwave transmission, so-called 'over-the-air' pay subscription television and multi point distribution services but excluding direct broadcasting by satellite and cable television.

Browser means software which allows computer based displays of web pages and other HTML text.

Bundling means the tying of one service or product to the supply of others, including some situations where the supply of services are linked through the use of discounts.

Cable Operator means a person providing a cable retransmission of a wireless broadcast[3].

Cable Retransmission means the reception and immediate retransmission by cable, including the transmission of microwave energy between terrestrial fixed points, of a wireless broadcast[4].

Cable Television means the transmission from a fixed point within the territory of an uplink signal from that point to a satellite and the retransmission of the same from such satellite to a beam aimed towards the territory for reception by the operators of receiving antennae and redistribution by such operators, either by cable to those households or other subscribers connected to such operators' relay systems, or by terrestrial re-broadcast by means of an encrypted signal or any closed circuit television system for reception by the occupants of dwellings and other buildings in multiple occupation but excluding Broadcasting Television and Direct Broadcasting by Satellite.

Cache means, commonly, the temporary storage of information for the purpose of speeding up the operation of network communications (as in cache copying).

Compact Disc Read-Only-Memory (CD-ROM) means a format which is able to record up to 65 Mbytes of computer data (software, data files, multimedia products etc) on a 12 cm disc.

Content Scramble System (CSS) means an encryption code designed to protect DVD's against unauthorised copying.

Copper Line is the 'narrowband' medium commonly used in telecommunications networks to connect telephone equipment to the local exchange. A copper line is unable to convey broadband type services unless used in conjunction with enabling technology such as DSL.

Crawler software means software applications which are designed to search the internet for particular types of data.

DBS means direct broadcast satellite.

DeCSS means software designed to circumvent copy protection afforded by CSS systems.

Digital means a method of representing information (such as text, audio or video) as a series of computerised signals (binary data bits) rather than in analogue form.

Digital Audio Broadcasting (DAB) means a radio signal which is transmitted in digital rather than analogue form.

Digital Compression means a process using computer analysis techniques to reduce the amount of information transmitted while still allowing reconstruction of a picture (sound or data) in the receiver.

Digital Programme Service Licensees (DPS) means the holder of a licence through a contract with a multiplex provider and subject to the multiplex provider's licence conditions.

Digital Rights Management (DRM) means the process of managing rights in the digital environment, via the implementation of systems designed to track and/or limit access to copyright works in accordance with pre-determined systems of rules.

Digital Satellite Television means the television services offered by digital satellite operators that offer a choice of more than 150 channels using a small receiving dish and receiver/decoder.

Digital Subscriber Line (DSL) means the technology which allows ordinary copper line to be used to send large quantities of information (such as the information necessary to convey moving audio visual pictures) to the user whilst also enabling a 'return path' (consisting for example of the kind of control channels necessary to establish interactive services) to be established.

Digital Terrestrial Television (DTT) means terrestrial broadcasting services by which channels are carried via Multiplexes.

Digital Video (DV) means a generic term for the use of digital binary data to represent pictures, used by some consumer equipment manufacturers to brand new digital TV products.

Digital Video Broadcasting (DVB) means an industry-led consortium of broadcasters, manufacturers, network operators, software developers, regulatory bodies and others committed to designing global standards for the delivery of digital television and data services.

Digital Video Disc (DVD) (aka 'Digital Versatile Disc') means a family of optical disc standards that have much greater capacity and flexibility than the Compact Disc (CD). They are typically used to store movies and use digital image compression technology.

Direct Broadcasting by Satellite means the transmission from a fixed point within a territory of an uplink signal from that point to a satellite and the retransmission of the same from such satellite in a beam for reception by those members of the general public possessing a satellite dish and/or any other receiving and decoding equipment necessary in order to receive the same in an intelligible form, but excluding Broadcast Television and Cable Television.

Direct to Home (DTH) Satellite Transmissions are those designed for reception by viewers via their own dish antennae and not via a cable programme service. They can be received over a very wide area – virtually the whole of Europe. The ASTRA satellite was the first satellite to provide such transmissions in Europe. Satellites can be used for delivering programmes directly to the public (DTH) or to designated users (such as cable operators and hotels) and (as with terrestrial broadcasts) the signal can be encrypted to prevent reception by unauthorised viewers.

Downlink means the signal sent from the transponder to earth.

Downloading means the process of copying a file onto a user's computer following reception from another source via a communication network.

E-commerce means the buying and selling of goods by electronic means e.g. the internet, interactive TV.

Encryption means scrambling the television signal in such a way that it can only be received by those who have the appropriate decoders.

EPG means 'electronic programme guide' a navigational aid allowing subscribers to view programme listings data and which may act as a gateway to other services, such as VOD, pay-per-view services, interactive services etc.

Footprint means the area of the earth's surface where the signal of the satellite can be received.

Framing means the actuation of a link from site (A) to (B), such that content from site B is displayed on the viewers screen, 'framed' by content (e.g. advertising) from site A.

Free Cable means a group of Cable Television channels selected by or supplied to any Cable Television subscriber with or without interactive services in consideration for which a single aggregate subscription or other fee is charged by the cable operator which is not allocated or apportioned to any channel.

Free-to-Air means a television service which is not encrypted and can be received without paying a fee.

Free-to-View means a television service which can be received without paying a fee, although transmissions may be encrypted and require use of a decoder and smart card. Reception may be deliberately restricted to certain geographical areas only.

Headend means the physical place from which a cable operator diffuses its signal to its subscribers.

Host means to provide a storage facility, typically a computer server, on which information is held.

Hyperlink means the functionality of linking between pages via the internet, by use of HTML code.

Hypertext Markup language (*HTML*) means the computer language used in the creation of web pages.

Information Society Service means a service 'normally provided for remuneration, at a distance, by electronic means and at the individual request of a recipient of services'[5].

Integrated Services Digital Network (*ISDN*) means an international communications standard for sending voice, video and data over digital telephone lines or normal telephone wires. ISDN lines offer high-speed access to the internet.

Interactive Service means any service or system (or any part of any service or system) which distributes transmits and/or exhibits audio and/or audiovisual programming and which allows the recipient to interrupt the linear reception of such programming and/or manipulate or interact with the content of the service or system but excluding NVOD and VOD.

Interactive Television: means TV programming with interactive content and enhancements, blending traditional TV viewing with the interactivity of a personal computer.

Internet Service Provider (*ISP*): means a company that provides individuals and organisations access to the internet, and other related services such as web site building and hosting.

Linking means the process whereby a web page (B) may be accessed from another web page (A) by means of the inclusion of HTML in page (A) code citing the relevant URL for (B). 'Deep linking' occurs where a link is made direct to content held on a third party site, bypassing any home page on that site.

Metatag means a 'tag' used to identify and order web pages.

MHEG-5 means a standardised method of providing digital text and simple interactive applications for digital television. Used in the UK for digital terrestrial television.

Microwave Distribution Video System (*MVDS*) means a television distribution service using microwave transmissions.

Microwave Frequencies means radio frequencies at the higher end of the radio spectrum, generally above 1 GHz (1,000 MHz).

Mini Disc (*MD*) means a re-recordable compact disc system for the domestic market. The MD carries up to 140 Mbytes of data, corresponding to 74 minutes of compressed digital audio programme.

MMDS means multichannel multipoint distribution system.

Modem means a device for connecting a computer or other device (e.g. a set-top box) to a network (usually a phone line). The modem converts the digital information that a computer uses into audio signals which can be sent along a phone line.

Multichannel Multipoint Distribution System (*MMDS*) means a system for broadcasting programme transmission using the UHF/SHF frequency bands. It provides low power, line-of-sight coverage to relatively small areas (sometimes referred to as a 'wireless cable network').

Multiple Systems Operator (*MSO*) means a cable operator running more than one system.

Multiplex means a single digital transmission comprising several programme services and sometimes additional data services.

Must-Carry means an obligation on cable systems to carry certain channels, usually the public service broadcast channels.

Narrowband means an old cable television system with a limited channel capacity, usually four or seven channels, or more frequently slower internet connectors (e.g. internet services utilised via a 56 kbps connection).

Near Video On Demand (*NVOD*) means a technique used in digital satellite and cable services using several channels to transmit a feature film with staggered start times.

Near Video on Demand means services on which the same programming is made available on a sufficient number of separate channels (at staggered intervals selected by the service provider) to enable the viewer to view the programme at short notice on demand.

Non Theatrical Distribution means distribution and exhibition to closed user groups, e.g. hotels, restaurants, bars, educational institutions (i.e. schools, public libraries, colleges, universities, dormitories and residence halls), churches, museums, summer camps, commercial premises, business and industry, the transportation industry (i.e. aeroplanes, ships and trains) and organisations of an educational, cultural, religious, charitable or social nature including drama groups, film societies and professional associations and to all other like entities.

Pay Per View or *Pay Per Period* means a service for which the viewer has to pay on a per programme or 'per period' (e.g. per day) basis.

Pay Television means any form of television for which the subscriber has to pay on a per channel basis.

Platform means a distribution system (e.g. terrestrial): through a ground-based transmitter to your aerial, (e.g. Freeview); via satellite to a dish aerial (e.g. Sky Digital); cable: (i.e. through the ground and cabled to your house or flat, e.g. NTL, Telewest and others); Digital Audio Broadcasting (DAB) from land based transmitters to your radio set, mobile telephony (e.g. Vodafone).

Premium Channels usually refers to more expensive channels which offer first run films or sports coverage where the programmes have a 'premium' over normal subscription channels. It can also be used to refer to pay-per-view channels.

Server means an individual computer on, for example, a LAN (Local Area Network), that acts as a service or resource provider to client computers, by sharing the resources within the network infrastructure.

Short Messaging Service (*SMS*) A text message service that enables short text messages of up to 160 characters in length to be sent and transmitted from a mobile phone.

SMATV means satellite (or small) multiple antenna television – that is, hotels, military camps, oil rigs, blocks of flats and other places of multiple occupancy which have antenna to receive satellite television for the benefit of their guests.

Streaming means the 'live' or 'as live' delivery of content.

Subscription Television means any Broadcast for which a premium is payable whether on a 'pay-per-view' 'pay-per-channel' 'pay' subscription or other periodic or other fee basis.

Teletext means the data system by which Teletext which uses the spare lines of the 625-line television signal to convey digital information and data to domestic television sets.

Terrestrial means a reception system where the signals are beamed from a ground (terrestrial) transmitter to an aerial.

Thumbnail means an image which is reduced in dimensions (usually to facilitate reproduction as part of, for example, a web page).

Transponder means that part of a satellite which receives a signal from earth and relays it back to earth.

TVRO means 'television receive only' and refers to the receiving station. Sometimes the expression 'earth station' is used to mean the same thing.

Uplink means the signal sent from the ground transmitting station to the transponder.

Uplink Station means the place from which programme-carrying signals are transmitted to a satellite.

Video means a tangible copy of recordings made on any disc, cassette or other storage device designed to be used in conjunction with reproduction apparatus which causes a picture to be visible to the viewer.

Video on Demand (*VOD*) means a service by which a particular programme may be sent to a single viewer (as distinct from, say, a group of subscribers) at the individual request of, and a time selected, by the viewer.

Watermark: means data embedded into digital content identifying the owner.

Wireless Application Protocol (*WAP*): means a standard for providing mobile phones, pagers and other handheld devices with secure access to email and text-based web pages.

Wireless Broadcast means a broadcast by means of wireless telegraphy[6].

Wireless Telegraphy means the sending of electro-magnetic energy over paths not provided by a material substance constructed or arranged for that purpose but does not include the transmission of microwave energy between terrestrial fixed points[7].

1   See **paragraphs 2.09** and **7.07**.
2   See **paragraph 2.10**.
3   Ibid.
4   CDPA s 144A(7).
5   CDPA s 144A(7).
6   CDPA s 178.
7   CDPA s 178.

Broadcasts and 'digital products' – ownership of copyright

Broadcasts

26.03   Issues of copyright ownership are considered in detail in **Chapter 10**, but in summary, the author of a broadcast will be the person making the broadcast and the broadcast will be one of joint authorship if more than one person is taken as making the broadcast. The criteria for establishing the maker are considered in detail elsewhere[1]. In brief, the maker will be the person transmitting the programme (if he is responsible for its content) and any person who provides the programme and makes the arrangements necessary for its transmission.

By way of example, satellite broadcasters, such as BSkyB, use their own transmitters or those of one of the companies licensed to provide uplinks (such as British Telecom). If, under the agreements with the programme providers for transmission services in transmitting the programmes, the programme providers agree not to transmit certain types of programming, such as obscene or defamatory programming, it could be argued that they have responsibility to some extent for the contents of the broadcasts. If this is correct, then the uplink operators would also be joint authors of the broadcasts with the companies providing the broadcasts.

1   See **paragraphs 2.01** et seq.

Digital products

26.04   Where a digital product is a 'multimedia' work comprised of a number of different copyright elements (such as literary, dramatic, musical and artistic works, films and sound recordings), each of these elements will be entitled to copyright protection in their own right (computer software included in the product will be protected as a 'literary work[1]). In other jurisdictions, visual components of some multi-media works have been construed as 'films' and that is also a possibility under UK law[2]. Taken as a whole, the collection of works will have no sui generis protection except to the extent that it may be construed as a compilation or a database (both categories of literary work) and/or as a database for the purpose of the database right[3]. In general terms, where the author of a digital product, consisting of a collection of other works, has invested skill and labour in its creation, so that it constitutes his own intellectual creation, his work will certainly be entitled to copyright protection. Additionally, the 'maker' of the database (i.e. the 'person who takes the initiative in obtaining, verifying or presenting the contents of a database and assumes the risks of investing in that obtaining, verification or presentation') will be entitled to exercise the quite distinct database right in the work[4].

In relation to the component copyright works, each of these will be created by an author, the identity of whom can be established according to normal copyright principles[5]. In essence, the author of any literary, dramatic, artistic or musical work will be the natural, qualifying, person who creates the protectable elements of the work[6], and that person will also as a general rule be the first owner of his work, the exception being where the author is an employee who creates the work during the course of his employment, in which event (in the absence of any agreement to the contrary) his employer will own the work[7]. Where the work includes films and sound recordings, the author of those elements will be the producer together with (in the case of a film) the director[8]. Like a film producer, the creator of a digital product will need to ensure that he has obtained adequate assignments or licences of all the 'underlying' works he wishes to include in his product which will be necessary to enable him to make and fully exploit his creation[9].

Particular issues arise in the context of computer-generated works. Where a literary, dramatic, musical or artistic work is computer-*generated* (i.e. as distinct from the situation in which the computer is simply used as a tool to assist human creativity), the author will be the person by whom the arrangements necessary for the creation of the work were undertaken[10].

1 See **paragraph 2.02**.
2 *Galaxy Electronics Pty Ltd v Sega Enterprises Ltd [1997] 145 ALR 21.*
3 See **Chapter 16**.
4 See **paragraphs 10.03 and Chapter 16**.
5 See **paragraphs 10.03 et seq**.
6 See **paragraph 10.02**.
7 See **paragraphs 2.02 and 10.11 et seq**.
8 See **Chapter 24** for a detailed analysis of the issues involved in this process.
9 See **paragraph 10.22**.
10 CDPA s 9(3).

Broadcasts and digital products: moral rights

26.05 Moral rights do not protect the authors of broadcasts. However, they do apply to the elements of a 'digital product' in the same way as, say, the elements of a film. Particular moral rights issues arise in the context of digital networks. In the context of digital media, where the rearrangement and re-purposing of copyright material is often of the essence of 'interactive' services, manipulation of content is common. Various acts take place which may be argued to infringe moral rights: a work may be 'cropped', reduced in size, framed with, or linked to, offensive material. English courts have not been asked, on the whole, to assess whether these activities infringe moral rights (although in one English case simply reducing an image in size was not enough to find summary judgment for a claimant who claimed that that use infringed his moral rights[1]). However, given the multi-jurisdictional nature of the internet, it will also be necessary to give appropriate consideration to the laws of other jurisdictions (such as France) where moral rights protection is enforced perhaps more vigorously than in the UK.

An electronic publisher will, for example, infringe moral rights if:

- he manipulates an author's works in circumstances where a moral right in the work arises and the act is sufficient to give, say, a derogatory treatment to the work[2]; so, for example, if he manipulates a work digitally in such a way as to change details or colours, he may infringe the author's moral rights;

- he fails to properly identify the author, or falsely attributes authorship of a work[3]. So, for example, if an on-line service or search engine makes available digital images of artistic works without crediting the artist, this may infringe the artist's right to be identified as author of a work (the 'paternity right').

It follows that publishers and other providers of such services must take care to ensure that they are free to manipulate the material they acquire without complaint from the author. In practice, this will require ensuring that suitable moral rights waivers are obtained from those involved[4].

The paternity right must be asserted by the person entitled to the right[5]. It follows that when acquiring rights from, say, a producer of material to be used by an electronic publisher or 'on-line' producer, it will be necessary to take appropriate warranties that waivers have been obtained from all relevant authors, and that no paternity rights have been asserted[6].

1　See **paragraphs 11.12 and 27.21**.
2　Ibid.
3　See **paragraphs 11.01 et seq.**
4　See **paragraph 11.29**.
5　See **paragraph 11.08**.
6　See **Chapter 11** for a full analysis of moral rights. During the life of this edition of the *User's Guide* the CDPA will be amended to introduce moral rights for performers. These are considered in detail at **paragraph 11.33**.

Duration of rights

26.06　The term of copyright in a broadcast (as distinct from any copyright work included in the broadcast) under the CDPA is 50 years from the end of the calendar year in which the broadcast is made. Repeating a broadcast does not extend the life of copyright[1]. It should be noted that this period may vary downward in relation to the protection afforded to broadcasts emanating from outside the EEA[2].

A 'digital product', will, where it is protected as a literary work (either as a compilation or a database), when taken as a whole, receive the same period of protection afforded to other literary works, namely 70 years following the end of the year of the author's death[3]. Any database right which may subsist in the digital product will continue until expiry of the later of 15 years after the end of the year of its completion, or 15 years after it is first made available to the public (provided that period starts within 15 years after the end of the year of its completion)[4]. Ordinary principles of duration of term will apply to the period of copyright in the components to the digital products.

1 See **paragraphs 6.16 and 6.17**.
2 See **Chapter 4**.
3 See **paragraphs 6.06 et seq**.
4 See **paragraph 16.07**.

Acquiring and licensing rights

26.07 Issues regarding the acquisition of rights in programmes intended for television broadcast are considered in more detail elsewhere in this *User's Guide*[1].

Licences or assignments of the owners of all copyright works included within a 'communication to the public' will be required. Reference should be made to the *Table of Incidents of Copyright* which summarises the incidents of these works[2]. So, the scenario or screenplay of a film, whether intended for television or otherwise, is a dramatic work. The scripts of documentaries or newscasts, or even lists of sports results, are literary works once they have been reduced to writing, and consequently it is not permissible to transmit communications to the public which are simply copies or readings of the sports pages of newspapers without a licence from the owner of the copyright. If, however, the sports results are communicated verbally to the television or radio station, there will be no copyright in the verbal communication and it can be used for the purposes of broadcasting without the need for any licence. Where a broadcaster purchases his own programming from an independent producer and other third party, the programme acquisition and licence agreement will impose obligations on the producer to ensure all underlying rights have been properly acquired for inclusion in the programme.

The position of the creator of a digital product is largely analogous to that of a film or television producer[3], although a number of additional issues should also be considered in the context of acquiring rights across digital networks:

- *Uncontemplated technologies*: in the context of rapidly advancing technology it may be difficult to ensure that the rights obtained are wide enough to include all the delivery platforms (such as the internet) which the user may require during the life of his rights in the product. Problems arise in the context of technologies not in the contemplation of the parties at the time of contract. In each case it will be necessary to construe the terms of a contractual licence to decide whether the wording is wide enough to include the new technology, an issue considered in detail elsewhere in this *User's Guide*[4]. Under UK law, this problem is avoided where an assignment of copyright is taken.

- *International issues*: when dealing with products intended for transmission via the internet, it will be necessary to take account of the fact that the service may be received internationally. This issue is considered in detail elsewhere in this chapter[5].

- *Collective licensing*: inclusion of music in an internet service will involve exploitation of music publishing rights and possibly sound recording rights. Considerations relating to the exploitation of such works are set out more fully elsewhere in this *User's Guide*[6]. The EU has encouraged the establishment of centralised clearing houses allowing the procedures of digital works a 'one stop shop' at which to clear rights. There have been several European initiatives in this regard (in the UK, the PRS/MCPS's *Music Alliance* is one example). The EU has also funded several pilot rights management systems, but is beyond the scope of this *User's Guide* to consider these projects in detail[7].

- *What terms will the service be available on?* If the digital product is to be made available 'on-line', will use be limited to a particular web site or service, and will that service be linear, interactive, on demand etc?

- *Ongoing obligations*: will a licensor have any ongoing obligations following delivery of materials (such as updating on-line databases provided)?

- *Underlying tools and software*: notwithstanding any grant of rights, there will be a category of rights which the publisher/provider will receive only a limited right to use. Any software or tools used to create or operate the digital product (e.g. to recreate interactive elements) will be copyright works[8] and the producer will need to ensure that any grant of rights he enters into is limited to such (usually non-exclusive) rights in the software and 'tools' necessary to use the digital work for the purposes envisaged by the agreement[9].

Granting rights to exploit copyright in a digital environment may raise novel issues as to whether, and if so when, it can be said that agreement is reached as between licensor and licensee. Although a detailed discussion of contract law principles is beyond the scope of this user's guide, basic contract law requires that in order to establish a binding contract the elements of offer, acceptance and consideration (i.e. the exchange of value) must be satisfied. No further formalities are required, although any assignment or exclusive licence of copyright should be in writing[10].

1   See **Chapter 24.**
2   See **Appendix 4**
3   See **Chapter 24**.
4   See **paragraph 10.31**.
5   See **paragraph 26.59**.
6   See **paragraph 13.01**.
7   See Dr Martin Schippan's overview of this issue. [2000] EIPR, issue 1.
8   Software is protected under the CDPA as a literary work, See **paragraph** 2.02.
9   Computer software is considered in detail in **Chapter 31**.
10   See **paragraph 10.24.**

Shrink wrap licences

26.08   In the case of off-line software purchases, it is common for licence terms to be enclosed within the sealed wrapping enclosing the purchased product. A notice in the wrapping may instruct the user not to open the product unless he agrees to the licence terms. The ability of such an arrangement to incorporate terms into a contract has not been tested before the English courts (on basic contract law principles, the time to incorporate terms into a contract is before the contract is accepted). It follows, that if the product has already been purchased before an opportunity to read the licence terms is offered, there is a clear argument that such terms are not incorporated into the contract. For obvious reasons, shrink wrap licences are not an option in the context of on-line services, although such licences may accompany software etc purchased 'off line' for use as part of on-line services (e.g. networked games).

Click wrap licences

26.09   More commonly, particularly in the context of on-line services, the user will be presented with an icon, clicking on which will constitute acceptance of the terms for use of the relevant material.

Browse wrap licences

26.10   Often, users will be invited to consult privacy and other licence terms as a precondition to viewing an on-line service. Commonly, web sites will include links to terms and conditions and notify the user that continued use of the site should be deemed to constitute acceptance of those terms, whether or not they have in fact been viewed. However, case law in the US has questioned the validity of such licences, unless the user is compelled to undertake some positive act of acceptance of the terms (such as clicking on an 'I accept' icon)[1].

1   *Specht v Netscape Communications Corpn. and AOL Inc, Case 00 Civ 4871 (AKH) US Dist. Court, Southern NY.*

Implied licences

26.11 Where material is made available on-line in an unrestricted manner, and knowing that certain acts restricted by copyright will be undertaken by any person viewing the content, then it may be argued that the person so making the content available does so together with an implied licence to undertake those acts. By way of example, any person viewing content offered on a web-page will make a copy of that content in his computer's memory. It follows that it may be implied that the person knowingly making the content available on that web-page should properly be taken to have authorised that act of copying. However, in implying licence terms, the law will not go further than is necessary to give 'business efficacy' to the relationship. It follows that it will be more difficult to argue, under English law principles, that simply making available content in this manner should be taken to have permitted other uses of the content (such as redistribution etc)[1].

Issues regarding the ownership and transfer of rights in copyright works are considered in further detail in **Chapter 10**.

1 See **paragraph 10.30** for a discussion of implied licences.

Broadcasts

Teletext services

26.12 Teletext transmissions[1], which are transmitted by broadcasters (including cable operators) as part of their programming, are entitled to copyright protection as a broadcast[2]. So, those supplying data which is for use on Oracle or Ceefax should bear in mind that they are entitled to be paid for a licence for the broadcasting of their work. The issues discussed in this chapter in relation to broadcasts therefore apply equally to teletext services.

1 Such as those made by Oracle and Teletext Ltd.
2 See **paragraph 26.02**.

Wireless broadcasts – overspill and the 'country of origin' principle

26.13 Terrestrial wireless broadcast signals intended for reception in a single country are often capable of reception in other jurisdictions. The concept is known as 'overspill'. So, for example, German television signals are received and relayed by cable stations in Holland, Belgium, Switzerland and Austria, and the signals of the UK broadcasters are capable of being received on the coast of mainland Europe. In the context of satellite signals the issue of overspill is much more significant. The 'footprint' of a satellite will cross many more borders than a terrestrial signal, to a much larger potential audience, although only a relatively small area of that footprint may be exploited. It is common for broadcasting agreements to acknowledge an acceptable degree of overspill and to provide for measures to limit its effect, usually by financially compensating the programme provider or by requiring that the signal is encrypted and decoders are not actively marketed other than in the territory of grant.

A foreign broadcast which is not protected in the UK will not be infringed by inclusion in, say, a communication to the public, although such inclusion may infringe any copyright material (e.g. literary, dramatic and musical works) included in the broadcast.

The CDPA contains provisions allowing the Government to apply copyright protection to works and people from countries to which the CDPA does not otherwise extend[1]. This is achieved by an 'Order in Council', implemented by Statutory Instrument. The latest such Order[2] protects broadcasts originating from a number of listed countries. These include, for example, all EEA states.

For the purpose of ascertaining whether a wireless broadcast is entitled to copyright protection under the CDPA, the broadcast is treated as being made at:

'the place where, under the control and responsibility of the person making the broadcast, the programme-carrying signals are introduced into an uninterrupted chain of communication (including, in the case of a satellite transmission, the chain leading to the satellite and down towards the earth)'[3].

This 'country of origin' principle was introduced into the CDPA by the 1996 Regulations, which implemented the Satellite and Cable Directive[4]. The position is varied in the case of certain satellite broadcasts, where the wireless broadcast is made from a country which is not an EEA state and where the law of that country fails to provide a specified level of copyright protection. In these circumstances, if the country in which the uplink station is an EEA state:

'(a) that place shall be treated as the place from which the broadcast is made, and
(b) the person operating the uplink station shall be treated as the person making the broadcast'[5].

If, on the other hand, the uplink station is not located in an EEA state, but a person who is established in an EEA state has *commissioned* the making of the broadcast:

'(a)   that person shall be treated as the person making the broadcast; and
(b)   the place in which he has his principal establishment in the EEA shall be treated as the place from which the broadcast is made'[6].

For these purposes, the specified level of protection, below which the non-EEA originating state must at least afford a level of protection, is as follows:

'(a)   exclusive rights in relation to the wireless broadcast, equivalent to those conferred by section 20 (infringement by communication to the public) on the authors of literary, dramatic, musical and artistic works, films and broadcasts;
(b)   a right in relation to live wireless broadcasting equivalent to that conferred on a performer by section 182(1)(b)(consent required for live broadcast of a performance); and
(c)   a right for authors of sound recordings and performers to share in a single equitable remuneration in respect of the wireless broadcasting of sound recordings'[7].

So, by way of example, if a US television broadcaster, which makes its programmes in the United States, uplinks its transmission from the USA to a satellite which is downlinked to Europe and the signal is retransmitted by an uplink station located in the UK, then the UK will be treated as the place from which the broadcast is made.

Section 6A(2)(b) of the CDPA (which provides that the person operating the uplink station is to be treated as the person making the broadcast) seems also to have the effect of making the UK uplink company the owner of the broadcast because the owner of the broadcast is the person making the broadcast[8]. In the debate in the House of Commons on the 1996 Regulations, a Government spokesman stated that this was not intended to be the case and he did not believe that a UK court would so hold. However, on the face of the wording of the CDPA, this does seem to be the proper construction.

If the transmission from the USA is not downlinked to an EEA uplink station for retransmission to the UK, but is downlinked for direct reception by the public as a single hop (i.e. there is an uplink from the USA and reception of the downlink from that satellite by the UK public), then it is necessary to establish whether the wireless broadcast has been 'commissioned'. If it was commissioned, then the commissioner is the person making the wireless broadcast and the place where the broadcast is made is that from which the commissioner has his principal establishment in the EEA.

'Commission' is not defined in the CDPA. An obvious case would be if the UK broadcaster requested an American broadcaster to transmit an NFL football game live from the USA and paid for the transmission. There would be no doubt in such a case that the UK broadcaster commissioned the broadcast.

In the case of a US broadcaster who uses an Atlantic satellite for direct to home transmissions in Europe, which he uplinks from the USA, there could be no suggestion that the wireless broadcast had been commissioned by a person established in an EEA state. In such a case the only conclusion would be that the place of making the broadcast was the USA and the person making the broadcast was indeed the broadcaster. In these circumstances one would have to look at The Copyright (Application to Other Countries) Order 1999 to determine if the CDPA extends[9]. The USA is not so listed and, therefore, the broadcast would have no copyright protection in the UK.

1   CDPA s 159.
2   The Copyright (Application to Other Countries) Order 1999, SI 1999/1751, See **paragraph 4.09**.
3   CDPA s 6(4).
4   See **paragraph 14.03**.
5   CDPA s 6A(2).
6   CDPA s 6A(3).
7   CDPA s 6A(1).
8   See **paragraph 4.09**.
9   Ibid.

Infringements[1]

26.14   To summarise, the acts restricted by copyright in relation to broadcasts are:

- *Copying*: this will include taking a photograph of the whole or a substantial part of an image (i.e. 'video grab')[2].
- *Issuing of copies to the public*: this applies to the first act of putting particular copies of the work into circulation within the EEA[3] (e.g. making a copy of a live broadcast by video and distributing the video to the public).
- *Playing or showing in public*: where a broadcast is shown or played in public to an audience (such as, for example, on a 'big screen' like those commonly displayed in sports and other bars), the copyright in a broadcast, or in any sound recording or film which is included in the broadcast, will not be infringed, provided the performance is before a non-paying audience[4].
- *Communication to the public*[5]: if a television station wishes, say, to

broadcast part of another broadcast as part of its own programming, it will need a licence from the other broadcaster to do so. So, for example, if a cable operator includes in his service a live transmission from the local flower show and this programme is relayed to the subscribers of a competitor in a neighbouring area, then the competitor will have infringed the copyright in the broadcast of the operator which originated the transmission from the flower show[6].

It is worth noting that the restricted acts of rental and lending and adaptation are *not* applicable to broadcasts, although they may well be applicable to the content featured on such transmissions[7].

An infringement will only take place if a 'substantial part' of a work is copied. The test for what constitutes a 'substantial part' is qualitative, not quantitative[8]; see, however, the exceptions to copyright infringement considered at **Chapter 9** and below.

1   The acts which may only be undertaken with the authority of the copyright owner are considered in detail in **Chapter 7**.
2   See **paragraph 7.03**.
3   See **paragraph 7.04**.
4   See **paragraph 7.06**.
5   See **paragraph 7.07**.
6   Although See **paragraph 26.12**.
7   See **paragraphs 7.05 and 7.08**.
8   See **paragraph 8.06**.

Broadcasts: acts permitted in relation to broadcasts

26.15   Most of the general exceptions to the restricted acts, apply to broadcasts[1]. A number of specific permitted acts are also authorised in respect of these categories of work. These are, in summary, as follows:

- making incidental copies for purposes of making broadcasts ('the ephemeral right')[2];
- making copies for the purposes of supervision and control of broadcasts[3];
- making copies for purposes of time shifting for private use[4];
- taking photographs of television broadcasts for private use[5];
- making free public showings of broadcasts[6];
- reception and retransmission of broadcasts[7];
- making and issuing to the public sub-titled copies of broadcasts[8];
- making copies for archival purposes[9].

1   See **Chapter 9**.
2   See **paragraph 9.31**.

3   See **paragraph 9.32**.
4   See **paragraph 9.33**.
5   See **paragraph 9.34**.
6   See **paragraphs 7.06 and 9.35**.
7   See **paragraph 9.36**.
8   See **paragraph 9.37**.
9   See **paragraph 9.38**.

Communicating to the public – live events

26.16   There is no copyright in a live event per se. So, if a communication to the public includes a live transmission of an event which is not protectable as a copyright work[1], and does not contain protectable performances[2], no licence will be required to transmit the event. A sporting event, for example, does not attract copyright, and sportsmen will not usually acquire performers' rights[3]. The fees paid by broadcasters to sports governing bodies for the 'broadcast rights' to sporting events are not to acquire copyright. What broadcasters pay for is the right to bring their cameras onto the premises to create live signals and films recording the event (the 'access right' – which is protected not by the law of copyright, but of trespass).

If an event contains copyright material or a protectable performance, these rights will need to be cleared. So, for example, a 'half-time show' featuring the display of a military band will require a licence of the copyright music and an appropriate performers' consent and assignment of performers' property rights[4].

In practice, however, it is almost impossible to conceive of a communication to the public which does not include some other protected works. A live music concert, which is so communicated, will, for example, include (at least) the copyright in the musical compositions which are included, and (where broadcast) the copyright in the broadcast itself (i.e. the programme carrying signal). Inevitably, there will also be a number of other rights to consider, such as the copyright in any artistic works used in set design, and any performer's property or non property rights arising in respect of performances rendered by the musicians.

Although internet-based transmissions to the public are not, on the whole, 'broadcasts', some such transmissions are included within the definition of a 'broadcast' set out in the CDPA, including the simultaneous transmission of live events[5]. It follows that if acquiring rights to transmit a live event on an internet streaming service, it is necessary to ensure that wide rights to 'communicate the work' should be obtained.

1   See **paragraph 1.02**.

2   See **Chapter 12**.
3   See **paragraph 12.02**.
4   See **paragraphs 12.19 et seq**.
5   See **paragraph 7.07**.

Broadcasts and public performance

26.17   A public performance of a broadcast may be effected by the operation of receiving apparatus (e.g. a television set or other monitor), but the person who sends the transmission is not responsible for such a public performance, and nor is a performer whose performance may appear in the transmission[1].

Although it is a restricted act applicable to broadcasts to play or show them in public, there is an exception which permits them to be shown in public so long as the audience have not paid for admission[2]. So, for example, to install a television set carrying a broadcast in the bar of a hotel to which the public have not paid for admission does not infringe the copyright in the broadcast, or in any sound recordings (unless the sound recordings are 'excepted sound recordings'[3]) and films included in it. If, however, such a performance takes place in the bar of a theatre, to which the public must pay for admission, the copyright in the broadcast (and its contents) will be infringed unless the performance is properly authorised. The infringement is caused by the theatre, which is then liable to be sued, not only by the broadcaster, but also by the owners of the copyright in all the works included in the broadcast.

If a hotel owner decides to install his own closed-circuit television set, and show a videotape of a film for the benefit of his guests, where there is a television set in a public part of the hotel, or in individual rooms, he will almost certainly be infringing copyright in the film and underlying works by undertaking the restricted acts of performing or playing the works in public[4] and including the film in a broadcast[5]. This use would constitute a public performance notwithstanding that only one guest might view the film on any single television set.

It is worth noting that this exception to copyright infringement only applies to broadcasts and not to any other communication to the public. So, for example, the proprietors of a bar which is open to members of the public who have not paid for admission will infringe copyright if they publicly show an 'on demand' transmission (such as a VOD film) in their bar without an appropriate licence to do so.

1   CDPA s 19(4), See **paragraph 7.06**.
2   See **paragraph 9.35**.
3   See **paragraphs 7.06 and 9.33**.

4 See **paragraph 7.06**.
5 See **paragraph 7.07**.

Broadcasts

Satellite broadcasts in the EEA

26.18 The provisions of the CDPA regarding the protection of satellite broadcasts referred to above[1] should be mirrored in the legislation of all EEA member states, since the 'country of origin' principle was introduced by the Satellite and Cable Directive[2]. The significance of the principle is that an owner or licensee of the rights in a copyright work in one member state can license the broadcast by satellite of the work from that state to a footprint covering the whole of the EEA. The DTH reception in countries where there are other copyright owners or licensees of the work does not infringe the rights of such owners and licensees[3].

This position is to be contrasted with the position in relation to cable retransmissions of these broadcasts[4].

1 See **paragraph 26.03**.
2 See **paragraph 14.03**.
3 Subject to the exception referred to at **paragraph 26.21** for co-production agreements.
4 Which are considered further at **paragraph 26.20**.

Cable retransmissions of local/national wireless broadcasts

26.19 Under certain circumstances, a wireless broadcast made *from the UK* (i.e. not from elsewhere in the EEA) may be received and immediately retransmitted by cable without infringing copyright in the broadcast, or works included within the broadcast[1]. The circumstances are set out in detail elsewhere on this *User's Guide*[2]. Where a cable operator has the right to retransmit under this provision, and the broadcaster has failed to clear the necessary rights in works which he includes in his service, the fact that a retransmission takes place under this provision is relevant when considering damages[3]. So, broadcasters must ensure that the appropriate retransmission right is cleared. PRS for example, factor such retransmissions into account when considering licences for musical works to be used in broadcasts.

1 CDPA s 73.
2 See **paragraph 9.36**.
3 CDPA s 73(3).

Cable retransmissions of broadcasts from other EEA states – the 'cable retransmission right'

26.20 Inclusion of a wireless broadcast in another communication to the public (e.g. a cable retransmission) will infringe the copyright in the broadcast[1]. However, the CDPA, as amended by the 1996 Regulations, contains special provisions in relation to the cable retransmission of broadcasts originating from elsewhere in the EEA, which impact upon the rights or copyright owners.

The CDPA recognises the right of the owner of any literary, dramatic, musical or artistic work, film or sound recording, to grant or refuse authorisation for cable retransmission of a wireless broadcast from another EEA member state in which the work is included[2]. This right is known, in the CDPA, as 'the cable retransmission right'[3]. However, each such owner (other than the maker of the broadcast) is required to exercise his rights against the cable operator only through a licensing body[4].

If the copyright owner has not transferred management of his cable retransmission right to a licensing body, the licensing body which manages rights of the same category (e.g. AGICOA for films, PRS for musical compositions, PPL for sound recordings) will be deemed to be mandated to manage his rights[5]. A number of other bodies have established collection services for members, including ALCS (writers) and ComPact (producers)[6]. The copyright owner will be deemed to have the same rights and obligations resulting from any relevant agreement between the cable operator and the licensing body as do copyright owners who have transferred management of their cable retransmission rights to that licensing body[7]. The copyright owner must exercise his rights against the licensing body within three years of the date of the cable retransmission[8].

This cable retransmission right does not contradict the local retransmission right referred to at **paragraph 26.19** because it only applies to wireless broadcasts from other EEA member states, whilst **paragraph 26.19** applies to 'local' broadcasts only.

An important exception to the principle of collective licensing is made in the case of rights exercisable by the maker of the initial broadcast, whether in relation to the broadcast itself, or any works included within the broadcast[9].

So, if a UK cable operator wishes to retransmit a Dutch satellite television broadcast which includes a film, only (a) the Dutch broadcaster (in respect of cable retransmission rights he controls), or (b) AGICOA or a similar body, could claim for breach of copyright in the

cable retransmission right and remuneration from the UK cable operator even though the film owner is not a member of AGICOA. The film
producer will be able to claim its share of AGICOA revenues attributable to the retransmission of the broadcast of the film under normal
AGICOA rules, within three years of the date of the cable retransmission as if it had been a member of AGICOA at that date.

Again, these provisions of the CDPA implement the Satellite and
Cable Directive and as such should be largely mirrored throughout the
EEA.

1   See **paragraph 7.07**.
2   CDPA s 144A(1).
3   CDPA s 144A
4   CDPA s 144A(2).
5   CDPA s 144A(3).
6   See **paragraph 13.01** and **Appendix 1** for contact details.
7   CDPA s 144A(4).
8   CDPA s 144A(5).
9   CDPA s 144A(6).

Satellite broadcasting of films and international co-productions

26.21   International co-production agreements for films normally provide that the respective production companies retain copyright ownership of the film in their own countries. The effect of the provisions
described in **paragraph 26.13** is to cut across such arrangements (since
one producer can license the broadcast by satellite of the film by
reception in homes across Europe including the country of the
co-producer, thus damaging the value of the film rights in that country).
The 1996 Regulations sought to alleviate the problem this created for
film producers by providing that, where a co-production agreement has
been concluded before 1 January 1995 between two or more
co-producers of a film, one of whom is a national of an EEA state, and
the provisions of the agreement grant to the parties exclusive rights to
exploit all communication to the public of the film in separate geographical areas, the person to whom the exclusive exploitation rights in
relation to the UK have been granted may not make any satellite
broadcast of the work from the UK without the consent of the other
party to the agreement 'whose language-related exploitation rights
would be adversely affected by that broadcast' if the agreement does
not 'expressly or by implication address satellite broadcasting from the
UK'[1].

So, if a co-production agreement came into existence before 1 January 1995 between a UK film production company and a French film
production company for the co-production of a film under which each

party retained the right to communicate the film to the public in its own territory, neither producer could exercise the satellite broadcasting rights in the film from its own territory by way of a DTH broadcast intended to be received by the public in the other producer's country without the other's consent. In practice, in circumstances where this provision may apply, it would be prudent for the person acquiring satellite broadcasting rights to procure the agreement of all co-producers to the broadcasting agreement in addition to the usual warranties and indemnities.

1   1996 Regulations, reg 29.

Encrypted transmissions

26.22   Some satellite television transmissions are encrypted and are intended for reception by cable television systems, hotels and designated SMATV systems only. Accordingly, decoders are not made available to the public. The reception of a broadcast includes reception of a broadcast relayed by means of a telecommunications system[1]. Since a cable television system is a telecommunications system, such transmissions are 'capable of being lawfully received by members of the public'. However, they do not come within the definition of 'broadcast' because the decoders for those transmissions are not made available to the public and, accordingly, the transmissions do not qualify for copyright protection as broadcasts. Nevertheless, the CDPA does protect such transmissions from fraudulent reception[2].

1   CDPA s 6(5).
2   See **paragraph 26.24**.

Satellite broadcasting and cable agreements

26.23   There are potentially at least five types of agreement which a channel provider usually enters into in relation to a satellite or a cable transmission which have copyright implications:

An agreement for the provision of services on a transponder or a transponder lease: the transponder lease may be made with British Telecom, or one of the other licensed UK uplink station operators, or more likely, directly with the satellite operator such as EUTELSAT or Société Européenne des Satellites (the owners of ASTRA). In the context of digital satellite transmissions, digital compression allows the transmission of several channels of television programming via each single transponder. The transmissions to the satellite must be from a single uplink station of all the channels intended for one transponder. However, the signals to the uplink station can be provided by different programme providers. Thus, the owner or lessee of a whole transponder may enter into sub-leases with other channel providers to take their digital transmissions to uplink to the satellite. Where these transmissions are of pay television services, it is necessary for the 'gateway holder' to provide subscription management systems to the programme providers and for a common encryption system to be used. So, the programme provider which is not itself a transponder lessee, will enter into a single multiplex agreement with the gateway keeper to cover uplink transponder services and the provision of a subscriber management system.

Although the transponder lease provides services to the lessee which are basically passive (in that the role of the transponder is to receive and retransmit the channel provider's signal from the uplink station), it is customary for the satellite owner and operator to impose certain conditions on the channel provider relating to the content of its programmes, for example, to ensure that the programming complies with the provisions of the Television Without Frontiers Directive. Indeed, the satellite operator may reserve the right to 'turn off' the transponder if the channel provider is in breach of these conditions.

The CDPA provides that the person making the broadcast is 'the person transmitting the programme, if he has responsibility to any extent for its contents, and to any person providing the programme etc'[1]. Whether or not the satellite operator is 'broadcasting' the channel provider's signal within the meaning of the CDPA depends on whether monitoring the programme and taking the right to close down transmissions for reasons relating to its content constitutes 'responsibility to any extent for its contents'. If so, the satellite operator will be one of the broadcasters and is liable to be sued by the copyright owners of the material in the signal who have not licensed use of their material in the broadcast by the programme provider.

Accordingly, the channel provider should be prepared to indemnify the uplink station operators and satellite operators against any actions that may be taken against them as persons making the broadcast in the event of the broadcasts constituting a breach of a third party's copyright.

It is normal in transponder leases for the lessor to take the right to record the channel provider's signals for monitoring purposes. The recording, by whatever means, of copyright work infringes the restricted act of making copies[2]. The CDPA provides that copyright is not infringed by the making of certain recordings for the purpose of monitoring and regulating UK television broadcasters[3]. However, these provisions do not extend to monitoring by a multiplexer or a satellite owner and operator. It is unlikely that the channel provider will be able to obtain any relaxation of this requirement by the satellite operator and accordingly will need to ensure that programme acquisition agreements, and indeed agreements with any copyright holder providing the copyright material which is used in broadcasts, give permission for copying for monitoring purposes.

An agreement with the uplink station to transmit the service to the satellite: the agreement between the uplink station and the channel provider will only have copyright consequences if, like the satellite operator, the uplink station can be said to 'have responsibility to any extent' for the contents of the programme. If the uplink station agreement contains warranties as to the content of the programme by the channel provider and the uplink station reserves the right to monitor the signals and to cut off the transmission to the satellite in the event of a breach of the warranties then it may be difficult for the uplink station to argue that it has no responsibility for the programme contents. In these circumstances, like the satellite operator, the uplink station will need indemnities from the channel provider against third party claims for breach of copyright contained in the programme signals.

Agreements with the suppliers of the programme material ('programme acquisition agreements'): programme acquisition agreements will include a number of restrictions on the use by the channel provider of the programmes. This is partly because the licensors may have limited rights in the copyright elements in the programme and partly because certain uses may trigger additional (or residual) union payments. If the agreement is for a satellite broadcast and the channel provider's signal is encrypted and intended for reception in a limited part of the satellite footprint, the channel provider should be required (insofar as possible within the boundaries of competition law)[4] not to issue nor to permit the issue of decoders capable of decoding the signal outside the licence area. The question of reception and relay by SMATV operators (other than via cable stations) will be a matter for negotiation. The channel provider will be well advised to seek the widest possible rights in this regard. If any country within the footprint introduces a levy on the sale of blank audio and video cassettes, it is possible that one of the beneficiaries of the levy will be the channel provider. The copyright owners of the programme may well insist that the channel providers pay to them the proportion of the levy attributable to the programme in question.

The contract should specifically permit copyright for technical monitoring purposes by uplink stations, satellite operators and cable stations.

Public performances before paying audiences will usually be forbidden, or subject to special terms.

Cable affiliation agreements: traditionally, a cable operator, when entering into an agreement with a channel provider, will be required to agree not to cut the channel's programmes, nor to record them and transmit them at a different time, nor to add anything to the programmes. He may be asked to ensure that the channel is not shown in public. In turn, the cable operator will require the channel provider to warrant that he has obtained all the necessary licences from all the copyright owners of the material in the channel's programmes, and to indemnify the cable operator against any copyright infringement proceedings that may be brought against the cable operator, consequential upon his transmitting materials supplied to him by the channel provider. If shops, hotels and other places are subscribers to the cable programme service, because of the likelihood of public performances taking place, the agreement should state that the programmes are licensed for such types of performances.

The cable operator must also enquire whether the channel provider has obtained blanket licences from the appropriate copyright collection societies which extend to the inclusion of the material in his programmes, failing which he will have to apply for such licences himself[5]. In practice it is common for the cable operator to impose the liability to obtain these licences on the channel provider.

Cable operators will (and should) require an exception from the restrictions upon the recording of any part of the programmes to permit them to record for monitoring, since cable operators are obliged to keep copies of all their programming for monitoring purposes. This exception is not, strictly speaking, necessary as a matter of law because the keeping of copies for these purposes will not infringe copyright in any work[6].

The channel provider will also require that the channel is given equal prominence on any EPG to other channels.

In the context of digital and interactive services, operators will need to reserve the right to enable subscribers to insert or overlay on the television screen (sometimes over the programme) the EPG, icons, text and other content identifying the channel and other interactive services. The channel provider will want to restrict the operator from overlaying these interactive elements itself (i.e. without the subscriber's prompt). The operator will need to re-size, re-position and frame content to the extent necessary to enable subscribers to access interactive content on the service.

Finally, an agreement with the subscriber management system operator is required. A detailed consideration of this agreement is beyond the scope of this *User's Guide*.

1   CDPA s 6(3)(a).
2   See **paragraph 7.03**.
3   See **paragraph 9.31**.
4   See **Chapter 14**.
5   See **Chapter 13**.
6   See **paragraph 9.32**.

Broadcasts and 'information society services' – fraudulent reception

26.24   The CDPA has long included provisions which make it a criminal offence to dishonestly receive broadcasts or cable programmes, and these were revised by the 2000 Regulations (which implemented in the UK the provisions of the Conditional Access Directive[1]), and by the 2003 Regulations[2].

The intention of the 2000 Regulations is to protect all broadcasting and 'information society services', offered to the public *within the EU,* which are subject to payment of subscriptions or other payments (including all forms of pay television, radio and 'on demand' services). Internet-based services which place conditions on access will also be included within this meaning.

To best comprehend the revised provisions, it is important to understand the terminology used. Following the 2000 Regulations, the CDPA[3] now contains the following definitions:

* *apparatus* is widely defined (as previously) to include 'any device, component or electronic data';
* *decoder* has the same meaning previously given by the Act: 'any apparatus which is designed or adapted to enable (whether on its own or with any other apparatus) an encrypted transmission to be decoded';
* *transmission* means any programme included in a broadcast service or 'information society service which is provided from a place within the UK or any other member state'[4];
* a decoder will now be considered 'unauthorised' if it enables an encrypted transmission 'to be accessed in an intelligible form without payment of the fee (however imposed) which the person making the transmission, or on whose behalf it is made, charges for accessing the transmission, or service';
* *conditional access technology* means 'any technical measure or arrangement whereby access to encrypted transmissions in an intelligible form is made conditional upon prior individual authorisation'.

A person now commits a criminal offence if he:

'(a) makes, imports, distributes, sells or lets for hire or offers or exposes for sale or hire, any unauthorised decoder; or

(b) has in his possession for commercial purposes an unauthorised decoder; or

(c) installs, maintains or replaces for commercial purposes any unauthorised decoder; or

(d) advertises unauthorised decoders for sale or hire or otherwise promotes unauthorised decoders by means of commercial communications'[5].

The provisions referred to at (b) to (d) cover activities prohibited by the Directive.

For example:

- If X, operating commercial premises, uses a decoder to obtain free access to an encrypted satellite broadcast of a movie without payment of the fee the broadcaster requires for reception, he will be guilty of an offence.

- If Y imports decoders from EU member state A to EU member state B so as to enable X to receive free access to encrypted broadcasts of a movie in circumstances where conditional access technology has been applied to prevent reception in EU member state B altogether, or to a restricted number of people not including X, he will be guilty of an offence.

Any person who commits one of the above offences will be liable to either:

- (on summary conviction) to imprisonment for a term not exceeding six months or a fine not exceeding the statutory maximum; or

- (on indictment) to imprisonment for a period of not more than ten years or an unlimited fine or both[6].

The defendant will have a defence if he can show that he 'did not know, and had no reasonable grounds for knowing, that the decoder was an unauthorised decoder'[7].

The rights and remedies available to the providers of information society services and conditional access services were also altered by the 2000 Regulations[8].

Any person who:

- charges for reception of programmes included in a broadcasting service provided from a place in the UK or other member state;

- sends the encrypted transmissions from the UK or other member state; or

- provides the conditional access services from the UK or other member state

will be entitled to the same remedies against the infringer as a copyright owner has, with regard to a breach of copyright (including delivery up and seizure)[9].

It is noteworthy that copyright holders themselves are not provided with a right of action, although where the copyright holder directly provides the service (e.g. through a password restricted web site providing access to his work) he is likely to be entitled to a remedy as an information service provider.

As in the case of a copyright infringement, the infringer will not be liable for damages if it can be shown that at the time of the infringement he did not know, and had no reason to believe, that his acts infringed these rights.

The CDPA was also revised by the Copyright, etc and Trade marks (Offences and Enforcement) Act 2002 to include:

- a power to issue search warrants authorising the entry and search of premises, using reasonable force as is necessary[10]; and
- a right to require forfeiture of unauthorised decoders[11].

These rights and remedies are available against any person who commits one of the criminal offences described above.

1   Directive 98/84 EC of the European Parliament on the legal protection of services based on, or consisting of, conditional access.
2   CDPA ss 297–299.
3   CDPA s 297A(1) and (3).
4   See **paragraph 26.02**.
5   CDPA s 297A(1).
6   CDPA s 297A(1).
7   CDPA s 297A(2).
8   CDPA s 298(1)–(4).
9   CDPA s 298(1), (2).
10 CDPA s 297B.
11 CDPA ss 297C (England, Wales and Northern Ireland) and 297D (Scotland).

Communicating to the public

Spoken words

26.25   Literary works include words 'written, spoken or sung'[1]. So, words spoken extempore (such as during an interview) will constitute a literary work at the time they are recorded, and the author of the literary work will be the speaker[2]. However, the CDPA contains an exception to copyright infringement, so that where a record of spoken words is made, in writing or otherwise, for the purpose of reporting current events or communicating to the public the whole or part of the work, the use of this recording (or copies of it) will not infringe the spoken 'literary work'[3] provided that a number of conditions are met[4].

We have considered the general exceptions to copyright infringement elsewhere in this *User's Guide*[5], but in essence, the reading or recitation in public by one person of a published literary or dramatic work, provided that it is only a reasonable extract from the work, will not infringe copyright, if it is accompanied by a sufficient acknowledgement[6]. Similarly, the making of a recording of such a public reading or recitation, or the inclusion of such a recording in a communication to the public will not infringe copyright in the literary or dramatic work, provided that the programme consists mainly of other material (i.e. public readings or recitations) the use of which is exempt from copyright infringement[7].

1   See **paragraph 2.02**.
2   See **paragraph 2.05**.
3   CDPA s 58(1).
4   See **paragraph 9.20**.
5   See **Chapter 12**.
6   CDPA s 59(1); see **paragraph 9.21**.
7   CDPA s 59(2); see **paragraph 9.21**.

Published editions in interactive or teletext services

26.26   Copyright subsists in published editions of literary, dramatic or musical works[1]. The term of the copyright is 25 years from the end of the calendar year in which the edition was first published[2]. Inclusion in a communication to the public is not a restricted act in relation to this subject matter.

1   See **paragraph 2.11**.
2   See **paragraph 6.21**.

Computer programs

26.27   Service providers may provide interactive services which include games or e-commerce opportunities. A computer program is protected as a literary work[1]. It follows that including a computer program in a communication to the public will require an appropriate licence from the copyright owner of the computer program concerned[2]. Similarly, the right to use any software conveyed to subscribers should be limited by the terms of a licence to the minimum content necessary to receive and utilise the service.

1   See **paragraph 2.02**.
2   For a detailed consideration of computer software generally, see **Chapter 30**.

Musical compositions

26.28   Communication to the public is an act restricted by copyright in relation to both musical works and literary works such as song lyrics[1], and these rights are vested in the PRS by virtually every UK composer[2].

1   See **paragraph 7.07**.
2   See **paragraph 22.07**.

Different collective licensing provisions applicable to traditional broadcasting and other networked uses

26.29   In the context of the broadcasting industry, PRS, in turn, negotiates 'blanket' licence agreements with broadcasters and cable operators which convey the right to broadcast *all* PRS music as part of their radio or television services.

The form of these blanket agreements is different in each case, and if agreement cannot be reached as to licence terms, the matter may be referred by the actual or prospective licensee to the Copyright Tribunal, which has the power to lay down terms[1]. Either party can appeal to the court on a point of law against a decision of the Tribunal.

PRS blanket licence agreements require licensees to keep detailed records of all music transmitted, so as to enable the PRS to divide its revenue between its members by reference to the number of times that its members' compositions are performed and the duration of each. Consequently, when it makes or acquires programming, the broadcaster needs to ensure that detailed 'cue sheets' identifying the music included in the programme are delivered, so as to enable it to make appropriate returns to PRS.

The basis of the royalty for the PRS blanket licence varies. For UK cable operators it is currently a charge per subscriber, per year and covers 'foreign' channels and 'local programming', which will be channels/services run by the cable operator. For the majority of television licences the royalty is a lump sum which may or may not be adjusted yearly. The exception to this is music channels which are charged on a percentage of revenue basis.

For commercial radio the PRS charge is based on a percentage of broadcasting revenue.

PRS fees are payable for the right to transmit the PRS members' compositions. The right to transmit sound recordings which embody those compositions is entirely separate and must be acquired separately from the PPL.

The right to copy a musical composition by making recordings of it, as distinct from the right to publicly perform the original composition or to include an existing recording in a broadcast, is also one of the restricted acts applicable to literary, dramatic or musical works. Most music publishing companies appoint the MCPS[2] as their agent to administer the right to record their musical compositions. A radio or television station which needs to record music (e.g. to include in a programme it intends to transmit) must pay a fee to the MCPS unless it is able to use the so-called 'ephemeral' right exception[3]. Television stations, BBC radio and some independent radio stations have blanket licence arrangements with the MCPS. Some independent radio stations rely on the ephemeral right, but on the whole, broadcasters are not prepared to rely on the exception because of the requirement to dispose of recordings within the requisite period.

The MCPS blanket licence does not apply to the recording of any complete dramatico-musical works, nor to excerpts from such works unless:

- the total duration is no longer than 20 minutes and does not involve a complete act;
- the use is not a 'potted version' of the complete work;
- the excerpt is not presented in a dramatic form.

Use of such works outside a blanket licence is usually licensed direct by the copyright owner or licensee of the work.

In each case, the broadcaster should ensure that his blanket licence will cover all his anticipated activities. To the extent that it does not cover such activities, further payments will be required to be made by the licensee broadcaster. It is worth noting that no licence is required by a cable operator for the inclusion in his service of the music in certain broadcasts which are intended for reception in the cable operator's area. However, unless the broadcaster has obtained a licence covering the cable operator's service, the cable operator will need a licence for out of area transmissions. Accordingly a South London cable operator which includes, say, Granada Television in its service may need a licence from the PRS.

The producer of any television programme will also need to take a licence from the copyright owner of the right to synchronise, or copy, any musical compositions he wishes to use on the soundtrack of the programme. This right is considered in detail elsewhere is this *User's Guide*[4].

In the context of the internet, different licensing models apply for the use of musical compositions; these are considered in detail at **paragraph 22.07**.

1   See **Chapter 13**.
2   See **paragraph 22.08**.
3   See **paragraphs 9.31 and 26.15**.
4   See **paragraph 24.10**.

Sound recordings of musical compositions and music videos

26.30   As with musical compositions, the acts restricted by copyright in relation to sound recordings include communication to the public[1]. A licence is therefore required to permit a television or radio station to broadcast a sound recording, and the broadcast rights in the great majority, if not all, of the commercial sound recordings produced in the UK are vested in PPL[2]. There are 'blanket' licensing arrangements in force between PPL and the broadcasting organisations, so that separate licences are not required in respect of each sound recording used.

To the extent that a broadcaster uses commercial sound recordings to accompany interactive service channels, a PPL licence will also be required to facilitate these uses[3].

Record companies produce videos principally (but not exclusively) for the purposes of exploitation on television. VPL issues licences for the dubbing and broadcast of such videos. Most of the terrestrial and satellite television stations have been issued with licences by VPL. The licences are sometimes on a 'pay for play' basis (dependent upon the requirements of the broadcaster)[4]. Licences for music videos can also be obtained direct from the record companies concerned.

Some doubts exist as to whether all necessary consents from session musicians are vested in PPL. To avoid problems, the broadcaster should seek warranties in their licences from PPL that all such consents have been obtained. If such warranties are not given (and PPL take the standard position that such warranties will not be provided) it may be possible to obtain clearances from the Musicians Union. VPL have requested a buyout, in perpetuity, with the MU regarding revise fees for music videos for broadcast and public performance.

Issues concerning the dubbing of commercial sound recordings into television programmes, and concerning PPL and VPL generally, are considered in detail elsewhere in this *User's Guide*[5].

Different issues apply in the context of taking licences to include sound recordings in internet and mobile telephony based services; these are considered in detail in **paragraph 22.02**.

1   See **paragraph 7.07**.
2   See **paragraph 22.22**.
3   See **paragraph 22.22**, any PPL licence regarding interactive services will be subject to certain limitations in relation to the use of the sound recording of part of such service.

4   See **paragraph 22.23**.
5   See **paragraphs 24.11, 22.22 and 22.23**.

Fair dealing

26.31   The restricted acts in relation to a broadcast, as with other categories of copyright work, include communication to the public[1]. So, it is a breach of copyright to include in a communication to the public any part of another broadcast, or other categories of copyright work, which have copyright protection in the UK, without the owner's consent.

An exception to this principle arises in respect of 'fair dealing'. In the context of making a communication to the public of a copyright work, 'fair dealing' for the purpose of criticism and review, and (except in the case of photographs) for reporting news events is permitted[2].

For these purposes, 'criticism' may extend to matters other than literary criticism, such as ideas contained in the work, or events surrounding it. In *Time Warner Entertainments Co Ltd v Channel 4 Television Corpn plc*[3], the inclusion of a film clip amounted to 'fair dealing' in the context of a programme that considered the merits of the decision to withhold a work from distribution in the UK. The question in each case will be whether the use is genuinely one of criticism or review[4].

In the context of news reporting, *BBC v BSB Ltd*[5] held that, in the circumstances, BSkyB's transmission of excerpts from BBC broadcasts of World Cup football matches, to which the BBC had the exclusive broadcasting rights in the UK, constituted fair dealing for the purpose of reporting current events. The excerpts varied in length from 14 to 37 seconds and were used in successive news bulletins over the period of 24 hours following the match in question. They were accompanied by a verbal report of the incidents and an acknowledgement of the source of the film. Scott J accepted that for the purposes of the CDPA, fair dealing is largely 'a matter of impression'.

This case led to the adoption of a non-legally binding code of 'off air' news access between the main broadcasters in the UK which, has subsequently been reviewed[6].

1   See **paragraph 7.07**.
2   See **paragraph 9.04**.
3   [1994] EMLR 1, CA.
4   See **paragraph 9.04**.
5   [1992] Ch 141.
6   Fair dealing is discussed in detail in **Chapter 9**.

Digital products – infringements

26.32 Digital products consist of other protectable works[1]. It follows that issues relating to the infringement of copyright works, moral rights and performers rights will all be relevant in considering whether a digital work infringements third party rights. These issues are considered in detail elsewhere in this *User's Guide*[2].

1 See **paragraph 26.02**.
2 See **Chapters 7, 8, 9, 11** and **16**.

Communicating to the public

Incidental inclusion

26.33 The incidental inclusion of copyright works in a broadcast will not infringe the copyright in such works. Nor is copyright infringed by the communication to the public of anything (e.g. a television programme) whose making is not an infringement of copyright because of the 'incidental inclusion' exception referred to above. However, where musical works are included, the position is qualified, so that a musical work will not be deemed to be 'incidentally included' if it is deliberately included[1].

1 See **paragraph 9.08**.

Linking and framing

LINKING

26.34 Internet sites typically contain links to other sites, providing immediate access to material made available on-line by third parties. Prior to the 2003 Regulations, there was controversy as to whether the act of linking was an act restricted by copyright. In *Shetland Times v Wills*[1], the *Shetland News* was providing links from its own site to stories featured on the site of the *Shetland Times*. In doing so the *Shetland News* copied the headlines from the *Shetland Times* onto its site and provided a direct link to the stories, bypassing the *Shetland Times'* home page and its advertising (i.e. 'deep linking'). The *Shetland Times* claimed that the linking arrangement resulted in copyright infringement in its headlines and that the *Shetland News* had included its copyright material (i.e. the headlines) in a 'cable programme service' (using the terminology of the CDPA prior to the 2003 Regulations – i.e. the internet web site). *Shetland News* argued that the headlines were not literary works, that since they were not copying or storing material, there was no infringement, and that in any event they were 'fair dealing'[2]. An application for an interim interdict (an injunction) was successful, although the case was settled before a full trial on the issues could take place, with the *Shetland Times* agreeing that linking could take place, subject to proper branding and attribution of the story to the *Shetland Times*.

This controversy has been resolved by the amended CDPA. Such links will clearly constitute 'communications to the public' within the ambit of the CDPA (as amended by the 2003 Regulations)[3].

Outside the UK, the issue of whether linking may infringe database rights in the web site to be accessed has been considered by the courts. In one case, involving an on-line employment agency which had allowed their users to 'deep link' to the site of another agency, thereby allowing its users to access employment advertisements offered by the other agency whilst by-passing its home-page, the court took the view that such repeated and systematic access infringed database rights, notwithstanding that a substantial part of the database had not been accessed[4].

A question also arises as to whether linking to a site which contains or enables users to make infringing copies of copyright works could itself be considered an act of copyright infringement. For the purposes of the CDPA it is worth noting that a copyright infringement occurs where a person commits an act restricted by copyright without proper authorisation, or where he 'authorises' another person to do such an act[5]. Although there is no case law which considers this issue in the UK, at least one case has considered the issue of 'authorisation' in the context of analogue 'tape-to-tape' machines, holding that the sale of such machines did not amount to an authorisation of copyright infringement, since the seller's advertising made it clear he had no authority to grant the required permission and had no control over the machines once sold[6]. Whether a person providing a link could be said to be 'authorising' infringement will depend on the facts of each case, but it is in the context of internet links, a web site provider should in any event be cautious about including links in his site to other sites which may contain infringing material. In any event such a web site provider would be well advised to ensure that the terms and conditions upon which his service is provided makes clear that he has no control over, and is not aware of, material appearing on sites to which his service is linked.

1   [1997] FSR 604.
2   See **Chapter 9** for a detailed consideration of the exceptions to copyright infringement.
3   See **paragraph 7.07**.
4   *Stepstone v Ofir Case No. Az 208 0692/00 Landgericht Koln 28 February 2001.*
5   CDPA s 16(2), See **paragraph 7.02**.
6   *CBS Songs Ltd v Amstrad Consumer Electronics plc [1988] 2 All ER 484, HL.*

FRAMING

26.35   Another method of providing connections between sites is 'framing'. A web page may be subdivided into different portions, enabling the user to, for example, view a second site through a 'window' in a portion of the screen. Inevitably, the 'framing' of content in this way enables the operator of the first site to add its own material (often advertising) in the 'frame' around the window to the second site, and to cover up material featured on the second site. Similar copyright issues arise in the context of such links to those mentioned at **paragraph 26.34**. However, there are also enhanced possibilities for material to be juxtaposed in a way which confuses the user as to the origin of the material in question, or constitutes a derogatory treatment, and as such issues of passing off and moral rights infringement are also relevant[1].

See **Chapters 5 and 11** for a detailed consideration of 'passing off' and moral rights.

Search engines and metatags

SEARCH ENGINES

26.36   Search engines provide a necessary means of navigating the content made available via on-line networks such as the internet. Such engines are themselves databases of information, relating to the content of other sites and derived from a variety of sources, such as ISPs, and by using crawler or similar software.

Since search engines reutilise material held on other sites, and may in themselves duplicate part of copyright works in order to function, their operation may involve a prima facie act of copyright infringement in any material copied by the engine provider. Their functioning raises similar issues in relation to the accessing of material from databases (i.e. web sites, to the extent that they are protected as such), as those discussed in connection with linking[1].

No cases have considered this issue in the UK and several of those in other jurisdictions have been argued on the basis of infringements other than copyright infringement[2]. However, one case, involving the reutilisation of images as thumbnails for a visual search engine, was held to constitute copyright infringement, albeit that such use was justified under the US doctrine of 'fair use'[3]. In our view it is unlikely that a UK court would also find that an infringement had occurred (the images where reduced in size but nevertheless contained a reproduction of substantially all of the work from which they were copied). However, since the UK doctrine of 'fair dealing' is much less expansive that its US counterpart, 'fair use', it is unlikely that on the facts a successful argument of fair dealing could be run[4].

Similarly, in the UK it would be open to the author of the relevant copyright material to enforce his moral rights to paternity and integrity. However, in that regard, the operator of the search engine may well have a valid defence, if he is able to show that his engine is a 'collective work of reference'[5].

Given the significance of search engines to the operation of the internet, it is possible, but unlikely, that public policy could intervene to deny copyright protection in this instance[6].

1   See **paragraph 26.34.**
2   E.g. *eBay Inc v Bidders Edge Inc, US Dist.Court, ND California 24 May 2000,* which was determined on the basis of the US doctrine of trespass to chattels.
3   See *Kelly v Arriba Soft,* discussed at **paragraph 9.06. At the time of going to press, Google was involved in ongoing litigation in the US with the Association of American Publishers over the search engine's decision to scan library books onto its system in order to create a searchable catalogue of books from which extracts may be extracted by users of Google's 'Print for Libraries' project. Google relies on 'fair use' arguments too support its actions. For a detailed consideration of this case, see, e.g. 'Google in new suit', Copyright World, November 2005.**
4   See **paragraph 9.06** for further discussion.
5   See **Chapter 11** for a fuller discussion of moral rights.
6   See **paragraph 2.16.**

METATAGS

26.37   Metatags appear in the HTML code of web sites and facilitate the searching of content by reference to key words included in the tag. Those key words may in themselves be protectable. Commonly, for example, they may include names or brands in which trading goodwill has been established or which are registered as trade marks. If so, the inclusion of such marks in a metatag may infringe such rights[1]. However, it is unlikely that words or phrases included in a metatag could amount to an actionable infringement of copyright[2].

1   See, for example, *Road Tech Computer Systems Ltd v Mandata (Management and Data Services) Ltd [2000] ETMR 970.*
2   See **paragraph 3.02.**

Digital rights management systems

26.38 It is generally accepted that the controlled exploitation of copyright works on-line can only be achieved within a framework of secure digital rights management ('DRM'). The acronym 'DRM' refers to the digital management of rights, and is not to be confused with the separate, but nevertheless key, process of managing digital rights.

Managing digital rights is all about achieving three principal objectives which help to ensure consumption of content always occurs within a rights owner's permitted framework, and that the chances of piracy are (in theory) non-existent:

- First, there is a need to *identify* content, ensuring that each and every piece of content is associated with a unique number or code. This is not a new concept and has been around in sectors such as publishing for some time, with the ISBN and DOI systems.
- Secondly, there is a need to *describe* data. By attaching 'meta data' to digital content, it is possible for the rights holder to indicate information about that content such as the author or the date and place of publication. This is useful for consumers, but also facts such as copyright information are key data in association with *rules*, the final aspect of managing digital rights.
- Thirdly, it is necessary to attach *rules* to the accessing and exploitation of data. Rules about the flexibility of each piece of content need to be set by the rights owner. These can range from simple statements such as 'do not copy' to complex logic formulations involving content-expiry and redistribution parameters. Setting digital rules is the technical implementation of the law, applying control mechanisms which closely detail the permitted activities falling under the scope of the licence of intellectual property. The total freedom in the sphere of rule, setting to go beyond the black letter of the law in regulating possible activities of the consumer, is what some groups regard as inconsistent with our fundamental copyright laws.

In practical terms, DRM may assist content owners with any or all of the following:

- filtering/classification – distinguishing certain types of content from others;
- authentication – being confident that only authorised users can access the content;
- broadcast monitoring – by embedding codes in the works, monitoring the timing and frequency of their appearance in broadcast signals;

- forensic tracking – allowing the work to 'remember' where it has been accessed, or to report home with these details;
- copy prevention – resisting (or restricting) attempts to duplicate the work;
- e-commerce/linking – triggering transactions or suggesting other transactions upon access; or
- copyright communication – ensuring end-users are aware of the identity of the rights holder.

DRM in the technical sense is the term given to any method of 'wrapping' content in order to achieve one or more access-related objectives. It is used primarily to encrypt content in order not only to prevent unauthorised access (necessary where unauthorised re-distribution is likely) but also to provide all parties in the delivery chain with a guarantee of integrity and authority via the use of digital signatures and/or watermarking. In respect of the latter it might be useful to be able to prove, as is possible, the source of the content and to integrate a mechanism for tracking content which might be 'in the wild' and otherwise reproduceable.

Figure 1 is a diagrammatic representation of a potential DRM framework for mobile super-distribution.

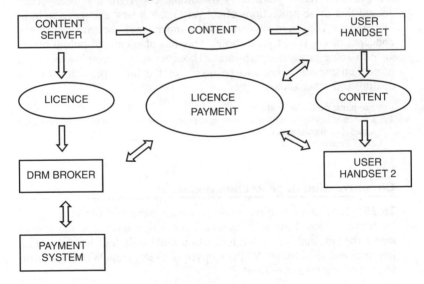

Figure I

In this system, the content (for example, video) starts its life on the content server (top left) operated either by the rights owner or its licensee. Consumers may download the content, which is encrypted and contained within a DRM wrapper, over the internet to their mobile handset. However, the content is unwatchable until activated by calling upon a third party DRM broker, acting under licence from the operator of the content server to issue the end user with a licence for the video file. The consumer acquires an individual licence (with whatever restrictions the content owner chooses) in return for payment. Rights holders can be comfortable with the consumers being able to forward the content to other handset users, as the content will remain in the DRM wrapper requiring the purchase of a separate licence for each consumer (the licence is invariably attached to the consumer's computer or the consumer himself, rather than each instance of the content).

DRM systems are only useful where they are effective. If an encryption technology is hacked, and either modified, to allow free access, or content meta data is changed, the system is rendered useless to rights holders. Consequently, the 2003 Regulations include various provisions to support use by content owners of DRM systems[1].

This anti-circumvention legislation serves as a technical addition to the exclusive rights granted by traditional copyright law. Many have argued that these protections effectively grant a new exclusive right of 'access' for copyright owners, which moves well beyond traditional concepts of copyright protection[2]. This has also created public resistance to some protection measures. Those wishing to employ technical protection measures need to be aware of the law's provision of fair dealing and other access rights[3].

1 See **paragraphs 26.39 et seq.**
2 Lawrence Lessig is one well-known academic whose published works discuss such issues. See **paragraph 1.14**.
3 See **Chapter 9.**

Circumvention of protection measures

26.39 New anti-circumvention provisions were laid out in the 2001 Directive, which deals with technical protection measures and implements the anti-circumvention legislation previously legislated for at an international level by the WIPO Copyright Treaty[1] and WIPO Performances and Phonograms Treaty[2]:

- *Article 6.1* of the 2001 Directive required that member states provide adequate legal protection against the circumvention of any effective technological measures, which the person concerned carries out in the knowledge, or with reasonable grounds to know, that he or she is pursuing that objective.

- *Article 6.2* of the 2001 Directive required member states to provide adequate legal protection against the manufacture, import, distribution, sale, rental, advertisement for sale or rental, or possession for commercial purposes of devices, products or components or the provision of services which:

  '(a) are promoted, advertised on the market for the purpose of circumvention of, or

  (b) have only a limited commercially significant purpose or use other than to circumvent, or

  are primarily designed, produced, adapted or performed for the purpose of enabling or facilitating the circumvention of any effective technological measures.'

- *Article 9* of the 2001 Directive emphasised that the provisions of the Directive were to be without prejudice to other legal provisions in this sphere. Thus, rights holders must continue to respect data protection law (for example, when tracking usage information by reference to individual identities) and the provisions of other relevant EU legislation such as the Conditional Access Directive[3], which prohibits the manufacture and distribution of pirate decoders.

For the purpose of the 2001 Directive, the expression 'technological measures' means any technology which in the normal course of its operation is designed to prevent or restrict acts, in respect of works or other subject matter, which are not authorised by the rights holder of any copyright or any right related to copyright. In practice, examples of technical measures would include the use of CSS and region coding in commercial DVDs; the Macrovision anti-copying system; encryption systems employed by satellite TV broadcasters; encryption on e-books; copy-proof CDs and digital rights management protection on music files.

Technological measures are to be deemed 'effective' where the use of a protected work is controlled by the rightholders through application of an access control or protection process, such as encryption, scrambling or other transformation of the work which achieves the protection objective[4].

These requirements were implemented into the 1998 Act by the 2003 Regulations. Sections 296ZA to 296ZD of the CDPA now provide for a new civil remedy against the actual act of circumvention against a person carrying out such an unauthorised act. The new provisions create new civil and criminal remedies against a person carrying out an unauthorised act in relation to the activities listed in Art 6.2(a), (b) and (c) above. The following paragraphs consider the UK provisions in further detail.

1 WIPO Copyright Treaty of December 20, 1996 – http://www.wipo.int/treaties/ip/wct/index.html.
2 WIPO Performance and Phonograms Treaty of December 20, 1996 – http://www.wipo.int/treaties/ip/wppt/index.html.
3 EU Directive 98/84 – November 1998.
4 These definitions are, in effect, duplicated in the CDPA, s 296ZF.

The CDPA and protection against circumvention

26.40 The amended CDPA contains a number of provisions designed to protect copyright owners against devices which are designed to circumvent any protective technology measures they have taken to prevent piracy and track copyright usage (implementing requirements set out in the 2001 Directive)[1].

1 CDPA s 296 of the CDPA already provided protection against those manufacturing and trafficking devices designed to circumvent copyright-protection. The effect of the 2003 Regulations was to enhance this protection. Section 296 now relates only to computer programs. New ss 296ZA–296ZG apply where technological measures have been applied other than to a computer program, including s 296ZE which provides remedies to a user where a technological measure prevents lawful acts.

Circumvention of technical devices applied to computer programs

26.41 Under the CDPA, as amended by the 2003 Regulations, copyright owners and exclusive licensees of copyright of software programs, together with persons authorised to issue or communicate the same to the public[1], have rights analogous to those of copyright owners, in respect of an infringement of copyright, where a technical device has been applied to a computer program and a person knowing or having reason to believe it will be used to make an infringing copy:

'(a) manufactures for sale or hire, imports, distributes, sells or lets for hire, offers or exposes for sale or hire, advertises for sale or hire or has in his possession for commercial purposes any means the sole intended purpose of which is to facilitate the unauthorised removal or circumvention of the technical device; or

(b) publishes information intended to enable or assist persons to remove or circumvent the technical device.'

In one recent case concerning the Sony Playstation, an English court considered the issue of whether it could be said that an article had the 'sole intended purpose' of unauthorised circumvention of a technical device where (in addition to such unauthorised circumvention) the device could also have a legitimate purpose (such as the making of a back-up copy under the exception at s 50A(1) of the CDPA)[2]. In that case, it was held that nothing had been pleaded which would allow such a defence to come into play. Unlike earlier, more unstable, software carriers, such as magnetic floppy discs, the storage devices on which Playstation Games are held (CDs and DVDs) were robust and could not be wiped clean and, in the unlikely event that they were damaged or destroyed, Sony agreed to replace them[3].

1   CDPA s 296(2).
2   See **paragraph 9.13**.
3   *Sony Computer Entertainment Inc v Ball [2005] FSR 9*, p.159.

Circumvention of other technical measures

26.42   In the context of copyright works other than computer programs, the CDPA, as amended by the 2003 Regulations, affords copyright owners and exclusive licensees of copyright, together with persons authorised to issue or communicate the same to the public[1], rights analogous to those of copyright owners in respect of an infringement of copyright, where effective technical measures have been applied to a copyright work and a person does anything which circumvents those measures and 'knowing, or having reasonable grounds to know, that he is pursuing that objective'[2].

The right does not apply to circumventions 'for the purpose of research into cryptology' unless the research, or information deriving from it, prejudicially affects the copyright owner[3].

Additional rights are afforded to the same categories of person where effective technical measures have been applied to a copyright work (other than a computer program) and where a person:

'manufactures, imports, distributes, sells or lets for hire, offers or exposes for sale or hire, advertises for sale or hire, or has in his possession for commercial purposes any device, product or component, or provides services which:

(i)   are promoted, advertised or marketed for the purpose of circumvention of; or

(ii)   have only limited commercially significant purpose or use other than to circumvent; or

(iii)   are primarily designed, produced, adapted or performed for the purpose of enabling or facilitating the circumvention of those measures'[4].

1   CDPA s 296ZA(3).

2   CDPA s 296ZA(1).
3   CDPA s 296ZA(2).
4   CDPA s 296ZD.

Criminal sanctions regarding devices and services designed to circumvent technical measures

26.43   Anyone who manufactures for sale or hire, imports (otherwise than for his private and domestic use), or (in the course of business) sells, lets for hire, offers, exposes or advertises for sale or hire, possesses or distributes 'a device, product or component which is primarily designed, produced or adapted for the purpose of enabling or facilitating the circumvention of effective technical measures' commits an offence[1]. The same offence is also committed if a person distributes any such device other than in the course of business 'to such an extent as to affect prejudicially the rights of the copyright owner'[2]. It follows that, under the CDPA (as amended), the operator of, say, a hacker web site via which circumvention software codes are distributed will be guilty of an offence, even where he does so in a non-business environment, where the *effect* of his action prejudices the copyright owner.

Similar offences are committed by a person who provides, promotes, advertises or markets a 'service the purpose of which is to enable or facilitate the circumvention of effective technical measures'[3]. The offence will arise if the activity takes place in the course of a business or otherwise (again, provided that, in the latter case, the activity is conducted to such an extent as to prejudicially affect the copyright owner)[4]. An exception is made for activities undertaken for the purpose of national security or in the detection of a crime[5].

A person accused of an offence under this part of the CDPA has a defence if he can establish that he did not know of or have reasonable ground for believing that, the relevant device, product, component or service enabled or facilitated the circumvention[6]. It follows that if a person wishes to rely on such a defence the burden will be on him to prove his lack of guilt.

The penalties for this form of activity are (on summary conviction) imprisonment for a term not exceeding three months and/or a fine not exceeding £5,000, and (on indictment) imprisonment for a term not exceeding two years and/or an unlimited fine.

1   CDPA s 296ZB(1).
2   Ibid.
3   CDPA s 296ZB(2).
4   Ibid.
5   CDPA s 296ZB(3).
6   CDPA s 296ZB(5).

Case law considering s 296

26.44 In one UK decision[1] regarding s 296 and the circumvention of technical protection measures, the court found in favour of the claimants, who sold a popular video games system which incorporated technical protection to prevent the use of unauthorised game discs. The defendant had imported and sold devices for use with the plaintiff's system which allowed the playback of unauthorised game discs. The court held that the devices were circumventing devices for the purposes of s 296, and that it did not matter that they had other uses which did not permit copyright infringement.

1   *Kabushi Kaisha Sony Computer Entertainment Inc and others v Edmunds (t/a Channel Technology) [2002] All ER (D) 170 (Jan), ChD.*

Fair dealing and circumvention

26.45 Article 6.4 of the 2001 Directive provides a remedy to a party where technical protection measures have been applied by a rights holder to a copyright work (other than a computer program) with the effect of restricting that party's ability to exercise fair dealing in respect of the work. The 2003 Regulations implemented that remedy into UK law by providing that, in such circumstances, a party prevented from exercising fair dealing can issue a notice of complaint to the Secretary of State, who in turn can direct that a rights holder make access available to the party giving notice. Notably, this remedy is NOT available in respect of works made available via an on-demand service. Failure to comply with any directions from the Secretary of State will amount to a breach of statutory duty by the rights holder.

Rights management information

26.46 In addition, the 2001 Directive required additional protection to be made available to protect rights management information (Art 7):

Article 7.1 of the Copyright Directive requires member states to provide for adequate legal protection against any person knowingly performing without authority any of the following acts:

- the removal or alteration of any electronic rights management information; and
- the distribution, importation for distribution, broadcasting, communication or making available to the public of works or other subject matter from which electronic rights management information has been removed or altered without authority, if such person knows, or has reasonable grounds to know, that by so doing he is inducing,

enabling, facilitating or concealing infringement of any copyright or any rights related to copyright.

For the purposes of the Directive, the expression 'rights management information' means any information provided by rights holders which identifies the work, the author or any other rights holder, or information about the terms and conditions of use of the work. Removal or amendment of this information may allow the work to be accessed or copied outside of the term of any express or implied end user licence. In some cases, tampering with rights management information could amount to liability for circumvention of protection measures (see above).

These rights are now incorporated into the CDPA by new s 296ZG. This provides in relation to Art 7.1 a new civil remedy against a person carrying out such unauthorised acts.

Peer to peer (P2P)

26.47 P2P refers to any relationship in which multiple, autonomous devices interact as equals. The traditional structure of the internet in the narrowband world consisted of two types of machine, each with defined roles. Millions of 'client' computers are used by individuals as devices to access the internet using dial-up modems; in essence they merely request data, whether that takes the form of web pages, music, video or any other content. Simultaneously, thousands of 'servers', usually connected to the internet via high-bandwidth links, store the content and await request from software such as web browers running on client computers. As Figure 2 indicates, in this simple arrangement, it is clear which party is the service or content provider.

A P2P network is a grouping of computers in which any of the participating machines may act as clients (requesting data), servers (offering data) and/or 'servents' (both a client and a server). Once part of a P2P network, users are able to share both content and computer resources by virtue of direct connections between machines (without the use of central servers). The immediate advantage of P2P sharing is that content spreads much more quickly due to its availability from multiple sources.

The adoption of always-on, high speed internet connections (such as consumer-targeted DSL services in the UK) has led to exponential growth in the popularity of software applications enabling participation in P2P file-sharing networks.

Centralised P2P

26.48   There are several different types of P2P network architecture. Historically, the most popular was that of a centralised network.

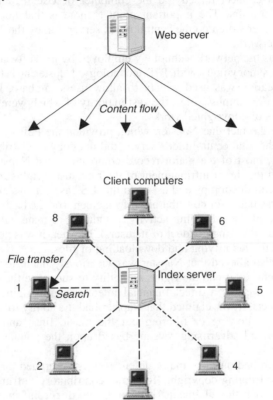

Figure 2

With this architecture, when, for example, user 8 runs P2P software on his client machine, a connection is made to a central index server that the user (who is identified by a unique nickname) has logged onto the system. At this stage, user 8's machine automatically sends to the index server a list of shared content (music, films etc) and information about its exact location on the internet (the IP address). User 1, who has also connected to the network, may use the P2P software to search for a copy of a particular film. The search request is sent to the index server, which returns a list of all users currently on the network with the correct file. Assuming User 8 has the correct file, by selecting the appropriate option, User 1's computer has the correct information to locate and connect directly to the computer of User 8, and the file begins to transfer. The important point to note is that no infringing content is ever stored on the central index server, run by the operator of the P2P network.

This was the network technology employed by the software application most synonymous with P2P technology, Napster at a time when that application was used widely to allow users to share, locate and download digital music files, the vast majority of which were unauthorised copies of copyrighted works.

Despite the fact that Napster, which provided the P2P software and operated the vital central index server, did not copy or distribute music files itself, most of the major record companies sued Napster Inc for facilitating the direct infringement of their exclusive rights of distribution and reproduction by end users. In this US case[1], it was alleged that Napster was liable for contributory infringement (on the basis that, with knowledge of the infringing activity, it induced or materially contributed to the infringing conduct of its users). Napster, it was pointed out, facilitated the identifying and downloading of files.

It was also alleged that Napster was vicariously liable for its users' infringements as it had the right and ability to supervise the infringing activity, as well as a direct financial interest in prolonging them. In these respects, it was claimed that Napster had the ability to *control* the activity, by allowing or filtering out the music files, and also that Napster earned advertising revenue based upon the popularity of the service.

Napster relied on three major defences. First, it argued that its users were not infringing copyright. To show 'contributory' infringement, it suggested that the claimants had to show direct infringement by Napster users themselves. Napster argued that swapping files between users fell within the defence of 'fair use' contained in US common law and US statute[2].

The court found that the activities of Napster's subscribers militated against a finding of 'fair use' because they were essentially receiving free music in circumstances where they would otherwise have had to pay for it and were therefore 'reaping economic advantage' from their use of Napster. Also, given the vast number of people using the service, their use could not be said to be 'private' in the traditional sense.

The second defence argument was that even if its users were infringing copyright, Napster could not be liable for contributory or vicarious infringement because not all of its subscribers were using the service for infringing purposes. Users could also use the service to listen to samples, swap files of recordings by unsigned artists and 'space shift' their collections from CD to computer. Napster relied on the decision of the Supreme Court[3] which ruled that Sony's sale of betamax video recorders could not be banned because they were 'capable of substantial non-infringing uses'.

The court did not agree, finding that '… any potential non-infringing use of the Napster service was minimal or was connected to the infringing activity. The substantial or commercially significant use of the service was, and continues to be, the unauthorised downloading and uploading of popular music, most of which is copyrighted.'

Napster's third argument was that as an ISP, it should be entitled to take advantage of the 'safe harbour' provisions of the US Digital Millennium Copyright Act ('DMCA'). These grant immunity to ISPs where they, essentially, act as a conduit for material. Depending on the nature of the ISP's activities, there may also be additional requirements (such as a notice and take down procedure).

Again, the court was not convinced. It held that Napster could and would have to control or supervise consumers' use of its service and questioned whether Napster could qualify as an ISP in any event.

Although there have been no court decisions in the UK involving Napster or similar P2P services, it is logical to assume that the outcome, as in the *Napster* case, would be a finding of liability on the part of the operators of any centralised P2P index server. The reason for this is that, whilst the circumstances of Napster seem to echo those surrounding the case of *CBS Songs v Amstrad Consumer Electronics plc [1988]*[4], an important distinction is the issue of Napster's required involvement in the ongoing operation of the centralised P2P network (by running the index server).

1 *A&M Records Inc v Napster Inc, 114F: Supp 2d 896 (NC Cal 2000).*
2 'Fair use' is a general statutory exception to copyright infringement available in the US by which copyright is not infringed by copying for purposes such as (but not only) criticism, comment, reporting, scholarship and research. However, such copying must be within certain parameters in order to enjoy this exception to the general copyright rules. In determining this, the US court will look at: (i) the character and purpose of the copying – was it, e.g., for commercial, non-profit or educational purposes? (ii) What is the nature of the work in question? (iii) How much of the work was used; was it a substantial part of the work? and (iv) What is the effect of the use on the potential market for the work? In addition, the US Audio Home Recording Act of 1992 contains a particular 'fair use' provision allowing music to be recorded for 'private' or 'non-commercial use'.
3 *Sony Corporation v Universal Studios Inc, 446 US 417 (1984).*
4 See **paragraph 7.02**.

Decentralised P2P

26.49 Given the outcome of the Napster litigation, it was fairly clear that there is no future for centralised networks sharing unauthorised copies of works, mainly because of the existence of a legal entity controlling the network to 'bite' on in order to shut down the service. However, other types of P2P network (e.g. those employing the Gnutella protocol) emerged using an alternative architecture where there is no central server, where every computer has equal status as both a client and a server to the network.

In order to share files using a decentralised protocol, users require an internet-connected computer with an appropriate P2P software application. Search queries are forwarded to several other computers on the network, which in turn forward the queries to everyone to whom it is connected. This process is iterated until a computer with the correct file is reached, after which a direct connection is made to the original requester in order to transfer the file. This is the network architecture used by Gnutella protocol applications such as BearShare, Limewire and Gnucleus. As decentralised frameworks do not rely on a central server, they are more robust than their centralised counterparts such as Napster-type networks. However, obvious disadvantages relate to the time taken to conduct searches, as queries may need to travel through hundreds of users before positive results are obtained.

Hybrid P2P

26.50 Some newer P2P networks have architectures based in part on both centralised and decentralised networks, as shown in Figure 3.

This approach, adopted by the likes of KaZaA, removes the need for central index servers, instead borrowing on a dynamic basis a handful of users' own client machines to maintain indices of content (so-called 'super-nodes') which effectively act as gateways for the other computers on the network. The allocation of super-nodes occurs transparently and can alter, depending on network conditions. In this model, each client machine forwards a list of its shared files to its local super-node, along with any of the user's search requests. The super-node will then forward the request to other super-nodes. When a successful match is found, the requesting machine connects directly to the machine with the desired content and begins to transfer the file.

Unsurprisingly, record industry bodies in more than one country have launched actions against the operators of the P2P networks using these 'hybrid' systems. However in March 2002, a Dutch appeal court held that KaZaA BV could continue to distribute its file-sharing software, refusing to impose liability on the company. The court recognised

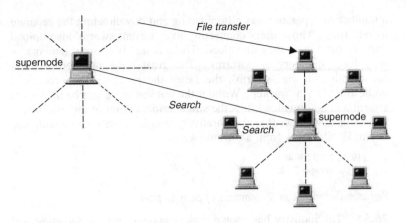

Figure 3

important practical and legal distinctions between the technology behind KaZaA and that incorporated into previous file-sharing applications such as Napster, and accepted the argument that, unlike Napster, the operation of KaZaA was not dependent on ongoing participation by KaZaA BV. Given that lack of control over users, it is also arguable whether a UK court would regard KaZaA as 'authorising' infringements following *CBS v Amstrad*[1]. Secondly, unlike in the *Napster* case, the Dutch court accepted evidence that KaZaA was being used for the exchange of a great deal of non-infringing material and that acts of copyright infringement, if they were occurring, were being conducted wholly by users, and not KaZaA BV[2].

As we write, one of the most widely used applications for the dissemination of infringing material is BitTorrent. BitTorrent alone accounts for a very substantial portion of all internet traffic – and that traffic comprises largely of unauthorised downloads of copyright material. In the television context, for example, popular television shows are commonly 'capped' (i.e. copied from the legitimate broadcast) and communicated to the public on-line soon after broadcast using BitTorrent (amongst other applications). In practice, a 'capping' group will upload the file to a secure web site. The file is then readied for communication (usually by members of an IRC (Internet Relay Chat) channel as a 'torrent' of smaller files. These 'torrent files' (which include instructions on how to receive the material via BitTorrent), are set out in the IRC channel and also on an accompanying web site. The user visits the web site hosting the small torrent files and commences a download process by which the user connects into a torrent swarm (i.e.

a number of separate users all uploading and downloading the separate torrent files). Those users connecting to a 'torrent swarm' also upload parts of the file as they download. There is no 'BitTorrent network' – only large numbers of 'swarms'. The greater the number of users participating in the 'swarm', the faster the process. The process is orchestrated by a 'tracker'. Without the tracker, there can be no torrent swarm and no download. It is the single critical point of any BitTorrent swarm or download. It is comparatively simple to track downloads and obtain IP addresses from a torrent swarm.

1   [1988] 2 All ER 484.
2   See **paragraph 7.02**.

Rights enforcement in the context of peer to peer

26.51   The industry has shown a clear appetite for the targeting and neutralisation of large-scale commercial operations facilitating online piracy. However, as P2P networks move away from centralised models, there may be a lack of potential defendants (i.e. those operating the P2P systems) to target in order to end trading of illegitimate copies. Targeting end users themselves raises many other peripheral issues, including privacy and data protection.

In recent years, entertainment companies have taken legal action against some organisations that have developed file-sharing software11, and also against some individuals who are using this software to upload content files.

Under the provisions of the CDPA, for example, the use of applications such as BitTorrent may involve several acts restricted by copyright:

● Those persons *uploading* unauthorised material engage in copyright infringement by means of their unauthorised copying[2]. Users of downloading services such as BitTorrent (where, as part of the network participating in the torrent swarm, they are uploading as well as downloading pieces of files), infringe copyright not only by downloading but also by uploading.

● Those persons who create and disseminate (e.g. through host web sites) software akin to that used by BitTorrent may arguably be authorising copyright infringement and/or be liable as a 'secondary infringer' of copyright[3]. The question of whether the work is being used to make infringing copies will depend upon the character of the activity undertaken by the downloader, and in particular whether that downloader's actions themselves amount to an infringement of copyright (see below).

● Those persons downloading material will clearly be undertaking the restricted act of *copying*[4]. It is unlikely that any 'timeshifting' defence to copyright infringement will now be available to such downloaders[5].

In the US, the most recent actions undertaken by the RIAA and MPAA have focused on end-users and against operators of those servers which point to the files available for download. In this regard the MPAA has had notable successes (SuprNova, the most popular BitTorrent provider, ceased business in late 2004).

1   US Supreme Court, June 27, 2005, in which the US Supreme Court took the view that two P2P firms, Grokster and Streamcast, were guilty of encouraging users to infringe copyrights.
2   It may be that in some circumstances, such as capping, the uploader may be able to rely on a defence such as timeshifting, but once uploaded via an application such as BitTorrent, the copy will be an infringing copy. These issues are discussed in detail at **paragraph 19.33**.
3   See **Chapter 7**.
4   See **paragraph 7.03**.
5   See **paragraph 9.33**.

Tracking infringers

26.52   The commonly held belief in relation to the internet is that users are protected by a veil of anonymity. In practice, the effectiveness of that veil is determined solely by the extent to which a user's ISP is prepared to co-operate or not with any request from rights holders for identification of users. This, in turn, will rest on the interplay of the ISP/customer agreement (including the acceptable use policy), privacy issues and data protection law, all battling to preserve users' anonymity in the absence of a court order requiring the ISP to disclose information.

IFPI Belgium discovered these problems some time ago, when it used purpose-built software to track illegal file sharing on the Napster network. The Belgian Privacy Commission held that users' IP addresses harvested by IFPI's software constituted personal information for data protection purposes and could not be used outside the context of judicial proceedings. IFPI was therefore not permitted to use the information to communicate the identities of users to their respective ISPs for warnings against copyright infringement to be issued. Nevertheless, IFPI Belgium has already made good its threats to a hundred or so users who repeatedly ignored warnings by passing their details to the police, who were poised to raid homes.

Under UK data protection law, to obtain access from an ISP to a subscriber's name and address, a rights holder will need to convince the

ISP to disclose such information. The ISP is entitled to disclose, without consent from its subscriber (the 'data subject'), where:

'the disclosure is required ... by order of the court ...or ...for the purpose of, or in connection with, any legal proceedings (including prospective legal proceedings) ... or is otherwise necessary for the purpose of establishing, exercising or defending legal rights.'[1]

US ISP Verizon Communications battled with the Recording Industry Association of America (the 'RIAA') in a Washington court over whether it had to disclose the identity of an alleged KaZaA user who had been facilitating copyright infringement by offering more than 600 recordings to other users on the network. The RIAA argued that the DMCA should be interpreted to provide authority for subpoenas in order to learn the identity of individuals who are using ISPs solely as a conduit for P2P trading.

The dispute was not actually so much about whether Verizon could be forced to reveal the identity of a suspected copyright infringer (who downloaded more than 600 songs in a single day), but about which legal mechanism was most appropriate (the RIAA preferring to rely on the DMCA's cheaper and faster subpoena process). Verizon argued that, because it is only a conduit and is not hosting the material, the DMCA did not apply. Many ISPs were concerned that if the RIAA were successful in pursuing their claim, the privacy of internet users would be endangered.

The judge ruled that the DMCA required the RIAA to submit to a subpoena to reveal the subscriber's identity. Verizon has appealed the decision and refused to give out the name, for fear of the chilling effect such disclosures could have on file sharing and other communications service indirectly supported by its services. In response, the RIAA issued further subpoenas insisting Verizon reveal even more names. At appeal Verizon was successful and the RIAA are no longer able to sue file-swappers by name. Instead the RIAA are required to discover the names of pirates through court-issued subpoenas.

1   S 35 of the Data Protection Act 1998.

Direct action

26.53   Recently there have been attempts to introduce a legal right for content owners harmed by P2P services to fight back in a more direct manner. In the US, Congressmen Howard Berman and Howard Coble had backed a change in law to allow copyright owners to use technological tools to secure or repossess their property. They argued that changes were needed to avoid rights holders who 'fight back' otherwise facing potential, if unintended, liability under a variety of state and federal laws.

Under the proposed P2P Piracy Prevention Act (the 'P2P Act'), rights holders would receive a limited 'safe harbour' from such liability, leaving them free to use technological measures to impair P2P piracy via decentralised networks where they have a 'reasonable basis' to believe such piracy is occurring. Although rights holders would have been able to block distribution of copyrighted files, the proposed P2P Act stopped short of allowing them to hack into the computer of a P2P user and remove files. Many were concerned that the draft P2P Act did not specify exactly which impairment methods could be used, and despite the absence of an ability for rights holders actively to delete files, it also limited the rights of individuals to sue if files were accidentally erased during the process (part of the draft P2P Act stated that the electronic intrusion may not cause 'economic loss of more than $50 per impairment to the property of the affected file trader').

As might be expected, the proposed P2P Act attracted much criticism, with commentators asking whether P2P file trading is really so bad that those pursuing infringers ought to be granted immunity from more important legal protections relating to computer security, privacy and fraud. Not only could the P2P Act inadvertently affect legitimate content (either due to mislabelling, or the file sitting on the same network node which has been the subject of an authorised attack), but it may have created widespread 'vigilante' justice not only by large companies owning IP rights, but also small rights holders with less integrity.

Ultimately, the controversial proposal died in Congress and Berman is not expected to revive such P2P legislation, as a result of heavy scepticism not only from consumer advocates, but also Hollywood itself, whose enthusiasm for the Bill was dimmed by Berman's insistence on imposing new liabilities on copyright holders that go too far in attacking pirates.

Under present UK law, the Computer Misuse Act 1990 makes it a criminal offence to obtain unauthorised access to any program or data on a computer, or to engage in modification of computer material (e.g. impairing access to or the operation of files). Thus, any form of direct action by rights holders would itself be illegal.

P2P as a legitimate distribution platform

26.54 None of the existing P2P networks appear currently to offer suitable platforms for the legitimate distribution of content. This is because rights holders will not sanction delivery of unsecure content to users who might be able to undertake unauthorised copying and redistribution.

P2P is not a viable option in the absence of a strong DRM solution[1]. With security in place to guarantee the prevention of piracy, films or video clips may well be shared with the blessing of rights holders, secure in the knowledge that 'locked' content may only be accessed by acquiring a licence from a central online 'broker'. This would also allow the content/service provider to define the relevant set of access rights and payment terms.

1   See **paragraph 26.38**.

Liability of internet or mobile service providers

26.55   In practice, the role of an internet or mobile service provider may be rather like that of a broadcaster (i.e. creating a series of web pages which are placed on line and accessed in exchange for a subscription or 'pay per view' fee, or supported by the sale of advertising). On the other hand, the role may be more akin to a post office, acting as the passive recipient or communicator of information made available by others. More commonly, the service provider will be both: a 'hub' for the supply of original commissioned or licensed content, and a 'host' for the services of, or for material posted to forums and 'bulletin boards' by, third parties.

One of the central questions which vexed industry and legislators has been: to what extent should a service provider be liable for illegal or infringing material included within its service?

In relation to the material he is providing in his role as 'quasi broadcaster' in respect of which he therefore has control, the answer to this question is simple: the service provider must ensure that his content does not infringe the rights of others. In making available material 'on-line' he will be undertaking a number of restricted acts[1]. In so far as he creates original content, or licenses content, he must ensure that his agreements contain assignments or grants of rights adequate for his proposed exploitation, and take appropriate warranties and indemnities to safeguard against liability in the event that his assignor/licensor does not have the rights he claims to have.

The position changes in the context of the service provider as 'host' or 'intermediary'. Where a person 'posts' infringing material to a bulletin board operated by a service provider, the person posting the material may be difficult to locate, or be located in a remote jurisdiction which would provide an inconvenient location for a legal action, or be without resources to pay damages, or a minor, and consequently, the possibility of taking infringement proceedings against the service provider becomes attractive to the victim of infringement, since his activities may include:

- a communication to the public of data[2];
- copying onto the server (including 'caching')[3];
- 'authorising' the copying of copyright works by third parties (both by the transitory copying of information onto the computer of the recipient necessary to view the material, and any more permanent copies retained by the recipient of material he has downloaded)[4];
- secondary infringement[5].

The situation changed in the UK on 21 August 2002 when it implemented Directive 2000/31/EC through the Electronic Commerce (EC Directive) Regulations 2002. One of the concerns that the Directive tried to allay was the apparent disparity between the laws of separate member states in relation to the liability of service providers and how this could detract from the smooth functioning of the Internal Market. The Directive gives defences for information society service providers[7] in respect of the following three forms of activities:

- acting as a mere conduit;
- caching; and
- hosting.

These activities are considered in more detail in the following paragraphs.

1 See **Chapter 7**.
2 See **paragraph 7.07**.
3 See **paragraph 7. 02**.
4 CDPA s 16 and **paragraph 7.02**.
5 See **paragraph 7.09** and in particular s 24(2).
6 For the purposes of the 2002 Regulations, a *service provider* is defined as any person providing an information society service (where an information society service covers any service normally provided for remuneration, at a distance, by means of electronic equipment for the processing (including digital compression) and storage of data, and at the individual request of a recipient of a service).

Acting as a mere conduit

26.56 When information simply passes through a telecommunications network, a service provider is not liable for the content of the information, provided that the service provider did not initiate the transmission, select the receiver of the transmission or select or modify the information contained within it.[1] In this situation a server provider is '*acting as a* *mere conduit*'. This exclusion of liability only applies to information that is not stored (whether automatically, or in an intermediate or transient form) for any longer than reasonably necessary, or for any other purpose, than that intrinsically relating to the transmission of the information. As a result this defence is not relevant to the majority of ISPs, like web site hosting, which deliberately store information for other purposes.

1   Art 12 of the 2000 Directive.

Caching

26.57 'Caching' is the process whereby service providers place information in temporary storage to improve the efficiency of the transmission of information. The reasoning behind such a defence to infringement is that the service provider has neither the knowledge nor control over the information that is transmitted and subsequently stored and the responsibility, therefore, should be shifted from the service provider. However, for the defence to apply, there are a number of conditions that need to be satisfied. The service provider must:

- not modify the information transmitted;
- comply with conditions on access to information and any rules in relation to the updating of information (in accordance with those recognised and used in the industry);
- not interfere with the lawful use of technology to obtain data on the use of the information;
- immediately react, by removing or disabling access to cached information, once it has actual acknowledge that the information at the initial source of the transmission has been removed from the network, or access to it has been disabled, or that the removal of, or disabling of access to, the information has been ordered by the courts.[1]

1   Reg 22 states that when a court is considering whether a service provider has actual knowledge, it should take into account which appear relevant in the circumstances and shall have regard to whether the service provider received a notice and whether this notice included the name and address of the sending of the notice and the details of the location of the information in question and the reasons behind why the information is unlawful.

Hosting

26.58 When the service provider stores information for the recipient of its service, it is 'hosting' this information. A good example of which is where a service provider hosts a web site containing a message board that is used by a subscriber to its services. On the basis that the recipient of the service was not acting under the authority or control of the service provider, then the service provider is not liable for the storage of information, or activities carried out by the subscriber, as long as it does not have actual knowledge that this stored information is infringing material. A service provider should be aware, however, that, in order to escape a claim for damages, it must immediately remove or disable any information as soon as it obtains knowledge, or is aware that, it is hosting such infringing material.

Unlike the other two defences, damages may still be recoverable from a service provider if the service provider is party to information that would give it objective knowledge of infringing material or activities. In other words, would a reasonable person, in possession of the same information have concluded that the activity or information was illegal and therefore have removed, or disabled access to it.

Similar defences appear in the USA, where the Digital Millennium Copyright Act 1998 (DCMA) introduced 'safe harbour' protection against copyright infringement for service providers who act as an unknowing conduit for infringing material, without controlling or supervising the material in question. The US legislation requires service providers to act expeditiously to remove offending material upon receipt of a notice in terms prescribed by the DCMA, and consequently, an infringement notice forwarded to a US based service provider can be an extremely effect method of ensuring that infringing material is removed from a web site.

Further protection for ISPs was introduced by the 2003 Regulations. These provide that copyright in a literary work, other than a computer program or database, or in a dramatic, musical or artistic work, or in the typographical arrangement of a published edition, or in a sound recording or a film, is not infringed by the making of a temporary copy which is transient or incidental, which is an integral and essential part of the technological process and the sole purpose of which is to enable a transmission of the work in a network between third parties by an intermediary, or a lawful use of the work, and 'which has no independent economic significance'[1].

1   See **paragraph 9.02.**

Applicable law and jurisdiction

26.59 The internet is a worldwide medium. Mobile services, although addressable, permit subscribers to 'roam' into different jurisdictions. Where a service is capable of being received in a territory, it is possible for liability to arise in that jurisdiction.

Broadly, in the case of copyright infringement, the law applicable to determining whether an infringing act has taken place will be the territory in which the act actually takes place.

Exactly where a case will be tried is a difficult issue when considering whether or not to bring an action against an infringer. There are particular problems in applying legislation conceived for print publishing to on-line exploitation of audio-visual works.

The basic rule of jurisdiction in the EU[1] and the European Free Trade Area[2] countries is that a respondent should be sued in his country of domicile[3].

In England, the service of process (i.e. the equivalent of what was known as a writ) on a person is the basis of the court's jurisdiction in the matter. This means that only if the claim can be legally served on that person can the court accept jurisdiction. If the infringer is domiciled within England (including if it only has a subsidiary office in England), the claim can always be served on him. If the infringer is domiciled outside England, it may still be possible to serve process on him. There are two categories of such service: service without permission, and service with the permission of the court.

- *Service without permission:* in the courts of EU countries and the EFTA countries, the Brussels Convention[4] and the Lugano Convention[5] (together, the 'Conventions') govern jurisdiction. For the purposes of this section, countries which are signatory to one of the Conventions will be termed 'Convention countries'. If (i) the Conventions apply to give an English court jurisdiction over a matter; (ii) there are no existing proceedings relating to the same acts and between the same parties within any Convention country; and (iii) at least one respondent is domiciled within a Convention country, then the claimant can serve proceedings in that matter without the court's permission[6].

  The basic rule under the Conventions is that the respondent should be sued in its country of domicile: that is, in the court nearest to where the defendant resides or does business or (if the respondent is a company) where it is incorporated[7]. (The nationality of the respondent is not relevant.)

  However, in cases of tort (which would include copyright infringement) the Conventions additionally confer jurisdiction on the courts of the Convention country where the infringement was committed and on the courts of the Convention country where damage (such as loss of profit) caused by the infringement occurred. These may therefore be alternatives to suing the defendant where he is domiciled.

- S*ervice with permission*: if there are existing proceedings in a Convention country which relate to the same acts and are between the same parties, or if none of the respondents are domiciled within a Convention country, permission will be required before an action can be validly served. There are detailed grounds on which permission will be given. The grounds most relevant to copyright infringement (although others may be relevant on the facts of each case) are that:
  - an injunction is sought to restrain or compel acts within England;
  - damage has been sustained within England; or
  - damage has resulted from an act committed within England.

In the context of the internet, for example, if a party places infringing material on a server outside England, an English court may have jurisdiction in relation to that infringement. If, for example, the party is domiciled in England (including if it only has a subsidiary office in England) it can be sued there; and if the infringement causes harm in England, the claimant can bring proceedings there.

Internationally, there has been a movement away from the simple approach that because a service is capable of reception in jurisdiction B, that country should have jurisdiction to hear an action brought in connection with a web site transmitted from jurisdiction A. Increasingly, courts have focused on issues such as: which territory is the service targeted at? Is the site marketed in the territory in which jurisdiction is claimed? In the US, the issue has been the subject of a significant amount of litigation, a detailed examination of which is beyond the scope of this edition of the *User's Guide*.

1 See **Appendix 3** for a list of members.
2 Austria, Finland, Iceland, Liechtenstein, Norway, Sweden and Switzerland.
3 Broadly speaking, a person is domiciled in a place where he regards it as his main place of residence permanently or indefinitely. A company is domiciled in the country where it is incorporated.
4 Brussels Convention on Jurisdiction and the Enforcement of Judgments in Civil and Commercial Matters 1968.
5 Lugano Convention on Jurisdiction and the Enforcement of Judgments in Civil and Commercial Matters 1988.
6 Civil Procedure Rules r 6.19.
7 Brussels Convention Art 2.

Practical protection measure: 'geoblocking' etc

26.60 In the case of internet exploitation it is very difficult to control who is accessing what content and where, and there is as of yet no

100% guaranteed way to avoid liability in a foreign jurisdiction. However, there are steps which may minimise risks for publishers of online content:

- *Subscription-based services.* It is possible to refuse subscriptions to persons outside the target area by barring certain postal addresses or countries of origin for credit cards. Unfortunately the fact that there are subscribers can also work against the publisher. For example, the judge in one Australian case[2] used the fact that the service provider was a subscription service to dispute Dow Jones' argument that it had no control over who read the features on its service.
- *Use of IP addresses.* It is possible to bar access to certain IP addresses by checking the country of origin of such addresses. However, this mechanism can never be 100% successful as users can manipulate their address, for example by using proxy servers, which make a web site think the IP address originates from a different country that from which it really originates.

1 May 2000, TGI Paris.
2 *Dow Jones & Company, Inc v. Gutnick M3/2002 (28 May 2002) (Australia).*

The EU Enforcement Directive

26.61 The objectives of the EU Enforcement Directive are to harmonise national laws on the means of enforcing intellectual property rights and to establish a general framework for the exchange of information between the responsible national authorities. It is designed to ensure a level playing field for rights holders in the EU and to reinforce measures against offenders and thus act as a deterrent to those engaged in counterfeiting and piracy. Its scope is restricted to infringements 'for commercial purposes or which cause significant harm to rights holders'. The Directive is considered in detail elsewhere in this *User's Guide.*

1 See **paragraph 8.22**.

Domain names: definition

26.62 Domain names are internet addresses facilitating the contact of users on the worldwide web. The domain name is the key part of the system which provides a user with an electronic name/address. The domain name system converts readable domain names into an internet protocol number which enables domain names to communicate. Essentially, the domain name system is a directory consisting of domain names from which companies or individuals can be identified. Inevitably, domain names have become valuable trading tools.

Ownership of a domain name is exclusive, leading to potential scarcity and an as a result their potential increased value. There are however different domain name suffixes available on the internet. This means that for an individual or company with the same name there is opportunity for both to use their identical name but with different suffixes; e.g. '.com' or '.co.uk'. One useful role which domain name suffixes play is to indicate the location or geographical area where the domain name holder's business is registered or where they reside. For example, '.com.au' domains indicate that the business is registered in Australia. Such domain name suffixes as '.com.au' or '.co.uk' are known as country code top-level domains ('ccTLDs').

Top-level domains ('TLDs') can be sub-divided into ccTLDs and generic top-level domains ('gTLDs'), the latter being available universally on a global level with no (or very limited) restrictions.

The most recognised and commonly sought after TLDs are '.com' (which relates to corporate and commercial organisations), '.org (relating to non-commercial organisations) and '.net' (these are available to internet service providers). Other TLDs include '.biz' and '.plc'. If any restrictions do apply, they usually relate to purpose/specific use restrictions; for example, a non-profit-making organisation such as a statutory body may be restricted from using the '.com' TLD.

Domain names: registration

26.63 The internet operates on a global level and there is no regulation of it by a central authority. In the UK, for '.co.uk' domain names, registrations are administered by Nominet UK Limited, whereas in the United States, where '.com', '.net', '.gov' and '.org' domains are allocated, administration is by Network Solutions, Inc, and a number of other providers such as 'register.com'.

The domain name registration procedure is straightforward and conducted on a 'first come first served' basis. Applicants are able to register a domain name even though they may have no association with the registered name. Unsurprisingly, registration by people who have no connection with the name being registered has led to a number of disputes. Companies, some of which have commercially valuable global brands, view the availability of domain names with the corporate name/brand as an essential part of their marketing and general brand strategies.

Registration rules for registering a ccTLD vary from country to country with some rules specifying that only businesses/individuals registered or residing in that particular territory can use them.

Information about who owns, and who is responsible for, the domain name is made publicly available. This is achieved by placing the details on a 'Who is the registrar' site. The reason for this is twofold: first, to allow for the swift resolution of technical problems, and secondly to enable intellectual property rights to be enforced. Registration in total lasts for ten years and within that period the Registrar may offer initial and renewal registrations of one year.

Most elements of registration (such as price, method of registration and renewal periods) differ from Registrar to Registrar.

Domain names: cyber squatting

26.64 A new series of cases has emerged dealing with passing off in the context of 'cyber squatting', the practice of registering internet domain names consisting of the names or marks of other businesses with the intention of selling the domain name on to that business.

Cyber squatters register domain names generally to disrupt the on-line capabilities of an organisation which has a legitimate interest in the registered domain name (mainly by directing web traffic to their domain/web site) and not to the 'legitimate' organisation's web site, or by selling the domain name to such an organisation at an inflated price. This is often done with fraudulent intent.

High prices are named by the cyber squatters for domain names because of the value that organisations place on them. A domain name which reflects an organisation's business name or trade/service mark will greatly enhance the activities of an organisation that wants to offer on-line services, move into the e-business market, or promote its goods or services via the internet. The universal appeal and high profile of the internet and its accessibility means that cyber squatters attempt to command high prices which greatly exceed their own costs in registering the domain name in the first place.

One of the first cases on this subject in the UK[1], concerned a defendant which had, without authorisation, registered domain names of numerous well-known enterprises, including Virgin, Sainsbury's, Marks and Spencer and Ladbrokes. The domain names were up for sale. The claimants sought an injunction to restrain passing off and trade mark infringement. The court found that the main purpose of the defendant's registrations was systematically to prevent registration by the owners of the goodwill in the name and extract money from the proper owner with the threat of either using the name or allowing someone else to do so. With regard to passing off, it was held that the proper owner was entitled to a final injunction to restrain such use, together with an order for the names to be assigned to the correct owners. In granting the injunction, the judge placed emphasis on the fact that the court was entitled to infer from the evidence that the registration itself (without any trading using the name) amounted to equipping the defendant with an 'instrument of fraud', because it inherently lead to passing off.

However, the above decision does not create this presumption in all potential cases. In another case[2], the defendant was an internet consultant who registered the domain name 'fcuk.com.'. French Connection had registered the same initials as a trade mark and used them in an advertising campaign, and applied for summary judgment for passing off. The application was refused because on the evidence the judge was not satisfied that there was no reasonable prospect of a defence to passing off (the defendant having claimed that the name was commonly used on the internet to denote pornography and that he had plans to use the name to attract traffic to his own site). The case illustrates that the courts will be reluctant to deal with 'cyber squatting' by way of summary judgment, except in flagrant cases[3].

A second case involving Marks and Spencer[4] was brought before the court along similar lines. An individual had pursued a consistent action of copying Marks and Spencer's web site and reproducing it onto domain names he had registered with remarkably similar names to that of Marks and Spencer's official web site. This understandably caused confusion amongst consumers using what they thought to be the official Marks and Spencer's site. The confusion extended to consumers using their credit cards on the sites, allowing their details to be used fraudulently.

The court found these web sites to be in breach of Marks and Spencer's intellectual property rights and that the imitation of domain names could constitute both trade mark and copyright infringement.

This case did, however, highlight that court orders which restrict the registration of a particular domain name may potentially be circumvented by cyber squatters registering similar, but equally misleading, domain names.

If the defendant can show some other legitimate purpose as to why he registered the domain name, then the domain name may not be an instrument of fraud. A defendant may thereby avoid liability in passing off even though the domain name is identical to a trade name of the claimant[5].

A domain name can still be an instrument of fraud, even if it is not inherently likely to lead to passing off because it is not so similar to the claimant's trade mark, if the get-up of the web site in total is adapted to be used for passing off and is intended to be so used[6].

1   *British Telecommunications plc, Virgin Enterprises Ltd, J Sainsbury plc, Marks and Spencer plc, Ladbroke plc v One in a Million Ltd [1999] 1 WLR 903, CA.*
2   *French Connection Ltd v Sutton [2000] ETMR 341.*
3   Details of ICANN and the ICANN dispute resolution procedure are set out at in **paragraph 26.65.**
4   *Marks and Spencer plc v Craig Cottrell and others (unreported, 26 February 2001, High Court).*
5   *French Connection Ltd v Sutton, [2000] E.T.M.R. 341.*
6   *EasyJet Airline Co. Ltd v Tim Dainty t/a easyRealestate, LTL, February 28, 2001.*

Domain names: ICANN and dispute resolution procedures

ICANN

26.65 All of the Registrars for the current TLDs – '.biz', '.com', '.info', '.name', '.net' and '.org' – subscribe to the Uniform Domain-Name Dispute-Resolution Policy ('UDRP'). There are procedures available whereby aggrieved parties can file a complaint with one of a number of approved dispute-resolution service providers.

A complainant can either pursue a remedy through the courts, or particularly in the case of 'cyber squatting', file a complaint with an approved dispute-resolution service provider.

The UDRP was adopted by ICANN in August 1999 and now applies to the registries allocating gTLDs. UDRP became fully operational in early 2000, and in adopting this policy, the gTLD Registrars incorporate the UDRP into their Registration Agreements thereby binding applicants to this means of dispute resolution.

The UDRP provides that a Registrar will cancel or transfer a domain name registration if the current domain name owner authorises them to do so, or if the Registrar receives a court order or binding arbitrator's decision. A Mandatory Administrative Proceeding is also incorporated into the UDRP. This procedure is invoked if a complainant alleges:

- the registered domain name is identical or confusingly similar to a trade mark in which the complainant has rights;
- the registered domain name holder has no legitimate rights or interests in that domain name; and
- the domain name was registered and is being used in bad faith[1].

1   This is reproduced from the web site www.icann.org/UDRP/UDRP-policy-24oct99.htm, which offers a fuller explanation.

The World Intellectual Property Organisation

26.66 The WIPO service first began in December 1999. In administering its service, the WIPO Centre applies the UDRP.

The complainant can file a complaint to WIPO and then the respondent has 20 days in which to file a response. Once a defence is filed or the period for filing a defence expires, either two or three panellists (the 'Panel') are appointed by the WIPO Centre. The Panel then considers the facts of the case and arguments put forward by the respective parties, before delivering its decision. This decision is distributed to the parties, the relevant Registrar, and ICANN.

If the Panel decides that a domain name should be cancelled or transferred then this must be carried out by the relevant Registrar. However, as discussed above, such dispute resolution service is in addition to any court proceedings that can be commenced, and there is a 10-day period after the Panel's decision is delivered, within which the losing party can commence court proceedings.

The service provided by the WIPO Centre is regarded as an effective and cost-efficient alternative to court proceedings. Proceedings are usually concluded within two months, and there is a fixed fee for the dispute resolution service which can increase depending on the number of panellists involved and number of domain names being disputed.

WIPO is one of a number of organisations that conduct dispute resolution under the UDRP and ICANN. The other organisations include the National Arbitration Forum ('NAF') and the CPR Institute for Dispute Resolution ('CPR') which are both based in the United States, and the Disputes.org/eResolution Consortium ('DeC') based in Canada.

The Nominet UK dispute resolution procedure

26.67 Another alternative to commencing court proceedings involving disputed '.co.uk' domain names is available through Nominet.

The Nominet resolution procedure differs from the UDRP, placing an emphasis on getting parties to resolve the dispute at the outset.

Before any sort of arbitration is entered into or party submissions invited, the first stage involves Nominet attempting to investigate whether the parties can reach agreement. They do this by contacting the holder of the domain name in dispute to see if an amicable solution can be reached.

If this fails, stage two of the process is undertaken. This sees Nominet decide unilaterally whether they should cancel the domain name. Their decision is then communicated to both parties in writing.

In common with the UDRP, either party can appeal the Nominet decision, although court proceedings are the only viable option if UDRP avenues have been exhausted. However, where the Nominet process differs is that only when the appeal process, stage three, is invoked, does an independent expert become involved. The expert's role is to review any documentation submitted during the dispute resolution process so far, and to possibly request further written submissions from each party. The expert will then submit a decision to Nominet and both parties, indicating whether Nominet's original decision should be upheld or not. It is important to note however that Nominet does not have to follow the independent expert's decision.

Chapter 27

Artists, photographers, art galleries, art dealers and museums

Introduction

27.01 This chapter focuses on 'artistic works' and their exploitation. The phrase 'artistic work' has a technical meaning under the CDPA, and it is worth prefacing this chapter by saying that modern artists frequently use works in their art which do not fall within the technical definition of 'artistic work' (e.g. films, sound recordings, etc). Where it is the intention to use one of these other works, we recommend reference to the particular parts of this book dealing with issues arising in respect of those categories of work[1].

1   See in particular **Chapters 22 and 24**.

Definitional issues

27.02   Under the CDPA, the phrase 'artistic work' means:

'(a)   a graphic work, photograph, sculpture or collage, irrespective of artistic quality;

(b)   a work of architecture being a building or a model for a building; or

(c)   a work of artistic craftsmanship.'[1]

In rare cases, an artistic work which is libellous, obscene, immoral or irreligious, may be in copyright but may not be entitled to rely on copyright law for its protection[2].

1   CDPA s 4(1), see **paragraph 2.06** for a detailed discussion of this definition.
2   See **paragraph 2.16**.

Ownership and infringement

27.03 It is important to distinguish between the ownership of the object of art (e.g. the painting or sculpture) and the copyright in the 'artistic work' which the object of art embodies. Ownership of one does not entail ownership of the other[1].

Where a gallery or museum acquires a work of art, its ability to make use of that work will depend upon the copyright it has acquired. It is therefore vital for the gallery or museum to ensure that it properly acquires the rights it needs and catalogues any rights it has acquired, and any which are reserved to other people[2].

In relation to infringement issues, in order to establish whether there has been a copyright infringement of an artistic work, it is necessary to establish that the 'infringed' work falls within one of the categories of work in which copyright exists[3], that the term of copyright for the 'infringed work' is still ongoing[4], that a restricted act has been undertaken without the authorisation of the owner (i.e. a primary infringement has been committed)[5] and/or that an act which amounts to a 'secondary infringement' has been committed with 'guilty knowledge'[6], and that no exception or defence to copyright infringement is available to the defendant[7].

1   See **paragraph 10.01**.
2   See **paragraph 27.15**.
3   See **paragraphs 2.01 et seq**.
4   See **Chapter 6**.
5   See **paragraphs 7.02–7.08**.
6   See **paragraphs 7.09–7.13**.
7   See **Chapter 9**.

Restricted acts – general

27.04 The acts restricted by the copyright in an artistic work are:

- *copying* the work in any material form[1];
- *issuing copies* of the work to the public[2];
- *renting or lending* the work to the public (other than a work of architecture in the form of a building or a model for a building, or a work of 'applied art')[3];
- *Communication to the public*[4].

It should be noted that exhibiting or selling an artistic work is not a restricted act. The copyright owner of an artistic work cannot prevent the work being exhibited without payment being made to him; nor is he entitled to any payment when the work is resold, unlike artists in countries where the 'droit de suite' exists[5].

1   See **paragraph 7.03**.
2   See **paragraph 7.04**.
3   See **paragraph 7.05**.
4   See **paragraph 7.07**.
5   See **paragraphs 14.03** and **27.23**.

Restricted acts – copying (two- and three-dimensional)

27.05   Copying an artistic work means reproducing it in any material form. This includes storing it in any medium by electronic means (e.g. in the memory of a computer[1]). The reproduction of an artistic work in any size, or the reproduction of a substantial part of an artistic work[2], will infringe copyright in the work, but there must be *actual* reproduction. The *re-use* of a copy of an artistic work made by someone else does not itself amount to reproduction and the use will not infringe copyright in the artistic work unless another restricted act (such as issuing to the public) is undertaken. So, it will not infringe copyright in an artistic work to make and sell a collage consisting of pictures of different artistic works cut out of magazines. However, if the collage maker, for example, takes copies of his own work embodying the other artistic works, or issues those copies to the public, he will be infringing copyright in the underlying artistic works which form part of his collage[3]. A collage which utilises other copyright works may also result in an infringement of the moral rights of the earlier artist, if the use amounts to a derogatory treatment[4].

Reproducing a two-dimensional painting, drawing or engraving in three-dimensional form is an infringement of the copyright in the two-dimensional original (e.g. toys; dolls; dresses; waxwork model tableaux; a tableaux vivant of a painting). Similarly, making a two dimensional graphic work representing a three-dimensional work of art such as a sculpture, a work of artistic craftsmanship, the model of a building, or the taking of photographs of such works, infringes the copyright in them. There is an exception for such works when on permanent public display, and the exception applicable to buildings is expressed broadly, making infringement in this manner very unlikely[5].

1   See **paragraph 7.03**.
2   See **paragraph 8.06**.
3   See **paragraph 27.06**.
4   See **paragraphs 11.12 et seq** and **27.22**.
5   See **paragraph 9.24**.

Restricted acts – issuing copies to the public

27.06   Under the CDPA, *issuing copies* is deemed to include issuing the original[1]. However, once the artwork has first been issued to the public, the author's right will be deemed exhausted, and further sale of the work will not infringe the artist's copyright[2]. An art gallery can, for example, exhibit original photographs or engravings without infringing the copyright in those artistic works. However, if the gallery wished to reproduce copies of the works in, say, a catalogue which is issued to the public, this would infringe copyright in the artistic work unless appropriate authorisation is obtained, unless the gallery can bring its use within the exemption from copyright infringement in relation to advertisements for the sale of artistic works[3]. A gallery may also wish to sell postcards or posters of the artistic work. Again, this will constitute an infringement both because it is a reproduction[4], and because it involves issuing copies to the public. Consequently any contract between a gallery and the artist should set out in detail the rights the gallery wishes to exploit in the artist's work, and the means by which the artist will be remunerated for that exploitation. In the case of architecture, issuing copies means selling casts or models of the original – it does not include issuing photographs of the sculpture[5].

1 CDPA s 18(4).
2 See **paragraphs 7.04 and 14.06.**
3 See **paragraphs 9.24 and 27.09.**
4 See **paragraph 27.05.**
5 This restricted act is considered in detail at **paragraph 7.04.**

Restricted acts – rental and lending of artistic works

27.07   The rental or lending of copies of artistic works to the public are acts restricted by the copyright in artistic works, subject to exceptions in the case of works of architecture and applied art[1]. Again, the making available of works for the purpose of exhibition in public does not constitute rental or lending[2], and the reference to the rental or lending of *copies* includes the rental or lending of the originals[3].

It should be noted that lending does not include making available artistic works between 'establishments which are accessible to the public'[4]. Therefore, galleries can lend artistic works to each other without the consent of the artist whether or not the purpose of the loan is public exhibition[5].

1 See **paragraph 7.05.**
2 CDPA s 18A(3)(b).
3 CDPA s 18A(6).
4 CDPA s 18A(4).
5 For the definitions of 'rental' and 'lending' and a discussion of this restricted act, see **paragraph 7.05.**

Restricted acts – communication to the public

27.08 Communicating an artistic work to the public is an act restricted by copyright[1].

1   CDPA s 16, see **paragraph 7.07**.

Exceptions and defences to copyright infringement

27.09 Fair dealing with an artistic work for the purpose of research for a non-commercial purpose and private study or for the purposes of criticism or review will not infringe copyright[1] provided that it is accompanied by a sufficient acknowledgment. A number of specific exceptions also apply to artistic works. The most significant of these which affect art galleries appear in the CDPA at ss 62 (representation of certain works on public display) and 63 (advertisement of sale of artistic works)[2].

- *Works on public display*[3]: in the case of buildings (including any part of a building, such as a room), and sculptures, models for buildings and works of artistic craftsmanship (i.e. not a graphic work, photograph, sculpture or collage) which are 'permanently situated in a public place or in premises open to the public'[4], copyright is not infringed by:

  '(a) making a graphic work representing it;
  (b) making a photograph or film of it; or
  (c) making a broadcast of a visual image of it'[5].

  Issuing copies to the public, or communicating to the public anything made in accordance with s 62 is also permitted without infringing copyright[6].

- *Advertisement of sale of artistic work*[7]: it is not an infringement of copyright in an artistic work to copy it, or to issue copies to the public, for the purpose of advertising the sale of the work[8]. It is worth noting that this provision does not apply to the advertising for sale of a *copy* of an artistic work. So, for example, this exception applies to the sale of a drawing but not the sale of a book which includes a copy of that drawing.

If a copy of a work permitted to be made pursuant to s 63 is subsequently 'dealt with' for another purpose (i.e. it is sold or let for hire, offered or exposed for sale or hire, or exhibited in public or distributed[9]), then that copy will be treated as an infringing copy with regard to that dealing and for all subsequent purposes. The provisions on secondary infringement of copyright will then apply[10]. Accordingly, whilst an art gallery may make copies of works for sale for the purpose of advertising them, it cannot sell copies of the sales catalogue after the sale, without the permission of the copyright owners of the works reproduced in it.

1   See **paragraphs 9.03 and 9.04**.
2   See **paragraphs 9.24 and 9.25**, exceptions and defences to copyright infringement generally are considered in detail in **Chapter 9**.
3   CDPA s 62.
4   CDPA s 62(1).
5   CDPA s 62(2).
6   CDPA s 62(3).
7   CDPA s 63.
8   CDPA s 63(1).
9   CDPA s 63(2).
10   See **Chapter 7**.

Galleries' condition of right of entry

27.10   Owners of museums, galleries and other premises who want to prevent visitors reproducing photographs, paintings, drawings, or engravings of sculpture, works of artistic craftsmanship or models of buildings they are exhibiting, do so by making it a condition of entry to their premises that visitors may not take photographs nor make drawings etc. This condition should be printed on admission tickets and notices to the same effect should be prominently displayed, particularly near entrances. Although this will not give any copyright protection to the gallery owner or the artist, the condition will form part of the contract under which the visitor enters the premises. Breach of this contract may give the owners of the premises the right to sue for an injunction preventing reproduction of the photographs, drawings etc and also a right to damages. With the potential value to museums and art galleries of the publication right[1], it is particularly important that they control photographers and the use of photographs of their exhibits.

1   See **paragraph 27.24** and **Chapter 6**.

Incidental inclusion of artistic works in other copyright works

27.11   There will be no infringement of the copyright in an artistic work if it is included incidentally in a film, broadcast or other artistic work or if the resulting work is issued, played, showed or communicated to the public[1].

So, paintings, drawings, and other artistic works can form part of the dressing of a set of a film or televised drama without requiring any licence from the copyright owners, if the inclusion is incidental. Reproductions of the paintings of an artist in a television programme about that artist would probably not constitute incidental use.

1   See **paragraph 9.07**.

Artists' reserved right of reproduction

27.12   If an artist sells the copyright in one of his works, he has a special right to continue to reproduce it in later works. He must not, however, repeat or imitate the main design of the earlier work. This special right extends also to the use of moulds, casts, sketches, plans, models or studies made for the purposes of the earlier work[1].

1   CDPA s 64; see **paragraph 9.26**.

Duration of copyright

27.13   The term of copyright in artistic works is the life of the author plus 70 years. In the case of an artistic work of unknown authorship, copyright expires at the end of the period of 70 years from the end of the calendar year in which it was made. If during that period the work is made available to the public, then copyright expires at the end of the period of 70 years from the end of the calendar year in which it is so made available[1]. For these purposes 'making available to the public' of an artistic work includes:

'(a)   exhibition in public;

(b)   a film including the work being shown in public; or

(c)   communication to the public'[2].

No account is to be taken of an unauthorised act. This produces a curious situation. The public exhibition of an artistic work is not a restricted act requiring the licence of the copyright owner. Usually the sale of an artistic work does not include the sale of the copyright in the work. The question therefore arises: is the authority required under s 12(5) that of the copyright holder? The better answer is probably that it is that of the copyright holder. The rules relating to photographs taken prior to 1 August 1989 are considered elsewhere in this *User's Guide*[3].

1   Duration of copyright is considered in detail in **Chapter 6**.
2   CDPA s 12(5).
3   See **paragraph 6.08**.

Ownership of copyright

27.14 Ownership of copyright generally, including artistic works, is generally considered in **Chapter 10**, but several points are particularly relevant to artistic works:

- *Commissioned work*: prior to the CDPA one of the exceptions to the general rule that the author is the first owner of a copyright was that copyright in commissioned photographs, portraits, engravings and sound recordings belonged to the commissioner, subject to any agreement to the contrary. Although the commissioner's copyright in photographs etc was removed by the CDPA, under the transitional provisions of the CDPA, copyright in photographs made after commencement (i.e. 1 August 1989) still belongs to the commissioner if the work is made in pursuance of a commission made before commencement.

- *Ownership of photographs*: prior to the CDPA, the owner of a photograph (which had not been commissioned) was the person who, at the time the photograph was taken, was the owner of the material on which it was taken. The CDPA did not repeat this, and the position is now governed by the general rule that the author is the person who created the work. This will normally be the person who actually takes the photograph. However, there may be circumstances where this is not the case. It might be the person who chose the camera angle, the type of film stock, the exposure and aperture setting but did not actually press the button to activate the shutter. It follows that, if he wishes to ensure that he is the sole owner of copyright, the photographer would be well advised to ensure that his arrangements with those other people collaborating in the creation of the photograph confirm his ownership of the resulting copyright[1].

So, under the CDPA, copyright in, for example, wedding photographs which have been commissioned by the bride and groom will belong to the photographer as the author (or maker) of the photograph. However, the bride and groom still have some protection by virtue of the moral right of privacy[2].

For the purposes of determining the period of copyright attributable to a photograph taken before 1 August 1989, the author of the photograph is deemed to be the photographer, whether or not the taking of the photograph was commissioned.

1 See **Chapter 10**.
2 See **paragraph 11.24**.

Dealing with copyright in artistic works

27.15 Whenever a photograph or a work of art is commissioned, and it is intended that the person commissioning it should own the copyright in the work, as well as the object itself, it is essential that there should be an assignment of copyright in writing signed by the owner. This does not have to be in any special form – a letter will suffice, providing that it is written in clear and unambiguous language[1].

The sale of an object does not automatically include the copyright in that work of art[2]. Thus a gallery, or dealer, which acquires a work of art which is still in copyright, does not necessarily acquire the right to reproduce it, or do any of the other restricted acts. To acquire such rights exclusively, there must be an assignment or exclusive licence of the copyright (or the relevant part of the copyright) in the work in writing, signed by the copyright owner. If a non-exclusive licence is required (e.g. to reproduce the work in a catalogue) it is still advisable to obtain a written licence, although a verbal licence (which is capable of proof, and which is sufficient to amount to a contract) will be legally enforceable. A licence may also, depending on the circumstances, be implied by conduct[3]. If, for example, the copyright owner knows that a catalogue is being produced and allows the publisher to incur printing and distribution expenses before refusing a licence, it may be held that the copyright owner's failure to take action by warning the publisher when he first knew of the gallery's intentions, constitutes an implied licence. Relying on an implied licence is never recommended[4].

As we have noted, if the catalogue is purely for the purpose of advertising the sale of the artistic work, no licence will be required[5].

The rules regarding ownership of works produced in the course of employment apply to artistic works with no special exceptions[6].

In practice, galleries and museums have moved away from the practice of acquiring assignments of copyright. It is therefore crucial that the gallery ensure it is contractually entitled (by licences of copyright) to exercise those rights it needs.

1   Issues to be considered when dealing with an artistic work are considered in detail in **Chapter 10**.
2   See **paragraphs 10.01** and **27.03**.
3   Implied licences are considered at **paragraph 10.30**.
4   See **paragraph 10.30**.
5   See **paragraph 27.09**.
6   See **paragraphs 10.11 et seq.**

Collective licensing

27.16 If a museum or gallery wishes to sell postcards reproducing paintings or drawings or reproductions of sculptures in its collection, it will need a licence not only from the owner of the copyright in the object concerned but also a licence or assignment of copyright from the person who produced the postcard or made the reproduction. The Design and Artists Copyright Society Ltd (DACS) has as members, artists, designers and photographers and their estates, and collectively administers their copyright. DACS has published scales of fees for reproduction of its members' works. It grants licences to the principal art publishers, broadcasters, poster printers and distributors and those who reproduce artistic works on merchandise (such as the Royal Academy of Arts) etc[1].

1 See **Appendix 1** for DACS' contact details.

International protection

27.17 As with the other copyright works, artistic works do not have to be registered to acquire copyright protection[1]. Strictly speaking, works of art need not carry the © symbol with the date of publication and the copyright owner's name to acquire protection under the Universal Copyright Convention. However, if there is any possibility of copies of a work of art being made available to the public in one of the few countries that are not parties to the Berne Convention, the requisite notice should, as a precaution, be affixed to the work, whatever its nature, to avoid the possibility that copyright protection may be lost in that country[2]. In every case the symbol should be affixed to reproductions of the work, if copies of the work are issued to the public. Accordingly, engravings, lithographs, sculptures and other works of art of which a number of copies are made for sale to the public should bear the © symbol etc. The safest course is to affix the © symbol etc to all works of art[3].

1 See **paragraph 10.21**.
2 See **paragraph 4.16**.
3 International protection for copyright works is considered in detail in **Chapter 4**.

Photographs

27.18 The following additional points regarding photographs and photographers should be noted:

- *Use of photographs*: as long as a photograph has not been commissioned for private and domestic purposes, and is therefore subject to the right to privacy of such photographs[1], there is nothing in copyright law nor any other express provision in English law to prevent a photographer taking and publishing a photograph of whomsoever he wishes, without making any payment to or obtaining any consent from the persons appearing in the photograph. The only restrictions arise under the general law. So, for example, to photograph a policeman in the company of a well-known criminal and to publish it in such a way that it appears the policeman is receiving a bribe from, or socialising with him, where that is not the real situation, may be defamatory of the policeman.

- *If invited to a celebrity's house as a private guest*: it may be a breach of confidence to publish a photograph of the celebrity in compromising circumstances[2]. But to take the same photograph from nearby premises with a telephoto lens and publish it, would give rise to no offence in law as the law currently stands. There are indications that the UK may be moving towards the 'invasion of privacy' laws that are to be found in some other countries, especially France and the USA.

- *Copies of other photographs*: even a snapshot is entitled to copyright protection[3]. However, if a photograph consists entirely of another artistic work, such as a photograph of another photograph, it will infringe the copyright in the artistic work by reproducing it in a material form[4]. The second photograph will not be entitled to copyright protection, if it lacks the elements of originality and sufficient skill and labour that must be applied to it for it to acquire copyright protection[5]. To take a photograph of an identical scene is not a breach of copyright[6].

- *Positives and negatives*: the positive as well as the negative comes within the definition of a photograph in the CDPA, and positives made from the negative will constitute reproductions of the photograph for the purposes of the infringing act[7].

- *Videograb*: copying in relation to a film or broadcast includes making a photograph of the whole or any substantial part of *any image* forming part of the film or television broadcast[8]. However, an exception is made under the CDPA where the photograph is taken for private use from the television[9].

1   See **paragraphs 11.24** et seq.
2   See **Chapter 5**.
3   See **paragraph 3.03**.
4   See **paragraph 7.03**.
5   See **paragraph 3.03**.

6   See **paragraph 3.06**.
7   See **paragraph 7.03**.
8   See **paragraph 7.03**.
9   See **paragraph 9.32**.

Parodies

27.19   A work of art which is a satire or parody of another work in copyright will infringe the copyright in the original work if it uses substantial part of the original[1]. So, if a portrait were to be copied, and changed only by the addition of a moustache and spectacles, the copyright in the original portrait will be infringed. The question whether or not the copyright in the original is infringed depends upon the extent to which the copy uses the actual original and the extent to which it merely uses the concept – the idea – of the original.

If a sufficient degree of skill and labour and originality is devoted to the changes then the new work – the satire or parody – will itself acquire copyright protection as an original work of art notwithstanding that it infringes the earlier work[2].

1   See **paragraphs 8.05 and 8.06**.
2   See **paragraph 2.15**.

Use of film and music in exhibitions

27.20   The use of films, videograms, music and sound recordings in museums and galleries will require the licence of the copyright owners of the films or videograms, music and sound recordings because their use as part of an exhibition constitutes public performance[1].

Licences are required from the PRS for the performance of music (whether or not in a record or tape), from the PPL for the performance of sound recordings and the VPL (or from the record company direct) for the performance of music videos[2]. The transfer of music onto specially prepared records or tapes (for example, compilations for the purposes of the exhibition) will require a licence from the MCPS[3].

1   Issues concerning performance of copyright works are considered in detail at **Chapter 25**. See also **paragraph 7.06**.
2   See **paragraph 22.23**.
3   See **paragraph 22.08**.

Moral rights and artistic works

27.21   The following moral rights are applicable to artistic works generally[1]:

(a) the paternity right or the right to be identified as author of the work[2];
(b) the integrity right or the right to object to derogatory treatment of a work[3];
(c) the false attribution right[4];
(d) the right to privacy of certain photographs[5].

There are important exceptions to each of these rights and these are discussed in further detail in **Chapter 11**. Moral rights can be waived by the author in writing or otherwise[6]. It is also worth noting the following points:

● The author of an artistic work has the right to be identified as such unless the artist or photographer died before 1 August 1989, or the copyright first vested in a person other than the author or unless the author parted with the copyright before 1 August 1989. In these cases, the author need not be identified, because the act coming within the circumstances giving rise to the right of identity (or paternity) is deemed to be done with the permission of the copyright owner.

● Of particular importance to those organising exhibitions of works of art are the provisions of the CDPA concerning the persons bound by the right of paternity[7]. The CDPA deals specifically with the way in which the right may be asserted in relation to the public exhibition of an artistic work[8]. A public exhibition is any exhibition to which the public are admitted; not only exhibitions in public galleries and museums. In the case of an artistic work, the author's moral right of paternity is asserted when the author (or other first owner of copyright in it) parts with possession of the original, or of a copy made by or under his control, on which the author is identified. The author may equally be identified, and therefore assert the right, by having his name on the frame, mount or other thing to which the artistic work is attached[9].

In addition, the paternity right may be asserted in a licence by which the author or other first owner of copyright authorises the making of copies of the work. To assert the right in relation to public exhibition of such copies, the licence must state that the author asserts his right to be identified in the event of the public exhibition of a copy made pursuant to the licence[10].

Anyone into whose hands comes the original or copy of an artistic work in respect of which the right to be identified in relation to public exhibition of the work, is bound by the assertion[11]. This applies whether or not the identification on the work at the time the right was asserted is still visible.

However, if the artist who is asserting his right to be identified has specified a pseudonym, initials or other particular form of identification, that form should be used.

The CDPA does not specify any particular way in which authors should be identified except to say that any reasonable form of identification may be used[12].

It is suggested that exhibition organisers should request the person providing an artistic work for exhibition to state in writing whether or not to his knowledge the right to be identified has been asserted and whether a particular form of identification has been specified by the artist.

If it is desired for some reason to omit the identity of the artist, then a written waiver of the right should be obtained from the artist himself – not the owner of the work – or, if he is dead, from the person to whom the right of identity has passed[13].

In *Tidy v Trustees of the Natural History Museum*[14], in considering whether the reduction in size of the plaintiff's cartoons by the Museum constituted a derogatory treatment, the court treated the question as being whether this was either a distortion or was otherwise prejudicial to the author's honour or reputation.

The moral right to privacy of photographs applies to the public exhibition of photographs[15]. Therefore, exhibition organisers should obtain a written statement from those providing photographs for exhibition to the effect that the photograph was not commissioned for private and domestic purposes. If, however, it was so commissioned, then consent for its exhibition must be obtained, not from the copyright owner (whose consent is not required in any event) but from the person who commissioned the taking of the photograph.

1   Moral rights are considered in detail in **Chapter 11.**
2   See **paragraphs 11.02–11.11.**
3   See **paragraphs 11.12–11.20**.
4   See **paragraphs 11.21–11.23**.
5   See **paragraphs 11.24–11.26**.
6   See **paragraph 11.29**.
7   See **paragraphs 11.02** et seq.
8   **CDPA s** 78(3).
9   See **paragraph 11.08**.
10   See **paragraph 11.08**.
11   CDPA s 78(4).
12   CDPA s 77(8).
13   See **paragraph 11.29**.
14   (1997) 39 IPR 501.
15   See **paragraph 11.24**.

Directive on Artists' Resale Rights[1]

27.22   On 13 October 2001 the Directive on Artists' Resale Rights came into force. The aim of the Directive is to harmonise the market in modern and contemporary art by applying a resale right throughout the European Union. An artist's resale right allows artists and, after their death, their heirs/beneficiaries to receive, during the copyright period in the work, a royalty payment on a work of art each time it is resold by an art market professional such as an auctioneer, a gallery or any other art dealer. The right does not apply to sales by private treaty. EC Member States must transpose the Directive into national law by 1 January 2006, but this may be extended until 1 January 2010 by those Member States that do not already apply resale rights and for a further two years, subject to consultation with the Commission. The UK plan is to have a rolling programme of consultation. Patent Office consultation documents were originally intended for publication in 2002 and then at the end of 2003, but both deadlines were missed. The consultation document was finally published on 22 February 2005 and it therefore, at the time of going to press, looked likely that the UK would miss the 2006 deadline.

1   2001/84/EC.

Publication right and museums and public galleries

27.23   The publication right, which was introduced into UK copyright law by the 1996 Regulations, is of particular importance to museums and public galleries[1].

The publication right applies to works which have been in copyright but where copyright protection has expired. It only applies to such works if they are previously unpublished. There is some ambiguity as to whether or not a work which has been exhibited in public is in fact unpublished, but on balance, such exhibition is likely to constitute publication when deciding whether or not the work is unpublished for the purposes of the 1996 Regulations.

Where a museum or art gallery owns works which have never been the subject of publication, it will be entitled to a publication right in the work. The publication right gives the owner of an unpublished manuscript or other object embodying a work in which the copyright has expired the right to publish the work for a period of 25 years from the end of the year in which the work is first published[2]. This is an exclusive right akin to copyright and the same exceptions and rights apply to publication right as apply to copyright in an artistic work[3]. To qualify, it must be first published in the EEA and the publisher at the time of the publication must be a national of an EEA state[4].

It follows that museums should be extremely cautious before allowing publishers of art books to publish photographs of works in their collection, whether they be works of sculpture or works of artistic craftsmanship or graphic works, because by so doing they may lose the publication right which could otherwise be a useful source of revenue. If a museum decides to grant a publisher a right to publish the work, it should enter into a publishing agreement under which the museum is assigned the publication right (or reserve it on the grounds that the museum is exercising the publication right by arranging for the publisher to effect publication) and be paid appropriate royalties or other consideration.

Equally, museums and art galleries when allowing photographers and publishers to take photographs of works in their collection should ensure that copies of these photographs are deposited with the museum or gallery and that the rights of publication in such photographs should be clearly stated (by an agreement signed by the photographer or publisher) to be reserved by the museum or gallery.

1   See **paragraphs 6.20** et seq.
2   See **paragraph 6.22**.
3   See **paragraph 6.21**.
4   See **paragraph 6.23**.

Chapter 28

Architects and architecture

Introduction

28.01   Works of architecture (i.e. buildings and models for buildings) are subject to a number of special provisions in the CDPA, which are considered in this chapter.

Definitions

28.02   The definition of 'artistic work' under the CDPA includes 'a work of architecture, being a building or a model for a building'[1], and a 'building' includes 'any fixed structure and a party or building or fixed structure'[2].

The plans, sketches, and drawings upon which works of architecture are based are also artistic works which have their own separate copyright[3], as do the notes prepared by the architect, which are protected as literary works[4].

Although there is no definition of 'fixed structure' in the CDPA, one decision which pre-dates the 1956 Copyright Act held that a garden, in that case a somewhat elaborately laid out garden, was a 'structure' and therefore a work of architecture[5].

The definitions of 'artistic work' and 'literary work' are so wide that they cover all the typical output of an architect's office: design sketches, blueprints, descriptive diagrams, working drawings, final drawings, artistic presentations, notes, both alphabetical and numerical, and reports.

1   CDPA s 4(1)(b).
2   CDPA s 4(2); see **paragraph 2.06**.
3   See **paragraphs 2.06 and 27.02**.
4   See **paragraph 2.02**.
5   *Meikle v Maufe [1941] 3 All ER 144.*

Restricted acts

28.03 The acts restricted by copyright applicable to works of architecture are the same as those applicable to any other artistic works[1], with certain special exceptions[2].

1   See **paragraph 7.02**.
2   See **paragraphs 28.11–28.14**.

Originality and artistic content

28.04 A work of architecture will not receive copyright protection unless it is original. However, the test for originality is not onerous. In essence, for these purposes 'originality' means 'originating from the owner'[1].

For architectural works, the inclusion of some distinctive design detail will certainly make the architect's task of proving infringement much easier. In the case of *Stovin-Bradford v Volpoint Properties Ltd*[2], the courts were influenced by the fact that although many details of the architect's drawing were not reproduced in the constructed buildings, 'a distinctive diamond-shaped feature which gave a pleasing appearance to the whole' was reproduced.

Some distinctive design feature may also be important when it could otherwise be proved that the person sued was without any knowledge of the plaintiff's prior design, and that he produced identical solutions because of a similarity in circumstances. In the US case of *Muller v Triborough Bridge Authority*[3], for example, the US Supreme Court held that a copyright of the drawing showing a novel bridge approach designed to disentangle traffic congestion was not infringed by copying, because the system of relieving traffic congestion shown embodied an idea which could not be protected by copyright and was only the obvious solution to the problem.

1   See **paragraph 3.01**.
2   [1971] Ch 1007.
3   43 F Supp 288 (1942).

Duration of copyright

28.05 The protection of copyright in an artistic work extends for the lifetime of the author and a further period of 70 years from the end of the calendar year in which he died[1].

In the case of joint works, the 70 years begins to run from the end of the calendar year in which the last of the joint authors dies[2]. A joint work is one in which the work is produced by the collaboration of two or more authors in which the contribution of each author is not distinct from that of the other author or authors[3]. So, if a building is designed by two architects, but one is exclusively responsible only for the design of the doors and windows, so that it is possible to distinguish between the contributions of the two architects, the building will not be a joint work.

1   See **paragraph 6.06**.
2   See **paragraph 6.23**.
3   See **paragraph 10.08**.

Qualification

28.06   In order to qualify for copyright protection in the UK, the qualification requirements of the CDPA must be satisfied either as regards the author or the country in which the work was first published[1].

1   See **paragraphs 4.01** et seq.

Publication in relation to artistic works, such as architecture

28.07   Under the CDPA, 'publication' essentially means the issue of copies to the public. However, in relation to works of architecture in the form of a building or an artistic work incorporated in a building, construction of the building is treated as equivalent to publication of the work[1].

The issue to the public of copies of a graphic work representing a building, or of photographs of a work of architecture in the form of a building, or a model for a building, a sculpture or a work of artistic craftsmanship, does not constitute publication for the purposes of the CDPA. Nor does the exhibition issue to the public copies of a film including the work, or the broadcasting of an artistic work. The inclusion of a model of a building in a public exhibition such as the Royal Academy Summer Exhibition, for example, would not amount to publication, nor would the inclusion of photographs of the model in a book[2].

1   See **paragraph 4.05**.
2   See **paragraph 4.06**.

Ownership of architectural works

28.08 Ownership of copyright in architectural works will usually first reside with the architect who actually drew the plan, drawing, sketch or diagram[1]. Property may be transferred in accordance with the principles referred to in **Chapter 10.**

However, it is possible for someone who did not actually put pen to paper to be a joint author of an architectural work. In *Cala Homes (South) Ltd v Alfred McAlpine Homes East Ltd*[2] an employee of Cala Homes supervised in detail the drawings for the designs and plans for houses which were actually undertaken by employees of a firm of technical draughtsmen. Notwithstanding he had not actually drawn anything, it was held he could be a joint author. This is, however, a rare case[3].

1 Unless he is an employee; see **paragraph 28.09** and **Chapter 10.**
2 [1995] FSR 818.
3 See **paragraph 10.09** for a detailed analysis of this issue.

Employees and sub-contractors

28.09 As with any other artistic work, the copyright in architects' drawings, buildings or models produced by an employee in the course of his employment automatically vests in his employer, whether the latter is an architect in partnership, a limited company, or a public authority, in the absence of any agreement to the contrary[1].

Frequently, architects employ independent architects and artists to carry out parts of the drawing service as was the case in *Cala Homes*. Such persons are rarely employed under 'a contract of service' as distinct from 'a contract for services'[2]. Employer architects should make it an express term of any sub-contractor's appointment that any copyright arising out of his work should vest in the employer.

Where a work is made by an officer or servant of the Crown in the course of his duties, the Crown will be the first owner of the copyright in the work[3].

1 See **paragraphs 10.11** et seq.
2 See **paragraph 10.12**.
3 See **paragraph 10.09**.

Ownership of drawings

28.10 Ownership of copyright in drawings should be distinguished from ownership of the actual material upon which they are drawn[1].

Although on payment of the architect's fees the client is likely to be entitled to physical possession of all the drawings prepared at his expense, in the absence of any agreement to the contrary, copyright remains with the architect, who also has a lien on (i.e. a right to withhold) the drawings until his fees are paid. If all copyright *is* assigned to the client, he may make such use of it as he wishes. Even if an architect does assign his copyright, he may reproduce in a subsequent work part of his own original design, provided that he does not repeat or imitate the main designs[2]. This provision enables an architect to repeat standard details which would otherwise pass to the client upon assignment of copyright.

1   See **paragraph 10.01**.
2   CDPA s 64; see **paragraph 9.26**.

Exceptions from infringement of architects' copyright: photographs and graphic works

28.11   Frequently, photographs of buildings designed by architects appear as part of advertisements by the contractors who constructed the buildings. As a matter of courtesy, the contractor usually makes some acknowledgement of the design, but he is not required to do so. Copyright in a work of architecture is not infringed by:

'(a)   making a graphic work representing it;
(b)   making a photograph or film of it; or
(c)   make a broadcast of a visual image of it'[1].

Copies of such graphic works, photographs and films can be issued to the public without infringing the copyright in the building as built. It remains an infringement to copy the drawing or plan from which the building was constructed.

1   CDPA s 62(2), see **paragraph 9.24**.

Reconstruction

28.12   Copyright in a building, or any drawings or plans from which a building is constructed (with the authorisation of the owner) will not be infringed by anything done for the purpose of reconstructing the building[1].

1   CDPA s 65, see **paragraph 9.27**.

Fair dealing

28.13 A defence to any alleged infringement of copyright in an artistic work is 'fair dealing' for the purpose of criticism or review, provided that a sufficient acknowledgement is made to the earlier work[1] and provided that the work has been made available to the public[2]. As reproduction by photograph is the most likely method of illustrating a review and as a photograph of a building is specifically exempt from infringement[3], this defence of 'fair dealing' would appear to be needed only in the case of photographs or copies of *drawings* of buildings. A 'sufficient acknowledgement' is an acknowledgement identifying the building by its name and location, which also identifies the name of the architect who designed it. The name of the copyright owner need not be given if he has previously required that no acknowledgement of his name should be made. As certain self-appointed groups have now taken to awarding prizes for ugliness in design, some architects might find themselves in the unusual position of wishing to have no acknowledgement made of their connection with a design, although perhaps such publicity would hardly be 'fair dealing'.

Fair dealing with an artistic work for the purposes of research for a non-commercial purpose and private study is also a defence to an alleged copyright infringement provided that it is accompanied by a sufficient acknowledgment. However, there are limits on how, and how many, copies may be made[4].

1 See **paragraph 9.04**.
2 For further information on what constitutes making work available to the public see CDPA s 29 (1A).
3 See **paragraph 28.11**.
4 See **paragraph 9.03**.

Special exceptions

28.14 Special exceptions are contained in the CDPA for copying for educational purposes and copying by libraries and archives and by public administration. These are considered in detail elsewhere in this *User's Guide*[1].

1 Generally, see **Chapters 9 and 20**.

Infringements

General

28.15 In brief, to prove infringement, a plaintiff must show:

- copyright subsists in his work;
- the copyright is vested in him;
- the alleged infringement is identical to his work in material particulars;
- the alleged infringement was copied from his work[1].

It is in the nature of architects' copyright that the alleged infringer must have had access directly or indirectly to the drawings. Infringement can therefore take three forms, considered in detail below.

1   Infringement of copyright is considered in detail in **Chapter 8**.

Copying in the form of drawings

28.16   It is rare for drawings to be copied in every detail and copyright will be infringed in a drawing if a 'substantial part' is infringed[1]. This issue is considered elsewhere in this *User's Guide*[2], but in brief, the word 'substantial' in this context refers to quality rather that to quantity. So, the reproduction of a distinctive diamond-shaped detail from a building design was enough to constitute infringement in the *Stovin-Bradford* case[3].

1   CDPA s 16(3)(a).
2   See **paragraph 8.06**.
3   See **paragraph 28.04**.

Copying the drawing in the form of a building

28.17   Reproduction of a drawing in the form of a building infringes the copyright in the drawing, even if no copy of the drawing itself is made by the infringer[1].

1   See **paragraph 7.03**.

Copying a building in the form of another building

28.18   How much of a work of architecture must be reproduced before there is an infringement? This is always a matter of degree and of examination of the facts in the particular case. It will be necessary to show that the subsequent building appears to substantially copy the earlier building[1]. The copyright in a building which is of an unusual design, and has considerable special detail, is more easily infringed than that of a very simple building using traditional forms and which is without much detail. The construction of a building with the same number of windows and doors and of approximately the same proportions in the case of, for example, a normal semi-detached house will not of itself constitute infringement. There must also be a causal connection – that is, the architect must have seen the original building, or a photograph or drawing of it[2].

Details of a building can also be infringed by reproduction. For example, a complex chimney arrangement, stair design or the like which is still in copyright may not be reproduced in a different building without a licence from the copyright owner (not necessarily the owner of the house). On the other hand, if the architect of a later chimney or staircase can show that he had drawn his inspiration from a common source, such as an even earlier building which is no longer in copyright, there will be no infringement.

1 See **paragraph 8.06**.
2 See **paragraph 3.05**.

Copying a building in the form of drawings

28.19 Copyright in a work of architecture is not infringed by two-dimensional reproductions which are graphic works or photographs[1].

1 See **paragraphs 9.24**.

Licences: express licence

28.20 The Royal Institute of British Architects[1] publishes a Standard Form of Agreement for use in the appointment of an architect which was in connection with fully designed building projects[2]. The Conditions of Appointment which are appended to this Standard Form provide that: 'the Architect owns the copyright in the work produced by him'[3].

The standard form also provides that the architect asserts his right to be identified as the author of the artistic work/work of architecture which constitutes the architectural project[4].

In each case, the standard form agreement provides that the client shall have:

'a licence to copy and use and allow other consultants and contractors providing services to the architectural project to use and copy drawings, documents and bespoke software provided by the architect in performing the services … but only for purposes related to the project on the site or part of the site to which the design relates'[5].

This licence is expressed to extend to the 'operation, maintenance, repair, reinstatement, alteration, extending, promotion, leasing and/or sale' of the project, but, unless a licence fee is agreed beforehand, the licence is not deemed to extend to use of the design for any extension built onto the architectural project, or to any other project[6].

The licence is also subject to a number of provisos. Most significantly, the architect is entitled to suspend the licence if the client is in default of paying fees[7].

RIBA also publishes amendments to the above terms for use in a 'design and build' situation, although these do not alter the copyright position as between client and architect referred to above.

Copyright may be expressly assigned to the client at some later stage, but it is usual to grant a licence authorising use of copyright subject to conditions rather than an outright assignment of all the architect's rights. An increasing number of public and commercial clients make it a condition of the architect's appointment that all copyright will vest in the client, but the architect should not consent to this without careful thought. It would seem reasonable that a client should not be prevented from extending a building and incorporating distinctive design features of the original building so that the two together should form one architectural unit.

So far as drawings are concerned, it must be remembered that drawings are the subject of copyright 'irrespective of artistic quality'[8] so that a prior express assignment of copyright to the client could theoretically grant him copyright in respect of even the most simple standard detail contained in the drawings.

1   RIBA, Tel: 020 7580 5532; Fax: 020 7255 1541.
2   Last updated in April 2004 SFA/99.
3   Conditions of engagement 6.1.
4   Conditions of engagement 6.1.
5   Conditions of engagement 6.2.
6   Conditions of engagement 6.2.
7   Conditions of engagement 6.2.3.
8   See **paragraph 2.06**.

Licences: implied licence

28.21   Courts will not imply a contractual term (including a licence) unless it is necessary to give efficacy to the intention of the parties[1]. Application of these rules of an architect's engagement would suggest that an architect may impliedly be said to consent to the client making use of his drawings for the purpose for which they were intended (i.e. creating a building). If, therefore, the nature of the engagement is not a full RIBA service but, for example, obtaining outline planning permission and no more, the architect may be said to impliedly consent to the client making use of his copyright to apply for such permission. Again, if an architect is instructed to prepare drawings of a proposed alteration for submission to the client's landlord, the client may use the drawings to obtain a consent under the terms of his lease but not for any other purpose, and certainly not for the purpose of instructing a contractor to carry out the alteration work. Reliance on implied licences is never recommended.

1   See **paragraph 10.30**.

Alterations to architect's drawing and works of architecture

28.22   If a client alters an architect's plans or the completed building, the probability is that he will not therefore be in breach of the architect's copyright[1]. However, the client may not 'sell or hire' such buildings or plans as the unaltered work of the architect[2].

1   *Hunter v Fitzroy Robinson & Partners [1978] FSR 167.*
2   See **paragraph 28.26** below on moral rights.

Remedies for infringement: injunction

28.23   An injunction can be obtained to prevent the construction of a building that would infringe the copyright in another building, even if that building is part-built.

However, there is a general principle of law that an injunction will not be granted if damages are an adequate relief. It is probable that a court would, in most cases, apply this rule in the case of an injunction to prevent the demolition of a building when the construction has substantially commenced. The decision of the court will depend upon all the facts and circumstances of the case[1].

1   See **paragraph 8.14**.

Remedies for infringement: damages

28.24   In the case of *Potton Ltd v Yorkclose Ltd*[1] the defendants admitted that they had constructed 14 houses, in infringement of the plaintiff's copyright in a style of house named 'Grandsen'. The defendant's houses were substantial reproductions of the plaintiff's 'Grandsen' drawings and they had copied the drawings for obtaining outline planning permission and detailed planning permission. It was held that the plaintiffs were entitled to the profits realised on the sale of the houses, apportioned to exclude profits attributable to:

- the purchase, landscaping and sale of the land on which the houses were built;
- any increase in value of the houses during the interval between the completion of the houses and their sale; and
- the advertising, marketing and selling of the houses.

In the case of *Charles Church Developments plc v Cronin*[2] the defendants admitted that they had had a home built based on plans which were the copyright of the plaintiff. The distinction between this case and *Potton Ltd v Yorkclose Ltd* is that in the former case the houses were built for sale and had been sold, whereas in this case the house had not been sold and the plaintiffs had obtained an injunction to prevent its sale. In the former case the plaintiffs sued for an account of profits. In the latter case the claim was for compensatory damages for the loss caused by the infringement. The judge held that the measure of damages was a fair fee for a licence to use the drawings, based on what an architect would have charged for the preparation of drawings. The architect's fee should be calculated on the basis that the architect would have provided the whole of the basic services – in that case, 8.5 % of the building costs.

The court may award additional damages as the justice of the case may require in cases of flagrant infringement, taking into account any benefit accruing to the defendant by reason of the infringement.

In the *Cala Homes* case[3], Mr Justice Laddie held that the breach of Cala's copyright had taken place flagrantly. He therefore held that it was an appropriate case for the court to exercise its discretion to award additional damages under the provisions of s 97(2) of the CDPA[4]. The damages would 'be designed to allow the court to register in terms of a financial penalty its disapproval of the behaviour of the infringer'.

1   [1990] FSR 11.
2   [1990] FSR 1.
3   See **paragraphs 8.12** and **28.08**.
4   See **paragraph 8.12**.

Industrial designs

28.25   The law on this subject is complicated and technical. It is not proposed to deal with this area at length in this *User's Guide*, but merely to warn architects, who may be commissioned to design articles or components capable of mass reproduction, to seek professional advice before entering into any agreement commissioning the design of such articles or components or assigning or licensing the rights therein.

Moreover, any architect who does design such articles or components should seek professional advice as to what steps should be taken to protect them. Industrial design falls mid-way between copyright (not registrable in the UK), which is concerned with 'artistic quality', and patents, which must be registered and are not concerned with artistic quality but with function and method of manufacture.

Moral rights

28.26 There are four basic categories of moral rights contained in the CDPA:

- the *right to be identified* as author;
- the right to object to *derogatory treatment* of work;
- *protection from false attribution* of work;
- the *right of privacy* of certain photographs and films[1].

The author of a work of architecture in the form of a building or a model for a building, has the right to be identified whenever copies of a graphic work representing it, or of a photograph of it, are issued to the public[2].

The author of a work of architecture in the form of a building also has the right to be identified on the building as constructed, or, where more than one building is constructed to the design, on the first to be constructed[3].

This right must be asserted by the author on any assignment of copyright in the work or by instrument in writing signed by the author. In the case of the public exhibition as an artistic work (for example, the inclusion of a model of a building in an exhibition), the right can be asserted by identifying the author on the original or copy of the work, or on a frame, mount or other thing to which the work is attached. If the author grants a licence to make copies of the work, then the right can be asserted for exhibitions by providing in the licence that the author must be identified on copies which are publicly exhibited[4].

There are certain exceptions to the right, of which the most important is that it does not apply to works originally vested in the author's employer[5].

The author of an artistic work has the right to object to his work being subjected to derogatory treatment[6].

In the case of a work of architecture in the form of a model of a building, the right is infringed by issuing copies of a graphic work representing it or of a photograph of a derogatory treatment of the work.

However, and most importantly, the right is not infringed in the case of a work of architecture in the form of a building. Nevertheless, if a building is the subject of a derogatory treatment, the architect is entitled to have his identification on the building as its architect removed[7].

In the case of works which vested originally in the author's employer, the right does not apply.

Similarly, in the case of an artistic work, a person has the right not to have its authorship falsely attributed to him. Thus, an architect can prevent a building which he has not designed being attributed to him as its architect[8].

1   Moral rights are considered in detail in **Chapter 11**.
2   CDPA s 77(4)(c).
3   CDPA s 77(5).
4   See **paragraph 11.08**.
5   See **paragraph 11.10**.
6   See **paragraph 11.15**.
7   See **paragraph 11.15**.
8   Moral rights are considered in detail in **Chapter 11**.

Chapter 29

Advertising agencies

Introduction

29.01   Advertising agencies are involved with every type of copyright, and reference should be made to the relevant chapters of this *User's Guide* in relation to different types of work[1]:

- *literary works*: advertising in newspapers and magazines[2];
- *dramatic works*: scripts of advertising films and television commercials[3];
- *musical works*: radio commercials and the sound-tracks of television commercials[4];
- *artistic works*: posters and magazine and press advertising[5];
- *sound recordings*: radio commercials[6];
- *films*: promotional films and television commercials[7];
- *published editions of works*: publicity publications which constitute editions of typographical arrangements[8].

There are, however, certain copyright problems which have a special bearing on the advertising industry.

1   See, generally, **Chapter 2**.
2   **Chapter 18**.
3   **Chapter 23**.
4   **Chapter 22**.
5   **Chapter 27**.
6   **Chapters 22 (Part II) and 25**.
7   **Chapter 24**.
8   **Chapter 17**.

Copyright in advertisements

29.02   The fact that work appears in an advertisement does not detract from its right to protection under the CDPA. An advertising poster will be an artistic work (as regards its artwork) and a literary work (as regards any words and numbers appearing on it)[1].

Whether an advertisement is entitled to copyright protection, will depend in each case on whether the skill and labour applied to its creation is sufficient to justify protection[2]. It is not the idea, but the resolution of the idea into material form, which is entitled to copyright[3]. An analogy may be drawn to titles of books and films, which the courts have held are not entitled to copyright unless they are of a complicated nature and could not have come into existence except by the application of skill and labour[4].

Trade catalogues will be entitled to copyright protection, provided the criteria for protection are met. Although they are not 'literary' in the ordinary sense of that word, they will be treated as literary works in copyright law if they are in writing, and if original and skill and labour has been extended upon their production. Their literary or artistic quality or merit is immaterial[5].

A distinction should be drawn between those artistic works which, like posters, are intended to be enjoyed as artistic works and those artistic works which are intended to be applied to other articles, such as T-shirts, belt buckles, drinking glasses and the like. The law in such cases is complex, falling partly under copyright law and partly under design right[6].

1 See **paragraphs 2.02** and **2.06**.
2 See **Chapter 3**.
3 See **paragraphs 1.03** and **8.04**.
4 See **paragraph 3.02**.
5 See **paragraph 2.02**.
6 See **Chapter 15**.

Ownership

29.03 There are no special provisions in the CDPA regarding the ownership of copyright works produced for the purposes of advertising. It follows that the question of who owns advertising materials will be determined in accordance with the general principles outlined elsewhere in this *User's Guide*[1]. In brief, an advertisement which consists of literary, artistic, dramatic or musical works will vest in its author or (if the author is employed, there is no agreement to the contrary and the work is made in the course of employment) in his employer[2]. It follows that the 'default position' in the relationship between an advertising agent and his client will be (as between them) be that the agent owns the copyright in the advertisement.

If an advertisement produced by an agency substantially copies material provided by the client, the advertisement will nevertheless qualify for copyright protection provided that it fulfils the requirements for protection[3]. Although the agency will (as against the client) own the copyright in the advertisement on the principles set out above, any use of the advertisement which amounts to a 'restricted act' will infringe the copyright in the client's material unless the use is authorised by the client[4].

1   See **Chapter 10**.
2   See **paragraphs 10.11 et seq**.
3   See **Chapters 2** and **3**.
4   See **paragraphs 7.02 et seq**.

The client and copyright in advertising material

29.04   When the client changes its agency it is the custom of the industry for the advertising agent to assign the copyright in all the advertisements prepared by him for that client to the new agency.

However, in the case of *Hutchison Personal Communications Ltd v Hook Advertising Ltd*[1] the agreement provided that Hook would:

> 'assign to you all and any copyright in all material produced or created for your advertising as is vested in us … as and when requested in writing …'.

That case concerned the ownership of the material prepared by Hook for the 'pitch' for Hutchinson's work and which was therefore prepared before the agreement was made.

Hook's material included a rabbit logo. It did not include material created before the advertising agent had been appointed. The logo, having been created before the date of the agreement, was not material caught by the clause even though it formed part of the advertisement. To catch the logo, Mr Justice Arden said that the clause would have had to read:

> 'every copyright in all or any part of the material produced or created for your advertising'.

This case illustrates the importance of dealing explicitly with material created for the 'pitch' and with elements of the advertisement created for that client.

All employees of advertising agents should be engaged under written contracts of service which vest the copyright in all material created by them in the course of their employment in the advertising agency and, in addition, in all advertising material created by them at any time whilst they are employed by the agency, even if it is written outside working hours[2].

Similarly, when freelance artists, copywriters and other contributors are engaged, they should also be required to sign agreements with the agency vesting the copyright in their contributions in the agency[3]. In addition, a waiver of all moral rights in their contributions should be obtained from such contributors[4].

A well-advised client should carefully consider the ownership position in relation to material created for him by an agency. In the event that the client wants to appoint a different agency to represent him at any time, he will need the ability to use material created by the first agent without restriction. This either means taking an assignment of copyright from the agent on the widest possible terms, or else an enforceable agreement to assign copyright at a later date on agreed terms, in the event that there is a 'parting of the ways'. A well-advised client will also seek contractual warranties and indemnities from his agency against the possibility that the agent has not obtained the copyright in any contributions made in the advertising copy by its staff or freelancers, and may require those agreements to be in approved form.

The Incorporated Society of British Advertisers[5], the Chartered Institute of Purchasing and Supply[6] and the Institute of Practitioners in Advertising (of which the great majority of advertising agents are members) have issued suggested provisions for use in agency/client agreements[7]. Those standard terms suggest alternative possible approaches to the issue of copyright, namely: either the client is entitled to call for an assignment of copyright in the agent's work at any time, together with the work produced by third parties commissioned by the agency (at the cost of the client), or to call for an assignment of the agency's work at the end of the term of the agreement (subject to payment of use fees in the work if used later on by the client).

1   [1996] FSR 549.
2   See **paragraph 10.22**.
3   See **paragraph 10.11**.
4   See **paragraph 11.29**.
5   ISBA Langham House, 1b Portland Place, London, W1B 1PN, Tel: 020 7281 9020, Fax: 020 7281 9029.
6   CIPS Easton House, Easton on the Hill, Stamford, Lincolnshire, PE9 3NZ, Tel: 01780 756777, Fax: 01780 751610.
7   IPA 44 Belgrave Square, London SW1X 8QS, Tel: 020 7235 7020, Fax: 020 7245 9904.

Unsolicited copyright material

29.05   Agencies are the recipients from time to time of proposed advertisements or ideas for advertisements from members of the public.

There are dangers in using this material or even in allowing the agency's creative staff to see it. Employees of the agency may be working upon material very similar, if not identical, to that which has been submitted by a third party. In the event that that person subsequently alleges a breach of copyright, it could be difficult for the agency to prove that they had already begun to work on the idea before the material was received.

If the agency wants to use an idea submitted to it which is not entitled to copyright, it may still be in danger of being sued for breach of confidence by using the material[1].

It is therefore recommended that to avoid such situations, a system is instituted whereby all mail is sifted at an administrative (as distinct from creative) level, and that submissions from the public are automatically returned with a standard form letter explaining that the agency does not consider unsolicited ideas because it has its own creative staff.

1 See generally **Chapter 5**.

Passing off

29.06 Advertisements are commonly based upon other copyright material, in such a way that an idea is used or parodied, but without an infringement taking place (e.g. no 'substantial part' is copied[1]). There is no objection to this practice in copyright law. However, if the effect of the advertisement is to suggest that the goods of the client are those of another person, this will constitute passing off[2].

It is no defence to an action for copyright infringement to claim that the infringing material is a satire of the original and can clearly be seen by the public to be a satire. There will nevertheless be a copyright infringement if the advertisement uses a significant part of the original material[3].

1 See **paragraphs 8.05** and **8.06**.
2 See **Chapter 5**.
3 See **paragraph 8.05**.

Lyrics of commercial advertisements

29.07 The PRS[1] owns on behalf of its members the right to perform publicly and broadcast the music and lyrics of its members. Almost every working composer and lyricist resident in the UK is a member of the PRS. However, there is an exception to this rule in the case of certain lyrics written for commercial advertisements. 'Words written for a commercial advertisement which are sung to music specially written for a commercial advertisement or to non-copyright music and the song performance has a duration of less than five seconds' are not included in the broadcasting right assigned to the PRS by its members.

Thus, when commissioning such lyrics, an assignment can and should be sought by the agency and/or client of all the copyright in the work.

1   See **paragraph 22.07**.

Chapter 30

Computer software

Introduction

30.01 It is by means of 'programs' that a computer is instructed to undertake the tasks which are required of it – that is to say, the reception, storage, processing and retrieval of information.

'Computer software' is the expression used to include such programs and will include computer databases and files. 'Hardware' is a word coined by the computer industry to refer to items such as the chips and memory circuits used in the processors which store programs and information in the computer, and other similar storage devices, which, although part of the computer itself, have nevertheless been specially adopted for the particular program needs of that computer. This chapter deals with the protection available to computer programs, computer software generally and the information stored in computers.

Computer programs are expressly excluded from patent protection under the laws of most European countries (including the UK).

In 1991, the EU adopted the Software Directive[1] on the legal protection of computer programs, which provided that member states should legislate to protect computer programs as literary works, but not the ideas and principles which underlie them. The Software Directive was implemented into UK law by the Copyright (Computer Programs) Regulations 1992[2].

This Directive followed the Directive of 1986 on the legal protection of topographies of semi-conductor products which provided that member states should legislate to protect the topographies of semi-conductor products. The UK implemented this latter Directive by according design right protection for semi-conductor products[3].

The manuals and papers relating to the programming and operation of computers will be protected as literary and artistic works[4]. No particular copyright problems arise in connection with these documents. The special problems are to be found in relation to the programs themselves and the information stored in computers.

Copyright provides no protection for bare concepts, or ideas[5]. Therefore, the concept of a particular algorithm, or an idea for a method of retrieving information will not be entitled to protection although the extent of this doctrine and its application raises difficult questions.

1 Council Directive 91/250/EEC of 14 May 1991 on the Legal Protection of Computer Programs.
2 SI 1992/3233.
3 See **paragraph 14.03**.
4 See **paragraphs 2.02** and **2.05**.
5 See **paragraph 8.04**.

Definitions

30.02 A *'literary work'* is defined by the CDPA as including a computer program, and preparatory design material for a computer program[1].

'Computer generated' means 'a work generated by computer in circumstances such that there is no human author of the work'[2].

'Adaptation' in relation to a computer program means an arrangement or altered version of the program or a translation of it[3].

'Translation', in relation to a computer program, includes a version of the program in which it is converted into or out of a computer language or code, or into a different language or code[4].

The definitions of *'artistic works'* and *'sound recordings'* are considered elsewhere in this *User's Guide*[5]

Expressions such as *'computer'*, *'program'*, *'system control'*, *'software'* and other examples of computer terminology have no definitions in the CDPA, and the courts will accept the computer industry usage as the source for definitions of such words. WIPO has prepared Model Provisions on the Protection of Computer Software which contain useful definitions of *'computer software'*, *'computer program'*, *'program description'* and *'supporting material'*.

1 CDPA s 3.
2 CDPA s 178.
3 See **paragraph 7.08**.
4 See **paragraph 7.08**.
5 See **paragraphs 2.06** and **2.07**.

Types of work – literary and artistic works

30.03　Software, to the extent that it is recorded in writing or otherwise, will be protected as a 'literary work'[1]. For these purposes, 'writing or otherwise' has a very broad meaning, including any form quotation or code recorded in any medium[2].

Computer software, which is conveyed in the form of tapes or discs, even if it is never resolved into writing, will consequently nevertheless qualify for copyright protection as a literary work. The CDPA provides that preparatory design materials for programs are also protected as literary works[3]. It is irrelevant if the program is in a higher or lower form language; or that there are no words, only numerals being used or that only a machine can understand it – it will, nevertheless, be a literary work.

The same principles apply to 'hardware', 'wired in' or 'firmware' programs, memory circuits (read-only memories, random access memories, bubble memories, etc), silicon chips, and to the information in the data bases of a computer, stored in the form of abstracts. If the program or data has been recorded, 'in writing or otherwise'[4], it will qualify as a literary work.

A computer print-out or manual will also be a 'literary work' or an 'artistic work' quite apart from the program itself and will therefore be entitled to copyright protection.

Protection under the Registered Designs Act or design right protection under the CDPA is not available to computer software although the topography of semi-conductor products is protected under the design right provisions of the CDPA.

1　See **paragraph 2.02**.
2　See **paragraph 2.05**.
3　CDPA s 3(1)(c), but please note that this protection only applies when 'the nature of the preparatory work is such that a computer program can result from it at a later stage.'
4　CDPA s 3(2).

Copyright protection and originality

30.04　It is not necessary nor, indeed, possible to register a work in a copyright registry in the UK which has any standing in copyright law[1]. Nor is it necessary to publish a work for it to acquire copyright protection.

For a work to be entitled to copyright protection, it must be original. In short, its creation must originate from the author, and be the result of skill, labour or judgement[2].

If several companies work on the same problem at the same time, the one which arrives at the right algorithm first will be the owner of the copyright in that algorithm. Theoretically, other companies could arrive independently and spontaneously at the identical algorithm and also have copyright protection for their work, but this is unlikely[3]. Therefore, it is important to be able to prove the date upon which the algorithm – or any other element of the program – was first written. This can be done for example by depositing the material with a solicitor in a sealed package with a record of the date and time of receipt[4].

For software to be protected in the UK, it must satisfy several of the requirements of qualification set out in the CDPA[5].

The 'ideas' behind the software are also protected unless:

- they have no connection with the literary, dramatic, musical or artistic nature of the work; or
- they are not original or are so commonplace as not to perform a substantial part of the work, in other words the programming techniques are already well known and frequently used in software programming.[6]

1   See **paragraph 10.21**.
2   See **paragraph 3.01**.
3   See **paragraph 3.05**.
4   See **paragraph 10.21**.
5   See **paragraphs 4.01** et seq.
6   *Designers Guild Ltd v Russell Williams (Textiles) Ltd [2000] 1 WLR 2416*.

Copyright ownership of computer programs

30.05   The only categories of copyright work within which computer programs may be protected are literary works and artistic works.

The basic rule is that the first owner of a literary or an artistic work is its author[1]. The CDPA also provides that the author of a work which is computer generated is taken to be the person by whom the arrangements necessary for creation of the work are undertaken[2]. An object code program is a computer-generated work, as will be a computer database, (at least to the extent it is created by downloading from other databases).

Where a computer program is written by the programmer in the course of his employment under a contract of service, then the employer will be entitled to the copyright in the program, in the absence of any agreement to the contrary[3]. Where freelance programmers are used, copyright will vest in the freelancer. Accordingly, where appropriate, letters of engagement should specify that the copyright in material originated by freelancers will vest in and belong to the employer.

1   See **paragraph 10.02**.
2   CDPA s 9(3).
3   See **paragraph 10.11**.

Copyright in commissioned programs

30.06 It is usual for companies to employ computer bureaux or consultants to write program specifications and the programs for them. In the absence of any contractual arrangements to the contrary, the copyright will remain in the bureau or consultant[1]. Therefore, customers should ensure that the terms of the contract with the consultant or bureau provide that the copyright in any programs specially written for them becomes their own or that they have, at the very least, a licence in the copyright in the program for the full period of copyright[2].

1   See **paragraph 10.02**.
2   See generally **Chapter 10**.

Ownership of computer output

30.07 Computer output is the result of the interaction between program and input. Behind this simple statement lie a number of complicated technical processes, which can involve up to three types of program:

- *source code*, written by the programmer;
- *a compiler, or interpreter*, which may have been written by the programmer but is quite often written by a different programmer;
- *object code,* which is the result of the translation of the source code by the compiler.

The hardware, which a program uses to produce output, will have its own copyright if it was originally recorded in a written form.

The output will, therefore, be the result of the interaction of programs and the data input by the user, each having its own copyright and usually with different owners.

Although the computer itself can be categorised as a tool (like a slide rule or paint brush), the program, as we have seen, is entitled to copyright protection. Dependent on the degree of skill and labour involved in the preparation of the data input, the output would seem to belong to the data provider.

In some cases (such as in the use of music writing software), it is relatively easy to see output as the work of the user (the computer and its software being a tool used to give effect to the creative act of the user. In other cases (such as in the use of programs which create music automatically) the user may have little or no input other than purely functional. In these circumstances the author will be the person by whom the arrangements necessary for creation of the work are undertaken[1].

1   See **paragraph 30.05**.

Duration of copyright

30.08   The period of copyright of a literary work and therefore of a computer program is the life of the author and 70 years thereafter. But in the case of computer-generated works, the copyright expires at the end of the period of 50 years from the end of the calendar year in which it was made[1].

1   CDPA s 12(3), see **paragraphs 6.01** and **6.10**.

Restricted acts applicable to computer software

30.09   Computer software is usually protected as a literary work[1]. The restricted acts applicable to a literary work are:

- *copying* the work;
- *issuing copies* of the work to the public;
- *renting or lending* the work to the public;
- *performing, showing or playing* the work in public;
- *communicating* the work to the public;
- *adapting* the work,[2] or doing any of the above acts in relation to adapting the work.

1   As regards restricted acts generally, see **Chapter 7**.
2   See **paragraphs 7.02** et seq.

Infringement by copying

30.10   Copying includes storing the work in any medium by electronic means[1]. It also includes making copies which are transient or are incidental to some other use of the work[2].

It follows that using computer software will involve copying in the sense of the CDPA, since running a computer program or loading a program into a computer memory both involve making copies, (even though those copies may be transitory). As a basic principle, therefore, any use of software will need to be licensed[3].

In *IBCOS Computers Ltd v Barclays Mercantile Highland Finance Ltd*[4] a programmer who created programming for his employer later created similar programming (after leaving the company) in the same language. The court established that the new program contained elements copied from the old. Jacob J rejected the defendant's claim that the similarities were a consequence of his use of well-established programming routines and holding that in circumstances where the facts suggest copying his style, arguments that the similarities arose from style should not be accepted when supported by independent evidence. Copying was found both within the individual programs concerned and in the overriding architecture of the software.

Particular problems arise in the case of computer software, where the 'look and feel' of a program may be duplicated even where the underlying program is based on an entirely different programming language. In the US, a number of cases have considered this problem but there is little English authority on the issue. Addressing the issue in *John Richardson Computers Ltd v Flanders*[5], however, Ferris J considered the appropriate question to be whether the similarities between the two programs arose from the copying of a substantial part of the claimant's work. In answering this question Ferris J compared similarities between 'non-literal' aspects of the two programs, finding that copyright had been infringed. This decision has been subject to considerable criticism but remains good law.

1   CDPA s 17(2).
2   CDPA s 17(6), see **paragraph 7.02**.
3   However, please see **paragraphs 30.15** et seq in relation to permitted acts.
4   [1994] FSR 275.
5   [1993] FSR 497.

'Substantial part'

30.11   For copyright to be infringed, it is necessary that a 'substantial part' of the work be copied[1].

If less than a 'substantial part' is used, there will be no infringement of copyright. Since a substantial part is not necessarily a reference to quantity, but to quality then if an essential part (even though a small part) of the program is copied, this will constitute an infringement.

In one recent case, it was considered necessary when establishing whether a substantial part of a computer program had been copied, to assess the skill and labour involved in the design and coding of the copied section against the skill and labour involved in the whole program[2].

1 See **paragraph 8.06**.
2 *Cantor Fitzgerald International v Tradition (UK) Ltd [2000] RPC 95.*

Issuing copies of computer software to the public

30.12 This restricted act is considered in detail elsewhere in this *User's Guide*[1]. It is worth noting that the act is infringed by the importation into the UK or elsewhere in the EEA of copies of software which have been put on the market outside the EEA. In some parts of the world, computer software sells more cheaply than in the EEA, but this restricted act would be infringed by purchasing copies of programs put on the market in, say, the USA and reselling them in the UK without the authority of the copyright owner[2].

It is also worth noting that the CDPA contains a provision for the Secretary of State to grant licences where it seems the public interest requires it, based on the findings of any Competition Commission investigation[3].

1 See **paragraphs 7.04** and **14.06**.
2 See **paragraph 7.04**.
3 See **paragraph 13.09**.

Rental and lending of computer software

30.13 The restricted act of rental and lending is considered in detail elsewhere[1]. Because it is so easy to copy computer software, copyright owners often refuse to permit their programs to be rented. However, there are a number of exceptions to the lending right[2].

Copyright in computer software is not infringed by the lending of copies of the work by an educational establishment or by a prescribed library or archive (other than a public library) which is not conducted for profit[3]. In order to try to limit the danger of copies being made unlawfully by persons borrowing computer software from educational establishments or prescribed libraries and archives, copyright owners should place on the software itself and on its packing notices to the effect that copyright will be infringed if any copy of the software is made. The notice can point out that use of the software by running it, loading it etc constitutes copying for copyright purposes. It would be wise to include these terms on a notice which is usually attached to software to the effect that when the shrink wrap is removed, the purchaser is deemed to have accepted the conditions of sale. This might deter libraries, archives and educational establishments from buying computer software for lending purposes, knowing that by so doing they will inevitably be in breach of the terms, because no use can be made of the software without infringing the restricted act of copying. If no such notice is placed on the software at the time of sale, it is more than probable that a court would hold that there is an implied licence to make copies for the purpose of using the software when it is sold to bodies which have the right to lend them under the provisions of the CDPA as amended by the 1996 Regulations.

Shrink wrap notices can only be relied on by the copyright owner or licensee if the notice can be read on the outside of the packaging at the time of purchase[4].

1　See **paragraph 7.05**.
2　Generally, see **Chapter 9**.
3　As to what is meant by a prescribed library or archive, see **Chapter 20**.
4　See **paragraph 26.06**.

Infringement of computer software copyright by adaptation

30.14　In the case of computer programs, the CDPA provides that 'adaptations' means 'an arrangement or altered version of the program or a translation of it'.

By s 21(4) 'translation' in relation to a computer program includes 'a version of the program in which it is converted into or out of a computer language or code or into a different computer language or code'.

The reproduction of source code into object code effected by a compiler is a 'translation' for copyright purposes and will constitute an adaptation of a work[1]. The significance of this is to provide a copyright action to restrain unauthorised decompilation and compilation etc of programs, or 'reverse engineering', (i.e. the conversion of an object code into a source code enabling an examination of underlying programming techniques)[2].

1　See **paragraph 7.08** for a full analysis of the restricted act of adaptation.
2　Although note the fair dealing provisions at **paragraphs 30.15** et seq.

Fair dealing with computer programs

30.15　Fair dealing is considered in more detail elsewhere in this *User's Guide*[1]. However, in addition, the CDPA, in relation to computer programs, states that it is not fair dealing:

- to convert a computer program in a low level language into a version expressed in a higher level language; or
- incidentally in the course of so converting the program, to copy it.[2]; or
- to observe, study or test the functioning of a computer program in order to determine the ideas and principles which underlie any element of the program (unless these acts are in accordance with s 50BA)[3].

1 See **Chapter 9**.
2 CDPA s 28(4).
3 CDPA s 28(4A); see **paragraph 30.19** for the permitted acts defined in CDPA s 50BA.

Transfer of copies of works in electronic form

30.16 Purchasers of works in electronic form may copy, adapt or make copies of adaptations of them in connection with their use as if they had been purchased on terms which allow them to do such an act. The terms may be express or implied. The terms of purchase should expressly forbid such acts if the manufacturer does not want purchasers to copy or adapt such works[1].

1 See **paragraph 9.17**.

Back-up copies

30.17 It is not an infringement of copyright for a lawful user of a copy of a computer program to make any back-up copy which it is necessary for him to have for the purposes of his lawful use. A person is a lawful user of a computer program if he has a right to use the program. The right to use the program can be pursuant to a licence from the copyright holder or otherwise[1].

It is irrelevant whether or not there exists any term or condition in an agreement which purports to prohibit or restrict the act of making a back-up copy because such a prohibition would be void[2].

1 CDPA s 55A; see **paragraph 9.13**.
2 CDPA s 286A; see **paragraph 30.19** below.

Decompilation

30.18 It is not an infringement of copyright for a lawful user of a copy of a computer program expressed in a low-level language:

- to convert it into a version expressed in a higher level language; or
- incidentally in the course of so converting the program to copy it (that is, to 'decompile' it) provided that the following conditions are met[1]:

'(a) it is necessary to decompile the program to obtain the information necessary to create an independent program which can be operated with the program decompiled or with another program ("the permitted objective"); and

(b) the information so obtained is not used for any purpose other than the permitted objective'[2].

These conditions are not met if the lawful user:

'(a) has readily available to him the information necessary to achieve the permitted objective;

(b) does not confine the decompiling to such acts as are necessary to achieve the permitted objective;

(c) supplies the information obtained by the decompiling to any person to whom it is not necessary to supply it in order to achieve the permitted objective; or

(d) uses the information to create a program which is substantially similar in its expression to the program decompiled or to do any act restricted by copyright'[3].

Again, any term or condition in an agreement which purports to prohibit the act which is permitted under s 50B will be void[4].

1   CDPA s 50B(1); see **paragraph 9.13**.
2   CDPA s 50B(2).
3   CDPA s 50B(3).
4   CDPA s 286A.

Observing, studying and testing computer programs

30.19   It is not an infringement of copyright for a lawful user of a copy of a computer program to observe, study or test the functioning of the program in order to determine the ideas and principles which underlie any element of the program if he does so while performing any of the acts of loading, displaying, running, transmitting or storing the program which he is entitled to do.[1]

Where an act is permitted under CDPA s 50BA, it is irrelevant whether or not there exists any term or condition in an agreement which purports to prohibit or restrict such act.[2]

1   CDPA s 50BA(1).
2   CDPA s 50BA(2).

Other acts permitted to lawful users of software programs

30.20 It is not an infringement of copyright for a lawful user of a copy of a computer program to copy or adapt it, provided that the copying or adapting:

'(a) is necessary for its lawful use; and
(b) is not prohibited under any term or condition of an agreement regulating the circumstances in which his use is lawful'[1].

Moreover, it is not an infringement of copyright to copy a computer program or adapt it for the purpose of correcting errors in it[2].

However, CDPA s 50C does not apply to any copying or adapting:

- permitted by making back-up copies[3];
- made in the process of decompilation[4]; or
- made in the process of observing, studying and testing computer programs[5].

Certain terms or conditions in agreements for the use of a computer program are deemed void by the CDPA, in particular, terms or conditions which seek to prohibit:

- the making of any back up copy of the program which it is necessary to have for the purposes of the agreed use;
- the decompiling of the program when the conditions set out in s 50B(2) are met[6];
- the use of any device or means to observe, study or test the functioning of the program to understand the ideas and principles which underlie any element of the program[7].

1 CDPA s 50C(1).
2 CDPA s 50C(2).
3 CDPA s 50A.
4 CDPA s 50B.
5 CDPA s 50BA.
6 See **paragraphs 30.17** and **30.18**.
7 CDPA s 286A.

Moral rights not applicable

30.21 The rights to be identified as the author of a work and to object to the derogatory treatment of a work do not apply to computer programs[1].

1 See **paragraphs 11.10** and **11.18**.

Deliberate mistakes

30.22   The proof of infringement of a program by deliberate copying can be very difficult in practice. One mechanism is to place 'deliberate mistakes' or bugs in programs so that if the program is copied, the deliberate mistake or bug will also appear, so providing evidence of copying[1].

1   See **paragraph 8.02** for a general consideration of this issue.

International protection

30.23   The copyright position of computer software and firmware outside the UK differs almost from country to country. The WIPO Geneva Copyright Treaty of December 1996 provided that:

> 'Computer programs are protected as literary works within the meaning of Article 2 of the Berne Convention. Such protection applies to computer programs, whatever may be the mode or form of their expression'.[1]

Nevertheless, wherever international use is likely to be made of software, the owner of the copyright should seek to bolster his copyright protection with contractual protection. Contracts can go some way towards giving the same rights and remedies to a company supplying software and hardware as does copyright but only against the persons with whom such company enters into contractual relationships. Third parties making unauthorised use of the software are not affected by, and cannot be sued by, the owner of the copyright if the copyright law offers no protection in that particular country, irrespective of the copyright laws of the country in which the software originated.

In order to ensure maximum protection in countries not party to the Berne Convention, it is wise to affix the copyright symbol © plus the name of the copyright owner and the year of publication on all software[2].

The manufacturers of silicon chips usually put the copyright symbol etc on the actual chips themselves.

1   Art 4.
2   See generally **Chapter 4**.

Anti-spoiler devices

30.24   The computer industry (as well as the record and home video industries) uses devices which are designed to prevent the making of unauthorised copies of computer programs, sound recordings and films. These are known as forms of copy-protection, or spoilers. The CDPA contains provisions[1] intended to provide a cause of action to restrain the making, sale, importation or hiring of devices or means specifically designed or adapted to circumvent spoilers. Circumvention is dealt with in more detail elsewhere in this *User's Guide*[2].

1 CDPA s 286.
2 See **paragraphs 26.39 et seq.**

Chapter 31

Character merchandising

Introduction

31.01 Character merchandising refers to the business of using characters to sell goods or services. The 'characters' may be real or invented. Real characters may include: pop stars, sportsmen, film stars and television stars. Invented characters may include newspaper cartoon characters; animated cartoon characters, television characters; feature film characters and characters from books. The goods to which the descriptions or names of the characters are affixed, are of every imaginable description: from lollipops to bed linen, from watches to motor cars.

Character merchandising is now a multi-billion pound international industry. In some cases, character merchandising has earned more than the original film, cartoon, book, etc from which the character derived.

It is generally assumed that the owner of the character whose name or representation is merchandised has a special legal right to limit its use and may be paid a licence fee for such use. It is true to say that in the great majority of cases the owner of the character or name does receive licence fees for its use on goods, but *not* because of any legal right per se which entitles people to prevent others using a name one has inherited or invented.

In order to protect the use of a character and prevent others using it, it is necessary to make out a case either for:

- copyright infringement; or
- passing off; or
- trade mark infringement.

Copyright protection for names

31.02   There is no copyright protection for a name itself, for the same reasons as there is no copyright protection for a title[1]. The courts have, for example, held that there was no copyright protection for the names 'The Wombles' and 'Kojak' (although there may be protection in passing off). Therefore, copyright protection will only be available if the way in which the character's name or representation is used makes it an artistic work. Merely putting lettering on a T-shirt does not constitute an artistic work, but if the name is designed in an elaborate or distinctive style, then that design will be an artistic work. If the public become accustomed to seeing the name in that distinctive form, so that they associate the design with the character as much as the name itself, then the merchandiser will have solved one of the biggest problems he faces when merchandising a real person. A successful example of such a design is the Batman logo. An invented character, whose likeness is fundamental to his fame, like a cartoon character, a character from an illustrated book like Paddington Bear, a television puppet etc has an enormous advantage, because he originates as an artistic work.

In *Universal City Studios Inc v Mukhtar & Sons Ltd*[2] the use of a drawing of a shark on a T-shirt similar to the drawing of a shark used by the copyright owners of the film *Jaws* in their publicity, was held to be an infringement of the *Jaws* drawing.

In these days of digitisation, when it is relatively simple to recreate a person's physical appearance including the face, as a photograph or on film using animation techniques or by blending or adapting photographs and films, it may seem curious that it is established law that one's appearance is not protected by copyright.

1   See **paragraph 3.02**.
2   [1976] FSR 252.

Cartoon characters

31.03   In the case of cartoon characters protection is relatively easy: the original character is a drawing and therefore an artistic work (see the Table of Incidents of Copyright in **Appendix 4** for the copyright attributes of artistic works). There is no test of quality required to establish copyright in an artistic work[1].

So, the owners of cartoon characters can issue copyright licences giving manufacturers the right to reproduce likenesses of the characters on goods. They will be able to sue manufacturers who market goods bearing unauthorised representations of the characters for damages, for an injunction to prevent further unauthorised use of the drawings of the characters and delivery up of all offending goods in the possession of the infringing manufacturer. This last is a penalty which can be extremely onerous for the infringing manufacturer[2].

1   See **paragraph 2.06**.
2   See **Chapter 8** for further detail regarding the remedies available for copyright infringement.

Likenesses of real people

31.04   The copyright in the drawing of a real person will belong to the artist, or to his employer if drawn in the course of his employment[1]. The person whose likeness is drawn has no right in copyright law to prevent the owner using the drawing – although he will be able to prevent its use in a defamatory context, or may be able to prevent its use on the grounds of passing off[2].

1   See **paragraphs 10.03 and 10.12**.
2   See further *Re Elvis Presley Trade Marks [1997] RPC 543*, Laddie J. See also **Chapter 5** for a full consideration of passing off and personality rights issues.

Photographs

31.05   The position in respect of the use of photographs of real people is similar to the use of drawings[1].

1   However, the right of privacy of photographs commissioned for private and domestic purposes discussed in **Chapter 11** should be noted.

Three-dimensional representations

31.06   The CDPA provides that the making of a three-dimensional object based on a painting, drawing or other two-dimensional work, infringes that work[1]. The unauthorised manufacture of soap in the shape of Mickey Mouse would infringe the copyright in a Mickey Mouse drawing. But it would be very difficult, in most cases, to identify the photographs from which a bust of a real life character is made. The making of models of a real life person does not infringe any copyright or other right vested in that person – only the copyright in another three-dimensional object or in a two-dimensional artistic work from which it might be proved to have been copied.

1   See **paragraphs 7.03 and 27.05**.

Passing off

31.07 **Chapter 5** discusses the basic rules of the law of passing off in detail. It is important to note that this law is contained in cases and is, therefore, continually evolving.

The courts are reluctant to find in favour of a plaintiff in a passing off action unless there is a common field of activity between the plaintiff's business and the business which he claims to be passed off as his own.

Applying this principle to character merchandising, if the owner of the character has never sold any goods, except the original book, film, etc. from which the character derived, and the goods complained of are not a film, book, etc then the owner of the character will have great difficulty – indeed he will generally be unable – to prevent the use of the character on goods of a quite different nature. Thus in the case of *Wombles Ltd v Wombles Skips Ltd*[1], the owners of the copyright in the Wombles books and drawings were unable to prevent the use of the name 'Wombles' on skips because, although Wombles Ltd had licensed the use of the name Wombles on a number of different goods, none of them was at all similar to a skip.

The courts have, to some extent, moved away from the previously strict interpretation that they have given to common fields of activity. Nevertheless, at the present time it is difficult to prevent the use of a character upon goods of a dissimilar nature from those which the owner of the character has marketed or has licensed to be manufactured and sold.

The 'Kojak' case[2] is a leading case dealing with character merchandising. In that case, Tavener Rutledge had been manufacturing and selling lollipops called 'Kojak pops' for some months without any licence from Universal City Studios, the owners of the Kojak television series. Trexapalm Ltd obtained a licence from Universal to use the name 'Kojak Lollies' for the lollipops they intended to market. Tavener Rutledge had applied for trade mark registration of the word 'Kojak pops'. Tavener Rutledge sued Trexapalm for an injunction to prevent them marketing their lollies under the name 'Kojak Lollies' on the grounds of passing off and trade mark infringement. The court held that Tavener Rutledge had established a reputation for the lollipops they had marketed under the name 'Kojak pops', and that the use of the name 'Kojak Lollies' would cause confusion with the public. The sale of the cheaper 'Kojak Lollies' would moreover undermine the reputation of the 'Kojak pops'. The fact that Trexapalm had a licence from Universal City Studios was no defence, because there was not sufficient similarity between the trades of making television series and the manufacture and sale of lollipops. Therefore, there was no risk of confusion in the minds of the public between the actions of Tavener Rutledge on the one hand, and Universal City Studios on the other. The court also held that there is no property in a name or word, per se. The fact that the public might think that Tavener Rutledge had obtained a licence from Universal City Studios was not material in an action for passing off.

In *Mirage Studios v Counter-Feat Clothing*[3] the court was prepared to accept that a child purchasing a 'Mutant Turtle' would expect to get a genuine turtle. This interlocutory decision was doubted by Laddie J in *Re Elvis Presley Trade Marks*[4], who took the view that the purchaser of a toy of a well-known character would have no reason to care who made or licensed it.

1   [1975] FSR 488.
2   *Tavener Rutledge Ltd v Trexapalm Ltd [1977] RPC 275.*
3   [1991] FSR 145.
4   [1997] RPC 543.

Trade mark registration

31.08   The registration of a character name or a famous personality's own name as a trade mark can provide protection for goods to which the name is affixed. There are, however, some serious problems to be overcome before the trade mark registration is an effective protection for a character which is to be merchandised. See further *Re Elvis Presley Trade Marks*[1], where the judge found 'very little inherent distinctiveness' in the mark 'Elvis' enabling it to be registered as a trade mark. The name was merely a given name.

1   Per Laddie J, [1997] RPC 543.

Registered design protection

31.09   This subject is outlined in **Chapter 15**.

Conclusion

31.10   The protection of a character which is not entitled to copyright protection as an *artistic* work is not easy. Accordingly, whenever possible, an artistic work should be brought into existence associated with a character. One might market T-shirts with the name of a real character with a distinctive cartoon of the character associated with the name, or with the name designed in such distinctive lettering that the design of the name is itself an artistic work. Illustrations assist protectability. 'Paddington Bear' might be difficult to protect as a name, but the illustrations in the book have made a distinctive figure of the bear, so that it would be difficult for a would-be infringer to use 'Paddington Bear' on goods without infringing the copyright in the drawings of the bear.

Where no protection is possible on the grounds of an artistic work, the owners should ensure that application for a trade mark is made promptly and in as many classes of goods as possible. If the name which it is desired to protect is not sufficiently distinctive to entitle it to trade mark protection, then invented words (such as 'Kojak pops') should be registered as trade marks.

Chapter 32

Designers of consumer goods, fashion goods and spare parts

Introduction

32.01 Designers of consumer goods and fashion goods are not generally entitled to copyright protection in relation to goods made to their designs unless the designs can be regarded as 'artistic works'[1]. Such designers may however be entitled to protect such goods by registration as registered designs under the Registered Designs Act 1949, or by way of unregistered design right[2].

1 See **paragraph 2.06**.
2 See **Chapter 15**.

Designer goods

32.02 Works of 'artistic craftsmanship' and 'sculptures' manufactured industrially in three-dimensional form, such as designer jewellery, designer furnishings, designer porcelain, designer cutlery and designer furniture, will be entitled to copyright protection if they fall within the definition of 'artistic works'[1]. Copyright protection is not generally available for manufactured articles. 'Artistic works' are, by their nature likely to be limited in number and not mass-produced. So, for example, a David Linley cabinet may well be regarded as an 'artistic work' protected by copyright, whilst a suite of reproduction furniture will not. Similarly a unique item of designer jewellery, such as a tiara, may be regarded as an 'artistic work', whilst mass-produced jewellery would not be. In the fashion field, a creation by Jean Paul Gautier would be an 'artistic work' whilst an 'off the peg' dress would not be. The tests as to what is a work of 'artistic craftsmanship' are not easily definable, but it is well established that a degree of 'artistic attainment' by the designer or a 'conscious intent to create a work of art' are requisites.

The period of copyright for 'artistic works' manufactured by an industrial process is limited to 25 years from the date of marketing such articles in the United Kingdom or elsewhere[2].

In order to facilitate the enforcement of copyright in works of artistic craftsmanship it is advisable that all design documents and prototypes of the articles in question are retained for evidential use. It will then be possible to illustrate the genesis of copyright in the work and show the necessary requirement of 'originality' for copyright to subsist.

1   CDPA s 4(1).
2   CDPA s 52(2).

Consumer goods

32.03   Copyright protection is not generally available for this category of goods. Provided that the features of shape or configuration of articles made to the design are:

- novel;
- applied by an industrial process;
- appeal to and are judged by the eye;
- aesthetic considerations are taken into account to a material extent in acquiring or using the design;

the design of the article will generally be registrable under the 1949 Act. Examples of the designs of articles so registrable include toys, the outside design of consumer electronic goods such as audio equipment or televisions, furniture and furnishings, crockery, cutlery, the overall design of cars and boats and clothing.

Articles whose design is dictated solely by function, such as electric terminals, are not registrable, nor are household articles in which the appearance of the design is not material. Specific examples from decided cases of what is registrable or otherwise include the following:

Registrable	Not registrable
Toy bricks	Electric terminals
Toy bucket	Propeller
Brassiere	Circuit boards
Power-boat	Pre-printed web for a computer
Personal stereos	Water tank system
Design for a portable building	Baskets
Corsets and other items of clothing	

Specifically excluded from registration under the Registered Designs Rules[1] are wall plaques, medallions, printed matter primarily of a literary or artistic character (which would in principle obtain copyright protection) including book jackets, calendars, maps, playing cards and dress-making patterns.

1 SI 1989/1105.

Unregistered design protection

32.04 The protection of designs is considered in detail in **Chapter 15**.

Spare parts

32.05 Because copyright protection for articles made to designs is limited to those which qualify as 'artistic works', the 'British Leyland spare parts exception'[1] which excluded copyright protection for spare parts is no longer relevant to copyright law, although it is arguable that it may still apply to prevent the enforcement of other intellectual property rights (eg patents in genuine spare parts, such as exhaust pipes or body panels). The scope of the exception was doubted by the Privy Council in *Canon KK v Green Cartridge Co (Hong Kong) Ltd*[2]. Additionally, registered design and unregistered design protection is unavailable for designs which are dependent upon the appearance of another article. Thus body panels and windscreens would not be registrable or protected by unregistered design right, whilst wing mirrors as commercial articles in their own right have been held not to be excluded from registration. In addition, excluded from unregistered design right protection are the features of shape and configuration of an article enabling it to be connected to or placed in or around, over or against another article. This 'interface' exclusion would extend to the design of interfacing parts. A suggested example would include the interlocking features of a battery-charging mechanism on a power-tool[2].

1 See **Chapter 15**.
2 [1997] AC 728.
3 In 2004 a proposal was presented by the Commission to revise the EU Design Directive 1998 in order to remove design protection from spare parts in the after market. For a discussion of the proposal, see Joseph Straus, 'Design Protection for Spare Parts in Europe' [2005] EIPR, Issue 11.

Chapter 33

Piracy and counterfeiting

Introduction

33.01   Piracy and counterfeiting are not new problems. In the 19th century the operettists Gilbert and Sullivan suffered from pirate performances and publication of their works, and Sir Walter Scott's novels were frequently published in pirated editions. In recent years piracy has become a problem involving billions of dollars, organised by international crime syndicates.

- 'Piracy' is a term generally used to denote any form of illegitimate copying.
- 'Counterfeiting' is the term used to denote piracy when the goods are packaged so as to resemble the original.

With the advent of machines freely available and widely marketed which enable people to make copies of records and audio cassettes, and of television broadcasts, 'piracy' in the home has now become commonplace. The presence of reprographic machines in virtually every office has made unauthorised copying of written material an everyday occurrence. The unauthorised copying of computer programs by both home users of micro-computers and professional users is said to be doing serious economic damage to companies marketing computer programs. At one point in recent years, over 50% of all new audio compact discs were said to be pirated, originating mainly from the Chinese mainland.

The laws of copyright, passing off, breach of confidence, trade marks and patents are the principal bodies of law which are used to sue for infringement by piracy and counterfeiting. This chapter deals, however, only with copyright, passing off and breach of confidence. Although patents and trade marks are frequently infringed by pirated goods, such goods also infringe industrial design copyright and artistic copyright.

Passing off is a useful weapon where the pirated goods are represented as those of the goods of another company – for example, counterfeit copies of blank videotapes.

Breach of confidence is less often used as the grounds for suing pirates because it is primarily of value in cases where ideas are pirated – in a recent case it was held that the idea for a television series had been pirated, although this word was not actually used by the judge in his decision.

Piracy in the home

33.02 A very large proportion of the British population is from time to time guilty of copyright infringement. This takes two principal forms:

- the copying of sound recordings either by copying a gramophone record or compact disc onto an audiotape or by copying one audiotape onto another;
- the use of copying machines to make copies of literary works.

Home copying of sound recordings

33.03 There are no exceptions or fair dealing provisions (except for the purposes of criticism and review) which entitle individuals to make copies of sound recordings from other sound recordings save from broadcasts (see **paragraph 33.04**). Therefore, whenever an individual copies a sound recording, he is infringing the copyright in that recording and can be sued for damages. The criminal sanctions in the Copyright Act will not apply so long as the copies are used for private purposes only and not sold or hired. However, the extent of such copying is enormous now, and the offence is almost more theoretical than real. In a number of countries a levy is made on the sale of blank audio-cassettes, that is divided between copyright owners of music and sound recordings to compensate them for the loss of income due to home taping. However, in spite of considerable pressure from the music and record industry, the Government decided not to introduce such a levy in the CDPA. But the EC is probably going to propose a Directive on private copying that will require all member states to introduce legislation providing for such a levy.

Home copying of broadcasts

33.04 Everything which is in a television broadcast that has been pre-recorded is regarded as a film for copyright purposes. Everything in a radio broadcast that has been pre-recorded is a sound recording for copyright purposes. Only live broadcasts do not come within this category.

Section 70 of the CDPA permits the making for domestic and private use of recordings of broadcasts and cable programmes solely for the purpose of enabling them to be viewed or listened to at a more convenient time. Moreover, the making of such recordings does not infringe the copyright in the works included in the broadcasts. Thus, it is not a breach of civil or criminal law to make copies of films in television broadcasts or of records broadcast by radio if the purpose of the recording is for private and domestic time shifting. It is probably a breach of copyright to create libraries of films and records by off-air recording.

Home copying of computer programs and video games

33.05 Computer programs are sold in shops in the form of floppy discs and CD-ROMs. Copying programs is very easy. Computer programs have copyright protection in a variety of ways, but basically as literary works. The associated manuals are also literary works. The fair dealing exception for private study and research applies to literary works. However, it is submitted that this exception would not be a good defence to a copyright action in a case where an individual hired or borrowed a cassette or manual and copied it in its entirety for his own use. It might be a good defence if a reasonable part of the program only was copied. In all other respects the copies of computer programs are in the same position as the copies of a sound recording. If the program copied is a video game, then there may also be infringement of film copyright.

Commercial piracy and counterfeiting: industrial designs and artistic works

33.06 In the case of industrial designs and artistic works, counterfeiting is a very serious form of piracy. Counterfeit tennis rackets and golf clubs that are almost undetectable, even by the legitimate manufacturers themselves, shirts printed with patterns which copy registered designs, designer watches, pens, bottles of whisky, air brakes for aeroplanes – all these and many more are examples of the counterfeiting which has become increasingly common. Usually the goods are manufactured outside the United Kingdom in countries where labour costs are much lower and tax is non-existent or where tax rates are very low. The counterfeiters are skilful manufacturers with well-organised marketing arrangements who can flood the market with counterfeit goods, sometimes only a few months after the originals are first marketed.

CDs and CD-ROMs are manufactured in factories in many parts of the world where the enforcement of copyright laws is lax – China was, until put under great pressure by the USA, one such country.

Piracy of broadcasts and cable programmes

33.07 Sections 287–289 of the Copyright Act deal with fraudulent reception of transmissions. These provisions are considered in detail in **Chapter 26**.

Commercial piracy and counterfeiting: cinematograph films

33.08 The commercial piracy and counterfeiting of films takes a number of forms. The most common form is that of copying an original feature film from its 35 mm version onto videotape. It is said that at one time this was being effected by means of film-to-videotape transfer equipment installed in furniture vans which were drawn up outside private projection rooms, where films were being screened by the film makers and distributors. Whilst they were viewing one reel, another reel was being covertly duplicated in the furniture van.

A frequent form of piracy is for videotapes which were originally legitimately distributed under licence, to be copied by retailers who then sell or rent them at substantially lower prices than the legitimate article. Feature films and television programmes are taped from television broadcasts.

Another form of piracy is videotapes which have been marketed for private purchase or rental, being performed before paying audiences in pubs and similar places, without any licence for their performance from the copyright owner.

Civil remedies

33.09 Civil remedies for breach of copyright fall into two categories – primary infringement and secondary infringement. It will be recalled (**Chapter 8**) that primary infringement constitutes a breach of one of the restricted acts and that secondary infringement can be summarised as the importation, sale, hire or distribution of articles which have been made without a copyright licence. In the case of secondary infringement, it is necessary to prove that the infringer knew or had reason to believe that the articles had been manufactured without the proper copyright licence. The principal restricted act which is infringed by the pirate or counterfeiter is that of the unauthorised copying of copyright material.

The remedies for infringement are damages, or delivery up of the counterfeit or pirated goods and an injunction. Damages are calculated on the basis that the copyright owner is put into the same position that he would have been in had his copyright not been infringed. In addition, the court has power to award additional damages, in the case of blatant breaches of copyright.

Performers and persons having performers' recording rights have the same remedies in respect of illicit recordings of their performances.

Delivery up of infringing copies

33.10 The CDPA contains special provisions as to what is to be done with infringing copies in respect of which an order for their delivery up has been made[1]. The court can order that the copies shall be:

- forfeited to the copyright owner; or
- destroyed or otherwise dealt with as the court thinks fit.

If no order is made, then the copies will be returned to the person who delivered them up in the first place.

In deciding on what order (if any) to make, the court will consider what other remedies, such as damages, might be adequate to compensate the copyright owner. Similar rights are accorded to performers by s 195 of the CDPA.

1 S 114.

Search and seizure orders

33.11 The 'search and seizure' order (formerly known as an Anton Piller order) is the most powerful weapon that can be used against a pirate within the context of civil law. A search and seizure order essentially enables a plaintiff who suspects his goods are being pirated to search the premises of the alleged pirate and seize any goods which have been pirated. This measure is used frequently against pirates of sound recordings, cinematograph films and manufacturers of high-quality goods. It can be obtained from a High Court judge without even the need to issue a writ in very urgent cases.

In practice, it frequently happens that after an order has been obtained and executed and pirated goods have actually been seized, the pirate will settle the case by paying agreed damages and giving an undertaking to the court that he will discontinue manufacturing and/or selling pirated goods.

A class search and seizure order can be obtained where the plaintiff is able to prove to the court that a large number of pirated products are on the market. In this case, the order is obtained without naming any of the dealers who are alleged to be dealing in the pirated goods, so that if anyone is found to be dealing in these goods, the plaintiff is able to execute the order without having to go back to the court, even though the dealer in question was not named in the order.

Plaintiffs frequently also seek a 'freezing order' at the same time as they seek a search and seizure order. A freezing order (formerly called a 'Mareva injunction') ties up the assets of the infringer, so that if the plaintiff is successful in obtaining an order for damages against him, the infringer cannot sell his assets or remove them from the United Kingdom.

If a pirate refuses to comply with the search and seizure or freezing order, he can be committed to jail for contempt of court, with remarkable speed and lack of formality.

Right to seize infringing copies

33.12 Under s 100 of the Act there is a right of seizure not found in previous copyright legislation – a recognition of the serious problem presented by the proliferation of pirated and counterfeit articles. The right is available to copyright owners or those authorised by them.

It applies to infringing copies exposed or immediately available for sale: not, for example, to copies stored in a warehouse for distribution to retail outlets. It is intended primarily to deal with street traders. Accordingly, the person exercising the right of seizure may only enter premises to which the public has the right of access and which are not permanent premises. Moreover, he must not seize anything which is in the possession, custody or control of a person at a permanent or regular place of business (such as a shop or regular market stall). Force may not be used.

The local police station must be notified of the time and place of the proposed seizure. A notice must be left at the place of seizure, stating on whose authority or by whom the seizure was made, and the grounds for making it.

Similar rights are accorded in respect of illicit recordings of performances to performers and persons having performers' rights under s 196.

Criminal remedies

33.13   The degree of proof in criminal proceedings is greater than that in civil proceedings. In particular, it is necessary to prove that the accused knew or had reason to believe that he was dealing in goods which were infringing the copyright of other goods.

Criminal remedies are available against pirates under the CDPA[1], the Trade Descriptions Act 1968 and the Trade Marks Act 1994 and under the common law offence of conspiracy to defraud.

Trading Standards Officers have considerable powers of seizure and arrest and the penalties for infringement of the Trade Descriptions Act 1968 are severe. Counterfeit product infringes the Trade Descriptions Act 1968 because it necessarily involves a false description of a manufacturer. The use of this weapon against pirates has been most effective and has resulted in a considerable reduction in the amount of counterfeit activity, particularly in the field of videotapes.

The common law crime of conspiracy to defraud can be used when it can be proved that a number of persons were working together to infringe copyright. In the case of *Scott v Metropolitan Police Comr*[2], the accused were convicted of this crime for having bribed cinema employees to make available to them films for the purposes of illegal copying.

1   The criminal provisions in the CDPA appear in ss 107–110. They are outlined in **Chapter 8**.
2   [1975] AC 819, HL.

Presumptions

33.14   Because copyright pirates could deliberately prolong civil and criminal proceedings by forcing the plaintiffs to prove their copyright title, the CDPA provides (in ss 104–106) that certain matters relating to the ownership of copyright are to be presumed to be correct until the contrary is proved. These presumptions apply in all civil proceedings but the only criminal proceedings in which they apply are those for an order for delivery up.

To take advantage of these presumptions, copyright owners should make sure that:

(a)   the author's name appears on all copies of literary, dramatic, musical and artistic works;

(b)   the publisher's name appears on all copies;

(c)   the copyright owner's name and the date of first publication and the country of first publication appears on sound recordings and computer programs;

(d) the same details are included in films and on the containers of videogram films, plus the name of the author and director of the film.

Anti-counterfeiting devices

33.15 Because counterfeit copies are so difficult to detect from the original, a number of devices have been invented in order to enable solicitors executing search and seizure orders, police officers executing search warrants and Trading Standards Officers who are looking for counterfeit copies, to detect the genuine copy. The use of security labels has proved to be one of the most successful devices because the counterfeiters have had great difficulty in duplicating the security labels.

HM Revenue & Customs

33.16 In the case of literary, dramatic or musical works, sound recordings and films, notice can be given to Customs pursuant to s 111 of the CDPA requiring them to prohibit the importation of specified infringing goods. In the case of literary, dramatic and musical works, this provision applies only to printed copies of the works, thus excluding computer programs.

As regards sound recordings and films only, the notice must specify the time and place at which the infringing copies are expected to arrive in the United Kingdom.

In addition, Customs are given additional powers to seize, suspend the import, or prohibit the release for free circulation of counterfeit or pirated goods and destroy them. These powers are set out in EC Regulation No 31285/94 laying down measures to prohibit the release for free circulation, export, re-export or entry for a suspensive procedure of counterfeit and pirated goods which came into force on 1 January 1995. It has direct effect in the United Kingdom and does not need national legislation to implement it.

Trade associations

33.17 A number of associations have been very successful in using the civil and criminal law against counterfeiting and piracy. The principal ones are the BFPI, the Anti-counterfeiting Group, the Federation Against Copyright Theft, the Federation against Software Theft, and the Video Copyright Protection Society. In addition, the Motion Picture Association of America and the International Federation of Phonogram and Videogram Producers have formed special divisions to combat piracy and counterfeiting. A new body, AEPOC has recently been established under the aegis of the European Broadcasting Union to fight audiovisual piracy which is the result of 'hacking' of signals, decoders and smart cards.

Source identification codes

33.18 The collecting societies, led by the MCPS, are developing technical solutions for counteracting piracy, such as the source identification (SID) codes.

Part 3
Appendices

Appendices

Appendix 1

Relevant organisations

AGICOA
Rue de Saint Jean, 26
CH-1203 Geneva
Switzerland
Tel:+41–22–340–3200
Fax:+41–22–340–3432
e-mail: info@agicoa.org
website: www.agicoa.org

ASSOCIATION FOR STANDARDS AND PRACTICES IN ELECTRONIC TRADE (EAN
UK LTD): SEE E-CENTRE

ASSOCIATION OF PROFESSIONAL COMPOSERS
34 Hanway Street
London W1P 9DE
Tel:020 7629 0992
Fax:020 7629 0993
e-mail: a.p.c@dial.pipex.com

ASSOCIATION OF PROFESSIONAL RECORDING SERVICES LTD
PO Box 22
Totnes
TQ9 7YZ
Fax:01803 868600
e-mail: info@aprs.co.uk
website: www.aprs.co.uk

ASSOCIATION OF UNITED RECORDING ARTISTS
1 York Street
London W1U 6PA
Tel:0870 8505 200
Fax:0870 8505 201
website: www.ukmff.net/aura
e-mail : office@aurank.com

AUTHORS LICENSING AND COLLECTING SOCIETY (ALCS)
Marlborough Court
14–18 Holborn
London EC1N 2LE

Tel:020 7395 0600
Fax:020 7395 0660
e-mail: info@alcs.co.uk
web-site: www.alcs.co.uk

BRITISH ACADEMY OF COMPOSERS & SONGWRITERS
British Music House
25–27 Berners Street
London W1T 3LR
Tel:020 7636 2929
e-mail: info@britishacademy.com
website: www.britishacademy.com

BRITISH ACTORS EQUITY ASSOCIATION (KNOWN AS EQUITY)
Guild House
Upper St Martins Lane
London WC2H 9EG
Tel:020 7379 6000
Fax:020 7379 7001
e-mail: info@equity.org.uk
website: www.equity.org.uk

BRITISH ASSOCIATION OF RECORD DEALERS
1st Floor
Colonnade House
2 Westover Road
Bournemouth
Dorset BH1 2BY
Tel:01202 292 063
Fax:01202 292 067
e-mail: admin@bardltd.org
website: www.bardltd.org

BRITISH COPYRIGHT COUNCIL
29–33 Berners Street
London W1T 3AB
Tel:01986 788122
Fax:01986 788847
email: secretary@britishcopyright.org
website: www.britishcopyright.org.uk

BRITISH PHONOGRAPHIC INDUSTRY
Riverside Building
County Hall

Westminster Bridge Road
London SE1 7JA
Tel:020 7803 1300
Fax:020 7803 1310
email: general@bpi.co.uk
website: www.bpi.co.uk

COMPACT COLLECTIONS LTD
Greenland Place
115–123 Bayham Street
London
NW1 0AG
Tel:020 7446 7420
Fax:020 7446 7424
e-mail: info@compactcollections.com
website: www.compactcollections.com

COMPOSERS' GUILD OF GREAT BRITAIN
The Penthouse
4 Brooke Street
London
W1Y 1AA
Tel:020 7636 2929
Fax:020 7629 0993

COPYRIGHT LICENSING AGENCY
90 Tottenham Court Road
London W1P 0LP
Tel:020 7631 5555
Fax:020 7631 5500
e-mail: cla@cla.co.uk
website: www.cla.co.uk

DESIGN & ARTISTS COPYRIGHT SOCIETY
Parchment House
13 Northburgh Street
London EC1V 0JP
Tel:020 7336 8811
Fax: 020 7336 8822
e-mail: info@dacs.org.uk
website: www.dacs.org.uk

DIRECTORS GUILD OF GREAT BRITAIN
Acorn House
314–320 Gray's Inn Road
London WC1X 8DP
Tel:020 7278 4343
Fax:020 7278 4742
e-mail: guild@dggb.co.uk
website: www.dggb.co.uk

DLA PIPER RUDNICK GRAY CARY LLP
(Contact Nicholas Fitzpatrick)
3 Noble Street
London EC2V 7EE
Tel:020 7796 6046
Fax:020 7796 6586
e-mail: nick.Fitzpatrick@dlapiper.com

E-CENTRE [ASSOCIATION FOR STANDARDS AND PRACTICES IN ELECTRONIC
TRADE (EAN UK LTD), CREATED FROM 1998 MERGER OF ANA AND ELEC-
TRONIC COMMERCE ASSOCIATION (ECA)]
10 Maltravers Street
London WC2B 3BX
Tel:020 7655 9000
Fax:020 7681 2290
e-mail: info@e-centre.org.uk
website: www.ana.org.uk

EDUCATIONAL RECORDING AGENCY
New Premier House
150 Southampton Row
London WC1B 5AL
Tel:020 7837 3222
Fax:020 7837 3750
e-mail: era@era.org.uk
website: www.era.org.uk

GUILD OF RECORDING PRODUCERS
Directors and Engineers
PO Box 310
London SW13 0AF
Tel:020 8876 3411
Fax:020 8876 8252
e-mail: repro@aprs.org.uk
website: aprs.co.uk/repro/

MECHNICAL-COPYRIGHT PROTECTION SOCIETY LTD
Copyright House
29–33 Berners Street
London W1T 3AB
Tel:020 7580 5544
e-mail: info@mcpaonline.org.uk
website: www.mcpaonline.org.uk

MUSIC PUBLISHERS' ASSOCIATION
3rd Floor
20 York Buildings
London WC2N 6JU
Tel:020 7839 7779
Fax:020 7839 7776
e-mail: mpa@musicpublishers.co.uk
website: www.musicpublishers.co.uk

MUSICIANS UNION
60–62 Clapham Road
London SW9 0JJ
Tel:020 7582 5566
Fax:020 7582 9805
e-mail: info@musiciansunion.org.uk
website: www.musiciansunion.org.uk

NEW PRODUCERS ALLIANCE
9 Bourlet Close
London W1W 7BP
Tel:020 7580 2480
Fax:020 7580 2484
Email: queries@npa.org.uk
website: www.npa.org.uk

NEWSPAPER LICENSING AGENCY LIMITED
Wellington Gate
Church Road
Tunbridge Wells
Kent TN1 1NL
Tel: 01892 552837
Fax: 01892 525275

PERFORMING ARTIST MEDIA RIGHTS ASSOCIATION (PAMRA)
161 Borough High Street
London SE1 1HR

UK
Tel:+ 44 (0) 20 7940 0410
Fax:+44 (0) 20 7407 2008
e-mail: office@pamra.org.uk
website: www.pamra.org.uk

PERFORMING RIGHT SOCIETY
Copyright House
29–33 Berners Street
London W1T 3AB
Tel:020 7580 5544
Fax:020 7580 4455
e-mail: info@prs.co.uk
website: www.prs.co.uk

PHONOGRAPHIC PERFORMANCE LTD
1 Upper James Street
London W1R 3HG
Tel:020 7534 1000
Fax:020 7534 1111
e-mail: info@ppluk.com
website: www.ppluk.com

PUBLIC LENDING RIGHT OFFICE
Richard House
Sorbonne Close
Stockton-on-Tees
TS17 6DA
Tel:01642 604 699
Fax:01642 615 641
website: www.plr.uk.com

PUBLISHERS' ASSOCIATION
29B Montague Street
London WC1B 5BW
Tel:020 7691 9191
Fax:020 7691 9199
e-mail: mail@publishers.org.uk
website: www.publishers.org.uk

SAMUEL FRENCH LIMITED
52 Fitzroy Street
London W1T 5JR

Tel:020 7255 4311
Fax:020 7387 2161
website: www.samuelfrench.com

SOCIETY OF AUTHORS
84 Drayton Gardens
London SW10 9SB
Tel:020 7373 6642
Fax:020 7373 5768
website: www.societyofauthors.net

THOMSON & THOMSON
500 Victory Road
North Quincy
MA 02171 3145
USA
Tel:+800 692 8833/+617 479 1600
e-mail: support@t-t.com
website: thomson-thomson.com

UK PATENT OFFICE
Central Enquiry Unit, Room 1L02
Concept House
Cardiff Road
Newport
Gwent NP10 8QQ
Tel:01633 813930
Fax:01633 813600
e-mail: enquiries@patent.gov.uk
website: www.ukpats.org.uk

US COPYRIGHT OFFICE
Library of Congress
101 Independence Avenue S.E
Washington DC
20559–6000
website: www.copyright.gov

VIDEO PERFORMANCE LIMITED
1 Upper James Street
London W1F 9DE
Tel:020 7534 1400
Email: general@vpluck.com
Website: www.vpluk.com

Appendix I

WARNER CHAPPELL PLAYS LIMITED
129 Park Street
London W1Y 3FA

WRITERS' GUILD OF GREAT BRITAIN
15 Britannia Street
London WC1X 9JN
Tel:020 7833 0777
Fax:020 7833 4777
e-mail: admin@writersguild.org.uk
website: www.writersguild.org.uk

Appendix 2

Countries party to the Paris, Berne, UCC and Rome Conventions, Member Countries of WTO

	Paris	Berne	UCC	Rome	WTO
Albania	✓	✓	✓	✓	✓
Algeria	✓	✓	✓	–	–
Andorra	✓	✓	✓	✓	–
Angola	–	–	–	–	✓
Antigua and Barbuda	✓	✓	–	–	✓
Argentina	✓	✓	✓	✓	✓
Armenia	✓	✓	–	✓	✓
Australia	✓	✓	✓	✓	✓
Austria	✓	✓	✓	✓	✓
Azerbaijan	✓	✓	✓	✓	–
Bahamas	✓	✓	✓	–	–
Bahrain	✓	✓	–	–	✓
Bangladesh	✓	✓	✓	–	✓
Barbados	✓	✓	✓	✓	✓
Belarus	✓	✓	✓	✓	–
Belgium	✓	✓	✓	✓	✓
Belize	✓	✓	✓	–	✓
Benin	✓	✓	–	–	✓
Bhutan	✓	✓	–	–	–
Bolivia	✓	✓	✓	✓	✓
Bosnia and Herzegovina	✓	✓	✓	–	–
Botswana	✓	✓	–	–	✓
Brazil	✓	✓	✓	✓	✓
Brunei Darussalam	–	–	–	–	✓

	Paris	Berne	UCC	Rome	WTO
Bulgaria	✓	✓	✓	✓	✓
Burkina Faso	✓	✓	–	✓	✓
Burundi	✓	–	–	–	✓
Cambodia	✓	–	✓	–	✓
Cameroon	✓	✓	✓	–	✓
Canada	✓	✓	✓	✓	✓
Cape Verde	–	✓	–	✓	–
Central African Republic	✓	✓	–	–	✓
Chad	✓	✓	–	–	✓
Chile	✓	✓	✓	✓	✓
China	✓	✓	✓	–	✓
Chinese Taipei	–	–	–	–	✓
Colombia	✓	✓	✓	✓	✓
Comoros	✓	✓	–	–	–
Congo	✓	✓	–	✓	✓
Costa Rica	✓	✓	✓	✓	✓
Côte d'Ivoire	✓	✓	–	–	✓
Croatia	✓	✓	✓	✓	✓
Cuba	✓	✓	✓	–	✓
Cyprus	✓	✓	✓	–	✓
Czech Republic	✓	✓	✓	✓	✓
Denmark	✓	✓	✓	✓	✓
Djibouti	✓	✓	–	–	✓
Dominica	✓	✓	–	✓	✓
Dominican Republic	✓	✓	✓	✓	✓
Ecuador	✓	✓	✓	✓	✓
Egypt	✓	✓	–	–	✓
El Salvador	✓	✓	✓	✓	✓
Equatorial Guinea	✓	✓	–	–	–
Estonia	✓	✓	–	✓	✓
European Community	–	✓	✓	–	✓
Fiji	–	✓	✓	✓	✓
Finland	✓	✓	✓	✓	✓

Countries party to the Paris, Berne, UCC and Rome Conventions

	Paris	Berne	UCC	Rome	WTO
France	✓	✓	✓	✓	✓
Gabon	✓	✓	–	–	✓
Gambia	✓	✓	–	–	✓
Georgia	✓	✓	–	✓	✓
Germany	✓	✓	✓	✓	✓
Ghana	✓	✓	✓	–	✓
Greece	✓	✓	✓	✓	✓
Grenada	✓	✓	✓	–	✓
Guatemala	✓	✓	✓	✓	✓
Guinea	✓	✓	✓	–	✓
Guinea-Bissau	✓	✓	–	–	✓
Guyana	✓	✓	–	–	✓
Haiti	✓	✓	✓	–	✓
Holy See	✓	✓	✓	–	–
Honduras	✓	✓	–	✓	✓
Hong Kong	–	–	✓	–	✓
Hungary	✓	✓	✓	✓	✓
Iceland	✓	✓	✓	✓	✓
India	✓	✓	✓	–	✓
Indonesia	✓	✓	–	–	✓
Iran (Islamic Republic)	✓	–	–	–	–
Iraq	✓	–	–	–	–
Ireland	✓	✓	✓	✓	✓
Israel	✓	✓	✓	✓	✓
Italy	✓	✓	✓	✓	✓
Jamaica	✓	✓	–	✓	✓
Japan	✓	✓	✓	✓	✓
Jordan	✓	✓	–	–	✓
Kazakstan	✓	✓	✓	–	–
Kenya	✓	✓	✓	–	✓
Korea (Democratic People's Republic of)	✓	✓	–	–	–
Korea (Republic of)	✓	✓	✓	–	✓

Appendix 2

	Paris	Berne	UCC	Rome	WTO
Kuwait	–	–	–	–	✓
Kyrgyzstan	✓	✓	–	✓	✓
Lao People's Democratic Republic	✓	–	✓	–	–
Latvia	✓	✓	–	✓	✓
Lebanon	✓	✓	✓	✓	–
Lesotho	✓	✓	–	✓	✓
Liberia	✓	✓	✓	–	–
Libya	✓	✓	–	–	–
Liechtenstein	✓	✓	✓	✓	✓
Lithuania	✓	✓	–	✓	✓
Luxembourg	✓	✓	✓	✓	✓
Macau		–	–	✓	–
Macedonia (The former Yugoslav Republic of) (FYROM)	✓	✓	✓	✓	✓
Madagascar	✓	✓	–	–	✓
Malawi	✓	✓	✓	–	✓
Malaysia	✓	✓	–	–	✓
Maldives	–	–	–	–	✓
Mali	✓	✓	–	–	✓
Malta	✓	✓	✓	–	✓
Mauritania	✓	✓	–	–	✓
Mauritius	✓	✓	✓	–	✓
Mexico	✓	✓	✓	✓	✓
Micronesia (Federated States of)	–	✓	–	–	–
Moldova	–	–	–	–	✓
Monaco	✓	✓	✓	✓	–
Mongolia	✓	✓	–	–	✓
Morocco	✓	✓	✓	–	✓
Mozambique	✓	–	–	–	✓
Myanmar	–	–	–	–	✓
Namibia	✓	✓	–	–	✓

Countries party to the Paris, Berne, UCC and Rome Conventions

	Paris	Berne	UCC	Rome	WTO
Nepal	✓	✓	–	–	✓
Netherlands	✓	✓	✓	✓	✓
New Zealand	✓	✓	✓	–	✓
Nicaragua	✓	✓	✓	✓	✓
Niger	✓	✓	✓	✓	✓
Nigeria	✓	✓	✓	✓	✓
Norway	✓	✓	✓	✓	✓
Oman	✓	✓		–	✓
Pakistan	✓	✓	✓	–	✓
Panama	✓	✓	✓	✓	✓
Papua New Guinea	✓	–	–	–	✓
Paraguay	✓	✓	✓	✓	✓
Peru	✓	✓	✓	✓	✓
Philippines	✓	✓	–	✓	✓
Poland	✓	✓	✓	✓	✓
Portugal	✓	✓	✓	✓	✓
Qatar	✓	✓	–	–	✓
Republic of Moldova	✓	✓	✓	✓	–
Romania	✓	✓	–	✓	✓
Russian Federation	✓	✓	✓	✓	–
Rwanda	✓	✓	✓	–	✓
Saint Kitts and Nevis	✓	✓	–	–	✓
Saint Lucia	✓	✓	✓	✓	✓
Saint Vincent and the Grenadines	✓	✓	✓	–	✓
San Marino	✓	–	–	–	–
Sao Tome and Principe	✓	–	–	–	–
Saudi Arabia	✓	✓	✓	–	–
Senegal	✓	✓	✓	–	✓
Serbia and Montenegro	✓	✓	✓	✓	–
Seychelles	✓	–	✓	–	–
Sierra Leone	✓	–	–	–	✓
Singapore	✓	✓	–	–	✓

	Paris	Berne	UCC	Rome	WTO
Slovakia	✓	✓	✓	✓	✓
Slovenia	✓	✓	✓	✓	✓
Solomon Islands	–	–	–	–	✓
South Africa	✓	✓	–	–	✓
Spain	✓	✓	✓	✓	✓
Sri Lanka	✓	✓	✓	–	✓
Sudan	✓	✓	–	–	–
Suriname	✓	✓	–	–	✓
Swaziland	✓	✓	–	–	✓
Sweden	✓	✓	✓	✓	✓
Switzerland	✓	✓	✓	✓	✓
Syrian Arab Republic	✓	✓	–	–	–
Tajikistan	✓	✓	✓	–	–
Tanzania (United Republic of)	✓	✓	–	–	✓
Thailand	–	✓	–	–	✓
Togo	✓	✓	✓	✓	✓
Tonga	✓	✓	–	–	–
Trinidad and Tobago	✓	✓	✓	–	✓
Tunisia	✓	✓	✓	–	✓
Turkey	✓	✓	–	✓	✓
Turkmenistan	✓	–	–	–	–
Uganda	✓	–	–	–	✓
UK	✓	✓	✓	✓	✓
Ukraine	✓	✓	✓	–	–
United Arab Emirates	✓	✓	–	✓	✓
United States of America	✓	✓	✓	✓	✓
Uruguay	✓	✓	✓	✓	✓
Uzbekistan	✓	✓	–	–	–
Venezuela	✓	✓	✓	✓	✓
Vietnam	✓	✓	–	–	–
Zaire (Democratic Republic of Congo)	✓	✓	–	–	✓

Countries party to the Paris, Berne, UCC and Rome Conventions

	Paris	Berne	UCC	Rome	WTO
Zambia	✓	✓	–	–	✓
Zimbabwe	✓	✓	–	–	✓

Appendix 3

EU and EEA Member States

EUROPEAN UNION
Austria
Belgium
Cyprus
Czech Republic
Denmark
Estonia
Finland
France
Germany
Greece
Hungary
Ireland
Italy
Latvia
Lithuania
Luxembourg
Malta
Poland
Netherlands
Portugal
Slovakia
Slovenia
Spain
Sweden
United Kingdom

EUROPEAN ECONOMIC AREA
The following countries, in addition to the Member States of the EU:
Iceland
Liechtenstein
Norway

Appendix 4

Table of Incidents of Copyright

I. Type of Work	Definition section	II. Term of copyright subject to reg 15(1) of the 1995 Regulations (see Chapter 6 and Appendix 5)	III. Restricted acts	IV. First owner (except Crown, Parliamentary and certain international organisation copyright)
1 *Literary* (Books, newspapers, magazines, catalogues, letters, tables or compilations (other than databases), computer programs, preparatory design material for computer programs, databases)	3(1)	Life of author plus 70 years Exceptions: (i) works of unknown authorship: 70 years from the end of calendar year in which made, or if during that period it is made available to the public, 70 years from the end of calendar year in which first made available to the public; (ii) computer generated works; 50 years from end of calendar year in which work was made; (iii) works of joint authorship: life of last author to die plus 70 years (s 12)	(a) Copying the work, ie reproducing the work in any material form (b) Issuing copies to the public (c) Renting or lending the work to the public (d) Performing, showing or playing the work in public (e) Communicating the work to the public (f) Making an adaptation (g) Doing, in relation to any adaptation, any of (a) to (f) (s 16)	(a) Author (ie the person who creates the work), or (b) If made in course of employment under a contract of service, employer will be first owner of all copyright (ss 9 and 11)

I. Type of Work	Definition section	II. Term of copyright subject to reg 15(1) of the 1995 Regulations (see Chapter 6 and Appendix 5)	III. Restricted acts	IV. First owner (except Crown, Parliamentary and certain international organisation copyright)
Dramatic (Plays, operas, screen-plays, mimes, panto-mimes, choreo-graphic works, etc) *Musical* (Classical and popular songs, excluding words or action intended to be sung, spoken or performed with music. Does not include sound recordings of musical works) (s 3(1))	3(1)			

I. Type of Work	Definition section	II. Term of copyright subject to reg 15(1) of the 1995 Regulations (see Chapter 6 and Appendix 5)	III. Restricted acts	IV. First owner (except Crown, Parliamentary and certain international organisation copyright)
2 *Artistic works* (Graphic works, photography, sculpture, collages, architecture – buildings and models of buildings, works of artistic craftsmanship)	4	Life of author plus 70 years Works of unknown authorship, computer-generated works and works of joint authorship as 1 above (s 12)	(a) Copying the work, ie reproducing the work in any material form (b) Issuing copies to the public (c) Renting or lending copies of the work to the public other than: (i) a work of architecture in the form of a building of a model for a building, or (ii) a work of applied art (d) Communicating the work to the public	(a) Author, or (b) If made in course of employment under a contract of service, employer will be first owner of all copyright (ss 9 and 11)

I. Type of Work	Definition section	II. Term of copyright subject to reg 15(1) of the 1995 Regulations (see Chapter 6 and Appendix 5)	III. Restricted acts	IV. First owner (except Crown, Parliamentary and certain international organisation copyright)
3 *Sound recordings* (Recordings of sounds from which sounds may be reproduced, or a recording of a whole or part of a literary, dramatic or musical work from which sounds reproducing the work or part may be produced.	5A	(a) 50 years from the end of the year in which it was made, or (b) if released before end of that period, 50 years from end of calendar year in which released (s 13A)	(a) Copying the work ie reproducing the work in any material form (b) Issuing copies to the public (c) Renting or lending the work to the public (d) Playing or showing the work in public (e) Communicating the work to the public	The producer – the person by whom the arrangements necessary for the making of the sound recording are made (ss 9, 11(1) and 178)

I. Type of Work	Definition section	II. Term of copyright subject to reg 15(1) of the 1995 Regulations (see Chapter 6 and Appendix 5)	III. Restricted acts	IV. First owner (except Crown, Parliamentary and certain international organisation copyright)
4 *Films* (A recording on any medium from which a moving image may by any means be produced, and including the soundtrack)	5B	(a) 70 years from end of calendar year in which the death occurs of the last to die of: (i) the principal director; (ii) the author of the screenplay; (iii) the author of the dialogue; or (iv) the composer of music specially created for and used in the film (b) If the identity of (i) to (iv) is unknown, 70 years from end of calendar year in which the film was made, or if it is made available to the public during that period, then 70 years from the end of calendar year in which it is first so made available	(a) Copying the work, ie reproducing the work in any material form (b) Issuing copies to the public (c) Renting or lending the work to the public (d) Showing or playing the work in public (e) Communicating the work to the public	(a) The producer (the person by whom the arrangements necessary for the making of the film are undertaken) and the principal director (ss 9, 11 and 178) (b) The employer if the film was made by the producer or principal director in the course of their employment (s 11(2))

I. Type of Work	Definition section	II. Term of copyright subject to reg 15(1) of the 1995 Regulations (see Chapter 6 and Appendix 5)	III. Restricted acts	IV. First owner (except Crown, Parliamentary and certain international organisation copyright)
		(c) if there is no person falling within categories (i) to (iv), then 50 years from the end of the year in which the film was made (s 13B)		
5 *Broadcasts* ('An electronic transmission of visual images, sounds or other information ...'. NB definition limited as set out in paragraph 2.09)	6	50 years from end of calendar year in which broadcast was made (s 14)	(a) Copying the work, ie reproducing the work in any material form (b) Issuing copies to the public (c) Playing or showing the work in public (d) Communicating the work to the public	The person making the broadcast, or in the case of a broadcast which relays another broadcast by reception and immediate retransmission, the person making that other broadcast (ss 9 and 11(1))

I. Type of Work	Definition section	II. Term of copyright subject to reg 15(1) of the 1995 Regulations (see Chapter 6 and Appendix 5)	III. Restricted acts	IV. First owner (except Crown, Parliamentary and certain international organisation copyright)
6 *Published editions* (In the context of copyright in the typographical arrangement of a published edition, means a published edition of the whole or any part of one or more literary, dramatic or musical works, except to the extent that it reproduces the typographical arrangement of a previous edition)	8	25 years from end of calendar year in which edition was first published (s 15)	(a) Copying the work, i e reproducing the work in any material form – means making a facsimile copy of the work (s 17(5)) (b) Issuing copies to the public	The publisher of the edition (ss 9 and 11)

Appendix 5

Tabular Representation of the Duration of Copyright By Professor John N Adams, Michael Edenborough and James Graham

ORIGINAL WORKS

Literary, dramatic and musical works (known author)	
Works published during the author's lifetime	
Provided in copyright in another EEA state on July 1, 1995[1], date of publication immaterial	70 years pma[2,3]
Works unpublished at the author's death	
Published June 1, 1957–August 1, 1989	50 years from the end of the calendar year of publication, etc[4], if longer[5] than 70 years pma[6]
Unpublished at August 1, 1989	50 years from end of 1989[7] if longer[8] than 70 years pma[9]
Other unpublished works	70 years pma[10]
Artistic works, known author (excluding photographs and engravings)	
Whenever created, published or unpublished	70 years pma[11]
Photographs (excluding computer generated) and engravings with a known author	
Photographs with a known author	
Taken before June 1, 1957	50 years from end of the calendar year taken[12] or 70 pma[13] if longer[14]
Published June 1, 1957–August 1, 1989	50 years from end of calendar year of publication[15] or 70 years pma[16] if longer[17]
Taken after June 1, 1957 and unpublished at August 1, 1989	50 years from end of 1989[18] or 70 years pma[19] if longer[20]
All other photographs	70 years pma[21]

Engravings with a known author	
Published after death of author but before August 1, 1989	50 years from end of calendar year of publication[22] or 70 years pma[23] if longer[24]
Published before death of author	70 years pma[25]
Still unpublished	70 years pma[26] if longer[27] than 50 years from the end of 1989[28]

Anonymous or pseudonymous works, literary, dramatic, musical or artistic works (other than photographs but including engravings)

Published/made available to the public	
Published before August 1, 1989	70 years from end of the calendar year made available to the public[29]
Made available to public after August 1, 1989	70 years from end of the calendar year made available to the public[30]

Not published/made available to the public	
Existing but unpublished at August 1, 1989	50 years from end of 1989[31] or 70 years from end of the calendar year made[32], whichever is longer[33]
Made August 1, 1989–January 1, 1996	Possibly indefinite[34]
Made after January 1, 1996	70 years from end of calendar year in which made[35]

Anonymous or pseudonymous photographs

Published/made available to the public	
Taken prior to June 1, 1957	70 years from end of calendar year taken[36] or, if made available to the public in that period, 70 years from end of the calendar year made available[37]
Taken between June 1, 1957 and August 1, 1989	70 years from end of calendar year made available[38]
Taken between August 1, 1989 and January 1, 1996	70 years from end of calendar year made available[39]
Made after January 1, 1996	70 years from end of calendar year made available to the public[40]

Unpublished/not made available to the public	
Taken prior to June 1, 1957	70 years from end of calendar year taken[41]

Taken between June 1, 1957 and August 1, 1989	50 years from end of 1989[42] or 70 years from end of calendar year taken[43]
Taken between August 1, 1989 and January 1, 1996 but not made available to the public	Possibly indefinite[44]
Made after January 1, 1996	70 years from end of calendar year of making[45]

Derivative works

Sound recordings (other than film sound tracks)

Made before June 1, 1957	50 years from the end of the calendar year in which they were made[46] or, if released before that period expires, 50 years from the end of the calendar year in which released[47]
Made and published between June 1, 1957 and August 1, 1989	50 years from the end of the calendar year in which published[48]
Made after June 1, 1957 and unpublished at August 1, 1989	50 years from end of 1989[49] or if not released after August 1, 1989, then 50 years from the end of the calendar year in which released[50] so long as released within 50 years of being made[51], whichever is the longer[52]
Made after August 1, 1989	50 years from the end of the calendar year in which they were made[53] or, if released before that period expires, 50 years from the end of the calendar year in which released[54]

Cinematograph films

(It must be noted that the rules for films made prior to the commencement of the 1911 Act are significantly different, and are not dealt with here.)

Rules for films prior to January 1, 1996

Made before June 1, 1957	Protected as photographs and dramatic works[55] (see photographs and sound recordings)
Made after June 1, 1957:	

if registrable under (Part III of the Cinematograph Films Act 1938), Part II of the Films Act 1960	Until registered and thereafter 50 years from the end of the calendar year in which registered[56]
if not registrable	Until publication and thereafter for 50 years from the end of the calendar year of publication[57]
Films unpublished at August 1, 1989	50 years from the end of 1989[58]
Made after August 1, 1989	50 years from the end of calendar year made[59] or if released then 50 years from the end of the calendar year of release[60]

Current rules for films	
Films made after January 1, 1996, first qualifying for copyright protection after that date, existing copyright works, and films in which copyright had expired before that date but which were still in copyright in another EEA country[61]	70 years from the end of the calendar year in which the death occurs of the last to die of the following persons: (1) principal director; (2) author of the screenplay; (3) author of the dialogue; (4) the composer of the music specifically created for and used in the film[62]. If the identity of one or more of the above persons is known and the identity of one or more others is not, the reference in that subsection to the death of the last of them to die is to be construed as a reference to the death of the last whose identity is known[63]. If the identity of none of the above is known, then the term is 70 years from the end of the calendar year in which the film was made[64], or if during that period the film is made available to the public by being broadcast or included in a cable programme or service, the period is 70 years from when such making available to the public occurred[65]. Alternatively if the length pre-scribed under the 'Rules for films prior to January 1, 1996' is longer than that under the current rules then that longer period is preserved[66].

Film sound tracks under the Duration of Copyright Regulations
(The effect of the Duration of Copyright Regulations[67] is to apply the rules for the extension of copyright in films set out in the previous section, to film sound tracks, both existing at January 1, 1996 and created thereafter.)

Broadcasts	
Television or sound and cable transmission after June 1, 1957	50 years from the end of the calendar year in which the broadcast was first made[68]
Typographical arrangements	
Typographical arrangements of published editions	25 years from the end of the calendar year in which the edition was first published[69]

NOTES

1   The Duration of Copyright and Rights in Performance Regulations 1995, SI 1995/3297 ('the 1995 Regulations'), reg 16.
2   'Post mortem auctoris'.
3   Copyright, Designs and Patents Act 1988 ('CDPA'), s 12(1) unamended, now substituted by CDPA, s 12(2) as amended by the 1995 Regulations.
4   Copyright Act 1956 ('CA 1956'), s 2(3). CDPA, Sch 1, para 12(2)(a).
5   1995 Regulations, reg15(1).
6   CDPA, s 12(2) as amended by the 1995 Regulations.
7   CDPA, Sch 1, para 12(4)(a).
8   1995 Regulations, reg 15(1).
9   CDPA, s 12(2) as amended by the 1995 Regulations.
10   Ibid.
11   Ibid.
12   CA 1956, Sch 7, para 2; CDPA, Sch 1, para 12(2)(c).
13   CDPA, s 12(2) as amended by the 1995 Regulations.
14   1995 Regulations, reg 15(1).
15   CA 1956, s 3(4)(b).
16   CDPA, s 12(2) as amended by the 1995 Regulations.
17   1995 Regulations, reg 15(1).
18   CDPA, Sch 1, para 12(4)(c).
19   CDPA, s 12(2) as amended by the 1995 Regulations.
20   1995 Regulations, reg 15(1).
21   CDPA, s 12(2) as amended by the 1995 Regulations.
22   CA 1956, s 3(4)(a); CDPA, Sch 1, para 12(2)(b).
23   CDPA, s 12(2) as amended by the 1995 Regulations.
24   1995 Regulations, reg 15(1).
25   CDPA, s 12(2) as amended by the 1995 Regulations.
26   Ibid.
27   1995 Regulations, reg 15(1).
28   CA 1956, s 3(4)(a); CDPA, Sch 1, para 12(4)(b).
29   Fifty years from end of year of publication under CA 1956, Sch 2, para 1; CDPA, Sch 1, para 12(3)(a); CDPA, s 12(3)(b) as amended by the 1995 Regulations.
30   CDPA, s 12(3)(b) as amended by the 1995 Regulations.
31   CDPA, Sch 1, para 12(3)(b).
32   CDPA, s 12(3)(a) as amended by the 1995 Regulations.
33   1995 Regulations, reg 15(1).
34   CDPA, s 12(2) (unamended) only defined duration for works that were 'made available to the public' and not by reference to the date that the work was made. Thus

there is potential indefinite protection for such works which are preserved by reg 15(1). Further, these works are not caught by s 12(3) of the CDPA as amended by the 1995 Regulations because that section is not retrospective in action.

35 CDPA, s 12(3)(a) as amended by the 1995 Regulations.

36 Fifty-year period from when taken under the CA 1956, Sch 7, para 2 and preserved by CDPA, Sch 1, para 12(2)(c) second part; under CDPA, s 12(3)(a) as amended by the 1995 Regulations this period is extended to 70 years from when 'made' (which is arguably the same as when 'taken').

37 Fifty-year period from when taken under the CA 1956, Sch 7, para 2 and CDPA, Sch 1, para 12(2)(c); under CDPA, s 12(3)(b) as amended by the 1995 Regulations this period is extended to 70 years.

38 CA 1956, s 3(4)(b); 50 years from when published preserved by CDPA, Sch 1, para 12(2)(c); under CDPA, s 12(3)(b) as amended by the 1995 Regulations this period is extended to 70 years.

39 Fifty years from when made available to the public under CDPA, s 12(2); CDPA, s 12(3)(b) as amended by the 1995 Regulations this period is extended to 70 years.

40 CDPA, s 12(3)(b) as amended by the 1995 Regulations this period is extended to 70 years.

41 Fifty-year period from when taken under the CA 1956, Sch 7, para 2 and CDPA, Sch 1, para 12(2)(c) second part; under CDPA, s 12(3)(a) as amended by the 1995 Regulations this period is extended to 70 years from when 'made' (which is arguably the same as when 'taken').

42 CDPA, Sch 1, para 12(4)(c).

43 CDPA, s 12(3)(a) as amended by the 1995 Regulations this period is extended to 70 years.

44 These works are not subject to s 12(3) of the CDPA as amended by the 1995 Regulations, because these provisions are not retrospective, and CDPA, s 12(2) (unamended) only made the duration referable to 'making available to the public' and not the date of creation. Thus, there is potentially indefinite copyright which is preserved by reg 15(1).

45 CDPA, s 12(3)(a) as amended by the 1995 Regulations.

46 CA 1956, Sch 7, para 11; CDPA, Sch 1, para 12(2)(d) second part; CDPA, s 13A(2)(a) as amended by the 1995 Regulations.

47 CDPA, s 13A(2)(b) as amended by the 1995 Regulations.

48 CA 1956, s 12(3); CDPA, Sch 1, para 12(2)(d); CDPA, s 13A(2)(b) as amended by the 1995 Regulations assuming that 'publication' is subsumed within 'release'.

49 CDPA, Sch 1, para 12(5)(a) which is longer than the period provided by CDPA, s 13A(2)(a) as amended by the 1995 Regulations which is 50 years from when made, thus old duration is preserved by reg 15(1).

50 If unpublished at August 1, 1989 but then published between that date and the end of 1995 then the period of protection expires 50 years from the end of 1989. If published after 1993 under CDPA, s 13A(2)(b) as amended the period of protection becomes 50 years after publication.

51 CDPA, s 13A(2)(b) which defines the period in which the release must occur in order to take advantage of the extra term of protection.

52 The latter period will always be longer for works made after 1939 therefore if such works are released they will always get the extra protection.

53 CDPA, s 13(1)(a); CDPA, s 13A(2)(a) as amended by the 1995 Regulations.

54 CDPA, s 13(1) (unamended) and reproduced by CDPA, s 13A(2) as amended by the 1995 Regulations.

55 CA 1956, Sch 7, paras 14–16.

56 CA 1956, s 13(3)(a) as amended by Films Act 1985, s 7 and Sch 2 and CDPA, Sch 1, para 12(2)(c).
57 Ibid.
58 CDPA, Sch 1, para 12(5)(b).
59 CDPA, s 13(1)(a).
60 CDPA, s 13(1)(b).
61 1995 Regulations, regs 14 and 16.
62 CDPA, s 13B(2) as amended by the 1995 Regulations.
63 CDPA, s 13B(3) as amended by the 1995 Regulations.
64 CDPA, s 13B(4)(a) as amended by the 1995 Regulations.
65 Ibid.
66 1995 Regulations, reg 15(1).
67 CDPA, ss 5A and 5B as amended by the 1995 Regulations.
68 CDPA, s 14(2) as amended by the 1995 Regulations which reproduces CDPA, s 14(1) (unamended) and Sch 1, para 12(6).
69 CDPA, s 15 not amended, but note the publication right due to be introduced by the Rental and Lending Right SI from Art 4 of Directive 93/98 with provisional date December 1, 1996.

Appendix 6

Declarations (Libraries)[1]

FORM A

DECLARATION: COPY OF ARTICLE OR PART OF PUBLISHED WORK

To:

The Librarian of   Library

[Address of Library]

1. Please supply me with a copy of:

*the article in the periodical, the particulars of which are
[   ]
*the part of the published work, the particulars of which are
[   ]

required by me for the purposes of research or private study.

2. I declare that—

(a)   I have not previously been supplied with a copy of the same material by you or by any other librarian;

(b)   I will not use the copy except for research or private study and will not supply a copy of it to any other person; and

(c)   to the best of my knowledge no other person with whom I work or study has made or intends to make, at or about the same time as this request, a request for substantially the same material for substantially the same purpose.

3. I understand that if the declaration is false in a material particular the copy supplied to me by you will be an infringing copy and that I shall be liable for infringement of copyright as if I had made the copy myself.

**Signature

Date

Name

Address

*   Delete whichever is appropriate.
**   This must be the personal signature of the person making the request. A stamped or typewritten signature, or the signature of an agent, is NOT acceptable.

FORM B

DECLARATION: COPY OF WHOLE OR PART OF UNPUBLISHED WORK

To:

The Librarian/Archivist of   * Library/Archive

[Address of Library]

1. Please supply me with a copy of:

the *whole/following part [particulars of part] of the [particulars of the unpublished work] required by me for the purposes of research or private study.

2. I declare that—
(a)   I have not previously been supplied with a copy of the same material by you or by any other librarian or archivist;
(b)   I will not use the copy except for research or private study and will not supply a copy of it to any other person; and
(c)   to the best of my knowledge the work had not been published before the document was deposited in your *library/archive and the original copyright owner has not prohibited copying of the work.

3. I understand that if the declaration is false in a material particular the copy supplied to me by you will be an infringing copy and that I shall be liable for infringement of copyright as if I had made the copy myself.

**Signature

Date

Name

Address

---

*   Delete whichever is appropriate.
**   This must be the personal signature of the person making the request. A stamped or typewritten signature, or the signature of an agent, is NOT acceptable.

1   See **paragraph 20.04**.

Index

Index

Index

Index

Index

Index

Index

Index

Index

Index

Index

Index

Index

Index

Index

Index

Index

Index

Index